D0947002

AFRICAN SOCIAL STUDIES

A Radical Reader

AFRICAN SOCIAL STUDIES

A Radical Reader

Edited by

Peter C.W. Gutkind

and

Peter Waterman

MONTHLY REVIEW PRESS

NEW YORK AND LONDON

Copyright © 1977 by Peter Gutkind and Peter Waterman
All rights reserved

Library of Congress Cataloging in Publication Data
Main entry under title:
African social studies
Biography: p.
1. Africa—Social conditions—Addresses, essays,
lectures. 2. Africa—Economic conditions—Addresses,
essays, lectures. I. Gutkind, Peter Claus Wolfgang.
II. Waterman, Peter.
HN777.A37 309.1′6 75-43575 ISBN: 0-85345-381-0

First printing

Monthly Review Press
62 West 14th Street, New York, N.Y. 10011
21 Theobalds Road, London WC1X 8SL

Manufactured in the United States of America

Contents

PART V—SOCIAL STRUCTURE: THE PROCESS OF CLASS FORMATION

PART VI—IDEOLOGY: IDEAS AS A MATERIAL FORCE

PART VII—POLITICS: RULERS, MASSES AND POLITICAL POWER

PART VIII—A BIBLIOGRAPHICAL GUIDE

Preface

When this book was first conceived, Amilcar Cabral was alive, but Cabral's Africa and the whole of Southern Africa was under firm colonial-racist domination. For this reason—and also because of the impossibility of adequately covering all regions of the continent—relatively little space was given to that region.

The work moved from conception to a long and difficult gestation. One editor moved from Ibadan to Montreal and from Montreal to Edinburgh. The other moved from Zaria to The Hague. To the imaginable problems of communication were added those of handling very disparate manuscripts and sources, the authors of which were sometimes impossible to contact. It is for these reasons that there are shortcomings in the references and bibliography of some items. We hope that readers unable to refer to the original sources for full references will feel mollified by the lengthy bibliography with which the book ends.

The long gestation implies an accumulation of debts. First, for a contribution to the costs of publication from the McGill University Faculty of Graduate Studies and Research. Secondly, to Alice Gutkind in Edinburgh and Suzanne Parker in The Hague who shared with us the thankless task of proofreading. We hope that the appearance of the book will compensate them—as well as all those students and colleagues to whom we kept promising it.

As the work moved into its later stages, Cabral was murdered. But Cabral's Africa arose from his funeral pyre, the working class of South Africa and Namibia asserted itself in dramatic fashion, and the seemingly unshakeable edifice of racist domination began to fall apart. This swift and dramatic process, creating new types of African societies, vindicates the book's stress on class structure, class consciousness and the struggle for socialism. We do not need to dedicate the work to a murdered revolutionary. It is offered as a contribution to the 'second independence' that his work and life presaged.

P.G. and P.W.

PART I
Introduction: On Radicalism in African Studies

*Hide nothing from the masses of our people. Tell no lies. Expose lies whenever they are told. Mask no difficulties, mistakes, failures. Claim no easy victories . . . **

*The quotations used at the beginning of each part have been selected from Amilcar Cabral, *Revolution in Guinea,* Stage One, London, 1969.

On radicalism in African Studies

PETER WATERMAN

An earlier version of this paper was published in *Politics and Society*, **3**, 3 (May 1973), New York.

Over the last ten years or so there has appeared a clear and growing tendency away from the conventional wisdom enshrined in the bulk of writings and teaching on African history, sociology, economics, and politics in the West. The generic term used for this tendency is 'radical'. Yet it appears that no one has examined the phenomenon, to define its limits or catalogue its content. In a sense everybody knows what is meant by saying of a certain Africanist that he is a radical, or of a piece of work that it is radical. But if the phenomenon is important–and it is increasingly so–it deserves a certain attention. This introduction is an attempt both to open up the subject for debate and to preface the anthology that follows. No attempt will be made at rigorous definition. Instead there will be an examination of various aspects of 'radicalism' in African Studies. The first two sections deal with radicalism as a commitment and as an approach. The next deals with it as an interest. The current interests of radicals are illustrated by reference to the content of the book. The conclusion will attempt to suggest limits for the use of the term without destroying the popular understanding of it.

Radicalism as a commitment

Africanists are increasingly declaring or revealing in their writings an overt moral or political commitment. This is usually phrased in terms of opposition to imperialism (seen as a social system dominating Africa politically and exploiting it economically). And–more positively–in terms of a concern for Africa's masses, and of a preference for socialist economic and political strategies. As one such scholar puts it (Brett, 1973),

> I am primarily concerned with three aspects of change–those relating to the structure and size of economic production, the nature of the distribution of the social product, and the location of control over social processes. These concerns embody a set of related normative assumptions–that production be maximized, distribution equalized, and control decentralized.[1]

The same attitude is expressed more politically by the veteran radical Africanist, Basil Davidson (1971:8):

The basic problem for Africans is to find their own way of revolutionizing the structures of the past, and revolutionizing the colonial structures they've had imposed upon them, and which they inherited, in large part, when they have become politically independent. Africans need this dual revolution along African lines: they need it because they have to move on to new systems and modes of production... and it seems to me very clear indeed that this revolution will not be, cannot be, in the direction of capitalism. It must be in the direction of socialism.

Radical commitment can be much more specific than this. Thus, in his Presidential Address to the founding conference of the Nigerian Anthropological and Sociological Association in 1971, the veteran Zikist, Ikenna Nzimiro (1971), declared that the Association's members

must be committed to the problems of their nation; must study our institutions in order to help to eliminate those institutional obsoletes (sic) that lead to political instability in Nigeria and thus impede the development of a virile, prosperous, democratic, and just society.

This declaration suggests a 'nation-building' commitment that has come under fire from other radicals. Criticizing the call of an American liberal for policy-relevant research in Africa, Pierre van den Berghe (1971: 334–5) had this to say:

In the last analysis, relevant social research in Africa (and elsewhere) can be of two types. It can be a handmaiden to the government and the class it represents. That type of research, even when it is ethically innocuous enough, is typically pedestrian because it is conducted within a narrow conceptual and empirical frame-work. Alternatively, relevant social research can be based on a fundamental questioning of the social order, as indeed all social research *should be*, at least to some extent. The implications of such an independent search for relevance *need not* be revolutionary, but they often are, and such research often has a much more creative quality than the 'handmaiden' variety...

Criticism of 'nation-building' histories has been made from a liberal–humanist position by Christopher Wrigley (1971:123):

... the tendency of recent African historiography to celebrate the rise of states is evidence that it is being written almost exclusively from the point of view of Africa's present ruling class.

Nzimiro, to do him justice, did not in fact stop at a 'nation-building' position. While calling for a commitment to national unity and stability he suggested that this required explanation of the causes of economic inequality in Nigeria, and of the connection of this with social stratification and the pattern of political power.

The epitome of radical commitment is provided by Frantz Fanon, a man whose personal involvement, passion, integrity, and crystal vision has probably been the major single influence on the majority of young radical Africanists. While most liberal Africanists were concentrating attention on the 'modernizing élites', and most socialist ones were focusing on the trade unions and a problematic proletariat, Fanon addressed himself directly to the peasant masses, dubbing them 'the damned of the earth'. As one recent critic sees it (Beckett, 1972), Fanon's most positive message is

> his insistent and powerful perception that revolutionary, or even 'progressive' social thought in the African context, must be *about* the peasant masses of the African countries... He points up the permanent structural problem of the African countries, which is the relation of the state and associated urban centres to the rural reality of the country... (His) message insists that 'the last shall be first', the poorest regions favoured and, most basically, that the national life be by and for the rural masses, rather than simply based *on* them.

A sense of commitment in radical African Studies can thus apparently imply a declaration of personal values, as identification with a national interest, or with the masses within the continent. It can also mean acceptance of a given programme or framework of research. Such a framework appears to exist in Tanzania, where a radical nationalist régime is oriented towards economic self-reliance, social egalitarianism, and rural development. Much social research (see Collins, 1971) and historical writing (see Ranger, 1971) seem to take place within this perspective. Thus, when writing a paper on the agricultural history of Tanzania, John Iliffe (1970) takes as his starting point a statement of President Nyerere, although he does not allow himself to be limited by Nyerere's position.[2] The position adopted consciously and explicitly by researchers in Tanzania is being urged on those in Nigeria by Onigu Otite (1971:1), when he states that

> in order not to kill itself in Nigeria, social anthropology has to be macro-sociological, refraining... from concern with some exotic micro-system, or some zoo custom, or joking relationship unless the relevance of this can be shown in the solutions to the problems of the Nigerian national, political, and economic development and integration.

Commitment of this kind is taken to the limit by the many (though not all) Communist Africanists whose apparent aim is simply to illustrate a pre-existing theoretical or political position. This attitude is known in Russian as *parteinost* and translates most kindly into English as 'Party-mindedness'. An example is Solodovnikov's 'Some features of the African countries' non-capitalist development' (1971) which is devoted to demonstrating the *correctness* of a decision of an international Communist conference in 1969. Commitment need not be always conscious and explicit–that is at least the position of Basil Davidson (1971:4). He suggests that historians and archaeologists working on Africa in the late '40s were moved by the very nature of their enterprise away from their frequently neutral or conservative positions:

> ... many of those who... began to research the possible facts of African history, were themselves driven by the very pressure of what they were doing, to take up a stance in favour of the defence of African values–and so, by extension, in favour of what I would regard as radical positions... I can-think of a number for whom the discovery of African history has been a continuous means of political self-enlightenment.

One can think of others whose periodic up-dating of textbooks has represented little more than a process of minimal tactical adjustment to the demands of the time. But the point is an interesting one and will be returned to later.

Radicalism as an approach

The bulk of radical writings on Africa show a great interest in theory and method, these often being a matter of central concern. There are, however, a series of differences amongst radicals in their attitude towards theory. There is, firstly, a difference in the attitude taken towards conventional African Studies. It could be suggested that what distinguishes radical from *reformist* Africanists is the condemnation by the former of the *basic assumptions and methods* of mainstream 'Western' African Studies. There is, secondly, a difference, even amongst the so-defined radicals, towards the adoption of an alternative approach. While some are largely content to leave the proof of their pudding to its eating, others are concerned to present the recipe. There is, again, amongst the second group here, a distinction in terms of the relationship to Marxism. These differences will now be examined in turn.

Reformists and radicals
To distinguish between these two groups we may take a sample of each. In a paper claiming to lay out a 'radical approach' to change in Africa and elsewhere, Richard Sklar (1967:10) had this criticism to make:

> A functional approach to national integration, focusing upon the particular nation-state as a system-in-being, tends to point up the beneficial effects of such dependence [on the metropolitan countries—P.W.] upon that system's development.

Whilst Sklar considers that Western theory merely 'tends' to conservatism, others consider that it is fundamentally flawed and biased. Criticizing modernization theory, Edwin Brett (1973) says that

> Although it is argued that these constructs are 'empirical generalizations' derived directly from observation of reality rather than from the observers' subjective value system, this claim does not hold up under examination. They are not (and could not be derived from the observation of all advanced or traditional societies or of all aspects of behaviour in the societies which are so chosen, but are deliberately and systematically selective... The ideal types represent dominant beliefs (held by both actors in the society and by academic observers) about how people ought to behave, or as myths used to rationalize behaviour after the event...

And in a general criticism of positivism in African studies, Gavin Williams (1971)–borrowing from Marx–has this to say of its practitioners:

> ... they take as their starting point that which needs to be explained, the unequal appropriation of resources in society, and indeed today, the unequal appropriation of resources throughout the world, and the social relationships which flow from or are pre-supposed by this unequal appropriation of resources.

Pudding or recipe?

On the question of an alternative theory and method, we can consider first the attitude revealed in the work of Thomas Hodgkin and defended by Basil Davidson. This pair might well be considered as the founding fathers of radical Africanism in Britain.[3] Both have implicitly (and sometimes explicitly) rejected conventional Western attitudes and methodology. Thus, in a review of a history of Islam in Africa, Hodgkin (1963:95) has condemned the 'scissors-and-paste' empiricism that has been the major weakness of at least the English school of African history, and followed up his criticism by a full page of what could be called 'Marxist-type' questions that he considers Islamic scholars need to ask. For his part, Davidson (1971:5) has reported his own concern to 'analyse the economic connections which underlie the situation' and states that 'in this respect, of course, I *am* a Marxist'. Whilst both could therefore, be, taken as exemplifying in their work a radical approach, neither has to my knowledge ever attempted to lay out explicitly an alternative theory or methodology. There is probably a two-fold explanation for this. The first is that they were working on Africa at a time when radical theory was virtually monopolized by a Communism that neither accepted. The second is that they were both raised within a British intellectual tradition profoundly antipathetic to theory.[4] Concerning his theoretical position, therefore, Davidson has said (1971:14)

> One has only got a certain amount of time, and I myself am not concerned with arguing my credentials... the books are there, and they'll do it better.

Davidson and Hodgkin are now, however, rare birds in the radical aviary. A younger generation has matured during a period in which the major obstacle to *seeing* Africa has been the existence of a highly sophisticated and ubiquitous academic theology, and when the Communist monopoly of radical theory was evidently breaking down (see Hobsbawm, 1966). It has been maturing, moreover, in countries like France and the United States, which take theory *seriously*. One justification for an explicit theory has come from Amilcar Cabral (1969:75). Cabral first repeats Fanon's position on the necessity in Africa for ideology, and then extends it from the practical to the analytical plane:

> The ideological deficiency, not to say the total lack of ideology, within the national liberation movements—which these movements claim to transform—constitutes one of the greatest weaknesses of our struggle against imperialism, if not the greatest weakness of all... A full discussion of this subject could be useful, and would... make a valuable contribution towards strengthening the present and future actions of the national liberation movements...
> It is with the intention of making a contribution, however modest, to this debate that we present here our opinion... To those who see in it a theoretical character, we would recall that every practice produces a theory, and that if it is true that a revolution can fail even though it be based on perfectly conceived theories, nobody has yet made a successful revolution without a revolutionary theory.

Gravedigging

Amongst the theoretically inclined radical Africanists the greatest activity has been that of subverting or destroying conventional Western approaches. While much of this criticism is well-informed, original, and likely to impress adversaries there is a considerable danger here of repetition and sterility. If the horse is dying, does it really need such a flogging? Various thoughts of Marx come to mind here: that out-dated theories are defeated not so much by the attacks of opponents as by the increasing irrelevance of the questions they ask and answers they provide; that what is important is to recognize the truth of false ideology, to pick out what is of value in the position of an opponent, even when this opponent is the whole thought of the past.

This is a lesson still to be learned by some radical Africanists in the West. Thus, Bernard Magubane's unselective and undialectical attacks (1968, 1969, 1971) on liberal Africanists have brought down on him the largely justified protests of those he attacked (see van den Berghe, 1970; Epstein, 1971; and Mitchell, 1971). They also compare unfavourably with the more rigorous and balanced–though no less critical–examinations of colonial anthropology by Onoge (1971) and of pluralist theory by Legassick (1971). The danger here is revealed more fully, once again, in Soviet African studies. For Soviet Africanists, mention of Western sources seems to be almost invariably accompanied by undifferentiated condemnation as 'bourgeois', the few 'Marxist' exceptions being usually Communist works, whether serious or merely journalistic (see Letnev, 1970:23). An extreme, though not untypical, example will illustrate this style. A 237-page book by the Soviet historian Chernyak (1968) entitled *Advocates of colonialism*, contains 13 chapters with titles like 'The neo-colonialist historians' crusade...', 'Neo-colonialist distortion...', '... Neo-colonialist defenders', 'False opponents of colonial oppression', 'The reactionary falsifications of the history of the national liberation movements', and even 'Neo-colonialist literature on Neo-colonialism'. This kind of exercise is perhaps better understood in terms of the religious ritual of exorcism. Amongst Africanists its effect is likely to be not so much counter-productive as auto-destructive. What is beyond question is that it creates a barrier through which it is difficult to see the creative work of Soviet writers.

Marxism: implicit, official, and neo

The constructive work of the theorists is most usefully considered in its relationship to that mainstream of post-liberal and anti-bourgeois theory provided by Marxism. We may refer again to the position of Davidson. Following his statement, quoted above, that in one sense he is a Marxist, we find him stating (1971:5–6).

> I think that every serious student of Africa would have to be one. You must be familiar at least with the first volume of *Das kapital*, with *Pre-capitalist economic formations*, with *The civil war in France*, and some other of Marx's writings. And you must have thought about these matters with deep and constant care. Having said that, I would strongly resist the title 'Marxist'.

Explicit in Davidson, this attitude is implicit in much of Hodgkin's work. Davidson is, of course, in good company here: Marx himself denied that he was a Marxist. The shortcomings of what we might call Implicit Marxism are, however, revealed in part by his linking of a Marxist approach simply to economic analysis[5], and in part by the confusion created in the minds of Davidson's interviewers (predominantly young, black, American militants) by his explanations.

From the Implicit Marxists to the Official Marxists. Although there are other Party-Marxisms that share its characteristic short-comings, I will concentrate on Communist Marxism. Anyone interested in seeing the results of this approach should look up the numerous contradictory (and often self-contradictory) Communist analyses of the Nigerian civil war, replete with citations of Stalin on the national problem, Lenin on minorities, and examples taken from Europe in the nineteenth century (see, for example, Dutt, 1969; Kudryavtsev, 1967; Otegbeye, 1968; Zanzolo, 1969; Ledda, 1968; Woddis, 1970). I feel, however, that enough has now been said, here and above, in criticism of Official Marxism. Is there not something that can be said for it? It must, firstly, be borne in mind that with the exception of the South Africans and some Frenchmen, most Communist Africanists have been obliged to work either within the university libraries of Moscow and Leningrad (Potekhin, Olderogge, Kubbel), Leipzig (Markow), or outside them in such places as London (see Kartun, 1954; Cox, 1966; and Woddis, 1960, 1961, 1963). Marked, as it usually was, by dogmatism, eurocentrism, and political pragmatism, the Communists nonetheless preferred and practised a radically different approach to that of the Western establishment. They retained Marx's stress on the mode of production as a key to the understanding of historical development. They insisted on placing African societies within the holistic framework of world imperialism in crisis. They sought explanations for 'that which needs to be explained'–the political and economic inequality *in* and *of* Africa. Thus it is that even when Kubbel (1969) and Malowist (1966) are seeking feudalism in the great states of the Sudan, or Olderogge (1959) is finding early feudalism in pre-Jihad Hausaland, or Suret-Canale (1969) discovering Marx's 'Asiatic mode of production' in pre-colonial Africa, they had nonetheless something to say that was subversive of imperial ideology and that challenged conventional Western Africanists.

After the Official Marxists, a group that might be called Neo-Marxist, although the French *Marxisant* might be more appropriate. It seems to me that a primary source for this revived Marxism was, again, Frantz Fanon. Fanon's lack of interest in the sterile categories of Cold-War Marxism, his presentation of a very different reality from that of the Communists, made it possible and necessary for would-be Marxist Africanists to reconstruct their approach. The kind of re-interpretation this gave rise to may be seen in the socialist debate on Nkrumah's Ghana (summarized in Waterman, 1971). Here a deliberately Fanonist analysis opened long-closed questions, and gave rise to a series of creative reactions. The thought of Amilcar Cabral is much closer to that of Marx than is Fanon's, but his Marxism has a Fanonist cast. It is also refreshingly free of the debased axioms of textbook Marxism and has that independent attitude towards the classics that successful field experience so often brings. Writing in the midst of a revolution, he yet found time to comment critically on the Marxist concept of history (1969:77):

> ... does history begin only with the development of the phenomenon of 'class' and consequently of class struggle? To reply in the affirmative would be to place outside history the whole period of life of human groups from the discovery of hunting, and later of nomadic and sedentary agriculture, to the organization of herds and the private appropriation of land. It would also be to consider–and this we refuse to accept–that various human groups in Africa, Asia, and Latin America were living without history, or outside history, at the time when they were subjected to the yoke of imperialism.
> Our refusal, based as it is on concrete knowledge of the socio-economic reality of our countries and on the analysis of the process of development of the phenomenon 'class'... leads us to conclude that if class struggle is the motive force of history, it is so only in a specific historical period... It therefore seems correct to conclude that the level of the productive forces, the essential determining element in the content and form of class struggle, is the true and permanent motive force of history.

Amongst those who are moving away from the old simplifications we can find an Italian Communist Party official, Romano Ledda, and a leading Senegalese Communist, Majhemout Diop. Ledda's main contribution has been a destructive critique of Stalinist analysis (1969). And Diop has produced an original and sophisticated analysis of actual and possible political alliances in post-colonial Mali (1971). Many other radicals base themselves squarely within the Marxist tradition. One of the most prolific–and most cited–is Samir Amin (see, *inter alia,* 1965, 1970a, 1970b, 1973). Claude Meillassoux (1960) has made a major contribution to an area barely touched on by the classical Marxists, the role of the economic factor in pre-class societies. His empirical work inspired an important theoretical essay on the same subject by Emmanuel Terray (1972). Roger Murray (1966) has written an original theoretical study of the African military régimes. He also raised, in an article on Ghana (1965:68), a problem that Marxists writing on Africa have previously ignored or suppressed:

> Class structure is diffuse and 'politics' is a complex, criss-crossing inter-action of *horizontal* (class, status group, economic group) and vertical (regional, 'ethnic') allegiances and interests.

Although this problem had been raised in general theoretical terms by Rudolfo Stavenhagen in 1966 (see Stavenhagen 1975: 19–39), it was not until 1972 that Immanuel Wallerstein re-thought the theoretical problems arising from African conditions in Marxist terms. His treatment of the relationship between race, nation, and tribe on the one hand, and class on the other is certain to provoke discussion and controversy in the future. In line with Cabral's demand for a new look at the nature of African history, we find the British Marxist historian, V.G. Kiernan (1965), declaring that Marxist history has so far been a history without Africa, and stating that

> by trying to come to grips with Africa, European Marxists may come to learn more about history in general.

His point would seem to have been taken by Catherine Coquery-Vidrovitch, who was stimulated by the debate on the relevance of Marx's Asiatic mode for pre-colonial Africa (CERM, 1969) into producing her own independent characterization of an *African* mode of production. In her model there exists an economic base of subsistence agriculture, a dominant bureaucracy that draws tribute but does not intervene directly in production, and a dynamic consisting in West Africa not of the necessity for great works but for *trade* (see Coquery-Vidrovitch, 1969). Not only is this an original attempt to apply Marxist *method* (rather than Marx's findings) to Africa but it is likely to stimulate lively and fruitful debate in the future.[6] Other writers have addressed themselves specifically to the problem of method. One of these is Anouar Abdel-Malek (1970: 272) who, having criticized two conventional approaches to economic history, recommends a third group of studies

> which has developed recently, trying to combine the use of modern analytical tools with social analysis set in its historical perspective. The problems which are being tackled are, mainly, those of discontinuity, heterogeneity, and the specific character of economic development in different countries of the 'three continents'; the inter-relation between past history and present development, between ideology and socio-economic structure; the reasons for the uneven evolution of different countries; the role of voluntarism and political activism, etc.

Abdel-Malek would certainly consider himself within the tradition of creative Marxism, but in setting out his method he refers both to Marx and Weber who 'albeit in highly different ways, led the way', as well as to C. Wright Mills, whose book *The sociological imagination* he sees as a 'turning-point in the intellectual history of our time'. (Abdel-Malek, 1970:273.)

Syncretic radical theory

Abdel-Malek's paper provides an introduction to a distinct type of radical theory. Weber, if not Wright Mills, might seem incongruous with Marx as a source of ideas for radical Africanists. Yet in three recent radical studies of Nigeria alone we can find direct or indirect references to them alongside references to Marx. Thus, Osoba's study (1970) of the dominant group in Nigeria during the period 1952–65, uses Mills's concept of the 'power élite' in its very title. The Africa Research Group's analysis (1970) of the Nigerian civil war, refers to itself as a 'class-based probe', but then uses the concept of a dominant 'middle class' in ways that owe more to Mills's *White collar* (1951) than to Marx, Lenin, or Mao. Finally, a study of social stratification in Western Nigeria by Gavin Williams (1970) uses both Marxist and Weberian stratification theory, without treating either as subordinate to the other. Perhaps it is going too far to talk of a syncretic radical *theory*, as if its principles had already been worked out. But of the existence of such an *approach* there can be no doubt. It is implicit in the above-cited article of Christopher Wrigley (1971) which shares an approach with Marxists whilst specifically condemning a 'historicism' which it identifies with Marx.[7] It is explicit in Brett (1973) who, whilst admitting the difficulty of producing a 'coherent alternative approach which will lead to a viable programme of action', suggests that [my italics—PW]:

The basis for such an alternative exists in the *liberal, humanist,* and *Marxist* traditions which start from conflict assumptions and which have in some degree and at certain times referred to the 'negation' rather than the maintenance of the existing order.

Is this synthesizing of such apparently diverse thinkers and traditions mere eclecticism? Or is it a return to the Great Tradition of social theory and to the libertarian and humane philosophies of Europe? This latter thought is inspired by the argument of Andre Gunder Frank (1969:36-7) when he appeals to Weber as well as Marx against the narrowness, the abstractedness–and the crudely manipulative prescriptions–of American development theorists.

The theoretical enterprise of the radical Africanists, it would seem to me, can be criticized sometimes for its dogmatism, sometimes for its schematism, sometimes for its eclecticism, and frequently for its lack of rigour. What it cannot be accused of, however, is the asking of irrelevant questions. And it is the posing of urgent and probing questions that is most important at this stage.

Radicalism as an interest

Without necessarily accepting Davidson's suggestion that a discipline could itself be 'productive of radical positions', it is evident that there can be at one time or another some kind of frontline discipline in which problems that are of acute political significance are raised. Davidson states that in the 1950s this discipline was history. Assertion at that time that Africa had had its own states was both called for by the independence struggle and necessary for its conclusion. Since then, sadly, much African history has been concerned with simple assertion and expansion on this theme. The result today is that much African history is limited to producing the founding myths necessary for the present ruling groups. The front line would now seem to have shifted to anthropology and sociology. It is significant that Davidson should have himself shifted in this direction with *The Africans* (1969), the aim of which was to pose a new set of questions:

> The great need now is to put social and cultural *flesh* on the chronological skeleton–to round out the picture, to give it energy and life. It is not enough, for example, to say that Africans had kings. How did these kings get to be kings? Within what socio-cultural structures did they operate, and so on? Otherwise, we shall never really be able to plumb the depths of Africa's history, to see and to appreciate its inner subtleties and mechanisms, to enjoy and portray its specificity.

This movement can also be seen when one contrasts the rather staid activities of Nigeria's History Society with those of its Anthropological and Sociological Association, from whose first conference a number of references in this paper are drawn. (For a report, see Waterman, 1972.) It is notable, moreover, that the radical Nigerian historian, Segun Osoba, makes extensive use of sociological theory in his work. If we look, on the other hand, at Hodgkin's *African political parties* (1961), a radical work written before this new focus on sociology, we find that it largely depended on categories drawn from conventional Western political science, particularly the work of Duverger (see, on this point, Letnev, 1970). Once again, it seems, it is the political needs of the moment (now a break with the structures functional for the incumbent régimes) that puts one discipline to the fore and calls for fresh analysis. If sociology does hold a position at the forefront this does not imply the absence of central struggles *within* other disciplines. An examination of the literature over a period of about ten years, and coming from most of the major national sources, seems to reveal certain problems, areas or themes of special interest to radicals.

It is these that we have attempted to reflect in this collection. The production of any kind of reader naturally involves problems of representativeness, quantity, quality, the finding of items which are short enough or that can be reduced to an appropriate length. The major problem is not so much what is included as what must be excluded. We have attempted to compensate for such exclusions in the bibliography. But the book will stand or fall by its contents, its quality, and its organization of radical writings on African society. The structure of the book, beginning with methodology and ending with politics, is deliberate. And the mottos, taken from Cabral, are meant not merely to decorate but to indicate the keynote for each section.

Thus, the motto to the first section, *methodology,* reminds us of the necessity of a revolutionary theory if we wish to take revolutionary action. The item by Jean Copans is meant to show the historical and social context of African Studies and the theoretical and ideological nature of the concepts it has employed. He shows the intimate connection between these studies and the metropole–satellite relationship. The contribution of Onoge, already quoted from, enlarges on this theme, developing a bitter critique of mainstream sociology and anthropology. The piece by Legassick is concerned with one concept that became popular in liberal African Studies in the 1960s–pluralism. In a balanced but rigorous critique he distinguishes the different uses, shows the relationship between them in liberal scholarship, and contrasts them both with African reality and with a radical approach to this reality. The piece by Brett has also been quoted from. This not only challenges conventional approaches to historical change but also discusses in some detail a radical alternative. Finally, there is the contribution from Abdel-Malek. This is less a polemic than a discussion of the relationship between sociology and history, both liberal and Marxist, and illustrated by an examination of Egypt's past, present, and future.

The next section is naturally on *history,* since it is history that explains the development of present economic, social, ideological, and political structures. The motto from Cabral provides a warning against the vulgar class analysis that in the past was too often the only challenge to the reigning orthodoxy. The contribution by Coquery-Vidrovitch has been discussed above. That of Jack Goody will be referred to below. Like her piece, it is concerned with modes of production. It goes on to discuss the relationship of state forms to the means of production, differentiating Africa from Eurasia on this basis. Walter Rodney's contribution on the pre-colonial African economy provides a contrast with Goody's in its stress on the responsibility of pre-colonial

European trade for Africa's technological stagnation and economic distortion. Philip Ehrensaft's item is a classical piece of class analysis. Tracing the rise of a 'proto-bourgeoisie' in Yorubaland, he not only enables us to understand nationalism in class terms, but also to understand the ambiguous nature of this nationalism later. In his item on the economic effects of French colonialism in West Africa, Jean Suret-Canale complements and up-dates Rodney's piece, and presents an assessment that strongly contrasts with liberal writings on colonial modernization. Finally, John Saul makes a criticism of nation-building history, suggesting that specific socialist questions have to be asked if African historians are to rightly understand the past.

From here on we deal with present processes and structures. First, with the *economy*, which provides the base for all social life; the section being inspired by Cabral's succinct summary of the extent and limitations of capitalist development in Africa. The first of three short items on agriculture, that of Samir Amin, deals with capitalist agriculture in precisely these terms. Ann Seidman shows how post-colonial agricultural policies in Uganda led to virtual stagnation. And David Kom shows how co-operatives have helped capitalist development in Cameroun. Giovanni Arrighi's piece analyses the pattern of foreign investment in reference to the choice of techniques, of sectors, and the development potential implied. Leonnard Goncharov deals with the pattern, extent, and peculiarities of the capital drain from Africa. By analysing the cases of Egypt, the Maghreb and Ivory Coast, Samir Amin undermines arguments about 'the privileged worker' in Africa, stating that it is political relations between the metropolitan and local ruling groups that decides basic questions of income distribution in Africa. His contribution leads logically to Chris Allen's which deals with incomes policies and unions. It shows the importance of political analysis for economic policy, and reveals the repressive intent behind the incomes restriction arguments.

Two last items are based on the experience of Tanzania, the country considered by many radicals to demonstrate a non-capitalist road of development in Africa. The contribution by Shivji on the role of the 'parastatal' (mixed foreign and government) companies in continuing imperialist control in Tanzania provides a corrective to the over-optimistic view of Tanzania. Glyn Hughes presents the positive side, stressing the steps necessary if Tanzania and other African countries are to move towards socialism.

The motto which begins the section on *social structure* stresses a note common to the contributions, that all analysis of social groups must relate them to the colonial or post-colonial régimes and the national or international class struggle.

Cabral contributes an item on the social structure of Guinea which is not only outstanding as an analysis produced by a leading African politician but which is a model of analysis of a whole society. It is followed by two pieces on peasants. Atieno-Odhiambo deals with the development and decline of the peasantry in colonial Kenya. Whilst his piece is largely descriptive, that of Ken Post is theoretical, concerned with the process of 'peasantization' in the West African setting. Peter Gutkind is concerned with another major social group, the city unemployed, and their attempts at self-defence. Writing on Mali, Majhemout Diop deals with the structure of its tiny working class and the role it played within Modibo Keita's 'socialist' state. Jack Woddis reviews evidence on the nature of Africa's bourgeoisie and attempts to judge its potential. Wallerstein's piece on class and non-class stratification has been mentioned above and needs no further description or recommendation. Finally, Gavin Williams produces an analysis of class structure in post-colonial Nigeria that provides a number of interesting contrasts in content and conceptualization to that of Cabral on colonial Guinea.

Next, to *ideology*. Cabral's statement here refers to the necessity today for an ideology related to historical realities and necessities. The contributions deal with both current and past ideologies in this spirit. First, two items on religion. Basil Davidson criticizes the conventional Western attitude to Africa's local belief systems, and shows them as holistic ideologies, capable of both detailed description and prescription. Whilst the implications for non-religious ideologies are here only implicit, in Thomas Hodgkin's contribution they are explicit. Concerned with Mahdism and Messianism, Hodgkin refers to a third revolutionary ideology–Marxism–to throw light on them. Yves Benot deals directly with the impact of one variety of Marxist ideology–Stalinism–on radical African socialists, stressing how the very characteristics that gave it an appeal in colonial times disqualified it from having any value in the complex post-colonial situation. If Stalinism has lost appeal as well as value, this cannot be said for Populism. John Saul's item is an attempt to come to terms with populism, a political phenomenon that is widely spread but difficult to define. R.W. Johnson deals with Sékou Touré, a man whose ideas apparently moved from the first of these patterns to the second. Finally, a savage but pointed critique is made by Otonti Nduka of the attitudes underlying the egalitarian pretensions of the intellectual élite in Nigeria, as revealed by the universities' submissions to a wage commission.

Lastly, to *politics* and the struggle for state power. Here, most of all, there is expressed the cold, hard view of Cabral on the reactionary nature of the post-colonial régimes, the two possible directions of development, and the role of leadership in the struggle for socialism. The section starts again with the peasants. Colin Leys is concerned with the question of whether peasantization in Kenya is likely in the near future to lead to the politics of class struggle or to remain within the framework of a patron–client relationship. His conclusion suggests the latter to be more likely. With Ian Clegg we examine an advanced form of social struggle, the attempt at workers' control in Algeria. Its failure leads him to important conclusions concerning the nature of both the class and its leadership. Two items on the ruling élites follow. Segun Osoba deals with the politicians and businessmen who inherited power–and an electoral system–from the British in Nigeria. Roger Murray is concerned with the military régimes that followed this and other parliamentary ones and are now in power in most African countries. Two items have to do with strategies of societal transformation. Gérard Chaliand's is a classical analysis of a form of struggle still growing in importance–that of guerilla warfare. Majhemout Diop's is an analysis of a form that has suffered almost total failure–that of revolution from above by a radical petty bourgeoisie. The concluding piece by Archie Mafeje poses Africa's basic political choices in terms of current world social structures and world historical development. The option is, he says, between neo-colonialism and state capitalism on the one hand and socialism on the other.

Conclusion: radicals or radicalism?

In the section dealing with approaches I drew a certain line between reformist and radical Africanists. Such a distinction seems reasonable when discussing theory and method but it is more difficult to maintain in reference to applied studies. We have here the problem of Africanists known from their writings, positions, or activities to be politically committed, but who frequently appear wearing an empiricist or positivist hat. We have, conversely, writers whose work and activities might fit them into the mainstream of Western academic African Studies and who yet produce work which one would like to call radical. Thus, Jack Goody, whilst in one case specifically–and justly–attacking the 'palaeo-Marxists' who find feudalism all over Africa, nonetheless uses, fruitfully, the Marxist concepts of 'mode of production' and 'production relations' (Goody, 1971:22). And Tony Hopkins, who starts off an article by dismissing Lenin's theory of imperialism (Hopkins, 1968), nonetheless shows us a process of economic crisis and the resulting concentration of ownership in European hands that not only undermines the school of 'uneconomic imperialism' but also seems consistent with a broad interpretation of Lenin's theses.

Do we have here an *unconscious radicalism* to add to our implicit Marxism? Or are we back to Basil Davidson and his 'radical positions'? The first proposition raises problems best left to philosophers–preferably Hegelian ones. The second has already been treated with a certain scepticism. And yet there is evidently something in what Davidson says. Perhaps the key to the riddle may be found in the second and less common use of the word 'radical'–*primary, fundamental, of the roots.* After all, a major characteristic of conservative African Studies is that despite their frequent sophistication and elegance, their findings are banal and trivial. In this sense, any work which ignores the superficial and epiphenomenal, which uncovers basic structures and root problems, can and should be considered radical. It would seem to me that any definition of radicalism must include this element if it is to be able to exclude the mere striking of political attitudes or mouthing of political platitudes. What one is concerned with, after all, in the development of African Studies is not vehement declaration but the uncovering of concealed realities. Such an understanding, moreover, is not merely an intellectual stance, it is a political programme which *looks out to* and *invites in* all Africanists. The sole criterion–although it might seem to some either pompous or idealistic to say so–is *truth*. This is what Cabral believed and it was why he had to be killed: those who conceal things from the masses, hide difficulties, and claim easy victories, live longer. Cabral here joins up with–and reminds us of–the great tradition of intellectual radicalism. We contemporary Africanists need only remember with Gramsci (who for believing so died in one of Mussolini's prisons) that truth is revolutionary and, with John Hus (who for stating so was burned by the Church), that it will conquer.

NOTES

[1] Brett's concerns closely follow the declared aims of Nigeria's 1970 Development Plan (Nigerian Plan, 1970:32), which states as its five objectives: national self-reliance, a dynamic economy, an egalitarian society, full opportunities for all, and democracy. Whether these aspirations are reflected in the body of the Plan is another matter.

[2] Iliffe actually states that 'the present paper has two objects. The first is to use the greater space available here to investigate and document the process the President has described, by showing how these changes actually occurred in certain areas of the country. The second object of the paper is to suggest that certain other changes have also been at work in Tanganyikan agriculture to reinforce or modify the changes analysed in *Socialism and rural development*.'

[3] Or should this honour be accorded to Morel? Professor Fage has suggested in conversation that it is to the Morel tradition that Thomas Hodgkin rightly belongs.

[4] Hodgkin was a member of the British Communist Party for a number of years before resigning. Davidson was the author (1957) of a condemnation of the Soviet suppression of the Hungarian uprising. As for the theoretical poverty of the British intellectual tradition, this is admirably analysed by Perry Anderson (1969).

[5] How much more Marxism is than its economic element has been brought out recently by numerous social theorists. A useful introduction to Marxism as method is provided by the papers collected in Berger (1969).

[6] Note here, however, Davidson's characteristically cautious note (1971:6): 'I still think it's another obfuscating label. If you *have* to have a label, I'd be content with "the mode of production in Africa"; it says very little, of course, but that's why I like it. It leaves the options open for further research and identification.'

[7] Wrigley has a feeling for whole societies and a sense of history that lifts him above the myopic apologists for neo-colonialism and links him–despite himself?–with the radicals. His unpublished paper (1968) on the collapse of the Balewa régime in Nigeria shows this, and it is often quoted by the younger radicals. All the more shame that he repeats Popper's distortions of Marxism. (For a convincing refutation of the Popper thesis, see Cornforth, 1968.)

BIBLIOGRAPHY

ABDEL-MALEK, A. —1970, 'Social and economic history: a mediation', Cook, M. (ed), *Studies in the economic history of the Middle East*, OUP, London.

AFRICA RESEARCH GROUP —1970, *The other side of Nigeria's civil war*, Africa Research Group, Cambridge, Mass.

AMIN, S. —1965, *Trois expériences africaines de développement: le Mali, la Guinée et le Ghana*, PUF, Paris.

—1970a, *The Maghreb in the modern world*, Penguin, London.

—1970b, 'Development and structural change: the African experience, 1950–1970', *Journal of International affairs*, **24**, 2, 203–25.

—1971, *L'Afrique de l'Ouest bloquée: l'économie politique de la colonisation, 1880–1970*, Editions de Minuit.

ANDERSON, P., 1969, 'Components of the national culture', Blackburn, R. and Cockburn, A. (eds), *Student power*, Penguin, London.

BECKETT, P. —1972, 'Frantz Fanon and sub-Saharan Africa: notes on the contemporary significance of his theories', *Africa Today*, **19**, 2, 59–73.

BERGER, P. —1969, *Marxism and Sociology*, Century Appleton Crofts, New York.

BRETT, E. —1973, *Colonialism and underdevelopment in East Africa*, Heinemann, London.

CABRAL, A. —1969, *Revolution in Guinea*, Stage One, London.

CERM —1969, *Sur 'le mode de production asiatique'*, Centre d'Etudes et des Recherches Marxistes, Paris.

CHERNYAK, Y. —1968, *Advocates of colonialism*, Progress Publishers, Moscow.
COLLINS, P. —1971, 'Ideology, policy and the political development of research in Tanzania', *Institute of Development Studies Bulletin* (University of Sussex), **IV,** 1, 35–42.
COQUERY-VIDROVITCH C. —1969, 'Recherches sur les modes de production africaines', *La Pensée*, Paris, **144,** April, 61–68.
CORNFORTH, M. —1968, *The open philosophy and the open society*, Lawrence and Wishart, London.
COX, I. —1966, *African socialism*, Lawrence and Wishart, London.
DAVIDSON, B. —1957, *What happened in Hungary?*, Union of Democratic Control, London.
—1969, *The Africans*, Longman, London.
—1971, 'An interview with Basil Davidson', *Ufahamu*, **I,** 3, 1–32.
DIOP, M. —1971, *Histoire des classes sociales dans l'Afrique de l'Ouest:* 1: *Le Mali*, Maspero, Paris.
DUTT, R. —1969, 'Britain and Biafra', *Labour Monthly*, London, **51,** 4.
EPSTEIN, B. —1971, 'Comment on Ben Magubane', *Current Anthropology*, **XII,** 4–5, 431.
FRANK, A. —1969, *Latin America: underdevelopment or revolution*, Monthly Review Press, New York.
GOODY, J. —1971, *Technology and the state in Africa*, OUP, London.
HOBSBAWM, E. —1966, 'The dialogue on Marxism', *Marxism Today*, London, **X,** 2, 43–6.
HODGKIN, T. —1961, *African political parties*, Penguin, London.
—1963, 'Islam, history and politics', *Journal of Modern African Studies*, **I,** 1, 91–7.
HOPKINS, A. —1968, 'Economic imperialism in West Africa: Lagos, 1880–92', *Economic History Review*, 2nd series, **XXI,** 580–606.
ILIFFE, J. —1970, 'Agricultural change in modern Tanzania: an outline history' (duplicated), East African Social Science Conference, Dar es Salaam.
KARTUN, D. —1954, *Africa! Africa!*, Lawrence Wishart, London.
KIERNAN, V. —1965, 'The new station states', *New Left Review*, London, **30,** 86–95.
KUBBEL, L. —1969, 'On the history of social relations in the Western Sudan in the 8th to the 16th centuries', *Africa in Soviet studies 1968*, Nauka, Moscow.
KUDRYAVTSVEV, V. —1967, 'African maturity test' (in Russian), *Izvestia*, Moscow, 10 November.
LEDDA, R. —1968, 'Biafra: classi e tribu', *Rinascita*, Rome, 30 August.
—1969, 'Some problems of analysis', *Marxism today*, London, **XIII,** 9.
LEGASSICK, M. —1971, Review of Kuper, L. and Smith, M.G., 'Pluralism in Africa', *Economic development and cultural change*, **19,** 4.
LETNEV, A. —1970, 'Political parties of Africa and Western historiography', *Social Sciences Today*, USSR Academy of Sciences, Moscow.
MAGUBANE, B. —1968, 'Crisis in African sociology', *East African Journal*, Nairobi, **V,** 12, 21–40.
—1969, 'Pluralism and conflict situations in Africa: a new look', *African Social Research*, Lusaka, **VIII,** June, 529–94.
—1971, 'A critical look at the indices used in the study of social change in colonial Africa', *Current Anthropology*, **XII,** 4–5, 419–45.
MALOWIST, M. —1966, 'The social and economic stability of the Western Sudan in the middle ages', *Past and Present*, **33,** 3–15.
MEILLASSOUX, C. —1960, 'Essai d'interprétation du phénomène économique dans les sociétés traditionnelles d'autosubsistance', *Cahiers d'Etudes Africaines*, **I,** 4, 38–67.
MILLS, C. —1951, *White collar*, OUP, New York.
MITCHELL, J. —1971, 'Comment on Ben Magubane', *Current Anthropology*, **XII,** 4–5, 434–6.

MURRAY, R. —1965, 'The Ghanaian road', *New Left Review*, London, **32**, 63–71.
—1966, 'Militarism in Africa', *New Left Review*, London, **38**, 35–59.
NIGERIAN PLAN —1970, *Second National Development Plan*, 1970–74, Federal Ministry of Information, Lagos.
NZIMIRO, I. —1971, Press conference held at the eve of the annual conference of the Nigerian Anthropological and Sociological Association (duplicated), Ahmadu Bello University, Zaria, 16 December.
OLDEROGGE, D. —1959, 'Feudalism in the Western Sudan in the 16th to 19th centuries' (in Russian), *Sovietskaya Etnografiya*, Moscow, 91–103.
ONOGE, O. —1971, 'Revolutionary imperatives in African sociology' (duplicated), Nigerian Anthropology and Sociology Association Conference, ABU, Zaria.
OSOBA, S. —1970, 'The Nigerian "power elite", 1952–65: a study in some problems of modernisation' (duplicated), History Society of Nigeria, 16th annual conference, Ibadan.
OTEGBEYE, O. —1968, 'Healing the wounds of the Republic', *Advance*, Lagos, 23 June.
OTITE, O. —1971, 'Anthropological responsibility in Nigeria' (duplicated), Nigerian Anthropological and Sociological Conference, ABU, Zaria.
RANGER, T. —1971, 'The "new historiography" in Dar es Salaam: an answer', *African Affairs*, **70**, 278, 50–62.
SKLAR, R. —1967, 'Political science and national integration–a radical approach', *Journal of Modern African Studies*, **V**, 1, 1–11.
SOLODOVNIKOV, V. —1969, 'The non-capitalist road of development in Africa', *Marxism Today*, London, **XIII**, 9, 278–82.
—1971, 'Some features of the African countries' non-capitalist development', *Social Sciences*, Moscow, **2**, 117–29.
SURET-CANALE, J. —1969, 'Les sociétés traditionelles d'Afrique et le mode de production asiatique', CERM.
TERRAY, E. —1972, *Marxism and 'primitive' societies*, Monthly Review Press, New York.
WALLERSTEIN, I. —1972, 'Social conflict in post-independence Black Africa: the concepts of race and class reconsidered', E.Q. Campbell (ed), *Racial tensions and national identity*, Vanderbilt University Press.
VAN DEN BERGH, P. —1970, 'Pluralism and conflict situations in Africa: a reply to Ben Magubane', *African Social Research*, Lusaka, **IX**, 681–9.
—1971, 'Research in Africa: knowledge for what?', *African Studies Review*, **XIII**, 2.
WATERMAN, P. —1971, 'Marxist critiques of Nkrumah's Ghana: implications for Africa', *Nigerian Opinion*, Ibadan, **XII**, 7–9, 85–8.
—1972, 'Whither Nigerian sociology?', *West Africa*, London, 18 February, 189.
WILLIAMS, G. —1970, 'The social stratification of a neo-colonial economy: Western Nigeria', Allen, C. and Johnson, W. (eds), *African perspectives*, Cambridge University Press, London.
—1971, 'Sociological explanation and neo-colonialism', Nigerian Anthropological and Sociological Association Conference (duplicated), ABU, Zaria, December.
WODDIS, J. —1960, *Africa: the roots of revolt*, Lawrence and Wishart, London.
—1961, *Africa: the lion awakes*, Lawrence and Wishart, London.
—1963, *Africa: the way ahead*, Lawrence and Wishart, London.
—1970, *Morning Star*, London, 12 and 13 February.
WRIGLEY, C. —1968, 'Some aspects of the political economy of Nigeria' (duplicated), Institute of Commonwealth Studies, London.
—1971, 'Historicism in Africa: slavery and state formation', *African Affairs*, **70**, 279, 113–24.
ZANZOLO, A. —1969, 'The struggle for Nigerian unity', *Political Affairs*, New York, **XLVIII**, 2.

PART II
Methodology: The Weapon of Theory

... we would recall that every practice produces a theory, and that if it is true that a revolution can fail even though it be based on perfectly conceived theories, nobody has yet made a successful revolution without a revolutionary theory.

African Studies: a periodization*
JEAN COPANS

From Jean Copans, 'Pour une histoire et une sociologie des études Africaines', *Cahier d'Etudes Africaines*, Vol., XI, No. 43, 1971, Mouton, Paris. (Translation © Heinemann Educational Books Ltd, 1974.)

In its preliminary stages this periodization draws inspiration from Leclerc's thesis. Later I put forward my own interpretation of the present evolution of African Studies. This periodization, obviously summary, aims at bringing to the fore two different kinds of phenomena; the historical and social context of the theoretical development, and the ideological and theoretical configuration of concepts. I shall proceed in a somewhat formal manner: definition and illustration of a principle, review and illustration of the problems.

Preamble

The evolution of theories and ideologies in African anthropology and sociology is bound up with the nature of the connections between the mother countries and Africa, between the place where the theory was elaborated and the area where it was applied. The form of the connection determines the scientific practice, which in turn justifies, then conceals, and finally calls into question the connection itself. (See Table 1.)

Two observations are necessary concerning this logical and chronological classification. First, the five periods shown in the table overlap one another; there are surviving theories which may remain to the fore long after their justification has vanished. For the theory always comes later than the ideological expression and even later still than the historical context. Second, the political–ideological–theoretical coherence is relative. There are major differences between the countries concerned, for instance between the French colonial policy and the British. And there is reciprocal re-forming of colonial ideological themes into 'scientific' themes, and of the latter into the former. Especially as both are dependent upon a common ideological and social configuration.

*Original English titles and texts have been translated from the French. (eds.)

Table 1

Date	Connection	Ideological–theoretical conformation	Dominating discipline
To 1860	Exploration of Africa	Exoticism of travel and adventure; origins of human society.	Literature, philosophy, accounts of travels
1860-1920	Colonial conquest	Justified by evolutionist theory; possibility of ethnology.	Ethnography, ethnology.
1920-45	Development	Self-justified. Ethnology describes the reality of development without questioning its principle: functionalism which deludes itself and is deluding.	Ethnology, applied anthropology.
1945-60	De-colonization	Massive entry of Africans into history and into science. Consideration of the colonial connection and preceding descriptions. Transition of anthropology to sociology and suppression of scientific exoticism.	Sociology; sociology of underdevelopment.
1960-?	Neo-colonialism	Discovery of illusions of independence. Radical criticism of the connection considered as economic mechanism (imperialism). Marxist revival (following de-Stalinization) which re-occupies the whole theoretical domain of African Studies and pursues unification of anthropology, sociology, and political economy (concept of mode of production).	Anthropology, sociology, political economy.

From origins to the Second World War: advent and domination of ethnology

I shall confine myself to a short study of the following three series of problems:

(a) The advent of ethnology in the field; the transformation of the colonial relationship into an original scientific relationship; basis of the ethnological advance.

(b) Differences between colonial policies and ethnological theories.

(c) Modes of transition from colonial ideology to ethnological practice; choice of themes or research and conditions of elaboration.

1. The functional evolution from the eighteenth century onwards was: traveller, explorer, missionary, soldier, administrator, ethnologist. The autonomy of the last is therefore relative. His function can be read into the pattern previous to the European penetration: traveller, explorer (exoticism); missionary ('civilizing mission'); soldier, administrator (representatives of the political power). Nor must the expedition be forgotten, that collective exploration with chosen aims, often deliberately chosen. This is the transition from the level of amateur dilettantes to that of organized professionals.

The particular importance of this last function should be noted: the physical occupation and its maintainance ('pacification', exploitation) made research possible, research freed of the constraints of maintaining order and *its own security*. The latter condition is indeed fundamental, as it ensured the material and institutional bases of ethnology. In this respect, Gough has every reason for saying, 'Anthropology is the child of Imperialism.'

Ethnology is not a pure or blameless science, and as a *science* it has filled (and continues to fill) a very special ideological function. To quote Leclerc:

> To the Victorians, anthropology was the parlance and the practice of a society which gave itself the alibi, the good conscience and the luxury of a 'scientificity' in its colonial experiences. To the anthropologist in the field, his position as a European has a precise scientific meaning and solely a scientific meaning (methodological): the understanding of social systems assumes a certain externality with regard to such systems. Only an outsider can grasp the entire structure of them. In a word, the anthropologist in the field still regards his European situation as a condition of the knowledge he aims to elaborate.[1]

There is a functional identity within the evolutionist theory (humanity passes through a certain number of necessary stages) which evaluates the superior product of this evolution: western civilization and the colonial ideology, and which justifies its application as a 'civilizing mission', as a transition from an inferior to a superior stage. The titles of books and articles of the period 1880–1910 which Leclerc gives in his thesis are symbolic of this.[2]

2. The differences and contrasts between the British and French schools of ethnology need to be explained in a scientific manner. To begin with, there is the contrast between the indirect rule of the British and the French policy of association and assimilation. The British method has clearly led to applied

anthropology, while in France the 'utilization' of research has never been institutionalized to that extent.[3]

The International African Institute (IAI) was founded in 1926 by Lord Lugard, one of the proponents of indirect rule: an obvious connection. In France, the institution which seems to have played a similar role is the Office for Scientific and Technical Research Overseas (ORSTOM), which only came into being in 1943.

But there are ideological and theoretical causes. British pragmatism led to a theoretical and comparative systematization (Frazer) and to fieldwork properly so-called (Malinowski). In France, on the other hand, there predominated a sociological tradition with a quite different philosophical inspiration. Research 'in the laboratory' (at home) survived much longer, and its preoccupations were chiefly metaphysical: 'elementary forms of religious life', 'mental functions in inferior societies', etc., The Institute of Ethnology was founded in 1926 (the same year as the IAI, which was already seeking results to apply). But it was not until 1931–33, with Griaule's Dakar–Djibouti expedition, that French Africa became a scientific field. (This expedition was a natural sequence to the major technical exploits of white men at this period– the Citröen rallies, Paris–Saigon, crossing of the Gobi Desert, etc. Dakar–Djibouti was the crossing of 'French' Africa, the supremacy of Western power. We had come a long way from simple ethnographical curiosity.)

So to the differences and contrasts between the two schools of ethnography must be added the backwardness of the French compared with the British. This leeway of some 15 years was not overcome until the early 1950s.

3.   Within these ideological and theoretical outlines there are three levels which constitute a coherent whole: the *themes* of research, the *form* of the work, and the *concepts* utilized.

(a)   Great Britain: applied anthropology, functionalism, and acculturation.

In a quite empirical manner the British defined the main branches of anthropology and sociology: economic and political anthropology, culture contact, and change. The functioning of the colonial system implied a minimum of knowledge of local societies and its effects upon them. The different theoretical tendencies (Malinowski, Radcliffe-Brown, Evans-Pritchard) had this in common: an approach to societies as collections of institutions, of functional relations, or productions. So there was an obvious tendency in this theoretical field to take, as far as possible the social totality as a *system* (whatever the manner, moreover, of explaining its functioning).

The need to find political continuity in African society in order to ensure a beginning of indirect rule was the reason for political anthropology. 'Find the chief', as Malinowski would have said; and in 1940 appeared *African political systems*. In another part of the world, Firth set forth the principles of economic anthropology. Acculturation in a wide sense had some success, and in the early 1930s the British examined the problems of migration and work in industry (the Rhodesian and South African mines). Hunter's *Reaction to conquest* was published in 1936. I do not intend to discuss the criticisms of this research–the misappreciation of the inequality of the acculturation phenomenon, the mechanism of the functional explanation, etc. But what should be borne in mind is the great interest given to the 'solid' problems of political and economic consequence, and the reference (even if illusory) to a world social situation, and the institutional form that research in Anglophone Africa was taking: development of institutes and universities which were autonomous though not independent (Rhodes–Livingstone Institute).

(b) France: monograph–catalogue, total social. fact, technology, and cosmogony.

Contrary to the pragmatism and empiricism of the British, French ethnology between the wars synthesized, paradoxically, the faults of philosophical idealism. The ideological and theoretical configuration described above, combined with a colonial administrative policy which was more direct, led French ethnology to grant the conception of the world as 'social facts', conveying the totality of social relations, in the manner of Hegelian logic.[4] French ethnology sought the principles of social life and not the nature of the relationships or the systems which constituted it. Moreover, after the founding of the Musée de l'Homme in Paris and the interest taken in a museographical collection, there was a descent to the formal level of the monograph–catalogue, facts presented according to a pre-established order which does not give the relationships between the various orders of phenomena.

At the conceptual level properly so called, the idealism of Griaule is obvious: the mind accounts for and is the basis of the social concept, and African societies are worthy of interest because their spiritual forthcomings are quite the equal of 'ours' (of Christianity, obviously).[5] To this idealism is added an ideological vision of the colonial phenomenon as a boon or blessing.[6] The ambiguous and mechanistic problem of acculturation has no place in this theoretical field–*it cannot exist*. Which is why the consideration of this problem resulted in a breach–the transition of ethnology to sociology– while in Britain things were much less decisive.

Advent of sociology and de-colonization (1945–60)

For an analysis of this period I shall take the French school as my basis almost exclusively; and for an obvious reason–it was in France that a sociology devoted to Africa clearly emerged. And the French school caught up on the British during the 1950s (in fact some people think that the French forged ahead). The forming of a new discipline devoted to African Studies was an important event; sociology was not just a new specialization, it constituted a complete break on several counts; empirically, as it was taking into consideration the real history of the African peoples; in scale, as it moved on from the village to national social groups (from 'mini' to 'maxi'); theoretically, as a materialistic and historical explanation took the place of Griaulian idealism which ignored the realities of colonialism. This break eventually allowed a fresh analysis of 'traditional' societies, as the theoretical re-formulation was brought to bear upon a new and defined subject, the modern sector and the consequences of the colonial phenomenon. The interest even to modernization turned into the sociology of underdevelopment.

The best example and the chief artisan of this break is obviously Balandier. The titles and themes of his published work between 1950 and 1955 speak for themselves.

The theoretical structure supporting these themes is based on three principles: a) African societies have a history ('traditional and modern') and are dynamic and contradictory; b) the social and ideological movements of the present reveal both the structure in the past and the modes of change induced by the colonial situation; c) the colonial situation is a global phenomenon and of an unequal nature. The colonial phenomenon is thus called in question through an examination of the movements which themselves question it: messianisms, syncretisms, ideologies, and political parties.[7] The position taken by Leiris in 1950 corresponds to this. In his *L'Ethnographe devant le colonialisme* he emphasized the significance of colonial exploitation and the scientific interest inherent in the study of the 'developing people'.[8]

It is not a figure of speech to explain the transition of ethnology to sociology interms of a break. This theoretical development corresponds to the rise of African nationalism (and of the Third World in general) and to the *break* in colonial relations which asserted itself as a constituent part of the study. A few dates, while being no more than indications, will demonstrate the maturity of the break: 1945, riots in Algeria; 1947, uprising in Madagascar; 1946–53, French war in Indo-China (Vietnam); 1947–49, strikes in French West Africa; 1952, Mau-Mau uprisings; 1947, independence in India; 1949, socialism in China; 1955, Bandung.

But other factors of a different nature intervened to determine the possibilities of a break, in particular the institutional framework of French research. Leclerc has rightly emphasized the 'freedom' of French anthropologists who were not engaged in (and so not controlled ideologically and institutionally) an applied anthropology whose explicit function was *the maintenance of the colonial connection*.[9] And there was also theoretical criticism of the implications and acquired knowledge of Griaule, which were quite unable to take account of the new social and historical dimensions of African Studies.[10]

However, during the late 1950s African sociology asserted itself. At the institutional level there was a general development led by Gurvitch. At the political and ideological level, the Algerian war made students and intellectuals sensitive to colonial problems of national liberation and underdevelopment. The early 1960s saw the spread of independence; and African sociology, which had already received recognition at research institutes, was given official support with the appearance of the *Cahiers d'etudes africaines* (1960) and the award of degrees in the sociology and history of Tropical Africa (1963).

But independence did not sound the end of history. It was the end of an epoch (colonialism) and the beginning of another (neo-colonialism). The coming to power of the African 'élite' partly changed the form of the problem. This new situation involved a theoretical radicalization. I shall now examine why this was so.

Unification of the human sciences and the Marxist problematic (1960 onwards)

The appearances of independence need to be explained–the underdevelop-

ment, the struggles for national liberation, and the class struggles in the decolonized countries. There was a collapse of anti-colonial unity. The political
alliances before independence practically disappeared, but the economic
exploitation continued and even became more intense. A new theoretical
field therefore asserted itself in Marxist terms (world economic market,
repression of struggles for liberation, military intervention): the world system
is an imperialist system. Capitalist economy induces a certain development
of social classes; traditional societies have an economic structure; African
societies can be analysed in terms of means of production.

There are three reasons for the approach to African societies in Marxist
terms only becoming possible after 1960:

(a) Marxist thought found new life after 1956. But as Africa had never
been a subject of reflection for the founders (Marx, Engels, Lenin) it was a
virgin theoretical field; and this was its great attraction, in conjunction with
the political support given to the movements for liberation and independence.

(b) Balandier's approach was close enough to Marxism for the transition
from a dynamist to a Marxist explanation to be made by filiation and not by
rupture (as previously). Whilst there was a contradiction between the dis-
avowal of the colonial system and its theoretical recognition, the use of
concepts of the imperialist system or modes of production was facilitated by
an explanation in terms of unstable arrangements and the dynamism of
contradictions.

(c) The characteristics peculiar to neo-colonialism led to research into the
economic roots of exploitation and into the *political and revolutionary* solutions for the overthrow of exploitation, and so to the adoption of a Marxist
perspective.

I shall endeavour to give the main outlines of the problems inherent in
African Studies today and the manner in which this new Marxist tendency[11]
(specifically French, it must be emphasized) attempts to resolve them. The
importance of what follows will escape no one, as it concerns the daily thought
and action of the specialists in African Studies. The basic problems arise
from three different fields or provinces:

(a) political awareness of the ideological and institutional context of the
research and its implications; (b) attempts to elaborate a Marxist problematic
relating to African societies (traditional and modern); (c) improvements in
methods of study and removal of barriers between the different human
sciences.

1.   The awareness (a) is in the first instance empirical, for Africanism is a
combination of ethnology, sociology and its variants, geography, and
semantics. From the time of independence (and even before, in fact) the
African leaders, political and intellectual, have been distrustful of ethnology,
likening it, rightly so, to the paternal concern of the West for the irresponsible
black child. Later, and for political reasons, the distrust extended to sociology,
which could describe the socio-economic and ideological bases of the existing
governing power[12], an additional reason for the low number of African
ethnologists and sociologists.

Despite independence, cultural inequality still exists–African Studies are
still the prerogative of the West. Moreover, the great majority of research

workers fail to see that they are a cause of this inequality and contribute to its continuance.[13] In general, for professional reasons (career) and because of local attitudes (governmental incapacity and distrust) the knowledge obtained is not re-employed on the spot. Scientific research, by its very objectivity, is participating in the cultural exploitation of the African people, and is both an alibi and an instrument for world imperialism.

The second International Congress of Africanists, held in Dakar in December 1967, was an occasion for a clear expression of this phenomenon by African and European research scientists. But the resolutions which were passed have scarcely produced any obvious effect so far; they were certainly no more than a concession by the majority of those attending the Congress, who represented the Western 'establishment' of African studies.[14]

2. The elaboration of a Marxist attitude to the problem was at first the work of a few lone researchers. And even at the present time it is of a select and heterogeneous nature, for the theoretical divergences between Marxists are as numerous as those between Marxists and non-Marxists. Moreover, many people call themselves Marxists without having read Marx. This elaboration covers the classic fields of ethnology and sociology: explanation of traditional social structures in Marxist terms (modes of production, social inequality, exploitation, ideological function, etc.), and definition of the inequalities of the colonial situation in imperialist terms, as a world system of economic and political exploitation.

To the extent in which the development of Marxist thought has been and remains the driving force of this elaboration, it has undergone all the general divergencies of an ideological, political and theoretical order. Thus the theoretical considerations of Althusser, Godelier, and Bettelheim have had more or less contradictory effects. In any case, it is impossible to understand the sense of certain divergencies, apparently of a purely scientific or theoretical order, without considering the larger context; for instance, that one Africanist, Suret-Canale, is a member of the central committee of the PCF (French Communist Party), another, Terray, leads the Maoist group within the PSU, while Meillassoux has no connection with either party.

It was Suret-Canale who, in 1958, inaugurated these new Marxist researches in the field of African studies. Later he concentrated on colonial history and the possible application of the 'Asiatic mode of production' to the societies of Black Africa. The other pioneer of Africanist Marxism was Meillassoux, whose theoretical considerations sought a basis for economic anthropology. In 1966 a Marxist from the Cameroons and leader of the UPC demonstrated the need for a scientific and political analysis of neo-colonial societies. That same year saw the publication of the work of Godelier, a contribution to the elaboration of an economic anthropology. Following this, Meillassoux produced an original theoretical analysis, though its principle was contested by Terray. Finally, the work of the economist Amin permitted a more precise definition of the nature of the economic and political problems with which African societies have to deal.

Since 1965 a more or less disparate body of researchers has identified itself with this new tendency, either partially or entirely; among them are Amselle, Augé, Althabe, Bonnafé, Copans, Dupré, Rey and Waast.[15] But before proceeding to the third problem (c), note should be made of the almost natural disappearance of the ethnology–sociology antinomy within this tendency.[16]

3. At the present time a quantitative and qualitative development of field studies is noticeable. On one hand there is a multiplicity–admittedly relative–of collective and inter-disciplinary studies; on the other, new themes of research are appearing for theoretical, ideological, and practical reasons– for instance, the study and the recording of oral traditions for historical, literary, or linguistic ends, and the study of barter and economic production at village and national level. These new themes, these new theoretical trends, imply the perfecting of new study procedures and the employing of modern techniques: aerial photography, audio-visual aids, computerized data, statistical refinements, etc. These new procedures and techniques provoke theoretical reflection. More than ever, the scientistic division of theory– practice (method–technique) appears deceptive. The new theoretical develop- ments cannot be isolated from their thematic specialization and their practical studies, and the opposite applies too.

Moreover, the re-shaping of themes raises the question of the classic division of disciplines.[17] For one thing, the political sciences need to widen their field to include agronomy, even pedology and climatology, for studies of agricultural production, and economics and statistics for studies of sectors of production (even villages).[18]Collaboration and discussion are bound to become essential for theoretical elaboration; the ethnologist or sociologist (or even the linguist) working alone becomes a thing of the past, and anthro- pological or sociological science is no longer possible in such conditions. Just as historical modifications of the subject studied impose unification on the human sciences and remove the isolationism of disciplines, so must the research worker drop the anti-scientific alibi of solitude and accept 'collective epistemological vigilance'.[19]

The final consequence of this phenomenon is to question the basis of ethnology–observation from without, from the exterior. This basis appears illusory for a) ideological reasons; b) a reason of principle, epistemological and theoretical–the unity of the human sciences corresponds to the unifica- tion of the laws of their functioning. The modes of functioning of each society do not refer to the particular theoretical principles but to different procedures; c) ethnologists and sociologists from the 'ethnological' societies challenge it.

NOTES

[1] One can compare this conclusion, which I fully endorse, with the point of view of Lévi-Strauss: '"A left-over from colonialism," is the remark sometimes made about my investigations. The two things undoubtedly have a common bond, but it would be false in the extreme to take anthropology as the final remnant of the colonial spirit—a shameful ideology possibly giving it a chance of survival. What we call Renaissance was a real birth for both colonialism and anthropology. In confrontation since their common origin, an ambiguous dialogue has been taking place for four centuries between the two. If colonialism had never come about, the advance of anthropology would have been less tardy, but perhaps anthropology would not have been driven, as has since happened, to question the whole of humanity in each of its specific examples.'

2 The titles given by Leclerc are: Mason, *The uncivilized mind in the presence of higher phases of civilization* (American Association, 1881); Wilson, G.S., 'How shall the American savage be civilized?' (*Atlantic monthly*, 1881); Bordier, *La colonisation scientifique*, (1884); Orgeas, *La pathologie des races humaines et le problème de la colonisation* (1889); Giraud, *De l'éducation des races; étude de sociologie coloniale* (1913); Saussure, L. de, *Psychologie de la colonisation* (1890).

3 For a detailed analysis of indirect rule and its consequences for anthropology, and of the French approach, the reader is referred to Leclerc's thesis. I quote two extracts which are very revealing of the difference–and of the fundamental sameness of these two colonial policies:

Governor Clozel wrote in a circular in 1909: 'We cannot impose upon our subjects the provisions of French law, which are obviously incompatible with their social condition. But neither can we tolerate that certain customs which conflict with our principles of humanity should be beyond all authority... Our firm intention to respect customs cannot be allowed to put us under an obligation to preserve them from the march of progress. With the aid of the native courts it will be gradually possible to introduce a rational classification, a generalization of practices, compatible with the social condition of the people, and to bring these practices more and more in line with our basic principles of natural law, the source of all legislation.'

Lord Lugard (who had been Governor of Nigeria) wrote in a political memorandum in 1919: 'The policy outlined in this memorandum must obviously be applied with sympathy and success–especially in the tribes which do not yet recognize a sovereign king. It is essential that these tribal organisms (*sic*) and social customs be not only fully included but also used as a framework on which to build. It is to be hoped that the purposes for which the many native societies–which have a great influence on the native mind–exist will be studied in full, considering that they can become valuable factors in a system of native administration adapted to these tribes.'

4 The total social phenomenon of Mauss had an immense theoretical success, and research scientists as different as Balandier and Lévi-Strauss refer to it. But does not this conception of a phenomenon, this reflection of the whole social relationship and structure, contain a large dose of Hegelian idealism (history is but the realization of the Mind and the result already existed before our origins)?

5 One has only to read the preface to *Dieu d'eau* to be convinced of this point of view: 'These men live on a cosmogony, metaphysics, and religion which put them on a level with the peoples of antiquity, and which Christology could study with profit.'

And here is an extract which explains the idealistic methodology of Griaule: 'Myths appear in layers like the coatings of a seed, and one of their reasons for existing is precisely to cover up something precious which apparently belongs to a valuable and universal knowledge. Myths find expression in various ways, not only verbally; they underlie all activities, civil and legal institutions, family, religious and technical institutions. By that I mean that customs in the legal sense, civil or religious rites, etc., and the agents of all the activities, therefore present panels of knowledge, panels which themselves fit together to form the panorama of the world from the point of view of the mind.'

6 Griaule was a Counsellor of the French Union from 1947 to 1956. The spirit of Griaulian ethnology can be judged by an extract from Leclerc which needs no comment: 'The self-complacency of some civilizers who have not studied ethnology condemns a little hastily a whole range of institutions which have stood the test of time... Not all the native customs and techniques need perhaps be rejected... otherwise the colonizing action, which ought to be a collaboration bearing fruit, will find itself shackled, slowed down, set aside by misunderstandings, errors and slight-

ings and mutual incomprehension... This is why Rivet said that there is no good colonization without well-conducted ethnology... It would be anachronistic to colonize gropingly when light shed by scientific observation permits it to be done with clarity and knowledge.'

(Record of Transactions of the International Congress of the Cultural Evolution of Colonial People, Paris, September 1937, pp. 15–16.)

[7] See the studies and researches of Mercier. The collaboration of Balandier in founding *Présence africaine* was due to his desire to provide a means for Africans to express themselves.

[8] Leiris took part in the Dakar–Djibouti expedition and participated in the research work of Griaule. There was a break there too.

[9] This context had a double effect and the contrary to the British context: a positive effect by the absence of applied anthropology and the relative freedom of the researcher with regard to the colonial system; a negative effect through a centralized system of research which greatly limited the Africanization of research and even of universities.

To the extent in which, after independence, the 'élite' took over the colonial institutions as they stood, Anglophone Africans were able (relatively) to take charge of the institutions of applied anthropology and even the universities. The Francophone universities, with the exception of Dakar University, are post-independence creations, and are therefore *directly* an element of the neo-colonial policy of cooperation; as such, the staffs are 75 percent French and the programmes 100 percent French. Moreover, the local institutes were less important than their British counterparts, and in any case are still run by French organizations and researchers.

Consequently it is not surprising that there should be a relatively large number of Anglophone sociologists, historians, and linguists as opposed to only a score or so of Francophone equivalents. There are other factors, too, which limit the number of research workers and university graduates in the political sciences in both Anglophone and Francophone Africa.

[10] This criticism, political and ideological as well as theoretical, was certainly new in the early 1950s, as the following quotation from a book on colonization clearly demonstrates: 'It is an absolute misconception to support autonomist theses with ethnological arguments. There can be no question of denying that the presence of the French is in the interests of the native populations. Everywhere in the overseas territories, instead of violence, civil war, and pillage there is now peace, the basis of all progress. There is not a single territory where the withdrawal of authority would not bring fresh outbreaks almost at once.'

[11] I shall emphasize later the heterogeneous nature of this tendency and the reasons for it. This is of course a personal interpretation. My tentative periodization aims at bringing to light the dominant tendencies in African studies; their appearance is given chronologically, but each new tendency does not cancel out the old, especially as in the present situation the method of filiation prevails over that of rupture, whereas in the 1950s it was the reverse.

[12] This distrust turned into ignorance in the linguistic field, due to the doubts as to the cultural ascendancy of the language of the late colonizing power. Finally, only geography came out of it not too badly; its latent positivism went very well with the prevailing ideology, which lacked the means of criticizing it and even vaunted a non-ideological attitude (analysis of the visible, the physical, the 'measurable').

[13] Here the objective function needs to be distinguished from the ideology of the objective function. Indeed, it is possible for an Africanist researcher to question the ideology which dissembles and accompanies its objective function, but his 'revolutionary' engagement does not for all that remove the system of domination of African research by Western research, *of which he is part whether wanting to be or not*. It is

not a case of extolling the virtues of the *status quo* in return, but of realizing that ideological criticism (the kind here being developed) does not suffice; we must proceed from 'weapons of criticism to criticism by weapons'.

[14] There was, for instance, the peremptory statement made by Forde, the chairman of the Congress and president of the IAI: 'It must be admitted that in many cases the colonial governments did much for the Africans.'

[15] This list is not exhaustive, neither is it selective; the names are merely those of friends and colleagues who are likely to accept such a grouping together.

[16] Balandier had already prepared the way for this disappearance, as his 'current sociology' is also ethnology. But this is going beyond the African scene, for it concerns the two disciplines in a world context. See the criticisms of Frank on this point.

[17] Meillassoux proposes a theoretical formation corresponding to the research problems and not in terms of the traditional cleavages.

[18] Economy is not meant here in the sense of classic political economy but that of theory of the capitalist economic system, therefore 'modern', which functions in Black Africa. See the comments of Godelier on the distinctions between classic political economy, and economy, and economic anthropology.

[19] Note the comments of Chodkiewicz, writing about the natural and the exact sciences: 'Although the Nobel Prize is awarded by scientists who ought to know all the circumstances, still no notice is taken of the profound changes brought about by the advent of two things about which even the ordinary public has become aware–the growth of big sciences which require much expensive equipment, and *the necessity in most disciplines of supplanting individual action by teamwork*.' (My italics.)

And the following extract from another work, which also gives a detailed analysis of the above-mentioned necessity, is of interest in this connection: 'By constantly confronting each scientist with a clear criticism of his work and its suppositions, and thereby obliging him to take it into account when communicating his findings, this "system of cross-control" will tend to form and maintain an aptitude for epistemological vigilance.'

BIBLIOGRAPHY

AFANA, O., *L'économie de l'ouest-africain*, Paris, 1966.
ALTHUSSER, L., *Lénine et la philosophie*, Paris, 1969.
AMIN, S., *Trois expériences africaines de développement: le Mali, la Guinée et le Ghana*, Paris, 1965.
AMIN, S., *Le développement du capitalisme en Côte d'Ivoire*, Paris, 1968.
AMIN, S., *Le monde des affaires sénégalais*, Paris, 1969.
AMIN, S., and COQUERY-VIDROVITCH, C., *Histoire économique du Congo, 1880–1968*, Paris, 1969.
BALANDIER, G., 'La situation coloniale: approche théorique', *Cahiers Internationaux de Sociologie*, **XI**, 1951.
BALANDIER, G., 'Contribution à une sociologie de la dépendance', *Cahiers Internationaux de Sociologie*, **XII**, 1952.
BALANDIER, G., 'L'anthropologie appliquée aux problèmes des pays sous-développés', Paris, 1954–55, 3 fasc. ronéo.
BALANDIER, G., *Sociologie des Brazzavilles noires*, Paris, 1955.
BALANDIER, G., *Sociologie actuelle de l'Afrique noire*, Paris, 1955.
BALANDIER, G., 'Tendances de l'ethnologie française', *Cahiers Internationaux de Sociologie*, **XXVII**, 1959.
BOURDIEU, P., CHAMBOREDON, J.-C., and PASSERON, J.-C., *Le métier de sociologue*, **I**, Paris, 1968.
CHODKIEWICZ, M., 'Le mât de cocagne', *La recherche*, 7 décembre 1970.

Iᵉ CONGRES INTERNATIONAL DES AFRICANISTES, 'Résolutions, Dakar, décembre 1967', *Présence Africaine*, 66, 1968.

COPANS, J., 'Le métier d'anthropologue', *L'homme*, **VII**, 4 1967, et **IX**, 4, 1969.

COPANS, J., 'Dossier sur les responsabilités sociales et politiques de l'anthropologue', *Les temps modernes*, 293–94, décembre-janvier 1970–71.

EVANS-PRITCHARD, E.E., and FORTES, M., *African political systems*, London 1940.

FORDE, D., 'Anthropology and the development of African Studies', *Africa*, **XXXVII**, 4, 1967.

FRANK, A.G., *Le développement du sous-développement*, Paris, 1970.

GODELIER, M., *Rationalité et irrationalité en économie*, Paris, 1966.

GRIAULE, M., *Dieu d'eau*, Paris, 1948.

HUNTER, M., *Reaction to conquest*, London, 1936.

KRISTEVA, J., *Recherches pour une sémanalyse*, Paris, 1970.

LECLERC, G., 'Anthropologie et colonisation (analyse et idéologie dans la théorie 'africaniste')'. Thèse de Doctorat de 3ᵉ cycle, Paris, EPHE, VIe Section, 1969, ronéo.

LEIRIS, M., 'L'ethnographe devant le colonialisme', *Les temps modernes*, 58, août 1959. (Republished in *Cinq études d'ethnologie*, Paris, 1969.)

LENINE, V., 'Matérialisme et empiriocriticisme', *Oeuvres*, **XIV**, Paris, 1962.

LEVI-STRAUSS, C., *Lecon inaugurale au Collège de France*, 5 janvier 1960, Paris, 1966.

MANDEL, E., *La formation de la pensée économique de Karl Marx*, Paris, 1967.

MEILLASSOUX, C., 'Essai d'interprétation du phénomène economique dans les sociétés traditionnelles d'auto-subsistance', *CEA*, 4, **I**, 1960.

MEILLASSOUX, C., *Anthropologie économique des Gouro*, Paris, 1965.

MEILLASSOUX, C., 'Elaboration d'un modèle socio-économique en ethnologie', *Epistémologie sociologique*, 1–5, 1964–68.

PIAGET, J., *Logique et connaissance scientifique*, Paris, 1967.

PIAGET, J., *L'épistémologie génétique*, Paris, 1970.

POIRIER, J., and LEROI-GOURHAN, A., *Ethnologie de l'Union Française*, Paris, 1953.

POULANTZAS, N., *Pouvoir politique et classes sociales*, Paris, 1968.

SAREVSKAYA, B.I., 'La *Méthode de l'ethnographie* de Marcel Griaule et les questions de méthodologie dans l'ethnographie française contemporaine', *CEA*, 16, IV–4, 1964.

SERRES, M., 'La réforme et les sept péchés', *L'Arc* (nᵒ consacré à G. Bachelard), 42, 1970.

SURET-CANALE, J., *Afrique noire occidentale et centrale*, Paris, 1958.

SURET-CANALE, J., *L'ère coloniale 1900–45*, Paris, 1964.

SURET-CANALE, J., 'Les sociétés traditionnelles en Afrique tropicale et le concept de mode de production asiatique', *La Pensée*, 114, avril 1964. (Republished in *Sur le 'mode de production asiatique'*, Paris, 1969.)

TERRAY, E., *Le marxisme devant les sociétés 'primitives'*, Paris, 1969.

WANE, Y., 'Réflexions sur la recherche sociologique en milieu africain', *CEA*, 39, X–3, 1970.

Revolutionary imperatives in African Sociology

O.ONOGE

Paper presented at the First Conference of the Nigerian Anthropological and Sociological Association Conference, Ahmadu Bello University, Zaria, Nigeria, December 1971.

The unilaterally decreed normative value of certain cultures deserves our careful attention. One of the paradoxes immediately encountered is the rebound of egocentric, sociocentric definitions.
There is first affirmed the existence of human groups having no culture; then of a hierarchy of cultures; and finally, the concept of cultural relativity. We have here the whole range from overall negation to singular and specific recognition. It is precisely this fragmented and bloody history that we must sketch on the level of cultural anthropology.

Frantz Fanon[1]

The history of Africanist sociology has very few redeeming features. In the main, it is perverse and counter-revolutionary from an African standpoint. And unless the new generation of Africanists achieve a radical departure from the past orientation, there can be no justification for the incorporation of the discipline in African universities and research institutes.

Only a skeletal review of this sordid history is possible here.[2] The review will focus on Africanist anthropology not because it is the most culpable, but because, unlike the case of Europe where the social sciences developed somewhat independently in a parallel fashion, in Africa, anthropology was the primary and omnibus discipline which provided the essential data on the African on which the other sciences depended as they reached the continent. The morbid perversion of much of Africanist anthropology has therefore been inherited by the Africanist manifestations of sociology, psychology, political science, and economics.[3]

The white man's burden

To be sure, the sociological sciences have never been immune from criticisms and reformulations from within. The very fact that we have had shifts in theoretical and methodological frameworks such as evolutionism, diffusionism, configurationalism, functionalism, and the like, testify to a certain internal dynamism in these disciplines. However, to my mind, the most significant diagnosis of the paralytic condition of the 'science of man' has been Kathleen Gough's famous essay in which she linked the evolution and subsequent methodological craft of anthropology to the rise of Imperialism.[4]

For her, the coincidence of empirical anthropology with the expansion of 'Western Capitalist imperialism' (to use her own terminology) was not a temporal accident. Rather, an essential harmony did develop between the two social movements–a harmony which is blatantly reflected in the offensive congruence between colonial cartography and the nationality of ethnographers.

> Before the Second World War, fieldwork was almost all done in societies under the domination of the government of the anthropologists own country; occasionally, under that of a friendly Western Power. In the Old World the imperial powers were clearly recognizable and predominantly European. The world of most American anthropologists was, of course, different from that of Europeans, for the primitive people chiefly studied by Americans were conquered Indian groups who had been placed in reservations.[5]

As anthropology followed the flag into Africa, the discipline and the allied sciences became an elaborate rationalization of the 'White Man's Burden.' To my mind, the white man's burden has been and continues to be the dominant aspect of Africanist social sciences. There have, of course, been changes in the rhetorical garb which Kipling's imperial slogan has worn in the development of Africanist social sciences.

Here come the Hamites

Initially, Africanist anthropology wore a relentless racialist garb in the search for Hamites. The tradition of fieldwork anthropology, we recall, developed as a reaction against the ethnological speculations of predominantly armchair Victorian evolutionists. The excesses of the evolutionists had rendered historicizing suspect among early fieldworkers. Yet in the initial confrontation between systematic anthropology and the African milieu, ruins such as Zimbabwe which indicated some past cultural achievements provoked a historical explanation. An orthodox evolutionist of Tylorian or Morgan's bent would have, in the first instance, attempted an ethnological explanation by placing the burden of these cultural developments on the autonomous inventive abilities of tropical Africans. As we know too well this did not happen. On the contrary, ethnologists like Seligman deflected the dynamic from tropical Africa and produced this scandal:

> indeed it would not be very wide of the mark to say that the history of Africa south of the Sahara is no more than the story of the permeation through the ages, in different degrees and at various times, of the Negroes and the Bushmen by Hamitic blood and culture. The Hamites were, in fact, the great civilizing forces of black Africa from a relatively early period, the influence of the Semites being late and in the main confined to the 'White' areas north of the Sahara inhabited by Hamitic peoples.[6]

As Olderogge pointed out long ago, the invention of the Hamites as an ethnographic category stemmed from a reactionary ideology of racialism and a refusal of bourgeois social scientists to confront the Marxian approach to socio-cultural development.[7]

What is equally important is the profile of the cultures of black peoples that was implicit in the Hamitic theory of African development. The image of the cultures of black peoples was one of total inertia. Blacks were engaged in an unreflective connubium with nature–especially its wild 'jungle' African manifestations–with neither the urge nor the will to break from this savage harmony. This first 'scientific' image of Africa was in every way congruent with the 'Darkest Africa' image which had sedimented in British thought in the nineteenth century.[8]

To be fair, the image was not exclusively British. It was general to Europe of the time. For had not Hegel said:

Africa proper, as far as history goes back, has remained for all purposes of connection with the rest of the world–shut up; it is the Gold-Land compressed within itself–the land of childhood, which laying beyond the days of self-conscious history, is enveloped in the dark mantle of night.
The Negro as already observed exhibits the natural man in his complete wild and untamed state. We must lay aside all thought of reverence and morality–all that we call feeling–if we would comprehend him; there is nothing harmonious with humanity to be found in this type of character.
At this point we leave Africa never to mention it again. For it is no historical part of the world; it has no movement to exhibit. Historical movement in it—that is in its northern part—belongs to the Asiatic or European world...
What we understand by Africa, is the unhistorical under-developed spirit, still involved in the condition of nature...
The history of the world travels from East to West, for Europe is absolutely the end of history, Asia the beginning.[9]

The functional amnesia of functionalism

Racialist interpretations of African development generally suffered an eclipse with the introduction of structural–functionalist anthropology. There were three reasons for this eclipse. First, not only did functionalist anthropology suspect history, it banished it entirely. Synchronic analyses therefore had no necessity to explain socio-cultural developments in Africa. Freed from this necessity, the Hamitic theory of development fell into quiet hibernation. We may point out, however, that synchronic a-historicism in Africanist anthropology carried the implication that the African past was itself *unknowable*. In this, the anthropologists had the support of bona fide historians who had dismissed oral accounts as inadmissible historical records. Second, functionalist anthropology had responded strongly to the climate of liberal tolerance in Europe by inventing the ethically neutral concept of 'Cultural relativity'. Guided by this concept, anthropologists conceded cultural integrity to all human groups. Third, as is now well established, the first bulk of anthropologists were in the employ of the colonial governments. Colonial governments were not interested in history but in pressing issues of the moment, such as law and order. These bureaucrat scholars, in their

African studies, reflected the social control/solidarity problematic faithfully.

Let us, in the first instance, mention some positive results, though unintended, that arose from the functionalist perspective. For example, the doctrine of cultural relativity gave early African nationalists some scientific room for arguing their case. They could, thenceforth, in face of the objective superiority of Western technology, argue that Africans nevertheless had rich cultures with humane emphasis, which were sufficient grounds for recapturing their freedom. We need not add that one of these cultural nationalisms–Senghorian negritude–has today become a reactionary fetter to African liberation.[10] Moreover, these a-historical ethnographies have ironically become sources for reconstructions in the works of several contemporary Africanist historians and African artists.

These gains aside, the consequences of Africanist functionalism were however more damaging. First the concession of cultural integrity was often more *formal* than substantive. The ethnocentric devaluation of non-European cultures and a corresponding inflation of European aesthetics and ethics intruded readily on every ethnographic page. As my colleague, Dr Ikenna Nzimiro has shown in a forthcoming article in *Theory and practice,* derogatory terms like 'savage', 'primitive', 'native', 'simple', 'uncivilized' were consistently used as modes of reference for the African by even the most liberal anthropologists.[11] The free use of these terms has created the irony of functionalists who, having castigated evolutionists for their 'stages of development' theories, have themselves introduced a new hierarchy. The only difference being the substitution of dichotomies–primitive/civilized, simple/complex, etc.–for the trichotomies–savagery/barbarism/civilization–which informed the works of the evolutionist anthropologists.

But by far the most disastrous consequence of the functionalist Africanists was their general amnesia over the objective social situation in which Africans were at the time implicated. I refer of course to the colonial situation. This amnesia was demonstrated in two major ways. First, the unit of study always remained the 'tribe'. The new colonial social systems in which these 'tribes' were encapsulated received cursory mention only as geographical benchmarks. The African reality for the functionalist cartographer remained a plurality of primordial 'tribes' whose mutual monadic isolation was periodically shattered by warfare in pre-colonial times. The practice of this exclusive focus of interest on the small unit without any substantive reference to the larger colonial socio-cultural milieu is especially revealing when re-situated in the very discipline which defined its boundary *vis-à-vis* other social sciences in terms of its special 'totalistic' or 'wholistic' approach. In practice, it was a partial totality that Africanist functionalists were willing to consider. References to the colonial presence and its consequences for the pre-colonial totality were perfunctory and prefatory, and not implicated, as one would have expected from the reified tower of structural–functional ideologies, in the substantive analytical experience.

For example, the sociological consequences of the brutal conquest of African peoples in the very process of their incorporation into the *Pax Brittanica* are calmly ignored by British anthropologists. The undeniable tragic consequences of imperial sadists like Cecil Rhodes are unheard of in the ethnographies on Zimbabwe Africans. Evans-Pritchard in his classic work on Nuer society which he described as 'organized anarchy' dissociated the following passage from his central analysis:

> In 1920 large-scale military operations, including bombing and machine-gunning of camps, were conducted against the Eastern Jikany and caused much loss of life and destruction of property. There were further patrols from time to time, but the Nuer remained unsubdued... From 1928 to 1930 prolonged operations were conducted against the whole of the disturbed area and marked the end of serious fighting between the Nuer and the Government. Conquest was a severe blow to the Nuer... [12]

Synchronic structural functionalism as we know has itself been subject to criticism from within the ranks.[13] This criticism has usually reduced to the charge that, in its concentration on harmonies, it produced a 'totalization without contradictions'. However, while not challenging the validity of this criticism, we must insist that at the time these 'traditional' communities were studied, it was not the contradictions among their supposedly pristine institutional clusters that should have received primacy but the very contra-diction of *life in a colony* which had become the fundamental existential datum. This central contradiction was hardly ever broached.

On the contrary, whenever it became impossible to retain a blissful amnesia over the colonial situation, this fact was introduced by way of several mysti-fications. For example, the very concepts of imperialism and colonialism with their harsh associations of *exploitation* were either written in quotation marks or tamed, chloroformed, and deflected into safe concepts like 'British Administration', 'Government', 'Social change', and others which in no way were suggestive of the raw quality of the black man's burden in the colonial setting. In a fit of applied anthropology, appropriate theoretical schema with ingenious ritual checks were developed to embrace the tabooed subject in a grand distortion. 'Natives' with 'backward sloping' labour curves and time orientations were invented to offer their 'cultural resistances' to the civilizing innovations of the 'culture–contact' wonderland.

Those anthropologists, like the Wilsons, who defected and insisted on a sociology of structures saw colonialism as a contact of systems of unequal scale. The micro-scaled African societies were in this contact milieu enjoying an expansion of scale. The only problematic of the contact was one of 'uneven-ness of scale'. This unevenness could and did produce 'maladjustments', 'ordinary oppositions', 'radical opposition', 'disequilibria'. However, the potential insights of a 'network' perspective were lost in an unforgiveable vulgarity. Consider the major example of 'radical opposition' or 'disequili-brium' offered by the Wilsons:

> The Nyakyusa, to take a simple facet of the disequilibrium in which they are involved, lay great emphasis on hospitality. Entertaining his friends is an obligation of a rich man enforced on him not only by conventional pressure–the stingy man loses prestige–but also by fear of witchcraft, 'the breath of men', legitimately used by his cheated neighbours. Hospitality is dependent upon polygyny, for only by the labour of more than one wife can a household grow and prepare enough food to entertain well. Christians

are thus in a dilemma. They value both monogamy and hospitality. If a Christian takes a second wife he is suspended from membership of the Church, probably lives in fear of hell fire, and is ashamed before Christians and pagans alike, for the conflict is not only between Christian and pagan, but within the Christian group itself. If he is inhospitable he is both afraid of witchcraft and again ashamed. Often we saw Christian wives struggling to get through more work than they could manage, in order to entertain as they wished to do. The opposition can only be resolved by social change, economic or religious. Either there must be greater division of labour so that the well-to-do may buy some of their food, more provision of water in the villages, mechanized milling to replace the laborious hand grinding, and the employment of servants; or, on the other hand the abandonment either of hospitality, or of monogamy. Radical opposition is even less tolerable than ordinary opposition, and social change always does and always must follow its occurrence. In BuNyakyusa, adjustment in the situation described was in fact beginning. A few well-to-do Christians employed youths to help in fieldwork, and in fetching wood and water; while coffee, requiring relatively little preparation, was offered to visitors rather than home-brewed beer.[14]

The upshot of applied anthropology was its speedy degeneration into applied colonialism.[15] Colonialism was defined as modernization. All that a liberal posture required was the advocacy of *Indirect Rule,* though without the racism of the *Dual Mandate.* This advocacy was to ensure minimal 'disequilibria' in the 'painful' process of a 'desirable' westernization. African peoples who showed some proclivity towards Westernization and individuation were heralded as 'progressives' in a series of 'receptivity-to-change' studies.[16]

As Marvin Harris has pointed out, functionalist anthropology proved unable to predict the rise of the national Liberation movements in Africa. They could not because they had defined colonialism as modernization and prepared themselves to serve its cause without any complexes. We do not exaggerate. In 1927, Malinowski, the father of applied functionalism in Africa was explicit:

> The practical value of such a theory (functionalism) is that it teaches us the relative importance of various customs, how they dovetail into each other, how they have to be handled by missionaries, colonial authorities, and those who economically have to exploit savage trade and savage labour.[17]

In 1950, the collateral ancestor of the theory, Radcliffe-Brown hoped that *African systems of kinship and marriage* 'will be read not only by anthropologists, but by some of those who are responsible for formulating or carrying out policies of colonial government in the African continent.[18]

Two years earlier (1948), the dean of applied functionalism in Africa, Lucy Mair, had expressed her apprehension of the national liberation movements in a paper with the revealing title, 'Self government or good government'. Warming up to the false dilemma she had posed, the only case she could make for African freedom was in Joyce Caryean terms:

> Everyone has a right to be miserable in his own way. If a people prefer to democracy, arbitrary justice to the rule of law, contaminated

water to drains, poverty with leisure to hard work and higher real incomes, it is no one else's business. From this position one can look on at communal massacres, dacoity, famine or near famine, and reflect that whatever sufferings these events may cause to however many individuals, they are as nothing to the recognition of the principle that every people has the right to conduct its own affairs in its own way. One may regret these events, but one has no right to invoke the argument that under colonial rule they would not have occurred...

The removal from key posts in colonial territories of a large number of persons who worship efficiency will have its effect on the way things are done in future in those territories. Will the result of their going be felt in the form of hardship? In a great many cases, probably not. If trains are not clean or punctual, surgical instruments not always sterilized, university qualifications not recognized as equivalent to those obtainable in Britain, this is a small price to pay for freedom and it may not even be felt as a price.[19]

For our part we draw attention only to the empirical reality of colonial Angola, Mozambique, Guinea-Bissau, South Africa, Namibia, and Zimbabwe where Africans are enjoying Lucy Mair's enchanted colonialism.

Caliban on the couch

The distortion of the colonial situation was not accomplished by structural functionalists alone. Anthropologists with a culture-and-personality persuasion and ethno-psychiatrists partook of the fraud. In a work which began with a declaration of the necessity for studying the 'human significance of colonial situations', Mannoni betrayed the promise by reducing *the situation* to an encounter between 'two entirely different types of personality'– the colonized and the colonizer.

For him the colonizer and the colonized do not elicit a contradiction but rather a felicitous blend of complementary personality needs. The colonized with his 'dependence complex' has a psychological hunger for passive servitude whereas the colonizer with an 'inferiority complex' in his own country has a psychological need to dominate others especially in the vacant world of non-European peoples. In the colony the will to dominate and the will to be dominated blend to provide a harmonious psycho-social system. Exploitation theories of imperialism are false, because according to Mannoni, 'there is no doubting the fact that colonization has always required the existence of the need for dependence. Not all peoples can be colonized: only those who experience this need.[20] Third World peoples already possessed collective unconscious expectations of rules from across the seas. And from his particular ethnographic study of Madagascar he reached the conclusion that national liberation struggles arise from the 'threat of abandonment' rather than from the desire to be free.

Other Caliban studies of Africans followed in which the 'inferiority' of the African is not derived from his race but on the cultural roots of his personality formation. Two of the most famous studies by Richie[21] and Carothers[22] sponsored separately by the Rhodes–Livingstone Institute and

UNESCO reach the same conclusions of a predominant infantilism in the adult African personality. They blame this 'lobotomized' personality not on race but on practically every African institution—the family, child-rearing practices, age-grades, initiation rites, and religion. There can be no mystery about the implication of these studies—which is that, as 'permanent children', Africans cannot be self-governing.

Continuity and change in Africanist sociology

The image of Africa in contemporary African Studies has shed a great deal of the racism and paternalism of colonial scholarship. Colonialism itself is now a dirty word and not many contemporary Africanists are in sympathy with it—at least in print. The changed intellectual climate is of course traceable to the changed political climate of independent African nations in which Africanists of various disciplinary backgrounds have now to work. The growing presence of assertive and articulate Africans in the fields of politics, history, and culture has also been a strong influence in the positive revision of the African image in the sociological sciences.

However, although black is now beautiful in contemporary Africanist literature, the contemporary social science has not moved beyond this expressive phase to provide the strategies that will assure black beauty with a black power base in the foreseeable future. In fact, the new sociology has not even begun to present an *honest* diagnosis of the objective problems of African nations. Instead, like its colonial past, the prescriptions of the new sociology are in the main diversionary and reactionary.

Consider the dominant theme of contemporary Africanist social science which goes by the names 'modernization', 'social change', or 'development'. The issue of macro *change* is not only valid in terms of the aboriginal linkage of these disciplines with social contention, but also, because the necessity for change is a pressing empirical reality in Africa. The true character of contemporary Africanist sociology is therefore decipherable from its approach to this theoretical and empirical issue.

The results of our diagnosis may be summarized in this fashion. Which is that modernization and development studies overwhelmingly engage in a psycho-cultural analysis. Like the case, in bona fide colonial scholarship, African cultures are held as the primary obstacles to development. Any incidental institutions (nucleated families, two-party government, de-politicized bureaucracy and the like) found in the advanced industrial capitalist societies are held to be part of the *sine qua non* for development. In short the vision of a developed Africa is a replication of Western culture and social arrangements. The contemporary crisis of these advanced capitalist states now being articulated by the youth movements is carefully hidden in the advocacy of the Western model of development.[23]

At a more psychological level there is now an intense interest in the examination of our cultures for traces of *achievement motivation*. In the specific case of Nigeria, an anthropologist has assured us that our development is predicated on the quality of our fantasy lives.[24]

Following Cold War rhetoric, contemporary Africanist social science assures us that what we have to prove is whether we can stem the incursion of 'totalitarian communism' by the development of 'democratic' institutions of the West. Responding to this challenge two generations of African states-men (civilian and military) as well as the African intellectual establishment announce Western democracy as their aims or, in a fit of petty nationalism, spend their intellectual energies in proving the democratic character of their cultural traditions.

The obstacle to political modernization and stability is cultural *tribalism*. The role of external counter-revolutionary squads openly located in foreign embassies and the inability of the internal neo-capitalist economies to deliver the goods are muted.

The issue that is never raised in the modernization movement is the objective historical sources of African underdevelopment. The slave trade is irrelevant! Colonialism is past! Neo-colonialism is a myth!

Towards a revolutionary sociology

Despite the prescriptions of the modernization movement and its easy access to the local centres of power in Africa in the form of a variegated corps of 'experts', Africa remains brutally wretched and with no foreseeable prospect of escape. For those of us who know this crushing poverty both intellectually and existentially, it is time to question the *received* theories, their diagnoses and prescriptions.

Frantz Fanon has already provided the guidelines for a sociology of African liberation. To escape from a sociology of conservation of our underdevelop-ment requires that we push these elementary facts into the threshold of consciousness.

First our cultures are not to blame. As Fanon has shown, our cultures are neither more mystical nor less rational than the cultures of other peoples.[25] If anything, the fragmented foci of contemporary Africa is not a derivative of our traditional cultures but a derivative of our ready adoption of a colonial mentality. Our poverty is traceable more profitably to the two traumatic historical experiences of the slave trade and colonialism. If received moderni-zation theories are silent on the contributions of the slave trade and colonial-ism to the modernization of the West, need we acquiesce in this? For 400 odd years the West received from the Third World free labour and free resources. No ethical posturing is called for on our part–although such posturing would not be baseless. All that is needed is to recall these historical experiences and we reach the inevitable conclusion that our interaction with the West since the fifteenth century has contributed to their rapid development and our *simultaneous* underdevelopment.

As Andre Gunder Frank has argued eloquently, during the colonial phase of our interaction with the West certain structures were introduced to faci-litate our incorporation into the capitalist social system. Our political inde-pendence and attempts to develop have been illusory because of the persist-ence of the exploitative metropole-satellite structures.[26] The subservience of our intellectual establishment, our literature, news media, and political behaviour to the West derives from this unequal power relations inherent in our asymmetrical structural bondage.

Today, we find that the historical circumstances in which we must develop are altered in this fundamental respect. We cannot, even if we wanted, have the benefit of free labour in the form of slaves or colonized natives to inject into our production process. Modernization theories that ignore this are scientifically defective in that respect.

If sociology is to be relevant to the contemporary African situation, it cannot be a sociology that runs around chasing mythical socio-cultural resistances to an even more mythical modernization, but a sociology that searches for the strategies for structural disengagement from the capitalist system. The only alternative to that is to constitute ourselves, as at present, into a service corps producing sales managers, personnel managers, and public relations men for the more efficient exploitation of our peoples by UAC 'developers', and the internal comprador élite.

Our position is not original. Political leaders like Nkrumah, Sékou Touré, Nyerere, and sociologists like Magubane[27]–to name only Africans–have reached these conclusions. Our purpose has been to ensure that they would not remain a perennial minority in a sea of false internationalism and reformist liberalism.

Political, intellectual, and financial obstacles will be put in the way of an Africanist sociology dedicated to this structural disengagement. But we ought not to retreat to the old position where Africans are important only as academic subjects. It is our duty to identify with their aspirations. If courage is what we need, there are several sources of inspiration in the African past. In 1890 when the Yao people were given the ultimatum of voluntary surrender or invasion by Hermann von Wissman, a German imperialist, their chief, Macemba, wrote back in Kiswahili in the following words:

> I have listened to your words but can find no reason why I should obey you–I would rather die first. I have no relations with you and cannot bring it to my mind that you have given me so much as a *pesa* (fraction of a rupee) or the quarter of a *pesa* or a needle or a thread. I look for some reason why I should obey you and find not the smallest. If it should be friendship that you desire, then I am ready for it, today and always; but to be your subject... I do not fall at your feet, for you are God's creature just as I am... I am sultan here in my land. You are sultan there in yours. Yet listen, I do not say to you that you should obey me; for I know that you are a free man... As for me, I will not come to you, and if you are strong enough, then come and fetch me...

NOTES

[1] Frantz Fanon, 'Racism and culture', in *Toward the African revolution,* Monthly Review Press, 1967.

[2] A detailed review entitled, *The 'native' as anthropologist: the colonial factor in the rise of the social sciences in Africa,* has been published under the auspices of The Nigerian Academy of Arts, Sciences and Technology, Ibadan, 1974.

[3] My colleague, Dr Dayo Akeredolu-Ale disagrees with this contamination hypothesis. On the contrary, he holds that all the sociological disciplines, regardless of the sequence of their emergence in Africa, derive from a common spring of Western intellectual prejudices.

[4] Kathleen Gough, 'World revolution and the science of man', in Theodore Roszak (Ed.) *The dissenting academy*, Random House, 1967.

(Her article appeared initially in *Monthly Review* under the frank caption, 'Anthropology, child of imperialism'.)

[5] Kathleen Gough, ibid. p. 128.

[6] C. G. Seligman, *Races of Africa*, London, 1961, p. 10 (3rd edn).

[7] D. A. Olderogge, 'The Hamitic problem in Africanistics' in *Soviet ethnography*, 3, 1949, pp. 156–170.

(Translated from the Russian by Mr P.O. Dada.)

[8] Philip D. Curtin, *The image of Africa: British ideas and action, 1780–1850*, London, 1965.

(This book systematically explores the process of sedimentation of negative images of Africa in British thought.)

[9] Quoted by Ngugi-wa-Thiong'o (James Ngugi) in his 'The writer and his past', *Mazungumzo*, **1**,2, Winter 1971.

[10] The definitive critique of Senghorian negritude and its Sartrean enthusiasts has been accomplished by the Dahomean philosophy professor, Stanilas Adotevi, in his famous paper, 'Strategies of culture', presented at the Pan-African Culture Festival in Algiers, 1966.

[11] Ikenna Nzimiro, 'Anthropologists and their terminologies' to be published in the forthcoming journal, *Theory and practice* (Journal of the Nigerian Academy of Arts, Sciences, and Technology).

[12] I owe this insight to Perry Anderson, 'Components of the national culture', *New Left Review*, 50, July–August 1968. Incidentally, Anderson in this same article argues that even this measure of holism in British Anthropology is a profound advance over the theoretical and methodological mould of British Sociology which stayed at home. According to him, Britain is unique in the Europo-American world for failing to produce either a classical or Marxist sociology with synthetic or global conceptual system. In its stead, British sociology was defined by an 'atomized empiricism'.

[13] Cited by Perry Anderson in *op. cit.*

[14] Godfrey and Monica Wilson, *The analysis of social change*, Cambridge, 1965, pp. 126–7.

[15] A detailed study of the works of three leading applied anthropologists, Lucy Mair, Audrey Richards, and Monica Wilson, is in preparation.

[16] It is interesting to note that in general societies which currently enjoy the appellation of 'progressive', 'democratic' in anthropology were the same societies that suffered from 'statelessness' at a time when African kingdoms enjoyed pride of place among earlier anthropologists.

[17] Quoted by Marvin Harris in his *The rise of anthropological theory*, New York, 1968, p. 558.

[18] Quoted by Marvin Harris, *ibid* p. 547.

[19] Lucy Mair, *Studies in applied anthropology*, The Athlone Press, London 1961, pp. 65–67.

[20] O. Mannoni, *Prospero and Caliban: the psychology of colonization*, Praeger, New York, 1964, p. 85.

(For a penetrating critique see Fanon's essay 'On the so-called dependency complex' in his *Black skins, white masks*, Grove Press, New York, 1967.)

[21] James Richie, *The African as suckling and as adult*, Rhodes-Livingstone Publication.

(It is interesting that an anthropologist of Max Gluckman's stature could claim in his preface to the paper that Richie's 'psychoanalytic' interpretations *complemented* his own sociological work.)

[22] James Carothers, *The African mind in health and sickness*, UNESCO, 1954.

[23] Incidentally, Malfred Halpern argues that the indices of modernization being prescribed by American social scientists were achieved most fully in Nazi Germany. See his 'A redefinition of the revolutionary situation' in Norman Miller and Roderick Aya (eds) *National liberation: revolution, in the Third World*. The Free Press, 1971.

[24] Robert A. LeVine, *Dreams and deeds, achievement motivation in Nigeria*, Chicago, 1966.

[25] On this issue of supposed cultural resistances, see especially Fanon's *Studies in a dying colonialism*, Penguin, 1970.

[26] Andre Gunder Frank is solid. On this issue see his famous critique of liberal theories, *Sociology of development and the underdevelopment of sociology*, Pluto Press, 1971.

[27] Magubane is, to my mind, the most exciting Africanist sociologist today. He has written papers on 'The crisis of African sociology' and in an issue of *Current anthropology*, he subjected the Manchester 'School' of urban anthropology to severe criticism.

PART II

The concept of pluralism: a critique
MARTIN LEGASSICK

Originally published as a book review in *Economic development and cultural change*, Vol., 19, No. 4, July 1971, University of Chicago Press, Chicago.

What is 'pluralism'? The contributors to this volume[1] which originated in papers presented to an interdisciplinary colloquium arranged by the African Studies Center, UCLA, in the spring of 1966, offer a variety of definitions and perspectives. But this variety is, perhaps, embraced by a definition along lines such as these: pluralism exists when diversity of culture and institutional practice or structure occur within a given society and where such divergences cluster to demarcate distinct and often virtually closed social sections. (Leo Kuper, indeed, introduces a conflicting notion of pluralism: as the concept used by some American theorists to denote that condition of multiple affiliations, intersecting lines of group cleavage, which is supposed to underpin 'liberal democracy'. The use of the same term by Kuper and other contributors for this diametrically opposed phenomenon is a confusing red herring.) Many of the issues of debate in the volume arise immediately from the definition. Few societies, for example, have an entirely homogeneous culture, with members sharing an identical system of institutions. (In pre-colonial Africa, as a masterly essay by M. G. Smith demonstrates, such was often not the case.) Hence, one needs to ask under what conditions a diversity of culture and institutional practice does produce social cleavage and under what conditions it does not. Furthermore, what holds societies together or, indeed, what constitutes a society under conditions of acute social cleavage? And what constitutes a society in the more general case? Smith, in an earlier essay, demonstrated how the tendency of social scientists to define culture and society in terms of each other made them not only unable to deal with pluralism, but also inadequately able to formulate a viable conception of a 'society'[2]. Moreover, what is the relationship between pluralism and social oppression? It is a curious fact that a valid and initially theoretical concern with the stability and continuity of social structures becomes transmuted by social scientists into a moral imperative. In other words, there is a theoretical distinction, at least, between social cleavage on a horizontal level, expressed at its maximal dimension by separate societies, and social cleavage which implies differential access of the social segments to socially valued resources.[3] The ideal type of the second case is the plural society, in which one social segment (a minority?) exerts total domination over other subordinate sections. Clearly, a solution in the first case is societal separation, whereas in the second case a solution is elimination of differential access. But where 'stability' is a moral imperative, social scientists find societal separation intolerable: 'intersectional conflict threatens the very existence of the society,' writes Kuper (p. 17), as if it were the continuance of the system of social relations, rather than the justness of the social relations themselves, that was the prime moral issue—hence, Kuper's fear of 'polarization' under conditions of pluralism, without reference to the content or context of that polarization. Finally—and 'polarization' is an example—there is the question of the distinction between 'objective' forms of social structure and the subjective perception of these and of whether, indeed, such a distinction can be made. Smith is criticized by several contributors for neglecting the subjective dimension, although even he is not consistent in this (see, e.g., pp. 30, 50).

One does not expect answers to these perennial questions to emerge in one book, although the contributions to this volume make plain that the concept of pluralism casts new and fruitful perspectives on them. The backbone of the book consists in three dense essays by Smith, in his customarily idiosyncratic style, and four by Kuper. Additional theoretical contributions are provided by Pierre van den Berghe, Ali Mazrui, Leonard Thompson, and Max Gluckman, while Pierre Alexandre (French-speaking Africa), Basil Davidson (Zambia), Hilda Kuper (Asians in South Africa and Uganda), and Michael Lofchie (Zanzibar) present case studies. It is not without interest that only one of these contributors is American-born and that most of the remainder have lived large parts of their lives in archetypal 'plural societies', at least five in South Africa. The volume is a rich one, containing a variety of insights on a range of theoretical and specific issues. A review such as this cannot do justice to such diverse contributions and my concentration on what appear to be the central themes and assumptions is by no means intended to disparage the remainder of the work.

The concept of the 'plural society' owes its currency to the writings of Furnivall on Asian colonies.[4] Furnivall was himself concerned with the nature of social relations and the forms of societal integration in conditions which Balandier would later define as the 'colonial situation'.[5] But, even within this volume, the concepts of the plural society and pluralism have been taken in a variety of directions. Kuper, for example, has directed himself primarily (though not entirely) toward a refinement of this analysis to the situation of white-settler societies such as South Africa and to the means by which peaceful evolutionary change can be achieved in such societies. All the authors are also aware of that rather different form of pluralism which exists in the 'new' African states: here, it is horizontal social cleavage rather than stratified pluralism which is regarded as the central problem, the solution to which emerges as 'national integration'. Smith, on the other hand, strongly influenced by Nadel,[6] attempts to integrate the concept of pluralism to a general theory of comparative institutions. In a rigorous, though constantly elaborated, treatment, he detaches pluralism from its colonial context to apply it to a wide variety of historical and contemporary societies. For him, pluralism becomes *one* mode by which collectivities may associate and is defined by their 'differential incorporation' into a 'common political society'. The 'collective character [of the system of differential incorporation] and the scope of its substantive differentiation, must be sufficiently rigorous and pervasive to establish an effective order of corporate inequalities and subordination by the differential distribution of civil and political rights and the economic, social and other opportunities that these permit or enjoin' (pp. 27–28, 91, 430). Furthermore, 'the decisive conditions that constitute and perpetuate social pluralism consist primarily in differences of institutional organization in the *public* domains of segregated collectivities identified as the basic corporate units of social structure' (p. 52; italics mine).

Undoubtedly, Smith has made the most inclusive, the most precisely formulated, and the most difficult attempt of all the contributors toward a theory of pluralism. The depth and range of his reading, as expressed in the descriptive and analytical material on which he draws, is truly stupendous: the effect of this and his style is to encourage total acceptance or total rejection by the reader. However, in trying to avoid either, the following may be noted: (*a*) although a society, according to Smith, is a 'self-sufficient, self-perpetuating and internally autonomous system of social relations' (p. 29), in practice Smith takes societies as *politically* defined, and politically in an often narrow sense; (*b*) Smith is a political determinist, and, hence, as a quotation above illustrates, it is by removing 'civil and political' disabilities that pluralism is eliminated; (*c*) for Smith, horizontal social cleavage without differential incorporation is not pluralism: indeed, he would define such cases as 'equivalent' incorporation by which society 'is constituted as a consociation of complementary or equivalent, but mutually exclusive, corporate divisions, membership in one of which is prerequisite for citizenship in the wider unit' (p. 434); (*d*) his typological approach excludes, as other contributors point out, an analysis of pluralism as a variable parameter; (*e*) in another dimension, his comparative and typological institutional approach excludes qualitative distinctions, for example, between pre-industrial and industrial societies or between pre-colonial and colonial societies. Smith's method forces him to treat colonial societies as 'arbitrary products of historical combinations' (p. 429) and to deny any form of qualitative social evolution.

There is a further dimension along which pluralism could be analysed, which is mentioned only parenthetically by Smith (p. 57) and which may relate to his ambivalence concerning the plural or equivalent status of such social relations as symbiosis (p. 94) and clientage (p. 56). This dimension, which it is difficult for Smith's corporate bias to include, would distinguish the level at which differential incorporation was instituted and enforced in the society. The extremes would constitute plural social relations, collectively established and maintained at the societal level from those which were instituted and enforced predominantly at the personal level (such as, clientage, some types of slavery, as well as many people would argue, the status of 'wife'). My own study of a South African frontier zone suggests that eighteenth-century frontiersmen did not act as a corporate group, except at an ideological level, in 'differentially incorporating' non-white dependants. The role of the British in the nineteenth century in giving these 'Hottentot' dependants equal civic status was then to transform this 'personal pluralism' to the level of collective enforcement. It would seem to be characteristic of white-settler groups to wish to maintain such personal pluralism. This is why the Trekkers complained of British 'interference in the relations between master and servant'. Davidson, quoting a twentieth-century Zambian white settler, substantiates the point nicely: the 'natives... are not governed in the sense that they are legislated for by the people, but they are governed by the people who employ them' (p. 221). To postulate such a transient situation of personal pluralism in the case of the creation of a colonial society might also clarify the problems raised by Alexandre (pp. 202–3), Davidson (p. 218), and Thompson (p. 353).

The theory of pluralism represented by the diverse contributions to this volume, not only attempts–at least in Smith's case–to provide a *total* and inclusive perspective on social relations, but also to prescribe valued forms of social structure. These are the 'heterogeneous' societies of Smith, the 'consensus pluralism' societies of Kuper, and the 'pluralistic or homogeneous democracies' of van den Berghe, as well as other similar definitions. Holland and the Scandinavian countries emerge as the purest types (p. 35). Such a prescription explicitly ignores the role of class–analysed in terms of the relations of production, distribution, consumption, and exchange–as constituting a form of 'differential incorporation' into the corporate groupings of the society and, hence, providing a basis for social cleavage as potent as any other form of pluralism. Indeed both Kuper and van den Berghe (pp. 77, 459, 477) do at times mention class as a possible base of pluralism, and the latter notes (p. 68) that 'to the extent that classes are corporate groups, they will develop subcultural differences and some class-specific institutional structures'. Smith, on the other hand, argues that the acquisition of 'citizenship, education, and effective industrial and political organization' by the 'hitherto disenfranchised' transformed the social structures of European nation-states from pluralism in the eighteenth century to heterogeneity in the twentieth. Such a statement both reflects his political determinism and is inconsistent with his approach to other societies, which stresses real and substantive rather than formal factors.

There are several reasons why the contributors minimize the significance of class. First, 'class' is more manifestly a source of cleavage today on the international than the national level (despite recent events in France and Italy); and only a few contributors even mention, let alone develop, the concept of a society broader than the nation-state: for example, Thompson (pp. 368–69), Hilda Kuper (pp. 279–80), Leo Kuper (pp. 462–64, 469). In other words, imperialism is totally ignored. Second, Kuper assumes that bases of pluralism other than class are more likely to induce 'primordial sentiment' or 'total identity' (p. 460). But, if the 'progressive compounding of collectivities' is a fundamental feature of historical process, as Smith follows Spencer in asserting (p. 93), then it would seem that identification with such a collectivity has been no more transcendental than identification with a class.

A third reason for the neglect of class and latent class cleavage stems from a more general inadequacy of social theory which the concept of pluralism was intended to modify. The assumption, explicit or implicit, of many of the contributors, an assumption derived from Durkheim, is that the functional specialization characteristic of 'advanced' societies leads to interdependence and, hence, cohesion and stability (see, e.g., p. 35). Were this the whole truth, it would still not say anything about the dimension of 'justice' as opposed to that of 'order', but it is not even this. This partial analysis is in itself loose: Gluckman's valuable contribution to the volume points out the lack of sophistication in terminology dealing with conflict and cohesion. But the analysis is also partial. It refuses to deal dialectically with contradictory aspects of the same phenomenon. Kuper is closer to the mark in referring to the 'dualism' characteristic of plural societies: their nature as societies gives them a 'unity', while their pluralism adds 'diversity'. It would be still more correct to consider this dualism characteristic of societies in general, and to apply this notion to the sort of questions which were raised in the first paragraph of this review. If Kuper recognizes dualism in plural societies, it is equally true that Marx, who is generally believed to have laid exclusive stress on conflict, was concerned with cohesive forces. In developing his analysis of surplus, accumulation, and exploitation, for example, Marx wrote of interdependence: 'personal independence, based on dependence on *things,* is the second great form [of social organization, i.e., capitalistic society] which for the first time allows the development of a system of universal social exchange, universal relations, universal needs, and universal wealth... [This] presupposes the universal dependence of all producers on one another. The production of every individual is dependent on that of all the others, and the conversion of his product into articles for his consumption has become dependent on the consumption of all the others... This universal reciprocal dependence of individuals who are otherwise indifferent to one another forms their social bond. This social bond is expressed in *exchange-value... money*'.[7]

Marx did, however, neglect the question of other cleavages in society and their relationship with those of class; it is a question Marxists have tackled, thus far inadequately, as "the national question." But in the last resort, pluralist theory, or Smith's version at least, does no better. For Smith, 'all institutions have two analytically distinct, intimately connected aspects: the cultural and the social', but, in addition, 'culture includes such systems as language, aesthetic styles, philosophies, and expressive forms which may be transferred across social boundaries easily and with little social effect' (pp. 34–35). The latter part of this assertion is highly question-able, and Thompson at least implicitly takes issue with it (pp. 354–68). But Smith is not even consistent with the first part of the statement, for, despite his concept of the intimate connection of culture and society through institu-tions, he argues that cultural pluralism can exist *by itself,* consisting 'in institutional differences to which no corporate social differences attach' (p. 440). The effect of this analysis is to make the existence of pluralism rather than heterogeneity depend on two essentially subjective assessments: (*a*) whether incorporation of collectivities is 'equivalent' or not (and by this, Smith means purely in the political sense, as with federalism); (*b*) whether the institutional diversity in question is in the *public* or *private* realm, where the distinction between these, in fact, varies with time and varies among different groups in the society. (E.g., there is an increasing number of people who would regard the family itself as a 'public' institution, in the sense that it is integral to the preservation of capitalist society.)

By a feat of legerdemain, therefore, Smith has succeeded in eliminating the initial problem of pluralism: under what conditions does cultural diversity in a society promote social cleavage? To which one might add, in what manner does cultural diversity interact with other dimensions of diversity, such as class, on the national or international levels? The areas where such questions are at present most acute are, except for South Africa, not dealt with in this volume: Biafra–Nigeria, inexcusably Ireland; the Middle East; and Breton, Scottish, Welsh, and French-Canadian nationalism, because they are not in the scope of the work. Nor, for the same reason, are the contributions informed in any way by consideration of that massive international 'voluntary pluralization' which constitutes the contemporary 'youth culture', which is, on the one hand, the most visible manifestation of the existence of a world plural society and, on the other, intimates that form of social organization presaged by Marx, of 'free individuality, based on the universal development of individuals and on their joint mastery over their communal, social productive powers and wealth'.[8]

Finally, if, indeed, social relations are characterized by the dualism which Kuper finds in plural societies, then the polarization of which he is in such great fear will, almost by definition, be promoting depluralization in another dimension. As Smith points out and as Kuper himself cannot quite forget, structural change requires collective action, and 'individuating processes' in Kuper's sense cannot eliminate social cleavages (see, e.g., pp. 50 ff., 183 ff., 483–86). But, in advanced societies, polarization of youth in a national context is promoting depluralization on the international level. Similarly, the revolutionary movement in Guinea-Bissau, by polarizing Africans against the Portuguese, is depluralizing the relations among ethnic groups.[9] Similarly, the analyses of South African society produced by the African National Congress and other groups, while encouraging polarization in one sense, have consistently promoted depluralization in other senses, sometimes across racial lines, sometimes across national lines (Pan-Africanism), and so on. Were Kuper, or for that matter Smith, to read such writers as Fanon (to whom Kuper devotes an entire, but one-dimensional, essay) or other 'revolutionaries' more carefully, they would notice a significant emphasis, not simply on violence or revolution, but on reconstruction, on the creation of a culture transcending the plural collective past. They might then understand that the 'uniform incorporation' which is the antithesis of the plural society is painfully created, not by simple acts of legislation (see pp. 60–61, 448–49) from the top down, but by the constant and patient re-evaluation of the relationships between man and man throughout the society and through the creation at the base of society of institutions which permit collective and equal participation, that is, uniform incorporation. Then, observing the 'anti-people's war'[10] which the United States is waging in Vietnam, observing the treatment accorded youth culture or the (anti-racist, one should note) Black Panthers, and without neglecting the treatment accorded a similar depluralizing régime in Czechoslovakia, it might be asked: in whose interest is the preservation of 'differential incorporation'–on lines of class or of culture?

NOTES

[1] Leo Kuper and M.G. Smith (eds) *Pluralism in Africa*, University of California Press, Berkeley and Los Angeles, 1969.

[2] M.G. Smith, 'Social and cultural pluralism', *Annals of the New York Academy of Sciences* **83** (January 1960), 763–77.

[3] This begs the question as to whether the separate sections will value some resources in common. However, there will always clearly be *some* commonly valued resources, related to the means of subsistence, and I argue below that those very bonds which create 'differential access' also imply some agreement on valued resources.

[4] See, particularly, J. S. Furnivall, *Colonial policy and practice: a comparative study of Burma and Netherlands India*, Cambridge University Press, London, 1948; idem, *Netherlands India: a study of plural economy,* Cambridge University Press, Cambridge, 1939.

[5] Georges Balandier, 'La situation coloniale: approche théorique', *Cahiers Internationaux de Sociologie* 11 (1951): 44–79.

[6] S. F. Nadel, *The foundations of social anthropology,* Cohen & West, London, 1951.

[7] K. Marx, *Grundrisse der kritik der politischen oekonomie* (Rohentwurf) (Berlin: Dietz, 1953). See Martin Nicolaus, 'The unknown Marx' *New Left Review* **48,** 41–61, March–April 1968. This important manuscript by Marx, which forms the temporal and theoretical transition between his earlier writings and *Capital,* was published in the Soviet Union only in 1939 and Nicolaus's article is a brilliant introduction to it and should be read by all those who have been introduced to Marx only in vulgarized American or Soviet form.

[NB the *Grundrisse* has now been published in the Penguin Marx Library and in an edition by D. McLellan (1971).]

[8] *Ibid.* p. 49.

[9] Basil Davidson, *The liberation of Guiné* (Baltimore: Penguin Books, 1969); G. Chaliand, *Armed struggle in Africa* (New York: Monthly Review Press, 1969).

[10] Noam Chomsky, 'After Pinkville,' *New York Review of Books* 13 (January 1970): 12; *I.F. Stone's Weekly* 17 (December 1969): 23.

Problems in analysing colonial change
E.A. BRETT

From E.A. Brett, *Colonialism and underdevelopment in East Africa*, Heinemann Educational Books, London 1973.

We can broadly distinguish two general tendencies in modern social thought. The behavioural school makes use of structural-functional categories with Parsons as its primary modern source, and Almond and Easton its leading exponents in political science. This school is primarily concerned with problems relating to the stability, persistence, or maintenance of given systems,[1] it uses the concept of a 'stable equilibrium' as 'a defining characteristic of structure'.[2] With this starting point 'all categories terminate in the existing order',[3] since systems must be evaluated in relation to their ability to adjust or adapt, rather than to change in any revolutionary way. The best that can be hoped for is a consideration of the possibility of a 'moving equilibrium', a dubious concept when one considers the need for radical transformation facing the countries of the Third World. The acceptance of this equilibrium model tends to reduce the ability to criticize the structure of power which has determined both the present and the past relationship between the colonial and colonized peoples; it serves to perpetuate their dependence and subordination. Its theoretical inadequacy and dangerous practical implication are clearly exposed in Frank's article.[4] But while it is relatively easy to reject these formulations, it is less easy to produce a coherent alternative which will lead to a viable programme of action. The basis for such an alternative exists in the liberal, humanist, and Marxist traditions which start from conflict assumptions and which have in some degree and at certain times referred to the 'negation' rather than the maintenance of the existing order.[5] It is no accident that the theories which have most readily been taken over from the West derive from this radical tradition, for example the Marxism of Lenin and Mao Tse-tung, and the revolutionary humanism of Fanon. These theories incorporate an understanding of the Western achievement, but start from the assumption that Western dominance must be destroyed before true liberation can occur; both of these elements must be present in some form before effective action can be taken.

Secondly, major theoretical problems have to be surmounted before Western institutions can be successfully transplanted from one society to another. The mere existence of a body of advanced technical knowledge does not provide any basis for advancement even where the capital is available to acquire the physical assets involved. The new technology will only make a

positive contribution where it is relevant to local needs and can be adapted
to suit local conditions. This is as true of welfare oriented institutions like
modern hospitals,[6] as it is of economic and political arrangements. The
technical knowledge which creates the ability to run machines or heal diseases
must be accompanied by 'practical knowledge'[7] of the circumstances of time
and place which will enable them to be utilized with greatest benefit. This
means that the understanding of Western models must be backed by an
equally profound understanding of the nature of developing societies—
unless this occurs, the result will be the creation of expensive but useless
monuments to Western technology. Carried out in this way, the adaption of
Western models is not an imitative and dependent activity; it is a creative
process which must ultimately result in the evolution of new social forms and
autonomous models of thought. When this is achieved the West in turn will
come to the Third World for models, witness even now the influence of
Ghandi, Mao, and Guevara on contemporary European thinking.

Any colonial history, if it is to transcend 'the horizon of the existing social
order',[8] should start from a theoretical position which refuses to accept the
actions of the dominant colonial classes at their own evaluation, but should
not induce an uncritical rejection of the achievements of the period since
these, however inadequate, must provide the foundations for the next generation. Bearing this in mind, it is now possible to suggest what appears to be
the most useful normative assumptions for the analysis of development
before going on to consider the critical factors involved in any process of
social change.

I am primarily concerned with three aspects of change—those relating to
the structure and size of economic production, the nature of the distribution
of the social product, and the location of control over social processes.
These concerns embody a set of related normative assumptions–that production be maximized, distribution equalized, and control decentralized. The
issues raised by these assumptions can be discussed in relation to the corresponding analytical categories–growth, equity, and autonomy.

Growth, however difficult to measure,[9] can be used in the sense familiar
in the literature on economic development, and taken to relate primarily
to growth in the monetary economy and therefore to the introduction of
modern technology and the expansion of production for the market. But
most economic analysis tends to focus exclusively upon the analysis of growth,
and to ask few questions about the distribution of its benefits. But such
questions are critical for an analysis which does not see development purely
in economic terms. Ethically it is possible to argue that economic growth is of
little value where its benefits are appropriated by a small minority. This
means that distribution must be judged in relation to its equity—its tendency
to equate performance with reward. It appears to be necessary to accept
quite large inequalities in rewards, especially during periods of rapid growth
(even Marx accepted that 'the cry for an *equality of wages* rests [...] upon an
absurd mistake)',[10] but it should be possible, however roughly, to determine
whether particular inequalities are in fact 'necessitated by genuine social
needs, technical requirements, and the physical and mental differences among
[...] individuals.'[11] Structurally the nature of the distribution of the social

product is critical because it exerts a fundamental influence upon the process of social and political change. A process of cumulative causation can be shown to operate in these matters,[12] those classes which are able to appropriate the bulk of the surplus will, by so doing, increase their ability to influence the future structure of production and the institutions of social and political control; those who cannot will find their influence progressively reduced. These processes of upward and downward mobility, resulting in class formation and social control operate in all societies, but are very visible and of critical importance in societies undergoing radical transformation of the kind induced by colonial penetration. Unless we understand the implications of last changes in this regard it is impossible to understand the contemporary disposition of political forces.

Autonomy is used here to incorporate the wide range of assumptions implied by words like 'independence', 'freedom', and 'participation'.[13] It defines a particular kind of exchange relationship, one in which complete equality prevails; in an autonomous situation neither party can impose its will upon the other. Its polar opposite is one of dependency in which one party determines the situation for the other–in this case the pure colonial situation. The use of this term raises a wide range of implications. Firstly, it must be positively defined; it does not simply imply the absence of 'overwhelming concentrations of power'[14] of the liberal tradition, but suggests the ability of any individual, group or State to act independently in a given situation because of an ability to control the techniques which structure that situation. An illiterate has no autonomy with regard to a trained bureaucrat or trader because he cannot understand their environments, yet depends upon their services. Thus that autonomy must be related to a given level of social and mechanical technology. Colonial populations were autonomous with regard to their pre-colonial structures, but dependent upon colonial structures which were imposed upon them and which depended upon skills which they had not acquired. This condition will only end when they have assimilated these skills and become 'truly masters of all the material means which make possible the radical transformation of society.'[15] Secondly, autonomy must depend upon the ability to innovate at the level of the most advanced technology. At present, innovation is virtually monopolized by the West. Since many of the benefits of 'growth industries can be virtually monopolized by the first country to innovate',[16] dependence will finally disappear only when the Third World, like Japan, has acquired the ability to produce new forms on equal terms with the developed world. This, of course, implies that colonial dependency relationships do not end with the termination of formal legal control, but continue for as long as the situation of substantive inequality persists.

The difficulties involved in the use of these three concepts are considerable. They each present major problems of measurement and are even more difficult to use together since they can come into direct conflict with each other. In the short term it might be necessary to sacrifice equality for growth by centralizing power in order to enforce maximum rates of saving and investment; alternatively it might be necessary to forego some measure of growth to maintain independence from external sources. But in the long term they can be shown to be functionally interrelated: autonomy must depend upon continued economic growth, this in turn will depend upon the ability to resist the dominance of groups whose interests are opposed to the changes which growth must bring. Both are only likely to continue where broad strata of the society can participate effectively in political, social, and economic development on terms which they accept as equitable. This degree of complexity makes simple definitions and refined measurement impossible– all we hope for are rough approximations and broad generalizations. But this seems preferable to the alternative of 'sacrificing the relevance of subject matter to the elegance of analytical method; it is better to deal imperfectly with what is important than to attain virtuoso skill in the treatment of what does not matter'.[17]

It is necessary now to consider the kinds of structures involved in the colonial situation, the way they relate to each other, and the dynamic factors which cause movement in one direction or another.

Interaction in the early stages of colonial administration was determined by the dominance which the agencies of foreign control were able to assert over the indigenous structures which they overran. The latter exhibited a wide range of social forms, but from the European point of view were all in relative terms small-scale, isolated, and technically backward. And their internal differences were of limited importance when compared with their general subordination to the dominant structures introduced in virtually every sphere of life by the new rulers. New administrative, economic, religious, and educational institutions were extended and consolidated, establishing new centres from which radical change in rural society was bound to flow. These centres were controlled by a new class of expatriate whose ends and methods were determined with reference to the European metropolitan centre; these, in turn, imposed new demands upon local society and established the limits within which the now dependent indigenous structures would be free to operate.[18] These pre-colonial formations were not entirely incorporated by the new colonial system–they were required to change in favour of new demands only up to the point but no further than that required for the purposes of the colonial political economy.[19] The dependent structures were expected to provide for the maintenance of law and order, the production of cash crops, the collection of taxes, and the unskilled labour required by the new economic and administrative system. Beyond this the new authorities encouraged the perpetuation of 'traditional' values, these being seen as fundamental to the maintenance of the 'traditional' or 'tribal' social order. The maintenance of this order, in some attenuated form, was fundamental to a system which did not have the desire or the resources to modernize the whole of its new domain in any basic way.[20] But the continued survival of these dependent structures should not be taken as proof of the continued existence of some earlier 'traditional' society. The changes imposed by colonialism were partial but fundamental–they undermined the old structures at their most vulnerable points. The chief might still command his people, but he now deferred to the district commissioner. When faced with a threat to his authority his ultimate resource lay with the colonial state, not the pre-colonial social and political sanctions. The old closed economy was broken open, the old verities challenged and new demands created by the authority of Western religion, education, and medical services. These dependent structures drew such independent authority as they had from the past, but they survived in the present only because the colonial power did not choose to destroy them. But their hold on the future was wholly problematical in the face of the changes introduced by the new institutions. For the future the critical question was not the nature of traditional values but access to the modern resources embodied in the dominant colonial structures. These were distributed very unevenly; their impact upon dependent society varied very sharply as a result. Their presence or absence in the form of roads, schools, etc., initiated chains of cumulative causation which led some individuals and groups to move forward very rapidly, others to stagnate or even regress in relation to the changes taking place in society as a whole. These movements were fundamental to the developmental process on all levels, it is only possible to come to terms with contemporary configurations when they are properly understood.

This suggests that we begin with a dualistic typology which assumes the existence of dominant colonial and dependent indigenous structures, the former introducing the dynamic element into the situation and deriving their objectives from the metropolitan centre, the latter serving the former and exercising an independent authority derived from earlier social forms only within the limits set by the demands of the metropolitan centre. In the period up to the Second World War this system gave every appearance of stability in most parts of tropical Africa. In its most enlightened guise it was characterized by the paternalism of the colonial agent on the one hand, and the apparently willing deference of the African subject on the other. As a system it lent itself to analysis in terms of equilibrium models and was so studied by anthropologists and other more or less academic advisers to the colonial authority. But this harmony was more apparent than real; the appearance of colonial law and order overlaid a deep-seated contradiction. I would wish to argue here that the original relationship can only be understood in relation to this contradiction, and that it was to be the forces which it released which were to create the need for 'the suppression of the old society by the new one'.[21] This, once again, requires some methodological explanation.

While much social analysis starts from equilibrium assumptions, I would argue with Leach that 'real societies can never be in equilibrium',[22] and further that the degree of conflict involved in colonial society was of a particularly intense kind. The relations between colonial and dependent structures were characterized by great inequality, however cordial the day-to-day interactions of the parties concerned. The expatriates might have been happy to exercise their paternalism indefinitely, but the African population could not be expected to accept their dependence in the same spirit. During the initial stages of penetration the indigenous populations were in no position to challenge this situation short of suicidal wars or rebellions like that forced upon the Zulu in Natal at the end of the nineteenth century. But the new situation was a dynamic one; the interaction between new structures and old gave rise to new structures and new forces which were bound ultimately to challenge the colonial political order. The colonial power was forced, in its own interests, to transfer certain skills and resources to the indigenous population; they built railways, roads, and schools, introduced new crops and revolutionized the system of economic exchange.[23] For the coming generation reality was not necessarily dominated by a system of monolithic and exploitative control, but incorporated some opportunities to acquire the skills required to exploit the new situation 'as a means of social advancement'.[24] Their success in so doing created new resources, new demands, and new classes, and so altered 'the structure of society itself'.[25]

But this process took place within a general framework of grievance derived from perceived exploitation. The emergent classes were given access to these opportunities on very unequal terms; where their interests conflicted with those of the colonial authorities the latter could be expected to use their power to ensure their own preponderance.[26] The emerging indigenous classes perceived reality in terms of inherited inequality, blocked economic opportunities, and social discrimination. This was bound to create a desire to resist and replace the colonial structure; the new skills gave them some of the resources with which to attempt this. Thus we can see the broad historical process in dialectical terms; during the first stage colonial and dependent structures were juxtaposed in conditions of intense but, after the period of initial colonization, for the most part unexpressed conflict, this relationship subsequently gave rise to new social forces which were ultimately to stand in opposition to both. Thus the first stage of colonialism terminated in a second during which the battle was to come out into the open and be fought on different terms. Originally the district commissioner and chief divided the territory between them; once this situation had matured both, from their different perspectives, faced the nationalist politician and the new forces which he represented. But it should again be noted that the process was not one of pure conflict, but an interaction in which 'convergent and divergent current [...] [were] inseparably interwoven'.[27] The emergent forces depended upon the resources made available by the colonial state; their opposition to it derived from the limits which that state sought to impose upon their ability to acquire them. It was the conjunction between these positive and negative elements which introduced the dynamic elements into the situation.

To understand the contemporary situation one must therefore understand the implications in structural terms of the first stage of this process, that of the period during which colonial control was consolidated and the new administrative and economic structure given its original form. This stage is critical in relation to the present because the foundation of the emerging indigenous structures which should be concerned to produce fully autonomous structures, in the sense of that term set out earlier, was created then. The distribution of modern resources by the colonial power determined the life chances of the rising generation; the emergence of a new political, economic, and social élite depended upon their allocation. The configuration of forces during the second stage of colonial control (and, indeed, after independence) depended upon the nature of this allocation and can therefore only be understood in relation to it.

Again it is important to note that this approach does not imply the existence of some inevitable 'law of historical development'. Western dominance was bound to induce conflict and change, but the scale, content, and direction of change depended upon particular circumstances–the nature of the colonial presence on the one hand and of the pre-colonial formations it confronted on the other. It would be reassuring but excessively optimistic to anticipate 'the inevitability of emancipation through social conflict'.[28] Emancipation occurs only where the circumstances are favourable: in many places the lack of physical resources, the dominance of reactionary classes, or the weakness of the colonial presence seem likely to hold up progress for as far ahead as anyone cares to look. Our problem is to identify both the positive and negative factors and thus improve our ability to make realistic assessments about future courses of action.

This leads into the consideration of a final methodological problem. I have suggested a model through which we can identify the fundamental interactions and the historical stages of any developmental process in a colonial situation. To take the analysis a step further it is necessary to identify and abstract the dynamic factors in the situation; the variables which will influence the actual outcomes of particular interactions in particular situations and produce movement in one direction or another.

At any point in time most social action will take place in relation to an established and unequal distribution of resources, regulated through a complex system of social control.[29] The bulk of these resources will be devoted to the maintenance of this existing structure, to 'simple reproduction' in the Marxist sense,[30] and will take the form of immobile capital assets, goods required to meet existing levels of consumption or values 'embedded in fixed, ascriptive, relations and groups'.[31] But in every society there will at some time at least be a margin between actual consumption and actual production; there will also be some possibility of moving existing resources from one use to another. The control, sources, and scale of these 'free-floating resources'[32] will determine the nature of the change process; allocated to particular purposes they will set cumulative growth processes in motion; taken from existing uses they will induce cumulative processes of decline. These positive and negative processes taken together will, over a shorter or longer period, revolutionize the whole structure of social relations. The critical factor in social change, therefore, is not so much the absolute level of production but the composition of the surplus which can be appropriated and put to new uses. Its size, sources, and allocation will determine the speed and direction of change and must therefore provide the primary focus for analytical attention.

The size of the actual surplus at any point in time will be determined by the difference between actual consumption and actual production. But it would be misleading to confine attention to the actual surplus as though this constituted an absolute social category. Any surplus, economic or otherwise, is not absolute but relative to the social situation. Its size will depend upon the prevailing interaction between values, power, and technological capacity, and will change with a change in any of them. A surplus can only come into existence where a new opportunity has been identified, it will actually be made available only where the relevant group has sufficient social control[33] to appropriate it, and it will produce new assets only where the technological capacity exists to exploit it. The interaction between the consciousness of new objectives, social control, and technical capacity will determine 'what things and how much a given society produces, who is responsible for production, how much is consumed and in what proportion by the various groups in the society [and] how much is saved or diverted from consumption and for what purposes... '[34] The identification of new needs, changes in institutional control, or technological innovation will alter the size of the surplus and its implications for the future. Thus the actual surplus appropriated at any time will only constitute a small part of the potential surplus available if under-utilized resources were brought into use, productivity increased without a corresponding increase in consumption, or vice versa.[35] The existence of a potential surplus is a critical factor in the competition between groups at any point in time–this will take the form of an effort to obtain control over the institutions through which these additional resources can be captured and redirected.

Changes in the movement of resources must therefore be understood in relation to both sacrifice and appropriation, that is to the transfer of assets from one part of society to another. Identification of the source of supply will suggest areas of likely relative downward mobility. Where one social category constantly gives up a larger relative percentage of its assets than it obtains in return, its relative position in the social structure will deteriorate. This will be true even where its absolute level of income is rising, but more slowly than that of other sections of the community:

> A house may be large or small; as long as the surrounding houses are equally small it satisfies all social demands for a dwelling. But let a palace arrive beside the little house and it shrinks from a little house to a hut [...]. Our desires and pleasures spring from society; we measure them, therefore, by society and not by the objects which serve for their satisfaction. Because they are of a social nature they are of a relative nature.[36]

The analysis must also take account of the fact that a surplus can be derived from internal or external sources, assets can be transferred from the metro-polis to the colony and vice versa. New resources can therefore be created at the periphery without any internal sacrifices; on the other hand internal resources can be sacrificed without creating any corresponding growth in local assets.

If the source of free floating resources indicates areas of downward mobility, their allocation determines potentialities for growth. Particular groups in society will appropriate some portion of the surplus and convert it into new productive resources in the form of 'additional capital'.[37] This ability will depend upon control over any or all of a wide range of factors–for example, access to military technology, religious sanctions, or socially necessary skills. Its effects will be to cumulatively expand the ability to control resources and hence to advance their relative social position.

This very bald statement requires some further development. Firstly, it is clear that concentration upon control over the surplus enables us to give concrete empirical content to the conflict model outlined earlier. Change occurs because certain groups are able to utilize the surplus and advance their position relative to that of others in the society. To understand this process we must be able to isolate the factors which provide them with this ability, the constraints within which they are able to operate it, and the scale and productivity of the resources to which it gives them access. This requires first that we identify the critical groups which are competing for resources within any given political system[38] (in this case the colonial, dependent, and emergent structures outlined earlier) and second that we establish the terms on which the leading groups are able to extract them from the rest. Any surplus will be derived from an exchange relationship–for example that between the tax collector and the peasant, the trader and his customer–to which both parties will make some sort of contribution. The critical question relates to the terms on which this takes place–what profit or loss does each party derive from the relationship? While it can be assumed that each is attempting to maximize his own interest, the degree of reciprocity involved can vary from a situation in which benefits are completely equalized to one in which one party is totally subordinated to the other. Secondly, a concern with control and the ability of some groups to grow at the expense of others should not lead to unrealistic assumptions about their ability to determine all the outcomes of particular decisions and therefore their own future social position. Control is always partial; even the governors of a totalitarian State cannot determine all the consequences of every decision in advance and have therefore to contend with some measure of uncertainty.[39] Dominant groups have to provide subordinate groups with some form of payment for their services–this can, over time, alter their relative positions. Decisions will always have 'unanticipated consequences',[40] which may again direct resources towards groups for which they were not originally intended. If this were not the case revolutions would never succeed because they depend upon a change in the distribution of social control which is necessarily against the interests of the ruling class. It is possible here to use the concept of in-direct influence to take account of the ability of subordinate groups to benefit from decisions taken either without any reference to their interests (as where they can make use of a road built essentially for some other group) or from those taken by other groups on their behalf whose interests coincide partially with theirs. The broader the issues and the longer the time scales involved, the lower the ability to predict and control outcomes. This is especially true in the general field of economic development where the ability to consciously shape the future is still exceedingly low. Thirdly, when assessing the ability of particular groups to control resources it is necessary to take into account factors built into the structure of the situation which are rarely questioned but which do in fact exert a decisive influence over the life chances of the groups involved. The fundamental assumptions which determine the relation-ships in any society are rarely brought to the surface, they lie 'hidden in the dim depths',[41] and produce unquestioning habits of deference and command. This is the area in which outcomes are determined by 'non-decisions',[42] however difficult, it is the task of the social scientist to bring them to the surface and make their implications explicit.

In conclusion it is perhaps worth trying to relate this discussion of change factors to the methodological considerations outlined earlier. I have argued that change occurs where groups are able to extract surpluses from society and apply them to new uses, and that the primary groups competing in the colonial situation are those which constitute the colonial, dependent, and emergent structures which make up the colonial political economy. Thus the nature of the change process will be determined by the relative ability of each of these to get control over free-floating resources; more precisely, it will depend on the terms under which they enter into exchange relationships with each other. Growth will depend upon the relative productivity of the resources transferred from one use to another. It has a general aspect, where it relates to the increase in total social product, it also has a particular aspect in relation to the expansion of one group in relation to the rest of society. This latter aspect leads to the consideration of questions relating to distribution, equity, and changes in social structure, since these can be quantified in relation to the scale and productivity of (or rate of return on) the transferred assets. It should be noted here that the level of conflict in the total situation will be heavily influenced by the tendency for total resources to expand or contract. Where total resources are expanding it will be possible for subordinate groups to be provided with an increase in absolute levels of consumption despite an increase in their relative deprivation. This will not eliminate conflict, as Marx points out in the passage cited earlier, but it may make it easier to contain. But it is important here not to allow the existence of high-living standards in absolute terms to blind us to changes in relative deprivation–this is likely to be highest among relatively well placed groups whose position is either deteriorating or cannot improve fast enough because of the opposition of entrenched competitors. Finally, it will be possible to determine the tendency for autonomous structures to evolve within the colonial situation by determining the ability of the emergent structures to establish favourable exchange relationships with the other structures in society and continuously increase their span of social control. Their ability to obtain the resources which determine the ability to modernize–access to capital, skills, and political structures–will determine the point at which they are able to eliminate the influence of both the dominant colonial structures and their indigenous subordinates.

NOTES

[1] See G. Almond and G. Powell *Comparative politics*, Princeton, 1966, where the tendency is less noticeable; see also D. Easton, *A framework for political analysis*, Englewood Cliffs, N.J., 1965, Ch. VI, and *A systems analysis of political life,* Englewood Cliffs, N.J., esp. pp. 14-15.

[2] *The structure of social action*, Parsons, McGraw-Hill, New York, 1937. p. 84.

[3] H. Marcuse, describing Hegel's system in *Reason and revolution,* New York, 2nd ed., 1954, p. 258.

[4] Frank, 'Sociology of development' in his *Latin America: underdevelopment or revolution*, Monthly Review Press, New York, 1969.

[5] Marcuse, *Reason and revolution,* p. 258, who confines his description to Marx.

[6] See, for example, M. King, 'Aspects of medical care in developing countries', Paper presented to Institute of Development Studies Conference in Social Planning, University of Sussex, April 1968 (mimeo).

[7] Oakeshott, pp. 7 ff., draws a useful distinction between practical and technical

knowledge. M.S. Oakeshott, *Rationalism in politics and other essays*, London, 1962.

[8] Baran, P.A., 'The political economy of growth', New York, 1962, p. 248.

[9] See P. J. D. Wiles, *The political economy of communism,* Oxford, 1962, Ch. XII on problems of measurement.

[10] K. Marx, 'Wages, prices and profit', *Selected Works,* I, p. 426. Emphasis is his.

[11] Marcuse, *One dimensional man,* London, 1968, p. 49.

[12] On this point, see Veblen, T., 'The preconceptions of economic science', *The place of science in modern civilisation*, New York, 1961; and Myrdal, G. *et al.* in A. and E. Etzioni, *Social Change,* New York, 1964.

[13] It is used in this way with regard to personality types by G. Jahoda, *White man,* London, 1961, pp. 107 ff.

[14] M. Oakeshott, 'The political economy of freedom', in *op. cit.,* p. 40

[15] Fanon, F., *The wretched of the earth,* Penguin, 1967, p. 250.

[16] R. Williams (Ed.), *May-day manifesto,* Harmondsworth, 1968, p. 61.

[17] Baran, p. 22.

[18] This analysis follows Frank in part (see *Latin America: underdevelopment...*).

[19] See Apthorpe, R., 'Two planning theories of social change', in E.A. Brett (ed), *Public policy and agricultural development in East Africa*, Nairobi.

[20] See S.N. Eisenstadt, *The political systems of empires*, New York, 1962, pp. 300 ff., for a discussion of the need to maintain traditional institutions during change.

[21] Mao Tse-tung, 'On contradiction', *Selected works,* II, p. 16.

[22] E. R. Leach, *Political systems of highland Burmah,* London, 1964.

[23] See, for example, K. Marx, 'The future results of British rule in India', *Selected works,* I, pp. 354-356; Mao Tse-tung, 'The Chinese Revolution and the Chinese Communisty Party', *Selected works,* III, pp. 74-82.

[24] Leach, p. 8.

[25] ibid.

[26] See G. Balandier, 'The colonial situation', in I. Wallerstein (Ed.) *Social change,* New York, 1966, pp. 36 ff.

[27] G. Stimmel, *Conflict,* Glencoe, 1955, p. 26. For a more extended version of my own position, see E.A. Brett, 'Politics, economics and rationality', *Social Science Information*, **VIII**, 2, 52 ff. April 1969.

[28] R. Sklar, 'Political science and national integration', *Journal of Modern African Studies,* **V,** 1, 1 1967.

[29] This discussion is drawn from my 'Politics, economics and rationality, *Social Science Information*, **VIII,** 2 April, 1969, pp. 59 ff.

[30] See P.M. Sweezy, *The theory of capitalist development,* London, 1942, p. 76.

[31] S. Eisenstadt, *The political systems of empires,* New York, 1962, p. 25.

[32] Ibid., esp. pp. 27 ff.

[33] E.A. Ross, 'Social control', R. Bierstedt (Ed), *The making of society,* N.Y., 1959.

[34] H. Pearson, 'The economy has no surplus', in K. Polanyi *et al.,* (eds), *Trade and market in the early empires,* Glencoe, 1957, p. 339.

[35] See Baran, Ch. II on the notion of 'potential surplus'.

[36] Marx, 'Wage, labour and capital', in *Selected works,* I, pp. 93-4.

[37] See Sweezy, pp. 79 ff., on the process of capitalist accumulation.

[38] Here the group theorists are likely to prove most helpful, notably A. Bentley, *The process of government,* Cambridge, Mass., 1908, and D. B. Truman, *The governmental process,* New York, 1951.

[39] See Brett, 'Politics, economics and rationality', p. 59.

[40] A. Kaplan, 'Some limits on rationality', in C.J. Friedrich (Ed), *Rational decisions,* New York, 1964, p. 60.

[41] Ross, *op. cit.* p. 341.

[42] See P. Bachrach and M.S. Baratz, 'Decisions and non-decisions', *American Political Science Review,* **LVII,** 3, September 1963.

PART II

Sociology and economic history: an essay on mediation

ANOUAR ABDEL-MALEK

From M.A. Cook (Ed) *Studies in the economic history of the Middle East, from the rise of Islam to the present day*, Oxford University Press, London, 1970, for the School of Oriental and African Studies.

Economic historians working on the Middle East–and more so perhaps on its modern period–have been submitted, for a generation or a little more, to the impact of the complex range of factors of change which has been re-moulding the hitherto remote fields of the social sciences (including economic history) and regional studies, understood as the study of the underdeveloped 'Three continents' (including the Middle East). From the methodological viewpoint–which can only be of a generally valid, scientific, type, not of the more restricted regional one–we have to question the uses and limits of economic history, not *per se*, but within the general framework of the social sciences; this analysis will have to bear upon the field under study–i.e., the modern Middle East, with special reference to Egypt–with its specific features, yet within the broader framework of Asia, Africa, and Latin America.

Such inadequacy as is currently perceived in the field of modern Orien-talistic studies has been mainly ascribed to the inadequate training and equip-ment of specialists in the 'modern'-type disciplines.[1] I would rather suggest that the central problem is that of a restricted vision of the problem. For methodology is but the prospecting head of different social philosophies as related to concrete reality.

I. Economic history and national development

The science of economics, or political economy as we know it today, retains but little of what classical figures, such as Plato and Aristotle, or a founding father, such as Ibn Khaldun, contributed to it. The starting point is currently admitted to be the transition period between feudalism and capitalism in Europe, between scholasticism and *The wealth of nations*. The rise of mer-cantilism and the coming of age of industrial capitalism had to tackle problems such as: the rationale of (apparently) economic obstacles to progress; the role of different factors in economic activity; the finality of this activity; the quest for moral and political justifications for this activity, etc. The happy pastoral interlude of the Physiocrats contrasts sharply with Adam Smith's work in 1776. A new socio-economic formation–capitalism–was seeking its way; a new class–the bourgeoisie and, later, the industrial sector of the bourgeoisie–was fighting ahead and finally coming to power with the victory of the French revolution.

Economic analysis or economic history? This question raised by *The wealth of nations* came again to the fore with *Das kapital* (1867–94). The narrow specialist's approach to the various fields of political economy and the rising social sciences was compelled to recant: here were two towering works that combined economic history, economic analysis, social analysis, and philosophy.[2] Their aim was not descriptive but interpretative: of the *Homo economicus*, as an entity, by Smith; of social causation and the dynamics of human history, not just fact-finding and the re-arrangement of evidence, in Marx's work. And yet, positivism was beginning to emerge as the logical sequel to empiricism and the dominant philosophy of the nineteenth century. Twice in modern times, and in the field of economics proper, Oscar Lange's thesis was thus illustrated, viz., that 'the existence and development of a scientific economic knowledge depends on the existence of a social class that would be interested to know really the economic relations and the laws that govern those relations, a class whose aspirations express themselves in a progressive ideology, an ideology that unveils reality'.[3]

The rise of the historical school (W. Roscher, B. Hildebrand, K. Knies, etc.) as from 1843, and the work of Richard Jones, nearly coincide with the beginnings of economic history, then understood as the history of economic ideas.[4] A brief survey of a century's work in the field of economic history shows that, under this title, three different types can be distinguished: (i) histories of economic ideas and systems; (ii) histories of the economic evolution, or development, of a single country or group of countries; (iii) histories of a specific field of economic activity (industry, transport, etc.).

Economic history relating to the 'Three continents', including the Middle East, recent as it is, lies within the field of the second type, sometimes with openings towards the third. Very seldom has a serious effort been made to analyse the movement of economic ideas and relate them to the general stream of the history of thought. Colonial countries, it was thought, could not evolve an autonomous body of theoretical thinking, let alone of economic theory. Broadly speaking, this was the situation obtaining in the major ex-colonial countries, for obvious reasons, till the 1930s. It is therefore important to elucidate the nature of the work achieved by the general body of classical European and North American economic historians, so as to put the work of their colleagues on ex-colonial countries in general, and the Middle East more particularly, in proper perspective.

The basic postulate of economic history, and indeed of all the social sciences, is that of the universal validity of patterns and concepts evolved in the advanced capitalist countries of Europe and North America. Clearly, the world did not consist of similar units. But differences were generally thought to be amendable to rationality, which would secure their 'normal' development, according to the model set by the vanguard countries. This basic postulate comes, it will be seen, from the general humanistic social philosophy and, perhaps more, from the evolutionary philosophy which entered the field of social studies during the late nineteenth century. It was reinforced by the tacit assumption that what was good for the best could not possibly fail to be a guiding-line for the rest of the world, i.e., the colonial countries: Europeo-centrism, came gradually to take the place of evolutionary humanism, as colonial countries came to the fore in their struggle for national liberation. The concentration of academic life and institutions in the Western world, late in the nineteenth century, led quite naturally to the strengthening of this tendency. Centres for specialized scientific education; libraries; publishing and the press; the leading thinkers and professors–such were the major elements of thought and action which contributed to assert the universalist postulate in the field under study. The whole conceptual framework of the social sciences was, and remains broadly to this day, Western in its origins and orientations. And this trend, in the field of economics, was much reinforced by the leading economic role of the major capitalist countries in world politics, by the creation of the world economic market and the forced integration of the colonial and dependent countries into it, by the hegemony of the West over that market. Traditional cultures and religions of a non-European type continued to obtain in the majority of the world; only in the field of economic activity were most peoples and countries compelled, at it were to go the path of the West.

Asa Briggs has recently pointed to the fact that 'it is primarily through the development of "sub-histories" that theory has been injected into history. Economic history provides one of the best examples.' The main influence is Marx's, followed by Max Weber. 'The theories will rest on "concepts", "frameworks", and "techniques of thinking": when the historian begins to study a particular problem he will start with these as with the data'.[5] This 'two-way traffic between history and economics' has been developing with growing intensity in (normal) works of economic history and theory; and specialists have found it necessary to co-operate with anthropologists, sociologists, psychologists, and other social scientists. For the problems to be studied gradually appeared as complex totalities, rather than split phenomena. Here lies the source of social history, as a discipline, which was soon to supersede traditional historiography, notably in France, with Marc Bloch's school of the *Annales*.

Economic change, its rate, type, and scale; economic growth and stagnation; economic welfare; economic development and social values–how did these theoretical notions and concepts fare when applied by economic historians to the 'Three continents'?

The nature of the problems encountered, first. They seem to lie within two different fields:

(i) The type of economic milieu. Everything goes to suggest that we have to deal with heterogeneous units and this at several levels. We are familiar with the 'two sectors' in underdeveloped, or developing, economies, i.e., the traditional and the modern, the archaic and the developed, forward-looking.[6] We now can see how 'economic development' can be combined with 'economic backwardness', though much remains to be explored if we are to rise to the level of meaningful analysis.[7] The contrast between old nation-states

(Egypt, China, Persia, Turkey, etc.) and other types of 'national formation', including the so-called 'new nations' and the problem of artificial colonial frontiers, have put to question the operational concept of the 'Third World'.[8] The image of large devastated areas, cornered by famine and death, looms large in manifestos, counsels, and guerillas and is coming to be accepted as part of our contemporary human condition.

Heterogeneity–and not only dichotomy. Not a combination of old and new, but, as a consequence of complex diverging factors active throughout the social texture of these countries, a basic unwholeness, a fundamental disquiet, trouble, and strife. *Homo economicus* could never be dreamt of in that realm of mankind.

(ii) And yet, in spite of this basic structure, chaos is being pushed aside, in a steady and decisive way, in the old nation-states; and the will to do so can be observed in the other categories. What is it, then, that makes for cohesiveness in spite of heterogeneity?

Specialists and public opinion alike in the West are gradually coming to realize that–beyond economic disparities and incoherence–there lies a whole stratum, deeply entrenched, of beliefs, customs, ways of living, ideas and systems of thoughts, a will-to-be, a collective, national, will at that. And, if this national will has clearly to be made explicit and forcefully set forth, its mainstay–the nerve-centre, as it were, of this depth-structure– can be accurately labelled 'implicit ideology',[9] the largely hidden part of the iceberg, far beyond statistics, surveys, pools, and the like–far more whole- some, a submerged socio-historical specific national structure that no social analyst can afford to neglect or underestimate. This will be, then, my working hypothesis, which this essay is trying to illustrate.

Meanwhile, we can proceed and, after the problems, consider the nature of the work achieved by economic historians in the field under study:

(i) A first set of books and studies provides factual surveys, mainly des- criptive, sometimes analytical. And, in this last instance, analysis is usually set against a sketchy 'historical background', unless it starts with general assumptions about Oriental religion in relation to economic activity. Under the influence of Colin Clark, a whole trend of economic thought has tried and still is trying, to evaluate the economic development of ex-colonial countries with a unified set of statistical, mathematically-regimented criteria, particularly international 'comparisons' of national income calculations:[10] accountancy and econometrics have resolutely pushed aside historicism and ignored the problems of specific national characteristics.[11]

(ii) Studies set against the 'historical background' usually start with general postulates about the inter-relation between Oriental religions and modern economic activity. Underdevelopment and prospects for the future are explained in terms of permanent structural units and learned considera- tions about *Homo Islamicus,* etc., are propounded to fill the gaps left inevit- ably by work done under (i).

(iii) There is, however, a third group of studies, which has developed recently, trying to combine the use of modern analytical tools with social analysis set in its historical perspective. The problems which are being tackled are, mainly, those of discontinuity, heterogeneity, and the specific character of economic development in different countries of the 'Three continents': the inter-relation between past history and present development, between ideology and socio-economic structure; the reasons for the uneven evolution of different countries; the role of voluntarism and political activism, etc.

Hypotheses are being formulated which provoke considerable theoretical discussions and are also geared to guide future practical activity. In both fields–theory and action–the work of this group now under way aims at putting the universal and the particular–science and national development–in a historically correct relationship, at the same time meaningful and efficient.

II. The uses of sociology

It has recently been argued with much force by Raymond Aron that the dividing line between the two sociologies–Western and Soviet, liberal-bourgeois and Marxist–is now in process of being replaced by a new cleavage, between the empiricist–experimental and the theoretical trends.[12] And though it seems that Marxist sociological writing stands more within the realm of theoretical sociology, major works by prominent Western-liberal sociologists (with R. Aron himself at the forefront) suggest that the two divisions inter-cross in many sectors and cases.

Clearly, if classical economic history, and its application to the 'three continents', lends itself to severe criticism for lack of theoretical insight into the *nationalitarian* process, such help as we are now seeking from sociology cannot be derived from its empirical–experimental sector. In fact, the theoretical sociology to which we now turn is not a philosophical digression on society, but, in a very precise way, the conceptual elaboration of sociological findings within the framework of history.

Marx and Weber, albeit in highly different ways, lead the way. And our generation, so different from their age, witnessing the appearance and growth of socialist states and the upsurge of national movements and revivals in the ex-colonial world, has evolved a body of sociology which is gradually coming to be recognized as more adequate than the hitherto prevalent schools and categories. Perhaps even more so in our specific field of study, so rich in new, non-classical, disruptive, disquieting, phenomena. Because of its scope of vision, eagerness, and penetration, let alone other classical scientific criteria, C. Wright Mill's *The sociological imagination* (1959) has appeared to a great many social scientists and non-specialists alike as a turning-point in the intellectual history of our time; and, for those working on the new problems raised by the profound transformations under way, as an inspiration and guide in method. Three points need concise discussion:

(i) Sociology has been currently regarded as two things at a time: a vision of things; a specialized body of study bearing on social institutions, material and spiritual. The first element–a vision of things–is now taking shape. 'The sociological imagination enables us to grasp history and biography and the relations between the two within society', by asking three types of questions: '(1) What is the structure of this particular society as a whole?

What are its essential components, and how are they related to one another? How does if differ from other varieties of social order? Within it, what is the meaning of any particular feature of its continuance and for its change? (2) Where does this society stand in human history? What are the mechanics of its change? What is its place within and its meaning for the development of humanity as a whole? How does any particular feature we are examining affect, and how is it affected by, the historical period in which it moves? And this period–what are its essential features? How does it differ from other periods? What are its characteristic ways of history making? (3) What varieties of men and women now prevail in this society and in this period? And what varieties are coming to prevail? In what way are they selected and formed, liberated and repressed, made sensitive and blunted? What kinds of 'human nature' are revealed in the conduct and character we observe in this society in this period? And what is the meaning for 'human nature' of each and every feature we are examining?... These are the kinds of questions the best social analysts have asked...–and they are the questions inevitably raised by any mind possessing the sociological imagination. For that imagination is the capacity to shift from one perspective to another–from the political to the psychological; from examination of a single family to comparative assessment of the national budgets of the world; from the theological school to the military establishment; from considerations of an oil industry to studies of contemporary poetry. It is the capacity to range from the most impersonal and remote transformations to the most intimate features of the human self–and to see the relations between the two.'[13]

I have quoted at length, as this first draft of the 'sociological imagination' cuts through nearly all the problems raised in section I, and clearly shows the spirit in which it is proposed to use sociology to overcome the difficulties now encountered by classical economic history.

(ii) The main point–once agreement is reached about the inter-relation between the different social sciences, and their respective subdivisions–is: how to integrate the historical dimension into social studies?

We are familiar with Ferdinand Braudel's distinction between the three levels of history: short-range micro-history at one end, faced by long-range structural history at the other; and between them, intermediate medium-range history ('conjoncturelle'). In his view, the second one unites history with sociology.[14] How could middle-range history, which is here our main concern, fail to show traces of this earlier symbiosis? Hence the wide audience of Wright Mills's thesis that 'history is the shank of social study–directly derived from Marx–and his conception that 'all sociology worthy of the name is "historical sociology"'.[15] For this intimate connection between history and sociology, several reasons are put forward that apply to all societies: 'In our statement of what-is-to-be-explained, we need the fuller range that can be provided only by knowledge of the historical varieties of human society.[16]... A-historical studies usually tend to be static or very short-term studies of limited milieux... Knowing that what we are studying is subject to change, on the simplest of descriptive levels, we must ask: What are the salient trends? To answer that question we must make a statement of at least "from what" and "to what"... Long-term trends are usually needed if only in order to overcome historical provincialism: the assumption that the present is a sort of autonomous creation.' A second thesis follows: If 'historical change *is* change of social structures, of the relations among their component parts', it follows that the social scientist, 'when he compares, becomes aware of the historical as intrinsic to what he wants to understand and not merely as "general background"'.

The third thesis is grounded in Marx's famous 'principle of historical specificity'. Could it mean that the past dominates and shapes both the present and the future? T. B. Bottomore has recently stressed the fact that the whole range of national phenomena (as well as the bureaucratic rationalization of society) remained unknown until Weber.[17] Marx's principle would therefore refer 'first, to a guide-line: any given society is to be understood in terms of the specific period in which it exists', and second, 'that within this historical type various mechanisms of change come to some specific kind of intersection'. But Wright Mills moves further, as he discovers Marx's ignorance of the scope and significance of the national process: 'It is, of course, quite clear that to understand a slow-moving society, trapped for centuries in a cycle of poverty and tradition and disease and ignorance, requires that we study the historical ground, and the persistent historical mechanisms of its terrible entrapment in its own history. Explanation of that cycle, and of the mechanics of each of its phases, requires a very deep-going historical analysis.' The reference here is to Asia, Africa, and Latin America; but also, in some ways, to North America: 'It is only by comparative studies that we can become aware of the *absence* of certain historical phases from a society, which is often quite essential to understanding its contemporary shape... A retreat from history makes it impossible–and I choose the word with care–to understand precisely the most contemporary features of this one society which is an historical structure that we cannot hope to understand unless we are guided by the sociological principle of historical specificity.'[18]

(iii) Historical specificity should not lead to immobility and stagnation. 'We must often study history in order to get rid of it... Rather than "explain" something as "a persistence from the past", we ought to ask, "why has it persisted?"' Hence, 'it is very often a good rule first to attempt to explain its contemporary features in terms of their contemporary function'.[19] For history, conceived as a non-revocable condemnation, can block the way to evolution, and render 'the present as history', in Paul Sweezy's very apt word, simply non-existent, as the present would be but a contemporary image of the historical past. 'The national mould of historical composition encourages the use of stereotypes, including stereotypes about national character': here lies the danger of Weber's 'ideal types', as Asa Briggs forcefully points out.[20]

Typology, and its application to the whole ex-colonial world: a veiled racialism. In place and lieu of this static approach, the principle of historical specificity, precisely as it introduces the notion of history, directly leads to the concepts of evolution and change; and these, in turn, require the tools of criticism. The central questions, as regards the present, become: 'why?'; and, as the future is concerned: 'how?'

How are we to conceive then the principle of historical specificity in the light of the sociological imagination for our specific purpose, i.e., economic history?

(i) Dealing, as we are, with a part of the world with a very old historical tradition of ethnic existence, and sometimes national cohesiveness, our first aim should be to study in depth the long history of these countries. Not as a record of events but a sequence of socio-economic formations. We should then try to discover those features that appear to be persistently present, distinguish carefully their shapes and the degree of their impact during different historical stages, and reach at what would appear to be the central nucleus, the *kernel*, of any particular historical tradition, i.e., the historical specificity of a given society.

(ii) This central nucleus is to be conceived as a factor of both continuity and change. Its influence on continuity is much greater and direct: in the final instance, this central nucleus is the very texture of national continuity. When it comes to change, the inter-relations are more complex. That central nucleus which makes for such persistent stability can only be viewed as giving the basic framework within which a certain limited range of patterns of change can take place.

(iii) Change, transformation, evolution–these are the key concepts and the general tone of modern scientific historical studies. Such changes as take place within the basic framework of any given historical specificity cannot but leave their mark on the basic framework itself. And this means that, by acting in a conscious, persistent, powerful manner on nodal elements of change (such as technology, institutions, the structure of social relations, at times, even more so, ideology), on such elements as appear to be the most vulnerable to modification and wide public acceptance of this modification, there is reasonable hope that the basic framework itself, the *kernel* of the historical specificity of a given society, can be, in its turn, slowly modified.

Neither change, any change, in a uniform, cosmopolitan, way–the hegemonic dream of the leading industrial societies–nor immutable stagnation, at which, ethno-racial typologies inevitably point. Rather, a specific range of possibilities and ways of transformation.

III. Egypt's past unto present and future

Let us now consider how these two series of considerations could be brought to bear upon certain concrete and reputedly complex problems of the modern economic history of Egypt. Reference will be made to a select number of studies to illustrate the analysis, and to help to detect significant questions which lie ahead.

A first problem is that of the transition from feudalism to capitalism. It is noteworthy that this problem, which belongs to the classical tradition of economic history, has only recently been raised under the impact of the ideological discussions around the nature of the Egyptian revolution–and not through autonomous academic channels. Social thinkers and political cadres alike had to assess the nature of Egyptian society around the Second World War, in order to frame an image of the future that was feverishly being sought by the national movement. Could it be that Egypt was predominantly a 'feudal' society for which a national-capitalist, bourgeois-democratic, revolution could be assigned as a national aim? Or was feudalism but a relic from the past, hence opening the path for more radical advances, perhaps even to socialism?

The economic system before 1952 was heavily based on agriculture. The ruling class and groups belonged, with few exceptions, to different sections of the landed aristocracy. Culture and traditions, the role of religion, the quality of inter-personal relations, the condition of women tended to confirm this backward, 'agrarian' pattern. Political denunciations of the overt or tacit alliance between the Egyptian ruling groups and imperialism naturally centred around the notion of the *iqtā iyyīn*, i.e., big landowners, or 'feudal' landlords as they were, and could at first sight be called, led by the ex-royal family. Several radical groups adopted this definition of Egypt's economic and social system, in spite of their difference of outlook and programme: the MDLN, one of the main communist organizations, as well as the Free Officers. By and large, public opinion and the press did not fail to concur; and there were several instances of this theme being used in the universities and learned circles. After the 1952 *coup d'état*, it became possible to describe the agrarian reform as tantamount to the liquidation of feudalism and the launching of the new, modern, phase in Egypt's economic and social history. The industrialists, in their turn, seized on this thesis to claim their share in the control and management of the economy and the State, pointing out that both the bourgeois-democratic and the socialist revolutions could be averted, the main thing, i.e., the destruction of 'feudalism' and the shift towards industrialization having been achieved. Economic history–mainly in the form of vulgarized essays and articles–took a curious shape of total discontinuity: a gap remained half-hidden, that of Egypt's social and economic history from Muhammad 'Alī till 23 July 1952.

The discussion of 'feudalism' started around 1944–46, only some years after the publication of A.E. Crouchley's pioneer work on *The economic development of modern Egypt* (1938). In 1944, two economic histories of Egypt were produced, one by Muhammad Fahmī Lahīta, the other by Rashid al-Barāwi and Muhammad Hamza 'Ulaysh. By then, discussion was starting seriously in the Marxıst political–cultural centres of Cairo and Alexandria. The adoption of what was then the classical Marxian periodization of socio-economic formations,[21] as applied to Egypt, could not but reveal that, at least since the institution of private landed property under Sa'īd and, still more, with the integration of Egypt into the world economic market precipitated by British rule from 1882, the whole socio-economic structure had shifted to a new level, i.e., capitalism, with its two (Marxian) characteristics of production for the market and wage labour. 'Feudalism' could no more be said to be the system obtaining in Egypt; and al-Barāwi's formulation, under the influence of the Left at that time, can be considered as the first academic admission of this trend of thought,[22] which has gained official (national) recognition with Husayn Khallaf's analysis of modernization in 1962.[23] The main work was done, however, during the years 1956–58, and greater attention given to the forms of transition from Oriental feudalism to capitalism, since Muhammad 'Alī, by a group of Marxist historians and theoreticians, the most important for our present purposes being Ibrāhim 'Amir.[24] A more sophisticated and relaxed study of the same problems was undertaken independently by C. Issawi and G. Baer, with basically similar conclusions.[25]

Not 'feudalism'; but then, if capitalism, of what type? The current formulation to define the immense and still very heavy legacy from the era of the great decay was 'relics of feudalism'. The aftermath of Suez stimulated research in two directions.

(i) The nature of Egyptian capitalism. Clearly, in Egypt as in other colonial countries, slowly emerging from underdevelopment and foreign domination, monoculture and 'export-oriented economy' (C. Issawi) contributed to shape a distorted version of Western capitalism. The very heavy predominance of the agrarian sector did not mean 'feudalism': it meant, however, that the other sectors–industrial, commercial, financial–were lagging behind. Therefore, the economic system prevalent in modern Egypt (from Ismā'īl till 1952) could be described broadly speaking as 'backward capitalism of the colonial type with a prominent agrarian sector'.[26] This definition could help to interpret the course of development, as from the 1930s, i.e., the struggle of the industrial and financial sectors of Egyptian capitalism to gain access to the power of decision in economic matters, with the aim of reshaping the whole power structure at the top in the final analysis. It could also help to interpret the economic history of Egypt under the new régime–from the agrarian reform to the massive nationalization of the modern sectors.

(ii) The second topic required much deeper insight, this time in the domain of sociology. How could it be that a society tightly integrated to the world economic market since the 1860s could present such a vast arsenal of 'feudal relics' at mid-twentieth century? A first explanation could be supplied by the greater persistence of the ideological factors as compared to the material ones (the 'infra-structure'). In the specific case of Egypt, a second explanation was suggested by studying one of the items of its historical specificity. The central, hegemonic, persistent, role of State religion, as ideology, meant that one could expect a similar situation in less important fields of ideology and culture, in the sociology of everyday life to which reference was made above. And this greater persistence was in turn reinforced by the exceptional intensity of ethnic and national unity obtaining in Egypt. Differences with, for instance, India–as regards the degree of integration into the world economic market and that of ethnic and national unity–could and should be clearly seen by economic historians and observers, seeking to find the diverging paths of the inter-relation between the universal and the specific–particular cases.

The second main problem is that of socialism. The history of the creation and growth of the public sector is impressive, from 1957 to 1963, and onwards. Mass media have tended to obscure figures provided by government sources: estimates for the 1962–63 Budget put the private sector's contribution at 65.8 per cent thus leaving only 34.2 per cent to the public sector; plan targets for 1964–65 indicate that the expected value added was 1.538 million pounds from the private sector, as against 375.7 million from the public one. Meanwhile, i.e., between 1963 and today, nearly 80 per cent of industry, transport, and commerce have been brought into the public sector, and by 1970 the bulk of agricultural output will be achieved within the framework of the producers' co-operatives.[27]

Three years ago, summing up 12 years of economic development, I wrote thus: 'The Egyptian economy appears as a mixed economy. It is still in many ways capitalistic: the land remains nearly untouched by nationalization: the public sector, though under the direction of managers (technocrats) is still ruled by the market and (public) profit incentive; and planning, and foreign aid particularly, tend to strengthen this pattern, at least in the short run. It is a relatively fast-growing economy with a central State-capitalistic sector (the public sector) of unusual proportions: but every new wave of nationalization, while it weakens the power of private capital, only provides more solidly entrenched positions and power to the technocrats.'[28] A more critical estimate had just been propounded by Hassan Riad.[29] And the careful study of Patrick O'Brien, in spite of its subtitle, chooses 'the term centralized market economy (as) more revealing than vaguer adjectives like planned and socialist'.[30]

These three estimates, as well as the recently published work of several specialists, all revolve about the key notion of centralization. I have tried to show that 70 centuries of centralization had not been limited to the economic sphere in that most compact of all 'hydraulic societies': the State controlled the Nile and, till the second half of the last century, owned the land; it had to concentrate a powerful apparatus in its hand, because of the geo-political situation of Egypt; and ideological homogeneity, often pointing to theocracy, is clearly perceptible throughout, from the Pharaohs to Sunnī Islam, including the Coptic era. Here, in this symbiosis, lies the central nucleus, the *kernel*, of Egypt's historical specificity. And from here, any analysis of its economic history should proceed and provide a rational, meaningful, interpretation, pointing to the future. Over-centralization is not in itself socialism. The central, hegemonic, role of the State does not constitute by itself a collectivist socio-economic formation. Neither is it any more a free market economy.

The approach to these two select problems of modern economic history has centred around the relationship between ideology and the economic structure, and the analysis of the short-term evolution related to the century-long historical specificity of Egyptian society. Ideology and historical specificity appear, thus, in the case of this exceptionally old nation-state, as factors of the first magnitude—what Louis Althusser recently called '*surdétermination*'[31] in another context; and these two factors themselves appear, in the final instance, to be shaped by the geographical and economic conditions which have put their indelible stamp on Egyptian history from its very beginning till today.

And yet, this very sociological approach to economic problems can throw light on some possibilities for a non-utopian future. The role-to-be of this over-centralization, in all spheres of social life, suggests at least two possible courses:

(i) The first one would be to use such a tradition to accelerate the building up of an even more powerful leading economic sector, as a spearhead to development. It would be interesting to study closely the impact of the world economic crisis (1929–32) on the Egyptian economy and society; the shift to the right and the imposition of the dictatorial rule of Ismāʿīl Sidqī against the Wafdist masses was coupled with protective tariffs for nascent industry and a whole policy designed to favour national capital, especially its industrial and finance sectors. But it could be argued reasonably that Egypt's present régime has already gone a very long way in this latter direction, and that the main obstacles to further economic development lie·in the deeply entrenched 'new class', and the bureaucratic, veiled sabotage of a wide array of government organs to the social dynamics–objective and not ideological–of the present national–radical policy. And it would be highly unrealistic to dream of a change in the very nature of the state that would enhance the role of the peasantry, the working-class, and the radical intellectuals in a decisive way.

(ii) The second course belongs to medium-range history. The nodal point would be the very texture of Egyptian society itself with its majority of *fallāhs*. Here lies the crux of the matter, as it does in the 'Three continents'. Underdevelopment, poverty, and illiteracy are still much greater in the countryside than in the cities, though notable progress has been realized since 1952. But the formidable efforts required to develop Egypt cannot be restricted to the technological and state levels; they require mass-mobilization of the people; and this mobilization, if it is not to take an ugly form, cannot be put to effect in a rational, humane manner unless carried out by institutions and organs emanating from the peasantry itself. Such appears to be the true meaning of the Kamshīsh affair (April 1966) and its sequels.

(iii) Attention should be drawn, finally, to the profound transformation of the socio-economic terrain itself, both at the level of infra-structure (economic institutions, living conditions of the working people), and ideology (the deep impact of the adoption of socialism as a national programme and ideology, in spite of vagueness and distortions). The intermediate level in the sociological pyramid–i.e., the state apparatus and the 'new class'–on the other hand, appears to be much more static; intentions are hardly coupled with action, for we are here at the very heart of the problem of power.

The 'principle of historical specificity', heavy as it is bound to be in such cases, is not, however, a stumbling block. Analysis shows its cohesiveness to be dynamic. And though the potential range of change variables is limited as regards future history–including economic history–for the near future the dialectics of Egyptian society, never dormant, have been at work in an intensified manner since 1939–46.

History, from curse to promise: such could be the uses of the sociological imagination.

NOTES

[1] Cf. *University Grants Committee: Report of the Sub-Committee on Oriental, Slavonic, East European and African Studies*, HMSO, London 1961. Latin America remains outside the scope of this report, as the linguistic factor (Spanish, Portuguese) oviously does not hinder research. Yet the nature of the problems is similar to those of Asia and Africa.

[2] A. W. Small, *Adam Smith and modern sociology*, I, pp. 235, 238, in H. Becker and

H. E. Barnes, (eds) *Social thought from lore to science*, (3rd ed.), New York 1961, II, pp. 523-6.

[3] *Economie politique*, French trans. by A. Posner, Paris 1962, I, p. 379.

[4] E. Roll, *A history of economic thought*, (revised ed.), London 1962, pp. 11-17, 303-18.

[5] 'History and society', in N. Mackenzie (Ed.), *A guide to the social sciences*, London 1966 pp. 33-53 (38-9).

[6] Literature from autochthonous social scientists abounds, especially from Latin America, viz., the work of Raul Prebisch, Celso Furtado, etc., and the recent issue of *Partisans*, nos. 26–7, c. 1966, devoted to 'L'Amérique latine en marche'; etc.

[7] Cf. the gathering of theses and discussion, especially those of T. Balogh and H. Myint, in (eds), K. Martin and J. Knapp, *The teaching of development economics*, London 1967; and the General Introduction by C. Issawi to *The economic history of the Middle East*, 1800–1914, *a book of readings*, Chicago and London 1966, pp. 3–13.

[8] Cf. A. Abdel-Malek, 'La vision du problème colonial par le monde afro-asiatique', *Cahiers internationaux de sociologie*, **XXX**, pp. 145–56, 1963, and 'Sociologie du développement national: problèmes de conceptualisation', *Revue de l'Institut de Sociologie*, 1967, pp. 63–78.

[9] This concept has been refined and applied recently by M. Rodinson, especially in his *Islam et capitalisme*, Paris 1966.

[10] E.g., on the basis of the purchasing power of the U.S. dollar in 1924–33.

[11] J. Weiler, 'Le passage de l'analyse à la sociologie économique', in G. Gurvitch, (Ed) *Traité de sociologie*, Paris 1962, **I**, pp. 357–82 (370–2); he mentions the similar criticism by J. Nef.

[12] Cf. his introduction to *Les étapes de la pensée sociologique*, Paris 1967, pp. 9–22.

[13] New York ed., 1959, pp. 6–7. J. Berque's approach to Arab studies has opened new perspectives for specialists by the use of what I would call 'prospective intuition'.

[14] 'Histoire et sociologie', in G. Gurvitch, *op. cit.*, I, pp. 83–98.

[15] For a survey of this subject as a particular field of sociology in the nineteenth century classical style, cf. H. E. Barnes, *Historical sociology: its origins and development*, New York, 1948.

[16] It is significant that the two phenomena selected by C. Wright Mills should be the role of the army and nationalism (*The sociological imagination*, 1959, p. 146).

[17] 'Sociology', in Mackenzie, *op. cit.*, pp. 79–94 (87–8).

[18] This case is argued, *inter alia*, by both A. Briggs and T. B. Bottomore in their contributions already quoted.

[19] All quotations are taken from ch. 8 ('The uses of history') of C. Wright Mills's work, (pp. 143–64).

[20] A. Briggs, *op. cit.*, p. 49; cf. A. Abdel-Malek, 'L'orientalisme en crise', *Diogène*, 44, pp. 109–42, 1963; and I. Sachs, 'Du Moyen-Age à nos jours: Européo-centrismetic découverte du Tiers-Monde', *Annales*, **XXI**, pp. 465–87; 1966, etc. The apex of this type logical approach is to be found in J. Austruy's books.

[21] Primitive classless society, slavery, feudalism, capitalism, socialism and communism. The gradual publication of Marx's *Grundrisse der kritik der politischen okonomie* (Berlin 1953) has stimulated discussion around pre-capitalist economic formations of the new European type, among them the so-called 'Asiatic mode of production'. Cf. E. Hobsbawm's illuminating introduction to K. Marx, *Pre-capitalist economic formations*, London, 1964, pp. 9–65.

[22] *Al-tatawwur al-iqtisādī fī Misr fī'l-'asr al-hadīth*, Cairo 1944, pp. 27–8. Leading centres at the time were 'Dār al-Abhāth al-'Ilmiyya' and 'Lajnat Nashr al Tham al-Hadītha'.

[23] *Al-tajdīd fī'l-iqtisād al-Misrī al-hadīth*, Cairo, 1962, pp. 431–41.

[24] *Al-ard wa'l-fallāh, al-mas'ala al-zirā'iyya fī Misr*, Cairo 1958. Other studies with

special attention to this field by Shuhdī A. al-Shāfi'ī and F. Jirjis. The whole discussion has been studied in A. Abdel-Malek, *Egypte, société militaire*, Paris, 1962, pp. 15–91.

[25] C. Issawi, *Egypt at mid-century*, New York, 1954, ch. 2 and 3; G. Baer, *A history of landownership in modern Egypt* 1800–1950, London, 1962; A. A. I. el-Gritly's *The structure of modern industry in Egypt*, Cairo, 1948, starts from a slight historical background, in sharp contrast with his very interesting *Al-sukkān wa'l-mawārid al-iqtisādiyya fī Misr*, Cairo, 1962.

[26] This is the formulation adopted in *Egypte, société militaire*.

[27] The first figure is from 'The UAR Budget estimates 1962–63', *National Bank of Egypt Economic Bulletin*, **XV**, pp. 108–25; 1962, the last item is from P. O'Brien, *The revolution in Egypt's economic system, from private enterprise to socialism* 1952–1965, London 1966, pp. 325, 317.

[28] A. Abdel-Malek, 'Nasserism and socialism', *The Socialist Register* 1964, pp. 38–55 (44).

[29] *L'Egypte nassérienne*, Paris 1964.

[30] *Op. cit.*, p. 316, and also: 'As a document, the First Five-Year Plan suggests, however, that almost all economic activity is centrally planned, but as implemented Egyptian planning includes no more than investment expenditure by the public and private sectors and the allocation of foreign exchange' (p. 319).

[31] *Pour Marx*, Paris 1965, pp. 85–128, 206–24.

PART III
History: Historical Stages and Transition

Those who affirm...that the motive force of history is the class struggle would certainly agree to a revision of this affirmation to make it more precise and give it an even wider field of application if they had a better knowledge of the essential characteristics of certain colonized peoples...

Research on an African mode of production
CATHERINE COQUERY-VIDROVITCH

Originally published as 'Recherches sur un mode de production africain', *La Pensée*, 144, Editions Sociales, Paris 1969. Translated in M.A. Klein and G.W. Johnson (eds), *Perspectives on the African past*. Little, Brown and Company, New York, 1972.

Until recently, African traditional societies have generally been studied in isolation and with emphasis on the particular. Economic anthropologists are only just beginning to understand the kinship structures of subsistence societies.[1] But by concentrating on the fact of subsistence, they have under-estimated the importance of the organization of production and of the social hierarchy. Subsistence, which is not autarchy, does not imply the absence of a division of labour or of elementary methods of exchange, in particular, local food markets. These are not 'class societies' as Marxists understand the term nowadays, and they differ from pre-capitalist Western societies in the absence of any private appropriation of the land. However, throughout Africa, they have gone beyond the stage of 'primitive community'. Even the economic organization of the Pygmies in the forest is based on an exchange of goods from hunting and gathering for the agricultural produce of sedentary tribes.

Thus, the problem of a mode of production arises, which even Soviet historians[2] hesitate to compare to one of the stages defined for Western Europe: slavery, feudalism, and capitalism. Since Marx and Engels had outlined another mode of production, the Asiatic, Marxists naturally thought of extending to Africa this concept hitherto used for societies of the Near East (Egypt and Mesopotamia) and Far East (China).[3]

The Asiatic mode of production presupposes villages based on collective production and bound to a 'higher unity' in the form of a state capable of compelling people to work. Behind this 'generalized slavery', a despot 'exploits these communities economically while he rules them'.[4] The State becomes an entrepreneur capable of massive public works despite a limited technical capacity: irrigation systems (the river states of the Near East), military defence (the Great Wall of China), or prestige (the pyramids).[5] In this extreme form, the Asiatic mode of production is clearly not found in Black Africa. Even if we could compare certain forms of African despotism with it, we would find ourselves without the dynamic element, the 'generalized slavery', which is found only perhaps in the massive constructions of the 'Builders of Stone' in Southern Africa (Zimbabwe, 11th to 18th centuries).

Conscious that some of the Asian characteristics mentioned by Marx are not found in Black Africa, researchers have been generally reluctant to push their analysis to its limits. Although they would be reluctant to admit it, their problem is an excess of respect for the master, who could not have analysed societies which were unknown in his time.

The most striking effort was Jean Suret-Canale's attempt to describe an Asiatic mode of production in pre-colonial Black Africa in terms of an evolution in three stages: the *primitive community* (which has, in fact, disappeared); the tribal or *tribo-patriarchal* structure of segmentary societies called 'anarchic' or 'stateless', where the basic social unit is the extended family, and which is the transition to clearly differentiated *class societies*, or *states* in which privileged aristocracies seem to have created the State above the patriarchal village.[6]

By elimination–since African societies were neither slave-based (as the term is used in ancient history) nor feudal–Suret-Canale compares their system to that of Asian societies. He has to recognize the absence of *despotism*, but is anxious to relate the African mode of production to his general plan, and hence gives a broad definition of an Asiatic mode of production: 'The coexistence of an instrument of production based on the rural community... and the exploitation of man by man in diverse forms... which consistently use the intermediary of the community.'

Suret-Canale assigns to the difference between 'a stateless society' and a State an importance which is now debated for Black Africa.[7] In addition, his definition of a surplus exclusively based upon the privileged class's appropriation of the products of village labour appears to be erroneous (we shall return to this later) and his definition of an Asiatic mode of production, if not false, is too general since it omits the essential point: the motivating factor of the exploitation of man by man, that is to say the kind of these 'diverse forms'.

A similar problem prompted Godelier, in a study of the Asiatic mode of production,[8] to distinguish between 'an Asiatic mode of production with public works'–and 'an Asiatic mode of production without public works'. The latter seems more debatable. Once again this limited definition omits the dynamic element from a mode of production, by leaving out its economic foundation at the level of production. In fact, public works, which surpass the means of particular communities, create the conditions of productive activity for these communities: 'The State and the ruling class directly intervene in the conditions of production, and the connection between productive capacity and production lies directly with the organization of public works.[9] These public works give rise to a bureaucracy and an absolute power, which is centralized and "despotic".'

Suret-Canale had already noted that the states of West Africa were set up differently: 'they were clearly based on the union of a tribal confederation (headed by a "king", the chief of the land), and a *market* to which the king gives security and from which he takes an important part of his revenue.'[10] Godelier is also aware that the rise of empires in tropical Africa (such as mediaeval Ghana, Mali, and Songhai) was not related to the organization of public works but 'to the control by tribal aristocracies of inter-tribal or inter-regional trade involving an exchange of precious products–gold, ivory, skins, etc.... between black and white Africa'.[11]

In completing his presentation, Suret-Canale unconvincingly eliminates the dynamic element in African history which stemmed from foreign contacts. He resorts to a local example rather than to scientific reasoning: his proof is the existence of the Mossi States in whose formation 'trade apparently played no role whatever',[12]–which remains to be verified. Godelier, on the other hand, accepts the consequences of his analysis. He proposes 'to add a second hypothesis to that of Marx... that there can be another path and another form for the mode of production, by which a minority dominates and exploits the community without directly interfering with their conditions of production, but by profitably taking a surplus in labour and in products.'[13]

We are in complete agreement with this, and the object of this article is to show why. We take exception to the comparison between the 'Asiatic mode of production' and the mode of production found in some African societies, and therefore will use the term 'African mode of production'. The only thing the two systems have in common is the existence of subsistence village communities. In Asia, however, it is a question of despotism and direct exploitation through generalized slavery, whereas in Africa, as we shall see, there is a superimposed bureaucracy which interferes only indirectly with the community. We do not see the necessity of examining these two types of production, which differ in so many respects, together. By considering the original features of both, and analysing the productive relationships in Africa, it will be possible to discern an 'African mode of production'.

Long-distance trading

One characteristic of African societies is that they were never truly isolated. The African continent has known two major phenomena: the mobility of its people and the volume of long-distance trade. Migrations–collective movements or progressive infiltrations–came to an end only in the colonial era when colonial régimes fixed populations for more effective police control or for such administrative goals as tax collection or the allocation of lots for private property. Previously, the history of Africa was indistinguishable from the movements of its peoples. These were partly attributable to the existence of low population densities and large, relatively open areas. Nearly everywhere, except along the coasts, the land is open to movement and even the dense forest is cut by large navigable rivers such as the Congo.

Examples of movement are numerous. The most spectacular was the Bantu expansion which overflowed most earlier populations in the central and southern part of the continent.[14] The Fulbe, who took refuge in the Senegalese Tekrur after prehistoric migrations from the Sahara, moved in the opposite direction from the 17th century. Today they are scattered from Senegal to Lake Chad. The history of the Fang since the early 19th century is that of movement from Cameroon toward the Atlantic.[15] Finally, there were Nilotic movements which spread south from the Sudan throughout eastern Africa between the 15th and the 19th centuries and perhaps their superior techniques reached the Lake Region, Katanga, and Rhodesia.[16] In brief, there is no ethnographic monograph which cannot present for the people studied a map of their origins marked with criss-crossing arrows, symbols of the complexity of its successive and often recent migrations.

Following these continual upheavals, African societies were at all times under foreign influence, which came from Egypt, from the Arab world, from Europe, indeed, even from Asia. The heritage of ancient Egypt spread into Nubia, to Napata and then to Meroe (the Kingdom of Kush, 600 B.C. to A.D. 300), and from there to Axum in Ethiopia. Southwest Asia looked to East Africa, which offered a reserve of manpower, a place for immigration, and numerous early ties. From the 9th century on, members of persecuted sects took refuge on the Coast. Kilwa, in Swahili country, is said to have been founded in the 10th century by a group of Iranians. Other places along the coast–Mogadiscio, Mombasa, Malindi, Pemba and, further south, Sofala (opposite Madagascar), which were great centres of Arab mercantile activity, at least until the Portuguese discovery, had a comparable origin. Indian merchants, between the 11th and 13th centuries, had enough influence to introduce their system of weights and measures, and their money practices to the region, and in Kilwa, enough to even bring an adventurer of their choice (Al Hasan ibn Talut) to power in the thirteenth century. In the South, even before Islam, Malayan canoes opened the way to the Comaro Islands and Madagascar, and Malacca had regular relations with the western coasts of the Indian Ocean from the ninth and tenth centuries. Finally, the Chinese at least twice made contact with East Africa, in 1417–19 and in 1431–33, and the archaeological discoveries of Chinese and Persian pottery are numerous enough for this to have been written: 'From the 10th century onwards, the buried history of Tanganyika is written in Chinese porcelain.'[17]

In West Africa, contacts with the Maghreb were even earlier: in 734 an expedition from the Sous reached Sudan. Contacts were established which were never broken: in 757–58 the founding of Sijilmassa in southern Morocco opened the Sudan road for the gold caravans. As for the Europeans, they moved along the coasts from 1434 (the date when Cape Bojador, opposite the Canary Islands, was crossed) to 1487 (when they doubled the Cape of Tempests, later the Cape of Good Hope).

These contacts led to long-distance commerce across the Sahara and the Indian Ocean. This cannot be reduced to external factors: the Arab conquest, the Portuguese Exploration, or the colonial impact. They profoundly affected the interior too by encouraging the collaboration of coastal kingdoms (slave-traders, for example), and of inland tribes who acted as intermediaries. In the Congolese basin, merchandise got through long before white men did, preceding the half-breed Portuguese traders, the 'pombeiros' who had been trickling toward the Pool along the caravan trails since the end of the fifteenth century. In the Gabonese back country, the people of the Ogooué had European-made textiles, pearls, and 'neptunes'[18] in their possession. The Fang of Woleu-Ntem, an area barely penetrated before the twentieth century (within the borders of southern Cameroon), had guns from trading before anyone there had ever seen a white man.[19] Likewise, during the mediaeval Sudanese empires, the people of the forest regions, including the Gold Coast, whose mines were opened in the mid-14th century by Mandé initiative, had received merchandise of Maghreb origin (glass beads, salt) in exchange for iron ore, ivory, or kola nuts which had been sent up North.

It was not necessary for trading to achieve a large volume in order to exercise great influence. History shows, however, that it often reached considerable proportions: gold and salt in mediaeval West Africa, or the gold and copper exported via the Monomotapa, rulers of an empire centred in the bend of the Zambesi river and Sofala on the Indian Ocean. In addition, there were slave traders. At least 10 to 20 million were sent to the Atlantic trade between the sixteenth and nineteenth centuries.[20] The trans-Sahara trade to the Ottoman empire was at about 10,000 a year in the nineteenth century (compared to 70,000 sent to America)[21] and in the same period, large numbers were being shipped from the Congo basin to Zanzibar and the Indian Ocean trade.

A critique of the traditional contrast in Black Africa: states *vs* stateless societies

The economic life of pre-colonial African societies was characterized by the juxtaposition of two apparently contradictory levels: the local subsistence village and international, even transcontinental commerce. This economic phenomenon is paralleled by and inseparable from a political one pointed out by Balandier, the conflict between a kinship-based tribal structure and a territorial organization with centralizing tendencies.[22] Does that mean we must link (as Suret-Canale implicitly does) first, subsistence to 'tribo-patriarchal' or stateless society and, second, long-distance trade and the more or less despotic state? The analogy is questionable. In order to show this, we shall limit ourselves to a few examples. Let historians and anthropologists make the case which will permit us to verify what in our present state of knowledge must be considered a research hypothesis.

Anthropologists have certainly proved to what degree kinship structures are associated with the economic structures of subsistence. Segmentary societies, until recently placed in the poorly defined and poorly studied category of primitive 'classless societies', show themselves on closer analysis to be rather diversified. Once again, it is Balandier who reminds us that in Black Africa 'all societies are heterogeneous to varying degrees'.[23] This primitive community is made up of 'social strata' which are involved in 'antagonism, competition, and conflict'.[24] In its simplest form, it is the domination of the elder over the younger, the elder controlling the means of production because they can demand that the younger 'remit the product of their labour'.[25] They can exclusively hoard or exchange 'prestige goods', which reinforce their position–and, thus, we have a process of accumulation in the villages, capable of developing and accentuating inequalities. This is not a full outline. It is sufficient to underline the danger of denying that subsistence is 'an economic, scientific, and Marxist category' because 'it is only a void, the absence of a market economy and market goods'.[26] Such a negative definition risks the rejection of 'all pre-capitalist societies... in the vague concept of traditional society', which would explain in part the lack of interest shown in this problem by Europocentric historians, including Marxists. We find no such strong refusal in Marx himself. On the contrary, he states that

> 'the specific economic form in which unpaid surplus labour is exacted from the direct producers... is the basis of *any form of economic* community... and, at the same time, the basis of its *specific political form*. It is always necessary to seek the hidden foundation of any *social edifice*, and consequently, of any political form which draws its relationship from sovereignty and dependence in the immediate relationship between the manager of the means of production and the direct manager (a connection whose different aspects naturally correspond... to a *certain degree* of productive social force'.[28]

Is it necessary, on the contrary, to associate long-distance trading and centralized power? This seems much more dubious. To be sure, the most striking examples have been studied within states: Ghana and Mali were tied to trade with Maghreb; Benin and Dahomey experienced a similar development with the slave-trade; Zanzibar flourished in the 19th century with slave and ivory trading in East Africa. But recent studies prove that long-distance trade influenced the most diverse societies. Along the Congo River and its main tributaries (the Oubangui, Sangha, Likouala, Alima, to mention only the north bank), trade was the only means of existence for certain segmentary peoples. In the 16th century trading took place between the Portuguese and the Kongo Kingdom situated on the south of the Congo. But, by 1850, the latter no longer existed. Beyond the Bakongo of the coastal zone, trade had reached the Bateke of Stanley Pool, and, further up-river, the Bubangi who lived where the Sangha and Oubangui rivers met the Congo.[29] There, the power of the chief rarely extended beyond the village or fraction of a village. Nonetheless, these river people, isolated on knolls along a complex system of lagoons, constituted a dynamic whole; unable to earn a living from the marshy soil, they turned to trade in local food products and in slaves. On the upper Alima, the Bubangi (locally called Lakuba) set up temporary encampments for the dry season and traded about 20 tons a day of manioc from the Batekes of the plateau and the Mbochi of the river. In return they offered the fruits of their activity: mats, pottery, paddles, nets, harpoons, and dried fish which they produced in large amounts.

With these activities, which were indispensable to the maintenance of their position in this strategic, though barren area, they combined their role as agents for long-distance Congolese trading: in exchange for European merchandise, they received ivory from Likouala. Further upstream came slaves, wood, ivory and, before long, rubber from the Sangha and the Oubangui. Important markets developed around Pool and along the rivers. These products were provided by similar segmentary groups operating further upstream. The inhabitants of the forest knew that the river came from 'the land of white men' armed with guns, who were certainly Arabs. This fact, among others, confirms the extent of Congolese trade which handled products and men over great distances.

No matter what society is examined, the permanence of trade transcends the traditional contrast between states and stateless societies. Balandier has already shown the coexistence of apparently contradictory elements at the heart of *all* African politics, state or stateless. In both, all forms of transition can be discovered. To be sure, there is a progress toward centralized organization, but the difference is qualitative rather than essential: even in the most 'despotic' societies (mediaeval Sudanese kingdoms, the Kongo in the sixteenth century, and Dahomey in the nineteenth century), the authority of the sovereign never replaced the tribe-patriarchal organization. At most, it involved a superimposed bureaucracy, which respected the structures of rural life. To recognize this trait common to all African societies is, at the same time, to seek its economic basis. One of the motives of African history is to be found in the dialectical interplay, or the absence of interplay, between apparently heterogeneous socio-economic levels within the same unit (the coexistence of communal clan structures and territorial entities, the superimposition of subsistence and long-distance trade). At any given moment, their history reveals a certain stage of development in these relationships, whose contradictions were perpetually generating disequilibrium and conflict.

Toward an 'African mode of production'?

By taking into account these specific traits it becomes possible to discern an *African mode of production* distinct from the classic model of the *Asiatic mode of production*.

Black Africa, as we have stated, never had an Asiatic type of despotism. That does not mean that there were no aristocracies or privileged classes. But the rulers who had power in various places were hastily identified as 'absolute monarchs' by European observers. The demands which they made with the aid of the ruling class were neither, nor exclusively, wrought on 'the hard-working peasantry, made up both of free men and captives', which was, in Africa, as elsewhere, 'the fundamental exploited class'.[30] To be sure, there were exceptions. In pre-colonial Senegal the families which had power also possessed rights to land and to work from the peasants (as a collectivity, however, with neither the exploiters nor the exploited considered as individuals).[31] In Burundi, property (livestock and pastures) was controlled by the *Tutsi* at the expense of the *Hutu*. This suggests a relationship of a feudal nature.[32]

However, it seems excessive to seek the only motive for this development of African societies in the productive forces of a subsistence economy. Such a statement, which seeks within African society the opposition of exploiters and the exploited reveals a lack of observation of the actual data. Black Africa is the one place in the world where agriculture was least liable to produce a surplus. Agricultural and craft techniques were particularly rudimentary (no wheel nor plow: the only tool was the hoe). The necessity of improving production with the aid of new tools or large public works was never felt. A rather sparse population was able to meet its needs without too much effort from land which was abundant, though not fertile. No ruler, in order to live, ever needed to take food from village production *in quantity*.

At most, he was content to organize for his own benefit the labour of his wives (the case of Dahomey, for example), and 'domestic' slaves, but this was not comparable to what has been called the 'slavery mode of production'. The tribute levied by the best-organized despots (the kings of the Kongo and Dahomey) does not seem to have been used as payment for services or to provide labour needed on tasks of public utility. It is not certain that tribute was regularly used to feed the people of the court, and nothing indicates that it was even used as a public aid fund to which those in need could appeal.[33] In the Kongo, the King and the nobles redistributed what they had received among vassals who requested it.[34] In Dahomey, the 'customs festival', an annual ceremony celebrated since the eighteenth century in honour of the royal ancestors, fulfilled the same function. It was an occasion for the sovereign to collect the tribute but, above all, to dazzle his assembled subjects for several weeks with the dynasty's wealth and bounty, either by the public sacrifice of hundreds of slaves,[35] or by the distribution of spirits, poured out in great quantities, or of cowries (local money) and cloth cast out from public platforms.[36] In brief, the fees demanded were, above all, of symbolic value, a guarantee of the social structure. Not that the relationship of exploiters to exploited did not exist; rather the African despot exploited his subjects less than the neighbouring tribes. In fact, it was long-distance trading which provided the major part of his surplus. From this point of view, the customs festival was not a retrograde institution which limited or paralysed European contacts–on the contrary, it stimulated the economic life of the country and encouraged the intense trading activity necessary to supply this 'fair' with all sorts of products (slaves in exchange for European merchandise). Let us not be reproached here for excessively favouring the *mode of circulation of goods* at the expense of the *mode of production*; the fundamental problem was not to transport merchandise but to procure it–in a certain sense to 'produce' it. It was evidently a bastardized form of production, both immediate and apparent, which was in fact ruinous, since, in the long run, it sterilized the country instead of enriching it. There were two ways of procuring goods: war (in the case of slave raids),[37] or peaceful exchanges with neighbouring peoples (the case of salt and gold in the Sudan), a type of externally oriented exchange comparable to a form of production and opposed to circulation within a given society.

Suret-Canale noted the basic role of trade in Black Africa, 'the decisive element in the consolidation of the first states in tropical Africa.'[38] He has not sufficiently explored its significance, however, because of his concern to establish *direct* domination of the aristocracy over the peasantry. The control of long-distance trading demanded the subordination of the bulk of the population to those who benefited from it. Yet the control exercised by the ruling class was manifested *indirectly*, by the exclusive possession of goods which were accumulated in a process analogous to the way 'prestige goods' are often amassed by the elders in a subsistence society: for example, red cotton fabric from Europe which the Bateke chiefs kept for their funerals[39] and weapons accumulated in the arsenals of the Sultans of Haut-Oubangui. Furthermore, indirect domination did not exclude its corollary, direct domination, especially in the case of the gun trade which conditioned them both.

In acquiring arms, the sovereign assured himself of control of military enlistment, the payment of tributes and the work of the plantations which in turn promoted the accumulation of an exportable surplus (for example, palm oil cultivated by the king's plantations in Dahomey since the mid-19th century). But, let us repeat, the major revenues came not from village communities, but from outside the territory, from the annual raids or from peaceful commercial transactions which secured products at rates much lower than their actual value. Thus, life in the kingdom of Dahomey was marked by military expeditions launched each dry season towards the Ashanti in the West or the Yoruba cities in the East, in order to bring back the slaves required by the economy. This was also true in the Kongo and probably in Benin. In central Africa, the Likouba (Bubangi) obtained manioc from the Bateke and the Mbochi 'at ridiculously low prices.'[40] At Stanley Pool they resold the red wood, the ivory and the slaves bought upstream at five or six times, indeed, perhaps ten times the price.[41] Even in the case of the empires founded on mineral wealth (gold from the Sudan or from southern Africa), the ruler's problem was not to impose on his subjects a collective effort to extract the ores. It was to obtain, at a low price, a metal sometimes located far from his territory. Neither the King of Ghana, nor the Emperor of Mali controlled the producers who probably operated within a hunting and gathering economy. They knew even less about them because of silent barter. This oft-described process forbade the two parties to enter into direct contact. The merchants who came from the North displayed their merchandise (salt) in a specific place and then they withdrew. The next morning, opposite each object they wanted to sell, they found an amount of gold-dust. If they thought the offer sufficient, they took the gold; if not, they touched nothing, until a supplementary amount was added or, if their demand was too high, it was all taken away. When the Emperor of Mali had one of the traders carried off in order to discover 'what kind of men did not allow themselves to be seen or to be spoken to,' the only result was the suspension of trade for three years.[42] In addition, Arab writers reported absurd stories about cannibals or deformed savages who worked the veins of gold after the rains. . . .[43] In southern Africa, the ore-bearing sites spread from Katanga to the Limpopo are more extensive than the ruins of the 'stone builders,' which testify to a political organization around Zimbabwe and Mapungubwe (South Rhodesia) and seem to corroborate an analogous hypothesis of 'production' by trade rather than by direct exploitation.[44]

The African mode of production is based then upon the combination of a patriarchal-communal economy and the exclusive ascendancy of one group over long-distance trade. The form of power at any given moment depends upon the nature of this group. If political authority was in the hands of the heads of kinship groups at the village level, their preeminence was then uncontested. In the case of the Fang or the Bubangi, it was only threatened by the rivalry of small groups involved in the same trade. In the middle Congo, the system collapsed only under the pressure of external factors: the intrusion of Europeans who seized control of trade for their own profit and eliminated the traditional middlemen.

If, on the other hand, in a more differentiated political system, a privileged class succeeded in controlling long-distance trade by means of a hereditary caste or because of an accumulation of capital, the régime combined the tribo-patriarchal system and a new kind of territorial ambition. The mediaeval Sudanese empires, for example, were characterized by the utilization of traditional animist structures by an Arabized aristocracy which controlled trade. It would be an error to imagine these to be Islamic states (especially since Ghana was already declining when Islam took root). The function of these empires was to control and exploit trade between the western Sudan and North Africa. Their goal was domination for profit and this economic objective allowed them to realize their political form. The ruling class was interested in presenting a Moslem facade, through the organization of its Courts and the pilgrimages, which would favour good relations with the Maghreb, a client and supplier. However, Islamic proselytizing would have threatened internal stability. We have no evidence that Islam had a solid base outside of the large cities; on the contrary, even within monarchical institutions the descriptions left by Arab geographers show that the leaders felt the need to graft their power onto a typically pagan structure, probably of Mandé origin. Hence the pomp which surrounded the King, the rites he had to follow (not to drink in public, not to converse directly with his subjects...), and the submissive demonstrations of his dignitaries (who prostrated themselves in the dust or performed sacramental dances in honour of the sovereign). To abandon these traditions would have provoked hostility, since the masses were attached to patriarchal forms. The evolution of the empires resulted from the equilibrium between these two antagonistic currents: in Songhai, for example, Sonni Ali (1464–92), a champion of militant paganism, aroused a Moslem reaction against himself. To be sure, he subdued the whole loop of the Niger river, but the history of the Empire became a constant competition between pagans and Moslems, which weakened the state and encouraged the Moroccan conquest in 1591. This resolved the conflict by uniting all in resistance in the name of the animist cause–but at the price of economic supremacy.[45]

The history of Dahomey reveals an attempt to resolve similar internal contradictions. The Kingdom expanded gradually by filling a political void left by the decline of the Aja traditional structures which were undermined by the slave trade. Superimposed on communal institutions we see a new notion of a State based upon territory, where each subject was to serve the King as well as the patriarchal chief. The paradox was that the Kingdom, which first developed in order to resist the corrosive influences of the slave trade, committed itself to an economic and administrative structure based upon the trade. This was the direction taken by Agadja (1708–40) whose transition to slave trader was the source of the flowering of the nineteenth century.[46] Power was narrowly bound to specific economic forms; Dahomean centralization was based on the ruler's absolute control of international trade, which was not integrated with local trade or involved in the market economy. It was a massive exchange of products rather than true trade. The King was not looking for profit as much as for merchandise from far-off lands: weapons (basic to his power and his supply of slaves), textiles, alcohol, and various trade merchandise, the basis of his generosity at the annual procession of treasures accumulated in trade. The Customs Festival thus assured periodic regrouping and redistribution of his Kingdom's riches.

The authoritarian administration of the trade explains the stability of prices, despite internal disorders and the frantic competition of various European nationals. On the Dahomean side, price variation, subject to the law of supply and demand, was limited by the ruler who determined prices according to environmental and military factors and the conditions of transport. For example, the standard price of a slave included a calculated estimate of his defaults, and the selection of 'packages', *i.e.*, assorted, coded, and priced lots of merchandise. Finally, the relatively stable value of the cowrie lasted for a century and a half (as a rule, 32,000 cowries to one ounce of gold). Right up to the colonial conquest[47] this shellfish from the Indian Ocean was used as money under a stable policy which regulated its use and avoided oversupply by authoritarian control of its import.

Thus, Dahomey realized the surprising union of a state with a high degree of monarchical organization in the service of the king and his chiefs along with absolute respect for the autonomy of village life. We must not be deceived by the seeming perfection of the financial and administrative system described by Herskovits[48] (census counts, tax collections, and military enlistments organized by the palace with the aid of pebbles placed in different sacks). The most recent studies suggest that this retrospective reconstruction by a European mind was very much idealized.[49]

When a privileged group or a despot lost control of long-distance trade this eventually led to the decline of his political power: this was the case in the Kingdom of the Kongo. At first it owed its cohesion to the King's mono-poly of long-distance trade which probably existed within central Africa from the twelfth century: lumps of sea salt were carried inland, as well as the 'zimbu' shellfish from the isle of Luanda which was used as money. On the other hand, raffia mats and ivory were received at the Pool from forest areas. When the ruler lost control of trade with Europe, he also lost control of outlying provinces. Chiefs on the coast from Loango and Soyo north of the river's mouth to Angola in the south profited by the distance from the capital to seize control of markets, with the aid of Portuguese merchants from Saô Tomé. From the sixteenth century on, these peripheral coastal peoples gradually freed themselves. The vassals became brokers, and from this trade they took a power which permitted them to compete with the authority they henceforth rejected.[50]

The examples presented do not in themselves claim to establish a general law. In the present state of our knowledge, they are simply an effort to explain the coexistence of contradictory political and economic elements. This coexistence was undoubtedly explained by the preference of the minorities in power to exploit their neighbours rather than their subjects. No African political régime, no matter how despotic, felt the need to eliminate communal village structures within their borders which did not interfere with their exploitation. As long as the village transmitted its tribute to the chief of the district or of the province, it ran the life of the collectivity as it pleased. The elders assured the worship of the clan's ancestors; the chief of the land allotted arable land to each family and to each generation; groups of women dominated the local food markets. There was no need to supply the ruler with a contingent of plantation labourers or porters, tasks generally performed by royal slaves seized in foreign countries. The most frequent obligations were limited to military service, or, as in Dahomey, the selection of some girls for the harem or the 'Amazon' corps, the élite female warriors of the King.

To be sure, in many African societies trade played a lesser role; this was the case of the Gouro of the Ivory Coast, even though kola markets existed and played a dynamic role. Trade was a way for the younger Gouro, who controlled it, to challenge the supremacy of their elders.[51] In any case, wherever trade was limited, it seems that nothing endangered the 'tribe-patriarchal' structures because nothing was capable of assuring enough of a surplus. As to the 'military hegemonies' which prevailed elsewhere, were they as extraneous to a long-distance trade economy as is said? For example, it would be necessary to study further the role played by the little known merchant class in the Mossi kingdoms. Elsewhere, pastoral occupations encouraged the development of the Fulbe, by favouring the accumulation of wealth in the form of livestock. Whatever might be said of them, their prosperity first manifested itself in active cattle markets. The Fulbe States, heirs to Ousman don Fodio, especially, controlled in the nineteenth century, and no doubt before that, the slave trade which supplied all of Sudan with slaves.[52] It is not necessary, however, to require identification of everything. We admit that in Africa there were several types of ascendency by a ruling class over the rest of the population: control of long-distance trade often implied military power (for example, the slave-trade kingdoms). No doubt the latter prevailed, sometimes by itself in certain 'parasitic military States' (Buganda, for example, where the State appeared to be a war machine designed to plunder slaves, cattle, and prestige objects destined for the chiefs, the military officers, and the bravest warriors, thereby making possible the mobilization of a large part of the population for two annual campaigns).[53] It would also be necessary to distinguish between West Africa and the inter-lacustrine zone. In the former, land was controlled collectively by the village community (only the King of Dahomey in the nineteenth century asserted his right of eminent domain, when he took over land for the palm plantations sought by Europeans). In the latter, phenomena akin to the appropriation of land by the ruling class are discerned quite early (the case of Ruanda, for example).

These examples prove the need for more case studies. It would be equally desirable to begin a comparison with other so-called subsistence societies, beginning with the Maghreb. There we also find this juxtaposition of two economic systems impervious to each other on the village and on the State level. Perhaps we could then also clarify the reasons for a dichotomy which has struck all African historians: the *invariability* of the communal bases of subsistence as opposed to the *instability* of the socio-political level. The second term, although inseparable from the first, could be explained by other factors. It might arise from the complex interplay of diverse elements. Among these, long-distance trade was among the most dynamic, but also the most vulnerable, since it was subject to external as well as internal factors.

We can see how much the African mode of production, which cannot be reduced to the pre-capitalist modes of production in the West, is also radically different from those of Asia, because there is no true despotism directly exploiting a peasant class. A final problem remains: the possible evolution of this mode of production. It has often been suggested that the Asiatic mode of production was doomed to stagnation. Godelier, on the contrary, insists that the movement of a society toward an Asiatic mode of production, revealing the emergence of a fluid class structure 'is the greatest advance of productive forces possible on the basis of early communal forms of production'. Evolution beyond this stage (providing that it is not petrified at this stage), could only come from the working out of its internal contradictions. Class structures would progressively take precedence over communal ones, through the development of private property.[54]

Can a comparable evolution of the African mode of production be conceived? Stagnation is more frequent than elsewhere, for the productive forces are not real forces. Founded upon war or trade, production is sterile. To be sure, a surplus is guaranteed for the privileged class, but it is an apparent surplus, whose long-term price is the impoverishment of the country. The Sudanese Empires disappeared without leaving a trace, as soon as commerce was reversed, the trade to the North of gold for salt, being redirected to the Guinea area discovered by the Portuguese, where gold and then slaves were traded for European merchandise. The States founded upon the slave trade were finally overcome by that which created their prosperity: the Kongo, starting in the seventeenth century, Benin, even before the eighteenth century, and the Ashanti Confederation (Gold Coast) in the nineteenth century. Is that to say that the African mode of production was condemned to be engulfed, or to be disintegrated? In one case at least, that of Dahomey, it was capable of evolution: King Ghézo agreed to renounce the increasingly uncertain slave trade in the middle of the nineteenth century in favour of a 'legitimate commerce', encouraged by Europeans and based upon actual production: palm oil and palm kernels.

Sufficient accumulation of capital allowed him to develop huge plantations under his direct control. It was the beginning of the passage to a mode of production having some characteristics of the *ancien régime* (most labour was servile, supplied by annual slave raids), and certain forms akin to feudalism, but with monarchy increasingly claiming the right of eminent domain over property. By the carefully maintained confusion between 'lands of the kingdom' and 'lands of the king', he proceeded to the private appropriation of land. The peasants were compelled to maintain trees and collect oil; the *topo* took care of applying strict regulations. Those who possessed palm groves were obligated to take care of the soil and harvest the fruit, under penalty of a fine or loss of land. They could not cut a palm tree without royal authorization. Palm oil made the king wealthy through taxes levied on trade. His subjects owed him a tax in kind on the oil sold, estimated at one-eighteenth of the harvest. Special officials, stationed in the various cities, collected the taxes which multiplied in Dahomey. In Allada, the former capital, every vessel which passed through 'the large and the small', was taxed.[55]

Would this development have been possible elsewhere? It seems to be outlined, at least, in the interlacustrine area–a system with feudal tendencies in Ruanda, based on the capitalization of cattle. All this was shattered by the conquest, which altered relationships between the colonizers and the colonized and caused African societies to move toward a capitalist system which was 'adulterated in that capitalist relationships were closely linked to more archaic forms to the greater profit of the privileged'.[56] However, these examples indicate that one African society was no less capable than any other of assimilating elements from the West, and of overcoming its contradictions, provided that she could control herself the transformation of her economy. By substituting the exploitation of the palm groves for the destructive slave trade, Dahomey was integrated into a new economic system without a shattering of its equilibrium. It began by altering the mode of production.

NOTES

[1] Especially Claude Meillassoux 'Essai d'interprétation du phénomène économique dans les sociétés traditionnelles d'autosubsistance,' *Cahiers d'Études Africaines*, 4, pp. 3–67, 1960, and *Anthropologie économique des Gouro de Côte-d'Ivoire* (Paris 1964).

[2] On the opening of the debate on the Asiatic mode of production in the Soviet Union, see J. Chesneaux 'Où en est la discussion sur le mode de production asiatique. II', *La Pensée*, 129 (1966).

[3] On this, see the synthesis of J. Chesneaux: 'Le mode de production asiatique. Quelques perspectives de recherche,' *La Pensée*, 114 (1964). 'Où en est la discussion sur le mode de production asiatique?' *La Pensée*, 122 (1965). 'Où en est... II,' 129 (1966). 'Où en est... III,' 138 (April 1968), pp. 21–42.

[4] J. Chesneaux: 'Le M.P.A. quelques perspectives...', *La Pensée*, 114 (1964).

[5] Ch. Parain: 'Protohistoire méditerranéenne et mode de production asiatique,' *La Pensée*, 127, pp. 26–27 (1966).

[6] Jean Suret-Canale, 'Les sociétés traditionelles en Afrique noire et le concept du mode de production asiatique,' *La Pensée*, 177, pp. 19–42 (1964).

[7] Whatever type of society is considered, political institutions are based upon principles of descent and two categories of relationships—lineage and political—always appear both complementary and antagonistic. G. Balandier: *Anthropologie politique*, Paris 1967, p. 61.

[8] M. Godelier: '*La notion de mode de production asiatique et les schémas marxistes d'évolution des sociétés*, C.E.R.M., Paris, 1963.

[9] Godelier, *op. cit.*, p. 29.

[10] Suret-Canale: 'Les sociétés traditionelles...,' *op. cit.*, p. 37.

[11] Godelier, *op. cit.*, p. 30.

[12] 'This hypothesis is invalidated by the existence of the Mossi States...,' Suret-Canale, *op. cit.*, p. 37.

[13] Godelier, *op. cit.*, p. 37.

[14] J. H. Greenberg: *Languages of Africa* (Bloomington, 1962).

[15] P. Alexandre: 'Proto-histoire du groupe beto-bulu-fang: essai de synthèse provisoire,' *Cahiers d'Études Africaines*, **V**, pp. 503–60 (1965).

[16] Oliver and Mathew: *History of East Africa*, chap. VI, 'Discernible developments in the interior, c. 1500–1840' (London, 1962), pp. 169–211. R. Oliver and J.D. Fage, *A short history of Africa* (London, 1962), p. 52.

[17] Sir Mortimer Wheeler, 'Archaeology in East Africa,' *Tanganyika notes and records*, 40 p. 46 (1955). G.S.P. Freeman-Grenville has done important studies of money found on the coast, which confirms commercial contacts with Yemen, Arabia

and Asia. Cf. 'East African coin finds and their historical significance,' *Journal of African History*, I, pp. 31–44 (1960). On the history of the contacts between East Africa and the Indian Ocean see Auguste Toussaint: *History of the Indian Ocean*. Tr. by Jane Guicharnaud (London, 1966). A. Villers, *The Indian Ocean* (London, 1952); J. M. Gray, *History of Zanzibar from the Middle Ages* (London, 1962); G.S.P. Freeman-Grenville, *The mediaeval history of the Tanganyika coast* (London, 1962); J-L Duyvendak, *China's discovery of Africa* (London, 1949).

18 Great plates of embossed copper which were used for money, especially for the payment of dowries (originally introduced by the Portuguese, they were in use until the 20th century).

19 Catherine Coquery-Vidrovitch (ed.), *Brazza et la prise de possession du Congo* (Paris: Mouton, 1970).

20 For a long time it was estimated at 20–50 million. Philip Curtin estimates that 10 million would be the maximum. See *The Atlantic slave trade* (Madison, 1970).

21 A. Adu Boahen: *Britain, the Sahara and the Western Sudan* (London, 1965).

22 G. Balandier: *Anthropologie politique, op. cit.*

23 Ibid. p. 93.

24 Ibid. p. 93.

25 Cf. Meillassoux: *Anthropologie économique des Gouro, op. cit.*, p. 217.

26 Suret-Canale, 'Structure et anthropologie économique,' *La Pensée*, 135, p. 99 (1967). In saying this, Suret-Canale evidently goes beyond his own line of thought, since he has devoted himself to an analysis of the 'tribe-patriarchal' society and has defined the *productive forces* based on communal agriculture: 'Les sociétés traditionnelles...,' *La Pensée*, 117, pp. 19–42 (1964).

27 Hence Godelier's contradiction; he reproaches Meillassoux while accusing him at the same time of over-emphasizing 'the fact of inequality... in most classless societies.' 'A propos de deux textes d'anthropologie économique,' *L'homme* (1967), p. 86.

28 Marx: *Le capital*, III, Ed. Soc., pp. 171–172. On this subject see, Parrain: 'Proto-histoire méditerranéenne...', *La Pensée*, 127, p. 26 (1966).

29 G. Sautter: *De l'Atlantique au fleuve Congo* (Paris, 1965), pp. 215–325. Also see: C. Coquery-Vidrovitch (Ed.), *Brazza et la prise de possession du Congo, op. cit.*, and J. Vansina: 'Long-distance trade routes in Central Africa.' *Journal of African History*, III, 3, 375–90 (1962).

30 J. Suret-Canale: 'Les sociétés traditionnelles...' *op. cit.*, *La Pensée*, 117, p. 30 (1964). Godelier expresses the same thing in an analogous, although less categorical, form; the aristocracy, 'assures the *bases* of its class exploitation by the deduction of a part of the communities' product (in work and goods),' *La notion de M.P.A....*, *op. cit.*, p. 30.

31 Kalidou Deme: 'Les classes sociales dans le Sénégal pré-colonial,' *La Pensée*, 130, p. 17 (1966).

32 J-J. Maquet: *The premise of inequality in Ruanda*, London, 1961.

33 Peter C. Lloyd: 'The political structure of African kingdoms,' *Political systems and the distribution of power* (London, 1965), p. 78.

34 W. G. L. Randles: *L'ancien royaume du Congo des origines à la fin du XIX^c siècle*, Chap. 5, 'La fiscalité', Paris, 1969.

35 About a hundred each year, and more than five hundred for the grand Customs Festival celebrated the year of the King's funeral.

36 Coquery-Vidrovitch: 'La fête des coutumes au Dahomey, historique et essai d'interprétation,' *Annales*, 4, pp. 696–716 (1964).

37 'War, *which is one of the forms of production*, in a characteristic fashion generates what is called "parasitic-military States" found in Ancient times as well as in the Middle Ages.' G-A. Melekechvili: 'Esclavage, féodalisme et mode de production

asiatique dans l'Orient ancien,' *La Pensée*, No. 132 (1967), p. 41.

[38] Suret-Canale: 'Les sociétés traditionnelles....,' *La Pensée*, No. 117 (1964), p. 36.

[39] G. Sautter: 'Le plateau congolais de Mbé,' *Cahiers d'Études Africaines*, No. 2, 1960, p. 37.

[40] From the testimony of European observers. C. Coquery-Vidrovitch (ed), *Brazza et la prise de possession du Congo*.

[41] A knife bought for 3 bars of copper in Ikelemba was resold for 60 bars in Bonga; a slave bought for 20 bars was resold for 400–500 bars. *Ibid*.

[42] A. Ca' da Mosto: *The Voyages of Cadamosto*. Tr. and ed. G.R. Crone (London, 1937).

[43] See the evidence in: Al-Bakri, 1068: *Description de L'Afrique*, trans. (Algiers, 1913), p. 381; Al-Omari, 1338: *L'Afrique moins l'Egypte*, trans. (Paris, 1927), pp. 70–1; A. Ca' da Mosto, *The Voyages*...

[44] See R. Summers: *Ancient Mining in Rhodesia* (Salisbury, 1969).

[45] J. D. Fage, 'Some thoughts on state formation in the Western Sudan before the 17th century,' *Boston Univ. Papers in African History*, **I**, pp. 17–34, 1964.

[46] A. Akinjogbin: *Dahomey and its neighbours*, 1708–1818, Cambridge, 1967.

[47] K. Polanyi: *Dahomey and the slave trade* (Seattle, 1966). The inflexibility of the system proposed by this writer must be balanced with other studies on the cowrie, such as: Marion Johnson, 'The ounce in the eighteenth century West African trade,' *Journal of African History*, **VII**, pp. 197–214 (1966).

[48] M. J. Herskovits: *Dahomey, an ancient West African kingdom* (New York, 1938), 2 vols.

[49] W. J. Argyle: *The Fon of Dahomey* (Oxford, 1966), pp. 94–5.

[50] W. G. L. Randles, Chap. IV, 'L'économie'; XI, 'Les conséquences de l'ouverture de la nouvelle frontière,' *op. cit.*

[51] Meillassoux: *Anthropologie économique...*, *op. cit.*

[52] C. Coquery-Vidrovitch: 'La politique francaise en Haute-Sangha,' *Revue francaise d'histoire d'outre-mer*, 186, pp. 29–31 (1965).

[53] D. Sperber: *Les paysans-clients au Buganda*, Communication au Colloque du Groupe de Recherche en Anthropologie et Sociologie Politique (CRASP) (Paris, 29 March 1968). However, this thesis assumes that Buganda was more independent of commercial relationships with the coast than Dahomey or Ashanti, which can be debated.

[54] M. Godelier, *op. cit.*, pp. 31–33.

[55] C. Coquery-Vidrovitch: 'Le blocus de Whydah (1876–1877) et la rivalité franc-anglaise au Dahomey,' *Cahiers d'Études Africaines*, **II**, p. 384 (1965).

[56] Y. Lacoste, *Géographie du sous-développement*, pp. 230–31, Paris, 1965.

Polity and the means of production

JACK GOODY

From Chapter 2 of Jack Goody, *Technology, tradition, and the state in Africa*, Oxford University Press, London, 1971. Originally as 'Economy and Feudalism in Africa', *Economic History Review*, 2nd Series, XXII (1969).

There appears little to be gained by thinking of African societies in terms of the concept of 'feudalism'.

But the usage and, indeed, debate, continues apace; the number of feudal states in Africa has proliferated even in the last few years, the authors of the accounts explicitly or implicitly rejecting my caveat about the use of this term.[1] I should make it clear that these doubts are not about the possibility of finding broad resemblances between the states of medieval Europe and those of pre-colonial Africa: there are plenty of similarities in the structure of monarchical systems of government, wherever they are found.[2] My queries had to do with the utility of any analysis that rested on such vague and all-embracing concepts; that approached the situation in terms of wide categories rather than sets of particular variables. But there are more precise reasons why the overall comparison with mediaeval Europe seems inappropriate and this has, initially, less to do with government and politics than with economics and technology. In my opinion, most writers about African social systems, particularly when they are dealing with class and government, have failed to appreciate certain basic differences between the economies of Black Africa and of the Eurasian continent, and this failure has led to superficial comparisons not only in relation to 'feudality', but also in relation to land tenure, property, inheritance, marriage, descent groups, and other important spheres of social action.[3]

Before I continue, I add a disclaimer. The identification of 'feudalism' in Africa has been associated with the left rather than the right. Palaeo-marxists accept a fixed progression, inherited from their nineteenth-century predecessors, from tribalism through feudalism to capitalism, though a greater element of flexibility is introduced with the recent publication of some of Marx's writings.[4] Others regard the discovery of the same processes in Africa that earlier occurred in Europe as crucial to the recognition of African history as a proper subject for academic discussion. Such an approach seems to me understandable, often correct, but in this case, misguided. We are here concerned with the utility of analytic concepts and whether 'feudalism' illumines more than it obscures. I suggest that we need to take a closer look at the means and organization of production in Africa and Europe instead of tacitly assuming identity in these important respects.

There are three inter-related aspects of the society I want to discuss, the system of exchange (that is, trade and markets), the system of production (especially the ownership of the means of production) and the military organization (and especially the ownership of the means of destruction).

My thesis is that while the pattern of trade showed little difference from Eurasia, and while the military organization displayed some similarities, at least in the savannah country of West Africa, productive relationships did differ in certain major respects. And secondly that these differences are relevant not only to the understanding of the past but to the present as well, and they need to be taken into active consideration when formulating development programmes.

First I want to stress that the difference between Africa and Eurasia does not lie in the presence or absence of markets and, in some spheres of activity at least, of a market economy. Much writing about non-European economics is based on the island communities in the Pacific–of the Trobriands, Tikopia, or Rossell Island. These communities are atypical in that certain primary features of the economy arise from the fact that they are small, relatively isolated groups rather than just 'simple societies'. The concept of non-monetary economics is hardly applicable to pre-colonial Africa, with the possible exception of certain hunting groups of minimal importance. Africa was involved in vast networks of wide-ranging trade long before the Portuguese came on the scene. For East Africa we have a late first-century sailors' guide to the trade along the coast, the *Periplus of the Erythrean Sea*. Long before the Europeans arrived there were trade routes from Madagascar up to the East African coast, through the Red Sea and into the Mediterranean, along the Persian Gulf to India, South-east Asia and Indonesia. Possibly there was a direct route by which cinnamon was brought from the Spice Islands.[5] By the time the Portuguese reached the eastern shores of Africa, the Chinese had already been very active there; before the development of the gun-carrying sailing ship on the Atlantic seaboard, the maritime commerce of the Indian Ocean made Western Europe seem like an underdeveloped area.[6] Indeed, the trade between Ethiopia, the Mediterranean and the Indian Ocean had much to do with the developments in the Arabian peninsula, possibly including the rise of Muhammad.[7]

In West Africa the mediaeval empires of the Niger bend were built up on the trade which brought salt, cloth, and beads south from the Sahara across to West Africa and took gold and ivory and slaves back to the Barbary coast and from there into mediaeval Europe. When the British defeated the Ashanti in 1896 they found a war shrine in Kumasi consisting of a bronze ewer and a jug. The jug now stands in the mediaeval section of the British Museum as one of the finest examples of English craftsmanship at that time. It bears the arms of England and the badge of Richard II, and is inscribed with the following proverbs:

> He that will not spare when he may
> he shall not spend when he would.
> Deem the best in every doubt
> till the truth be tried out.

If it were known, the story of how these vessels reached the tropical forest of West Africa would encapsulate much of the economic history of trans-Saharan trade.[8]

From the point of view of mercantile economy, parts of Africa were not dissimilar to Western Europe of the same period. Metal coinage was in use on the East African coast. In the West, currencies consisted of gold, brass, salt, but more especially cowrie shells which, coming as they did from the Maldive Islands off the south of Ceylon, filled most of the necessary attributes of money. In certain respects this was a monetary economy. Trade was highly organized and in kingdoms such as Dahomey and Ashanti important sectors of the economy were under state control, whereas in the savannah regions exchange was left largely in private (Muslim) hands. Most of the kinds of economic operations that were found in pre-industrial Europe were also to be found in Africa; even in the stateless societies of the interior, barter had been superseded by more complex forms of exchange, and production was rarely limited to subsistence alone; the extensive use of cowries from the Maldives and carnelians from Gujerat shows that they were all in some degree part of the economic system of the Old World. The impact of long-distance trade on social organization of course depends upon the degree to which productive activity is diverted to serve the purposes of external demand. My point is that, except in the special fields of the wine and wool trade, the differences between the external exchanges of Africa and early mediaeval Europe appear to have been relatively slight.[9]

If mercantile activity was not vastly different from that of mediaeval Europe, what about other aspects of the productive system? As we have seen, some writers have claimed that land tenure in African states was feudal in kind; others dispute this contention, denying the utility of the concept of a landed fief in Africa. Most of this discussion has taken place on a politico-legal level. But there is one crucial and obvious difference which has been largely overlooked. It is a difference which means that African land tenure (and hence vassalage and landed fiefs) was unlike that which obtained in much of Europe and indeed in much of the Eurasian continent generally; and it has to do with the means of production rather than with productive relations, though its influence upon these relations is of considerable importance. Basically Africa is a land of extensive agriculture.[10] The population is small, the land is plentiful and the soils are relatively poor. Moreover, one fundamental invention that spread throughout the Eurasian continent never reached Africa south of the Sahara, with the exception of Ethiopia. I am referring to that Bronze Age invention, the plough.

What effect does the plough have? In the first place it increases the area of land a man can cultivate and hence makes possible a substantial rise in productivity, at least in open country.[11] This in turn means a greater surplus for the maintenance of specialist crafts, for the growth of differences in wealth and in styles of life, for developments in urban, that is, non-agricultural, life.[12] In the second place, it stimulates the move to fixed holdings and away from shifting agriculture. Thirdly (and not independently) it increases the value (and decreases the availability) of arable land.

In Africa, then, there was little use of machines, even elementary ones;

agriculture has meant hoe farming which was carried out by men or women or both, depending upon the particular society. Indeed animal power, that drew the Eurasian plough, was not used for any other form of traction. One immediate reason was that the wheel,[13] though it crossed the Sahara, both in the West (as evidenced in the two-wheeled chariots liberally engraved upon Saharan boulders) and in the East (in Ethiopia and in the early Sudan), never penetrated pre-colonial Africa (or rather was never adopted there). Nor was this because of the lack of a metal technology. While Black Africa escaped the civilizing influence of the Copper and Bronze ages, the smelting of iron diffused rapidly from the Mediterranean down both sides of the continent.

In the East the technique of iron-smelting travelled to the Sudan, where Meroë has been described, with some exaggeration, as the 'Birmingham of Africa'; the metal began to be known there in the sixth century B.C., roughly the same time as iron was found in Ethiopia. From there it spread to Chad in the first century A.D., possibly brought across by horsemen using a long lance. In the West, iron was transmitted from Carthage and the Barbary Coast to the Niger towns in the third century B.C. The technique of iron-working, which followed later, spread through West and East Africa. By 'the first few centuries A.D.' it had been introduced to Zambia by a number of small related groups of immigrants who brought not only metallurgy, but also food production and pot-making from the area west of Lake Tanganyika. Copper and bronze were employed in many parts of pre-colonial Africa, but before the coming of iron the extent of this use was negligible.[14]

The absence of the wheel meant that man was not only unable to make use of animal power, but of the power of wind and water as well. This is why the recent introduction of the lorry, the bicycle and the engine-driven mill has had such a revolutionary effect upon the rural economy of Africa. But the lack of the wheel had another consequence for agriculture, since it limited the possibilities of water control. In the drier regions of the Eurasian continent the wheel has played a dominant part in raising water from wells to irrigate the land. Simple irrigation there is in Africa, as almost everywhere agriculture is practised. Some of the inhabitants of the settlement of Birifu (LoWiili) in northern Ghana channel the water from a permanent spring to run among their fields, and thus get two crops a year in place of one. The Sonjo of Tanzania practise more developed water control. Rice growing in the Western Sudan, and it should be remembered that some of the rice used here (*Oryza glaberima*) was domesticated independently of Asian rice in the Senegal–Mali region, demands yet more positive measures.

There are other means of water control that do not involve the wheel, that is, using various techniques of temporary storage. Methods of this kind did of course exist. Everywhere there was some improvement of natural pools. In Gonja and in neighbouring areas of northern Ghana there are many ancient cisterns hollowed out of the laterite; in the famous market town of Salaga, the city of 1000 wells, these are cylindrical in form and do not seem wholly dependent upon surface water. But these storage systems are very different from the village tank of South-east Asia; while there is no lack of water in Africa, the problem of its distribution is enormous. And in terms of agriculture what is lacking, apart from the *shaduf* of the Saharan fringe, which uses the lever principle, is any mechanical device for drawing water, such as is used in the Middle East and even in the Saharan oases.

One further highly important effect of the technological gap between Africa and Eurasia lay in the military field. When the Portuguese spearheaded European expansion into other continents, they succeeded largely because of their use of gun-bearing sailing ships.[15] Through these they could dominate their African opponents who were armed only with sword, spear, and bow. But, by the end of the fifteenth century, when the expansion of Europe began, their guns were also far in advance of Asia as well. These technological innovations soon spread from Europe, just as simpler forms of gunpowder and 'cannon' had earlier diffused there from China and the Middle East. But the way in which they did so is of great interest. Beachy notes that 'the Africans never seem to have learnt to make fire-arms as good as those of the Europeans, unlike the sixteenth- and seventeenth-century Japanese and Sinhalese, who soon achieved virtual parity with the Portuguese in this respect'.[16] Already in the mid-sixteenth century the Japanese were producing matchlocks and they soon were followed by the Koreans; Ceylon had become a centre of production by the end of the sixteenth century, when muskets and cannon were made at many different points in the Indian subcontinent. By the seventeenth century the inhabitants of the Malabar coast were exporting muskets to Arabia.[17] The reason for the failure of Africans successfully to take up the manufacture of this powerful new weapon is a simple one. They did not possess the requisite level of craft skill in iron-working. As a result, Africans were at an enormous disadvantage when the scramble for their continent began, since they had to fight against the very people who were supplying them with arms.[18]

What does all this add up to in socio-economic terms? Firstly, in Africa rights in land were less highly individualized than in most of Europe, partly because land was not a scarce commodity.[19] Among the Bemba of Zambia rights in the productive use of land, other than the small proportion under cultivation at any one time, hardly existed; the same is still true among the Gonja in northern Ghana. Under such conditions neither individuals nor kin groups bother to lay specific claims to large tracts of territory, since land is virtually a free good. Elsewhere, among the LoWiili and Tallensi of northern Ghana, for example, the population densities are around 100–200 per sq. m and rights in land more highly developed; these rights tend to get tied down to small kin groups, such as minimal lineage segments, although residual rights are vested in larger descent groups which often see themselves as property-holding corporations. But in fact rights to these assets are divided up among the smaller units, which are themselves constantly splitting and reuniting, depending upon the distribution of the births of male children.

But, overall, people were thin on the ground. Even today, the total population for Black Africa is not much more than that of the United States, although the surface area is four times as great. Not only was land plentiful, it was also less productive than in Eurasia, partly because of the technological limitations, and partly because tropical soils are often of poor quality. Moreover, since processes of soil regeneration (either by manure or by special

cropping) were limited in nature, the fertility of land soon fell off. Under
these conditions, the answer usually lay in moving one's farm (though not
necessarily one's residence) to a new site, that is, in shifting cultivation.

The social consequences were two-fold. Politically, chiefship tended to be
over people rather than over land; these a leader had to try to attract as well
as restrain. The conditions for the forms of domination that obtained in the
European Middle Ages hardly existed, except for slavery itself.[20] In slavery,
labour is controlled by political force; in serfdom, economic controls, such
as land tenure, are of equal importance. It is highly significant that only in
Ethiopia, which had the plough, was there any landlordism in Africa; here
in true medieval fashion, estates in land supported a nobility that filled the
important offices of state, both in the staff and line organization, a nobility
that was at the same time a leisure class in Veblen's sense. Besides the nobility
one also found ecclesiastical landlordism–functionaries whose time was
devoted to the glory of God (though individual commitment to the monastic
life was often temporary rather than permanent in character) and who
derived their 'living' from the church with which God had been endowed.[21]

If you have landlords, you can also have tenants and serfs; unfree tenancies
mean little unless land is highly valued and your peasantry has nowhere else
to go.[22] Under conditions of shifting cultivation, it means little. Slavery was
important throughout most of Africa: war captives were given household or
agricultural work to perform for their captors or their purchasers. But ties
of subordination arose not out of shortage of land but as the result of purchase or conquest, thus giving rise to slavery rather than to serfdom.

Though there were no landlords, there were of course lords of the land–the
local chiefs of centralized states, who, from the standpoint of food production,
were in a sense carried by the rest of the population; we may either look at
this as a return for services rendered or as the exploitation of the weak, for
there is, I think, no real test. On the one hand chiefs could not be expected
to sit around hearing complaints on an empty stomach. Their families did
better than those of commoners; they often rode where others walked. But
in general, due to the limited nature of the technology, to the relatively low
differentiation in the terms of levels of consumption, it seems that standards
of living, as measured by the usual tallies, were not markedly different.
Gluckman has remarked of Zulu chiefship that one man can only eat a limited
amount of porridge; the rest that he accumulates has to be distributed.[23]
Probably the maximum differentiation in terms of what Weber called 'styles
of life' was to be found in the trading states of the coast, in the empires of the
Niger bend and in the emirates of northern Nigeria, where there were certain
modes of behaviour that distinguished the urbanites of the capital (the
dynasty, the merchants, the learned men, the specialist workers, and
the hangers-on) from the rural population. But in most cases such differentiation was confined to chiefs themselves rather than spreading to the whole
dynastic descent group, being a function of roles rather than social strata;
and the most noticeable aspect of the difference lay in control over women
and slaves, and guns and horses, rather than goods and land.[24] The exceptions
were to be found in the coastal strips, where ruling and merchant groups
financed themselves out of the European and Asian trade: there are certainly

some sumptuary distinctions reported by travellers from Dahomey and Ashanti. But these differences do not approach those of mediaeval Europe, nor even of Ethiopia, where a series of sumptuary rules confined to the nobility the playing of certain musical instruments, the brewing of honey wine, and similar forms of behaviour that were by definition of high prestige.[25]

I have been suggesting that while there were local chiefships (a line organization) supported partly out of agriculture, partly from trade, there was nothing equivalent to estates in land of the European kind. I should perhaps modify this statement and say 'save only in some places and under limited conditions'. Because if you turn from line to staff organization, Colson suggests that the large-scale development of central government, which as Weber had argued involves the creation of appointive (as distinct from hereditary) office, was possible only in a few African states because of the land situation that I have described.[26] The southern Bantu failed to develop in this way. But some states, she maintains, succeeded. Among those that did were the highly centralized kingdoms of Buganda,[27] of Barotseland (Zambia), and of Dahomey. In each of these cases special conditions existed. In Buganda, the banana provided the basis for continuous cultivation; in Barotseland, there were the fertile lands of the Zambezi flood plain; in Dahomey there was the development of some plantation agriculture.[28] In each of these kingdoms you got a system of 'office estates' (rather than fiefs proper), that is, estates attached to the staff rather than the line organization.

Limited estates in land, sufficient to support appointive offices, were only rarely built up under conditions of this kind and in any case did not give rise to the kind of landlord–tenant (or serf) relationship characteristic of Europe. But was it possible to use benefices of a different kind in a similar way? In Ruanda, estates in cattle were employed to create relationships of subordination that resembled the cattle clientage of early Ireland.[29] Such estates are less easy to assign for the support of appointees to offices. They easily become fused with the personal property of the incumbent; and in any case, support by livestock is the formula for a very much looser polity than the predominance of appointed office suggests; it is difficult to centralize cows.

A more likely form of benefice to substitute for the estate in land is one based upon the allocation of income from tax or trade, which also provided one of the bases of support in Western Europe. Few states of Africa were not involved in long-distance exchange. In the case of coastal trade with Europeans (as in Dahomey and Ashanti), goods could be channelled through the machinery of government. Trading privileges could be granted directly by the king, and taxation held few administrative problems.[30] But even in the savannah kingdoms where state import–export systems did not exist, the trading communities could be forced to contribute to the support of office-holders in a variety of ways–by market taxes, customs dues, and transport charges.

Other more problematic methods of endowment did exist. These lay in the field of military organization, which is the third aspect of the social system to be considered. Here, at least in the savannah country of West Africa, the military technology resembled that of feudal Europe, since war was dominated by the use of horsed cavalry. In this connection it is relevant to turn to the thesis elaborated by Heinrich Brunner concerning the relationship of feudalism and cavalry in Europe. Brunner maintained that the great change from infantry to cavalry fighting came in the eighth century, some time after the Frankish king, Charles Martel, faced the Saracens and their horsemen near Poitiers in 733. In this battle Charles was victorious but lacking cavalry he was unable to follow up his success and Brunner held that the change to cavalry occurred shortly after this event and marked the beginning of feudalism. White agrees that this 'was essentially military, a type of social organization designed to produce and support cavalry'. But he doubts whether it was the Saracen invasions themselves that produced the change, for the redistribution of lands had already begun by 732 and moreover the Muslims made little use of horses. It was rather the advent from the East of a technological device that made mounted warfare possible, namely, the foot-stirrup. The traditional Frankish arm had been infantry. The stirrup however enabled the horseman to gain greater control on horseback so that he could wield a sword or charge his enemy with lance at rest. With the coming of the stirrup, the *francisca*, the distinctly Frankish battle-axe, and the *ango* or barbed javelin, disappear. The long sword comes into use and so too does the spear with a heavy stock and a spur below the blade to prevent too deep a penetration. This kind of horsed warfare led in turn to developments in the sphere of defence, especially the use of increasingly heavy armour.

This new form of combat required a considerable capital outlay; the military equipment for one warrior cost about 20 oxen, or the plough-teams of at least ten peasant families. To maintain cavalry of this kind there had to be some pay-off for those making the investment. In France the redistribution of church lands appears to have met this need, providing an income, a pasture, and a training ground for 'the feudal class' which, as White remarks, 'existed to be armed horsemen, cavaliers fighting in a particular manner which was made possible by the stirrup'.[31] The original and basic knight's service was mounted shock combat; it was around the cavalry that notions of chivalry arose, that there developed a knightly ethic based upon *loiautee* to leader and *proesce* in arms. 'The feudal aristocrat might, indeed, be a ruler, but this was incidental to his being a warrior'.

The horse penetrated early into Africa up the Nile valley, into the Sudan, and across the Sahara to the region of the Niger and Lake Chad. So later did the stirrup–the toe-stirrup in Ethiopia, but elsewhere the foot-stirrup. But there was no later changeover to heavy cavalry equipment; the heavy lance never replaced the javelin, and the coats of kapok, mail, and Koranic leather charms worn by the horsemen were mainly a protection against infantry rather than against opposing cavalry.

The failure to develop heavy cavalry was no doubt partly due to the weaker economic base, which inhibited the accumulation of the required capital. But in any case lighter cavalry was characteristic of the Berbers of North Africa, who also were not directly faced with Christian arms; and furthermore the lighter cavalry of the Turks and other Muslim powers had the advantage of speed, in attack, in pursuit, and in escape.[32] The added mobility placed a premium on raiding rather than warfare. In Europe the cavalry reimbursed themselves in part from loot, slaving, and from the ransom for their more valuable captives; at other times they had their estates to sustain them. In Africa, the cavalry were maintained partly by taxes on trade, by tribute and protection payments, but largely from booty. The booty did not primarily consist of material goods, for there was little to seize from the average farmer except his family. The pay-off was in human booty, captives to be sold as slaves. Booty was indeed part of the productive system of the ruling class. A measure of this close interdependence of cavalry and raiding is the situation that obtains today in the eastern Gonja capital of Kpembe, the twin city of Salaga. A cavalry headquarters at the end of the last century, it now boasts only one horse; yet on the wall of every entrance-hut hangs the dusty and disintegrating harness that tells of former glories.[33] The establishment of colonial over-rule spelt the end of the external raiding and the internal control, thus undermining the economic position of the ruling estate. When the British authorities seized power and monopolized the use of force, the Gonja had no further use for the animal on which their domination had largely depended. The economy and power of the ruling estate largely collapsed; their authority was restricted by the new rulers. But they retained enough to carve out a place for themselves in the colonial and independent régimes that followed.

Although there was no development of heavy cavalry in Africa, the military system had nevertheless some basic similarities with that of medieval Europe. Here I refer not so much to the trappings of war, some of which were indirect borrowings, but rather to associated features of the political system. For the very nature of cavalry warfare imposes certain patterns upon the social organization.

In the first place the cavalry usually provide the ruling strata, since they also provide the means of destruction, the means of conquest, the means of booty. Unlike military technologies based upon the bow and arrow or upon iron infantry weapons, there is a built-in stratification between horse-soldier and foot-soldier.[34] Secondly, horsed warfare demands a considerable investment of skill as well as of money–a long training in horsemanship which again tends to make for differences in 'class consciousness', for ideas of nobility and the knightly ethic. While these were less marked with light cavalry, they were not altogether absent.[35] Thirdly, the investment of skill and capital was not a free gift to the nation. Not only was there a pay-off in booty but there was also a political increment. Since military power was centred upon the cavalry, they were well set to demand a share in political power. This they might achieve by acting as kingmakers, or else as strong divisional chiefs. But in West Africa the diffuse government characteristic of European feudalism often took the different form of a system of succession by which the paramountcy passed between the various segments of the ruling estate.[36]

Cavalry states have certain common features both in feudal Europe and in the circum-Saharan Africa, though the difference between heavy and light cavalry remains important. But most of Africa was unsuitable for the horse which is more sensitive to tsetse fly than other livestock. Not only is the animal absent from all forest areas; it never penetrated south of the Sudd marshes of the Sudan. Consequently the structures of East African kingdoms display a number of differences from those found in the West. Even in Buganda, where war was an economic activity, it required little investment of skill and goods;[37] no large-scale endowment of land and peasant services was needed to support a permanent body of knights. Nor was there the sharp dichotomy between horse-owners and agriculturists that existed in the savannahs of West Africa, though the rigid stratification that marked Ruanda and some other inter-lacustrine states of central Africa had a similar root in the division between a ruling estate whose economy was based on livestock, and a conquered group who worked the land.

I have argued that the social systems of Africa and Eurasia displayed some broad differences which were closely linked to the productive technologies, more especially in the rural sector. In Africa, there was virtually no use of rotary motion nor of animal traction; there was almost no application of machinery to cultivation, to water control, or to transport. Practically the only machine was the loom.

NOTES

[1] See Loeb, 1962; Beattie 1964: pp. 25–35; Cohen, 1966; Lombard, 1965. For an extreme position, see Gravel, 1965. Gravel's article is based on field work in 1960–1; in it he 'purports to describe certain *specific* aspects of life on a small "manor" in eastern Rwanda, and to show how remarkably similar they are to the same aspects of life on a baronial manor of mediaeval continental Europe' (p. 323), especially with regard to the absence of 'true markets', the 'economy of subsistence' and the 'self-sufficiency of the community'. For a view much closer to my own, see Steinhart, 1967. In general these discussions place very little emphasis upon the basic technology of mediaeval Europe, the use of mills, animal traction, etc.

[2] For a discussion of some of these similarities, see my introduction to *Succession to High Office*, 1966.

[3] See Goody, 1969.

[4] See Marx, 1964, and the comment by M. I. Finley, 1968.

[5] See Miller, 1969.

[6] Cipolla, 1965; Serjeant, 1963.

[7] The early trade in the Indian Ocean had important consequences for the population of Madagascar, the spread of Asian food crops to Africa, and for the changes in the social organization of the coastal areas of Eastern Africa and parts of the Arabian peninsula prior to the rise of Muhammad. Some aspects of these latter changes are discussed by Wolf, 1951.

[8] *Guide to mediaeval antiquities*, 1924, fig. 156. See also the fourteenth century bronze ewer, in the same museum, which was 'the great war fetish of the Ashanti Nation' (*Brit. Mus. Quarterly*, **viii**, p. 52 (1933). For the European side of the trans-Saharan slave trade, see Verlinden, 1955.

[9] For mediaeval trade, see Carus-Wilson, 1954.

[10] The difference between extensive and intensive modes of agricultural production is clearly relative, and one that has to be related to the nature of the soils, the labour force and the terrain; shifting cultivation continued in less fertile and less accessible parts of mediaeval Europe long after the plough dominated the agricultural scene, and the same is of course true of Ethiopia today.

[11] In forests the plough clearly has many limitations. Nor does it improve vegeculture to the same extent as it does the cultivation of cereals. The main point however was effectively made by V. G. Childe. See also McNeill, in *The rise of the*

West: 'The harnessing of animal power for the labor of tillage was a step of obvious significance. Human resources were substantially increased thereby, since for the first time men tapped a source of mechanical energy greater than that which their own muscles could supply. The use of animal power also established a much more integral relation between stock-breeding and agriculture. Mixed farming, uniting animal husbandry with crop cultivation, was to become the distinguishing characteristic of agriculture in western Eurasia. It made possible a higher standard of living or of leisure than was attainable by peoples relying mainly or entirely upon the strength of merely human muscles' (1963: 25–6).

[12] Urban centres of course existed in pre-colonial Africa; they ranged from the Agro-cities of the Yoruba to the polyethnic trading and administrative towns of the Saharan fringes and the coastal regions.

[13] Animal disease was another factor limiting the use of the plough. Of Ethiopia, which may have obtained the plough from South Arabia or Egypt even in pre-Semitic times (about 1000 B.C.), F. J. Simoons has written: 'Where there are animals suitable for ploughing, both Cushites and Semites use the plough; but where, as along the Sudan border, these animals are excluded by disease, even Semites turn to the hoe or digging stick for preparing their fields' (1965: 11). Iron-working however appears to have arrived from South Arabia at about the same time as writing, that is, in the fifth century B.C. (Anfray 1968: 352).

[14] See Mauny, 1952 and 1961.

[15] I use the term 'gun' in a general way. At first they depended upon the cannon on their floating castles; later upon the hand-gun. See Cippola's useful discussion where he quotes Pannikar as saying that by 1498 'the armament of the Portuguese ships was something totally unexpected and new in the Indian (and China) seas and gave an immediate advantage to the Portuguese' (1965: 107).

[16] Review of B. Davidson, *J. African Hist.*, **iii** (1962), p. 510.

[17] See Cipolla, 1965: 127–8 and Al-Djamuzi's history in Serjeant, 1963: 117: 'These Malabaris are Muslims: the Munaibāri muskets are called after them'.

[18] The position was not quite as desperate as at first appears, since one European power was quite willing to benefit at the expense of another; the sources never entirely dried up. And even within the same political unit (*e.g.* the British-administered Gold Coast), the interests of merchants and administrators were often at odds. It should be added that, though sulphur had to be imported, there was certainly some manufacture of local gunpowder (*e.g.* in northern Ghana) but this was recognized to be of inferior quality (because it was not 'corned'). Equally, guns could be repaired.

But there is no evidence of any extensive manufacture of components. Even today imported bicycle frame tubes are often used to replace barrels. The one exception may have been the late nineteenth-century Mandingo warrior Samory. In 1898 Nebout was reported to have been shown a small-arms factory 'capable of turning out three repeaters a week'. The gun is described 'as a wonderfully close copy of the French article, but not bearing near inspection as to its details, more particularly in the matter of rifling (Dir. Mil. Intell. to C.O., 14/1/1898 C.O. Confid. Print, African (West) No. 549). Legassick quotes a similar report (1966: 104). Peroz and Binger, who separately visited Samory in 1897, make no mention of locally-made guns; Henderson, who was captured in 1897, writes only of a cartridge factory. Local *numu* blacksmiths may have learnt new techniques from the invaders, but it is difficult to see how the low-temperature forge could be used for the manufacture of guns from scratch, as distinct from the kind of repair work that Binger describes (1892: i, 191–2). In Europe the temperatures needed to merge from the wrought-iron phase were first produced in the fourteenth century by using water-powered bellows for blast purposes, and this in turn depended upon rotary motion. But whether or not Samory succeeded in manufacturing firearms, his continued attempts to secure imported guns by exchanging captives or by more direct methods indicate that his efforts in this direction met with little success. Indeed right to the end the military economy of his empire-building was based upon the necessity of acquiring sufficient income from booty to import guns, powder and percussion caps (Goody, 1965: 75–8).

[19] The tendency for rights in land to be more highly individualized the greater the population density has been noted by Meek, 1946: 149–50. See also Jones, 1949: 313, and Goody, 1956: 37. Of course land shortage is always relative to the available resources of labour, etc. But the tractor can create a shortage more easily than the plough, the plough more readily than the hoe. In my view there is no doubt that the 'communal' nature of African land tenure must break down rapidly with the introduction of plough or tractor, just as the economy of larger households must tend to fragment when individual members acquire their own pay-packets, by selling their labour outside the domestic group.

[20] Edward Miller points out that there is another situation which leads either to serfdom or to plantation slavery. Both institutions can emerge under conditions where 'land is relatively plentiful and where it is necessary to prevent the escape of rent producers or labour producers which a chief or landlord requires. Perhaps an extreme form of this is the slavery found in pioneer settlements in certain parts of early mediaeval Europe.' In Africa labour requirements led to slavery but not serfdom; trading towns like Kano and Bida in northern Nigeria, or Salaga and Bole in northern Ghana, were surrounded by villages of slaves which supplied the ruling and commercial groups. Domestic slaves, dependent kinsfolk and clients filled other servile roles, but the supply of land and the degree of control made it difficult to exploit labour by anything other than slavery. In Middle America, despite ample land, the Spanish conquerors imposed on the population a system of peonage, which was something less than slavery. But the conditions of productivity (the plough, soil, crops) and control (guns and horses) were very different.

[21] In Ethiopia the Church was the largest landowner after the Emperor. Some of these lands were worked by the monks; others were farmed by peasants. The landlord's rent, lay or ecclesiastical, could be enormous. At the end of the eighteenth century. Bruce noted that the tenants of Tigre usually surrendered at least half their crop, the landlord supplying the seed. But it was 'a very indulgent master that does not take another quarter for the risk he has run' (see Pankhurst, 1961: 193–5). A similar situation existed in Egypt with regard to the *waqf* lands. See for example Ibn Khaldun's reference to chieftains who 'are wont to build Mosque schools, shrines and almshouses and to endow them with Waqf [Mortmain] land...' (Issawi, 1950: 144). Of course monasticism could also be supported by other means than land, by 'taxes' on trade, or by providing services for travellers. But this was not, I think, possible to any great extent under pre-colonial conditions in Africa.

[22] The reduction of population in relation to resources can have the opposite effect on serfdom. When in the fourteenth century land in Europe became relatively plentiful (either through the Black Death or other causes), rents were halved in a decade, wages doubled and the institution of serfdom was greatly weakened.

[23] Gluckman suggests that the failure of the southeast Bantu to develop more extensive political units before the time of Dingiswayo at the beginning of the nineteenth century may have been due to the limited technology and to the availability of land, so that there was possibly little point in building up power. 'The tribal economy was simple and undifferentiated; even in a good year the available technology did not allow a man to produce much beyond his own needs. There was little trade and luxury, so even a conqueror could not make himself more comfortable than he had been before. One cannot build a palace with grass and mud, and if the only foods are grains, milk and meat, one cannot live much above the standard of

ordinary men' (Gluckman, 1960: 157–68). In West Africa the economy was more developed in these respects, particularly the military economy in so far as it depended upon cavalry and the importation of firearms and gunpowder. But the general point still holds.

[24] In Hausaland, as elsewhere in the western Sudan, trading too produced great differences in wealth.

[25] Levine notes that the upper stratum of Abyssinian society 'created and shared what might be called a "gentry sub-culture", even though it was not so differentiated from the general culture as was the case in Europe and China' (1965: 156). It should be added that sumptuary laws in the strict sense often arise when certain individuals or groups are challenging the prestige behaviour of old-established classes; they are, Edward Miller points out, 'a defensive mechanism to help maintain the existing social hierarchy'. See for example Edward II's Ordinance against extravagant house-keeping, 6 Aug. 1316 (Stubbs, 1882: 238–9).

[26] Colson (1958) speaks of the variable as the 'attitude to land' but the context of her remarks allows us to give this a more concrete reference.

[27] See Wrigley, 1957.

[28] And more importantly perhaps, the European trade.

[29] Maquet, 1961: 129 ff.; E.M. Chilver, 1960: 390.

[30] Busia, 1951: 79 ff.; Wilks, 1966: 215–32; Herskovits, 1938.

[31] White, 1962: 28. Parts of White's thesis seem too rigidly tied to the stirrup, but the connection of European feudalism with cavalry is clear. For a criticism of White's thesis, see Hilton and Sawyer, 1963.

[32] Cipolla, 1965: 91.

[33] See Braimah and Goody, 1967.

[34] The horsemen are particularly useful for fighting peasants and collecting captives, but the archers still had an advantage at close range, behind defensive positions. The layout of buildings and settlements in the Western Sudan was profoundly influenced by cavalry. (For examples of fortifications, see Binger, 1892: i, 93, 171.) With the advent of the horse, the cavalry became the offensive or predatory arm of states, whereas the bow was employed mainly for defence, though from the later sixteenth century it was supplemented by imported firearms, initially in very short supply.

[35] However, the exclusiveness of classes was limited by the open marriage system and by the limitations of the agricultural technology; for a discussion of this point, see Goody, 1970.

[36] See Coulbourn (Ed.), 1956. For an analysis of rotational systems, see Goody, 1966.

[37] War brought 'women, slaves, cattle and ivory into the elaborate system of gift-exchange centred on the Court' (Chilver, 1960: 386–7).

BIBLIOGRAPHY

ANFRAY, F. —1968, 'Aspects de l'archéologie éthiopienne', *J. African Hist.*, **IX**, 345–66.

BEATTIE, J.H.M. —1964, 'Bunyoro: an African feudality?', *J. African Hist.*, **V**, 25–35.

BINGER, L. —1892, *Du Niger au Golfe de Guinée*, Paris.

BRAIMAH, J.A. and GOODY, J. —1967, *Salaga: the struggle for power*, London.

BUSIA, K.A. —1951, *The position of the chief in Ashanti*, London.

CARUS WILSON, E.M. —1954, *Medieval merchant venturers*, London.

CHILVER, E.M. —1960, '"Feudalism" in the interlacustrine kingdoms', *East African Chiefs* (ed A.I. Richards), London.

CIPOLLA, C.M. —1965, *Guns and sails in the early phase of European expansion 1400–1700*, London.

COHEN, R. —1966, 'The dynamics of feudalism in Bornu', *African History* (ed Butler), Boston Univ. Papers on Africa, vol. II.

COLSON, E. —1958, 'The role of bureaucratic norms in African political structures', *Systems of political control and bureaucracy in human societies* (ed V.O.F. Ray), Proc. Am. Eth. Soc., Seattle.

FINLEY, M.I. —1968 'Slavery', *International Encyclopedia of the Social Sciences*, **XIV**, 307–13.

GLUCKMAN, M. —1960, 'The rise of a Zulu empire', *Scientific American*, CCII, 157–68.

GOODY, J. —1956, *The social organisation of the LoWiili*, London.

—1966, 'Circulating succession among the Gonja', in *Succession to High Office*, Cambridge.

—1969, 'Inheritance, property and marriage in Africa and Eurasia', *Sociology*, **III**, 55–76.

—1970, 'Class and marriage in Africa and Eurasia', *Am. J. Sociology*, December 1970.

GRAVEL, P.B. —1965, 'Life on the manor in Gisaka (Rwanda)', *J. African Hist.*, **VI**, 323–31.

HERSKOVITS, M.J. —1938, *Dahomey, an ancient West African Kingdom*, New York.

HILTON, R.H. and SAWYER, P.H. —1963, 'Technical determinism: the stirrup and the plough', *Past and Present*, **XXIV**, 90–100.

ISSAWI, C. —1950, *Ibn Khaldun: An Arab philosophy of history*, London.

JONES, G.I. —1949, 'Ibo Land Tenure', *Africa*, **XIX**, 1, 44, 309–23.

LEGASSICK, M. —1966, 'Firearms, horses and Samorian army organisation 1870–98', *J. African Hist.*, **VII**, 95–115.

LEVINE, D.H. —1965, *Wax and Gold*, Chicago.

LOEB, E.M. —1962, *In Feudal Africa*, Bloomington, Ill.

LOMBARD, J. —1965, *Structures de type 'féodal' en Afrique noire*, Paris.

MAQUET, J.J. —1961, *The premise of inequality in Ruanda*, London.

MARX, K. —1964, *Pre-capitalist economic formations* (ed E.J. Hobsbawm), London.

MAUNY, R. —1952, 'Essai sur l'histoire des métaux en Afrique Occidentale', *Bull. IFAN*, **XIV**, 545–95.

—1961, *Tableau géographique de l'Ouest Africain au Moyen Age*, Mém. IFAN, No. 61, Dakar.

MCNEILL, W.M. —1963, *The rise of the West*, Chicago.

MEEK, C.K. —1946, *Land law and custom in the colonies*, London.

MILLER, J.I. —1969, *The spice trade of the Roman Empire*. Oxford.

PANKHURST, R. —1961, *An introduction to the economic history of Ethiopia*, London.

SERJEANT, R.B. —1963, *The Portuguese off the South Arabian coast*, Oxford.

SIMOONS, F.J. —1965, 'Some questions on the economic pre-history of Ethiopia', *J. African Hist*, VI, 1–13.

STEINHART, E.I. —1967, 'Vassal and fief in three lacustrine kingdoms', *Cah. d'Études Afr.*, **VII**, 606–23.

STUBBS, W. —1882, *Chronicles of the Reigns of Edward I and Edward II*, vol. I, London.

VERLINDEN, C. —1955, *L'Esclavage dans l'Europe médiévale*, Bruges.

WHITE, L. —1962, *Medieval technology and social change*, Oxford.

WILKS, I. —1966, 'Aspects of bureaucratization in Ashanti in the nineteenth century'. *J. African Hist.*, **VII**, 215–32.

WOLF, E.R. —1951, 'The social organisation of Mecca and the origins of Islam', *South-western J. Anthrop.*, **VII**, 329–56.

WRIGLEY, C.C. —1957, 'Buganda: an outline economic history', *Econ. Hist. Rev.*, **X**, 69–80.

Technological stagnation and economic distortion in pre-colonial times

WALTER RODNEY

From Chapter 4 of Walter Rodney, *How Europe underdeveloped Africa*, Bogle L'Ouverture Publications, London, and Tanzania Publishing House, Dar es Salaam, 1972. (Also Howard University Press, Washington, 1974.)

In the fifteenth century European technology was not totally superior to that of other parts of the world. There were certain specific features which were highly advantageous to Europe–such as shipping and (to a lesser extent) guns. Europeans trading to Africa had to make use of Asian and African consumer goods, showing that their system of production was not absolutely superior. It is particularly striking that in the early centuries of trade, Europeans relied heavily on Indian cloths for resale in Africa, and they also purchased cloths on several parts of the West African coast for resale elsewhere. Morocco, Mauretania, Senegambia, Ivory Coast, Benin, Yorubaland, and Loango were all exporters to other parts of Africa–through European middlemen. Yet, by the time that Africa entered the colonial era, it was concentrating almost entirely on the export of raw cotton and the import of manufactured cotton cloth. This remarkable reversal is tied to technological advance in Europe and to stagnation of technology in Africa owing to the very trade with Europe.

Cloth manufacture in the world went through a stage of handlooms and small-scale craft production. Up to the sixteenth century, that was the general pattern in Africa, Asia, and Europe: with Asian cloth makers being the most skilled in the world. India is the classic example where the British used every means at their disposal to kill the cloth industry, so that British cloth could be marketed everywhere, including inside India itself. In Africa, the situation was not so clear-cut, nor did it require as much conscious effort by Europeans to destroy African cloth manufacture, but the trend was the same. Europe benefited technologically from its external trade contacts, while Africa either failed to benefit or actually lost. Vital inventions and innovations appeared in England in the late eighteenth century, after profits from external trade had been re-invested. Indeed, the new machinery represented the investment of primary capital accumulated from trading and from slavery. African and Indian trade strengthened British industry, which in turn crushed whatever industry existed in what is now called the 'underdeveloped' countries.

African demand for cloth was increasing rapidly in the fifteenth, sixteenth, and seventeenth centuries, so that there was a market for all cloth produced locally as well as room for imports from Europe and Asia. But, directed by an acquisitive capitalist class, European industry increased its capacity to produce on a large scale by harnessing the energy of wind, water, and coal. European cloth industry was able to copy fashionable Indian and African patterns, and eventually to replace them. Partly by establishing a stranglehold on the distribution of cloth around the shores of Africa, and partly by swamping African products by importing cloth in bulk, European traders eventually succeeded in putting an end to the expansion of African cloth manufacture.

There are many varied social factors which combine to determine when a society makes a breakthrough from small-scale craft technology to equipment designed to harness nature so that labour becomes more effective. One of the major factors is the existence of a demand for more products than can be made by hand, so that technology is asked to respond to a definite social need–such as that for clothes. When European cloth became dominant on the African market, it meant that African producers were cut off from the increasing demand. The craft producers either abandoned their tasks in the face of cheap available European cloth, or they continued on the same small hand-worked instruments to create styles and pieces for localized markets. Therefore, there was what can be called 'technological arrest' or stagnation, and in some instances actual regression, since people forgot even the simple technique of their forefathers. The abandonment of traditional iron smelting in most parts of Africa is probably the most important instance of technological regression.

Development means a capacity for self-sustaining growth. It means that an economy must register advances which in turn will promote further progress. The loss of industry and skill in Africa was extremely small, if we measure it from the viewpoint of modern scientific achievements or even by standards of England in the late eighteenth century. However, it must be borne in mind that to be held back at one stage means that it is impossible to go on to a further stage. When a person was forced to leave school after only two years of primary school education, it is no reflection on him that he is academically and intellectually less developed than someone who had the opportunity to be schooled right through to university level. What Africa experienced in the early centuries of trade was precisely a loss of development *opportunity*, and this is of the greatest importance.

One of the features associated with technological advance is a spirit of scientific enquiry closely related to the process of production. This leads to inventiveness and innovation. During the period of capitalist development in Europe, this was very much the case, and historians lay great emphasis on the spirit of inventiveness of the English in the 18th century. Socialist societies do not leave inventions merely to chance or good luck–they actively cultivate tendencies for innovation. For instance, in the German Democratic Republic, the youth established a 'Young Innovators' Fair' in 1958, calling upon the intellectual creativity of socialist youth, so that within ten years over 2,000 new inventions were presented at that fair. The connection between Africa and Europe from the fifteenth century onwards served to block this spirit of technological innovation both directly and indirectly.

The European slave trade was a direct block, in removing millions of youth and young adults who are the human agents from whom inventiveness springs. Those who remained in areas badly hit by slave-capturing were pre-occupied about their freedom rather than with improvements in production. Besides, even the busiest African in West, Central, or East Africa was concerned more with trade than with production, because of the nature of the contacts with Europe; and that situation was not conducive to the introduction of technological advances. The most dynamic groups over a great area of Africa became associated with foreign trade–notably, the Afro-Portuguese middlemen of Upper Guinea, the Akan market women, the Aro traders of the Bight of Biafra, the mulattos of Angola, the Yao traders of Mozambique, and the Swahili and Wanyamwezi of East Africa. The trade which they carried on was in export items like captives and ivory which did not require the invention of machinery. Apart from that, they were agents for distributing European imports.

When Britain was the world's leading economic power, it used to be referred to as a nation of shopkeepers: but most of the goods in their shops were produced by themselves, and it was while grappling with the problems posed by production that their engineers came up with so many inventions. In Africa, the trading groups could make no contribution to technological improvement because their role and pre-occupation took their minds and energies away from production.

Apart from inventiveness, we must also consider the borrowing of technology. When a society for whatever reason finds itself technologically trailing behind others, it catches up not so much by independent inventions but by borrowing. Indeed, very few of man's major scientific discoveries have been separately discovered in different places by different people. Once a principle or a tool is known, it spreads or diffuses to other peoples. Why then did European technology fail to make its way into Africa during the many centuries of contact between the two continents? The basic reason is that the very nature of Afro-European trade was highly unfavourable to the movement of positive ideas and techniques from the European capitalist system to the African pre-capitalist (communal, feudal, and pre-feudal) system of production.

The only non-European society that borrowed effectively from Europe and became capitalist is that of Japan. Japan was already a highly developed feudal society progressing towards its own capitalist forms in the nineteenth century. Its people were neither enslaved nor colonized by Europe, and its foreign trade relations were quite advantageous. For instance, Japanese textile manufacturers had the stimulus of their own growing internal market and some abroad in Asia and Europe. Under those circumstances, the young Japanese capitalist class (including many former feudalist landowners) borrowed technology from Europe and successfully domesticated it before the end of the nineteenth century. The use of this example from outside of Africa is meant to emphasize that for Africa to have received European technology the demand would have had to come from inside Africa–and most probably from a class or group who saw profit in the new technology. There had to be both willingness on the part of Europeans to transfer technology and African socio-economic structures capable of making use of that technology and internalizing it.

Hunting for elephants or captives did not usually induce in Africa a demand for any technology other than firearms. The lines of economic activity attached to foreign trade were either destructive as slavery was, or at best purely extractive, like ivory hunting and cutting camwood trees. Therefore, there was no reason for wanting to call upon European skills. The African economies would have had little room for such skills unless negative types of exports were completely stopped. A remarkable fact that is seldom brought to light is that several African rulers in different parts of the continent saw the situation clearly, and sought European technology for internal development, which was meant to replace the trade in slaves.

Europeans deliberately ignored those African requests that Europe should place certain skills and techniques at their disposal. This was an element in the Kongo situation of the early sixteenth century, which has already been mentioned. It happened in Ethiopia also, though in Ethiopia no trade in captives was established with Europeans. A Portuguese embassy reached the Ethiopian court in 1520. Having examined Portuguese swords, muskets, clothes, books, and other objects, the Emperor Lebna Dengel felt the need to introduce European technical knowledge into Ethiopia. Correspondence exists between the Emperor and European rulers such as kings Manuel I and John III of Portugal and Pope Leo X, in which requests were made for European assistance to Ethiopian industry. Until late in the nineteenth century, Ethiopian petitions to that effect were being repeated with little or no success.

In the first half of the eighteenth century, there were two further examples of African rulers appreciating European technology, and stating their preference for skills and not slave ships. When Agaja Trudo of Dahomey sought to stop the trade in captives, he made an appeal to European craftsmen, and he sent an ambassador to London for that purpose. One European who stayed at the court of Dahomey in the late 1720s told his countrymen that 'if any tailor, carpenter, smith or any other sort of white man that is free be willing to come here, he will find very good encouragement'. The Asantehene, Opoku Ware (1720–50), also asked Europeans to set up factories and distilleries in Asante, but he got no response.

Bearing in mind the history of Japan, it should be noted that the first requests for technical assistance came from the Ethiopian and Kongo empires, which in the sixteenth century were at a level undoubtedly comparable to most European feudal states, with the important exception that they had not produced the seeds of capitalism. During the eighteenth century the great African states of Dahomey and Asante became prominent. They had passed out of the communal stage and had a somewhat feudal class stratification along with specialization in many activities such as the working of gold, iron, and cloth. Asante society under Opoku Ware had already shown a capacity for seeking out innovations, by going to the trouble of taking imported silk and unravelling it so as to combine the silk threads with cotton to make the famous *kente* cloth. In other words, there would have been no difficulty in such African societies mastering European technical skills and bridging the rather narrow gap which existed between them and Europe at that time.

Well into the nineteenth century, Europe displayed the same indifference to requests for practical assistance from Africa, although by that period both African rulers and European capitalists were talking about replacing slave trade. In the early nineteenth century, one king of Calabar (in Eastern Nigeria) wrote the British asking for a sugar refinery; while around 1804 King Adandozan of Dahomey was bold enough to ask for a firearms factory! By that date, many parts of West Africa were going to war with European firearms and gunpowder. There grew up a saying in Dahomey that 'He who makes the powder wins the war', which was a far-sighted recognition that Africans were bound to fall before the superiority of Europeans in the field of arms technology. Of course, Europeans were also fully aware that their arms technology was decisive, and there was not the slightest chance that they would have agreed to teach Africans to make firearms and ammunition.

The circumstances of African trade with Europe were unfavourable to creating a consistent African demand for technology relevant to development; and when that demand was raised it was ignored or rejected by the capitalists. After all, it would not have been in the interests of capitalism to develop Africa. In more recent times, Western capitalists had refused to build the Volta River Dam for Ghana under Kwame Nkrumah, until they realized that the Czechoslovakians would do the job; they refused to build the Aswan Dam for Egypt, and the Soviet Union had to come to the rescue; and in a similar situation they placed obstacles in the way of the building of a railway from Tanzania to Zambia, and it was the Socialist state of China that stepped in to express solidarity with African peasants and workers in a practical way. Placing the whole question in historical perspective allows us to see that capitalism has always discouraged technological evolution in Africa and blocks Africa's access to its own technology. As will be seen in a subsequent section, capitalism introduced into Africa only such limited aspects of its material culture as were essential to more efficient exploitation, but the general tendency has been for capitalism to underdevelop Africa in technology.

The European slave trade and overseas trade in general had what are known as 'multiplier effects' on Europe's development in a very positive sense. This means that the benefits of foreign contacts extended to many areas of European life not directly connected with foreign trade, and the whole society was better equipped for its own internal development. The opposite was true of Africa not only in the crucial sphere of technology but also with regard to the size and purpose of each economy in Africa. Under the normal processes of evolution, an economy grows steadily larger so that after a while two neighbouring economies merge into one. That was precisely how national economies were created in the states of Western Europe through the gradual combination of what were once separate provincial economies. Trade with Africa actually helped Europe to weld together more closely the different national economies, but in Africa there was disruption and disintegration at the local level. At the same time, each local economy ceased to be directed exclusively or even primarily towards the satisfaction of the wants of its inhabitants; and (whether or not the particular Africans recognised it) their economic effort served external interests and made them dependent on those external forces based in Western Europe. In this way, the African economy taken as a whole was diverted away from its previous line of development and became distorted.

It has now become common knowledge that one of the principal reasons why genuine industrialization cannot easily be realized in Africa today is that the market for manufactured goods in any single African country is too small, and there is no integration of the markets across large areas of Africa. The kind of relationship which Africa has had with Europe from the very beginning has worked in a direction opposite to integration of local economies. Certain inter-territorial links established on the continent were broken down after the fifteenth century because of European trade. Several examples arose on the West African coast down to Angola, because in those parts European trade was most voluminous, and the surviving written record is also more extensive.

When the Portuguese arrived in the region of modern Ghana in the 1470s, they had few commodities to offer the inhabitants in exchange for the gold coveted by Europe. However, they were able to tranship from Benin in Nigeria supplies of cotton cloths, beads, and female slaves, which were saleable on the 'Gold Coast'. The Portuguese were responding to a given demand on the 'Gold Coast', so that a previous trade must have been in existence between the people of Benin and those of the 'Gold Coast', particularly the Akan. The Akan were gold producers, and the people of Benin were specialist craftsmen who had a surplus of cloth and beads which they manufactured themselves. As an expansionist state with a large army, Benin also had access to prisoners-of-war, while the Akan seemed concerned with building their own population and labour force, so the latter acquired female captives from Benin and rapidly integrated them as wives. When the Portuguese intervened in this exchange, it was subordinated to the interests of European trade. As soon as Portugal and other European nations had sufficient goods so as not to be dependent on the re-export of certain commodities from Benin, then all that remained were the links between the 'Gold Coast' and Europe on the one hand and between Benin and Europe on the other.

Probably, Benin products had reached the 'Gold Coast' by way of the creeks behind the coast of what is now Dahomey and Togo. Therefore, it would have been more convenient when Europeans established a direct link across the open sea. As pointed out earlier, the superiority of Europeans at sea was of the greatest strategic value, along with their organizational ability. This was illustrated in several places, beginning with the Maghreb and Mauretania. After the Portuguese took control of the Atlantic coast of North-West Africa, they were able to secure horses, woollen goods, and beads, which they shipped further south to West Africa for gold and slaves; up to the early sixteenth century, the most important article brought by the Portuguese for trade in Senegambia was the horse. In exchange for one horse they received as many as 15 captives. North African woollens and beads were also utilized by the Portuguese in buying gold on the river Gambia and as far south as Sierra Leone.

It needs to be recalled that the Western Sudan had links with the West African coast and with North Africa. Long before the European arrival, horses were moving from North Africa to be inter-bred with local West African stock. Long before the European arrival, the Arabs and Mauretanians travelled to the river Senegal and further south to meet the Mandinga Djola traders and hand over to them products such as beads made in Ceuta and cloth spun from the wool of North African sheep. With the advantage of rapidity of transport by sea as opposed to overland across the desert, the Portuguese were in effect breaking up the economic integration of the region. As with the Benin–Akan example, the point to note is that after the Portuguese became middlemen they had the opportunity of developing a new trade pattern by which both North West Africa and West Africa looked to Europe and forgot about each other.

A similar situation came into existence on the Upper Guinea coast, and this time the European exploitation was aided by the presence of white settlers in the Cape Verde Islands. The Portuguese and the Cape Verde settlers broke into the pattern of local Upper Guinea trade ever since the 1470s. They intervened in transfers of raw cotton and indigo dye from one African community to another, and the Cape Verdean settlers established a flourishing cotton-growing and cotton-manufacturing industry. They used labour and techniques from the mainland, and exported the finished products along the length of the coast down to Accra.

The Portuguese also took over the trade in cowries in the Kongo and its off-shore islands, the trade in salt along the Angolan coast, and the trade in high-quality palm cloth between northern and southern Angola. In some instances, they achieved dominance not just because of their ships and commercial skills but also by the use of force–providing they were operating on the coast and could bring their cannon into use. In East Africa, for instance, the Portuguese used violence to capture trade from the Arabs and Swahili. The disruption of African commerce between the 'Ivory Coast' and the 'Gold Coast' followed that pattern. A strong coastal canoe trade existed between these two regions, with the people of Cape Lahou (modern Ivory Coast) sailing past Cape Three Points to sell their cloth as far east as Accra. The Portuguese set up a fort at Axim near Cape Three Points to service gold trade with the hinterland; and one of its functions was to chop the east–west coastal African trade. They banned Axim residents from going to Cape Lahou, and they stopped canoes from 'Ivory Coast' from travelling east beyond Axim. The purpose was obviously to make both areas separate economic entities exclusively tied to Europe.

The above-mentioned African commerce proved to have deep roots. The Dutch found it still going on when they took over Axim in 1637. The servants of the Dutch West India Company which was operating on the 'Gold Coast' wanted to put a complete stop to the African trade; and when that was not achieved they tried to force the people of the 'Ivory Coast' to buy a certain amount of Dutch goods. The Dutch ruled that each Axim canoeman going to Cape Lahou should carry Dutch goods worth at least 4 ounces of gold. The purpose was to convert a purely inter-African exchange into a European-African trade.

What was doubly detrimental to African attempts to integrate their own economies was the fact that when Europeans became middlemen in local trade networks, they did so mainly to facilitate the extraction of captives, and thereby subordinated the whole economy to the European slave trade. In Upper Guinea and the Cape Verde islands, the Portuguese and their mulatto descendants engaged in a large variety of exchanges involving cotton, dyes, kola nuts, and European products. The purpose of it all was to fill the holds of slave ships. In Congo and Angola, the same picture emerges. The salt, cowry shells, and palm cloth that came into Portuguese hands made up for their shortage of trade goods and served to purchase captives on different parts of the coast and deep in the interior.

The element of subordination and dependence is crucial to an understanding of African underdevelopment today, and its roots lie far back in the era of international trade. It is also worth noting that there is a type of false or pseudo integration which is a camouflage for dependence. In contemporary times, it takes the form of free-trade areas in the formerly colonized sections of the world. Those free-trade areas are made to order for the penetration of multi-national corporations. From the fifteenth century onwards, pseudo integration appeared in the form of the interlocking of African economies over long distances from the coast, so as to allow the passage of human captives and ivory from a given point inland to a given port on the Atlantic or Indian Ocean. For example, captives were moved from Congo through what is now Zambia and Malawi to Mozambique, where Portuguese, Arab or French buyers took them over. That was not genuine integration of the economies of the African territories concerned. Such trade merely represented the extent of foreign penetration, thereby stifling local trades.

The West African gold trade was not destroyed, but it became directly dependent on European buyers by being diverted from the northward routes across the Sahara. Within the savannah belt of the Western Sudan, the trans-Saharan gold trade had nourished one of the most highly developed political zones in all Africa from the fifth century onwards. But it was more convenient for Europe to obtain its gold on the West Coast than through North African intermediaries, and one is left to speculate on what might have occurred in the Western Sudan if there had been a steady increase in the gold trade over the seventeenth and eighteenth centuries. Nevertheless, there is something to be said in favour of African trade with Europe in this particular commodity. Gold production involved mining and an orderly system of distribution within Africa. Akan country and parts of Zimbabwe and Mozambique sustained flourishing socio-political systems up to the 19th century, largely because of gold production.

Certain benefits also derived from the export of ivory. The search for ivory became the most important activity in several East African societies at one time or another, sometimes in combination with the trade in captives. The Wanyamwezi of Tanzania were East Africa's best known traders–acquiring their reputation through carrying goods for hundreds of miles between Lake Tanganyika and the Indian Ocean. When the Wanyamwezi gave their attention to the export of ivory, this sparked off other beneficial developments, such as increased trading in hoes, food, and salt between themselves and their neighbours.

Yet, ivory was an asset that was rapidly exhausted in any given region, and the struggle to secure new supplies could lead to violence comparable to that which accompanied the search for human captives. Besides, the most decisive limitation of ivory trade was the fact that it did not grow logically from local needs and local production. Large quantities of ivory were not required by any society inside Africa, and no African society turned to elephant hunting and ivory collection on a big scale until the demand came from Europe or Asia. Any African society which took ivory exports seriously, then had to re-structure its economy so as to make ivory trade successful. That in turn led to excessive and undesirable dependence on the overseas market and an external economy. There could be growth in the volume of commerce and the rise of some positive side-effects, but there was decrease in the capacity to achieve economic independence and self-sustaining social progress. Besides, at all times one must keep in mind the dialectical opposite of the trade in Africa: namely, production in Europe or in America under European control. The few socially desirable by-products of elephant hunting within Africa were chicken-feed in comparison with the profits, technology, and skills associated with the product in Europe. In that way, the gap between Africa and Europe was constantly widening; and it is on the basis of that gap that we arrive at development and underdevelopment.

The rise of a proto-bourgeoisie in Yorubaland
PHILIP EHRENSAFT

From Philip Ehrensaft, 'The political economy of informal empire in pre-colonial Nigeria, 1807–1884', *Canadian Journal of African Studies*, **VI**, 3 (1972) Montreal.

In the Yoruba region of what is now the Western State of Nigeria, thousands of Africans acquired 'modernized' skills in the spheres of commerce, education, technology, and administration. This 'proto-bourgeoisie' was produced by the conjunction of large numbers of freed slaves or their descendants returning to Western Nigeria and the political economy of informal empire. The proto-bourgeoisie's development was temporarily reduced and deflected by the imposition of a colonial régime, but the very process of discrimination and repression of these skilled Africans created the nucleus of Nigerian nationalism. This group of 'modernized' Africans is termed a proto-bourgeoisie for two reasons: 1) though numbering in the thousands and performing an essential intermediary role in the political economy of informal empire, the group was nowhere near large enough to exercise economic, political, and cultural hegemony *vis-à-vis* other indigenous elements; 2) the range of resources and organizational skills it possessed was not wide enough to exercise all the functions of hegemony exercised by a typical metropolitan bourgeoisie. Both quantitatively and qualitatively, the Nigerian group constituted the small, potential core of a bourgeoisie. Thus, the term 'proto-bourgeoisie' is employed.

To chart the origins and characteristics of Nigeria's proto-bourgeoisie, one must first know something of the politics of Yorubaland before the introduction of informal empire. Oral tradition indicates that the Yoruba were originally an inland people who moved south from the savannah into the forest belt. Few Yorubas migrated as far south as the coast. Among the major Yoruba towns, only Lagos, however, was founded some centuries after the other kingdoms and was not important until the eighteenth century.[1] During the eighteenth century, the Kingdom of Oyo was predominant in the area, covering over one-half of Yoruba territory.[2] Oyo was probably founded in the fourteenth century. It was located 200 miles from the sea, on the transition line from forest to savannah. The kingdom was already enmeshed in the trans-Saharan trading network when Atlantic trade began. Oyo was situated such that it linked coastal trade with the Western Sudan. On the basis of this strategic location, the kingdom flourished from trans-Atlantic trade. By the late seventeenth century, Oyo was exporting slaves on a large scale. In return, the kingdom received iron, salt, cutlasses, and luxuries such as cloth and mirrors. Fire-arms were not an important component of imports from Europe until the early nineteenth century.[3]

Oyo's fortunes declined during the last quarter of the eighteenth century. The kingdom had expanded beyond its administrative capacity, a phenomenon typical of pre-capitalist empires. The central government was weakened over disputes concerning succession. From 1754 until 1774, the throne was usurped by a man not eligible for the position by established criteria. By these criteria, the king had been first among equals within the governing class. Now kings began to assume more power for themselves, leading to dissension and resentment. Simultaneously, generals in the field set themselves up as independent powers. Internal strife at the centre also weakened its control over the provinces, where effective rebellious leaders began to appear.[4]

Before the nineteenth century, the Yoruba had been sufficiently well-organized to see that their neighbours to the north suffered most from the slave trade, not themselves. Disintegration of the Oyo empire precipitated civil wars, bringing the full impact of the slave trade to the Yorubas for the first time.[5] From 1821 onwards, Yorubaland was wracked by civil wars. Part of this process involved the expansion of the Hausa–Fulani empire into Yorubaland. The ruler of Ilorin, the northernmost Yoruba kingdom, made an alliance with the Muslims from the north in order to strengthen his hand against Oyo. The alliance was made open in 1824, following which the Muslims took over top political positions. They made military incursions towards the south and succeeded in destroying the capital of Oyo. Yorubas responded to these invasions by moving southwards, seeking European fire-arms, and developing closer relations with the Europeans (e.g., by admitting missions).[6]

The Egba kingdom of southwestern Yorubaland was the group which forged the closest relationships with Europeans. In 1839, the first group of returned slaves and their descendants left Sierra Leone and disembarked at Badagry, a coastal location just south of Egbaland and a short distance west of Lagos. The first European mission in Western Nigeria was established in 1842 at Badagry. That same year, the missionary Thomas Birch Freeman reached Abeokuta, the capital town of Egbaland. The ruler of Egbaland saw an opportunity to use an alliance with Europeans as a bulwark against pressures from rival Yoruba groups and also Dahomey to the west. Thus he was liberal in his policies towards Christians. In addition, Freeman was also encouraged by the presence of Christian returned slaves who had migrated to Abeokuta from Badagry following the first landing in 1839. Freeman had a vision of Christian 'civilization' spreading from Abeokuta into the interior. In 1846, the Anglican Church Missionary Society established itself in Abeokuta. It was followed in 1847 by a Wesleyan mission.[7] Missionaries became a vocal interest group supporting the Egba's claims *vis-à-vis* other African groups. Traders and soldiers often clashed with the missionaries over this support. The former groups were inclined to make bargains with any group that would further Great Britain's economic and strategic interests. Support for the Egba on any particular issue was contingent on these objectives.

The Egba viewed Europeans in terms of certain advantages to be gained through establishing relationships with them. They always had a wariness with regards to British intentions, a wariness increased by the conquest of Lagos and then intensified when the island kingdom was formally annexed. This last event demolished the basis for missionary influence in Abeokuta. In 1865, the United Egba Board of Management was organized by G. W. Johnson, a returned slave from Sierra Leone. The purpose of the Board was to equip Abeokuta with skills characteristic of the industrial revolution, skills which would enable the Egbas to preserve their independence *vis-à-vis* both Europeans and other Africans. Finally, Europeans were expelled from Abeokuta in 1867, their missionary buildings sacked and printing press destroyed.[8]

The role which returned slaves and their descendants played in other areas of Yorubaland continued, however, to be closely related to the missionary enterprise. Policies adopted by the first European missionaries in Nigeria encouraged support of African efforts towards self-help and self-development. Henry Venn, the General Secretary and leading spirit of the Church Missionary Society from 1841 until 1872, thought that a new evangelical approach had to be taken towards Africans. Venn believed that self-supporting, self-governing, and self-propagating churches should be established in West Africa. The basis for expanding Christianity would be an African bourgeoisie. Consequently, missions supported the development of trade in order to encourage the formation of this social group. In part, one must attribute this policy to the realities of the West African situation: the European mortality rate was high due to the climate, staffing missions with Africans would be less expensive than importing Europeans, and there was little support from the British government.[9] However, the aim of creating an independent, African bourgeoisie was often pursued deliberately and for its own sake. This notion had power as an ideology for missionaries like Venn which went beyond its practical suitability for the West African situation.[10]

Spontaneous movement of liberated Africans back to their homelands in Nigeria offered promising soil for the missionary goal of creating an African bourgeoisie. Churches in Great Britain gave these movements wide publicity.[11] Here was the nucleus of the desired class. Tens of thousands of liberated Africans who had acquired at least some of the linguistic and commercial skills of industrial Great Britain could penetrate the interior and carry progress and Christianity to their brethren. Supporters of British intervention in Lagos used the presence of liberated Africans as support for their argument: British presence would protect these people against re-enslavement and open the way for these people to reach their former homes.[12] The combination of an estimated 40–50,000 liberated Africans to their Nigerian homelands plus the particular stance of the European missionaries who strongly supported the 'Saros' (liberated Africans from Sierra Leone) and Brazilians (liberated Africans from Brazil) had important consequences for the development of Nigeria's contemporary social structure:

The emigrants had an importance in Nigerian history out of all proportion to their numbers. Left to themselves, and scattered all over the whole country, they might have had no more significance than a band of ex-servicemen, people who had taken part in a nightmarish experience, with a useful stock of strange tales, and a stock of other arts for which there was not much scope at home. But the missionary movement kept most of them together in a few focal centres, gave them scope and encouragement. For the Sierra Leoneans, they offered commercial opportunities, employment as catechists, evangelists, and schoolmasters; for the Brazilians, houses to build, roads to construct, and other facilities to practise the arts they had acquired. It was the emigrants who introduced the missions into the country, and they were an essential part of the mission movement.[13]

Important as missionary support for liberated Africans was, however, this support was not unqualified. Liberated Africans' activities were evaluated in terms of facilitating European goals. When the liberated Africans' conceptions of development through partnership differed from that of the missionaries, Europeans accused them of backsliding, deviation from the true faith, and so on. From the earliest days of the missionary endeavour, there were Europeans who did not agree with Venn's new ideas. Furthermore, European traders and administrator–soldiers had different ideas as to what partnership with indigenous peoples entailed. All these divisions of opinion were important determinants of relationships between liberated Africans and Europeans on the coast. In order to trace the dynamics of these relationships, one must go back to the earliest years of the Europeans' physical presence on the coast of Western Nigeria.

During the forties, missionaries were the spearhead of Great Britain's penetration into Western Nigeria. Among the African peoples in the hinterland immediately adjacent to Badagry, the Egba were receptive to missionary presence, while the Ijebu and Dahomey rebuffed them. Consequently, the CMS operated as a vigorous pressure group whose goal was to induce Great Britain to intervene in favour of the Egba when they clashed with Dahomey or the Ijebu. British traders were less concerned with the spread of Christianity than the flow of trade. Traders wished to negotiate with the Ijebu and Dahomey, whatever their religious preferences. Tension between the goals of traders and missionaries was solved in the former's favour. After the formal annexation of Lagos island in 1861, the missionaries' initiative in penetrating the interior began to recede. By 1863, CMS agents were following the penetration of European political–military authority, rather than leading it as was the case during the forties.[14]

Despite this shift in initiative, missions remained crucial in the formation of contemporary Nigeria's social structure. First of all, missions started and maintained all schools in Nigeria until 1882.[15] Even after government entered the educational scene, missions continued to educate most Nigerian students. Missions provided employment opportunities for a sizeable number of educated Africans. Consequently, missionary attitudes and policies toward Africans were quite important. From the beginning of the missionary enterprise in Nigeria, there was tension among the Europeans concerning Venn's ideas. The policy of partnership was one set in London. There was tension between the evangelical bureaucracy in London and missionaries operating in Africa, parallel to the tension between government officials in London and 'the man on the spot'. Basically, the white missionaries did not wish to relinquish control to the Africans they trained.

Venn's plan was to transform the mission into a church, *i.e.*, Europeans would vacate top positions and control of policy when enough indigenous people were available to make this transfer practical. Europeans who established congregations desired to remain as pastors and begrudged moves at later stages of life to difficult frontier conditions in the hinterland. The appointment of a Saro, Samuel Crowther, as the first African Bishop in 1864 was opposed by certain local missionaries who wanted the appointment to go to a white. Older missionaries finally agreed to the appointment, but a younger group refused to work under Crowther. Furthermore, Crowther was not appointed as an independent bishop with an established revenue. His formal position was that of a missionary bishop on the Niger River, which meant that he was financially dependent upon the CMS and subject to its control.[16]

European missionaries expected liberated Africans to be loyal agents in furthering their white mentors' interests. Loyalty was defined as acting just as the Europeans wished. Even where Africans acted in such a fashion, many white missionaries regarded blacks as less than equals. Most liberated Africans, however, did not act exactly as missionaries thought they should. They found themselves located in a developing nexus of ethnic, class, and political relationships which led to an independent assessment of liberated African interests. From 1861 onwards, returning Africans established ties with the tribes from which they originated. Hinterland groups came to view some of the liberated Africans as reliable spokesmen and advisers whose primary identity and loyalty was to the ancestral group. Saro merchants and traders were especially inclined towards tribal loyalty, since their commercial success depended upon contacts with Africans in the hinterland.[17] Such contacts were best established and maintained with one's ancestral group. Thus sentiments of loyalty were buttressed by the structure of modern commerce.

Within the colony of Lagos, liberated Africans divided into ethnic factions, each faction supporting the Yoruba group from which they originated. Ethnic associations were formed and direct contract was maintained with tribal leaders in the hinterland. Ethnic organizations served the hinterland primarily as sources of military supplies and other forms of support.[18]

Perhaps the most effective Lagos–hinterland ethnic ties were organized by the Ekiti and Ijesa proto-bourgeoisie. Liberated Africans from Sierra Leone and the Americas who were of Ekiti and Ijesa origin and a number of Ijesa–Ekiti men who had been captured and sold as slaves, but not shipped away from Lagos, formed the Ijesa Association during the 1850s. The name was changed to the Ekitiparapo Society in 1876. It began as a Christian group holding weekly prayer meetings but gradually became preoccupied with politics, especially ameliorating the lot of their compatriots in the hinterland. The Ekiti and Ijesa peoples were under the strong yoke of the Ibadan. As time went on, the Ekitiparapo Association became convinced that only an armed uprising against Ibadan would alter the condition of their people. The association influenced hinterland politics through visits by members from Lagos and through a number of liberated Africans who had settled permanently at home.[19]

During the second half of the 1870s, a new trade route from Lagos to the Ijesa and Ekiti countries was opened via Ondo. Previously, trade with these areas had to pass through Ibadan, where it was closely scrutinized for items such as fire-arms. Now a great proportion of the Lagos–hinterland trade via the Ondo road came into the hands of trader members of the Ekitiparapo Society, who served mainly as agents and factors for the big Lagos merchants.[20] Ekitiparapo merchants in Lagos used their influence and commercial-contacts to procure modern weaponry such as breech-loading guns with rifled barrels for the confederated Ekiti–Ijesa armies. Ibadan responded by sending strong letters to their own section of the Lagos proto-bourgeoisie, the Oyo, appealing that they emulate the Ekitiparapo and obtain the same rifles for Ibadan. At other times, Ibadan asked that its proto-bourgeoisie influence the Governor of Lagos to stop the activities. No effective results came from these letters or later efforts by the Oyo proto-bourgeoisie. Unfortunately, available materials seem inadequate to explain the differences in organizational success achieved by the two sections of the Lagos proto-bourgeoisie. The Ekitiparapo also organized a fairly strong rifle corps trained and led by volunteers and representatives sent up from Lagos.[21]

Formation of urban–rural ethnic bonds such as those organized by the Ekitiparapo were part and parcel of the formation of an African proto-bourgeoisie. As mentioned above, traders were most inclined to solidify tribal bonds. Since most of the liberated Africans in Lagos became small-scale traders, the majority of these people were enmeshed in the simultaneous and intertwined formation of class and ethnic networks. Class and ethnicity were not contradictory but mutually reinforcing: the more 'modern' one became, the more one became 'tribal'.

Small-scale liberated African traders became the middle-men between European merchants on the Western Nigerian coast and the Yoruba hinterland under the system of informal empire. They frequently served as commercial agents representing European firms in the interior. Others operated as independent agents, gaining commercial advantages from their ability to reach producer groups before the Europeans. From the point of view of European businessmen, small-scale African traders exercised important functions: they demonstrated European commodities in the interior and thus stimulated demand for imports; African businessmen transported commodities into the hinterland at a time when transportation was difficult for Europeans; through the agency of indigenous traders, European importers on the coast were able to divide large bulks of commodities into smaller units for sale in dispersed hinterland markets.

Not all liberated African businessmen operated on a small scale. A few became large traders, possessing an advantage over Europeans from hinterland contacts but at a disadvantage due to lack of access to capital on the scale available to whites. African entrepreneurs viewed themselves and were viewed by others as part of an entire group of businessmen which included both blacks and whites. They supported the demands of European traders upon the colonial government in Lagos to take actions facilitating commerce. Allies were chosen on the basis of common economic interests rather than colour.[22] Nigeria's proto-bourgeoisie was thus simultaneously bound to the various ethnic groups and the European bourgeoisie. Without the ethnic network, the proto-bourgeoisie could not achieve commercial success. If it joined with white capital to pursue the interests of business in general, there were occasions on which common class action violated the interests of tribes in the hinterland. Such actions could alienate hinterland leaders and thus undercut the African proto-bourgeoisie's position. On the other hand, common action with hinterland tribes would, on occasions, violate the class interests of business in general. Were such actions to alienate European businessmen who occupied the peaks of the trans-Atlantic trading system, the prosperity of Nigerian entrepreneurs could be endangered. The structural location of the Nigerian proto-bourgeoisie forced this group to perform a delicate balancing act. As an intermediary class, it had to define its own interests and act upon these interests in a manner which did not alienate either of its necessary networks of social support. The proto-bourgeoisie also had to attempt to influence both tribe and class not to act in a manner which would endanger its intermediary position.

Besides trading in the Yoruba hinterland, large numbers of liberated Africans also became active in commerce along the Niger River. African traders booked passages in European steamships which began to ply the Niger regularly from the 1850s onwards. They bartered goods produced in the factories of Manchester for common articles of native make such as cloth, mats, beads, shoes, sandals, pipes, lamps, calabashes, and potash. These were products which the large European companies were not interested in acquiring.[23] Some Africans also rose within the ranks of the European companies. Bishop Crowther invested CMS funds in shares of Holland Jaques and Company, one of the most important trading companies on the Niger at the end of the 1860s. During the next decade, Bishop Crowther's son, Josiah, was put in charge of Holland Jaques' trade on the Niger, Josiah Crowther replaced all the Europeans on the company's ships with African staff, except for engineers and ships' captains.[24] Another son, Joseph, became the general agent for the West Africa Company, another major trading company. Yet another son, Samuel, was appointed trading master of WAC. Bishop Crowther's daughter, Mrs. Macaulay, was active in commerce between Lagos and the kingdom of Nupe, located on the Niger just above its confluence with the Benue River. In 1880, the Crowther brothers went one step further and placed their own steamer on the Niger.[25] Clearly, the Nigerian proto-bourgeoisie which was developing out of the nucleus of liberated Africans exhibited great energies and a willingness to innovate. Under the system of informal empire, there was considerable latitude for them to exercise their talents and initiative.

Liberated Africans also rose to high position within the administrative system of the colony of Lagos. At the turn of the century, 15 years after the collapse of Great Britain's policy of informal empire, Africans still occupied approximately 20 of the 90 senior positions in the colonial administrative system.[26] However, the British government's recruitment of African officials was a pragmatic solution to immediate needs. There was little of the ideological beliefs held by men like Venn, which made the commitment of some missionaries to the concept of development through partnership more than just a practical policy for the moment. From the beginning, British policy-makers in West Africa wanted to staff their administration with as many Europeans as finances would permit. Furthermore, British officials were also uneasy about the allegiance of African officers if the government decided to act against the interests of their ancestral groups in the hinterland.[27] This unease later resulted in the wholesale, discriminatory displacement of Africans from top administrative positions when the colonial system was established and more Europeans were available.

From the evidence above, one sees that liberated Africans occupied a significant minority of the top economic, political, and religious–educational positions within the system of informal empire. Middle and lower levels of the 'modernized' sectors of informal empire were staffed by thousands of liberated Africans or new indigenous converts. Through their education in missionary schools, this proto-bourgeoisie became imbued with ideas of development through partnership and preparation for self-government. The British presence was welcomed as a necessary prelude to the creation of a new Africa which the proto-bourgeoisie would lead to industrial prosperity. During the 1860s and 1870s, these notions permeated the air. There were Nigerian engineers building roads and bridges on their own, architects, masons, and sea captains piloting their own vessels from Lagos to trade on the Niger.

Liberated Africans agitated for what they defined as their rights and interests from the first days after the formal annexation of Lagos. During the 1860s, a number of newspapers exposed the African point of view. These newspapers were small and short-lived operations, selling several hundred copies at 6d.[28] In 1872, African businessmen agitated for representation on the Legislative Council of Lagos and the colonial government acceded to their pressures. Wealthier businessmen also began to send their sons to Great Britain in order to further their education in universities. Young, university-educated Africans returned to Lagos imbued with British concepts of parliamentary representation. In 1883, liberated Africans established the Lagos *Eagle*. This newspaper's editorials expressed some of the earliest arguments for the development of African loyalties wider than that to particular ethnic groups. In 1886, shortly after the beginning of the collapse of informal empire, the Lagos proto-bourgeoisie led the population of the city in a protest against the imposition of a 'house tax' by the colonial government. It was the forerunner of later protest movements linking the proto-bourgeoisie and the masses, protests which ultimately resulted in the attainment of formal, political independence three-quarters of a century later.[29] With the introduction of colonialism to Nigeria, Africans were discriminated against and expelled from top economic, political, and religious–educational positions. A frustrated and angry proto-bourgeoisie then formed the nucleus of a nationalist movement against colonial domination.

NOTES

[1] Robert S. Smith, *The Kingdoms of the Yoruba* (London: Methuen, 1969), p. 45.

[2] I.A. Akinjogbin, 'Dahomey and Yoruba in the ninetéenth century', in Ajayi and Espie (eds), *A thousand years of West African history*, Ibadan University Press, Ibadan, 1965, p. 216.

[3] Smith, *op. cit.*, p. 45.

[4] R.C.C. Law, 'The constitutional troubles of Oyo in the eighteenth century', *Journal of African History*, **XII**, 1, 25–44 (1971); A.A.B. Aderibigbe, 'Peoples of Southern Nigeria', in Ajayi and Espie, *op. cit.*, pp. 191–2; Thomas L. Hodgkin, *Nigerian perspectives* (London: Oxford University Press, 1960), p. 36.

[5] Aderibigbe, *op. cit.*, pp. 191–92; Anene, J.C., *Southern Nigeria in transition 1885–1906*, Cambridge University Press, Cambridge, 1966, p. 107.

[6] J.F.A. Ajayi, *Christian missions in Nigeria: The making of a new elite* (Evanston: Northwestern University Press, 1965), p. 19; Hodgkin, *op. cit.*, p. 48; see Akinjogbin, *op. cit.*, pp. 317–18, for a summary of the civil war and R. Smith for a full account.

[7] Saburi O. Biobaku, *The Egba and their neighbours*, 1842–72, Clarendon Press, Oxford, 1957, p. 26–9.

[8] F.I.A. Omu, 'The "Iwe irohin", 1859–67', *Journal of the Historical Society of Nigeria*, **IV**, 1, 43 (1967).

[9] J. Burton Webster, *African churches among the Yoruba* (Oxford: Clarendon Press, 1964), pp. 3–5.

[10] Ajayi, *Christian missions*, p. 17.

[11] Ibid.

[12] Jean Herskovits Kopytoff, *A preface to modern Nigeria* (Madison: University of Wisconsin Press, 1965), p. 63.

[13] Ajayi, *Christian missions*, pp. 51–2.

[14] Kopytoff, *op. cit.*, p. 229.

[15] Ibid, p. 143.

[16] Webster, *op. cit.*, p. 7.

[17] Kopytoff, *op. cit.*, pp. 199–200.

[18] Ibid, pp. 194–5.

[19] S.A. Akintoye, *Revolution and power politics in Yorubaland*, 1840–1893 (London: Longman, 1971), p. 82.

[20] Ibid., p. 82.

[21] Ibid., pp. 118–20.

[22] Kopytoff, *op. cit.*, pp. 95–7; 132–3.

[23] Emmanuel A. Ayandele, 'Background to the "duel" between Crowther and Goldie on the Lower Niger, 1857–85', *Journal of the Historical Society of Nigeria*, **IV**, No. 1, 1967, p. 48.

[24] John E. Flint, *Sir George Goldie and the making of Nigeria*, OUP, London, 1960, p. 26.

[25] Ayandele, *op. cit.*, p. 48.

[26] I.F. Nicolson, 'The machinery of the federal and regional governments', in John P. MacIntosh (Ed), *Nigerian government and politics* (Evanston: Northwestern University Press, 1966), p. 147; a similar situation existed in the Gold Coast: see David Kimble, *A political history of Ghana* (London: Oxford University Press, 1963), pp. 93–98.

[27] Kopytoff, *op. cit.*, pp. 263–4.

[28] Omu, *op. cit.*, p. 43.

[29] For a summary of political protest during the period of informal empire, see Kopytoff, *op. cit.*, pp. 203–17.

The economic balance sheet of French colonialism in West Africa

JEAN SURET-CANALE

From Jean Suret-Canale, *French colonialism in tropical Africa*, 1900–1945, C. Hurst and Company, London, 1971, and Universe Books, New York, 1971. Paperback Heinemann Educational Books, 1976.

It is now time to draw up a balance sheet of this economic situation but the balance will not be a favourable one. The very limited funds provided by capitalist investment were applied not to progress in production or in technical fields, but essentially to the extraction of high profits with no modification whatever of pre-colonial techniques–in other words, principally by intensifying the work demanded of the population.

The result was a growing disequilibrium between the techniques–consisting of the local populations' traditional ways of working, mainly in agriculture–and the demands of production, which called for an ever-increasing quantity for export, over and above what was needed to ensure the people's subsistence.

(a) Pauperization

It is claimed as an element of progress that these exports were compensated for by corresponding imports, placing new products in the hands of the Africans, and so raising their standard of living; but this argument is illusory. Rather it should be said that increasing imports of manufactured goods led to the decline and eventual ruin of the traditional crafts of the smith and the weaver. While export products were, in their entirety, the fruits of indigenous labour (the 'independent peasant' workers on plantations and forestry), the imported products were destined only in part for the local indigenous population. Part of the imported items provided facilities destined not to improve the people's lot, but to perfect the manner of their exploitation–building materials for shipyards and trading posts, vehicles, and so on. Moreover, an important part of the consumer goods were intended for the Europeans–officials and settlers–whose purchasing power was out of proportion to their limited number: this applies particularly to luxury articles. To appreciate the importance of this point: in the absence of data prior to 1940, we can cite those of 1951, given by Capet and Fabre, who estimated the percentage of the gross national product applicable to the Europeans in

French West Africa, at that time fewer than 50,000 as against 17,000,000 Africans, at 15 per cent.[1]

As we have seen, the foreign trade of the tropical African countries did not represent equal exchange: thus it was at the level of foreign trade, and not that of production or the share-out of the alleged national income, that the process of exploitation was chiefly concentrated. There was far greater instability in the prices of export goods as compared to imports. All shortfalls had to be borne by the producer, while rises in prices were largely absorbed by intermediaries.

After the end of the First World War the following variations occurred in the general wholesale price index of staple colonial products in the franc, allowing for an average variation of ± 10 per cent:

	per cent
Rubber	35·5
Coffee	24·6
Palm kernels	17·7
Palm oil	17·7
Cacao	14·7

By contrast, the variation for rice was 9·7 per cent, and for cement 3·9 per cent.[2] On the whole, the terms of trade developed unfavourably, with marked depressions between the crisis and the war, followed by upswings, which rarely regained the previous purchasing power except for very brief periods. This was already the case in French West Africa after the 1921 crisis. While between 1913 and 1922 the coefficient of price increases in cotton fabrics, known as 'Guinea cotton', was 5·7 and in other fabrics 5·0, those in export

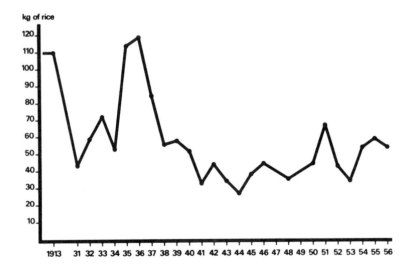

commodities were only 1·6 for groundnuts, 1·8 for palm kernels, and 2·2 for palm oil.

The natives' purchasing power has thus fallen heavily, to the direct detriment of the consumption of imported fabrics.[3]

If we follow the evolution of prices in the so-called period of 'prosperity' and up to the crisis, the results will be similar. Between 1913 and 1927 the prices of groundnuts and fabrics moved respectively at coefficients of 7·5 and 9·4—which is to say that purchasing power expressed in terms of fabrics came close to its 1913 level. But in October 1930, the coefficients dropped respectively to 3·4 and 7·6 and in the first half of 1931 to 2·6 and 7·0.[4] Native groundnuts show the same trend in relation to imported rice. The graph above, which expresses hundreds of kilos of groundnuts as against kilos of rice, reveals that the purchasing power of groundnuts dropped from 110 kilos in 1913 to 42·8 kilos in 1931. It did not exceed 100 except in the two years of recovery, 1935 and 1936, and never again regained that level.

The producers' losses naturally reached their peak in the crisis years. Governor-General Brévié gave the following as their losses for 1930, as compared with a figure of 400,000,000 francs for 1927, divided by products as follows:

	Millions of francs
Groundnut producers	285
Cacao producers	57
Palm-kernel and palm-oil producers	47

and by colonies:

Senegal	274
Ivory Coast	67
Dahomey	35
Guinea	9
Other colonies	15

The price of cacao dropped from 10,000 francs per tonne in 1927 to 3,000 in September 1931; coffee from 12,000 to 4,000 in the same period and cotton from 13,000 in 1927 to 4,500 in August 1931.[5] The upswing in 1935–36 did little to restore the former purchasing power to the producers. Reports from the subdivision of Faranah in Guinea give us the following prices paid by traders to producers in 1927 and in April 1936:[6]

The price of imported merchandise, by contrast, regained and even exceeded its earlier level. The 'minor crisis' of 1937–38 led to a new drop in prices, which was first apparent in October 1937, but affected only tropical produce. In the Cameroons, from October 1937 to July 1938, the drop in prices amounted to 27 per cent for palm kernels, 67 per cent for palm oil, 83 per cent for cacao: at the same time the price of rice rose by 43 per cent,

	1927 *Francs per kilo*	1936 *Francs per kilo*
Rice	2.00	0.65
Rubber	7.50	5.00
Indigo	0.75 to 1.00	0.50
Wax	12.50	5.00

that of salt by 93 per cent and of salted fish by 112 per cent.[7] Production, it is true, rose considerably, but the number of producers for the market grew simultaneously at the expense of the traditional subsistence economy. Progress in export production was also brought about–mainly in Senegal–at the expense of traditional food production, of which the shortfall was not made good by consumption of imported rice. It should be noted that, except in Senegal, the peasant continued as formerly to produce his own food, and imports supplied only manufactured goods.

The pre-colonial crop system, within the tradional social setting, provided a complete and permanent equilibrium between man and nature. Compelled thereafter, with means which were unchanged, to provide for his own subsistence and to furnish a surplus of export products as well, the peasant succeeded only in reducing this subsistence to a minimum, or even below: reserves kept back for traditional feasts or bad years disappeared. Every year there was famine. Malnutrition became a permanent feature. Any natural or economic catastrophe, such as a bad harvest or falling prices naturally resulted in famine, as in the Sudan in 1913–14. This malnutrition was accompanied by intensified exploitation of labour: there were greater areas to be cultivated, an increased demand by the administration for forced labour, and a shortage of manpower resulting from requisitioning and conscription.

On the eve of the Second World War, the peasants of French West Africa had to furnish each year, according to Governor-General Delavignette: 175,000,000 francs in poll-tax and cattle-tax, 21,000,000 days of statute labour and 12,000 soldiers.[8] This catalogue is not complete. To the taxes were added supplementary payments, 'customary' or otherwise, levied by the chiefs; debts paid to the provident societies (in Senegal loans of groundnut seeds were repayable with 25 per cent interest within *three months*; in fact, dishonesty often raised this to nearly 100 per cent, and annual quotas even higher); 'presents' to employees at processing plants; commodities 'requisitioned' for the entertainment of administrators, chiefs on tour and their hangers-on; sales of compulsory crops below cost price; and repayment at extortionate interest rates of seasonal debts–bad times forcing the impoverished peasants to pawn their loin-cloths, jewellery, and so on, as pledges for loans at 50 per cent interest, for a minimum of three months. Days of statute labour represented only a fraction of forced labour, excluding extra labour for the chiefs and recruitment for big public works and private enterprise.

This perhaps helps us to put in the right perspective claims that the under-nourishment of the Africans was due to the vagaries of nature or to their own laziness and lack of foresight. In presenting his report on the state of nutrition among the peoples of French West Africa in 1949, Colonel Pales wrote:

> With the exception of a few small and scattered regions–the coastal lands (Lower Casamance, the Baga country, etc.), the banks of the great rivers (fishermen on the Niger at Bozo and Somono) and a few areas in the savannah and the forest, true granaries of millet, rice, or tuberiferous roots–it can be said that the people in the whole territory lack balanced nutrition;[9] and this is a *permanent state.*[10]

Naturally, as there were regions where conditions were above the average, in others such as Upper Volta and Fouta–Djalon relative over-population was added to conditions that were basically poor.

The same author stated even more clearly:

> The harvest time is one of ease and fullness–in a very relative sense. It is followed by a period of deficiency as regards quality, and later by a period of shortage.
> This unbalanced diet leads first to a state of mild sub-deficiency (in vitamins C, A, etc.), followed by quantitative and qualitative deficiency combined–this affects roughly 40 per cent of persons.[11]

H. Labouret writes of this period of 'shortage', which 'runs from the moment the old harvest is exhausted until new agricultural products become usable', as follows:[12]

> During this interval, the peasant cheats his hunger by consuming wild plants of little nutritive value, taken chiefly in their natural form or as soups or spinach.[13]

The daily ration of a rural worker dropped from approximately 3,250 calories after the harvest to 750 and sometimes far below by July.[14]

> The daily ration of an adult might even go down to 208 calories per day, not during famines but simply at times of shortage. So great was the surprise of the personnel in charge of these calculations in France that they suspended their work, believing it an error on our part. There was no error.[15]

The urban workers, apart from the annual famine, suffered from monthly ones, or rather one every fortnight: the daily ration of 2,500 calories in October and November dropped to 1,500 in June and July, but went up, and then down again to 1,250 calories every other fortnight when wages were exhausted.[16] There was a particular shortage of the nitrogenous matter to be found in meat; and this could not always be made up by fish.

> Consumption of meat was barely a kilo per inhabitant per year on the Lower Ivory Coast and in Lower Dahomey; it varied from 3 to 5 kilos over a large part of Senegal and the Sudan, from 5 to 8 kilos in Guinea, to over 20 kilos in Mauritania and the north of the Sudan.[17]

In French Equatorial Africa we find the same state of affairs. In Ubangi, Pierre Kalck noted that the average ration everywhere was below the 3,000 calories considered the minimum necessary for a man doing even light work.

It was generally less than 2,000 and badly balanced, consisting almost entirely of cassava paste. Meat and fish, formerly eaten on a wide scale, became rare in the two generations following colonial penetration. 'The people of Ubangi were once great hunters, and fresh meat was abundant.'[18] Forced labour had compelled the people of Ubangi to abandon millet, which was rich in fats, for cassava, which required less care in its cultivation; compulsory cotton cultivation worsened this situation by preventing crop rotation. The shortage of salt (sold at 100 francs C.F.A. per kilo, or 5 francs per teaspoonful, though it cost 2 francs a kilo at Cap Vert) was greatly felt. These data, applying to the period after the Second World War, were equally valid for the preceding period.

For the Congo we can mention the following statement quoted in the general report on French Equatorial Africa presented to the Dschang Conference, and extracted from a medical report on the Kouilou region:

The prisoners are remarkably healthy since they are the best fed of all the African population.[19]

In view of the 'average' state, one can well imagine what famines were like. In 1924–6 a famine occurred in Gabon which coincided with the forest 'rush' and the vicious recruitment operated on behalf of the forest exploiters. Food crops were abandoned in the coastal regions, all available manpower being used in the forests; in the interior, the requisitioning of food for the forest workings led to the same result. The 1931 famine in Niger and the neighbouring regions, as well as in Upper Volta, was caused by the destruction of the harvest by locusts: but it is clear that the economic crisis aggravated it.[20] One author writes of 'some 15,000 dead of hunger in Niger'.[21] Even at the end of 1933 the Governor-General of French West Africa attributed the budget deficit in Upper Volta and Niger to the 'famine', and to 'deaths in the preceding period'.[22] Over a large part of French West Africa, famine and misery, the outcome of the crisis, made their effects felt between 1930 and 1936, in spite of an overall improvement in the economic situation after 1934. Investigations made in Senegal at the end of 1930 showed that in numerous cantons 'the situation appears as critical [in 1931] as in 1930. To pay taxes, the natives are obliged to sell all their products and part of their cattle.'[23] 'In the Diet-Salao canton, even by selling their harvest and their animals, they can only pay part of their dues to the administration. Moreover, they have to reimburse the advances granted by traders and money-lenders...'[24]

In the Baol circle, in January 1931, millet was sold at 4·50 francs a kilo, and the people were in danger of having neither reserves nor resources for a period of three to four months. The Fulani had already sold everything.[25] In the Foss canton, one of the most deprived of the Louga circle, the administrator while on a tour in September 1934 noted that 'the Wolof cultivators have done no sowing, but have eaten the larger part of the groundnut seed crops'; taxes were in abeyance.[26] In the neighbouring Mérinaghen canton the same administrator noted that on 31 May, after officially selling part of the cattle, he did not recover more than one-third of the debts of the canton, where a year's taxes were owed, and in places even a year and a half's or two years'. In Fouta the cattle population decreased by between a quarter and a half, and a strong wave of emigration moved towards the neighbouring colonies, Portuguese Guinea and Sierra Leone. The population did not manage to pay the taxes. The canton chief's henchmen, the *batou-labé*, lived in garrisons, confiscating and selling off cheap all that could be sold, down to kitchen equipment and korans. Even children were pledged to raise ready money.[27] The situation did not improve until 1937.

(b) Africa, a dying land

The system of cultivation was not modified, and the imbalance in living conditions spread to the exploitation of the soil. Under pre-colonial conditions a prolonged fallow period generally ensured recovery of the richness of the soil, which received no manure. The obligation to produce more without being able to use any supplementary acreage, and often over an area reduced by concessions to European settlers and classified forests,[28] led to a speeding-up in rotation, a decline in yields, and often the permanent ruin of the soil along with a reduction in pastoral land.

The effect on production did not make itself felt everywhere for, as we have seen, the market economy had not penetrated deeply except in limited zones, and there remained considerable possibilities of extending cultivation; thus, overall, production continued to grow. But certain regions (the first to be affected by groundnut speculation) such as Oualo and Cayor in Senegal were greatly affected.[29] From 1936, the advance of groundnuts in Senegal was due to the penetration of pioneers into the relatively fertile lands of Casamance, and the far less hospitable areas on the eastern and southern fringes of the Baol–Saloum region. The virgin lands were fertile, but the cultivator had to work far from home, the work of clearing the ground was hard and there was a scarcity of water, or rather of the equipment necessary for digging wells. These had to be dug to a depth of 40, 60, and even 80 metres. In a village of 200 people, with 200 oxen and 100 sheep teams working round the clock, less than one-third of the required water supply could be drawn.[30]

The general misery and the ruin of the soil were taboo subjects until the Second World War. After the war, the inability of the colonial countries to give the impetus necessary to raise essential production so that the local economies would benefit brought to the agenda what later became known as 'underdevelopment'. An answer to this question was given in 1947 in a book by Pierre Gourou, known in its English translation as *The tropical world*.[31] In his book, which cites numerous examples and provides many new insights, Gourou advanced the view that the tropical countries of Africa are doomed to a retarded civilization and a low level of life, owing to natural conditions unfavourable to human life and activity.

His thesis can be summarized as follows. The population of the tropical countries is numerically small and in bad physical condition; hence its productive capacity is limited. Its bad state is due to the unhealthiness of the tropical countries, where the climate is hot and damp, for at least part of the year, favouring the rapid multiplication of harmful micro-organisms. The large number of endemic diseases, especially malaria, lead to a high mortality rate, and open the way to other illnesses by lowering physical resistance. Add to this sleeping sickness, yellow fever, and parasitic and bacterial diseases. Natural resources are limited. The tropical soil, contrary to its acquired reputation, has a low fertility, and is quickly affected by erosion or desiccation. It is poor in useful chemical substances. Yields, even in intensive agriculture such as irrigated rice paddies, are greatly inferior to those common in the temperate zone. Traditional agriculture on burnt land devastates the soil, and European methods, like ploughing and continuous cultivation, lead to results worse than the evil they claim to rectify–as, for example, accelerated soil erosion. Intensive stockbreeding, generally apart from agriculture, yields poor returns and leads to equal devastation. Ill-nourished by natural pastures of low quality and weakened by diseases such as sleeping sickness and parasitosis, the animals are inadequate as a source of food and almost useless for work. As to whether these unfavourable conditions can be overcome, the author is sceptical. Industrialization cannot be considered urgent, as there is insufficient manpower even for agriculture, and the material resources are inferior, the forests are of little use, and there is no coal.

The introduction of modern agriculture, based on continuous cultivation with artificial fertilisers and the association of stock-breeding and agriculture at farm level, envisaged by well-known tropical agronomists like Auguste Chevalier, seem to him utopian.

> ... To seek to improve [techniques of cultivation] in imitation of European techniques is perhaps a bait.[32]

Only in the ninth chapter does the author touch on the 'problems posed by European intervention', where 'damage involuntarily inflicted on nature and tropical humanity... damage directly due to the spirit of profit and violence' on the one hand, and 'the good effects' on the other, seem to cancel each other out. The conclusion is pessimistic:

> The improvement of living standards among the tropical peoples poses very great problems; it may raise many more than it actually solves. Ultimately, at the root of all these difficulties, shall we not find that the poverty of the tropical soils will not permit those who use them to reach the same standard of life as agricultural workers in the temperate zone?[33]

Gourou does not envisage agricultural progress except in plantations and irrigated rice paddies, which preserve the soil. The tropical countries will keep their vocation as providers of 'colonial commodities' to the temperate industrialized countries, which, in return, will provide them with manufactured goods.

Gourou's authority and the wealth of his documentation strongly influenced the geographers of the period.[34] His arguments are scarcely tenable today, and in later works he has considerably altered his position. Even at that period, however, a cursory examination could have shown the weakness of his argument.[35] In studying the characteristic features of tropical countries, Gourou examined only the natural geographical features–climate, the soil, etc.–and left economic and social factors, in other words the hard core of colonial enterprise, in the background. Starting from true facts, copious and often of great interest, the author compromised his position from the start by comparing what cannot be compared. Can one seriously compare the demography and hygiene of the peoples and the yields and results of agriculture in the present tropical countries *today* with the same characteristics of Europe *today*? Yet was the hygiene of European peoples in the Middle Ages, and even at the beginning of the eighteenth century, so different from that of the pre-colonial African peoples? Was their food richer and better balanced?

The results of tilling burnt land with the hoe in tropical countries invite comparison with *analogous* techniques in temperate countries. More than the yields of contemporary temperate agriculture, however, it would be relevant to consider those of mediaeval agriculture, before the agricultural revolution; but, in spite of the fact that mixed cultivation and the plough existed then, we cannot be certain that the yields of rye or buckwheat on the 'frozen lands' of western France were much higher than those of traditional tropical agriculture.

The tropical soils are fragile, more so than the arid lands in temperate countries. In the United States, the ravages of soil erosion are well known. The content of chemical elements is not of great importance, while biochemical processes play a decisive role in matters of fertility; the sandy soils of Senegal, which give good groundnut yields, would be completely sterile in Europe.

Finally, the failure of any attempt at modernization of tropical agriculture is due, not to its intrinsic nature but to its economic and social setting. The automatic application of methods used in temperate climates, and only valid there, can only have catastrophic results. After the First World War, an attempt was made in West Africa to introduce tillage with the plough, and oxen were requisitioned for this purpose. The chiefs in charge of the operations kept the best for themselves, while the remaining animals did not take to breaking in or stabling, and soon died. The robust imported 'Brabant' ploughs sterilized the soil within a few years. For some years Governor Poiret in Guinea tried energetically to extend the use of the plough, and when he left the colony, the Governor-General saluted him as 'father of the plough'. However, what he achieved has almost completely vanished. The use of tractors designed for Beauce or Picardy, produced similar results. Is ploughing by means of either animals or tractors therefore impossible in tropical countries? What is certain is that methods and materials have to be improved before it can be used. But no one–even including the official agricultural services–ever had the means of achieving such improvements, though in the 1950s and 1960s great progress in this respect was recorded. Technical improvements in agriculture are not limited to the methods and the hardware, but apply equally to the species of crops grown. Gourou discusses tropical fodder plants likely to play a role similar to trefoils, lucerne, and root-crops in the European agricultural revolution of the eighteenth century. But, even in Europe itself, did the varieties that existed before that epoch play the same role as the tropical plants today? And have the improvements brought about during the last two centuries in crop species cultivated in Europe ever been calculated?

Last and most important of all, techniques cannot make progress unless the social and economic conditions are ready for them. In Europe it was the capitalist farmer and the big landowner, not the small traditional cultivator, who brought about the agricultural revolution. The advance of commerce and the beginning of modern industry provided a stimulus by enlarging the market. In tropical Africa, the native peasant does not have the means of improving his techniques, capitalists show no interest in investing capital in agriculture, and commercial exploitation enlarges yields with fewer risks. Leaving aside the flimsy arguments of opponents of industrialization in Africa–although Africa is poor in coal it is rich in potential water-power, in uranium-bearing minerals and, no doubt, in oil, and even more in mineral raw materials. In this area it seems privileged by comparison with Europe. But natural resources, while they ease the process of industrialization, are not indispensable for it. Here again economic and social factors are paramount. Japan and Italy, while short of fuel and power and raw materials, have nevertheless become great industrial powers.

Clearly this does not mean that in Africa either the transformation of agriculture to modern standards, or industrialization, can easily be brought about. But the backwardness maintained and aggravated by the colonial system is the root cause of all these difficulties; it has nothing to do with nature. The thesis of Gourou ends–involuntarily no doubt–by exonerating, at nature's expense, the colonial system, which he reproaches only for a few abuses and 'blemishes'. This conclusion seems to justify the perpetuation of the system whereby the only vocation open to the colonial countries is to be that of being the supplier of 'colonial' goods.

NOTES

[1] M. Capet and J. Fabre, 'L'économie de l'Afrique occidentale francaise depuis la guerre', *Annales africaines*, 1957, pp. 435–94. The *Comptes économiques de l'Afrique occidentale française*, 1956 (unpublished document) give 17.5% and 27%, if one only considers the money resources, excluding tribal consumption. For French Equatorial Africa (1958) the official data make it possible to evaluate the taxes corresponding to 20% and 35%. In Cameroon (1959) the part of the money revenue attributed to the European population was a quarter to one-third of this revenue (*Marchés tropicaux*, 21 November, 1959).

[2] Josué de Castro, *Le Livre noir de la faim*. Paris, Editions Ouvrières, 1961, pp. 80–1.

[3] *L'Afrique française*, 1923, p. 435.

	1913	1922
Average price of a metre of Guinea cotton	0.39	2.25
Average price of a kilo of other cloth	4.72	24.34
Average price of 100 kilos of groundnuts	33.00	52.60
Average price of 100 kilos of palm kernels	37.42	66.60
Average price of 100 kilos of palm oil	49.52	111.78

[4] Price evolution:

			1st term
	1927	1930	1931
	(francs)	(francs)	(francs)
Tons of groundnuts	2500	1150	875
Kilos of cotton fabric			
(other than percale)	44.63	36.28	33.59

(Address by J. Brévié to the Council of Government of French West Africa, session December 1931, *L'Afrique française, Revue coloniale*, 1932, No. 1.)

[5] Same source.

[6] Faranah Archives. D.1. Rapports d'ensemble, 1921–38.

[7] George R. Manue, *Cameroun, création française*, Paris, Sorlot, 1938.

[8] Robert Delavignette, *Les vrais Chefs de l'Empire*, Paris, Gallimard, 1939.

[9] Inter-African Conference on Food and Nutrition (Dschang, Cameroon, 3–9 October, 1949), Paris, *Documentation française*, 1950, p. 152.

[10] Underlined in the text.

[11] *Documentation française*, p. 152.

[12] H. Labouret in 'Le Travail en Afrique noire', *Présence française*, Paris, 1952, pp. 125–6.

[13] H. Labouret, ibid.

[14] L. Pales, *L'Alimentation en Afrique occidentale française*. Dakar, O.R.A.N.A., 1955, p. 71.

[15] L. Pales, *Le Bilan de la mission anthropologique de l'Afrique occidentale française*, Dakar, 1948, p. 22.

[16] L. Pales, *L'Alimentation en Afrique occidentale française*. Dakar, O.R.A.N.A., 1955, p. 71.

[17] *Encyclopédie coloniale et maritime: Afrique occidentale française*, vol. II, p. 28.

[18] P. Kalck, *Réalités oubanguinnes*, Paris, Berger-Levrault, 1959, p. 131.

[19] Inter-African Conference at Dschang, op. cit., p. 163.

[20] H. Labouret in his pamphlet *Famine et disette aux colonies* (Paris, 1938) mentions it without explanation. The Report of the Cameroons to the Dschang Conference attributes it to locusts. The address of Governor-General Brévié to the December 1931 session of the council of government of French West Africa mentions in its general picture of the economic crisis 'the famine in Upper Volta and in certain areas of Niger'.

[21] R. Monmarson, *L'Afrique noire et son destin*, Paris, Ed. Frances, 1950, p. 95.

[22] Speech by Governor-General Brévié to the council of government, session of December 1933 (*L'Afrique française*, 1934, No. 1, pp. 19–27).

[23] Senegal Archives, Dossier *Semences*.

[24] ibid.

[25] ibid. Discussions at Diourbel (January 1931).

[26] Senegal Archives, 1 D 2/28, Report on the circles, 1933–4.

[27] G. Vieillard, 'Notes sur les Peuls de Fouta-Djalon', *Bulletin de l'I.F.A.N.* 1, 1940.

[28] Which represented, in the savannah country, not 'forests' in the proper sense of the term, but areas where cultivation was prohibited.

[29] The impoverishment of the soils in those regions is not as evident as it might seem: in this field one must be sceptical of any simplifying explanations. The study of documents does not reveal in Cayor a lowering of yields, but a far greater irregularity. The abandonment of Cayor was far more an economic phenomenon, due to the lure and higher yields of Baol and Sine-Saloum, regions towards which the cultivators moved as soon as they became accessible by railway. The erosion of Ouala was more evident but it was probably in relation to modifications of the system and the course of the Senegal (cf. for Cayor, J. Suret-Canale, 'Quelques aspects de la géographie agraire au Sénégal', *Cahiers d'outre-mer*, 4, pp. 348–67, 1948). On the other hand, there were the regions where the ruin of the soil is evident through the introduction of colonial crops and too intensive exploitation of means used. For cotton growing in Chad cf. J. Cabot 'Le problème des Koros' *Annales de géographie*, 1961, pp. 628–9, and *Les pays du Moyen-Logone*, Paris, Orstom, 1965, pp. 173–4.

[30] Annual Report of the Agricultural Service in Senegal, 1938.

[31] Longmans, Wiley.

[32] op. cit., p. 117.

[33] ibid., p. 181.

[34] In particular J. Richard-Molard in his *Afrique occidentale française*.

[35] Cf. J. Suret-Canale, 'L'exploitation coloniale est-elle une réalité géographique?' *La Pensée*, 16, pp. 103–4 (January-February 1948).

Nationalism, socialism, and Tanzanian history
JOHN SAUL

From Lionel Cliffe and John Saul (eds), *Socialism in Tanzania: an inter-disciplinary reader* (*volume* 1: *politics*), East Africa Publishing House, Dar es Salaam, 1972.
This review article has also been published in A. Mazrui and Y. Tandon (eds), *African international*, Volume I (London and Nairobi, Oxford University Press, 1971).

This article is, in the first instance, a review of *A history of Tanzania*, edited by Isaria Kimambo and Arnold Temu and published in 1969 by East African Publishing House.[1] However, I have used this occasion to present a number of broader arguments about Tanzanian historiography and its relation to the needs of contemporary Tanzania as well. I am conscious that in so doing I cannot hope to do full justice to many of the positive features of the book; nonetheless, I hope that the urgency of the larger problems of method and approach which are discussed will be seen to provide sufficient warrant for a somewhat one-sided emphasis.

I. The problem

A history of Tanzania is an important book, a milestone in Tanzanian historiography. With chapters written by four Tanzanians and by six expatriates (whose experience in the country and commitment to many of its aspirations are readily apparent) it is designed to cover certain major aspects of the historical development of the area which comprises present-day Tanzania during the period 'from Olduvai to the Arusha Declaration' (as the editors put it in their introduction). Moreover, it seeks quite explicitly to break with the dominant themes of 'imperial' history and to write Tanzanian history more from the 'inside', i.e. from the standpoint of the African population itself.

The latter is, of course, a particularly laudable aim–identified by the former Professor of History at the University College, Dar es Salaam, Terence Ranger, (in his remarkable Inaugural Lecture[2]) as 'the attempt to recover African initiative in Tanzanian history'–and it has characterized much of the other work emerging from the History Department at the College (now University) besides that which appears in the book under review. Such an emphasis does involve certain dangers, however, some of which have been mentioned by Professor Ranger in his lecture, but not all of which have been avoided in the preparation of the present volume. As these can be expected to have important implications, beyond the academic community, for Tanzania's current efforts to construct a socialist society, it will be useful to refer specifically to the most important of them at the outset.

The main dangers inherent in too straightforward a focus 'on the African himself' (to use the editors' phrase) are:

(1) that this can shift attention too far away from the overall imperialist framework within which African initiatives are taken, and

(2) that it can encourage a blurring of relevant distinctions and differentiations within the African community itself,

(3) with the result that the full *meaning and significance* of African initiatives is lost and, moreover,

(4) the accomplishments of Africans (unity, nationalism, and political independence) are, therefore, over-valued, at the expense of a frank discussion of the very real challenges which remain (the realization of socialism and self-reliance, and the fulfillment of the country's productive potential).

In short, what must be critically scrutinized are the very questions scholars ask when examining the historical record. The contention of this essay is that the questions which underlie the Kimambo–Temu volume are too exclusively those relevant to a nationalist perspective on Tanzanian history, at a moment when a socialist perspective and a set of socialist questions are increasingly imperative.[3] Obviously it will be necessary to elaborate upon the four points tabled above, and to examine some aspects of the book itself in greater detail, before accepting this assertion and commenting upon its possible implications.

We shall see that the selection of an outspokenly nationalist emphasis can subtly distort discussion even of the earliest periods of 'Tanzanian' history, but its weaknesses are the more graphic the closer the historian moves to the present day. This is so chiefly because the major outside force impinging upon the people of what is now Tanzania during the last century or more has been the international capitalist system and it has affected developments here in a wide variety of complex ways. So pervasive has been its impact that economic initiatives taken by Africans, either because of external forces (including many forms of compulsory tax) or in response to various incentives, generally conform to terms dictated by the logic of this world-wide economic system. This means that, as economic growth takes place, its cumulative effect will be the further subordination of the colony to the requirements of metropolitan Europe and the creation of an increasingly *dependent* economy. Some economists have defined this process as 'the development of under-development'[4], and certainly the economic relationships with the outside world which result remain the major constraint upon genuine development in Africa. Moreover, formal education (mission and government schools) is part and parcel of this larger environment and inevitably reflects and inculcates its values–those of the 'possessive individualism' characteristic of advanced capitalist societies–even while communicating skills, technical capacity, and/or the key to salvation.

Paradoxically, these economic and educational forces are those which, at one and the same time, both tie an emerging country like Tanzania more tightly into the international capitalist system *and* create the conditions for a nationalist challenge to formal colonial rule. Numbers of Africans, freed by economic activity and/or education from a narrow focus upon their own locality and the subsistence economy, increasingly act on a territorial scale, and realize the frustrations to their own advancement characteristic of colonialism.[5] Moreover, in confronting the latter system, they can often expect to enlist mass support, itself the by-product of disruption of traditional ways inherent in the colonial-cum-capitalist impact.[6]

But it should be apparent that a challenge to formal colonial rule is not necessarily a full-fledged challenge to imperialism. Given both the fact that the economies of the 'colonies' have developed into dependencies of the world-wide system and that the new African leaders (politicians and bureaucrats) are themselves often active participants in such economies (while having, in any case, absorbed its values through the educational system) the imperialists have had little to fear from decolonization.[7] Once having sensed the initial stirrings of discontent the colonial government characteristically has begun to evolve a *strategy of decolonization* on the basis of which it can bargain with an African group eager to agree to marriages of convenience all along the line. The resultant successor-state, as Fanon has stressed, could represent merely a change in the colour of those in positions of authority, while maintaining its internal socio-economic structure and major links with the outside world more or less intact.

It will already be apparent that an understanding of the full complexity of these links with imperialism, their historic roots and present implications, must go hand in hand with a concern to identify the growing differentiations in African society. This is a process of historical evolution which begins even before colonialism, as we shall have occasion to mention later, but it is particularly graphic in the later period when indigenous classes can become more obviously the domestic guarantors of continued international subordination as well as exploiters in their own right. One dimension of the pre-independence political activism of 'leaders' will generally have been a desire for advancement as individuals and as group or class in any case. Once in power they soon come to realize all the more clearly that any attempt to challenge the imperial *status quo* in a more fundamentally threatening manner could involve both short-term disruption within the existing system and the necessity to arouse popular energies more powerfully. This in turn might unleash forces prejudicial to the retention of their own relatively privileged positions, however, and, therefore, could not be a realistic option for them. It is clear, in short, that whatever may be the popular mythology encouraged by contemporary leaders, Africa has moved some way from the communalism of the traditional past, and the serious historian must look for the first seeds of class formation as assiduously as he traces the initial sparks of nationalist consciousness! Nor should this concern with inequality be seen merely as an exercise in moralizing–far from it. Historically, patterns of inequality and class formation have been related in crucial ways to the process of economic development, sometimes facilitating, sometimes hindering, the expansion of the productive forces in a society. By focusing upon classes we are, in fact, carried to the very heart of the development problem.

Of course such an emphasis should not be allowed to boil away the idealism and the vigour which often characterized the nationalist impetus in Africa. If one dimension was inevitably more narrow and self-interested than is sometimes admitted, another undoubtedly consisted of an identification with larger goals and more popular aspirations. Nor need other African achievements be downgraded by virtue of hindsight, even if it is now apparent that their accomplishment did serve, in time, to define a fresh set of problems for Tanzanians. What *is* necessary is to insist upon the reality of those deeper currents of socio-economic change which give a fullness of meaning to events; otherwise the latter, taken in isolation, would remain obscure in its significance or, more dangerously, further mystify the understanding of the current generation.

In this context we can return to the theme of nationalism–a significant accomplishment, but also a potent myth with great potentiality for good and evil in contemporary Africa. Unity, an achieved national identity, such as had characterized the emergence of Tanzania, can minimize and displace the dangers of internecine ethnic conflict. Control of the state by indigenous personnel is an important pre-condition for future action along various lines, including socialist ones, if other factors permit this. For these reasons, among others, a clarification of the processes through which these ends were achieved, as well as an emphasis upon them, are important. But to the extent that a 'united' society benefits one or several classes at the expense of others, and to the extent that 'self-determination' ultimately confirms rather than challenges the hegemony of imperialism, then one may suspect that to such an extent nationalist slogans have succeeded only in rationalizing the socio-economic *status quo* and anaesthetizing the mass of the population. And under such circumstances an extreme form of patriotic, nationalist historical writing can, even with the best of intentions, come primarily to service a bankrupt balance of forces.

It may help to place this problem of method in comparative perspective; fortunately an instructive parallel with recent trends in American radical historiography offers itself. One school, led by Staughton Lynd and others, has tried to demonstrate the importance of viewing American history 'from the bottom up' (compare the use of the phrase, 'the African initiative'), and in so doing has seized upon the impressive wave of labour activity in the 1930s in the United States as a powerful testimony to the vitality of radicalism. Yet as James Weinstein has observed of this emphasis[8]

the possibility that the workers were... militant in behalf of a trade unionism that tied them closer to the system, that integrated their lives more tightly with that of the corporation, never occurred to Lynd. To him it was sufficient that the workers, those at the bottom, were engaged in militant activity.

The overarching structures of capitalist (read, in Africa, 'imperialist') domin-

ance remained unperceived and unchallenged; union leaders could be absorbed into the system, gradually transforming their relationship with the mass
base which had given substance to their challenge to the establishment.

> ... This illustrates the fault of Lynd's concept of history from the bottom
> up: it cannot explain or understand the *meaning* of actions taken by those
> at the bottom because it does not examine their relationship to the actions
> and consciousness of those at the top. For just as the meaning of ruling
> class thought and action cannot be understood without knowing what was
> going on in the under classes, neither can the activity of the under classes
> be understood except in the context of the actions and consciousness of
> the upper classes.

American trade unionism, like African nationalism, was an accomplishment but not one that cut down to the deeper currents of capitalist development, be it domestic or world-wide. To the extent that it failed to do so 'the
ruling class [was] left in a position to steer militancy (and radicalism) in the
direction advantageous to itself...'. Then the very accomplishments of the
movement can serve merely to deposit institutions and social relationships–
bureaucratized unions and leadership with vested interests (compare, in
Africa, 'states' and 'parties')–whose major role is to defend the *status quo*,
which stand, in fact, in the way of further advance.[9] For American radical
historians of the period there is a temptation similar to that which presents
itself to the 'patriotic' historian in Africa:

> [Such history] is too busy celebrating successful tactics and militant actions,
> too busy attempting to give 'radicals' 'their own history'–which is to say a
> false sense of accomplishment, and therefore a pious satisfaction with the
> past... [There is] a one-dimensional glorification of motion...

Weinstein concludes by questioning 'the usefulness of the concept of
radicalism, now that a socialist consciousness is widespread in the new left.
Both in history and in the movement radicalism, 'has no content. It is purely
formal'. Again there is a parallel, though it is by no means exact. It would be
too much to say that 'nationalism' in Africa has no content, nor is it purely
formal. Nonetheless, it is *too formal*, and it certainly lacks sufficient content
to be adequate to the task of ordering historical investigation. Moreover,
the solution to many of the weaknesses of such a perspective lies in a programme of historical inquiry premised upon 'a socialist consciousness'!

II. The book itself

The fact that the Tanzanian leadership has itself taken cognizance of these
deeper currents and, with the Arusha Declaration and other attendant initiatives, moved some way to challenge the realities of economic and cultural
dependency and internal class formation distinguishes this country from much
of the rest of the continent. It also means that there is every reason for the
concerns stressed in the preceding section to be less profane knowledge here
than is the case elsewhere. Yet this is precisely where the book under review

is to be found most wanting. For, on one level, a generally undiluted ethos of nationalism pervades the book, so that even its earlier chapters contribute to an uncritical celebration of political achievement. Possible complementary themes concerning hierarchy and exploitation are muffled and the multi-faceted nature of growing dependency is blurred. The mind of the reader is encouraged, in short, to follow a single track.

But it is not only this general ethos that discourages a crystallization of socialist consciousness and concern. Specific issues of immediate relevance to policy-making, which cry out for the addition of an historical dimension in order to illuminate them, also fail to surface. What is the exact character of dependency as it has emerged over time? Only in such a context can one evaluate the strengths and weaknesses of recent nationalizations and other steps taken to define new directions. What is the precise texture of differentia-tion in Tanzania? This is important at the national level where the quality of instruments available for socialist construction needs continuous discussion. It is even more the case at the local level where the distinctions of rank characteristic of a number of different epochs overlap each other and must be understood if meaningful strategies for implementing rural socialism are to be developed. But enough of generalization: let us now give some specific examples.

Kimambo deals with a period which long antedates colonialism and the rise of nationalism (chapter 2). He presents what is, in many of its particulars, an exemplary account of developments in the region now comprising Tanzania prior to 1800. In stressing the growth of more centralized political systems during the period, he finds this to be clear evidence of 'the efforts, initiative and even success achieved by the people of Tanzania even in the distant past'–citing, for example, 'the efforts *of the people of Ugweno* in evolving a system which achieved centralization and unification' (emphasis added). This is merely one instance of 'the Tanzanians of that period' being 'able to create political ideologies which suited their own environments and needs'. Kimambo concludes that 'it is from the realization of such achievements that the Tanzanians of today must draw inspiration and courage as they strive in developing a modern nation founded on their own culture'.

It would seem, however, to be of at least equal importance to suggest that this political 'creativity' was in part a reflex of the establishment of more hierarchical, quasi-feudal socio-economic systems that weakened the simpler forms of egalitarianism characteristic of pre-feudal systems. Not that this would necessarily be a wholly negative occurrence; presumably many emer-gent patterns of exploitation were linked with the growth of the productive forces in Tanzanian society and it is upon such a base that even higher forms of economy and society could be constructed in the future. Unfortunately, Kimambo's account does not help us much with this sort of query. Moreover, as with other, more recent periods, it may be safer to characterize such changes as the work of groups and classes within societies, rather than overemphasiz-ing the role of that mystical entity, 'the people'. It will already be apparent that these are not mere academic points. An identification of such changes may cast a searching light on any too simple generalization about the collec-tive, 'socialist' nature of 'traditional' African society, for example, and thereby sharpen socialist debate. As suggested above, a clarification of the legacy of structures from this period may also be of some help to contemporary socialist planners in identifying likely points of support and resistance in particular localities. But, more generally, once it is emphasized that an interest in the 'chiefdoms' of this period is linked not merely to investigating processes of state-formation but also to questions of hierarchy and equality, exploitation, productive capacity, and the like, then we may feel certain that these issues are becoming a central preoccupation of every Tanzanian concerning all periods.

Andrew Roberts (chapter 4) is, perhaps, a little less sanguine about the results of the processes of political centralization as it continued into his period of reference–the nineteenth century. 'Increasing external contacts multiplied the opportunities for leaders to obtain men and weapons with which to enforce their authority' and this process was '[not] necessarily progressive'. For example, 'often it involved a great deal of fighting, raiding, and brutality'. But even his subtle account of political changes seems to call out for further complementary analyses of the various modes of production of the peoples concerned (as well as any shifts in productive capacity which might be involved). This could help save the investigation from becoming too exclusively preoccupied with undifferentiated 'peoples' on the one hand and heroic individuals on the other, as is sometimes the danger in this chapter.

As for the expansion of trade which both Roberts and Edward Alpers, in another valuable chapter (chapter 3), take to be a key variable during the period, one senses that something more is required than to see this (as Roberts does) as involving simply 'greater access to the material and intellectual resources of the world outside' or to conceptualize it, straightforwardly, as 'a world of expanding horizons'. To be sure, Alpers is more concerned with the external links of this trade but even he sees the most important effect of the caravan trade to be 'the germ of unity which it planted in the middle of those who were involved in it'. Again the non-specialist senses that the theoretical framework is not adequate to the task, for even at this early date it seems probable that the economic development of Tanzania is being distorted by the manner of its insertion into the world economy. The long-term result is dependency; what questions must be asked to find its seeds in this period?[10]

Gilbert Gwassa deals with the German period (chapter 5) and, significantly, deals with it almost exclusively from the angle of African resistance to the imposition of colonial rule. His is a dramatic and inspiring story, to be sure, and does not require the somewhat strained definition of resistance he is prepared to adopt ('adaptive resistance') in order, for example, to absorb Merere, in fighting with the Germans against Mkwawa, into the pantheon of national heroes. It does not make imperialism any less reprehensible to say that indigenous individuals, groups, and classes can ally with it for their own gain. Indeed this is a common pattern on the continent to the present day, and might better be identified at the outset as such. Other moments might appear more ambiguous if greater attention were paid to distinctive aspects of the overarching process of absorption into the world economy introduced during the period. It is easier to present Abushiri and Bwana Heri

simply as patriots if their complex links to the declining slave trade are not
mentioned, and the statement that 'German occupation threatened the
existence of their power politically but especially economically' could well
be enlarged upon to capture more clearly the essence of the German colonial
presence and the socio-economic changes it introduced.

Moreover, only a brief concluding reference is made to the emergence of
inequalities during the period; thus, the practice of education for the civil
service of a limited number of Africans is seen to have 'created privileged
groups in a society that had in the past stressed egalitarianism in communities'. Nothing is said to document the degree of egalitarianism in, say,
Mkwawa's armed camp. Nor is the scope of the new inequality (as between
regions, individuals, or classes) introduced by educational and economic
change identified clearly or evaluated in terms of its implications for future
Tanzanian socio-economic development. The focus upon the legacy of resistance and the seeds of unity, visible, in particular, in Maji-Maji, virtually
crowds out all other concerns.

Iliffe's chapter on 'the age of improvement and differentiation (1907–45)'
(chapter 6) is probably the strongest in the book for it brings together more
of the components necessary to clarifying the movement of Tanzanian society
than any other. As befits the general tone of the book the main motif remains
that of identifying the roots of unity, national consciousness, and political
achievement. But Iliffe is careful to trace other significant aspects of the life
of the period, most notably that of novel and emerging differentiation and
division, the latter including, as he notes, 'divisions of education and wealth,
divisions of culture and belief'. In particular, 'looking backward, signs of
economic class formation can be seen', and he provides a rich store of observation about this process in both urban and rural areas.

Even with Iliffe, however, the full logic of imperialism is consistently
blurred, so that there is little sign of that deepening dependency upon the
economies of the metropolitan centres which now seems so striking a
characteristic of colonial development. Yet a recognition of dependency
would render those efforts at 'improvement' which Iliffe emphasizes as being
the characteristic feature of the period more ambiguous than they can ever
appear in the absence of such an overarching framework. For Iliffe 'education, economic development, and the modernization of local government'
are the instruments of 'improvement' which Tanzanians are using at this
time to prepare their challenge to external control. But what if the kind of
economic development that is taking place serves the needs of the imperial
power in such a way as to make Tanzania's realization of self-sustained
growth and genuine independence at a later stage more difficult.[11] Iliffe also
attributes to his 'men of improvement' a 'deep commitment to education,
Christianity, and the Western variety of civilization'. But what if such values,
absorbed while achieving education, in fact define the terms of continued
subservience and create a hegemonic culture which narrows the range of
alternative development strategies likely to be contemplated. Such results
would indeed be ironic; yet something of the sort was occurring in Tanzania.

Thus, Iliffe's 'modernizers' were 'modernizers' perhaps, but almost inevitably this meant being 'capitalist modernizers', the qualifier being of very

great importance. Of course they are not, therefore, to be seen as 'just the stooges of an alien Government', as Professor Ranger correctly observes in a related chapter on the movement of ideas during the period (chapter 7); indeed, 'many of them had to fight hard to get the opportunity to improve'.[12] But, more subtly, they were increasingly part of the same underlying system as that 'alien government', and there was, therefore, a growing tendency for the interests of such 'capitalist modernizers' (and for the character of the society and economy which they were, in effect, constructing by their efforts) to become complementary to those of the alien economy and culture. Not conspiracy, but a particular pattern of uneven and combined development is the key![13]

This is the irony of 'improvement', then, that Iliffe fails to catch, though his chapter brilliantly, but in the last analysis, uneasily combines a portrait of the modernizers as both nationalists *and* as class-in-formation. The reason for this is a familiar one: Iliffe is too committed to writing 'nationalist' history to follow unflinchingly the logic of his own evidence. What is of central importance to him is that such efforts are 'heroic' in their own way–they are a valued component of the tradition of resistance. Improving within the framework of colonial rule, overcoming 'the problem of ignorance', is necessary for the time being in order for 'Tanzanians' to gather strength for a future confrontation; 'they had to sacrifice their own freedom for that of their children'.

That imperialism might be consolidating its position even while the seeds of challenge to formal colonialism were being sewn is a possibility unlikely to emerge from a framework so singlemindedly in search of resistance. Equally important the formation of classes takes on a particular texture when viewed from this perspective. As noted, Iliffe is well aware of the latter pattern; he is also aware, with Professor Ranger, that some protests against such developments were manifesting themselves during the period. But it remains, in effect, the accidental by-product of unevenly distributed resistance to European rule and/or nationalist strivings, rather than the inevitable result of capitalist development which, therefore, manifests the spirit of entrepreneurial aggrandizement and possessive individualism attendant upon such a process.

In reality it is perhaps something of both, but it is difficult not to feel that in this case nationalist consciousness has been ascribed a little too uncritically to all comers in the period, not only as the major clue to the larger significance of their activity, but even as to the content of their intention. One may feel as well that such an emphasis has the effect of blunting and softening contradictions which can then be admitted without being brought centre-stage; praise displaces a perception of process and subtly denatures the kind of challenge to future generations which is involved. Iliffe stresses, of course, that nationalism is still in embryo here but having subtly elided resistance and improvement, he is quite prepared to assimilate the latter to nationalism. He does so by emphasizing strongly (and probably over-emphasizing) the centrality of 'the dream of unity' which he sees to be an increasingly potent force in the period and, moreover, a further guarantee that 'improvers' of various sorts are, first and foremost, to be considered 'nationalists' working for the common good.

As usual with Iliffe the evidence is carefully marshalled and impressively synthesized. And, in the last paragraph, the reality of class formation (if not dependency) *is* passed on intact to a later chapter as one of several crucial problems which face the emergent nationalist movement. To the extent that Iliffe's chapter is missing certain crucial nuances it at least forces one to recognize the subtle shadings that will eventually be necessary in any definitive history for a socialist Tanzania. Unfortunately, this is not as true for Arnold Temu's chapter on 'The rise and triumph of nationalism'. Here the dangers which one struggles to isolate and label in Iliffe's complex argument appear much more starkly, though they are in certain important respects identical.

The litany of resistance is duly recited by Temu, with continuity all the more heavily emphasized. There is throughout the book a tendency to discuss 'Tanzania' prematurely, assuming the entity even while it is in the process of formation. This tendency underwrites a second and even more important one: that of making 'the Tanzanian people' (once again a somewhat amorphous and mystical entity) the crucial motor of change. With Iliffe, for example, the idea that 'Tanzanians' were overcoming the problem of ignorance was the essential key to the 'improvers' educational advancement, thereby subtly distorting other important features (class formation, cultural transformation, dependency, and so on) of that occurrence. Temu seems to take his cue from this and is even less hesitant to interpret historical patterns in Tanzania as being primarily a product of the corporate activity of 'Tanzanians'. Maji-Maji is one early effort at resistance undertaken by Tanzanians. 'Self-improvement' (Temu's phrase) is another, for '*implicit* in this was that self-improvement in education and economic self-sufficiency would place them in a better position to fight against the British who had replaced the Germans in Tanzania' (emphasis added).

The emergence of the nationalist movement, and the interpretation of its implications, poses no problems for such a model. It is merely the culmination of the corporate activity previously traced, for Tanzanians have learned from their past mistakes and laid the groundwork well. Temu actually argues that 'it was largely these early failures that determined the way in which the people of Tanzania were to be mobilized for *uhuru* later on'! As compared with Iliffe even less is heard of emergent groups and novel classes among the Tanzanian populace whose varied interests might be expected to 'determine', in some part, the nature of the colonial political process at its various stages of development. And as little is said about the character of the imperial power's relationship to the colony, and any possible changes in its own calculations as a factor affecting the activities of the nationalists. Tanzanians are merely trying a new tactic against a familiar enemy, a tactic that this time is supremely successful.

This is not satisfactory. For one thing such a formulation provides no room for the bargaining role of the colonial government mentioned much earlier in our analysis. The Germans in 1905 and the British in 1960 become interchangeable terms with, apparently, a similar and single-minded ambition: political oppression of the African people. Temu notes, for example, 'that the associations kept African politics alive through discussion and dialogue at a time when the colonial administration did the best it could to stifle any political activities aimed at opposing either central or local administration'. But why was a more concerted effort not made to stifle TANU. The British were prepared to use military force in Malaya, Kenya, Guyana, South Arabia to safeguard their position or to guarantee a palatable successor; the Portuguese resist even armed assault upon their direct colonial hegemony to the present-day, just as the Americans continue the work of the French in Indo-China. The British would not have left without a push but had their interests so dictated they would have been a more active antagonist. What does this tell us of dependency and of British (and international capitalist) views concerning the degree of menace manifested by their successors? What interests, what linkages, really were at stake? The nationalist movement was important then, but it did not merely drive the British out in a straight-forward and unambiguous manner, as Temu seems to imply for much of his paper. That version is stirring stuff, but, as argued previously, one result may be to over-emphasize the accomplishment of nationalism and de-emphasize the continuing challenge.

A second point is equally important in this regard. Nyerere has written that for TANU 'the aim was *Uhuru*, pure and simple... It made everything simple. We deliberately refused to answer the question as to what we would do after *Uhuru*, because the moment we had started to do that we would have got our forces divided about future plans and that would have been wrong. Instead, from 1954 onwards, we were absolutely clear in our singleness of purpose.'[14] For a nationalist leader like Nyerere this may have been both a legitimate and a necessary tactic at the time, but such an agnosticism about the detailed motives and long-term goals of participants in the nationalist movement is not something that a historian of the period can permit himself. In fact Nyerere himself has forged subsequently some of the alternative questions which are of relevance. He writes that[15]

> ... many of the leaders of the independence struggle saw things in these terms. They were not against capitalism; they simply wanted its fruits, and saw independence as the means to that end. Indeed, many of the most active fighters in the independence movement were motivated—consciously or unconsciously—by the belief that only with independence could they attain that ideal of individual wealth which their education or their experience in the modern sector had established as a worthwhile goal.[16]

The mass of the population partake of this general ethos and 'simply (demand) the replacement of white and brown faces by black ones... Capitalism was the system which the masses knew in the modern sector, and what they had been fighting against was that this modern sector should be in alien hands'.

For Nyerere the denouement to such a process comes as no surprise:

> Once in power, some of the leaders whom the people have learned to know and trust will think their nationalism demands expropriation of non-Africans in favour of African citizens; the more sophisticated may deny this but think of economic development in terms of expanding capitalism with the participation of Africans.
> Such leaders as these may well identify the progress they have promised the people with the increasing wealth of the few; they will point to African-

owned large cars and luxurious houses and so on, as evidence of growing prosperity and of their own devotion to the cause of national independence.[17]

In fact, 'the most active, and, therefore, the most popular, of the nationalist leaders may have been people without a socialist conviction. They may either have never had an opportunity to study the problems and possibilities of social and economic organization, or they may have been people who were motivated by a personal desire for the fruits of capitalism.' To such people 'exploitation was only wrong when carried out upon the masses by people of a different race'.

As for the masses the carry-over of nationalist enthusiasm, complemented by defections from their ranks to those of the privileged, may lead to a short-run acceptance of this emergent *status quo*:

> The perpetuation of capitalism, and its expansion to include Africans, will be accepted by the masses who took part in the independence struggle. They may take the new wealth of their leaders as natural and even good–for a time they may even take reflected pride in it... This public acceptance of African capitalism will be obtained because the people have learned to trust their nationalist leaders, and wish to honour them. Also there will inevitably be new jobs and opportunities for a good number of the most active, vocal and intelligent of those who might otherwise have led criticism.[18]

In sum:

> Everyone wants to be free, and the task of the nationalist is simply to rouse the people to a confidence in their own power of protest. But to build the real freedom which socialism represents is a very different thing. It demands a positive understanding and positive actions, not simply a rejection of colonialism and a willingness to co-operate in non-co-operation.

Yet, as Nyerere stresses, by escalating racialism, apotheosizing opportunistic politicians, and single-mindedly emphasizing the significance of the achievement of formal independence, '*the anti-colonial struggle will almost certainly have intensified the difficulties*' of building 'this real freedom which socialism represents' (emphasis added).[19]

Unfortunately, there is more wisdom about the paradoxes and ambiguities of nationalism in these few pages by Nyerere than in the bulk of the book under review. Temu celebrates the political leadership, rather than situating its strengths and weaknesses within a complex and multi-dimensional analysis of the overall decolonization process. Nor is anything heard of the character and significance of rising African bureaucrats and entrepreneurs outside the immediate circle of political activists, though these are as much the inheritors of the fruits of independence as the 'leaders', more narrowly defined. The contribution of the workers to nationalist resistance is identified, though a deeper analysis both of their relationship to the socio-economic transformations of the period and of the actual basis of their protest might have revealed the roots of the conflict between government and trade union which was to emerge in the post-colonial period. Similarly, drawing upon the earlier investigations of Cliffe, Temu stresses the peasant contribution to successful nationalism, but neither is this analysed in such a way as to explore the quality and diversity of peasant consciousness.[20] In short, all 'opposition' is reduced to its lowest common denominator, and a relatively undifferentiated effort by all Tanzanians to reclaim their liberty becomes the sum total of relevant occurrence during the period.[21]

The possibility of contradiction having been more or less banned from the preceding discussion, one is startled to learn, in Temu's final paragraph, that 'the replacing of the colonial administration did not mean a complete break with the British or with their institutions. . . It was at first more a change of personnel in the top echelons of government and the civil service than a change in our institutions, attitudes, and thinking.' However unexceptionable, this conclusion seems arbitrary in context; what has preceded has not pre-prepared the ground for such a dilemma so baldly stated.[22] A 'nationalist' history of nationalism has failed, in other words, to aid in the identification of those barriers to 'real freedom' which are being erected by class formation, dependency, and the like during the very period of nationalist achievement. Whether some form of internal class struggle may be necessary to advance such a situation, on what novel fronts and with what degree of urgency imperialism is now to be confronted: such questions acquire little currency from such an investigation.

But if the historical genesis of barriers to further advance is slighted here as elsewhere in the book, a second and more novel danger becomes apparent in this particular chapter. For the characteristic method of the book tends to encourage oversimplification concerning the emergence of the socialist initiative itself! A careful reading of Temu's final paragraph, quoted above, suggests that socialism has become merely the next historic task for the corporate Tanzanian. Socialism is, in its turn, assimilated (even reduced) to nationalism, becoming for Temu, and perhaps for other participants in the book, merely an inevitable stage in the great tradition of resistance. Tanzanians learn, in effect, that formal independence is not enough, that socialism is, logically, the next tactic. Again, subtly, one is encouraged to think that such a transition can be smoother, more straight-forward, more unanimous, than it is ever likely to be.

This is not to deny the possible existence of genuinely positive links between nationalism and socialism; it is merely to insist, among other things, upon the centrality of such ambiguities as Nyerere's paradigm of decolonization helps to underscore. For it must be emphasized that nationalism has not tended to have this denouement elsewhere on the continent. What combination of historical forces and historical phasing can have led to the somewhat unlikely development of a serious socialist impulse here?[23] And, in light of such factors, how strong is it likely to be? Thus, despite the many merits of Temu's chapter and of the book as a whole, both the positive and negative sides of the current situation–and the tense contradiction between constructive socialist effort and hostile objective conditions which is the drama of contemporary Tanzania–remains blunted and mystified. The situation continues to cry out for further scientific illumination and the application of a fully effective historical perspective.

III. The challenge

Several remarks might be made by way of conclusion. The first is more narrowly methodological. For part of the problem of Tanzanian historiography, as exemplified in this book, may arise quite simply from too narrow a focus upon the purely political dimensions of Tanzanian history. It is significant that the editors, in stating their determination in the introduction to focus on 'the African himself', further note that 'there has been no attempt to deal with colonial administrative structures'. Perhaps if they had been more self-conscious about the fact that imperialism involves economic and socio-cultural dimensions of even greater importance than 'colonial administrative structures' they would not have been so eager to discard the imperial factor from their African-centred history or to make more difficult an identification of the subtle dialectic between external and internal factors by removing one of its terms. The early development of a school of economic historians in Tanzania is one major imperative which suggests itself from this. But even this may be misleading, for it has been apparent throughout our essay that institutions and culture, social structure and productive capacity, must all be understood to interpenetrate. More important, therefore, is the development of an increasingly sophisticated methodology, specifically tailored to Tanzanian needs (and preferably by Tanzanians) but drawing upon world-wide canons of left debate (in particular, one may suggest, the Marxist tradition), which stresses the complex and inseparable interplay of political, economic, and socio-cultural variables.

It is worth repeating that there are strengths in this book, nonetheless–a less illuminating book would not be worth discussing at this length. We have already noted that in Africa an achieved nationalism like that of Tanzania is of great importance and that African seizure of state power is also of great potential significance. Another more complicated factor is at stake: in a world where white dominance and white racism have worked for centuries to degrade and humiliate black men, it is no small thing to write history which emphasizes African accomplishment and, thus, makes available a sense of pride and self-confidence to black men in general and Tanzanians in particular. This is probably a more valid excuse for some slight tilting of the scale of the historical record than one could find for the sort of over-simplified radical history which we have seen Weinstein to be denouncing. But clearly a balance must be struck between the burden of the past and the stark imperatives of the future. On officially accepting a copy of the book under review President Nyerere himself 'called on African historians to refrain from exaggerating facts about Africa simply because their alien counterparts played them down or excluded them from the annals of history in the pre-independence era'.[24] In the last analysis problems and contradictions do not disappear by ignoring them and the most responsible and progressive nationalism may be that which is most conscious of this fact.

The positive contributions of a historiography which raises questions of pressing importance to socialist Tanzania in its examination of the past will not bear extended recapitulation here; continued mention of these has been made throughout the text. In fostering a general spirit of critical inquiry (alive, in particular, to the realities of exploitation and dependency), and in further clarifying both the obstacles which contemporary socialist planners must face and the forces to which they may look for support, there lies a clear challenge. Nor should historians mistake their role. Honesty and rigour are essential, but the past does not interpret itself; it springs to life in the present only in relation to the questions it is asked. And there is evidently enough life in socialist questions about the past to engage the energies of several generations of Tanzanian historians. Those who accept this challenge can expect to play a vital role in raising the level of consciousness of their countrymen and contributing to 'the Tanzanian revolution'.

NOTES

[1] I. N. Kimambo and A. J. Temu, *A history of Tanzania* (Nairobi, 1969).

[2] T. O. Ranger, *The recovery of African initiative in Tanzanian history*. The University College, Dar es Salaam, Inaugural Lecture Series, No. 2, (Dar es Salaam, March, 1969).

[3] Alternative perspectives or combination of perspectives could be imagined, but one such alternative is not that positivist will-of-the-wisp, 'objective history', which imagines that data interprets itself in the absence of evaluation and commitment. On this subject, see Hugh Stretton, *The political sciences* (London, 1969).

[4] The phrase is that of Andre Gunder Frank; see his *Capitalism and under-development in Latin America* (New York, 1967) and *Latin America: underdevelopment or revolution* (New York, 1970). For a more detailed elaboration of this and other aspects of the present author's choice of emphases see G. Arrighi and J. S. Saul, 'Socialism and economic development in Tropical Africa', *Journal of modern African Studies* **VI**, 2 (August 1968) and Arrighi and Saul, 'Nationalism and revolution in sub-Saharan Africa', *The Socialist Register 1969* (London, 1969).

[5] Liberalism, in itself a by-product of capitalist development, becomes a tool in their hands at this point—at once stimulating and rationalizing the drive for self-determination.

[6] For a case-study of this and other aspects of decolonization see Martin Kilson's valuable *Political change in a West African state* (Cambridge, Mass., 1968). But see also my review of Kilson in 3 (October, 1968), *Journal of Modern African Studies* **VI**, p. 141.

[7] The rise of the United States to a position of hegemony within the international capitalist system is also of importance here, for she had little, if anything, to gain from the perpetuation of formal colonialism with its accompanying barriers to her economic penetration.

[8] This and the succeeding quotations are from James Weinstein, 'Can an Historian be a Socialist Revolutionary?' *Socialist Revolution* **I**, 3 (May–June, 1970).

[9] Significantly, Nyerere himself has recently written to the effect that 'the anti-colonial struggle will almost certainly have intensified the difficulties' of building socialism. This may seem to many readers a startling statement, particularly coming from Nyerere; it is one to which we shall return in due course.

[10] More could also be done by both these writers to link the growth of trade and the creation of a new territorially defined (though externally dependent) mode of production with changes in the mode of production at the local (regional/ethnic group/village) level.

[11] More recently Iliffe has made certain of these questions more central to his concern; see his suggestive paper 'Agricultural change in modern Tanzania: an outline history' (cyclostyled draft, Dar es Salaam, 1970).

[12] As Iliffe phrases this point, 'improvement was not something Europeans did for Africans. It was something Africans did for themselves'.

[13] Unfortunately in this chapter, as in others, there is relatively little said about the pattern of penetration of European companies and banks and of the Asian trading community, or about the overall pattern of overseas trade, though these would be necessary to the more rounded picture which we have in mind.

[14] J. K. Nyerere, 'Introduction' to Kathleen Stahl, *Sail in the wilderness* (London, 1961).

[15] This and succeeding quotations are from Nyerere's introduction to his *Freedom and Socialism— Uhuru na Ujamaa* (Dar es Salaam, 1968), the section of the introduction entitled 'The problems of building socialism in an ex-colonial country', pp. 26–32. It is also reprinted in J. K. Nyerere, *Nyerere on Socialism* (D.S.M., 1969), pp. 52–8.

[16] It is worth noting the President's parenthesis here to the effect that 'it was not always selfishness which made leaders think only in terms of Africanizing the capitalist economy of the colonialists; often they had no knowledge of any alternative'. This may remind us of the need to see these developments not as a conspiracy but as a process, a particular process of capitalist development.

[17] As he further notes: '... it was on this basis, for example, that some Tanzanian leaders criticized the Arusha Declaration'.

[18] He continues ominously: 'But, sooner or later, the people will lose their enthusiasm and will look upon the independence government as simply another ruler which they should avoid as much as possible!'

[19] Cf. footnote 9, above.

[20] The reference is to Cliffe, 'Nationalism and the reaction to enforced agricultural change during the colonial period', paper presented to the EAISR Conference, (December, 1964). This has recently been published with a brief postscript by the author in *Taamuli* 1 (Dar es Salaam, July, 1970). I have briefly discussed the issue of 'the quality and diversity of peasant consciousness' in my 'On African populism' in G. Ionescu and E. Gellner (eds), *Populism* (London, 1968).

[21] The institutions of nationalism would make another interesting focus; in exploring the character of TANU, for example, with an eye to evaluating its likely strengths and weaknesses with relevance to subsequent tasks, points about its historical character would be likely to emerge which might otherwise be missed.

[22] It is worth noting that Cliffe's concluding chapter (in the book from which this item is drawn), more an exercise in contemporary analysis than an historical contribution, does raise a number of basic issues which parallel the concerns of this paper. But most of his emphases are not anticipated or illuminated in the historical sections, and that is the major point of the argument here.

[23] An attempt to explore this subject further will be found in the present author's forthcoming paper 'African socialism in one country: Tanzania,' in G. Arrighi and J.S. Saul, *Essays on the political economy of Africa* (Monthly Review Press) New York, 1973.

[24] From a report (under the headline 'Be honest, Nyerere tells historians') in *The Standard*, Tanzania, 11 November 1969.

PART IV
Economy: The Political Economy of Colonialism and Neo-Colonialism

We will not condemn nor justify imperialism here; we will simply state that as much on the economic level as on the social and cultural level, imperialist capital has not remotely fulfilled the historical mission carried out by capital in the countries of accumulation... We must however recognize that in certain cases imperialist capital or moribund capitalism has had sufficient self-interest, strength, and time to increase the level of productive forces (as well as building towns) and to allow a minority of the local population to attain a higher and even privileged standard of living, thus contributing to a process which some would call dialectical, by widening the contradictions within the societies in question. In other, even rarer cases, there has existed the possibility of accumulation of capital, creating the conditions for the development of a local bourgeoisie.

Development and stagnation in agriculture

SAMIR AMIN, DAVID KOM, ANN SEIDMAN

From Samir Amin, 'Development and structural change: the African experience, 1950–1970', Permission to reprint by the Trustees of Columbia University in the City of New York, from *The journal of International Affairs*, **XXIV**, 2 (1970), is gratefully acknowledged to the editors of the *Journal*. David Kom, *Le Cameroun: essai d'analyse économique et politique*, Editions Sociales, Paris, 1971. Ann Seidman, 'The agricultural revolution', *East Africa Journal*, **7,** 8 (August 1970).

SAMIR AMIN

The dynamic and limitations of agrarian capitalism in Black Africa

The Pearson Report (see footnote 10) stresses the decisive role of agricultural progress at the start of industrialization. One cannot but agree with it on this point. At the start of industrialization, agriculture alone, which employs the majority of the people, provides an important market for industry, just as it must feed the urban population. (Otherwise, it becomes necessary to import food supplies, which obstructs industrialization itself.) It is only at a later stage of industrialization that this double function loses its relative importance, with industry and tertiary activities becoming more and more the essential outlets for industry.[1]

Both during the long period from 1900 to 1966 and the more recent period from 1960 to 1967, agricultural progress in the Third World has been extremely inadequate. Such stagnation slows down possible industrialization, *even when it is inward-looking*.[2] Especially since 1960 the growth rates of both light *and* heavy industry have declined in the Third World for this reason. The agricultural productivity index (net calorie production per active male farmer), calculated by Bairoch for the entire Third World (excluding China), on the index of 100 in 1909–13, fell to 96 for the period from 1953 to 1957, and to 95 from 1960 to 1964. Moreover, this productivity was already 30 per cent lower than that of the developed countries on the eve of the Industrial Revolution.[3] Certainly the situation in India (which produces roughly 30 per cent of the cereal in the Third World) showed considerable improvement in 1967–8 after the 1965–6 setback. But this is jumping much too quickly to the conclusion that the miracle of a 'Green Revolution' is occurring and the first hurdle has been cleared, as the Pearson Report pretends.[4]

In the Third World there was a deficit of 23 million tons of grain in 1966 (9 per cent of the total production of the developing countries). This is in direct contrast to the 11 million tons of food grains exported from the Third World in 1938. The Pearson Report itself reminds us that while agricultural growth in Latin America, which was 3.5 per cent per annum from 1950 to 1967, exceeded the growth of the population (2.9 per cent), in Africa the rate did not exceed 2 per cent (less than the growth of population), and in India it just kept pace (2.5 per cent). In the case of Pakistan, although the rate has been 3.2 per cent since 1960, this followed a period of stagnation from 1955 to 1960 (1.4 per cent). It is nonetheless true that there will probably be a spurt in agriculture there, at least in certain areas of Western Pakistan.

Similar stagnation can be observed in Africa, although there it was the agricultural export trade (and not grain) that experienced a rapid start *in certain areas*. In fact, the idea that very poor or zero average rates of agricultural productivity growth, either in the Third World as a whole or in vast sections of it, such as Africa, indicate stagnation of the rural world, is completely erroneous. These average rates have no *significance* because they include immense areas of stagnation, and occasionally even recession, along with minor areas of rapid growth. It is essential to study the conditions that determined these localized spurts of activity. I have already begun to do this in the case of Black Africa and I believe it possible to show the obvious relationship between the growth of agricultural productivity and the establishment of agrarian capitalism.[5]

There seems to be a close correlation between those areas which did experience rapid spurts of activity and the development of a black rural bourgeoisie. The development of such a bourgeoisie requires that four conditions be met. The first of these conditions seems to be the existence of a traditional society sufficiently hierarchical so that certain kinds of hereditary chiefs possess enough social power to appropriate to themselves important parcels of tribal land. It is in this way that traditional tribal heads of Ghana, southern Nigeria, the Ivory Coast, and Uganda were able to create, to their profit, a plantation economy. However, it should be noted that very strict hierarchies of a semi-feudal nature, such as exist in the Islamic savanna, have not been favourable to the development of a rural bourgeoisie.

The second condition is an average population density of the order of ten to 30 inhabitants per square kilometre. Any lesser density makes the private appropriation of lands ineffective and the potential supply of paid labour insufficient. The mechanism of proletarianization is considerably facilitated when there is a convenient source of foreign labour, as is the case with Upper Volta and the Ivory Coast. At a second stage, the younger members and dependants of the families of the original planters can in turn be proletarianized.[6] Densities that are too great, as in Ruanda and on the Bamileke plateau in Cameroon, make it difficult for the chiefs to seize control of sufficient land.

The third condition is the presence of fertile soils, making it possible, with very little mechanization and, hence, with the low rate of productivity in an agriculture that is still largely extensive, to produce per man acre an adequate surplus from the very start of development. It is in this manner that cotton in Uganda or peanuts in the Serer country,[7] and, generally speaking, food produce with low production rates, preclude what coffee and cocoa have made possible elsewhere.

Finally, the fourth condition requires that the political atmosphere not be detrimental to this kind of spontaneous development. The relative ease of private appropriation of land, the freedom of work, and the credit awarded individual farmers have everywhere played an important role in the establishing of this rural bourgeoisie. Very characteristic of this was the abolition of forced labour in the French colonies in 1950. The typically middle-class demand for freedom of work allowed the Ivory Coast planters to profit from a flood of immigrants unparalleled in strength by the number of workers recruited by force and, up until then, assigned solely to the French planters. It also made it possible to organize a great political battle in the country, with the peasant victims of forced labour backing the native planters. On the other hand, in certain areas, such as the lower Congo, the paternalism of the Belgian *paysannats* undoubtedly played a negative role in checking the tendency toward the development of a bourgeoisie. Is it not noteworthy that, when the political structure of the *paysannats* was swept away after independence, such a bourgeoisie was able to clear the way for its own development? In six years, from 1960 to 1966, commercial food production in the lower Congo quadrupled. It should be noted that for the first time on a large scale the course of capitalist development had stemmed not from export goods, but from food products stimulated by the demand from Kinshasa. It should certainly also be noted that another condition–the possibility of using foreign labour–was finally met in the lower Congo in 1960, thanks to the influx of refugees from Angola. The politics of apartheid and 'preserving African traditions', practised in South Africa and Rhodesia, are obviously obstacles to the progress of a rural middle class.

Does the same hold true for the policies regarding rural mobilization, organization, and co-operative development? These policies, practised everywhere according to the same naive paternalistic formulas, which undoubtedly arise from the utopian desire to see the whole country advance at an even, sustained pace, have neither hindered the development of the plantation system wherever it was possible nor brought on any considerable qualitative transformation elsewhere.

In fact, there remain huge areas still outside the movement, because the conditions that make change possible have not been met; this is the Africa that 'didn't get off the ground' or 'was unable to get off ground'. This is also the rural Africa 'without problems' in the sense that it can adapt to its demographic growth without modifying its structures, simply by extending its traditional subsistence economy. The insertion of this Africa into the colonial world inevitably meant a very limited development of crops for export, often imposed by the authorities for tax purposes. Occasionally, when the terms of exchange between export goods and legally purchasable manufactured goods broken down, or simply whenever the administrative force which imposed them became weakened, these crops were given up in favour of subsistence agriculture. To call such abandonment a regression is superficial, because rationality here was on the side of the peasants and not the administration, which wanted to impose uneconomical crops. The development of a parasitic urban economy and the inflation it entails are often at the bottom of this breakdown in exchange terms, of which the economic setback of cotton production in the Congo (Kinshasa) provides the most spectacular example.[8]

Exceptional growth rates occasionally occur in the agriculture of some areas. Rates of 7 per cent annually are not uncommon. There is no doubt that the transformations undergone by these rural areas in Africa in the course of three decades contrast with the relative immobility of the oriental rural world. We are closer here to the conditions of certain areas of Latin America.

This is why it is a mistake to make the kind of universal statements which are common to United Nations literature. The analyses of the Food and Agriculture Organization (FAO) adopted by the Economic Commission for Africa underline the fact that, on the average, African food production growth has been very poor (2 per cent as compared to 3.5 per cent for agricultural export goods, which gives 2.4 per cent for agriculture as a whole). But the 'exceptions' to which the document draws attention are more interesting: corn in Kenya (3.9 per cent), rice in Egypt (3.8 per cent), livestock in all the savanna countries.[9] For all these products, *destined for the domestic market,* better prices have been possible. (This was a necessary, but insufficient condition.) The Pearson Report stresses the necessity of this condition. For once I share its opinion. For it is quite obvious that cereal production in Western Pakistan and rice production in Thailand could not have been undertaken without it.[10] However, the analysis is not carried far enough by the Report, as it neglects to mention all the *other conditions.* From this kind of compelling analysis, completely absent in the Pearson Report, of the problems relating to the transformation of the structures of the rural world (including, of course, its social structures, which cannot be studied apart from its economic structures). I am led to form conclusions almost always diametrically opposed to those of the Report.

Demographic *pressure* is not always an *obstacle* to the growth of productivity, as is suggested by the very superficial sort of analysis which consists of dividing the growth of production by that of the population and saying 'if the latter had been lower, the growth of progress per capita would have been greater'. On the contrary, demographic pressure is often the engine that sets the intensification and progress of productivity in motion.

Agrarian capitalism based on small family properties (of sufficient size, however, to be able to support a capitalist form of production, i.e., recourse to wage labour) is potentially more dynamic than that which results from the transformation of the big pre-capitalist (feudal) properties into capitalist estates. This second form of agrarian capitalist development is the one which occurred most frequently outside Black Africa for historical reasons (the structure of the pre-capitalist social formations of the Orient and that of the capitalism of the Latin American periphery instituted during the age of mercantilism). In Black Africa, in particular in the Islamic savanna, the precolonial 'semi-feudal' formations led, as a result of integration into the world market, to the development of less dynamic forms (such as the Nigerian

Sultanates, the brotherhoods–Mourid, Ansar, Ashiqqa, etc.). It is this system of land estates which has presented the principal obstacle to agricultural progress–the monopoly held by the great landowners did not compel them to modernize in order to retain their economic privilege. Thus the *political alliances* between the local ruling class and the foreign ruling capital have delayed and are still delaying vital agrarian reforms. It is significant that all the reforms which come under that heading have run up against open hostility from the West. The limited progress realized in this sense (as in Mexico, Egypt, Algeria) has opened the way to the subsequent development of the agrarian capitalism of the rich peasantry. Developments of this nature, in opening up certain areas of Pakistan, India, and Thailand, have brought about the current limited progress.

Whenever the conditions listed previously are met–and only under these circumstances–economic stimuli (improvement in the relative prices of farm products) will be effective. On this point I agree with the Pearson Report, pronouncing the paternalistic 'boy scout' policies advocated and practised in Black Africa a complete failure. Nonetheless, even on this point, the Pearson Report neglects to analyse the origin of these policies. For the transferring of the *world-wide structures of relative prices* from the centre to the periphery–more precisely through that international market which the Pearson Report so adamantly defends–is certainly at the bottom of the failure of the production stimuli. The devastating competition of American 'relief aid' is to be noted here. Because international prices are imposed upon the periphery, where today the internal relationship between agricultural productivity and industrial productivity is so different from what it is at the centre, the farmers are in fact systematically discriminated against. It is this world-wide transferring of price structures which orients producers toward export commodities, thus limiting any possible progress.

Consequently, the path of progress based on agrarian capitalism is narrowly limited by integration into the international market on which it depends. The nature of the peripheral social systems in fact allows the centre to appropriate to itself, through the breakdown of exchange terms, productivity gains made in agriculture on the periphery. The Pearson Report remains silent on this subject. The deterioration of these terms for peripheral trade as a whole has been 10 per cent since 1954. For agricultural products the percentage is higher.[11] Moreover, the economic stimuli have had only limited effects, since they are of interest only to a minor fraction of the rural population. In the concrete conditions of the Third World at present, the increasing predominance of the rural poverty-stricken masses (and it is here that the new phenomenon of demographic pressure comes into play) indicates the dire need for rapid progress. This demands the mobilization of the masses. *The direct contradiction between economic stimuli and mass mobilization defines the real conditions of the framework into which rapid agricultural progress must fit.*

NOTES
    [1] This thesis was brilliantly demonstrated by Bairoch in *Révolution industrielle et sous-développement*, Paris, 1963. Adam Smith had already understood this problem,

which the later Ricardian analysis was to overlook. See Palloix, *Problémes de la croissance en économic ouverte.*

[2] The word used in M. Amin's original French text is *auto-centre.* There is no exact translation in English; 'inward-looking' is closer than 'self-centered' or 'autonomous', and has been used throughout the translation.—Ed.

[3] Paul Bairoch, *Révolution industrielle et sous-développement,* p. 12.

[4] Gunnar Myrdal is considerably less 'optimistic' than the Pearson Report. See his *Asian drama* (New York: Twentieth Century Fund, 1968).

[5] Samir Amin, 'Le développement du capitalisme en Afrique noire, l'Homme et la Société 1968,' in *En partant du capital* (Paris: Collection Anthropos, 1968).

[6] See my study, *Le développement du capitalisme en Côte d'Ivoire* (Paris: Editions de Minuit, 1967).

[7] District of Senegal which, in contrast to the Wolof country, has retained less hierarchical systems of social organization.

[8] The International Monetary Fund, in helping to institute a convertible zaire, contributed greatly to making this delicate recession equilibrium possible. See B. Ryelandt, *L'Inflation Congolaise,* 1960–1968 (Kinshasa: Unpublished thesis, Lovanium University, 1969).

[9] UN Economic Commission for Africa, *The economic situation in Africa in recent years,* UN Document ECN. 14/435, 1969, New York, p. 67 ff.

[10] Pearson *et al., Partners in development: report of the Commission on International Development,* Praeger, New York, 1969, pp. 302–17, 330–37.

[11] See, for example, the figures relating to the UDEAC countries for the period 1960–1968 in Samir Amin and C. Coquery, *Du Congo francais à l'UDEAC*–1880–1968 (Paris: Collection Anthropos, 1969).

DAVID KOM
The Co-operative movement in the Cameroons

The experiment of the capitalist co-operative movement in the Cameroons proves that it cannot extricate the mass of peasants from their present poor economic situation.

Agricultural co-operatives first appeared in the Cameroons during colonial times, more so in the region under French mandate than that under the British. This co-operative movement was essentially the work of French colonists and was intended particularly for the processing of agricultural produce from the farms of Europeans; and so it assumed basically an industrial character (1932–3). In 1937 a co-operative was established for the treatment, drying, and sale of coffee in the home and export markets.

Before the Second World War a system called *indigénat* or 'citizenship rights' existed in French African colonies, by which the villagers and peasants were obliged to provide a certain number of days' work, without payment, for the benefit of the colonial administration. Formed into gangs, they were sent to work at building sites, on road-mending or the railway, down the mines (for instance, the gold-mines at Bétaré-Oya), or on the extensive plantations of colonists (at Mélong, Foumbot, Dizangué, etc.).

After the imperialist war, with the spread of the trade union movement and the rising demands for national independence, the peasants' co-operative movement developed and took hold.

But both before and during the war there were organizations which passed for co-operatives. These were the Sociétés Indigènes de Prévoyance (SIP)–Native Provident Societies. They were usually organized on a village basis or by parts of large villages. Each SIP was in the charge of a headman to whom the peasants had to pay a tax, at one time called a contribution; but it was, in fact, a 'head' tax.

Despite their pseudo-democratic appearance, the SIPs were fundamentally bureaucratic bodies, conceived by the colonial administration and set up in order to have better control over the peasantry of the Cameroons. In fact, with the growth of an agricultural proletariat, and the creation and spread of the trade union movement, the colonial authorities had every interest in taking the still ignorant peasantry in hand, to protect them from the 'virus' of Marxism and nationalism.

Nevertheless some kind of evolution towards a co-operative system took place within the SIP. The peasants began to realize the necessity of uniting as a class in order to ensure an improvement in their crops, especially as the monetary system was penetrating the peasant world and the cultivation of crops such as coffee and cocoa, (which were exported and, therefore, brought in money) became more widespread. But the accumulation of capital tends to develop a bourgeois mentality. And the peasant or small farmer, being a producer and owner of the means of production–and of a small initial capital–is increasingly absorbed by the world capitalist market, even if he produces much of his own food (less than in the past, however), for he tends more and more to aim at that market.

This seems to have been one of the defects in the capitalist co-operative movement. The rudimentary co-operatives like the SIPs became increasingly societies which accumulated capital. The capitalist mentality became more general; a peasant no sooner joined a SIP than he grew crops with the main aim of 'getting capital together' or of increasing, of 'putting to work' capital already held. It became the aim of such a peasant to assert himself socially by economic means; to increase his income, to 'make a place for himself', as they say in a capitalist bourgeois society.

But at a higher level a steady evolution was taking place; the co-operative system grew stronger every day, and the SIPs became effective nuclei of the co-operatives. The SIPs stood for the interests of the peasants to some extent and they gradually became credit institutions. More precisely, there was a division within the SIP movement which led to the establishment of a credit organization for peasants.

In order to develop his plantation, a peasant no longer counted solely on the labour contributed by the workers who formed the SIP, but counted more and more on a contribution in material, in capital. And the administrative authorities linked up the SIP with the colonial credit and finance system to an increasing extent. Thus the agent who was the representative of the treasurer–paymaster's office also became the official who collected the SIP tax. He therefore controlled two funds: the state coffers and the credit facilities.

In the early 'fifties, when the nationalist movement became stronger, the SIPs began to be outmoded and were superseded by the African Provident Societies (SAP). However, very little difference was noticeable in their set-up and social–economic functions.

It should be mentioned, however, that the SAPs were organized in a more systematic manner. They instituted a policy of investment and initiated several operations: mobile teams were sent out to plantations to aid with the work, advise on disease, select species and seed, and gather the harvest. And to facilitate financial operations, the SAP tax was merged with income tax. These measures gave new life to the co-operative movement, and all over the rural districts there sprang up peasants' co-operatives which endeavoured to throw off the SAP domination. These were the circumstances which led the colonial government to discard the SAP in favour of a new controlling agency, the Sectors of Modernization (SEM).

The part these were to play was set out by the French Ministry for Co-operation in *Economie et Plan de développement, République fédérale du Cameroun:*[1]

> The reduced role of the SAP results from the creation of the Sectors of Modernization (SEM). Established by a decree dated 26 September 1950, their areas of activity were extended to the whole of the territory during the period 1953–8... The original idea of the SEM, one for each particular crop, was to give the peasant additional help that was strictly specialized; but its evolution tended towards competition with and then *replacement* of the SAP in its work of popularization. (Author's italics.)

In any case, the SIP, like the SAP and later the SEM, was established at a time when the colonial government had most need of them. The authorities were endeavouring to maintain a tight hold on the peasantry and at the same time to restrain productivity and avoid a state of anarchy in production. These attempts, as can be seen in the light of the economic situation in the Cameroons, were quite illusory.

The co-operative movement in the Cameroons underwent the greatest development possible in the early 1950s. And this was no accident. As already emphasized, the pressure of the national liberation movement forced the colonists to look for new means of economic influence. The colonial authorities established co-operatives among the native peasants, both wealthy and poor, in order to obtain fresh political support, whose main task would be to oppose the spread of the anti-colonial movement.

The same aim is being followed today by the reactionary and pro-imperialist governing circles. These have remained opposed to their own people and have tried to create in rural areas a social class or body of the population on whom they could rely as a base for their policy directed towards capitalist development.

There were more than 2000 co-operatives in the Cameroons in 1959–62.[2] They operated at various levels. Unfortunately the statistical data available are not sufficient to determine their activities. However, it is possible to suggest that they were little different from co-operatives of the capitalist kind. These had been created for finance, for communal work, and for mutual purchasing. For instance, French specialists said of the former kind:

Established and managed by the leaders of the sectors of modernization, the co-operatives had a membership of 12 to 30 planters who had each to take at least one share costing 500 francs, and then had the right to a credit ten times the value of the shares held.[3]

This shows that in order to join a co-operative and obtain credit, it was necessary to purchase at least one share. Such a principle seems anti-democratic, for it allows the wealthy farmers to obtain much more credit than the poor peasants, whose need is greater. Therefore it must be emphasized that the co-operatives mentioned above are directed towards the development of capitalism in agriculture and the proletarianization of the peasantry. Some relevant remarks on the subject were made by V. P. Loguinova, writing from within the co-operative movement in the Cameroons:

The average percentage of the population in the co-operative movement is low: in 1961–2 it barely reached one per cent in the Eastern Cameroons and three per cent in the Western. Co-operative systems of marketing and credit prevail. The co-operatives, once established, are organized in general by the wealthy elements in the countryside and used by them to enrich themselves.[4]

All this proves that the co-operative movement does not enjoy a sufficiently widespread development, in the sense that the great mass of the peasantry is not included; and that it is limited to the wealthy planters, native and foreign, whose sole aim is to exploit the poor peasants more intensely and to quicken the development of capitalism in agriculture.

NOTES

[1] Paris, 1956, 2nd, ed., p. 45–6.

[2] From data supplied by Alexandrovskaya (cf. *Economie mondiale et rapports internationaux*, 3, p. 41 (1963), there were 2,582 co-operatives in 1959; but figures supplied by French specialists give only 2,000 in 1961–62. The difference is explained by the fact that the co-operative movement was passing through a major crisis due to the effects of the worsening international situation. An insight is obtained by the following extract from a French business periodical circulating among firms with 'special interests' in Africa (*Bulletin de l'Afrique noire*, 344, p. 6984 (Paris, 1964): 'Co-operation is deteriorating in the cocoa sector, leaving planters in a worse situation than that obtaining in traditional markets; the distribution of credits was so reduced that at one time they ceased altogether.'

[3] République fédérale du Cameroun. *Etude des structures rurales: analyse et diagnostics,* p. 133, Yaounde, March 1962.

[4] *Afrique* 1961–5, Nauka, Moscow, 1965, p. 141.

ANN SEIDMAN

Agricultural stagnation in Uganda

In Uganda estate agriculture was never as important as in Kenya. Small-scale African cash crop production had been extended over a major part of the arable land area. By the time independence was attained, it was estimated that about a fourth of the cultivated land was devoted solely to cash crops, and another fourth was used for cash together with subsistence farming, while the remaining half was devoted solely to subsistence. Population pressure on the land was, as yet, only a serious problem in local areas: Kigezi, Sebei, Bugisu, and parts of Buganda, Teso, and Bukedi.

The two-fold goals for agriculture set forth in the Second Five Year Plan were to draw more and more farmers into the monetary economy through production of cash crops; and to increase the yield per cent to avoid the emergence of more serious land shortages over time. Post-independence policies, following recommendations made by the World Bank Mission, emphasized smallholder tea and tobacco production in Uganda, as in Kenya and Tanzania.

There are a few areas in Uganda where moisture deficit is an overriding problem; perhaps a half a million acres of land might attain increased productivity with irrigation. The British initiated the Mubuku Pilot Irrigation Project near Kases in Tororo Kingdom in 1961 and a Uganda Development Corporation subsidiary, Agricultural Enterprises Ltd, started another 1000-acre pilot project with United Nations' assistance. There appeared to be some doubt, however, whether the heavy overheads would permit these projects to become commercially viable at the present stage of development.

Much of the increased agricultural yield was expected to result from increased education and extension work to introduce improved agricultural practices, including use of fertilizers, weed killers, and other new farming techniques. The Uganda Department of Agriculture continued the British-initiated policy of directing extension assistance and credit primarily to the 'progressive' larger African farmers who, in Uganda, already constituted a significant group.

1. Group farms

The primary institutional development in the post-independence plans for agricultural development appeared to grow out of a desire to accelerate the use of mechanized equipment. Almost a fourth of the Central Government expenditure on agriculture, aside from dairy farming and livestock, was to be spent on group farms. These had been first favourably considered in 1954, but in the post-independence era much more attention was given to providing them with tractors.

The group farms were supposed to be designed to enable a concentrated nucleus of people to unite in one economic activity so that, by pooling land, tractors, and other mechanical equipment, these could be used economically. At the same time, it was anticipated that many services, such as health, education, electricity, and water could be provided more efficiently to farmers gathered in groups than to scattered individual families.

A significant amount of agricultural expenditure was to be directed to establishing tractor hire services for individual farmers on their separate plots as well as to group farms. About 1250 more tractors were to be made available for hiring by 1971, 800 of them on group farms, the remaining 450 to be hired to private farms.

Two group farms were established in 1963 as a direct result of a cabinet decision, and the number of such farms increased steadily until in 1966 there were reported to be 37 of them, involving about 3500 participants. The farms varied, of course, but a typical one might have 60–100 members, each cultivating about 15 acres. Of these, perhaps two acres would be used for a house and food crops, and the rest would be part of a planned rotation. A member might cultivate nine acres a year, three acres single cropping, and three acres double cropping. Of these nine acres, three might be cotton and the rest finger millet, sorghum, maize, simsim, groundnuts, or beans. Most operations that were amenable to it were carried on mechanically. The cost of these operations, about shs 160 an acre, was covered by credit from the Uganda Commercial Bank through the Co-operative Credit Scheme at an interest rate of 12 per cent. The Co-operative Society sold the crops and deducted the loan repayments including the interest before paying the farmers.

A number of problems emerged as the group farms spread. Not a few farmer members kept their house and subsistence plots separate from the group farm, waiting to see how the project would work out. Apparently when there was a choice between work on the group farm plot and on the home plot, the home plot not infrequently won out; it was nearer, and the crop was not mortgaged to pay off the tractor hire loan. Considerable incentives in the form of amenities such as water and electricity were necessary to make members transfer from their old *shamba* to a new plot on a group farm, and the provision of these was expensive.

Despite the Government's declared determination to diversify agricultural output, moreover, a large proportion of these farms were engaged primarily in cotton production. When the Plan was written, cotton prices appeared relatively stable. In 1965, the U.S. policy of increasing sales of its cotton surpluses on world markets led to a sharp decline in world prices. Uganda's Lint Marketing Board exhausted its surplus funds by attempting to maintain the previously prevailing producer price. By 1967 the Board was forced to reduce the producer price by 30 per cent to 40 cents (Ugandan) a pound. One effect of this was a sharp reduction in the number of group farms, many of which had been growing cotton. In 1967, only 30 group farms, with about 1800 members, were reported to be still operating.

Other reasons which have been given for the post-1966 decline in group farms included problems in using mechanized equipment economically; sociological factors; and organizational deficiencies. One of the most serious problems was that of providing adequate management. The British, who supplied most of the tractors for credit (at a 7.5 per cent rate of interest) also provided group farm managers. For the most part, the managers did not speak the local language, although much of their effectiveness depended on relationships with the farmers, elected committees, and the attitude of the farm members. Where management was effective, and members had traditionally worked communally, as in Lango, results were apparently more successful. In a few cases, cotton yields averaged as much as 1000 pounds per acre, compared with a national average of 300–500 pounds. Apparently on many other farms, however, management was unable to establish efficient working relations with the members.

Furthermore, there were difficulties in ensuring full-time use of the tractors. In the peak planting season, tractors were utilized to the full; for the remainder of the year they stood idle a large portion of the time, so that charges for the time they were actually used covered barely half of their actual recurrent costs. It was estimated that in the good year of 1963 the Government tractor hire service lost Shs 13/63 on every tractor hour worked, not taking into account depreciation and administrative overheads. The hire service never became sufficiently viable to turn it over to private commercial enterprises as had originally been planned. Even with the subsidized hire service, however, it appears that the group farms only remained viable while the producer price for cotton remained relatively high.

By 1968, after the sharp reduction in producer prices for cotton, the original aim of establishing 120 by the end of the plan period had been virtually abandoned. The total expenditure on hire services and group farms from 1962 to 1967 had been about £4 million out of the actual total Agricultural Development and Recurrent Budget of about £15 million. Yet it has been estimated that government tractor services affected only about 1 per cent of the farming population. The addition to national cotton production as a result of the schemes was estimated to be in the region of only about 3 per cent.

2. The dairy and meat industry

The Ugandan Central Government planned to spend about £5 million for developing the dairy and meat industry. Almost half of this was to be spent to establish 100 new dairy farms a year (to continue for ten years) and to upgrade local cattle by importing exotic semen and cross-breeding after dipping and spraying schemes had brought tick-borne diseases under control. It was hoped, ultimately, to end imports of dairy products from Kenya, which, in 1966, provided more than half of Uganda's total estimated consumption of these items.

In 1967, Parliament established the Dairy Industry Corporation to regulate production, marketing, pricing, processing, and manufacturing of milk and milk products. By the end of 1967, the amount of milk collected at the Central Kampala milk plant had multiplied about ten times, from 400 to 4,000 gallons a day.

A 1967–8 survey of six districts indicated that a relatively small number of larger farmers produced a major portion of the milk delivered. Over half the farms had less than 10 head of cattle. Fewer than 10 per cent of the farms had between 30 and 100 head of cattle. The mean yield per cow was 29 gallons a month in farms with fewer than 30 cows, compared to 40 gallons for farms with over 30 cows. The larger farms had a higher proportion of cows in milk. The profit per cow was somewhat more than twice as high for the largest farms as for the smaller ones.

Two major bottlenecks reportedly hindered further expansion of the dairy industry. One was the inadequate number of extension veterinary workers. The other was said to be the fragmentation of farm areas, especially among the tenants in Buganda and the lack of secure title against which credit could be obtained from the predominantly private commercial banks. Given the apparent economies of scale, the need for creating larger sized farms seemed evident; but there seemed to be little available evidence and few efforts made to determine whether such larger scale farms should be created as private ranches, co-operatives, or state farms.

Expansion of beef production was considered one of the most promising prospects for diversifying the agrarian economy of Uganda, so large-scale private commercial ranches were established with extensive United States and Uganda Government assistance. In 1966 United States AID initiated a programme to settle some 50 large-scale ranchers in Ankole under an agreement by which AID provided $650,000 including $500,000 for local costs, and the Uganda Government provided counterpart funds of $500,000. The Government cleared the tsetse fly, put in roads and fences, and supplied a valley tank for each ranch. Each rancher received 5 square miles of land and was required to maintain effective tick control. It was evident, however, that the expenditure of about £8,200 a farmer was much higher than could be sustained on a national level; the rather expensive scheme appeared more likely to benefit only a tiny handful of large capitalist farmers, furthering the pattern of skewed income distribution, rather than contributing to increased productivity and raising the living standards of all Ugandans.

3. The possibilities of resettlements?

Initially, the Ugandan Government dropped the Resettlement Programme which had been started by the Colonial Administration in the post-war period. The original purpose of the programme had been to achieve an organized redistribution of population, rendering both land and people more productive than before by moving about 56,000 people from South Kigezi to less crowded areas elsewhere. Many young men had long found it necessary to leave overcrowded and fragmented farms in South Kigezi to seek employment as migratory labourers. Population densities there ranged from 108 to 580 persons per square mile in 1959.

The British had developed the programme in the post-war period to move the Bakiga initially to North Kigezi and, at a later date, to Ankole and Toro. Some efforts were made to enlist the support of the chiefs, but apparently, especially in the earlier phase, young men were actually compelled to resettle. Little planning accompanied the early stage. The settlers were given little in the way of equipment or assistance, but they were allowed to farm relatively large areas. Later, as more detailed planning was introduced, the amounts of land allocated were smaller, but the farmers were given greater assistance.

The cost per family of six gradually increased beginning with £6 in the earlier northern Kigezi schemes to as high as £30 in the later Ankole and Toro schemes.

Spontaneous resettlement, involving no government assistance, apparently followed the earlier official efforts. The later settlers moved both to the official resettlement area and to southern Ankole, mainly in Rwampara and Isingiro counties, which had not been officially a resettlement area.

Only recently have efforts been made to assess these early resettlement programmes. One involved a study of four samples, one from the most densely populated sub-country of southern Kigezi, the others from north Kigezi, Toro, and southern Ankole to represent each of the phases of the resettlement programme. Although the independent Ugandan Government did not initially attempt to pursue the resettlement programme, perhaps because of resentment caused by earlier compulsory efforts, it would appear that if the results of this study are valid, a new approach to resettlement might contribute to increased agricultural output in the country. This might be linked with planned creation of industries in crowded areas like Kigezi.

In sum, Uganda's post-independence agricultural programme did not, as yet, seem adequately directed to providing the essential foundation needed to restructure the inherited dual economy. The inadequacy of efforts to diversify agriculture left the economy essentially stagnant, with total GNP rising at a rate slower than the growth rate of the general population. The inadequacy of planned industrial growth to provide poles of growth, essential farm inputs and consumer necessities, and increased processing of agricultural raw materials for domestic consumption was a feature of the general failure to reshape the economy on an integrated, balanced basis. The continued distortion of farmer incomes, with only a handful benefitting from heavy government expenditures for agricultural development, appeared likely to limit the domestic market even for the few consumer necessities which were produced.

Foreign investment patterns
GIOVANNI ARRIGHI

From 'International corporations, labour aristocracies and economic development in tropical Africa' in Giovanni Arrighi and John S. Saul, *Essays on the political economy of Africa*, Monthly Review Press, New York, 1973.

We shall analyse the emerging pattern of foreign investment in Tropical Africa with particular reference to the choice of techniques and of sectors implicit in that pattern and to its developmental potential. The growth of oligopoly as the dominant structure in the advanced capitalist countries has been accompanied by a relative decline in importance of *rentier* capital as an independent centre of economic and political power, and of competitive capitalism as a dynamic factor of growth. Small competitive firms still exist but in a subordinate position with respect to the large manufacturing or distributive corporations.[1] The latter, on the other hand, are increasingly able to take care of their investment needs from internal financing (especially depreciation allowances),[2] thus freeing themselves from outside financial control. The reciprocal recognition of strength and retaliatory power on the part of competitors, suppliers, and customers, characteristic of oligopolistic structures, enables the corporations to protect their profit positions through adjustments in prices, techniques, and employment. The long time-horizon in investment decisions that the financial independence of the corporations makes possible, and the greater calculating rationality of corporate managers enable the oligopolies to approach new developments with care and circumspection and to calculate more accurately the risks involved.[3] These changes in the competitive structure of the industrial centres have, since World War II, been reflected in the pattern of investment in the periphery.

The declining relative importance of *rentier* capital has been matched by a decline in portfolio investment in the periphery relative to direct investment on the part of the corporations.[4] At the same time, the vast financial resources available to the corporations favoured further vertical integration while oligopolistic behaviour encouraged the formation of consortia in mineral extraction and processing.[5] These tendencies were strengthened by the process of 'decolonization'. The 'colonial preserves of European imperialism' were opened up to American capitalism,[6] in which the oligopolistic corporation plays a more central role than in French or British capitalism. More important still was the outflow of small-scale, competitive capital that accompanied independence. In fact, de-colonialization was, among other things, the result of a conflict between the dynamic elements (the big companies) and the backward elements (marginal enterprises, small planters, small trading houses, small semi-artisanal workshops) of colonial capitalism.[7] Independence favoured the outflow of the latter. For example, the accession to independence of French-speaking Africa was accompanied by capital outflow in the sector of small colonial enterprises and trading houses and a capital inflow in mining, manufacturing, and industrial agriculture.[8] Similar tendencies were at work in English-speaking countries: the flight of small-scale colonial enterprise was undoubtedly an important factor in the drastic fall of British private investment in Sterling Africa from £30 million in 1960 and £33.4 million in 1961 to £8.8 million in 1962, £2.5 million in 1963 and *minus* £9 million in 1964.[9] The upshot of these changes has been the emergence of a new pattern of foreign investment in which financial and merchanting interests and small-scale capital (mainly in agriculture but also in secondary and tertiary industries) have declined in importance relative to large-scale manufacturing and vertically integrated mining concerns. The typical expatriate firm operating in Tropical Africa is more and more what has been called the 'multinational corporation'[10] or the 'great interterritorial unit',[11] i.e., an organized ensemble of means of production subject to a single policy-making centre which controls establishments situated in several different national territories.

An analysis of the factors determining the investment policies in the periphery of such multinational corporations is therefore necessary in order to assess the impact that foreign investment is likely to have on the process of development of Tropical Africa. It is useful to break down the analysis into two problems: (1) The sectoral distribution of investment; and (2) the type of techniques adopted in each sector. As we shall see, the two problems are inter-related but, as a first approximation, their separate treatment is analytically convenient.

There is a lack of basic quantitative evidence on the *sectoral distribution of foreign investment* in Tropical African countries. Most of what exists is aggregated in such a way as to be of little use for our purposes. There is, however, considerable agreement on a few broad generalizations:

1. The colonial pattern of capital investment in production for export has has basically remained unaltered: investment in mining and petroleum absorbed the preponderant amount of private funds in the last decade.[12] What has changed in this respect is that complementary investment in the infrastructure, which used to be undertaken by private interests, is now the responsibility of the public sector. Private capital is now invested in more directly productive enterprises.[13]

2. Industrial investment other than in mining has been almost entirely concentrated either in primary products processing for the export market[14] or in import substitution in the light branches of manufacturing such as food, beverages, textiles, clothing, footwear, furniture, soap, and other consumer goods. More recently, the development of import substitution has begun to move gradually into branches of manufacturing industries producing intermediate goods (cement, non-metallic mineral products, and, less often, fertilizers and chemical products).[15]

3. Notwithstanding these developments, heavy industry in Tropical

Africa is either non-existent or, being export-oriented, is totally unrelated to the structure of the national and supranational African economies in the sense that it can hardly constitute a basis for the production of the capital goods required for the industrialization of the areas in which it is located. Rhodesia is possibly the only exception to the generalization. This situation is in sharp contrast with that of South Africa, where metallurgy, chemicals, and rubber are relatively advanced, and, to a lesser extent, with that of some North African countries, where chemicals and some basic metal and metal products industries have been developed.[16]

This sectoral pattern of foreign investment is likely to change slowly or not at all for reasons that are partly technological and partly political-economic. The sectors in question (mainly heavy engineering and chemical industries) are those in which economies of scale and the advantages of operating in an industrial environment (low costs of buying, erecting, maintaining, and operating machinery) are greatest. Hence the very under-development and the 'Balkanization'[17] of Tropical Africa hinder the development of an organic capital-goods industry.

However, as Barratt-Brown[18] has pointed out, there are more fundamental reasons than these:

> The main reason for the failure of capitalism to invest more in the industrialization of the less-developed lands has arisen from a real doubt about the possibilities of success, and, therefore, of a profitable return. Investment in heavy industry is a big business, on which a return may only be seen in the very long term. There must be good reasons to believe that the whole overseas economy will develop in such a way as to nourish a market for capital goods... It is not surprising that capitalist firms and financiers... should prefer to wait and see how the establishment of light industries and the development of power supplies and a marketable surplus of food goes, before wishing to sink their capital in heavy industry.

Bearing this in mind it would seem that the greater calculating rationality and the greater care and circumspection in approaching new developments of the modern international corporations, relative to competitive capital and to chartered companies and finance capital of old, are an important obstacle to the development of capital-goods industries in the periphery. The oligopolistic structure of advanced capitalist countries, however, plays a more direct role in favoring the bias of investment in the periphery against the capital-goods industry. As we have seen, oligopoly favours the reciprocal recognition of strength and retaliatory power. This means that when a large-scale manufacturer is deciding whether to invest in a new area, he will take into consideration, among other things, the effect of the decision on: (1) his own export interests, (2) his competitors' export interests, and (3) his customers' export interests, if any.[19] A textile manufacturing concern, for example, will take into consideration only (1) and (2). A manufacturer of capital goods, on the other hand, will also consider possible effects on his customers' interests which may be impinged upon by the growth, in the periphery, of a competing industry induced by the local production of capital goods. In consequence, quite apart from its effects on the level of investment to be discussed later on, the oligopolistic structure of the industrial centres strengthens the other factors mentioned above in producing in Tropical Africa a sectoral pattern of foreign investment biased against the capital-goods industry.

With regard to *choice of techniques*, it seems fairly well-established that foreign investment in Tropical Africa has a capital-intensive bias.[20] This bias is sometimes due to technological constraints. In mining, for example, the nature of the deposits may be responsible for differences in capital intensity. The scattering of Rhodesian gold deposits favoured labour-intensive techniques while the concentration of high-grade copper deposits in Zambia favoured capital-intensive techniques.[21] In the latter case, even if highly labour-intensive techniques exist, such as those used by Africans prior to European penetration, the technological gap is too great for such techniques to develop the industry on a significant scale.[22] However, even in extreme cases like the one in question, alternative techniques are always available,[23] though within a relatively limited range. Thus technological constraints are only one factor in determining the capital intensity of investment, and, in the case of many industries (e.g., light industries) in which foreign investment shows an equally strong bias toward capital-intensity,[24] they are rather unimportant. Other determinants have to be sought. Somewhat related to technological factors, management constraints have to be mentioned. Techniques of management, organization, and control have evolved in the technological environment of the industrial centres and cannot be easily adapted to the conditions in the periphery.[25] Often, therefore, either the conditions in the periphery can be modified, at least partially, to make capital- and skill-intensive investment possible or no investment at all will be under- taken by the multinational corporations.[26] In other words, the spectrum of techniques taken into consideration by the multinational corporations may not include labour-intensive techniques.

There is another reason, probably more important than management constraints, why labour-intensive techniques may be disregarded. As Perroux and Demonts[27] have pointed out, the multinational firm applies to all its branches technical methods corresponding to its capital, whatever the importance of the factors at work in the territories where it settles. There is a tendency in discussions of underdevelopment to overlook the fact that a shortage of finance is an important impediment to the growth of the small enterprise and of the public sectors of African economies, but it is no problem for the multinational firms. The latter not only have access to the capital markets in the industrial centres,[28] but, as we have mentioned, they are in a position through their pricing and dividend policies (in the industrial centres as well as in the periphery) to build up large accumulated reserves of capital for their investment programmes. Financial strength makes the large firm adopt capital-intensive techniques, not only in the industrial centres but also in the periphery.[29]

In a way, capital intensity is favoured also by the qualitative characteristics of the labour force in Tropical Africa. The problem is too often over-looked because of insufficiently clear definitions of the various categories of labour.[30] Let us classify labour as follows:

1. *Unskilled labour*, characterized by versatility (in the sense that it can be

readily put to varied unskilled activities), and by lack of adaptation to the discipline of wage employment.

2. *Semi-skilled labour*, characterized by specialization, regularity, and identification with the job.

3. *Skilled labour*, characterized by relative versatility (in the sense of having complex skills), e.g., carpenters, mechanics, supervisors, etc.

4. *High-level manpower*, characterized by specialization and by educational qualifications other than, or besides, training on the job, e.g., maintenance and production engineers, purchase and sales experts, designers, cost and accounting personnel, etc.

Capital-intensive techniques will not only require less labour for each level of output, but they will also require a different composition of the labour force than labour-intensive techniques, as they make possible the division of complex operations, which would need skilled labour, into simple operations that can be performed by semi-skilled labour. In other words, labour-intensive techniques are associated with a pattern of employment in which labour of type (1) and (3) predominates whereas capital-intensive techniques are associated with a pattern of employment in which labour of type (2) and (4) predominate. As we shall see in the next section, provided that employers take a sufficiently long time-horizon in their wage and employment policies, it is easier, under African conditions, to provide the remedy for a shortage of the latter types of labour than it is to do so for a shortage of skilled labour. Thus, from this point of view as well, the longer time-horizon of the multinational corporations favours the adoption of capital-intensive techniques.

These two biases of the pattern of investment emerging in Tropical Africa (i.e., in favour of capital-intensive techniques and against the capital-goods sector) reinforce each other. The choice of capital-intensive techniques within each industry favours the use of specialized machinery and consequently restrains the growth of demand for capital goods that could be produced in the periphery. The lack of investment in the capital-goods sector, in turn, prevents the development of capital goods embodying a *modern* labour-intensive technology which may reduce the bias in favor of capital intensity. This double bias has many implications for growth, development, and class formation in Tropical Africa that will be examined in the following sections. What must be considered here is *the relationship between the pattern of investment* just discussed and *the size of the internal market* that is a key determinant of foreign investment in the region.

The development of the capital-goods sector performs the double function of expanding both the productive capacity of the economy and the internal market. The latter function was emphasized by Lenin in a controversy with the Narodniks on the subject of the possibility of the '*internal* expansion of capitalism'. The development of the internal market, Lenin argued, was possible despite the restricted consumption by the masses (or the lack of an external outlet) because to expand production it is first of all necessary to enlarge that department of social production which manufactures means of production, and it is necessary to draw into it workers who create a demand for articles of consumption. Hence, 'consumption' develops after 'accumulation'.[31] The crucial assumption in the argument is that the demand for capital goods is largely autonomous, *i.e.*, that it is not induced by the pre-existing size of the market and its growth. However, this autonomous development of the capital-goods sector presupposes a type of behaviour which may characterize competitive capitalism, but which cannot be expected from the modern corporations.[32] These corporations tend to expand productive capacity in response to market demand and in consequence restrain the endogenous generation of growth stimuli.

In the case of Tropical Africa and the periphery in general, the position is made worse by the fact that the multinational corporations (whenever the nature of the productive process permits it) usually prefer to expand productive capacity in the industrial centres where they are more secure and where they can take advantage of operating in an industrial environment.[33] Expansion in the periphery is usually undertaken by a foreign concern in response to protectionist policies on the part of national government in order either to protect its own export interests, or to establish itself anew in the area.[34] In other words, the existence of a local market for the production of the foreign concern, though a necessary condition, is not sufficient for the actual establishment of a plant. This presupposes the ability of individual governments either to set up production in competition with foreign interests or to play one oligopoly off against the other. The fact that this ability on the part of the governments of Tropical Africa is most limited in the case of capital-goods industries is an additional factor strengthening the bias of the emerging pattern of investment against such industries.

It follows that the emerging pattern of investment is unlikely to reduce the basic lack of structure of the Tropical African economies. Growth in these economies continues to depend on the growth of outside markets. In fact, the dependence is even greater than it used to be in view of the fact that industrialization tends to take a capital-intensive path which presupposes the importation of specialized machinery. For this reason the integration of the modern sectors of Tropical Africa (due to the need of the multinational concerns to operate on a supranational scale) is accompanied by their greater integration with the industrial centres.

NOTES

[1] Cf. C. Wright Mills, *White Collar*, New York, 1956, pp. 23–38.

[2] Baran, P.A. and Sweezy, P.M., *Monopoly capital*, New York, 1966, pp. 102–5; S. Tsuru, (ed), *Has capitalism changed?* Tokyo, 1961, pp. 51–3.

[3] Baran and Sweezy, op. cit., p. 50.

[4] R. Vernon, 'The American Corporation in Underdeveloped Areas,' in E.S. Mason, ed, *The Corporation in Modern Society* (Cambridge, Mass, 1959), pp. 238–39; W.A. Chudson, 'Trends in African Exports and Capital Inflows,' in M.J. Herskovits and M. Harwitz, eds, *Economic Transition in Africa* (London, 1964), pp. 349–50; M. Barratt-Brown, *After Imperialism* (London, 1963), ch. 8; Baran and Sweezy, op. cit., pp. 196–97.

[5] Cf. Nkrumah, *Neo-colonialism: the last stage of imperialism*, New York, 1965.

[6] Ibid., pp. 58–60.

[7] E.R. Braundi, 'Neo-colonialism and Class Struggle,' *International Socialist Journal*, no. 1 (1964), pp. 55–56.

[8] Ibid., p. 60. See also the staff paper by G. Benveniste and W.E. Moran, Jr. (Stanford Research Institute, International Industrial Development Center), quoted in S.F. Frankel, 'Capital and Capital Supply in Relation to the Development of Africa,' in E.A.G. Robinson, ed., *Economic Development for Africa South of the Sahara* (London, 1964), pp. 431–32.

[9] D.J. Morgan, *British Private Investment in East Africa: Report of a Survey and a Conference* (London: The Overseas Development Institute, 1965), p. 6.

[10] 'Multinational Companies, a Special Report,' *Business Week*, 20 April 1963.

[11] Cf. M. Byé, 'La Grande unité interterritoriale,' *Cahiers de l'I.S.E.A.*, quoted by F. Perroux and R. Demonts, 'Large Firms–Small Nations,' *Présence Africaine*, no. 38 (1961), p. 37.

[12] Chudson, op. cit.

[13] Loc. cit.

[14] UNESCO, *Policy Aspects of Industrial Development in Africa: Problems and Prospects*, E/CN. 14/AS/II/2/K/1 (1965), pp. 22–27, mimeographed. In some cases increases in manufacturing activities merely represent classification changes. Cf. R.E. Baldwin, *Economic Development and Export Growth: A Study of Northern Rhodesia, 1920–60* (Berkeley and Los Angeles; 1966), p. 181.

[15] UNESCO, *Policy Aspects of Industrial Development in Africa.* See also G. Hunter, *The New Societies of Tropical Africa* (London, 1962), pp. 161–62.

[16] UNESCO, op. cit.

[17] Intermediary and capital goods industries generally require, especially in non-industrialized countries, supranational markets. The possibility of using protectionist policies or setting up competing units in neighbouring countries increases the risks of, and therefore discourages, investment in each country. This consideration points to the possibility of conflicts of interest within international capitalism concerning the balkanization of tropical Africa.

[18] Barratt-Brown, op. cit., p. 419.

[19] We are assuming that the new plants will not compete in the national market from which the investment originates. The argument holds *a fortiori* if this assumption is not made.

[20] Cf. Hunter, op. cit., pp. 60–61. See also H.A. Turner, *Wage Trends, Wage Policies, and Collective Bargaining: The Problems of Underdeveloped Countries* (Cambridge, 1965), p. 21; and below.

[21] Baldwin, op. cit., pp. 79–80.

[22] Loc. cit.

[23] Ibid. This is also shown by the fact that the copper mines of Uganda have a lower degree of mechanization than the Katangese mines. Cf. A. Baryaruha, *Factors Affecting Industrial Employment: A Study of Ugandan Experience, 1954–64* (Nairobi, 1967), p. 58.

[24] Cf., for instance, Baryaruha, op. cit., and Hunter, op. cit., pp. 60–61.

[25] Cf. Vernon, op. cit., pp. 253–54.

[26] See below.

[27] Perroux and Demonts, op. cit., p. 46.

[28] Cf. D.J. Viljoen, 'Problems of Large-Scale Industry in Africa,' in Robinson, op. cit., pp. 253–54.

[29] Capitalist enterprises always tend to adopt those techniques which 'maximize' the surplus. Such techniques are relatively capital intensive (see Section 3). However, financial stringency prevents the smaller firms from taking a long time horizon in their investment decisions and therefore from adopting capital intensive techniques.

The large corporation, on the other hand, is to a large extent free from financial constraints upon its investment decisions.

[30] One notable exception is W. Elkan, *Migrants and Proletarians: Urban Labour in the Economic Development of Uganda* (London, 1960).

[31] Quoted in Hamza Alavi, 'Imperialism old and new', *The Socialist Register*, London, 1964, pp. 106–7.

[32] Degree of competition is not the only variable in this context. As already mentioned, the calculating rationality of the capitalist concerns is equally relevant, giving rise to the discrepancy in the behavior of the chartered companies and concessionaries of old and that of the modern corporations.

[33] Cf. Alavi, op. cit., p. 121. This point is discussed more fully in Section 3, where the determinants of corporate investment in the periphery are dealt with.

[34] Cf. Vernon, op. cit., pp. 248–49; Barratt-Brown, op. cit., pp. 273–76; Morgan, op. cit., p. 47.

On the drain of capital from African countries
LEONNARD V. GONCHAROV

Originally published in *Mirovaya Ekonomika i Mezhdunarodnye Otnosheniya*, 11 (Moscow 1968). Translated and republished in *Studies on developing countries*, 42 (1970), Centre for Afro-Asian Research of the Hungarian Academy of Sciences, Budapest.

The build-up and development of a national economy requires the summoning of all available financial resources both inside the country and from abroad. In recent years the view has been gaining ground, that it is impossible to solve the economic problems facing newly liberated countries without calling for foreign aid–in credits, subsidies, technical assistance. The disintegration of the colonial system and its replacement with a multinational Third World has given rise to a number of new characteristic features, involving such problems as the flow of long-term capital between the developed and developing countries. One such feature is the steadily increasing drain of capital from the developing countries to the highly developed capitalist ones.

At first sight it may seem paradoxical, that with the common knowledge of the fact that funds flow from economically highly developed countries to those which are poorly developed, an outflow of capital in the opposite direction now comes into focus.

But, indeed, there is nothing so remarkable about it. Capital is being exported from highly developed imperialist countries into the developing countries, not actually with the aim of providing aid to the latter, but with the express purpose of deriving the highest possible profit. This does not mean that we should blame the exporters of capital for any particular wickedness: the laws of international capitalist economy exert an unrelenting pressure, and if investment of capital in the developing countries did not result in an outflow of funds from them, capitalism would not be capitalism. This is the conclusion we shall reach if we treat factors inherent in world capitalist economy as objective reality.

But mere recognition of the objective nature of things does not mean ceasing or abstaining from the struggle to eliminate or at least attenuate their vicious consequences. Moreover, it is hardly possible to overestimate the political significance of exposing the plunder camouflaged by the imperialists as assistance. Today, when the newly liberated countries are faced with the choice of the trends of their social and economic progress, to expose the nature, the motive force and stimuli of exporting capital under the new conditions, means to deal a blow on neo-colonialism.

So, how is capital drained from developing countries? What is its relative and net volume? What are the peculiarities of the process, as compared to the period when the countries that are now known as developing ones, were colonies of imperialist powers? Let us discuss these questions as applied to African countries.

If we go back to the time when the economic and territorial partition of the world was being completed (late nineteenth century), we'll notice a comparatively low rate of penetration of foreign capital into Africa. Only those countries which had vast mineral resources (South Africa, Rhodesia, the Congo) attracted the attention of imperialistic monopolies. The outflow of capital from Africa in the form of profit, dividend, or interest was likewise low.

The role of Africa as a place for foreign capital investment became much more prominent after the second World War, particularly due to the lack of some important raw materials which could be produced in Africa on the world market. Within the first decade after the war large capital investments were made into the mining of copper in Northern Rhodesia and the Belgian Congo; chromium in Southern Rhodesia; diamonds, gold, and polymetallic minerals in South and South-West Africa; tin and columbite in Nigeria; manganese and gold in Ghana; iron ore in Liberia and Guinea; etc. In subsequent years, as large ore and oil deposits were discovered in other African countries, foreign companies forced their greedy fingers into all, even the remotest, parts of the continent.

For some companies the extraction of a raw material or other in one or more African countries was the sole activity, while for others Africa was another sphere of investment, in addition to their old interests in Asia, Latin America, Australia, and elsewhere.

The supply of capital to individual countries and to the continent as a whole, has been far from uniform. This refers to either private capital or official loans and subsidies. In view of the fact that most African countries support from one to two-thirds of all development programmes from external sources, one can well imagine how tight the reins held by imperialist powers in these countries are. A reduction in the flow of capital from abroad, or excessive outflow of funds to redeem foreign loans, or as income to private foreign investors, poses a threat and not infrequently prevents the realization of these plans.

According to publications for 1964, the net outflow of income to foreign investors from 55 developing countries was $3,700,000,000. About half this sum came from seven oil-extracting countries, while in the other half about 60 per cent of the income came from Latin America and about one-sixth from 10 African countries (other than South Africa).[1]

A correlation of data for a number of years shows that the outflow of income on invested capital tends to increase in all the countries listed in Table 1, except Morocco. But we must not restrict our analysis of this trend to merely comparing the numerical values through a number of years for income outflow alone. It is important to relate the outflow of income on capital to the inflow of capital for the same years. Such a comparison leads us into believing that for most African countries the increment of income on foreign capital transferred abroad goes ahead of the inflow of new foreign investments. This is particularly true of direct private investments.

Occasional years see the transfer of income on foreign capital accompanied with repatriation of capital already invested rather than inflow of new capital. This usually takes place in periods of instability and political upheavals in the recipient country, as capital is then invested at greater risks. For Ghana such were the years 1956–58 and 1961, for Kenya, 1963–64, for the late Federation of Rhodesia and Nyasaland, 1963–64.

Here is some information on the relationship between inflow and outflow of long-term capital for some African countries.

Table 1
Net Outflow of Income on Investments, 1960–64.
(million US dollars)*

	1960	1961	1962	1963	1964	1965	1966**
Ethiopia	4	7	4	6	6	4	4
Ghana	15	15	14	25	18	27	20
Zambia					3	4	4
Malawi	144	120	114	137	54	...	...
Rhodesia					97	64	...
Morocco	20	29	29	21	17	29	39
Nigeria	13	11	25	48	78	147	208
Sudan	−1	−2	3	3	6	7	9
Tunisia	−2	−2	−2	1	4	8	14
UAR	−6	−4	6	11	18	16	10
Total for ten countries.***	187	174	193	252	301	306	308

*Approximated figures. Minus stands for inflow.

**Preliminary data.

***Nine countries in 1965 and eight in 1966.

Source: External financing of economic development of the developing countries, N.Y., V. 26, 1967, pp. 27–28.

Income on direct foreign investments in Ghana during 1955–59 was annually taken abroad to the tune of £3,200,000, on an average. At the same time there was an adverse balance of private capital movement (minus £1,700,000), while the net outflow in direct investments was an average of £3,000,000 each year.

In 1960–64 the average annual exported income on direct investment from Ghana grew two and a half times over the 1955–59 period to reach £8,100,000, which was $4\frac{1}{2}$ times as much as that of the annual inflow of new direct investment in the country (£1,800,000). In 1965 and 1966 the profit by direct investment somewhat dropped to £5,500,000 and £5,000,000 respectively. With the net inflow of direct investments £8,000,000 in 1965 and £21,300,000[2] in 1966. Such a steep increase in 1966 is directly related to the reactionary coup in the country and the guarantees offered foreign private investors by the new government.

In East African countries the '50s were characterized by a considerable excess of net new imported capital over exported income on such capital, while the '60s showed a reverse picture.

The sum transferred from Tanzania in 1961 as income on foreign capital, exceeded two-thirds of net capital inflow to the country (both private and loans by the central government). In 1962 this figure was 2.7 times as great as net capital inflow, in 1963, 1.7 times, in 1964, 1.6 times. During all of these years the movement of private capital showed an outflow rather than inflow (see Table 2). Thus, the inflow of official capital due to loans by the central government was insufficient to compensate for the outflow of funds as income on capital. It was not before 1965, as a result of efforts by the central government which contributed considerable national funds ($17,400,000) and due to some reduction in private capital outflow (from $5,600,000 in 1964 to $1,700,000) that the outflow of income on investment was somehow made up for, though even in that year it reached as high as two-thirds of the net inflow of new capital ($10,400,000 out of $15,700,000).

In Kenya exported income on investments and sums under the clause 'Private Capital Movement' amounted to almost double the incoming official funds supplied by the central government (mostly received as foreign loans). In 1964, closely following the gaining of independence, the outflow of income on capital amounting to $27,400,000 was accompanied by an outflow of private capital and official capital provided the central government to the sum of $39,300,000. Foreign private investors did not restore their 'trust' in the country before 1966, until the government of Kenya had proved its liberal attitude towards foreign capital. Yet that year the drain of profit on investment was equal to the inflow of new private capital and reached about half the total inflow of private capital and that mobilized by the central government (see Table 2).

Greater drain of income on foreign capital compared with net inflow of new capital can be also observed in a number of other countries.

In the former Federation of Rhodesia and Nyasaland the passive accounts balance of income on private foreign investment in 1950–54 averaged £29,000,000 a year, while the net inflow of new private capital was £72,000,000. In 1960–63 the balance of exported income on private capital averaged £32,200,000 a year, while the mean annual net inflow of private capital was negative (outflow) £600,000. The respective figures for 1964 were £41,800,000 and £2,900,000.[3] In 1965 £22,800,000 in income on foreign investment was exported from Zambia alone, while the net inflow of private capital and capital loaned by the central government reached £27,700,000.[4]

The huge profits derived by foreign companies from African countries enable these companies not only to export large sums from these countries, but also to re-invest a considerable portion of their income. On the other hand, as has been shown above, the incoming new capital is much inferior to the outgoing funds in the form of income on capital.

Thus, if one summarizes the inflow and outflow of capital for a number of years, one can see that the total inflow of new capital (net increment of investment) is nothing else but re-investment of profit derived, less the portion transferred from the developing countries which goes into the pockets of

Table 2
Movement of Capital Versus Income on Investments
(million US dollars)

	1961		1962		1963		1964		1965		1966		1967	
	Tan-zania	Kenya	Tan-zania	Kenya	Tan-zania	Kenya	Tan-zania	Kenya	Tan-zania	Kenya	Tan-zania	Kenya	Tan-zania	Kenya
Income on investments	−7·3	...	−8·4	...	−15·4	−25·8	−10·6	−27·5	−14·4	−25·1	−15·8	−34·1	...	−29·7
Movement of capital	−10·6	...	3·0	...	0·9	−0·5	7·9	−44·3	7·5	19·8	19·6	35·4	...	33·6
including:														
Private...	−1·1	...	−2·2	...	−0·8	−18·7	−5·6	−42·8	−8·8	−0·1	12·9	5·0	...	17·1
Official, by Central government	11·7	...	5·2	...	1·7	18·2	13·5	...	16·3	19·9	6·7	30·4	...	16·5

... no data available.
Source: *International financial statistics*, September 1967, p. 111, November 1967, pp. 109, 204, December 1967, p. 192.

Table 3
Profits Derived by US Investors on Direct Investments in Africa
(million dollars)

| Year | Gross profit | Including: | | New capital inflow (fromUSA) |
		transferred to USA	non-distributed	
1952	126	60	62	32
1953	117	54	61	14
1954	104	83	21	56
1955	129	76	53	57
1956	106	67	42	51
1957	94	41	47	38
1958	51	8	44	48
1959	55	7	42	39
1960	33	−17	50	81
1961	31	−3	34	125
1962	81	34	47	158
1963	166	123	42	109
1964	346	301	42	141
1965	380	332	47	160
1966	417	341	74	87
1967	418	364	44	176
Total	2654	1871	752	1372

Source: Survey of current business (Washington), for the years quoted.

foreign investors. For example, we shall cite same figures on US profits from direct investment in Africa and on the increment of such investments in the course of 16 years (see Table 3).

It is clear that, as a rule, income on direct investment transferred from Africa exceeded the inflow of new capital, and in the 16 years this difference was $499,000,000. During the same years the undistributed profit, which is the source of re-investment, reached another $752,000,000. Yet the incoming new capital in these 16 years was only 52 per cent of the total sum of profits derived over these years ($1,372,000,000 out of $2,654,000,000).

Besides the export of income on foreign investments, payments to redeem foreign loans are an important element in the outflow of long-term capital from African countries. In most of the countries such payments annually make up from one-sixth to two-fifths of newly acquired loans. Yet in some countries redemption payments reach or even exceed half the loan spent in a given year (see Table 4).

Table 4
Loans Received by Central Governments
(million US dollars)

	Used		Paid out	
	1965	1966*	1965	1966*
Ethiopia	24·6	31·1	−6·5	−8·6
Ghana	99·5	53·9	−52·4	−6·9
Nigeria	38·1	42·0	−7·6	−32·5
Sudan	34·1	38·5	−16·9	−11·2
UAR	239·9	200·1	−100·5	−113·2

*Preliminary estimate.
*Source: International flow of long-term capital and official donations 1961–
1966, N.Y., 1967, May 23, p. 15 (Doc. B/4371).*

According to the International Bank for Reconstruction and Development, payment by African countries in 1966 on account of external national indebtness (paying out debt plus interest) amounted to about $190,000,000.[5]

The ever increasing outflow of capital from African countries is a heavy burden on their economies: it depletes their scanty financial resources and retards the implementation of started development programmes. In the long run, the drain of capital acts as a brake on overcoming the economic backwardness and attaining economic independence.

These countries find themselves in a kind of vicious circle: the solution of the economic problems facing Africa is impossible without drawing on foreign capital; the drawing on foreign capital results in a growing outflow of funds from Africa; the drain of funds retards the solution of economic problems.

Many African countries see an alternative solution to this sort of situation in the state control over foreign capital, in subordinating the activities of foreign companies to the national interests, while ensuring these companies a reasonable margin of profit. The Foreign Investments Statutes adopted by a number of countries regulate the terms of attracting foreign capital, as well as conditions of its outflow in the form of profit, dividend, and interest, and also conditions of repatriation.

A Statute adopted in 1962 in the Republic of Guinea grants priority terms for investment which are of special importance for the economic development of the country. These include investments into such branches of the economy, the extension of which tends, in the first place, to reduce the dependence of Guinea on the imports of commodities,[6] thus saving foreign currency, and promoting the utilization of mineral resources and boosting exports. Also covered here is capital investment into power production and construction projects.[7] The Statute stipulates that investors should submit information on their plans for capital investments, expenditure in Guinean currency, scale of production, indicating the physical volume and cost of manufactured goods, as well as import and export plans. In addition, information should be given on labour requirements, with reference to the kind of vocational training and social benefits the workers are to receive.

Authorized capital investments enjoy certain privileges in tax and customs duty. At the same time, as the statute reads, 'foreign capital is ensured protection and necessary security within the framework and necessary observance of the laws and regulations'. Foreign investors are entitled to transfer abroad annually all the interest and up to 20 per cent of their share of net profit on operations. Foreigners employed at enterprises are not allowed to transfer abroad more than 30 per cent of their salaries.[8]

A number of developing countries have regulations on the utilization of the income on investment which is not to be taken out of the country. In Tunisia, for example, such incomes are placed on blocked accounts; in Ghana and Mali investors are recommended to invest such profit assets into state bonds and other securities, the income on which can be transferred abroad.

In Algeria the export of current incomes on investment, and of recovered sums in case of anullment, requires authorization by the Central Bank.

The Republic of Zambia passed a decree in April 1968, imposing state control over 26 foreign firms. This covered companies in the transport business, residential building, timber and fishing industries, wholesale and retail trade, brewing. The government's share in these companies is from 51 per cent to 71 per cent. Though this measure did not include at that time mining companies, certain restrictions were imposed upon them, too, as well as upon other foreign companies. At present they can transfer abroad not in excess of 50 per cent of net profits in the form of dividend. The remainder is to be used to promote economic development within Zambia.

This decision limited to a certain extent the scale of exploitation to which the country was subjected by foreign mining companies. The following data show how high their profits are.

In the fiscal year 1958–59 Nchanga Consolidated Copper Mines derived a profit of £7,800,000 (before tax), and in 1966–67, £19,800,000. The gross profit of the company in these nine years reached as high as £170,000,000.[9] The dividend paid by Nchanga to its shareholders was from 33 to 62 per cent annually. The company enters the group Zambezi Anglo-American, which, in its turn, is controlled by one of the largest corporations operating in Africa: Anglo-American Corporation of South Africa. With his headquarters in Johannesburg, the chairman of all the three companies (Nchanga, Zambezi Anglo-American, and Anglo-American Corporation) is Mr Harry Oppenheimer who is closely linked with Rothschild of London.

Further restrictions upon mining companies were imposed in August 1969. The Government is to acquire a 51 per cent share in the mining companies, following President Kaunda's decision. Other restrictions are in the field of royalties and export tax.

Under certain conditions, no doubt nationalization may become the most expedient solution to the problem of foreign capital in the developing countries.

As is well known, a number of countries have already nationalized the enterprises which are essential for their national economies.

Thus, the United Arab Republic has nationalized a great majority of foreign companies by sequestration and buying out. The foreign sector in the country's economy has been practically reduced to nought.

In the Republic of Guinea the power and water supply systems, the enterprises of the gold and diamond mining industries, and some others have been nationalized.

The course taken by the government of the Algerian People's Republic towards expanding participation of the state in economic management has found expression in the nationalization of mining enterprises, insurance companies, a number of oil companies, and residential buildings in towns and cities. Here the first to be nationalized are those foreign companies that refuse to make equity investments and evade state control.

The Arusha Declaration adopted in 1967 by United Republic of Tanzania was a starting point in the nationalization of foreign banks, and also of major foreign trade and industrial companies.

Steps to nationalize foreign property have been also taken in the Republic of Ghana, the Republic of Mali, and some other countries.

Yet experience shows, that nationalization becomes an effective lever in the struggle for economic independence, only when it has been thoroughly prepared and all the necessary prerequisites have been created. Thus, of great importance for successful nationalization are such factors as technical know-how and the availability of national specialists capable of managing industry, and of trained labour; also important is a guaranteed market for the goods made and availability of raw materials for the smooth running of the industries, etc. The fact is that a drastic measure like nationalization incites the monopolists into desperate attempts at disrupting the economic life of the country which ventured such a step. The monopolies resort to economic discrimination, boycott, recall of technical advisers and administrative personnel, etc. Hence, a country must well prepare in good time to face these difficulties, if winning economic independence is to be ensured, and not merely played with as a short-lived political speculation. In countries where conditions for nationalization have not yet ripened, it is advisable to consider the task of controlling the activities of foreign capital and inviting it on terms that are conducive, and not detrimental, to the progress of national economy.

NOTES

[1] U.N. Economic and Social Council, Doc. E/4374, p. 26.

[2] The estimates are based on *Balance of payments yearbook*, Washington, for the years quoted.

[3] Based on *Monthly digest of statistics* (Salisbury: Lusaka). Data for 1964 do not include Malawi.

[4] *International financial statistics*, November 1967, p. 350.

[5] International Bank for Reconstruction and Development, *Annual report for 1966–67*, p. 30.

[6] Enterprises in the food and light industries primarily using local agricultural products; the manufacture and assembly of domestic appliances, etc.

[7] *Investment laws and regulations in Africa*, New York, 1965. United Nations, p. 39; *Board of Trade Journal*, 22 May 1964, p. 1131.

[8] *Investment laws and regulations*, p. 39.

[9] *Beerman's financial year book of Southern Africa*, 1963, II, p. 463, ditto, 1967, II, p. 342 (Cape Town).

Income distribution and the 'privileged' worker
SAMIR AMIN

From Samir Amin, *L'accumulation a l'échelle mondiale,* Editions Anthropos, Paris 1970. Translated and published as *Accumulation on a world scale,* Monthly Review Press, New York, 1975.

The distribution of incomes (wages and others) has only rarely been subjected to statistical observation. I have worked it out myself, in a systematic way, for four African countries (Algeria, Tunisia, Morocco, Ivory Coast) and borrowed, for the Egyptian example, from the works of Hassan Riad. This analysis will enable me to explain the different inequalities by showing the factors mentioned. This will lead us to re-examine certain 'fashionable' views which have, it seems to me, been put forward rather too hastily, such as the view that the wage earners as a group are a 'privileged' category in the Third World.

The case of Egypt

The average income per capita appears to be more than four times as much in the towns as in the rural areas.[1] If, however, we plumb deeper than the gross figures, we find that these differences are connected with differences in both productivity and rate of employment, and that they do not always work in favour of the wage earners, alleged to be 'privileged' as a category.

a. Massive unemployment (two-thirds of the potential theoretical labour force) affects the masses of the people who make up 80 per cent of the rural population, but only 56 per cent of the population of the towns. Allowing for these different rates of employment, income for a full year's work for the mass of the people is only 2.5 times as much in the town as in the country.

b. If the average income seems to be only one-quarter as much in the country, the reason is, apart from the lower rate of employment and lower average productivity of labour (lighter techniques as regards use of capital), that the intermediate strata are relatively less numerous there (15 per cent of the rural population, as against 40 per cent of the town population), and that the average income of the privileged strata (4 to 5 per cent of the population) is less than a quarter as much in the countryside. These differences also reflect the fact that the urban economy, being more advanced, draws on a labour force that includes relatively many more skilled workers: permanently employed workers, office workers, middle and higher cadres, members of the liberal professions, and entrepreneurs.

Table 1

Categories	Total population	Income per capita per year in £E
A. Rural areas:		
1. Masses		
10: landless	14 000 000	3.5
11: cultivating less than 1 *feddan**	1 075 000	6.1
2. Intermediate strata		
(cultivating 1–5 *feddans*)	2 850 000	26.8
3. Privileged strata		
31: from 5 to 20 *feddans*	875 000	87.4
32: over 20 *feddans*	150 000	773.3
Total and average	19 000 000	17.1
B. Urban areas:		
1. Masses		
10: without recorded employment	2 983 000	0
11: domestic servants	934 000	21.4
12: subproletariat	186 000	26.8
13: traditional wage-earners	400 000	40.0
2. Proletariat	790 000	60.8
3. Petty-bourgeois elements		
30: minor office-workers	1 117 000	105.6
31: traditional entrepreneurs	736 000	127.7
32: middle cadres	614 000	133.5
4. Bourgeoisie	240 000	845.8
Total and average	8 000 000	73.4

*One *feddan* = 0.47 hectare

c. Among the working people of the countryside, the wage earners are not at all a privileged group; on the contrary, they make up the bulk of group A1, the most poverty stricken in Egypt (£E 11 per capita, for a theoretical year of full employment). The average annual income per capita of the unskilled urban workers (groups B11, 12, 13) is not much better: £E 26. Allowing for differences in price levels, and for the fact that the rural incomes are understated (production for self-subsistence, etc.) and that the expenses needed for living in town include items that do not appear in the countryside (transport; lodgings–which, even though wretched, cost a lot to rent; etc.), then, in terms of standard of living, the popular strata of the towns are not much better off than those of the countryside.

d. The 'privileged' element thus appears to be confined to the skilled workers in the towns, of whom about 75 per cent are wage earners (categories

B2, 30, and 32, in part, category B31 being composed of independent workers and heads of enterprises). The average income per capita of this group of wage earners is four times that of unskilled workers in the towns. This hierarchy, from 1 to 4, is largely due to differences of skill. Nevertheless, because the absolute standard of living of the lower strata is low, and because this poverty is aggravated by the very high rate of unemployment among the unskilled, differences of income which are in any case much greater than in the industrialized countries assume a special socio-political significance.

e. Finally, among the urban bourgeoisie (category B4), an increasing proportion is made up of wage earners, apart from the higher cadres of the state and the economy; the nationalizations carried out have caused a considerable number of the highest incomes in the category 'incomes of enterprise' to move into the category of wage-earners.

The hierarchy of urban wages in 1960 was as follows:[2]

Table 2
Average Annual Income, in £E

	Unskilled labourers	Skilled workers	Minor office workers	Middle cadres	Higher cadres
State:					
Civil administration	—	120	230	350	1350
Transport and telecomm.	—	125	230	350	1550
Suez Canal	—	180	—	530	2300
Modern enterprises:					
Industry, transport	60	145	—	290	1330
Commerce, services	—	—	113	360	1200
Traditional enterprises:	—	90	—	—	—
Domestic servants	50	—	—	—	—

Even apart from the employees of the Suez Canal organization, whose relative advantages, still considerable in 1960, seem to have now disappeared the differences in reward are more pronounced than in the industrialized countries.

During the last century the gap between the average income in town and country has increased, the ratio having moved from 3:8 in 1914 to 4:3 in 1960. At the same time it is to be noted:

a. that the progressive reduction in the average income in the countryside is wholly attributable to the progressive reduction in the level of employment, the percentage of landless poor having risen from 40 per cent in 1914 to 80 per cent in 1960.[3]

Table 3
Average Rural Income Per Capita (in £E, 1960 value)

	1914	1958
Landless and poor	6.7	3.8
Intermediate strata	20	27
Privileged strata:		
5 to 20 *feddans*	98	87
over 20 *feddans*	465	789
Average	28	19

b. that the stability of the average urban income conceals an increasing disequilibrium, the rate of underemployment having increased, so that the increases in productivity have been made up for by the reduction in employment.[4]

Table 4

	1914	1960
Average urban income (in £E, 1960 value)	80	78
Labour force employed	728 000	1 930 000
Per cent of employed population to total urban population	32%	22%

Whereas, between 1914 and 1960, the product of non-agricultural activities increased by 2.9 per cent per year, employment increased by only 2.0 per cent per year. The advance in productivity was marked in industry, the crafts– where numbers were reduced from 150,000 to 60,000–having given place to large-scale industry, where numbers increased from 20,000 to 280,000. In commerce and services the progress of productivity was much more modest:

Table 5

	Increase in manpower (%)	*Increase in production* (%)
	(*annual rates* 1914–1960)	
Industry, crafts	1.4	3.5
Commerce	3.3	3.5
Transport	2.3	2.6
Administration	4.5	4.7
Services	1.5	1.2
Total	2.0	2.9

Thus, over a long period: (1) productivity has been stagnating in agriculture while increasing in the urban economy, especially in modern industry–hence the increasing gap between the average rewards of workers employed in the two sectors, traditional and modern, and (2) the gap between the average incomes of the urban and rural populations as a whole is the combined result of the increasing gap in productivities and the different evolution of rates of employment.

The case of the Maghreb. In 1955 the ratio between agricultural and non-agricultural incomes per capita was, for the Maghreb as a whole, 1/2.1. But the gap between the average incomes per capita for the Moslem population was only 1/1.3.[5] The divergences were thus very much smaller than in Egypt. This was certainly due to (1) a smaller degree of relative underemployment of the rural population in the Maghreb as compared with Egypt, and (2) the existence of a highly productive modern agriculture (the *terres de colonisation*).

Table 6

Rural community	(OF = old francs)
Agricultural income	503 billion OF
Agricultural income: Moslems	373 billion OF
Occupied rural population	2 485 000
Average income per capita: overall	200 000 OF
Average income per capita: Moslems	150 000 OF
Urban community	
Nonagricultural income: Moslems	2 940 OF
Nonagricultural income: Europeans	6 020 OF
Occupied population: Moslems	1 270 000
Unemployed	195–365 000
Occupied population: European	580 000
Average incomes:	
Europeans	1 040 000 OF
Moslems (excluding unemployed)	230 000 OF
Total (excluding unemployed)	495 000 OF
Total (including unemployed)	420 000 OF

Within the rural community, inequalities of distribution were much less marked in the Maghreb than in Egypt. Here, however, the wage earners, being nearly all employed in the high-productivity sector (the European estates), did not stand out, as they did in Egypt, as the pariahs of rural society. The average wages of the permanently employed agricultural workers were higher (by 50 per cent) than the incomes of the poorest third of the cultivators. However, the wages of the non-permanent workers, five times as numerous, were lower, and comparable to the incomes of the poorest cultivators. Allowing for this, and for the fact that the productivity of the modern agriculture that employed these wage earners was higher than that of traditional agriculture, the agricultural workers of the Maghreb did not deserve the charge of being a 'privileged' section.

Table 7
Agricultural Incomes in 1955[6]

	Algeria		Tunisia		Morocco	
	Man power (000)	Income per capita (000 OF)	Man power (000)	Income per capita (000 OF)	Man power (000)	Income per capita (000 OF)
Workers:						
Permanent	100	100	25	120	415	70
Seasonal	500	50	110	65	—	—
Moslem cultivators:						
Poor	210	60	80	90	100	110
Medium	210	200	105	150	450	200
Rich	50	560	45	450	85	900
Total for Moslem agriculture	1070	110	365	140	1050	190

Among the Moslem population of the towns, the hierarchy of incomes and wages is much less marked than in Egypt: the scale extending from the lowest category, 'workers' (whether skilled or not), to the category 'higher cadres and heads of enterprises', goes from 1 to 8 for Algeria and Tunisia and from 1 to 13 for Morocco, as against 1 to 22 for Egypt.

The numbers of Moslems in the higher categories are, however, comparatively fewer than in Egypt, the higher appointments and positions of heads of enterprises being occupied by Europeans who, moreover, receive higher incomes for the same skill.[7]

Allowing for the non-Moslem population, the hierarchy of incomes extends from 1 to 14–from 1 to 20 if we consider only the Moslem workers in the lowest category and only the non-Moslems in the highest category. The wage earners within Moslem society in the colonial period could therefore in no way be regarded as privileged persons.

During its historical development, colonial society in the Maghreb experienced only minor qualitative changes: income per capita of the Moslem population remained stagnant. The progress of modernization, reflected in the spread of the modern sector in both town and country, made possible an increasing settlement of colonists, which monopolized almost all the benefits of productivity.

Table 8
Urban Moslem Incomes, 1955[8]

	Algeria		Tunisia		Morocco	
	Man power (000)	Income per capita (000 OF)	Man power (000)	Income per capita (000 OF)	Man power (000)	Income per capita (000 OF)
Unemployed	150–230	—	25–55	—	20–80	—
Workers	225	150	118	160	300	150
Office workers	90	270	35	300	106	250
Craftsmen, middle cadres	135	270	53	300	183	270
Higher cadres, heads of enterprises	7	1250	2	1250	11	2000
Total: Moslems	460	230	210	210	600	240
Total non-Moslems	305	950	80	950	195	1200

Table 9

	Manpower		Income per capita (000 OF)	
	Moslems	Non-Moslems	Moslems	Non-Moslems
Workers	650000	150000	150	400
Office workers	230000	150000	270	530
Middle cadres	370000	220000	280	1200
Higher cadres	20000	60000	1700	3200
Totals	1270000	580000	230	1040

Table 10
Evolution of Average Income (in 000 OF, 1955 value)[9]

	Algeria		Tunisia		Morocco	
	1800	1955	1910	1955	1920	1955
Moslem countryfolk	22	22	17	23	27	32
Moslem townsfolk	30	30	28	35	35	42
Non-Moslem townsfolk	200	320	200	320	200	320

The situation changed with independence, between 1955 and 1965. The exodus of non-Moslems benefited a minority of the local population: the numbers employed in the public services increased 9.5 times, whereas the increase in productive employment was only 30 percent. Although the remuneration of cadres and public officials was lower than that received by their non-Moslem equivalents in the colonial period, a new 'privileged' group appeared, for which there was little justification either in their qualifications or in the state of the economy. It is the rise of this 'privileged' group that has led observers to say, hastily and superficially, that wage earners as a whole form a privileged category.

Table 11

	Urban Moslem Employees[10] (000)		Income per capita (000 OF)
	1955	1965	In 1965
Economy:			
workers	640	770	250
office workers	170	290	330
craftsmen, etc.	330	480	430
cadres	60	100	650
Administration	70	660	450
Totals	1300	2300	390
Unemployed	600	600	—

Similarly, in the case of agriculture, I have shown that more pronounced differentiations have appeared because, while incomes have remained unchanged in traditional agriculture, privileged minorities have inherited the colonists' estates: the permanent workers of the management committees in Algeria, small proprietors organized in co-operatives in certain cases in Tunisia, bourgeois absentee owners in certain cases in Tunisia and Morocco, and latifundia owners in Morocco. Where Algeria is concerned it is true to say that the government wage earners in agriculture have become a privileged section.[11]

As regards the Maghreb, then, it can be concluded: (1) that, generally speaking, differences in remuneration, especially wages, are largely due to differences in productivity and skill; (2) that the chief cause of discrimination not based on productivity, namely, national origin, has been eliminated; (3) that, as a whole, wage-earners are not a privileged section, either in agriculture, where the bulk of them, made up of non-permanent workers, belong to the most poverty stricken strata of society, or in the urban economy (although in the latter case, probably owing to better trade-union organization and a lower level of unemployment, the hierarchy is less unequal than in many underdeveloped countries, such as Egypt), and (4) that the only 'privileged' groups of wage earners are to be found among the holders of the increased number of administrative appointments, together with, in the case of Algeria, the permanent workers who share in the benefits of collective management of the former colonists' estates. The special privileges of these sections clearly have a definite political significance, but they do not apply to the wage earners as a whole.

The case of the Ivory Coast. In the Ivory Coast, income per capita seems to be even more unequally distributed between town and country, although the difference was progressively reduced from 1/9 in 1950 to 1/7.5 in 1965.[12]

Because the overwhelming majority of urban occupations are on a wage basis it is too quickly and simply deduced that wage earners are a 'privileged' category.

In the agricultural economy the wages of the 120,000 labourers (20,000 francs per year), though they may seem very high in comparison with money incomes in the subsistence economies of the areas from which the wage earners come, are far from excessive when compared with the money incomes of the planters who employ them. These planters obviously benefit from the reserves represented by the subsistence economy areas and in this way annex for themselves the greater part of the increased productivity due to the transition from subsistence to plantation economy.

Table 12
Ivory Coast

	1950	1965
Population		
Rural	2 010 000	3 230 000
Urban	160 000	650 000
Product: (billions, 1965 value)		
Agriculture	33.5	77.8
Other activities	24.4	117.9
Product per capita (1965 frs)		
Rural	16 500	24 000
Urban	150 000	180 000

The same degree of inequality between wage earners, on the one hand, and planters, on the other, was a feature of the plantation areas in 1950. The alteration that has taken place here is expressed not in qualitative changes but only in the extension of the plantation areas, which increased 3.9 times in fifteen years.[13]

In 1965 the urban economy offered 164,000 jobs to Africans (to which should perhaps be added 20,000 jobs as unregistered family help) and 12,500 to Europeans and Lebanese, 142,000 of these being wage earning posts. For the African ones the distribution of remuneration was as follows:[14]

Table 13
Incomes in Plantation Areas in 1965[15]

	Number of production units (000)	Male labour		Total income (billions)	Wages (billions)	Income per cultivator (000)
		Family* (000)	Labourers (000)			
Native planters						
Small	40	100	—	4.8	—	120
Medium	40	150	40	9.2	0.8	210
Large-scale	20	110**	80	9.2	1.6	380
Foreign planters***	110	190	—	9.3	—	83
Totals	210	550	120	32.5	2.4	145

*planters and dependents
**planters excluded
***Africans from outside the plantation areas.

Table 14

	Jobs	Average income (frs)
Non-craft economy:		
Labourers	23000	150000
Workers	36400	240000
Office workers	17000	280000
Cadres	600	1800000
Draft economy	47000	280000
Domestic servants	9000	150000
Public-service officials	31000	550000
Total	164000	330000

The hierarchy of wages, rising from 1 to 12, from the labourers to the higher cadres, is more or less similar to that of the Maghreb, but the hierarchy of incomes is much less unequal than it is in Egypt, because urban incomes for Africans, other than wages, are negligible in the Ivory Coast, a situation that reflects the absence of a local private bourgeoisie.[16]

The incomes of the non-African population are obviously more substantial, and taking them into account increases the degree of inequality.

Table 15
Non-African Urban Employment, 1965[17]

	Numbers	Average income
Heads of enterprises and urban independent workers	2 100	7 700 000
Wage earners:		
Public service	2 500	1 600 000
Economy	7 400	1 850 000
Total	12 000	2 800 000

Finally, a substantial proportion of the non-agricultural income is not distributed at all inside the Ivory Coast. The exclusion of this income, which makes up 20 per cent of non-agricultural income, also intensifies the inequality.

Taken as a whole, then, African wage earners are not in the least a 'privileged' section, if we allow for differences in price levels between town and country, and the peasants' resources for self-subsistence. Here, too, differences in remuneration largely reflect differences in productivity. However, the fact that income of enterprise goes almost exclusively to foreigners, and is to a large extent distributed outside the Ivory Coast, causes the relatively privileged position of the public officials to stand out prominently. This fact is obviously significant in explaining socio-political behavior. This distribution structure, which is found over practically all of Black Africa, is not qualitatively different from that which prevailed in the Ivory Coast in 1950, change being expressed here in the spread of this type of urban economy without any alteration in proportions and relations.[18]

What conclusions can we draw from all these observations?

First, the very large divergences that are sometimes to be seen in the underdeveloped countries, between 'average wages' and 'average income' of the most deprived strata, especially the peasantry, are the inevitable consequence, under the capitalist system, of the juxtaposition in these countries of two economic systems belonging to different ages, with levels of productivity that are not to be compared. The hasty conclusion ought not to be drawn from this that 'the wage earners are a privileged section'–and, still less, that one of the purposes of economic policy should be to reduce the level of wages. A higher level of productivity not only makes possible a better wage but also, to a large extent, *requires* it. The Marxist concept of the 'value of labour power' brings out this connection. This is why comparisons between standards of living, when incomes are very different in kind, are of dubious validity, as are comparisons between levels of satisfaction, welfare, or happiness, which too often draw economists out of the realm of science. It is not only price levels that differ very greatly between rural and urban areas in the underdeveloped countries. There are the foodstuffs provided by a food-gathering economy which is very easily carried on in certain parts of tropical Africa, but which are sold at very high prices in the towns; the cost of housing in urban areas, which is very high even for tiny, unsanitary rooms in shanty-towns; the products of food-gathering or hunting that do not figure in the national accounts; and so on. There is also the way of life, which, when a countryman goes to live in a town, becomes transformed, involving as it does new requirements such as fares, entertainment, etc. The intensity of labour also must be taken into consideration. It is often forgotten that the income of the traditional peasant corresponds to 100 working days per year, whereas that of the urban wage earner corresponds to 300 working days. When all these factors are taken into account, the comparison between recorded incomes, in which the divergence is sometimes of the order of 1 to 10, often loses its dramatic quality.

Second, the problem of the 'privileged wage earners' lies elsewhere than in these too general comparisons. The hierarchy of wages is, on the whole, more pronounced in underdeveloped countries than in industrial ones. In the modern economy, whether plantation or urban, the mass of unskilled wage earners (notably agricultural workers and town labourers), who are relatively more numerous, make up the most deprived group in the nation. It is in relation to this mass and even more so, where unemployment in the towns and the underemployment of landless peasants reach disquieting pro-portions, in relation to this mass of underemployed persons, who are often also unskilled–that the wages of the skilled workers (manual and office workers alike) give a feeling of 'privilege' which, even when such wages are justified in terms of productivity, dictates certain socio-political attitudes. The same applies to the public service/official categories, especially when the feeling prevails that their numbers are too large and their recruitment dictated by the socio-political pressures of the 'little society of the towns', anxious for jobs. If, in addition, incomes of national capitalist enterprise are non-existent, these 'privileges' become significant.

Third, must the disparity become greater or must it shrink? According to one well known view, the disparity should increase, in the underdeveloped countries, between the average income of the mass of the workers, the growth of which is bound to follow the slow growth of the national product, and that of the most highly skilled categories, for whom the demonstration effect of the incomes of similar categories in the developed countries is fully opera-tive. In this form, this thesis seems fairly acceptable, but its implications are restricted to members of the most highly skilled categories, who are in a position to transfer themselves abroad ('brain drain'). Intuition, and the little information available for making long-term estimates of these changes, suggest that the gap was very wide at the start, perhaps as wide as it is today, especially where the absence of mutual permeation between the two spheres, the traditional one and the modern one, established by colonization, caused the supply of labour in the modern sector to be insufficient. Little by little the gap gets narrower for the unskilled masses in the modern sector, in pro-portion as migration from the country to the towns develops, whereas it gets wider for the more highly skilled categories.

Fourth, wages have, in the underdeveloped countries, a political dimension different from what they have in the advanced countries. In the latter, the wage earners represent the bulk of the working people, between 60 and 90 per cent of the occupied population. Consequently, over a long period, the average wage cannot evolve very differently from the way national production per capita evolves. Besides, in the industrialized countries, the working class is, as a whole, through its trade unions, comparatively solid as regards unity in struggle–except where, owing to racial differences (between black and white in the United States, for instance) or national once (between French and foreign workers in France and some other countries), this solidarity has been broken or at least impaired. The rate of growth of wages therefore tends to be fixed uniformly, for workers in all branches of the economy, around the average growth rate of productivity, rather than around the very varying growth rates of productivity in each separate branch of industry. Under these conditions, wages policy is a fundamental element in national policy on income distribution. The situation is very different in the underdeveloped countries, where wage earners make up only a small fraction of the occupied population–from 1 per cent (Niger) to 20 per cent (Congo–Kinshasa) or 30–40 per cent (Egypt, etc.)–and where, moreover, solidarity among the workers is less strong, owing to the backwardness of trade unionism and the distance separating the rural world from that of the towns.

In these circumstances there is no obvious relation, in the underdeveloped countries, between the long-term evolution of wages and that of the national product. Thus we find, in certain countries, a very low or medium growth of the national product (from 0.2 to 3 per cent) accompanied by a very fast fast growth in real wages (over 6 per cent per year in Jamaica and Colombia 4.5 per cent in Ceylon, over 8 per cent in Zambia, Rhodesia, Nigeria, and Tanzania); or, on the contrary, very low rates of growth of real wages (even negative rates) even in countries where the growth of production per capita has been relatively better (Taiwan, Burma, South Korea, India, the Philippines, etc.).[19] Phenomena such as this are not open to simple explanations, for there is not the slightest correlation between the movement of wages and the pace of industrialization, or even the movement of profits. In some instances (Congo–Kinshasa, Puerto Rico, etc.), the steady rise in wages has stimulated enterprises to make more efficient choices which have increased profits and quickened the pace of industrialization.[20] As regards response to chronic inflation, we find every possible case: belated adjustment of wages, steady increase in real wages, or, on the contrary, progressive reduction real wages. Elastic behavior, upward and downward, in real terms, is only possible, of course, because the problem of wages does not constitute the main axis of income distribution, and this can be explained only as part of a general theory of the stages of development of the Third World of today, a theory that can be worked out only for groups of countries whose initial structures, natural resources, and types of exploitation are comparable (Central America, the West Indies, South America, Black Africa, the Arab world, Southeast Asia, etc.), and which must integrate both real phenomena (structures of the sectoral distribution of growth, bottlenecks in the external balance, etc.) and the monetary phenomena (chronic inflation, etc.) that accompany them.

Fifth, the important gaps, both absolute and relative, between the levels of remuneration of the different categories of workers in the underdeveloped countries, notably between those of the rural and those of the urban spheres, between the skilled and the unskilled, between workers employed by certain big firms and the rest, although perfectly explicable on strictly economic grounds (differences in productivity, etc.), constitute an obstacle to the building of a coherent nation. It is thus conceivable that an economic policy of development might aim to work systematically *against* the 'natural laws' of the economy, seeking to reduce these gaps in order to ensure national cohesion. This policy can be justified, of course, only if the reduction in the remuneration of privileged categories which it undertakes to achieve is not affected for the benefit of other categories of income (in particular, incomes of private enterprise, whether national or foreign), but genuinely for that of the community as a whole, and provided that the categories affected by this policy possess a clear understanding of it, based on political conviction.

An egalitarian policy of this kind is politically quite reasonable, the aim of national cohesion being essential for successful development. But it must be clearly realized that it means the adoption of a price system very different from that of actual market prices. The actual price system in the underdeveloped countries is largely determined by the one that prevails in the advanced countries, through international competition and the substitution of products. This system thus corresponds to a relatively uniform distribution of productivities. Given the much greater spread between productivities in the underdeveloped economies, a uniform reward of capital and labour, respectively, would result in a very different price system. If a price system like this is to be aimed at, in the name of a particular rationality, namely, national cohesion, it must be appreciated that such a system is not rational from the standpoint of economic calculation, of the sectors of the economy that ought to be developed. Two price systems would then be adopted, the rationalities of which would exist on different planes: one, a system of actual prices, aimed at eliminating inequalities in reward and ensuring national cohesion, and another, a system of reference prices, serving the requirements of economic calculation. As development proceeded, of course, unevennesses in productivity would be reduced and the two systems would draw closer together.

It is the nature of the political revelations between foreign capital, the local business bourgeoisie, the 'privileged' strata of wage earners, and the administrative bureaucracy that ultimately determines important aspects of the evolution of this social distribution of income. Where there is no business bourgeoisie, as is often the case in Black Africa, the privileged wage earning strata may become, together with the administrative bureaucracy, the chief transmission belt of domination from without.[21] But this does not always happen. In Congo-Kinshasa, for example, between 1960 and 1968, it was the bureaucracy that grabbed the lion's share, while the condition of the working class was worsened, as was that of the peasantry.[22]

NOTES

[1] Hassan Riad, *L'Egypte nassérienne*, p. 41.

[2] *Ibid.*, pp. 46–60.

[3] *Ibid.*, p. 148.

[4] *Ibid.*, pp. 158–60.

[5] Samir Amin, *L'économic du Mahgreb*, **I,** Editions de Minuit, Paris, 1966, pp. 130 *et seq.*

[6] *Ibid.*, p. 130.

[7] *Ibid.*, p. 181, 185.

[8] *Ibid.*

[9] Samir Amin, *op. cit.*, tome II, pp. 157 *et seq.*

[10] Samir Amin, *op. cit.*, tome II, pp. 157 *et seq.*

[11] Samir Amin, *op. cit.*,II.

[12] Samir Amin, *Le développement du capitalisme en Côte d'Ivoire*, Edition de Minuit, Paris, 1967, Tabl. annexes pp. 285 *et seq.*

[13] *Ibid.*, pp. 89–92.

[14] *Ibid.*, pp. 155–78.

[15] *Ibid.*, pp. 292–3.

[16] *Ibid.*, pp. 175–8.

[17] *Ibid.*, pp. 155–78.

[18] *Ibid.*, pp. 298–9.

[19] A.D. Smith, *Apercu général des tendances des Salaires dans les pays en voie du développement*; Collaque d'Egelund, Tabl. III, VI et IX.

[20] J. L. Lacroix, *Industrialisation en Congo*, Mouton 1966; and Lloyd G. Reynolds and Peter Gregory, *Wages, productivity and industrialization in Puerto Rico*, Illinois, 1964.

[21] G. Arrighi, *Communication en Congrés des études africaines de Montreal*, October 1969.

[22] F. Bezy, *Situation économique et sociale du Congo Kinshasha, Cultures et développement*, Volume I, number 3, Louvain.

Incomes policy and union power
CHRISTOPHER ALLEN

From Christopher Allen, 'Unions, incomes, and development', in *Developmental trends in Kenya*, Centre of African Studies, Edinburgh, 1972.

Despite an earlier concentration on the frailty of unions in Africa, those economists that have dealt with their effects on wage levels recently have argued that they have been able to 'blackmail' (Lewis, 1967) or otherwise induce governments to grant large increases in real wages, which the private sector (usually under union pressure) then matches. As a result, an essential component of most incomes policies has been a set of measures to circumvent or suppress union activity.[1] To be valid, however, the economic arguments supporting such measures must include the following assumptions:

—wage increases occur as a result of union action.
—unions represent the recorded labour force, and are socially homogeneous (if not ethnically or politically): the importance of this assumption is that it implies that the interests of all union members are the same.
—workers not organized in unions cannot bring about major changes in their earnings.

To be feasible in addition, the measures must also assume that it is possible for governments that do not clearly represent the interests of the urban and rural poor to divert unions into a productionist strategy.

(i) The validity of incomes policies

Not only are none of the above assumptions true in practice, but the argument from them to a policy of control of union activity is itself invalid, since even if it is true to say that union activity causes wage increases, it does not follow logically that the absence of action will prevent increases.[2] Only when it is true that wage increases occur if and only if unions set about obtaining them, will the arguments underlying union control become valid. The policy of control may, of course, work whether the argument is valid or not; but then union control becomes a policy based not on economic reasoning and imperatives, but on political experience and expediency.

More important, however, is the falsity in general of the listed assumptions. The effect of union action on money and real wages has been lengthily examined in the case of Nigeria.[3] The debate in this case has been essentially over the extent to which wage determination in Nigeria has been primarily the result of government response to the electoral or political threat of discontent mobilized by union leaders. The supporters of the view that the determinants of wage changes are political[4] have been able to show that in certain cases the regional and/or federal governments have granted wage increases after public displays of worker discontent, or in order to gain votes. They have also shown that unions have played an articulative and representative role in the process, but not that economic factors are unimportant (with the obvious exception of changes in real wages). Their opponents,[5] particularly Weeks, have argued that economic factors are decisive in determining the broad timing and level of wage increases, and that no essential union role has been demonstrated. More recently Weeks (1971) has argued that the rival positions are complementary, and are best represented by the following disjunction:

> The argument of Cohen and those who agree with him fails to draw the crucial distinction between the *forms* or *mechanisms* of wage setting, and the underlying forces of wage determination. His argument deals only with the mechanisms of wage determination in Nigeria, which he correctly identifies as political, but by thus restricting himself, he is diverted from the causes of wage movements, which are economic.[6]

In Hegelian terminology, the role of unions in wage determination is therefore accidental, rather than necessary; they are–as it happens–the institutions used by employees to present their views and demands, and to negotiate on their behalf. But the success of their activity, which is in any case the activity not of unions *per se* but of union leaders, depends on the workers, including non-unionists, and on the economic situation.

If this is, as I believe it to be, applicable to all African trade unions (with modifications for special situations such as the presence of European skilled manual workers), then an incomes policy based on (partially) eliminating unions and union action in the wage bargaining process will not necessarily succeed. It may make bargaining less organized and more time-consuming; but by itself it will not reduce real wages.

The second assumption I have listed concerns the relationship between workers and union leaderships. In studies of unions, it is common both to substitute discussion of union leaders for that of workers as a whole, and to assume that leaders fall into the same social and economic class as their members. The first of these is obviously improper and confusing, leading to failure to account for the political activities of organized workers and their leaders in a satisfactory fashion.[7] The second needs more discussion, as it is bound up with the policy of co-opting union leaders in an attempt thereby to control unions.

Union membership falls into three categories:

(a) the rank and file, consisting largely of inexperienced workers (often unskilled and new migrants), and the apathetic;
(b) the 'shop-floor' leadership, consisting of experienced workers, with several years in the same or related enterprises. These men do not necessarily become members of workers' committees, *délégués du*

personnel, or shop stewards, as their functions are not simply those of representation and negotiation. They are more often to be found playing leadership and integrative functions during moments or periods of tension;[8]

(c) union officials, who–especially at the national level–differ from the other categories by being more frequently urban-born, more literate in English and better educated, and by enjoying a higher standard of living. Often they are from families of some existing status, and have no direct experience of the industries from which their membership comes; or they may be clerks.[9]

Socially therefore union leaders differ from their members but not from the urban élite,[10] and their ambition is very often to use their official positions to achieve at least the income of the élite, if not also membership of it. There is no space to prove this assertion; we may note, however, Friedland's finding that even minor union officials tended to have been born in towns, and the frequency with which union officials have become civil servants, or industrial or industrial relations officers in private firms,[11] as well as becoming important figures in governing parties.[12] We may also note the widespread evidence of excessive salaries for, and of corruption by, union officials, the former often justified by assertions that union officers must not appear inferior to those with whom they negotiate.[13]

Co-option of union leaders has a long history, and is concisely described for Kenya by Sandbrook (1970, pp. 254–5):[14]

African governments have usually preferred to obtain their acquiescence through less risky, informal bargains rather than solely through coercion. These bargains may involve 'trading-off' a certain degree of union independence in exchange for such benefits as compulsory 'check-off' and/or union shop systems; union leaders thus gain financial security in exchange for greater state direction. The bargain, on the other hand, may be on a more personal level. In this case, ambitious trade unionists are co-opted into the political élite (and, hence, often into the economic élite too) in exchange for their co-operation. Co-optation may take the form of a seat in the National Assembly or a position on an important government board or commission.

It is clear from my earlier remarks, however, that far from being repressive, (or even an example of repressive tolerance), such activity simply fulfills the ambitions of the bulk of union officials, and leaves the other categories of union membership untouched. Interestingly, there is some evidence that rank and file unionists are not only aware of this,[15] but have also begun to try to prevent it, by removing such leaders at the local level.[16]

The third assumption–that only through unions can workers achieve wage increases–is to some extent a corollary of the first, and has therefore been dealt with by implication. It is worth mentioning, however, that in West Africa, where control, suppression and co-optation have a longer history, worker activity increasingly bypasses the national union centres and their leaderships, or actively opposes them (as, *e.g.*, in Senégal), leaving union leaders with at best the role of negotiating after their members and other employees have obliged the government and employers to agree to negotiate and make concessions.

(ii) The feasibility of incomes policies

That the assumptions discussed above are not in general true does not imply that a policy of wage restraint and control of union activity will not succeed. The outcome of such a policy is an empirical matter, and it may well be true that 'what has motivated governments has not been the economic imperative postulated by economists, but rather. . . a political imperative, the economists' arguments serving as usual only as rationalizations'.[17] In such a case the invalidity of the economists' arguments is beside the point, and the feasibility of the policies they were meant to require becomes of greater importance.

A policy ceases to be feasible if it cannot be implemented, or will not achieve its stated aims. Implementation will be difficult both when the aims of the policy will not be achieved, and when they could better be achieved by different policies. Both difficulties apply to a policy of union control and wage restraint that has as its aims a reduction in townward migration, and increase in wage employment, and greater equity in income distribution. As I have already argued, wage restraint, in so far as it implies declining real per capita incomes, simply leads to the overall impoverishment of both urban and rural poor, and may not affect migration rates at all. Should migration be reduced, per capita rural incomes may well decline and become more unequal, preventing greater equity in income distribution. Lower real wages will not necessarily lead to increased private sector employment, though they will allow more jobs to be created in the public sector; but this will simply encourage further migration, as well as enhancing maldistribution of income by increasing profits.

Thus the aims of the policy are incompatible; they are also better achieved by different policies. Reduction of migration by making towns less attractive is a slower, more uncertain, and politically more dangerous policy than is one of reduction through increased rural investment. Income equity as a policy goal applies far more obviously to the very great differentials between the poor and the rich than it does to those between the poor, which, where they exist, can be resolved by increasing rather than reducing incomes. And creation of new jobs should surely be based on an analysis of all the factors that cause stagnation or slow growth in employment, rather than on one relatively minor factor.[18]

There are obvious answers to these trite points. They amount to saying that these alternative policies are equally impractical, given the nature of governing élites and the economic relationships that link industrialized and African economies. Thus the choice of wage restraint and union control is based on a calculation that the political power of workers is less than that of other interested urban parties. While this is true in terms of policy formulation and administration, workers may be able to prevent implementation of the resulting policies. . . Wage earners are likely to continue to demand higher wages as their per capita real incomes fall, and as élite incomes rise. Union leaders who try to prevent or divert them are likely to find themselves by-passed or replaced, at least at the local level. Wage policies are essentially repressive, and while the experience of Ghana, Senegal, Zaïre and Nigeria at various times during the 1960s shows that such repression can be successful, their more recent experience shows that success is only for a limited term.

NOTES
[1] For a useful East African discussion see Sandbrook (1970); and for West Africa, Rimmer (1970), 39–51.

[2] This logical fault is quite common in arguments supporting economic policy, as, for example, in discussions of the effect of wage increases on the propensity to consume imports. It does not follow, from the fact that at a given time those above the minimum wage consume a higher proportion of imported goods than those at the minimum, that an increase in the latter will lead to an increased tendency to consume imports. To show that this will be so, it is necessary to compare expenditure by the same group before and after (a) an increase solely in the minimum wage and (b) an all-round wage increase.

[3] Summarized in Cohen (1971b), Ch. 5.

[4] Warren (1966; 1969); Kilby (1968; 1969); Cohen (1971a).

[5] Berg (1969); Weeks (1971d).

[6] Weeks (1971d), 165; for a discussion see Cohen (1971b), 269–74.

[7] Allen (1971).

[8] For a description, see Peace (1972).

[9] See e.g. Grillo (1968), Ch. 11.

[10] This is not wholly true of Ghana and Guinea in the early 1950s; but in these cases, the local leadership of the party was drawn in part from non-elite groups.

[11] Friedland (1969), 75–76 and Appendix 3; Scott (1966), passim.

[12] 'Many union officials are not firmly committed to trade unionism, but view it as a convenient springboard into politics', Sandbrook (1970), 283.

[13] Most recently given me by a Ghanaian career union official with a B.A., and earning over £2000 p.a. My remarks on corruption are based on research in West Africa, expecially Ghana.

[14] For further discussion, see Sandbrook (1971, 1972); for Sierra Leone, see Conway (1968).

[15] See e.g. Pfefferman (1968), 265–8.

[16] Peace (1972).

[17] Rimmer (1970), 1; see also Weeks (1971b), and Sandbrook (1970), passim.

[18] '...basing wage policy on an employment expansion goal is rather like asking an airline passenger to go on a crash diet because the plane is overweight' (Weeks, 1971b).

BIBLIOGRAPHY
ALLEN, C.H. —1971, 'Some problems in the analysis of trade unionism in A.O.F.', paper delivered to the Social Science Seminar, Zaria, November.

BERG, E.J. —1969, 'Urban real wages and the Nigerian trade union movement, 1939–60; a comment', Economic development and cultural change, 17, pp. 604–17.

COHEN, R. —1971a, 'Further comments on the Kilby–Weeks debate', Journal of Developing Areas, 5, pp. 155–64.

COHEN, R. —1971b, The role of organized labour in the Nigerian political process, Ph.D. thesis, Birmingham. (Publ. 1974 as Labour and politics in Nigeria 1945–71, Heinemann Educational Books, London.)

CONWAY, H. —1968, Industrial relations in Sierra Leone, Ph.D. thesis, London.

FRIEDLAND, W.H. —1969, Vuta Kamba, Stanford.

GRILLO, R.D. —1968, African railwaymen, Ph.D. thesis, Cambridge.

KILBY, P. —1968, 'A reply to John F. Weeks's comment', Journal of Developing Areas, 3, pp. 19–26.

KILBY, P. —1969, Industrialization in an open economy: Nigeria 1945–66, Cambridge.

PEACE, A.J. —1972, 'Industrial protest at Ikeja, Nigeria', paper delivered to the British Sociological Association Conference.

PFEFFERMAN, G. —1968, *Industrial labour in the Republic of Senegal*, New York.

RIMMER, D. —1970, *Wage politics in West Africa*, Birmingham University Faculty of Commerce and Social Science, Occasional Paper No. 12, February.

SANDBROOK, R. —1970, 'The state and the development of trade unionism' pp. 252–95 of *Development administration: the Kenyan experience*, G. Hyden *et al.* (ed), Nairobi.

SANDBROOK, R. —1971, *Politics in emergent trade unions*, Ph.D. thesis, Sussex.

SANDBROOK, R. —1972, 'Patrons, clients, and unions', *Journal of Commonwealth Political Studies*, **10**, 1, 3–27.

SCOTT, R.D. —1966, *The development of trade unions in Uganda*, Nairobi.

WARREN, W.M. —1966, 'Urban real wages and the Nigerian trade union movement', *Economic development and cultural change*, 15, pp. 22–36.

WARREN, W.M. —1969, 'Urban real wages... a rejoinder', ibid., 17, pp. 618–33.

WEEKS, J.F. —1971b, 'The problem of wage policy with special reference to Africa', *Economic Bulletin of Ghana*, NS 1.

WEEKS, J.F. —1971d, 'Further comments on the Weeks Kilby debate', *Journal of Developing Areas*, 5, pp. 164–75.

The mixed sector and imperialist control in Tanzania

ISSA G. SHIVJI

From Issa G. Shivji, 'Tanzania: the silent class struggle' in Lionel Cliffe and John Saul (eds), *Socialism in Tanzania: an inter-disciplinary reader*, (*II. Policies*), East Africa Publishing House, Dar es Salaam 1972.

Tanzania does not definitely fall under the heading of bureaucratic capitalism. This is because the bureaucracy does not appear to have an upper hand and certainly does not wield political power. This may be due to the fact that the top leadership of the Party is dedicated to socialism. Neither does Tanzania fall under the type... termed state capitalism because it does not have a bourgeoisie of its own.[1] Rather, Tanzania appears to be in a situation of flux–a situation of latent but definite class struggle. *On the one hand, there is the economic and political bureaucracy (objectively backed by the international bourgeoisie, the country being still in the neo-colonial framework), and on the other are the workers and peasants as represented in their most vocal and conscious elements–largely small groups of intelligentsia, including a few enlightened leaders.* The economic bureaucracy does not have a definite upper hand as would be the case under bureaucratic capitalism. But the fact that the economic bureaucracy is a powerful force can be gleaned from the attitudes of the parastatal management generally towards what may be called 'socialist measures'. This attitude has facilitated the perpetuating of neo-colonial interests. 'Services industry'–tourism, hotel-building; running entertainment houses, breweries, etc.–has loomed large in N.D.C.'s investments policy. By the end of 1968, for example, roughly one-third of N.D.C.'s investments was concentrated in luxury items: breweries, cigarette production, hotels, and tourism[2] while only about one-tenth per cent was invested in subsidiaries and associated companies producing *consumer necessities*. This accords well with the investment policies of the international corporations, which are fighting desperately to maintain their hold on the Tanzanian economy, in order to ensure that it remains within the neo-colonial web.

This may be done in various ways. Of late, many foreign monopoly corporations have entered into partnerships with N.D.C. in various projects; they also manage and operate many projects on behalf of N.D.C.; they supply management and consultants[3] and act as technical advisers. They even undertake the so-called feasibility surveys, making huge profits on all these activities.[4] Let *Jenga*, the monthly magazine of N.D.C., itself take up the story:[5]

The basis on which a partnership is established, taking the Arusha Declaration guidelines into account, varies according to negotiations between N.D.C. and the potential partner. This is reflected by the fact that N.D.C.'s holdings in its subsidiary and associate companies ranges from 100 per cent of the shares in five companies to nine per cent in one company (although Tafco holds another 15 per cent of the shares in this company).

In establishing complex industries involving a large capital investment, such as the fertililer plant and the proposed sisal pulp plant, N.D.C. hires a firm to act as technical consultant–conducting extensive industrial tests, market surveys, and feasibility studies. Sometimes a second consultant is hired to evaluate or do a completely new study.

The technical consultants may invest in the equity of the new company, taking a minority shareholding, and continuing to supervise technical aspects of production. This was the case at Mwanza Textiles Ltd with French consultants, Tanzania Bag Corporation, with Italian consultants, Tanzania Tanneries Ltd, with Swedish consultants, as well as other projects.

In addition, N.D.C. often enters into a management agency agreement with the foreign firm. This generally involves a management contract for an agreed number of years, a share of up to 50 per cent of the equity by the company, possibly an agreement for the foreign partner to import surplus production and possibly also an agreement whereby the partner looks for financial backers for the project.

Besides the fact that management agreements, etc., ensure the foreign partners' profits,[6] they also protect the regional interests and markets of the monopolies. Going into partnerships with public corporations gives them political security and helps them to get concessions on import duties, to bar competitive imports and get markets for their machine goods at inflated prices. Over and above that, the interests of the management representing the foreign partner may not in most cases coincide with national priorities. Thus, 'In the case of the Dar es Salaam Portland Cement plant the management recommended that the required second plant be built near the first to double output to meet growing national demand. It is possible that a preferable location might have been in north-eastern Tanzania but the plant management with interests also in its Kenya plant may have wished to reduce competition with Kenyan supplies imported by rail.'[7] Furthermore, to fit in with the national plan it may be necessary to sell cement at lower prices than would be acceptable to the foreign partner who would be interested in maximum returns on his 49 per cent holding. It is not surprising, therefore, that the parastatals[8] and N.D.C. subsidiaries continue to function as individual entities without the co-ordination and integration which are so necessary for a comprehensive industrial strategy and National Planning.

The neo-colonial web

We have said that Tanzania's economy still remains entangled in the neo-colonial web; we have also pointed out some of the ways in which this is done. Here below, we give some typical examples, chosen at random, to illustrate this:

The N.D.C. has a 67 per cent holding in the Coastal Dairy Industries Ltd

(C.D.I.L.). Under a technical co-operation agreement, the Swedish[9] Development Authority provided two technicians to assist in the installation of the plant. The Tanganyika Creameries Ltd have been acting as its (*i.e.* C.D.I.L.'s) managing agents and 'in addition to these duties will assume responsibilities for marketing when the plant opens'.[10] The Tanganyika Creameries Ltd (it has been recently wound up) itself has an interesting story behind it. The N.D.C. held 33 per cent of the shares of this company. It operated as managing and marketing agents for Northern Dairies Ltd, Arusha, as marketing agents for the National Dairy Board and Wafugaji wa Mara Co-operative Union in Musoma and as distribution and selling agents for Kenya Co-operative Creameries Limited (K.C.C.). But the Tanganyika Creameries itself was managed by the K.C.C. under an agreement to last for five years. It was to provide top management. The K.C.C. Ltd is a Kenya-based Co-operative Society with Lord Delamere (who holds some 13 directorships in various companies) as one of the six European directors on its board. Besides the Tanganyika Creameries Ltd, K.C.C. has a number of subsidiary companies in East Africa: the Uganda Creameries Ltd, the East African Creameries Ltd, The Milk Producers Company Ltd, and the Penguin Dairies Ltd.

The Penguin Dairies Ltd manufactures ice cream in Kenya. Recently the K.C.C. interests in the Penguin were bought out by Lyons Maid (E.A.) Ltd, thereby Penguin became a wholly owned subsidiary of the Lyons Maid. The Lyons Maid (E.A.) Ltd, is a U.K. subsidiary of J. Lyons and Co. Ltd, a British catering group, which ranked 88 in 'The Times 300'. In 1966 they recorded a profit (before taxation) of B£3,584,756 (capital employed, 1967, B£56,988,000). The Eskimo Ice Cream Company, (a Nairobi concern), which was the other company producing ice cream in Kenya, was also bought out by the subsidiary of Lyons Group. Thus the latter became the sole supplier of ice cream in Kenya. The Lyons products have a market in Tanzania as well.

Thus far we have been showing the K.C.C.'s East African interests only. But that is not the whole story. K.C.C. is also associated with *three other giant global dairy organizations–Nestlés, Glaxo,* and *Unigate.*

Nestlés, a Swiss-based company, is the biggest dairy concern in the world with some 300 creameries in many countries. The Nestlé Company Ltd, its British subsidiary, ranks 110 in 'The Times 300' of 1967 with B£43,588,800 capital employed. In 1967 Nestlé was making plans to buy its raw materials from the K.C.C., for !he manufacture of its own products in Kenya.[11]

Glaxo Ltd ranked 94 in 'The Times 300' of 1967, with capital employed at B£51,630,000. Glaxo Ltd, in association with the Allenburys, manufactures baby foods and pharmaceuticals in Kenya, the raw materials for some of which come from K.C.C.

Unigate is a British dairy giant, combining United Dairies with the Cow and Gate group. It ranked No. 77 in 'The Times 300'. In 1967, they recorded profits for the year at B£13,546,000 (capital employed B£64,068,000) yielding a dividend of 14 per cent. Unigate has Cow and Gate (E.A.) Ltd and the East African Milk Products Ltd in East Africa as its subsidiaries. They manufacture Cow and Gate brand baby foods.

In the May, 1970 issue of *Jenga,* it was reported that the Tanganyika

Creameries has been wound up and that the N.D.C. may soon acquire 100 per cent shares in the Coastal Dairy Industry Ltd. Thus the K.C.C. has almost gone out of the picture as Managing Agents. But interestingly enough, the same issue reports that 'negotiations are being carried out with *NESTLE* of Switzerland with a view to appointing them managing agents of the company'. *The intermediary K.C.C. has been dislodged–instead the dairy business has come more firmly, under an international dairy giant, Nestlés!*

Let us next explore the international connections and links of our up-and-coming 'tourist industry' which has recently engaged national interest and attention. The recent 'tourism debate' in *The Standard*,[12] if anything, has uncovered a lot of confusion that pervades our intelligentsia so far as socialist thought is concerned. Phrases like 'imperialism', and 'neo-colonialism', and 'international monopoly capital' are rejected as slogans.[13] One half-baked bourgeois 'scholar' had even the temerity to suggest that 'sloganeering' and 'confused thinking' of the 'students'–*i.e.* the authors of original articles on 'tourism'–was due to faulty grammar![14]

Be that as it may: coming back to the international links of our 'tourist industry', one name that looms large in this area is that of *Hallmark Hotels* (*Tanzania*) *Ltd*. This is an associate company of the N.D.C., which holds 30 per cent of its shares. It specializes in hotel management, providing managerial and consultancy services to most of the N.D.C. hotels, including the new projects like the New Africa Hotel, Kunduchi Beach Hotel, Bahari Beach Hotel, Zanzibar Fishing Lodge, Lake Manyara Hotel, Ngorongoro Wildlife Lodge, Seronera Wildlife Lodge, and Lobo Wildlife Lodge. The remaining 70 per cent of *Hallmark's* shares are held by the *Hallway Hotels Overseas Ltd*, a hotel management firm, linked with the Trust Houses Group of U.K. and the *United Transport Overseas Ltd*. The shareholders of the Hallway Hotels are the Commonwealth Development Corporation (C.D.C.), United Transport Overseas Ltd. (U.T.O.S.), and Mr Eric Hall.

The C.D.C. is a well-known corporation. It was originally established in 1949 (then called the Colonial Development Corporation)[15] as a British statutory corporation to make investments in the colonies with a charter requiring it to make profits.[16] The C.D.C. had a portfolio of investment commitment in Eastern Africa (including off-shore islands, Malawi, Zambia, etc.) of B£29,167,000 of which K£16,600,000 is committed to Kenya. An analysis of the overall C.D.C. functional distribution of investments reflects in miniature the new methods employed by foreign private interests to attain old aims in Africa. 53 per cent of its investments is for basic development, meaning 'infrastructure'[17] for the exploitation of natural resources, 21 per cent for primary production (agriculture, forestry, and mining) and 26 per cent for commerce, indstry, development companies, and hotels. The Working Party (set up under the auspices of the Department of Christian Education and Training of the National Christian Council of Kenya) could not help making the following observation–though typically in its mild, Christian language:[18] 'The C.D.C. has to borrow at the rates current in London, and toward the end of 1966 was paying seven per cent on all the money it borrowed from H. M. Government. Investment at such a stiff rate of interest means that a heavier burden has to be borne at the Kenya end, and this is inevitably reflected in, for example, higher rents and debt-servicing charges in the projects supported. This "plusage" on the cost of capital received through C.D.C. reflects the situation of the British economy up to the end of 1966; in other words, if we in Kenya want British capital, we have to pay quite dearly for it.'

One of the other shareholders in the Hallway Hotels Overseas Ltd is the United Transport Overseas Ltd (UTOS), a giant transport concern incorporated in England. UTOS dominates the urban and long distance passenger business in East Africa through its following subsidiaries: Kenya Bus Services Ltd, of Nairobi; Kenya Bus Services (Mombasa) Ltd, *Dar es Salaam Motor Transport Co. Ltd* (DMT, now nationalized); Uganda Transport Co. Ltd; Tanga and District Transport Ltd; Kampala and District Services Ltd; and East African Road Services Ltd UTOS has some 55 subsidiaries and associated companies with some 13 in Rhodesia and 18 in South Africa. In 1966 it made net profits after tax of some B£1,759,759 (capital employed over B£14½ million). In 1967, it became one of the partners (the others being the Kenya Tourist Development Corporation, Wilken Aviation Services Ltd, and a New York firm, Lindblad Travel Inc.) in an air charter company, *Wilkenair Ltd* to provide 'best possible facilities' for tourists.

UTOS itself is one of the 43 subsidiaries of the *United Transport Company* (UTC), which with its subsidiaries had assets of B£22,287,458 at the end of 1965, and made a profit (after tax) of over B£2,000,000. UTC owns 60 per cent of the shares in UTOS: The 40 per cent belongs to the *British Electric Traction Omnibus Company Ltd* (BET) of London. With a capital amounting to B£57,812,000 BET ranks 87 in 'The Times 300'. On 8 June 1967, the Chairman of BET announced a net profit after taxation of B£1,368,000 and made the following remark about the overseas operations of UTOS. 'Any who take dramatic reports of political stresses and strain to represent the sole valid picture of Africa are plainly a long way wide of the mark. Over a ten-year period, total revenues have expanded two-and-a-half times, and gross profits five times. Total capital employed by the companies is now little less than £11 million.' The *United Touring Co. of Africa Ltd* is an 'associated company' of UTOS. Among its family members are UTC (Uganda) Ltd., UTC (Tanganyika) Ltd and Nairobi Travel Services Ltd.[19] In its fourth annual Report the N.D.C. announced that it had entered into discussion with Riddoch Motors and United Transport Overseas Limited (UTOS) with the intention of forming a *Tanzanian* touring company,[20] presumably, to make the 'tourist industry' really 'Tanzanian' and 'socialist'!

Once some economic activity has begun, it gathers its own momentum and snow-balls. It becomes self-propelling notwithstanding the wishes and ideals of its authors. So is the case with the Tanzanian 'tourist industry'. After the Kilimanjaro International Air Port, (to be built by Italian firms—Ital Consult and Impresa Ing. Fortunato Federici–with a loan of 70 million shillings from Italy)[21] there are plans to build a Hilton Hotel costing over 30 million shillings.

The story of 'Hilton and tourism' is a good illustration of the economic causes behind the development of tourism as an industry on the world stage. It also illustrates how, within the international capitalist mode of production, the international bourgeoisie is a dominant social class pulling the strings of its satellite economies in the so-called underdeveloped world. The petty bourgeoisie of the underdeveloped countries may pat itself on the back for striking a 'goldmine' in the money-minting tourist trade. The truth, however, is that it is not their ingenious discovery to offer their wild animals[22] on sale (or *notionally* as an 'export commodity'–bourgeois economics like bourgeois law abounds in notions which have long lost contact with reality!) that has developed world tourism: World tourism has developed partly because of the problem of surplus accumulated[23] in the hands of the international capitalist class but mainly because of the rapid development of global aviation in the last few decades. It is not 'historical accident' that the international airlines own and run chains of hotels–Hilton Internationals by Trans-World Airlines (TWA); Inter-Continentals by Pan American; etc.[24]–and through the International Union of Official Travel Organizations (I.U.O.T.O.) encourage tourism. Let *The Economist* itself speak:

> TWA's object in buying the 38 Hiltons outside the U.S. is to have sufficient rooms to bed down passengers likely to be coming off its 500-seat aircraft in the 1970s. The airline that can't provide hotel accommodation runs the risk of losing traffic to the airline that can, whenever the destination is a slightly off-beat one where the first-time visitor is suspicious of local hoteliers' standards. Hilton is expanding fast, with eight hotels being built and ten more 'in development'. This will put TWA ahead of Pan American, whose Inter-continental Hotels subsidiary has been in the business since 1949, and now runs 36 hotels round the world.[25]

And the most authentic organ of the international bourgeoisie, *Fortune*,[26] said:

> Airlines continue to strengthen their hotel interests, infusing a new element of marketing sophistication. Inter-continental Hotels Corp., founded by Pan American World Airways, and Hilton International Co., owned by Trans-World Airlines 1967, have announced expansion plans. Eastern Air Lines is in the hotel business in the Caribbean and Hawaii. Braniff Airways, with Western International Hotels Co. as one of its partners, plans to become a major force in Latin-American hotels.

What began as an appendage of the international air transport business, has itself become profitable. Thus in the past 'Inter-Continental... built some hotels that fitted Pan American's needs... Some were built because a developing country would grant Pan-Am landing rights only if it provided a prestigious hotel. Others were built because Pan-Am thought a first-class hotel would help it to increase traffic on a new route. That strategy is changing. In the future, Inter-Continental will build hotels only if they can be profitable in their own right.'[27] In 1968, Inter-Continental had a net income of $1,600,000 from its 42 hotels with a total of 12,264 bedrooms. 'And because of Pan American's extraordinary sensitivity to local political problems Inter-Continental has typically favoured partnership with local investors.'[28] On the other hand: 'Hilton International's hotels are usually owned by local investors, who contract with Hilton for management services. The contract normally gives the owners two-thirds of the gross profits, and requires Hilton to make only minimal investment: "We like the investors to supply even the egg cups", says President Curt Strand. *That technique has been highly profitable.* In 1968 the 41 hotels, with a total of 13 930 bedrooms, produced a net income for Hilton International of $6,200,000.'[29]

What has been said about the international links of the two cases above, in fact holds true for many other N.D.C. subsidiaries. Unfortunately, the names of N.D.C.'s foreign partners, and especially the terms of partnership and management contracts with them, are so well-guarded, that it is difficult to trace their international links.

What are the economic effects of the pattern of 'joint ventures' we have described above? Firstly, the foreign 'partners', being global monopolies, have a very strong bargaining position *vis-à-vis* Tanzania. The partnership being between unequal partners–and especially when one of the partners is a capitalist corporation–it does not need much economics to see that the weaker partner stands to lose. A neo-colonial economy essentially remains a trading economy. It remains an export-oriented economy whose industrial units are vertically integrated with parent industries in the metropolis with no or very little integration with other industries or sectors in the neo-colony itself. Thus it may make sense and is economically rational for the Brook Bond–Liebig Group, which operates on a global level, to have a plant– the Tanganyika Packers–exploit Tanzania's livestock (raw material) and process it into meat and export for *its* markets in Bahamas, Europe, Jamaica, Borneo, etc.[30] But it makes no sense and is economically irrational for the Tanzanian economy to have Tanganyika Packers, if (as it is now) only five per cent of its products are consumed locally. Again the high prices fixed for the canned products of the Tanganyika Packers may be completely in accord with the Brooke Bond–Liebig's international market but may not at all be justified for the Tanzanian home market. It is, in fact, possible (even desirable) for the Tanzanian socio-economic plan to require that the prices of canned meat should be fixed at a low level so as to raise the nutritional level of the country's industrial proletariat–a real asset for development.

At one time the colonial countries used to be encouraged to grow cash crops for export to the metropolis. In many colonies this meant neglect of food products, thus resulting in malnutrition and starvation.[31] Now the policy of the international corporations appears to have changed to some extent. They are interested in *processing* raw materials, again for the export market. The economic history of resultant malnutrition is repeating itself at a different level!

In fact, to establish packaging, assembly and processing plants[32] is a new investment strategy of the international corporations. This is fully attested by the organ of the international bourgeoisie, *Fortune.*[33] Let us quote it at some length:

International corporations originally invested in resource-based production–mines and plantations–for export to their home markets... As this placed foreigners in... control of basic natural resources, it was... hated and in some cases nationalized. In the era of import substitution, foreign investment began to assume an entirely different character. To protect infant local industries, governments had erected high tariff barriers or imposed stringent controls on a wide range of imports. Since foreign industrial companies could not export to developing countries over these barriers, they moved inside them. Foreign investment in extractive industries was supplemented by extensive outlays in, among other things, chemicals, pharmaceuticals, paper, automobiles, and farm machinery. Like the first-wave... into extractive industries–the third-wave investment will be specifically export-creating. Unlike investment involving ownership of natural resources, however, it probably will not elicit violent nationalistic reaction. The developing countries' contribution to this activity will be reserves of low-cost and teachable labour. The international corporation's input will be capital, of course, but also technical knowledge, global commercial intelligence, and marketing expertise. With products where labour is a substantial part of total production costs and economies of scale are not especially great, the combination can be commercially successful. Such goods would include canned and frozen fruits and vegetables, textiles, clothing, leather products, furniture and other wood products, sewing machines, component and spare parts, forged hand tools, small motors, electrical parts and assemblies, and lathes and other simple machine tools.

This investment pattern of the international corporations is clearly reflected in the nature of N.D.C. investment which in itself is evidence enough that the foreign enterprises are the *dominant* partner dictating terms. Thus at the end of 1968, N.D.C. investment in its subsidiaries and associates was as shown in the table below.[34]

Issued capital	NDC Investment
25.2% in Raw materials for export	(44.6%)
12.7% in Produce: goods	(10.6%)
1.9% in Necessities ⎱ for domestic	(10.0%)
38.0% in Luxuries ⎰ consumption	(33.0%)
20.5% in Export processing	(7.3%)
1.4% in Tourism	(3.9%)

This means that N.D.C. investments are hardly helping the country to construct an integrated economy and a strong industrial sector which is a *sine qua non* if the country is really to develop. The large portion of the surplus generated by the hard toil of the masses finds its way to the metropolis through these foreign partners. What remains with N.D.C. is partly eaten up by the petty bourgeois and the bureaucratic stratum and partly invested. But as the economic structure is as described above, this investment is done mainly in export-oriented activities–whose basic character is 'commercial'. Thus there is dominance of commercial capital which is not 'transformed' into industrial capital.[35] This is the characteristic of underdevelopment. And it is this basic economic reality (the nature of productive forces) which gives rise to petty bourgeois, bureaucrat, and comprador strata, rather than an industrial bourgeoisie (production relations and class structure). In the words of Fanon: 'The psychology of the national bourgeoisie is that of the businessman not that of a captain of industry...'

NOTES

[1] In October 1967, the President himself made the following remarks '... there are only ten people in our whole country who have an income of Shs. 300,000 or more in a year...' [Nyerere, *After the Arusha Declaration,* p. 10]. Before nationalizations, it was largely the foreign corporations and the Kenya and Uganda based capitalists (e.g. Madhvani and Mehta groups) who were controlling large sectors of the economy.'

[2] The N.D.C. Fourth Annual Report, p. 35.

[3] The 1968 (No. 3) issue of *Jenga,* the N.D.C. magazine, reported: 'N.D.C. has recently commissioned McKinsey & Company, Inc., an international firm of management consultants, to study the Corporation's management information system' (p. 9). Elsewhere the same issue notes that 'almost half of the five hundred largest United States industrial companies are present or former clients of McKinsey & Company'. And this company is expected to advise N.D.C.—an instrument for building socialism!

Another U.S. private company of international 'fame', whose name looms large in Tanzania as adviser and consultant is 'Arthur D. Little'. This was the company which made a study of Tanzania's industrial potential in 1961 under a contract with U.S.A.I.D. (Agency for International Development). Many of its recommendations to attract foreign investment—tax holidays, government financing, repatriation of profits, etc.—were incorporated in the First Five Year Plan. Foreign investment, alas, was not attracted! Arthur D. Little is responsible for drawing up a master plan for the 'tourist industry'—a task which, no doubt, it is most competent to do!

[4] Unfortunately, no figures are available. But some information suggests that management fees under some contracts may be as much as or even more than 20 per cent of *gross yearly turnover* (not profits). And this does not include allowances, etc., paid to foreign executives.

[5] *Jenga,* 6 p. 41 (May 1970).

[6] 'Management contracts undertaken... may involve costs that are every bit as heavy as the costs to the economy would be if the corporation in question were fully under direct foreign ownership... Tanzania's bargaining strength is so weak that the cost of the servicing of human capital may well have risen considerably... Research upon the present terms of management contracts is urgently required. It is extremely difficult however, to obtain information about them. Both parties to these contracts guard their terms so carefully that this alone is grounds for suspicion'. G. K. Helleiner, 'New forms of foreign private investment in Africa', E.R.B., Paper 67, 12 (9 December 1967) quoted in Ann Seidman, 'Comparative industrial strategies in East Africa', *East Africa Journal,* **III,** 6, 39n (June 1970).

[7] Seidman, 'Comparative industrial strategies...' op. cit., p. 39. Another good example is that of the Tanganyika Packers. The international octopus Brooke Bond Liebig Group is 49 per cent shareholder and sales agent. It is not surprising, therefore, that only five per cent of the Tanganyika Packers' products is consumed locally. With proper forward and backward linkages one would have expected a factory like Tanganyika Packers not only to provide a market for ranches, etc., but to supply its products to the home market. Instead it appears to be vertically integrated with the foreign corporation network of the Brooke Bond Liebig Group, selling its products in Europe, Bahamas, Jamaica, Borneo, etc. [See *The Nationalist,* 10 August 1970]. The Chairman of the Company in fact conceives "the fundamental aim of this company (is) to produce a product which will enable us to earn some foreign exchange" (*ibid*).

[8] Thus N.I.C. has its own investment policy no different from that of a private insurance company [cf. Shivji, 'Insurance and development' in the forthcoming *East African Law Review*], N.D.C. has its own internal loan and credit system almost in

competition with the National Bank of Commerce and so on. cf. Loxley, 'The monetary system of Tanzania since 1967: progress, problems and proposals' mimeo.].

[9] As for the Swedish economy itself and its domination by American monopoly, see Vestbro & Persson, 'How socialist is Sweden?' in *Cheche*, 2.

[10] N.D.C. 4th Annual Report, p. 48.

[11] *Who controls industry in Kenya?* Report of a Working Party of the National Christian Council of Kenya, East African Publishing House, Nairobi, 1968, p. 37.

[12] Beginning with 15 May issue.

[13] Mental laziness and vested interests combine to make the petty bourgeoisie reject well-tested theories as 'slogans'. They instinctively know what social theories can be effective in practice and what are mere 'platitudinous rationalizations'. The former for them are slogans; the latter they promote!

[14] F. Mitchell, 'Evaluating the role of tourism in Tanzania', *The Standard* (Dar es Salaam) 15 June, 1970.

[15] As colonies became 'independent sovereign states within the Commonwealth', so the Colonial Development Corporation became the Commonwealth Development Corporation—everything else remaining constant!

[16] *Who controls industry in Kenya? op. cit.*, p. 196–7.

[17] The C.D.C. being a governmental corporation 'prepares' the infrastructure' for private capital. True to the Marxist analysis the state under capitalism is 'a committee for managing the day-to-day affairs of the bourgeoisie'.

[18] *Who controls industry in Kenya? op. cit.*, p. 197.

[19] *Ibid.*, p. 73, pp. 95–6.

[20] p. 80.

[21] *Jenga*, May 1970.

[22] If wild animals [and our 'short men'!—In the August 1970 No. 7 issue of *Karibu*, a monthly tourist guide published by the Tanzania Tourist Corporation, Mr. Athuman (65 years old) who is 3ft 3in. tall is proudly presented as a 'tourist hit' and 'the island's biggest tourist attraction'! (See the photograph on p. 25 of the magazine)] and natural beauty were really responsible for the development of tourism, then one would have expected a large number of tourists flocking to the underdeveloped countries. But tourist statistics speak the opposite. There is more touristic traffic and foreign exchange earning among the developed nations than the underdeveloped. In 1967, for instance, Europe and North America received 81 per cent of the total currency receipts while developing countries only six per cent of the 138 million visitors and only nine per cent of the S14.1 billion foreign exchange receipts. And these figures 'vary slightly from year to year' (cf. *Commonwealth co-operation in the development of tourism*, background papers prepared by Working Party of Commonwealth Experts on Tourism, Malta, October/November 1967, p. 14 and Appendix A).

[23] For an excellent analysis of the problems of 'surplus absorption' in the capitalist economies, see Baran & Sweezy, *Monopoly capital*, MRP, New York, 1966.

[24] A £300,000 investment in Serengeti Safari Lodges Ltd, a company developing tourist accommodation in northern Tanzania, is planned by BOAC Associated Companies Limited, a wholly owned subsidiary of BOAC. As a shareholder, BOAC-AC will be associated with Tanzania Hotel Investments Limited, representing the N.D.C., the Commonwealth Development Corporation and United Transport (Overseas) Ltd'. *The Nationalist*, 30 July 1969.

[25] 'Hotels in hot spot', *ibid.*, 29 April p. 495, 1967.

[26] 'Reveille sounds for the hoteliers', *ibid.*, p. 111, September 1969.

[27] *Ibid.*, p. 144.

[28] *Ibid.*, pp. 144–5.

[29] *Ibid.*, p. 144 (emphasis supplied—I.G.S.).

³⁰ See footnote No. 7 supra.

³¹ Professor De Castro, in his outstanding work *The geography of hunger* [which together with Baran's *The political economy of growth*, MRP, New York, 1957 deserve much more to 'be on the bedside table of all political leaders, as well as economists, in emerging nations' than Myrdal's *Economic theory and underdeveloped regions* (Duckworth, London, 1958) recommended by Dumont, (*False start in Africa*, p. 268 fn. 15)], analyses this situation in a masterly fashion. To quote just two examples: 'The one-crop culture of cane sugar in the Brazilian north-east is a good example. The area once had one of the few really fertile tropical soils. It had a climate favourable to agriculture, and it was originally covered with a forest growth extremely rich in fruit trees. Today, the all-absorbing, self-destructive sugar industry has stripped all the available land and covered it completely with sugar cane; as a result this is one of the starvation areas of the continent. The failure to grow fruits, greens and vegetables, or to raise cattle in the region, has created an extremely difficult food problem in an area where diversified farming could produce an infinite variety of foods'. (p. 97).

In Africa 'the first European innovation which worked to upset native food customs was the large-scale production of cash crops for exports, such as cacao, coffee, sugar and peanuts. We already know how the plantation system works... a good example is that of the British Colony of Gambia in West Africa, where the culture of food crops for local consumption has been completely abandoned in order to concentrate on the production of peanuts. As a result of this mono-culture... the nutrition situation of the colony could hardly be worse'. p. 215.

³² This activity, to make it appear respectable, is termed 'manufacturing'. Thus in a factory producing electric bulbs, everything—the base, filament and the glass are imported. The only 'part' that is 'manufactured' locally is the 'vacuum'.

In the *Fortune* article quoted below, South Korea is given as an example of a successful 'exporter of manufactured goods'. This 'export success', the article says, 'has been achieved largely with a pot-pourri of unglamorous goods, including plywood and veneers (16 per cent of manufactured goods in 1967) *and even wigs and false beards* (10 *per cent*)' [emphasis supplied]. Thus Union Carbide, a U.S. Corporation, 'exports Dynel to Korea, where it is made into wigs by local producers according to designs and specifications supplied by U.S. companies which market the wigs in the U.S. and Europe'. (p. 93).

³³ Sanford Rose, 'The poor countries turn from buy-less to sell-more', *Fortune*, p. 90 April 1970.

³⁴ From Seidman, 'Comparative industrial strategies...', *op. cit.*

³⁵ In Europe, on the other hand, large accumulation of commercial capital through plunder, slave trade, etc., was channelled into industrialization. It is the industrial capital which forms the basis of development.

Preconditions of socialist development in Africa
GLYN HUGHES

From *Monthly Review*, **22**, 1 (May 1970). Reprinted by permission of Monthly Review Press.

The central problem in the economic development of African countries is the creation of economic surplus and its allocation to productive investment. This is not purely an economic problem, however, but rather politico-economic, since the creation of economic surplus and the use to which it is put depend on the dominant political forces within the society.

Bourgeois economists tend to view the problem with some despondency. They argue that investment resources* can be increased in three ways: (a) by increasing exports, (b) by increasing domestic savings and, (c) by an inflow of foreign aid and investment. But, it is pointed out, increasing the volume of exports may be self-defeating, since it leads to lower prices; and, in so far as the privilege of supplying the developed countries with raw materials has already been rationed out through quota systems and bilateral agreements, this may in fact be a non-option. Similarly, domestic savings can hardly be increased when the majority of personal incomes are so low. To be sure, feudal plutocracies, where they exist, are fair game for the bourgeois economist, but he is reluctant to press his demands too hard on the business sector for fear of damaging 'incentives'. This leaves us with foreign aid, and here our economist waxes indignant at the niggardliness of the rich countries, exhorts them in the name of humanity to allocate even one per cent of their wealth to their poorer brothers, and ends with a vague threat of retribution by the Third World if something is not done soon.

But even if developed countries increased foreign aid to two per cent or even three per cent of their national product (reversing, incidentally, the present trend by which aid is growing more slowly than donor nations' national product), two conditions would have to be met for it to result in long-term growth for the underdeveloped countries. First, the aid would have to be in the form of direct grants or soft loans. Yet no one seriously envisages the capitalist industrial powers transforming themselves into

---

*This term is not of course synonymous with 'economic surplus' as used by socialist economists, but since the level of investment resources is partly determined by the economic surplus, the distinction is not crucial in this context.

charity organizations. Secondly, the political and economic structure of the receiving countries would have to be such as to make long-term economic growth possible. In very few underdeveloped countries is this condition at present fulfilled, and the countries which come near to fulfilling it are precisely those which are not going to receive a massive input of aid from the West.

A socialist approach to economic growth in underdeveloped countries must centre on the problem of economic surplus rather than foreign aid or exports, and this in turn requires an examination of two inter-related factors. The first is the 'latent surplus' of the agricultural sector. The low productivity of peasant agriculture, resulting from its primitive methods and small-scale nature, coupled with large tracts of under-utilized land in many African countries, indicate that the agricultural sector is capable of vastly increasing its output. We have already seen that agricultural expansion depends in part on the establishment of local capital-goods industry. We have also seen that the continued expansion of consumer-goods industry depends on an increasing demand from the agricultural sector for consumer goods. And, conversely, some of the incentive for peasant farmers to increase their output above subsistence level must come from the production of consumer goods. There are other factors which will affect development in the agricultural sector, and it is beyond the scope of this article to consider them in detail. But possibly the most important is the way in which agricultural production is to be organized. While it is true that the individual peasant holding has in most cases the potential for a greater output, it would soon reach a ceiling. Further increases can only be obtained by creating larger units of production. The form that these would take must depend largely on local conditions, and even within the same country one can envisage collectives, co-operatives, or state farms, for instance, proving suitable for different regions or crops. Interesting possibilities are raised by the Tanzanian experiment of 'ujamaa villages' in which production is being organized partly collectively and partly individually, but where overall planning and organization is in the hands of the community itself. But it must be stressed that no system of agricultural organization will produce the hoped for, long-term development except in in the context of a general economic strategy as considered above, which will take into account the interaction between the agricultural and industrial sectors.

It has been argued, even by some socialists, that the re-organization of the peasant sector can best be left to market forces and the emergence of capitalist farmers from among the ranks of wealthier peasants. This development is already evident in most African countries to a greater or lesser extent. But it seems hard to see how this could be a serious option for a country intent on socialist development. The point has been well put by Nyerere:

> If this kind of capitalist development takes place widely over the country, we may get a good statistical increase in the national wealth of Tanzania, but the masses of the people will not necessarily be better off. On the contrary, as land becomes more scarce we shall find ourselves with a farmers' class and a labourers' class, with the latter being unable either to work for themselves or to receive a full return for the contribution they are making to the total output. They will become a 'rural proletariat' depending

on the decisions of other men for their existence, and subject in consequence to all the subservience, social and economic inequality, and insecurity which such a position involves.[1]

The absurdity of deliberately creating a capitalist class so that at some time in the future its wealth can be expropriated hardly deserves further attention.

The second factor which must be examined in relation to the economic development of African countries is what we might call 'hidden surplus', that is to say, resources which are put to wasteful or unproductive uses. Five main types of hidden surplus can be identified: (1) high consumption levels, particularly of imports, of the national bourgeoisie and labour aristocracy, (2) investment in both the public and private sectors in 'prestige' projects and luxury housing, (3) remittances abroad of expatriates' salaries and pensions, (4) public debt service on foreign loans, (5) net outflow of foreign investment earnings.

Each of these will be dealt with in turn, an attempt being made where possible to arrive at some quantitative assessment of their significance for economic development. By the very nature of the statistics available it is impossible to arrive at exact values. The calculations which follow are estimates only, whose purpose is to establish the rough order of magnitude of the concepts we are dealing with in order to assess their significance. These forms of economic waste appear to be to a greater or lesser extent inseparable from the period of national bourgeois rule which most African countries are experiencing at the moment. Two questions, then, face us. What would be the effect on economic development if these resources were put to effective use? And in what circumstances *could* this misallocation of resources be rectified?

(1) The salary scales which the national bourgeoisie happily took over from its colonial masters have encouraged high consumer demand from this class, especially since the national bourgeoisie, with its bureaucratic rather than entrepreneurial interests, tends to put consumption before saving. This tendency is reinforced by strong social pressures, especially towards consumer durables. The cars outside the senior civil servants' houses get larger and shinier, and the government clerk, taking note, puts down his first payment on a scooter. A significant proportion of this demand for consumer goods is for imports. Table 1 (p. 221) shows the commodity composition of imports of developing Africa in 1960 and 1964. Perhaps the most revealing figures here indicate that these African countries, with economies based largely on agriculture, spend about one-fifth of their import bill on food, drink, and tobacco! And the proportion in 1964 had risen slightly since 1960. Some of this, of course, represents trade between the underdeveloped countries themselves, but this is not the major part. In 1964, for instance, 66 per cent of these imports of food, drink, and tobacco came from developed capitalist countries.[2]

Any attempt to distinguish between 'essential' and 'non-essential' imports must be arbitrary, since the use of the commodity may be as relevant as the type. Light planes can be used for executive joyrides or crop-spraying. In each of the commodity categories in Table 1 some non-essential imports could be found. However, national bourgeois consumption is most significant

Table 1

Commodity Composition of Imports of Developing Africa*

(*Thousands of U.S. dollars*)

	1960	%	1964	%
Food, beverages, & tobacco	1 137 840	17.8	1 441 170	20.2
Basic materials	277 995	4.3	358 500	5.0
Mineral fuels	471 945	7.4	509 070	7.1
Chemicals	465 480	7.3	552 090	7.8
Textiles	678 825	10.6	666 810	9.4
Metals	633 570	9.9	731 340	10.3
Machinery & transport equipment	1 622 715	25.3	1 849 860	26.0
Other manufactures	1 121 630	17.5	1 011 160	14.2
Total Imports	6 410 000		7 120 000	

*Excluding South Africa.

Source: *A Survey of Economic Conditions in Africa*, UN, 1968, p. 143.

in the categories 'food, beverages, and tobacco' and 'other manufactures', with the addition of a considerable expenditure on private road vehicles which would be included under 'machinery and transport equipment'. Ignoring the effects of all bourgeois consumption on the other categories, it is possible to make a very conservative quantitative assessment in these three fields alone to discover whether bourgeois import consumption is large enough to form a significant drain on potential investment resources. We have noted that, in the first category, two-thirds of the imports were from developed capitalist countries: this is equivalent to 13.5 per cent of all imports in 1964, or $961 million. A detailed examination of six countries indicated that passenger cars and spare parts (but not fuel) comprise around five per cent of total imports; while at a conservative estimate one-third of 'other manufactures'–4.5 per cent of total imports in 1964–could be classified as non-essential. These three import categories alone, therefore, would together constitute 23 per cent of total imports, or $1.64 billion in 1964. This sum is nearly equal to all official bilateral and multilateral aid received by developing Africa ($1.72 billion) in the same year.

(2) It is not possible to calculate with any precision the investment resources which are wasted in luxury housing and prestige building projects. Governments are major offenders: airports, universities, conference halls, superhighways are often built on a needlessly lavish scale for use by a minute section of the population. In the private sector, the expansion of the towns and growing demand for offices and living accommodation provide practically risk-free investment opportunities with a high return, particularly attractive to a non-entrepreneurial bourgeoisie. The duplication of resources inherent in capitalist economies accounts for another form of waste: the familiar phenomenon

of the 'one gas-station town' with three gas stations (often selling, in fierce competition, three brands of gasoline from the same refinery). At any rate, building construction forms a high proportion of capital accumulation in African countries, and a subjective view would indicate that a significant proportion of this is waste.

(3) In so far as expatriates employed in Africa set the pattern of bourgeois consumption, their effect on imports is similar to that of the national bourgeoisie. But they are responsible for a further drain in the form of salary remittances and pension payments to their own countries. The few figures that are available indicate that salary remittances are astonishingly large. 'These remittances do not only constitute a drain on foreign exchange earnings of African countries, but substantially reduce the funds available for domestic investment.'[3] How 'substantial' is this drain? The same UN publication from which that quotation is taken gives figures for 14 countries between 1959 and 1962. The 393,435 expatriates living in these countries remitted portions of their incomes varying from 10.7 per cent (Sudan) to 47.4 per cent (Gabon) and totalling $117 million.[4] This sum represented 0.8 per cent of the GDP's of these 14 countries.* Applying the same proportion to developing Africa as a whole would give us an estimate for expatriate remittances of around $0.22 billion for 1961. This does not include pension payments to ex-colonial officers, which many African countries generously maintain.

(4) The rapid increase in Africa's public debt in recent years, mostly through foreign loans, has frequently been commented upon. In seven selected countries between 1955 and 1962, public debt doubled from $0.7 billion to $1.4 billion.[5] But whereas total debt increased by 100 per cent in these countries, debt service rose by nearly 400 per cent, from $37 million to $143 million. The fast increase in debt service was due mainly to amortization (repayment) of loans, which has been rising faster than interest payments, due to the short-term nature of much foreign lending. There is evidence that this trend is continuing. By 1965 total outstanding public debt for developing Africa had reached $5 billion, and in 1964 and 1965 annual debt-service payments amounted to $0.3 billion.

(5) Aggregate outflow of foreign investment income from developing Africa is hard to assess, although, as Arrighi and Saul point out: 'It seems a well-established fact that foreign private investment in less developed economies (far from being an outlet for a domestically created surplus) has been, in the recent past, an efficient device for transferring surplus generated abroad to the advanced capitalist countries.'[6] They quote, for instance, data derived from U.S. Department of Commerce statistics indicating that in the years 1959–64, U.S. direct investments (excluding oil) in Africa amounted to $386 million and investment income to $610 million. Profits are certainly high. 'Since net returns of 15 to 20 per cent on the equity before tax are not abnormal for new investment in developed countries, foreign investors expect to earn more than this on equity investment in developing areas.'[7]

---

*For some countries the proportion was much higher. In Gabon, for instance in 1961 the 5220 expatriates sent home 13 per cent of the country's GDP!

Table 2
Estimates of Resource Wastage in Developing African Countries*

	% of GDP	U.S.$ billions
1) Non-essential imports (1964)	5.22	1.64
2) Local 'prestige' investment	n.a.	n.a.
3) Expatriate salary remittances (1961)	0.8	0.22
4) Public debt service (1964)	0.95	0.3
5) Net outflow of foreign investment earnings (1963)	1.76	0.51
Total	8.73	2.67

*Excludes South Africa. n.a. = not available.

There has been a sharp increase in recent years in the invisible payments section of most African countries' balance of payments, and the largest component of the deficit in the invisibles' account has been interest and dividend payments on foreign private investment.[8] A study of eight countries revealed that net outflow of private investment earnings in 1963 totalled $200 million, which was equivalent to eight per cent of their export earnings.[9] Applying the same proportion to developing African countries as a whole, we can estimate that total net outflow of private investment earnings was approximately 1.76 per cent of GDP in 1963, or $0.51 billion.

Table 2 summarizes our findings. It is again stressed that the figures are rough estimates only, although the figure of 8.73 per cent of GDP is almost certainly an underestimate of total resource wastage, since it excludes any allowance for item 2, and item 1 includes estimates for only three categories of imports. This could then be taken as a minimum estimate.

Table 3
GDP of Developing African Countries 1960–64[a]

	1960	1961	1962	1963	1964
GDP (U.S.$ billions)[b]	27.11	27.64	27.96	29.25	31.39
Capital Formation as % of GDP	16.6	16.3	14.7	15.1	16.0
Consumption as % of GDP	90.0	90.0	89.7	88.5	87.6
Exports as % of GDP	19.9	19.7	20.9	22.1	24.3
Less: Imports as % of GDP	−26.5	−26.1	−25.3	−25.7	−28.0

a Excluding South Africa
b At 1960 constant prices.

Source: *A Survey of Economic Conditions in Africa*, 1968, UN, pp. 22, 28.

How significant are these totals? Table 3 shows the composition of the GDP of developing African countries between 1960 and 1964. The important figures are those for capital formation, which stood at about 16 per cent of GDP during this period.

Economists generally agree that this figure of 16 per cent is much too low, and that one condition for even a moderate growth rate must be for capital formation to be increased to at least 25 per cent of GDP. What now becomes obvious is that these economies are perfectly capable of raising their capital formation to at least this level by employing some of the 'hidden' surplus which is at present being unproductively used. The 8.7 per cent of GDP which has been calculated as a minimum estimate would alone be sufficient to do this. There is, in fact, a way off the economic treadmill, without the intervention of massive foreign charity or some other *deus ex machina*.

NOTES

[1] J.K. Nyerere, 'Socialism and rural development', in *Ujamaa–essays on socialism,* Oxford University Press, 1968, p. 168.

[2] *A survey of economic conditions in Africa,* 1968, UN, p. 143.

[3] *Ibid.,* p. 156.

[4] *Ibid.,* pp. 161–2.

[5] Kenya, Uganda, Tanzania, Ethiopia, Rhodesia and Nyasaland, Nigeria, Sudan. These and subsequent figures are from *Economic Bulletin for Africa,* **6,** 2, UN.

[6] Arrighi and Saul, 'Socialism and economic development', *The Journal of Modern African Studies,* Vol. 6, no. 2, 1968, p. 149.

[7] *Economic Bulletin for Africa,* **7,** 1 & 2, pp. 15–16, UN.

[8] *Economic Bulletin for Africa,* **6,** 2, p. 12, UN.

[9] *Ibid.,* p. 30. The countries were Ethiopia, Ghana, Morocco, Nigeria, Rhodesia and Nyasaland, Somalia, Sudan, Tunisia.

PART V
Social Structure: The Process of Class Formation

... you will understand that... analysis has no value unless it is related to the actual struggle. In outline, the methodological approach we have used has been as follows: first, the position of each group must be defined–to what extent and in what way does each group depend on the colonial régime? Next we have to see what position they adopt towards the national liberation struggle. Then we have to study their nationalist capacity and lastly, envisaging the post-independence period, their revolutionary capacity.

Brief analysis of the social structure of Guinea-Bissau

AMILCAR CABRAL

From Amilcar Cabral, *Revolution in Guinea*, Stage 1, London 1969. *Condensed text of a seminar held in the Frantz Fanon Centre in Treviglio, Milan, from 1 to 3 May 1964.*

I should like to tell you something about the situation in our country, 'Portuguese' Guinea, beginning with an analysis of the social situation, which has served as the basis for our struggle for national liberation. I shall make a distinction between the rural areas and the towns, or rather the urban centres, not that these are to be considered mutually opposed.

In the rural areas we have found it necessary to distinguish between two distinct groups: on the one hand, the group which we consider semi-feudal, represented by the Fulas, and, on the other hand, the group which we consider, so to speak, without any defined form of state organization, represented by the Balantes. There are a number of intermediary positions between these two extreme ethnic groups (as regards the social situation). I should like to point out straight away that although in general the semi-feudal groups were Muslim and the groups without any form of state organization were animist, there was one ethnic group among the animists, the Mandjacks, which had forms of social relations which could be considered feudal at the time when the Portuguese came to Guinea.

I should now like to give you a quick idea of the social stratification among the Fulas. We consider that the chiefs, the nobles and the religious figures form one group; after them come the artisans and the Dyulas, who are itinerant traders, and then after that come the peasants properly speaking. I don't want to give a very thorough analysis of the economic situation of each of these groups now, but I would like to say that although certain traditions concerning collective ownership of the land have been preserved, the chiefs and their entourages have retained considerable privileges as regards ownership of land and the utilization of other people's labour; this means that the peasants who depend on the chiefs are obliged to work for these chiefs for a certain period of each year. The artisans, whether blacksmiths (which is the lowest occupation) or leather-workers or whatever, play an extremely important role in the socio-economic life of the Fulas and represent what you might call the embryo of industry. The Dyulas, whom some people consider should be placed above the artisans, do not really have such importance among the Fulas; they are the people who have the potential–which they sometimes realize–of accumulating money. In general the peasants have no rights and they are the really exploited group in Fula society.

Apart from the question of ownership and property, there is another element which it is extremely interesting to compare and that is the position of women. Among the Fulas women have no rights; they take part in production but they do not own what they produce. Besides, polygamy is a highly respected institution and women are to a certain extent considered the property of their husbands.

Among the Balantes, which are at the opposite extreme, we find a society without any social stratification: there is just a council of elders in each village or group of villages who decide on the day-to-day problems. In the Balante group property and land are considered to belong to the village but each family receives the amount of land needed to ensure subsistence for itself, and the means of production, or rather the instruments of production, are not collective but are owned by families or individuals.

The position of women must also be mentioned when talking about the Balantes. The Balantes still retain certain tendencies towards polygamy, although it is mainly a monogamous society. Among the Balantes women participate in production but they own what they produce and this gives Balante women a position which we consider privileged, as they are fairly free; the only point on which they are not free is that children belong to the head of the family and the head of the family, the husband, always claims any children his wife may have: this is obviously to be explained by the actual economy of the group where a family's strength is ultimately represented by the number of hands there are to cultivate the land.

As I have said, there are a number of intermediate positions between these two extremes. In the rural areas I should mention the small African farm owners; this is a numerically small group but all the same it has a certain importance and has proved to be highly active in the national liberation struggle. In the towns (I shall not talk about the presence of Europeans in the rural areas as there are none in Guinea) we must first distinguish between the Europeans and the Africans. The Europeans can easily be classified as they retain in Guinea the social stratification of Portugal (obviously depending on the function they exercise in Guinea). In the first place, there are the high officials and the managers of enterprises who form a stratum with practically no contact with the other European strata. After that there are the medium officials, the small European traders, the people employed in commerce and the members of the liberal professions. After that come the workers, who are mainly skilled workers.

Among the Africans we find the higher officials, the middle officials and the members of the liberal professions forming a group; then come the petty officials, those employed in commerce with a contract, who are to be distinguished from those employed in commerce without a contract, who can be fired at any moment. The small farm owners also fall into this group; by assimilation we call all these members of the African petty bourgeoisie (obviously, if we were to make a more thorough analysis the higher African officials as well as the middle officials and the members of the liberal profes-

sions should also be included in the petty bourgeoisie). Next come the wage
earners (whom we define as those employed in commerce without any contract); among these there are certain important sub-groups such as the dock-
workers, the people employed on the boats carrying goods and agricultural
produce; there are also the domestic servants, who are mostly men in Guinea;
there are the people working in repair shops and small factories and there
are also the people who work in shops as porters and suchlike–these all come
under the heading of wage earners. You will notice that we are careful not to
call these groups the proletariat or working class.

There is another group of people whom we call the *déclassés*, in which
there are two sub-groups to be distinguished: the first sub-group is easy to
identify; it is what would be called the lumpenproletariat if there was a real
proletariat: it consists of really *déclassé* people, such as beggars, prostitutes,
and so on. The other group is not really made up of *déclassé* people, but we
have not yet found the exact term for it; it is a group to which we have paid a
lot of attention and it has proved to be extremely important in the national
liberation struggle. It is mostly made up of young people who are connected
to petty bourgeois or workers' families, who have recently arrived from the
rural areas and generally do not work; they thus have close relations with
the rural areas, as well as with the towns (and even with the Europeans).
They sometimes live off one kind of work or another, but they generally live
at the expense of their families. Here I should just like to point out a difference
between Europe and Africa; in Africa there is a tradition which requires
that, for example, if I have an uncle living in the town, I can come in and live
in his house without working and he will feed me and house me. This creates
a certain stratum of people who experience urban life and who can, as we
shall see, play a very important role.

That is a very brief analysis of the general situation in Guinea, but you
will understand that this analysis has no value unless it is related to the actual
struggle. In outline, the methodological approach we have used has been as
follows: first, the position of each group must be defined–to what extent and
in what way does each group depend on the colonial régime? Next we have
to see what position they adopt towards the national liberation struggle.
Then we have to study their nationalist capacity and lastly, envisaging the
post-independence period, their revolutionary capacity.

Among the Fulas the first group–the chiefs and their entourages–are tied
to colonialism; this is particularly the case with the Fulas as in Guinea the
Fulas were already conquerors (the Portuguese allied themselves with the
Fulas in order to dominate Guinea at the beginning of the conquest). Thus
the chiefs (and their authority as chiefs) are very closely tied to the Portuguese
authorities. The artisans are extremely dependent on the chiefs; they live off
what they make for the chiefs who are the only ones that can acquire their
products, so there are some artisans who are simply content to follow the
chiefs; then there are other people who try to break away and are well-disposed
towards opposition to Portuguese colonialism. The main point about the
Dyulas is that their permanent pre-occupation is to protect their own personal
interests; at least in Guinea, the Dyulas are not settled in any one place, they
are itinerant traders without any real roots anywhere and their fundamental

aim is to make bigger and bigger profits. It is precisely the fact that they are almost permanently on the move which provided us with a most valuable element in the struggle. It goes without saying that there are some who have not supported our struggle and there are some who have been used as agents against us by the Portuguese, but there are some whom we have been able to use to mobilize people, at least as far as spreading the initial ideas of the struggle was concerned–all we had to do was give them some reward, as they usually would not do anything without being paid.

Obviously, the group with the greatest interest in the struggle is the peasantry, given the nature of the various different societies in Guinea (feudal, semi-feudal, etc.) and the various degrees of exploitation to which they are subjected; but the question is not simply one of objective interest.

Given the general context of our traditions, or rather the superstructure created by the economic conditions in Guinea, the Fula peasants have a strong tendency to follow their chiefs. Thorough and intensive work was therefore needed to mobilize them. Among the Balantes and the groups without any defined form of state organization the first point to note is that there are still a lot of remnants of animist traditions even among the Muslims in Guinea; the part of the population which follows Islam is not really Islamic but rather Islamized: they are animists who have adopted some Muslim practices, but are still thoroughly impregnated with animist conceptions. What is more, these groups without any defined organization put up much more resistance against the Portuguese than the others and they have maintained intact their tradition of resistance to colonial penetration. This is the group that we found most ready to accept the idea of national liberation.

Here I should like to broach one key problem, which is of enormous importance for us, as we are a country of peasants, and that is the problem of whether or not the peasantry represents the main revolutionary force. I shall confine myself to my own country, Guinea, where it must be said at once that the peasantry is not a revolutionary force–which may seem strange, particularly as we have based the whole of our armed liberation struggle on the peasantry. A distinction must be drawn between a physical force and a revolutionary force; physically, the peasantry is a great force in Guinea: it is almost the whole of the population, it controls the nation's wealth, it is the peasantry which produces; but we know from experience what trouble we had convincing the peasantry to fight. This is a problem I shall come back to later; here I should just like to refer to what the previous speaker said about China. The conditions of the peasantry in China were very different: the peasantry had a history of revolt, but this was not the case in Guinea, and so it was not possible for our party militants and propaganda workers to find the same kind of welcome among the peasantry in Guinea for the idea of national liberation as the idea found in China. All the same, in certain parts of the country and among certain groups we found a very warm welcome, even right at the start. In other groups and in other areas all this had to be won.

Then there are the positions *vis-à-vis* the struggle of the various groups in the towns to be considered. The Europeans are, in general, hostile to the idea of national liberation; they are the human instruments of the colonial state in our country and they therefore reject *a priori* any idea of national liberation there. It has to be said that the Europeans most bitterly opposed to the idea of national liberation are the workers, while we have sometimes found considerable sympathy for our struggle among certain members of the European petty bourgeoisie.

As for the Africans, the petty bourgeoisie can be divided into three sub-groups as regards the national liberation struggle. First, there is the petty bourgeoisie which is heavily committed, and compromised with colonialism: this includes most of the higher officials and some members of the liberal professions. Second, there is the group which we perhaps incorrectly call the revolutionary petty bourgeoisie: this is the part of the petty bourgeoisie which is nationalist and which was the source of the idea of the national liberation struggle in Guinea. In between lies the part of the petty bourgeoisie which has never been able to make up its mind between the national liberation struggle and the Portuguese. Next come the wage earners, which you can compare roughly with the proletariat in European societies, although they are not exactly the same thing: here, too, there is a majority committed to the struggle but, again, many members of this group were not easy to mobi-lize–wage earners who had an extremely petty bourgeois mentality and whose only aim was to defend the little they had already acquired.

Next come the *déclassés*. The really *déclassé* people, the permanent lay-abouts, the prostitutes, and so on have been a great help to the Portuguese police in giving them information; this group has been outrightly against our struggle, perhaps unconsciously so, but nonetheless against our struggle. On the other hand, the particular group I mentioned earlier, for which we have not yet found any precise classification (the group of mainly young people recently arrived from the rural areas with contacts in both the urban and the rural areas) gradually comes to make a comparison between the standard of living of their own families and that of the Portuguese; they begin to understand the sacrifices being borne by the Africans. They have proved extremely dynamic in the struggle. Many of these people joined the struggle right from the beginning and it is among this group that we found many of the cadres whom we have since trained.

The importance of this urban experience lies in the fact that it allows comparison: this is the key stimulant required for the awakening of conscious-ness. It is interesting to note that *Algerian nationalism largely sprang up among the émigré workers in France*. As far as Guinea is concerned, the idea of the national liberation struggle was born not abroad but in our own country, in a milieu where people were subjected to close and incessant exploitation. Many people say that it is the peasants who carry the burden of exploitation: this may be true, but so far as the struggle is concerned it must be realized that it is not the degree of suffering and hardship involved as such that matters: even extreme suffering in itself does not necessarily produce the *prise de conscience* required for the national liberation struggle. In Guinea the peasants are subjected to a kind of exploitation equivalent to slavery; but even if you try and explain to them that they are being exploited and robbed, it is difficult to convince them by means of an unexperienced explanation of a technico-economic kind that they are the most exploited people; whereas it is easier to convince the workers and the people employed in the towns who earn, say, ten escudos a day for a job in which a European earns between 30 and 50 that they are being subjected to massive exploitation and injustice, because they can see. To take my own case as a member of the petty bourgeois group which launched the struggle in Guinea, I was an agronomist working under a European who everybody knew was one of the biggest idiots in Guinea; I could have taught him his job with my eyes shut but he was the boss: this is something which counts a lot, this is the confrontation which really matters. This is of major importance when considering where the initial idea of the struggle came from.

Another major task was to examine the material interests and the aspirations of each group after the liberation, as well as their revolutionary capacities. As I have already said, we do not consider that the peasantry in Guinea has a revolutionary capacity. First of all we had to make an analysis of all these groups and of the contradictions between them and within them so as to be able to locate them all *vis-à-vis* the struggle and the revolution.

The first point is to decide what is the major contradiction at the moment when the struggle begins. For us the main contradiction was that between, on the one hand, the Portuguese and international bourgeoisie which was exploiting our people and on the other hand, the interests of our people. There are also major contradictions within the country itself, *i.e.* in the internal life of our country. It is our opinion that if we get rid of colonialism in Guinea the main contradiction remaining, the one which will then become the principal contradiction, is that between the ruling classes, the semi-feudal groups, and the members of the groups without any defined form of organization. The first thing to note is that the conquest carried out first by the Mandingues and then by the Fulas was a struggle between two opposite poles which was blocked by the very strong structure of the animist groups. There are other contradictions, such as that between the various feudal groups and that between the upper group and the lower. All this is extremely important for the future, and even while the struggle is still going on we must begin to exploit the contradiction between the Fula people and their chiefs, who are very close to the Portuguese. There is a further contradiction, particularly among the animists, between the collective ownership of the land and the private ownership of the means of production in agriculture. I am not trying to stretch alien concepts here, this is an observation that can be made on the spot: the land belongs to the village, but what is produced belongs to whoever produces it—usually the family or the head of the family.

There are other contradictions which we consider secondary: you may be surprised to know that we consider the contradictions between the tribes a secondary one; we could discuss this at length, but we consider that there are many more contradictions between what you might call the economic tribes in the capitalist countries than there are between the ethnic tribes in Guinea. Our struggle for national liberation and the work done by our Party have shown that this contradiction is really not so important; the Portuguese counted on it a lot but as soon as we organized the liberation struggle properly the contradiction between the tribes proved to be a feeble, secondary contradiction. This does not mean that we do not need to pay attention to this contradiction; we reject both the positions which are to be found in

Africa–one which says: there are no tribes, we are all the same, we are all one people in one terrible unity, our party comprises everybody; the other saying: tribes exist, we must base parties on tribes. Our position lies between the two, but at the same time we are fully conscious that this is a problem which must constantly be kept in mind; structural, organizational and other measures must be taken to ensure that this contradiction does not explode and become a more important contradiction.

As for contradictions between the urban and rural areas; I would say that there is no conflict between the towns and the countryside, not least because we are only town dwellers who have just moved from the country; everybody in the towns in Guinea has close relatives in the country and all town dwellers still engage in some peasant activity (growing crops etc.); all the same, there is a potential contradiction between the towns and the countryside which colonialism tries to aggravate.

The rise and decline of the Kenya peasant, 1888–1922

E.S. ATIENO-ODHIAMBO

From *East Africa Journal*, **9,** 5, Nairobi (May 1972).

Introduction

In an earlier paper, the present writer has argued that there is the need, in current studies of Kenya's colonial period, to move over from the study of Thuku and Owen into the study of African peasants. This plea was thrown back at me when the editors of the *East Africa Journal* invited me to provide a paper on the history of the peasants. The demand was to formulate the dimensions along which peasant studies could be done. The outcome is this attempt. As a prolegomenal study we shall concern ourselves first with the definition of peasantry, and then attempt a rigorous correlation between categorizations and the early history of colonial Kenya. We are simply spelling out a framework along which more study must be done.

Who is a peasant? In our context, our interest lies in identifying and explaining the patterns of change and development in early Kenya, and we are therefore concerned to use the term peasant as an effective concept within an analytical framework that usefully structures such an explanation. Our basic criterion for differentiating the peasants from other people is primarily economic. The amplifications of it are twofold. Firstly, our concern with the structural position of the peasantry suggests that it must be seen as being a certain stratum within a wider political and economic system. Secondly, our dimension centres on the importance to the peasant of the family economy. Along these lines we define peasants as 'those whose ultimate security and subsistence lies in their having certain rights in land and in the labour of family members on the land, but who are involved, through rights and obligations, in a wider economic system which includes the participation of non-peasants'.[1] The fact that for peasants ultimate security rests upon maintaining rights in land and rights in family labour will be seen to be an important determinant shaping and restricting their social productive equilibrium. The distinction between them and the settler capitalist farmer in this respect is that, whereas the capitalist farmer might have appeared to depend upon his land and even the family labour in some cases, he was not ultimately forced to rely solely upon these in the last instance; for he had the alternative potential and dynamic sources of governmental security and investment. What the peasant shared with them was the fact of their integration into a complex social structure characterized by racial stratification and economic differentiation. In fact it is precisely the characterization of the peasantry in terms of its position relative to other groups in the wider social system which is of particularly important explanatory value in our analysis.

Let us start with a statement of a few postulates. The creation of an African peasantry was primarily the result of the interaction between an international capitalist settler economic system and the traditional socio-economic systems within the context of the territorially defined colonial political system. A further postulate is that the logic of capitalist exploitation upset the rural economic equilibrium and therefore created both the rural and urban proletariats. Next, a few generalizations: The colonial situation everywhere exposed the local populations to new goods and services and subjected the natives to specific government-imposed economic and labour demands with the result that new needs were generated which could only be met by participation in the cash-based market economy. The two ways open for participation were sale of labour and sale of agricultural produce. These were in turn determined by such variables as the presence of centres of labour demand such as settler farms and international capitalist plantations; the presence or otherwise of a suitable local environment for the production of agricultural crops for sale combined with the degree of availability of marketing opportunities; the presence of an immigrant Indian *dukawallah* group and Indian wholesale and retail merchants; and the presence of an immigrant settler group of capitalist farmers who were market competitors with African producers.

These variables in turn operated upon a pre-colonial Kenya that was itself characterized by a large number of ethnic groups with varying styles of political and economic organization, subsisting in varying environmental potentials both pastoral and agricultural. The study of environmental potential is itself a critical factor, for it helps to define both the character of agro-economic systems as well as the subsequent responses. For the extent to which labour-exporting peasantries developed was both a function of the labour demand–economic need dimension and also a consequence, in instances, of the degree to which adult men were under-employed in the traditional agricultural system and hence the extent to which they could be absent without threatening the security of minimal subsistence production. The Kamba long-distance traders are a relevant example here. The numbers absent at a given cultivation period trekking to the coast must have been crucial in terms of the maintenance of the subsistence equilibrium. The fact also that Masai men were crucial in the herding and fighting economy was a regulatory factor as to how many men could be away at other jobs at any given time. Similarly, the extent to which a peasantry could respond to cash cropping also depended on the adaptability of the traditional agricultural system to the incorporation of new crops or the expanded production of established crops without threatening the security of minimal subsistence production. A case in point here is the failure of cotton to catch on in Nyanza in the same way as it did in Buganda and Eastern Uganda in the first two decades of this century. Cultivation in Luoland had been essentially a woman's job, and given the fact that large numbers of men were at other jobs in the settler plantations, there was simply not enough labour forthcoming from the womenfolk to cultivate both for subsistence and for cash surpluses.

It must be stated at the outset, however, that one is not thinking of the peasants, in the early decades of this century, as a class. Their objective situation is reminiscent of that other group of peasants that Marx studied in the mid-nineteenth century, the peasants of France.[2] The peasants of Kenya, like their earlier French counterparts, were a vast mass, the members of which lived in similar conditions but without entering into manifold relations with one another. There was no *empathy* (the word is Ali Mazrui's) between one peasant in Mumias and another in Wundanyi, because they just did not know of their commonality of interest (and perhaps did not even know of the existence of one another). Their mode of production isolated them from one another instead of bringing them into mutual intercourse. The isolation was increased by lack of communication and the self-sufficiency of each peasant community. At the fundamental level, there was no peasantry as a class in pre-colonial Kenya precisely because they did not live, in the traditional set-up, under economic conditions that separated their mode of life, their interests and their culture from those of other classes (since there were no other classes). Horizontally they merely had local interconnections that did not necessarily demand large-scale political organization among them. The peasantry as an analytical category was a creation of colonialism. In the early decades of this century, moreover, the peasantry did not articulate itself as a class. But it did manifest itself as a general pattern of social life, typified by ethnic living.[3] Fanon insists that even during the colonial period, the native peasantry lived against a background of tradition, for the traditional structure of society alone remained intact. The peasant who stays put defends his tradition stubbornly, and in a colonized society stands for the disciplined element whose interests lie in maintaining the social structure.[4] Arrighi's formulation from his studies of Zimbabwe (Rhodesia) supports Fanon's thesis, and both are applicable to Kenya. Arrighi contends that the peasant society is alone stable for the native in the colonial period by arguing that since the native was paid the wages of a 'boy' rather than a family man in Zimbabwe before the Second World War, and since employment was very unstable, the peasant who went to work in town always maintained the closest of links with his home community through a flow of goods, of cash, or of occasional labour. The real cost of the means for the subsistence of the migrant workers' families were borne by the peasantry even as the individual slaved away in the settlers' farms and mines.[5]

The rise of the peasant

The peasant as a social category, we have postulated, is a product of the colonial situation. The peasant in Kenya arose at the same time as the African proletariat emerged. In historical terms the creation of the peasantry is synonymous with the transition from a cultivating and herding non-capitalist economy to a colonial racial capitalist economic system. How did this come about? It came about because the consequence of colonial penetration was to throw the ethnic economies into disequilibrium. The submission here is that nineteenth century African societies in Kenya observed certain self-sufficiencies in their economic pattern that were a cause and a consequence of the internal economic stabilities. Three variables were responsible for this. The first was simply the abundant availability of land. All over the country there was enough land to go round and satisfy the needs of the society–and here there is no distinction being made about the *nature* of the ownership of land: freehold, leasehold, communal, or individual. Even the fringe elements in the community–the Kikuyu *ahoi*–had enough land to cultivate. Shortage of land in a particular area simply meant that the ethnic frontier moved on, peacefully or otherwise. There was, and this is the second variable, enough labour to cultivate, to fight, and to wage a war. Thirdly, there was plenty of game to supplement the diet; the diaries of hunters and early administrators towards the end of last century and at the beginning of this century affirm this categorically. Admittedly there were the usual vagaries of climate; but this was compensated for by the clearly understood communal responsibilities. And given the fact that societies were well fed, and that the populations increased, the devastating effects of inter-ethnic wars (so resonant in imperialist literature) must have on the whole not had a permanently crippling effect on all societies. If anything, famine was always a more lethal enemy. There was trade in agricultural surpluses up and down the country–in grain and potato vines, between the Kikuyu and Kamba, the Samia and Iteso for example. Non-cultivable resources–like iron, ivory, snake poison–served to boost this marketing of surpluses. Up and down the country, productivity was in evidence. By the 1890s Kikuyuland was regarded as one continuous cultivable garden. *Mahindi* (maize), bananas, mangoes, plus mutton, chicken, and guineafowl were abundant in Meru when the area was first colonized.[6] Mrs Whitehouse, accompanying her husband in a survey of the railway in 1898, saw evidence of the bounteousness of food all over the lakeshore in Western Kenya. At Port Victoria her party revelled in quantities of fresh milk. In Kadimo Bay the natives brought them eggs, flour, bananas, and sheep for sale. On the islands of Mfangano and Rusinga they saw *shambas* all around. In 'Cutch' (Nyakach) on the south-east corner of the Nyanza Gulf they saw huge fishing baskets. Plenty of flour and sheep were available in Kisumu, while Kitoto's village a few miles to the east was a major food supply centre for these railway-building caravans. Up in the Nanyuki area and all the way down to Nairobi the Somalis were conducting a booming trade with the early footloose Europeans, the former selling surplus cattle from the north-eastern part of the country to these people.[7] In the first two decades many settler herds were built up of these Somali cattle–most notably by Berkeley Cole and General Wheatley in the Nanyuki area.[8] The above examples serve to illustrate that there was abundant food to go round and even to be spared for surplus marketing. It must be emphasized that it was these surplus foodstuffs that fed the initial porter caravans of the invaders–and Kikuyuland, Ukambani, the Kitosh area, the Nyando Valley, and Wanga were important centres in this respect. Further, in their day-to-day marketing operations the natives clearly had control as to the disposal of their produce. In their day-to-day economic dealings with one another market considerations determined the patterns of resource disposal. The colonial presence was to deny the natives this control of the disposal of their produce and also of their labour.

The initial British entry into Kenya was by way of the Imperial British East Africa Company. The Company intended to build up a chain of forts along a route running from Mombasa to Uganda. From 1888–the year of its Charter–forts were built at Machakos, Fort Smith, Eldama Ravine, and at Mumias. The structuring of these forts offered new marketing opportunities for the natives of the surrounding areas. They willingly brought in their produce and exchanged for them some of the station goods such as beads and *Amerikani* cloth. This state of willing response to new opportunities was however but the first stage of colonial penetration. It was a time when names like Kinyanjui, Mumia, Kitoto, and Odera Ulalo were important, because they were volunteer collaborators. But the second stage was more important for the masses of peasants in Kenya. This came with the assumption of direct responsibility for the governance of the East Africa Protectorate and sub- sequently of Kenya by the British administration. This stage, which was to last until independence and beyond, saw the creation of the peasantry and the alteration of the relationship between them and the invaders. From a time of voluntary response to new opportunities, the peasants found their relationship with the new presences altered to being that of a subordinate relationship to the dominant imperialist aggressors. The salient point to be made here is that as regards their economy, the peasants suffered increasing loss of control of the disposal of their own produce to the Europeans and Indians. Non-market political and racial considerations were to determine the patterns of the cultivators' response with consequences that were to disturb the equilibrium recognizably. The single most critical factor in this alteration of relationships was the decision by the colonial government to invite white settlers into the highlands of Kenya. But the settler was also boosted by the increasing numbers of Europeans who entered the country as government officials, mining prospectors, and concessionaire speculators. A fundamental consequence of this invasion was that widespread migratory movements by the Africans were brought to a halt. The officials laid down that the natives were to stay put wherever their rulers found them; these areas were henceforth to be regarded as their tribal lands. Immediate conse- quences followed from this alone. Some people, like the Kikuyu *ahoi*, for the first time were faced with the fact of real landlessness. More importantly, those who remained on the tribal lands had to work on it over and over again. The result was the severe soil erosion that faced the country from the 1930s onwards. Ukambani and Kamasia were to be at the centre of this controversy. Yet it is true that prior to the onset of colonialism there was a steady balance of nature in Ukambani, and *no* soil erosion, which was clearly a result of the pegging down of their populations, the seizure of Kamba lands in the Donyo Sabuk area, and the lack of social attention by the colonizing authorities to these problems which their invasion saddled the Kamba with.

As Watt put it:

In the Kamba reserve in the nineties (1890s) the areas cultivated were small, and much of the wood cut down by the Akamba was replaced by natural growth in a few years. When taxation of the Africans started, their areas of cultivation were greatly expanded to raise money for to pay taxes. No care was exercised to prevent erosion in heavy rains by the natives or the Agricultural Department.[9]

Thus the reserves were saddled with a rural proletariat who could not live off the land. This same group of people moved into towns to look for employment. In spite of the yearning for labour by the settlers, salaries were low and the conditions for work insecure. In time the urban proletariat emerged. By 1902 this class was already manifesting itself in Nairobi as prostitutes, spivs, thieves, and idlers. At the same time in the first two decades of the century the white man supported by the colonial government was recruiting more and more labour for his farms and his 'pacification' wars from the reserves, at the same time raising food to feed these uprooted peoples partly from the reserves. The consequences were that the countryside was gradually penetrated and commercialized. To begin with, the natives did not want to go and work for the white man; the shortage of labour was a sure indication of both the virility of traditional subsistence cultivation and pastoralism and the success of native adaptation to the free-market conditions of the Company period. The white man therefore sought to alter these satisfactory conditions. To begin with much more labour was squeezed from the reserves–especially in Luoland, Luhyaland, and Kikuyuland–than was compatible with the continuity of the peasant equilibrum. And once taken away the men were paid unmanly wages. The young ADC in Kakamega, Storrs-Fox[10] got it right when he wrote back to his mother in 1920:

> The European settlers as a class are out to exploit the nigger. They try to drive him out of his reserve (where he certainly doesn't do very much work but cultivates his own bit of ground and lives quite happily) by the Hut Tax. Thus he is quite gently persuaded to go out and work for a white settler who pays him the princely sum of 5–7 rupees p.m. and as often as not takes no pains to look after his housing and comfort and treats him pretty harshly... It is the old capital and labour stunt, but labour can't stick up for itself here.

The consequence was the village–city nexus earlier observed. The consequence was also to make the whole system of peasant cultivation volatile and inchoate. Furthermore, the settlers knew that their number one rival as producers would be the African cultivator. Consequently the peasant, now clearly emergent because of his relation with the urban worker and the white settler aristocracy, was denied unlimited access to capital, credit, fixity of tenure, and to labour, factors that might have entrenched him as a genuine competitor. This stage might then be summarized as the stage of white capitalist demoralization of the Kenya peasant.

The decline of the peasant

The above stage can be regarded as having been reached by 1922. By this date all the legislation necessary for its retrenchment had been passed. Once attained it became a process that had a tendency to perpetuate itself. And it led to what may be called the emergence of peasant inferiority in relation to the urban worker, the emergent school teacher, the Indian and, more importantly, to the settler. In a word, this peasant inferiority can be summarized in the statement that the peasant became a poor man and consequently a ready source for the proletarization of the towns. This came about through a series of related processes. Most fundamental was the disequilibrium between land and population, brought about by the bringing to a halt of otherwise expanding boundaries, and by the settler acquisition of land. There was, secondly, the change from discretionary to necessary purchases: clothes and blankets for example. The white European community in Nairobi in particular, but also elsewhere, insisted on seeing the native wearing a piece of cloth or blanket, rather than nude. (It was said that Nilotic disingenuity was exhibited on one occasion by Luos wearing blankets wrapped around their heads, but otherwise naked as usual.) Next there were new expenses to be gone into like fees for the education of children. There were, furthermore, hut and poll taxes to think about. For those who had to, and quite a number moved around to resettle in the sparsely populated sections of the reserve, there were the costs of migration and settlement to be taken care of: fares to pay, nails to buy and, increasingly, wood and grass for thatch to pay for as well. The new marketing conditions also tended to work against the peasant producer. The Indian *dukawallah* and the white trading groups like the Boma Trading Company[11] in Nyanza conducted a monopolistic business in the reserves, being at one and the same time purchasers of local goods, guarantors of credit to any aspiring natives, forwarders of manufactured goods and the determinators of prices. Then there were the sins of omission by the colonial rulers of the peasants. There was in the reserves a gross lack of welfare facilities–lack of dispensaries, schools, water. Compared with the townships–in spite of their slumps–the welfare aspect of the reserves was even more wanting. Marx's 'idiocy of rural life' made a lot of sense. The government itself compounded this idiocy by its circumvention of native areas. The roads and the railways were built to provide an infra-structure for the European settlers. The peasants were relegated to the back-waters in the economic structure of the colonial authorities. All these, plus the depopulation of the reserves through guided migrant labour, the limitation of the market opportunities and the poor salaries paid to these migrant labourers totalled up to a state of constant poverty of the peasants.

Conclusion

By the third decade of this century, therefore, the phenomenon of the poor African had asserted itself. The reserves were by and large synonymous with poverty. The days had changed from the 1890s. The money that was circulating from the towns to the reserves was being used for subsistence functions. Ainsworth[12] estimated that there must have been three million shillings circulating in Nyanza alone by 1912. This amount was to increase. But the assets of the countryside hardly improved recognizably. The logic of the situation was obvious: the Kenya peasantry itself had become dependent on the subsidies from the migrant labour. In the onslaught of colonialism in Kenya were to be found the origins of the present day 'idiocy of rural life', the plaguing poverty of the Africans in their reserves.

NOTES

[1] John Saul and Roger Woods, 'African peasantries' in Teodor Shanin (ed), *Peasants and peasant societies*, p. 105, Penguin Books, 1971.

[2] Karl Marx,' 'The 18th Brumaire of Louis Bonaparte' in Karl Marx and Frederick Engels, *Selected works*, Lawrence and Wishart, pp. 170–5, London, 1968, in one volume.

[3] Teodor Shanin, 'The peasantry as a political factor' in *Sociological Review*, **14**, 1, pp. 5–27, (1966).

[4] Frantz Fanon, *The wretched of the earth*, pp. 88–9. Penguin Books, 1967.

[5] Giovanni Arrighi, *The political economy of Rhodesia*, Mouton, The Hague, 1967, pp. 19–35.

[6] Mrs Platts: *Papers*, Rhodes House, Oxford.

[7] Mrs Whitehouse: *Papers*, Rhodes House, Oxford.

[8] Major-General P. Wheatley: *Papers*, Rhodes House, Oxford.

[9] J. Stuart Watt: *Papers*, Rhodes House, Oxford.

[10] Storrs-Fox: *Papers*, Rhodes House, Oxford.

[11] *Coryndon Papers*, Rhodes House, Oxford.

[12] *Ainsworth Papers*, Rhodes House, Oxford.

Peasantization in Western Africa
KEN POST

From Ken Post, '"Peasantization" and rural political movements in Western Africa', *European Journal of Sociology*, **XIII,** 2, 223–24, Paris, 1972. Reprinted by permission.

My treatment will be concerned with two models, and more especially with the delineation of two processes. The first model is one of a mode of production made up of what, for want of a better term, may be called 'communal cultivators'. The second represents a mode based upon peasant farmers. The parallel parts of these models are set out below. It must be emphasized that, like all their kind, they are abstractions and simplifications, particularly unlikely to exist in their pure form in Western Africa. The two processes with which we will be concerned are closely related to them, since one is the process of change from communal cultivator to peasant and the other the process of the incorporation of communal and peasant societies into the world capitalist network. It must be stressed that both these processes have been occurring simultaneously in Africa in the last hundred years.

Communal cultivator	Peasant
(*a*) Communal land ownership: group or individual land use.	(*a*) Individual land ownership; group or individual land use.
(*b*) Social division of labour largely based on kinship.	(*b*) Separation between social division of labour and kinship.
(*c*) Markets absent or peripheral.	(*c*) Market principle in operation.
(*d*) Political hierarchy and obligations largely conterminous with kinship.	(*d*) Separation between political hierarchy and obligations and kinship.
(*e*) Largely homogeneous culture.	(*e*) Distinction between 'great' and 'little' cultures.

In discussing the differences between these two, we may concentrate upon three sets of relationships, between the producer and the land, the producer and the market, and the producer and the state. In terms of the first, there can be little doubt that the subject of land tenure and usufruct is one of the most difficult with which the student of Africa must grapple, and all I am able to do at this point is to offer little better than a series of random remarks. Marx and Engels and their successors have all put emphasis upon the question of ownership; Fitchin, for example, makes the following contrast:

Whereas in many tribal societies, particularly unilateral societies, ascribed membership in a permanent, indestructible kinship group determines the property rights and social relationships of the individual, in European peasant societies, property rights in land and other goods are the basis of formation of social groups, and inter-personal relationships are contractual and often temporary.[1]

This representation of 'tribal' societies is acceptable, and expressed in the above designation of 'communal land ownership'. In peasant societies there are two important forms of land ownership, either by the peasant himself or by a landlord from whom the peasant rents or sharecrops land (or upon whose land he squats without payment and consequently with no guarantee of tenure). The distinction between these forms is sufficiently important for them to constitute separate sub-types of peasant society.[2]

The African situation in these terms is a complex one. In both the precolonial and colonial periods it would seem that, from the point of view of the individual, land use rights must be treated as more important than property rights. The important point about the individual in pre-peasant societies is that his ownership is mediated through the communal group; what then becomes important is whether or not the products of his use of the land (i.e., of his labour power) become his private property. Writing to Vera Zasulitch in March 1881, Marx noted that in the case of contemporary Russia,

property in land is communal, but each peasant cultivates and manages his plot on his own account, in a way recalling the small peasant of the West. Common ownership, divided petty cultivation: this combination which was useful in remoter periods, becomes dangerous in ours.[3]

It may be argued that this contradiction is exactly that at work today in Western Africa. Certainly with the modern introduction of cash crops witness after witness has attested all over Western Africa to the tendency to use land as if it belonged to the individual farming it, to the point where communal ownership has even been superseded.[4]

In Africa, then, it is more important to look at the relationships between property rights in land and its use than to treat them as in effect identical. Moreover, it may further be emphasized that use is more important than property rights in this context, since the latter are only decisive when they actively determine the control which the producer has over the fruits of his labour. Thus in pre-colonial times the forms of ownership would be more important in societies with large slave populations, like the Hausa–Fulani kingdoms, than where, as in Benin, tribute was levied by the king from villages which were the effective landholding units, and the fact that in theory the king owned all land did not actually effect the process of production. In the colonial and neo-colonial periods it is evident that the forms of landed property have lagged behind the way in which it is used, a phenomenon noted by Marx himself when he commented on Lewis Morgan's point that kinship systems changed in form only after the actual structure of the family had altered, 'the same applies to political, juridical, religious and philosophical forms generally'.[5]

Turning to the relations between the individual producer and the market, it is obvious that market systems, sometimes elaborate ones, may be found as part of systems of communal cultivation. A useful analytical distinction here, however, may be that made by Bohannan and Dalton between 'market place' and 'market principle', the latter defined as follows: '[...] in an economy dominated by the market principle, market prices serve to allocate resources, incomes, and outputs. The market principle means price formation by impersonal forces of supply and demand.'[6] Thus it may be suggested that part of the process of peasantization is a movement away from the market place towards the market principle, again implying a declining control of the producer over the disposal of his product, this time in terms of its exchange value. Whereas the market place implies a limited pattern of exchange, direct exchange without the necessary intervention of money, and little speculation on changing marketing conditions, incorporation into wider (even international) exchange patterns, currency as a universal medium and speculation are indices of the growth of the market principle, or, in Marxist terms, the presence of merchant capital.

In terms of the role of the state, we have already accepted Wolf's linking of this with the emergence of classes of unequal power. This implies a political hierarchy based on territory rather than kinship, and above all the imposition of obligations upon the individual enforced by power–the ability to coerce–rather than through the influence of mutually recognized kinship duties. This is not to imply, however, that coercion by the state is the only tool of the ruling class. An aspect of Redfield's 'great' and 'little' cultures which he scarcely touches on is the manipulative capacity which those who control the former derive from being able to appeal to its higher authority: 'the will of the emir is the will of Allah', in the Hausa formulation.

If the presence together of certain tendencies in land ownership and use, market exchange and state formation (and it must be emphasized that all of them have to be present) indicates that a peasantry is forming, how does this process occur, and, more fundamentally, why? It has already been implied that what is common to all these tendencies is a diminishing control of the producer over what happens to his products. Let us try to make this formulation more precise, and to do so by beginning with the concept of surplus.

For Marxists this is already familiar in terms of 'surplus labour' in situations where labour power has become a market commodity. The concept has been extended, however, by Marxists and others to mean surplus *goods*, often surplus foodstuffs. Thus V. Gordon Childe defined surplus as 'food above domestic requirements' and found in it the causal factor producing neolithic trade and then civilization.[7] But, as Pearson has pointed out,

> Marx scoffed at the idea of a naturalistic surplus and spoke only of 'surplus value' which he attributed to the institutional features of capitalism alone. It is all the more ironic then that the facile rationalization of the development of economic institutions set in motion by the surplus concept should have been derived from Marx's surplus value.[8]

In the hands of the bourgeois scholars this emphasis on surplus commodities often becomes a sterile exercise in calorie-counting in order to define a basic dietary requirement, and hence, by deduction, what is 'surplus'.[9] This academic version of the fetishism of commodities serves to disguise what is the crucial point, namely that, like 'surplus labour', these surplus products are not really *things*, but *social relationships*. (Though this does not prevent things becoming part of social relationships through the process of reification.) Just as surplus labour is an asymmetrical power relationship between individuals and between classes which permits one to expropriate the labour power of the other, so these 'surplus' agricultural products are not things in themselves but a similar relationship, in a non-industrial setting. The basic difference is that in one case the relationship is centred directly upon labour power, in the other it is mediated through commodities produced by labour power. But both relationships involve expropriation of labour power, whether directly or indirectly.

Having established this, let us approach the problem from another direction, by listing the uses to which the communal cultivator puts his labour power either directly or in terms of himself and his immediate family, which is also an allocation to the perpetuation of his own labour power into the next generation through his children (indeed, if more than one of them survive, to its multiplication). There *is* a basic minimum here, but it is not some ideal calorific intake, but rather the amount of food necessary to keep alive and working, which can include conditions of persistent malnutrition. A second allocation of the product is the aid to needy kin which the cultivator is obliged to make. A third is that made periodically when equipment has to be renewed, either by a direct investment of labour power by the cultivator or by exchanging products for what he cannot make himself. The fourth is an allocation of labour power or products to ceremonial, weddings, say, or rites for the spirits of ancestors.

The question of the renewal of equipment has already raised the matter of exchange. It seems unlikely that in Western Africa many communities of communal cultivators were completely self-sufficient, though, on the other hand, this did not necessarily imply the emergence of market places, let alone the market principle. But once exchange is involved there is always a possibility of expropriation of goods (labour power) through unequal terms of exchange. This is one of the ways in which individual (but not yet class) differentiation occurs in a kin-based society. What we are interested in, however, is class differentiation, and the threshold between the communal cultivator and the peasant is crossed, the first step in the formation of classes, when the cultivator has to allocate part of his labour power to producing goods for which there is no necessary return. When he has to do this he is involved in an asymmetrical power relationship and exploitation. It may be suggested that such a condition takes three forms: unequal terms of exchange, as suggested, when the weaker actor has to give much to get little; the levying of taxes and other dues by the State; and the exaction of rent and other dues by landlords. The minimum prerequisite for speaking of a peasantry is the presence of the second of these, though even this is not sufficient in itself.

The peasant thus adds to the demands upon the labour power of the communal cultivator another kind of demand, over which he has virtually no control and to which he has to subordinate the others, by eating less, say, or by giving less to his kin. The question still remains, how does this come about? The answer lies in the fact of the social division of labour specialization.

Communities are unlikely to be completely self-sufficient, and individual households even less so. As a result there is exchange, and soon specialization. This is reinforced by the fact that individuals are unequal not only in their skills but in physique and health and even luck. If a man was too shortsighted to keep back enough yams for the next season's seed, or if pests destroy his young crops, he must get replacements. If he breaks his hoe in the middle of planting he must get another from the blacksmith. In all these cases he may suffer an unequal exchange. Hill's work on such factors of differentiation provides valuable insights. Thus the examples she gives may be broken down into a number of types.[10] First there are factors which differentiate on a personal level, such as the capacity for hard work, or poor health. Next there are what might be termed other biological factors–premature death of helpers, a lack of sons. Third there are inherited advantages or disadvantages, in the case of her Katsina farmers the amount of manured land handed down from father to son. Fourth we may discern the advantages to be derived from combining farming with a non-agricultural enterprise, such as trading or Koranic scholarship, and fifth the benefits of judicious loans (and the converse consequences of debt). Between the first three and the last two of these, it may be suggested, there lies a transition, and it is that between personal, or at least kinship, factors and those related to the social relationships implicit in exchange, the market principle, the division of labour and specialization. Polly Hill's work was on contemporary Hausa cash-crop farmers, but any of the above types of differentiating factor could apply in the pre-colonial period, and could apply with only a minimal development of exchange and especially the market principle, and without the existence of a state. Thus we may suggest that in any agricultural community of any complexity (i.e., not entirely self-sufficient) factors of social differentiation will be at work, and that these will expose individuals to unequal exchanges with those more shrewd, skilled, or fortunate than themselves. In these circumstances, what Hill calls the 'vicious circle of rural poverty' is likely to set in. Moreover, a cumulative imbalance in control over the distribution of products (mediated labour power) may easily lead to an imbalance of control over the means of production–land, animals, implements. ('Control' over land may not necessarily mean ownership.) At this stage we are well on the way to a class society. Two more things only are required–the perpetuation of class status from one generation to another, and the institutionalization of the class inequalities in power through the state, with the emergence of a 'great' culture as an ancillary to this.

If, then, there is an innate tendency for class differentiation and the state to appear in most agrarian societies, such an appearance may still take many forms. Differentiation may well stop short at that among lineages, rather than classes, and the state may be nothing more than the royalty of one, or even alternating, lineages. On the other hand, specialization of labour in the form of administrators grouped round the king, often initially eunuchs and slaves, may serve to crystalize out the institutions of the state. Even more important in pre-colonial Africa, however, seem to have been factors external to the society–long-distance trade and war–and the effects of migration, where the special skills needed for moving whole populations and settling in new territory gave new specialists their opportunity. The problem of class-formation and the emergence of the state in pre-colonial Western Africa is far too complex to enter here, and much work remains to be done by scholars.[11] Let it suffice to say that, on an admittedly cursory survey, the process of class and state formation, and therefore of peasantization, still had far to go even in the more developed kingdoms like Mali or Songhai. In terms of peasantization I would not even term these feudal; rather they belonged to Marx's category of Asiatic modes of production, with a state imposed over local communities based on kinship, and a benefice-based bureaucracy (in the Weberian sense). It is even a matter of dispute as to how far they possessed fully differentiated artisan classes, particularly if we regard caste as a transitional form between kinship and class.[12] The Yoruba kingdoms do not even come into this category; rather, they demonstrate how complex a state apparatus could emerge upon a lineage basis, with the political and administrative hierachy still founded on kinship and without the regular state levies found in the others, or in the Hausa kingdoms. Thus, in the Yoruba case it is scarcely possible to speak of peasantization.

It is suggested, then, that the process of peasantization–the first of the two major processes with which we are concerned–was both slow and uneven in pre-colonial Western Africa. The second of our processes–incorporation into the world capitalist economy–which has taken place over the last century was much faster and less uneven, at least in the sense that no group has escaped its touch. On the other hand, the introduction of cash crops in some areas has considerably advanced the market principle compared to others, with all the concomitant changes. The previously important external factors in class and state formation, long-distance trade and war, appeared in new guises, but the states which were formed were extensions of foreign states, not indigenous growths, and the new ruling classes were not African. The new colonial states sponsored the introduction of cash crops, but as a means of expropriating commodities and thus forming capital outside the bounds of Western Africa, which was thus affected by all the unevenness of development of the imperial powers, France, Britain, Belgium, Germany (for a time), Portugal, and Spain (peripherally). It is time that this differentiating impact was examined, not in the familiar hackneyed terms of 'direct' versus 'indirect' rule but in relation to economic structures and class formation; P. Anderson has given an important lead with his concept of Portuguese 'ultra-colonialism'.[13]

Whatever their differences, it is true to say that all the colonial powers in Western Africa greatly extended the market principle, to the point where the impersonal forces of the world market dominated the lives of millions, and imposed a state where none had been before, or to supersede indigenous ones. The African quest for western education and the issue of 'assimilation' amply demonstrate the presence of a new 'great' culture. It would appear, then, that many of the conditions for the existence of a peasantry were suddenly created, but from outside and quite independently of the processes of internal differentiation in origin, though the internal factors had important influences upon the final form of these conditions. This process was sometimes consciously undertaken by the colonial power, sometimes it was an unconscious result of the new presence and its demands.[14] In all cases what was being attempted was the use of pre-capitalist modes of production, peasant or communal, for the purposes of the word capitalist market.[15] The result of this use was to increase the speed and intensity of the process of peasantization, but in a very uneven way, so that elements of communal, slave, feudal (possibly), Asiatic, and capitalist modes of production existed side by side and in a multitude of relationships with one another. One particularly important capitalist element created by colonialism was wage labour, in the perspective of this essay agricultural wage labour, employed on plantations owned by non-Africans or by the bigger African farmers who were most highly oriented to the world market. Along with peasantization it is thus possible to speak of a parallel process of 'proletarianization'.

What rural classes, peasants or otherwise, have then begun to emerge in Western Africa in this situation of uneven and combined development? The establishment of this is one of our prime tasks though only preliminary suggestions can be made here. R. Stavenhagen suggests that the colonial impact has created three 'new social categories' in rural Black Africa, the migrant labourer, the labourer on big commercial plantations, and the individual planter, producing for export.[16] He states that

> if we can speak of systems of classes, it is within the framework of partial, not global, economic structures. The migrant labourer is defined in relation to a capitalist industrial system which has need of him, but also in relation to a traditional subsistence economy. For his part, the agricultural worker on the big plantations is defined in terms of an economic structure characteristic of underdevelopment (mono-culture for export), but which is only one aspect of the general economic framework of underdeveloped countries. Lastly, the planter is defined in relation to labourers, in so far as he is an employer, but also in relation to the international market and the trading companies as a producer. Furthermore, he is defined in relation to other planters with whom he identifies, or else from whom he is distinguished in terms of factors of differentiation already mentioned.[17]

We are faced, then, with a number of different problems. We have to relate these three classes of agricultural producers (if, indeed, they are the crucial three) to the overall, as opposed to partial, patterns of development in Western Africa, which means understanding their relations with one another. We have to see them not only in relation to world capitalism, which imposes the global pattern, but to other classes within Africa, the rural and urban bourgeoisies of traders and transporters, the middle class of professionals, and civil servants, and clerks, the urban working class, and so on.

All this cannot possibly be attempted here. What must be done is to bring out more clearly some aspects of the processes of peasantization and proletarianization. Thus, it is obvious that labourers on capitalitst plantations, assuming them to be permanent and not migrant, form an agricultural proletariat rather than a peasantry, though even this may be complicated by their ownership of small plots alongside the plantation. Migrant labourers, working, say, for Agni coffee planters or Ashanti cocoa farmers, are a problem. They represent a transitional group, it is often said (by Stavenhagen, for example), but from what to what? Usually, it seems likely, from communal cultivators to peasants, since they represent an attempt to use labour power to meet the new demands of the market and the state, into which colonialism incorporated them. Yet there is a contradiction here, since they are not meeting these demands by producing commodities which they sell themselves; often, indeed, they come from areas which produce little which the new market requires. Thus, they are not really responding like peasants, but by selling their labour power as a commodity, like proletarians. In this way they are gradually being separated from the means of production, in this case the land. Theoretically, then, their fate is to become permanent wage workers, but what sector of the Western African economies can absorb them?

As for the cash-crop farmers, what has been already evident for some time among them is a process of differentiation. As Stavenhagen, who has an interesting summary discussion on the Ivory Coast, puts it:

> [. . .] this class situation could be the basis for the formation not of one social class only but of several, depending on the extension of landed property wherever it develops, the quantity of marketed produce, the amount of labour employed, and also on the use the farmer makes of monetary revenues.[18]

In this way classes of poor, middle, and rich peasants might well be emerging, though in terms of their employment of labour and use of investment capital the last might perhaps better be called capitalist farmers. The tenacity of forms of communal property and of matrilineal inheritance has so far hampered the emergence of a landlord class, but should this occur (and it seems likely in some areas) then the peasantization is likely to be considerably accelerated.

The question of the tenacity of ancient forms of property and kinship brings me to the last issue I wish to raise in this selective treatment. It is necessary to emphasize once again the speed of change in the last seventy years and, conversely, the transitional and preliminary nature of that change. In that period what we have seen has been the first adjustment to the impact of world capitalism. Many of the social phenomena with which we are concerned, particularly organizationally, represent techniques for meeting new demands, rather than crystallizations of new class structures. Indeed, since these new techniques often incorporate traditional relationships, they may serve to perpetuate kinship and communality, rather than destroy them. Five types of such techniques (at least) may be discerned. First we may note the frequency with which the extended family seems to have been re-organized as a working unit, with extensions or changes in its own internal division of labour; this probably accounts for the tenacity of traditional kinship in the face of quite radical economic changes. M. Douglas has also made the interesting suggestion in the case of matrilineal systems that 'economic buoyancy, abundant opportunity, and steady expansion create the same favourable conditions for matriliny as a static, poor, undifferentiated economy'.[19] Thus we find adaptations of traditional allocations of 'male' and 'female' crops, or extensions of female trading activities, as in the case of the Hausa production of foodstuffs.[20] In the same case, it seems significant that there is a strong correlation between the wealthiest households and use of the *gandu* system, in which the father and his sons work together as a farming team.[21]

In terms of production, we should also note the deliberate specialization in the growing of crops in certain areas, going far beyond the general phenomenon of cashcropping and in fact becoming intensive capitalist farming. Examples of this are the Anlo shallot industry in South-East Ghana and the rice-farming at Abakaliki, in East-Central Nigeria. Another innovative technique connected with cash crops has been the systematic, organized opening up of new territory. This has inspired a number of organizational forms, from the different 'companies' of the southern Akan to the Murid brotherhood of Senegal.[22]

Much more attention needs to be paid in our studies to marketing systems, though the volume edited by Bohannan and Dalton was a valuable beginning. Of particular importance in terms of our concern with the uneven way in which external capitalism was introduced, is the point they make concerning the marketing of cash crops, that this has evolved often through structures quite separate from traditional market places.[23] A study of any examples of exceptions to this generalization might be particularly instructive.

A fifth technique by which large numbers of the rural population of Western Africa have attempted to meet the demands of capitalism and the colonial and neo-colonial state has been that already touched on above, the resort to migrant labour. In terms of organization, the impression generally gleaned is that this has been a random, individual matter, but more attention might be paid to this as a planned activity. There are indications that among certain sections of the Ibo, at least, the education of boys was deliberately sponsored with a view to sending them 'abroad' later to get good jobs and remit money home–a sort of internal colonization. It might be argued, of course, that this was not qualitatively the same sort of migration as that by someone with only his labour power to sell, and not such skills as literacy. The fact remains that much work has still to be done on the phenomenon of migration.

It is perhaps fitting that this section should end on the inconclusive note of an exhortation to research. I began with the question of the diffidence shown by many scholars concerning the use of the term 'peasant' in African studies. The answer is not an indefinite extension of analytical modesty, but to look systematically at any given place at any given time in terms of the question: 'Who is extracting labour power in the form of agricultural products from whom, and how?' This analysis will involve such matters as the influence of land tenure, the extent and nature of absorption into the world market system, relations with the state apparatus and those who control it, and class differentiations and relations among the rural populations. Such a list is a fairly obvious one, but a surprising number of writers fail to keep it in mind.

NOTES

[1] Fitchin. J., 'Peasantry as a social type', Viola E. Garfield (ed), *Symposium: Patterns of land utilization and other papers*, American Ethnological Society, 1961, p. 115.

[2] On the former see Karl Marx, *Capital*, III (New York, International Publishers, 1967), pp. 804–13.

[3] Letter reprinted in Karl Marx, *Pre-capitalist economic formations*, edited by Eric Hobsbawm (London, Lawrence and Wishart, 1964), p. 143.

[4] See, for example, the contributions in Daniel Biebuyck (Ed.), *African agrarian systems* (London, Oxford University Press for the International African Institute, 1963).

[5] Quoted in Friedrich Engels, 'Origins of the family, private property and the state', in Karl Marx and Friedrich Engels, *Selected works* (two volumes Moscow, Foreign Languages Publishing House, 1951), Vol. II, pp. 175–6.

[6] Bohannan and Dalton, *Markets in Africa*, Northwestern University Press, Evanston, 1962, p. 1.

[7] See V. Gordon Childe, 'The birth of civilization', *Past and Present*, II pp. 1–10, (1952).

[8] Harry W. Pearson, 'The economy has no surplus: critique of a theory of development', in Karl Polanyi, Conrad M. Arensberg and Harry W. Pearson (eds), *Trade and market in the early empires* (Glencoe, The Free Press, 1957), p. 334.

[9] See discussions in Pearson, *op. cit.* pp. 322–327, and Marvin Harris, 'The economy has no surplus?' *American Anthropologist*, LXI pp. 188–91, (1959).

[10] Hill, *Migrant cocoa-farmers of southern Ghana* (Cambridge, Cambridge University Press, 1963) pp. 153–4.

[11] Jean Suret-Canale, *Afrique noire, occidentale et centrale: géographie, civilisations, histories* (Paris, Editions sociales, 1968), is a useful beginning.

[12] Peter Waterman, 'The Western Sudan in its classical period—a review of Marxist research and analysis' [mimeographed, unpublished] (1969), pp. 3–4.

[13] Perry Anderson, 'Portugal and the end of ultra-colonialism', *New Left Review*, XV-LVIII (1962), 83–102, 88–123, 85–114.

[14] It may be suggested tentatively that France, Belgium, and Portugal fall into the first category and Britain into the second: this would be an interesting topic for further research, involving the question of the use of a concept of 'peasant' in the metropolitan country itself. It seems probable that the reluctance of many Anglo-Saxon scholars to use the term analytically in African studies stems from the same source.

[15] An important discussion of this phenomenon in another context is Ernesto, Laclau, 'Imperialism in Latin America,' *New Left Review*, LXVII (1971), especially pp. 30–38.

[16] Rodolfo Stavenhagen, *Les classes sociales dans les sociétés agraires* (Paris, Editions Anthropos, 1969), p. 153.

[17] *Ibid.* pp. 180–1. All translations in this essay are by Ken Post.

[18] Stavenhagen, *op. cit.* p. 180.

[19] Mary Douglas, 'Is matriliny doomed in Africa?', in Mary Douglas and Phyllis M. Kaberry (eds), *Man in Africa* (London, Tavistock Publications 1969), p. 131.

[20] See P. Hill, 'The myth of the amorphous peasantry: a Northern Nigerian case study, *Nigerian Journal of Economic and Social Studies*, 2 239–60, (1968).

[21] See *ibid*, table on p. 249, and P. Hill, *Studies in rural capitalism in West Africa*, Cambridge University Press, Cambridge, 1970, pp. 147–8.

[22] On the Akan see P. Hill, *op. cit.*; and *Studies in rural capitalism*; for the Murids, see Paul Pelissier, *Les paysans du Sénégal* (Saint-Yrieix Imprimerie Fabrègue, 1966), Chap. VI, and D. B. Cruise O'Brien, *The Mourides of Senegal* (Oxford, Clarendon Press, 1971), expecially Chaps VIII and IX.

[23] Bohannan and Dalton, *op. cit.*, p. 10.

Social organization of the unemployed in Lagos and Nairobi

PETER GUTKIND

From Peter C. W. Gutkind, 'The energy of despair: social organization of the unemployed in two African cities: Lagos and Nairobi', *Civilisations*, **17**, 3 and 4, Brussels, 1967.

The unemployed as a collective category exist at the margins of African urban society. Their hope of effective participation in this society is rapidly declining. While their political power has considerable potential,[1] economically they are weak due to the fact that most unemployed men are unskilled and thus not readily placed in employment. The prospects of absorbing the totally unskilled in a gradually increasing labour market are slim indeed. If this observation is correct, African urban society will before long show clear signs of stratification.[2] On the one hand, there will be those with the required skills, resources and opportunities, and, on the other, those to whom mobility is denied. For some time to come, this group will have to depend on aid from family and friends and, progressively, on their own ingenuity. Mutual aid and reciprocity is a two-way process. The more advantaged see their help as of only limited reciprocal value to themselves–as those whom they support can offer little in return–other than turn some of their dependents into servants. The probable consequences will likely be that the unemployed, the unskilled, the illiterate, and the primary and lower secondary school-leavers, will devote their energy–the energy of despair–to draw inward for their own salvation and as means of protecting their self-respect.

The social networks of the urban-based unemployed

1. *Kin-based networks*
Because the reasons why Africans migrate to towns, the qualifications they bring with them, the length of time they stay, the ethnic group they belong to, the kin or friends they contact, where they find shelter and the work they obtain all vary enormously, so do the social groups they form, the networks they enter or construct, and the general manner in which they perceive and adjust to an environment with which they are not familiar. The time it takes the migrant to understand, adjust, and learn how to manipulate this environment also varies greatly, and is influenced by a large number of variables

which urban anthropologists are now engaged in sorting out and classifying.

Whether or not migrants are 'pushed' out of the rural areas for environmental, economic, or social and personal reasons, or whether they are 'pulled' into the towns for similar reasons, they all come with the expectation of finding employment. Those able to write often take the trouble to give advance notice of their pending arrival by writing to a relative or friend asking him to secure work in advance. The following letter was received by a junior civil servant from his brother, a Luo from Western Kenya, who had been resident in Nairobi for just over two years. The writer had just finished primary school and had taken a three month typing course at a secretarial college in Kisumu (a town of some 24,000 in 1962).

Dear Ezikiel,

I hope that you are well. I hope that your health is good and that you are eating well. We have had much rain recently. My work is now completed and I am ready to job (sic). I have done my work of learning to type and have reached a speed of 97 words per minute. I think that I can do better. My shorthand is not so very fine because the teacher was not good and I did not learn so good (sic). I must now earn my own money but I have not been lucky to find job in Kisumu. I have used all the money. I had to put (sic) on bus tickets and now I have no more to buy new clothes. I would like you to sent (sic) some money to me so that I can buy my ticket to come to Nairobi. Please find work for me in your office. I want to come on saturday or monday and will come to your home. Samuel has told me that he will give me some food to bring to you. Please sent (sic) me money because I have no more shillings left in my pocket.

Charles[3]

Many unemployed men, particularly those in the age group of 18 and over, prefer to seek out friends rather than relatives. This is particularly so among those who on earlier occasions stayed with relatives while they looked for work. Many of these men found this experience undesirable and as a result they circulated from one willing relative to another, until such a time when they had exhausted this particular hospitality. They then often returned home, for a short time, and on their return to the town they began to circulate among school friends or among those whose acquaintance they had made on previous visits to Lagos or Nairobi. Many friendships are made at Employment Exchanges and outside factory gates.

Many of the younger men, the primary school leavers in particular, almost invariably stay initially with close or distant relatives. Arrangements to do so are often made by the parents who insist that an older brother or sister look after a younger sibling, or the parents approach their own brothers or sisters for help. However, tribal traditions play a major part here. Thus almost any Ibo who comes to town can almost certainly expect food and shelter from another Ibo whether they are related in some manner or not. The same is largely the case among the Luo in Nairobi. This perhaps is to be contrasted with the Yoruba among whom a very large number of unemployed men expressed the view that it was quite unpredictable even whether a relative would act as a willing or friendly host. Far more so than among other tribes in Lagos, many of the unemployed Yoruba school leavers felt that an older brother or sister, an uncle or an aunt, had turned the misfortune of the unemployed to their own personal advantage. Thus young Yoruba often complained bitterly that they had been turned into house servants, that they often had to suffer abuse, that they were not given adequate food and, in several cases, that their hosts had refused to have them in their own home. In several cases, senior civil servants who had grown tired of the demands made on them, had rented slum accommodation for their younger brothers and nephews. If, at this early stage of the research, a generalization is possible, it appears that the young Yoruba unemployed men are far more dependent on securing support from kin than the Ibo who have developed a complex network of non-kin-based associations which are particularly suitable to aid the new urbanite both during times of plenty and times of stress.

The above gives an indication that unemployed men are part of different social and economic networks at different times of their residence in town and under different situations. While men often move from one type of network to another, it is possible, nevertheless, to abstract and analyse these various networks and to describe their characteristics and their functions. Yet, different as these networks are in purpose and organization, they have certain common characteristics.

For an unemployed person, who is seriously trying to obtain employment, it is important not to be restricted in his associations. If members of his kin group are unable to help him he must be willing and able to make wider contacts. Furthermore, if he is rigid in his expectations, *i.e.* that he will accept only certain kinds of work, he has restricted himself to a narrow network of associations with limited mobility potential. Under such circumstances he is highly dependent on his close relatives and friends who, being unable to help him, tire of him readily. He consults the same individuals repeatedly, visits the same offices and factories and writes to the same employers. This is largely true of the Yoruba in Lagos. The average young Yoruba uses his kin-based network with expectation that this is the best way to secure not only a job but also a particular kind of job. Thus the information obtained in Lagos indicated quite clearly that a Yoruba, upon arrival in Lagos or Ibadan, restricted his contacts to close kin. He comes with the expectation that he will receive aid and support and, further, that his well-to-do relatives have already laid on a job for him. He has a clear expectation that his close relatives will help him rather than more distant kin. Furthermore, in the Lagos and Ibadan area, the political power of the Yoruba is such that the unemployed person assumes that if he can establish the right contacts, influence peddling will eventually secure for him desired employment. Employment through 'brotherization' is strongly established among all the unemployed.[4] Thus for many unemployed men, the first and most important network is kinship based.

Those who must, or wish to, use this network frequently circulate from one relative to the next. The length of time the job seeker stays is determined by many circumstances. Thus, if his first contact is with a relatively well-to-do relative who does not measure his support in terms of the advantage for himself, who lives alone or does not have to help numerous other relatives,

such a host may offer hospitality for a considerable time. But as others drift
in from the rural areas his own position and that of his host are threatened.
He might then move on, although still without work, and as a dependent
person. Being unwilling to give up whatever shaky foothold he has obtained,
i.e. the possible job contacts he has made, the fact that he has registered at the
Labour Exchange, the gatemen at the factories he has got to know, or the
friends he has made among office workers, he usually makes a great effort
to locate another relative who will look after him for a further few weeks.
But the circumstances of his second host are often very different as is likely
to be the attitude in providing continued support for somebody who failed
to obtain employment.

The housing and family circumstances of the host often place enormous
strain on both the host and the job seeker. Many hosts complain bitterly
that they must cut back on their own standard of living, and that of their
own family, to meet the expenses of their guest. While some of the latter
are sensitive to the additional burden they impose on their hosts, quite a few
feel that their relatives and friends owe them a living. Such an attitude readily
breeds frequent quarrels and their cumulative effect is that the guest moves
on to the next person willing to look after him. A Kikuyu who had been in
and out of Nairobi over a period of eight years, but had never managed to
secure more than unskilled and casual employment, graphically described
one of these quarrels which he had had with an older brother and which finally
convinced him that he should in future stay with friends rather than relatives.

> ... My brother is lucky because he has good work [as a skilled automobile
> mechanic] but he always abused me. I stayed with him [his brother was
> married and supported a wife and five children] for only three weeks.
> Every day he told me that I was lazy because I could work if I really tried.
> But I did try but I was turned away many times. I went to the Labour
> Department and they made promises but could not give me job. One day
> my brother refused to give me money to buy bread and tea for my food
> and I complained. He told me to leave his house and said that he had to
> buy clothes and good food for his children. But I begged him to let me stay.
> Then a few days later in the evening he kept me waiting for my food and
> when he gave it to me it was too little and he refused to give me more. I
> then left him in the middle of the night and went to my friend in the Mathare
> Valley. He gave me a place to sleep and gave me tea and bread in the morn-
> ing... I will never return to my brother but I will tell my father how he
> abused me.[5]

In this way many of the unemployed circulate from one relative to another.
During this time such persons use the network of family and kin to the fullest
possible extent. Many of them seek out links of consanguinity and affinal kin,
although more of the former than the latter, which are then activated only
to be broken again a few weeks or months later. While the job seeker moves
in this network he continues to be, to a certain extent, under the watchful
eye of members of the kin group. While this is so his contacts are more restricted and he feels highly dependent on them for help. Particularly older members
of his kin group generally demand that he submit to their advice and wishes.
Failure to do so may result in being reprimanded or expelled from the home

of the host. Many young job seekers resent that the greater authority of their host, and the often condescending attitude they display, results in their being exploited in the home. This is particularly so if they move into the home of one of their affines who not infrequently treats this situation as an indication that the family of their guest has not been successful in providing for a good education and a job for one of their members. This was a view held quite frequently among Ibo hosts who expressed strong criticism of the lack of initiative and enterprise not merely of their guest but also of his family. In this regard, girls were generally treated with greater respect as it was recognized that they had fewer opportunities to obtain work.

2. *Association-based networks*

When a man has exploited every possible aid that he could obtain from his relatives, over a period of months or several years, while he tried to find employment but failed, he then starts to cultivate friends and progressively turns his back on his kin. What contacts he continues to maintain with the latter in the urban area are generally restricted to occasional visits and to more formal occasions such as births, marriages, and deaths when his absence would have been noted.

When an unemployed person has decided to turn to his friends, rather than return to his village, he has made an important decision. He can now no longer expect or demand help but must adjust to a highly flexible structure. He is now incorporated into an association of persons most of whom care little for him. But at the same time he is free to go his own way. While he cannot make demands, his friends cannot order him about. Goodwill and a sympathetic attitude allows him to stay in the home of his host. Generally, friends accept fewer responsibilities for their guest. He can come and go as he pleases. Most often a friend will offer no more than a bed space, although some generous friends will also offer food and money. This rather depends on the previous duration and the quality of the friendship. If both host and guest have come from the same village or town, or if they have been to school together, the bond of friendship tends to be closer and the job seeker can expect some measure of preferential treatment. Many friendships, however, do not have these qualities; they are of a more casual nature having been contracted at the Labour Exchange, at a street corner, or a football game. Nevertheless, their quality is such that many unemployed men prefer them for it suits their purpose not to be tied too closely to any person or group: they wish to preserve the kind of flexibility which allows them to move about in search of work.

Being attached to a working friend means that the unemployed person has entered a totally different kind of network. Basically this involves an extension of his contacts with individuals and groups with whom he is in free association. The mutual aid and protection of the kin-based network gives place to a more pragmatically organized set of contacts and associations. The bond of reciprocity has been replaced by a greater emphasis on individual initiative and enterprise. What contacts a man makes are judged by him to promote his own interest and to give him an advantage in his efforts to obtain work. Thus he might join an ethnic or recreation association, a church, or a political party. This further broadens his contacts which he uses as a means to find work. Unlike the contacts he had within the limits of the kin-based network, his new associations constantly proliferate. His working host introduces him to his friends, and these in turn introduce him to their friends. The conscientious job seeker usually follows each of the leads suggested. Thus new contacts are made, new avenues explored and old contacts lapse. The search for work involves the job seeker in a network of contacts which vary in strength and durability. Yet these networks have continuity and the kind of flexibility which make them particularly suitable under urban conditions.

Men who have looked for work for more than a year have often given up hope that they will ever find employment. Their friends, and even their kin, who are fortunate to have jobs, gradually drift away from them and restrict their contacts. Class attitudes then begin to manifest themselves. This was clearly expressed by a Benin man, a highly placed civil servant in Lagos, who talked about his younger brother (who had not succeeded finding employment for over a year) in the following terms:

> I have done what I could to help Isole. He lived in my home for almost ten months and I gave him letters to my friends who were willing to help him. But he complained all the time that he wanted a better job than people were willing to offer him. When he lived with me in my home my friends asked me about Isole and wondered why I had not been able to find work for him. He was even begging money from my friends. He has now become lazy and there is nothing more that I can do to help him. I think that he must join his own friends.[6]

The unemployed person is not insensitive to such sentiments and, as the prospect of his upward mobility appears to diminish, he more readily interprets his predicaments in class terms. His comments are often mixed with considerable hostility.

> David was a 22-year-old Maragoli, from Western Kenya, who had completed, very successfully, his primary education. He was an ambitious young man who had trained to be a mechanic during the day and took typing classes at night. Although he wanted to work in an office, he soon discovered that his chances to do so were very small. He therefore concentrated his efforts on finding work as a mechanic in a garage. He had decided that he did not wish to go to Nairobi but stay close to his family and for several months he tried to get work in one of the smaller towns near his home. When he failed to secure a job there, he then went first to Nakuru, staying with a friend, and later to Nairobi. When interviewed he had been in Nairobi for almost one year. During this time he had had a job for three weeks replacing a car mechanic who had gone on leave. He had been told that he might be kept on but this did not work out, in part, he suspected, because he had not obeyed the instructions of an Asian foreman. Although he could have taken work elsewhere which was offered to him as a messenger in a large office, he refused because he said, 'I was trained as a mechanic and this is the work I like'.
>
>   While in Nairobi he stayed with a Maragoli friend who worked in a newspaper office repairing the printing presses. Although he had been registered with the Labour Exchange, no work came along. Almost every

day he did the rounds of the garages and when interviewed he had been waiting outside a large garage for three hours because he had heard that two or three mechanics might be hired. In the course of the interview he expressed the following views:

'I did not get as much education as I wanted. My father is just a poor farmer with many children. I did not want to farm because it is a poor life. . . . I now know that there are rich and poor people and that some people will always be poor. I see many people driving in big cars and living in big houses. Many of my friends say that they can get no help from the rich people who keep all the money in their own pocket. . . I voted for Kanu (Kenya African National Union) because they said that if we worked hard our life would be better. But all the politicians just talk and they forget about us. . . I want to marry but now I don't think that I can until I am 35.'[7]

A similar view was expressed by an Ibo in Lagos, who had not quite completed primary school and had no skills. He had been out of work for almost three years although he had obtained occasional casual work carrying head loads and washing buses in the main bus park. Several months before he was interviewed he had tried to organize the Unemployed Citizens of Nigeria Union. He had collected some 497 signatures on a petition which he had drawn up and which three officers of the association presented to the (then) Minister of Labour of the Federal Government of Nigeria. While he was collecting signatures outside the Labour Exchange and in the more congested areas of Lagos, he was interviewed by the police but no action was taken.

Industrial development can make little use of this vast pool of readily available manpower–and an increasing number of unemployed recognize this predicament. Such men are caught in the crises of development and as such, the more articulate among them demand social services and welfare measures at a very early stage of national development. Thus, when in Lagos a Labour Unemployment Association was formed in July 1966, the organizers of a petition to the Head of the (then) National Military Government suggested that the government set up an Unemployment Assistance Council which would give the unemployed £2 per week.[8] No government in contemporary Africa could even contemplate such expenditures. When the unemployed repeatedly suggest that the government must help them, that more factories must be constructed, they do not thereby deny that their own initiative is as important as any programmes governments implement to ease the problem of unemployment. The job seeker has only a very limited understanding of the economic and social forces which presently engulf him, yet he understands the implications when he or one of his friends is laid off because an automated process has taken over. A surprisingly large number of job seekers have had this experience.

When a job seeker has thus reached the stage when employers treat him as unemployable, and his relatives and friends no longer offer him dependable aid, he is relegated to a new social milieu. The network of his contacts and associations, his friends and the social groups he selects, now comprise predominantly other unemployed men. While he will continue to visit his working friends and relatives, the greater part of his time is spent on activities no longer designed to help him find employment. Thus many job seekers have given up calling regularly at the Employment Exchanges or visiting factories, offices, or ministries. Some might take to individual entrepreneurship such as petty street trading but the rewards are so small that many give up in frustration. Few can raise the capital to secure and expand their efforts. Those who peddle goods for others also gain little reward quite apart from needing some cash as a deposit with the owner of the merchandise. Some adjust their lives to the very irregular employment available and others lower their expectations, although for the primary school leaver this is somewhat unusual. Junior secondary leavers tend to spend their time scanning the newspapers for advertisements and writing applications (one such young person, an Ibo, had filed copies of some 131 applications written over a period of 14 months). Not an insignificant number of young men offer their services to political parties and political leaders. Thus it was said that during the 1965 political upheavals in Western Nigeria a large number of unemployed youth formed the core of numerous rival political gangs. In return for their services they received small payments, or simply food and shelter. Certainly the Employment Exchanges in Ibadan and Lagos registered a significant increase of applicants during the last two weeks of January 1967 after the (first) military *coup* had taken place!

However, many more young men spend their time visiting each other within the neighbourhoods in which they live, and pooling whatever knowledge they have about job prospects or otherwise passing the time. Many school leavers will try to obtain funds to pay for books, or the cost of correspondence courses, in the hope of gaining further skills and qualifications. But having started, many give up because they are unable to raise additional sums for continuation lessons or final examinations.

The totally unskilled, or those with just two or three years of primary education, represent an immobilized segment of urban African society. As a category, with certain common characteristics, they exist as lone individuals who are wholly dependent on charity or illicit pursuits. This is particularly true of the older men (above 40), some of whom no longer even express embittered sentiments about their predicament. Many exist on the most casual and irregular work and generally sleep out. Such men will be found at the bus parks, the markets, the parking areas, the docks, in the bowels of slums, near building sites, or stores hoping to earn a few pence a day. Younger juveniles try to earn some money helping drivers park their cars and look after the vehicles. Many wait for hours outside warehouses and shops hoping that they will be given a headload to carry. Others wait at the lorry parks and at the docks to pick up a few hours work. When new building construction commences, within hours hundreds of young and old will gather near the site. Not infrequently the police have to be called to disperse or control the crowd. When the foremen have hired all the men they need, the rest walk away slowly in a dejected manner to begin their eternal round of visiting other places.

Community of the poor: Mathere valley, Nairobi

Thus rejected and dejected some of these men take to begging or illicit pursuits.

Many young boys engage in the former as they follow pedestrians, half shyly and half slyly, or half-heartedly stretch out a hand as customers enter or leave shops. Some may sell a cabbage or a small bag of oranges which they obtain in ways not to be questioned too closely. Seasoned beggars, who have been unemployable for years, cripples, and the infirm, and the 'skidrow' types daily take up their appointed places and try to cultivate their benefactors. Clearly some job seekers take to stealing or, if they are juveniles, attach themselves to thieves.

Mathere Valley, really a series of three squatter settlements, can best be described as a community of the poor. It is of interest in the context of this paper simply because almost all the young men living there, unless they produce gin, are unemployed. A very small number of men, after they move into the Valley subsequently manage to find work outside the Valley and decide to stay on although it is approximately three miles from the centre of Nairobi. Such men could live elsewhere in better homes and under more sanitary conditions, which are extremely primitive in the Valley. Running water is not readily available, the climb to the main road is steep and during a heavy rain houses are washed away and rutted paths turn into slimy mud. It is a densely packed area with little privacy and ethnically very mixed although the majority of residents are Kikuyu, Luo, Embu or Meru. These groups comprise about 65 per cent of the population. Family life is well established in the Valley as women and children have come to join the men.

As a community, the settlements are extremely tightly-knit units both socially and politically. The driving force behind this organization is KANU (the Kenya African National Union)–Kenya's main political party–whose following in the Valley is very strong. A member of parliament, in whose constituency the Valley is located, has done much to organize the people, not merely politically but also in terms of co-operative and self-help efforts. 'Chiefs' and other officers were appointed for each settlement to guide and regulate the affairs of the people. By means of self-help, and with some 'external' funds, the residents built a nursery, a lower primary school, and a community centre. Such facilities have produced considerable residential stability and community integration.

Unemployed men, who have been searching for work for many months, often attach themselves to the gin brewers helping them to secure the raw materials, supervising the actual brewing and later acting as the distributors and sellers of the gin. For this service they are rewarded with food and shelter and occasionally money. As police raids are infrequent, life in the Valley is reasonably secure. Men enjoy taking it easy, talking to their neighbours, visiting friends in the other two settlements, playing cards, listening to a transistor radio, or dancing to the tunes of an itinerant musician. Residents claim that nobody who is accepted as part of the community, ever goes hungry. Should an emergency arise such as sickness or death, friends and neighbours do what they can to help. Such help ties the resident to a viable system without generating a sense of shame, humiliation, victimization, or degradation of the individual. As a style of life the residents develop a sense of self-respect despite their economic immobility as well as a strong sense of their political power potential. Each settlement contains a number of young men, almost all of whom are either unemployed or only have casual work, and who are members of the KANU youth wing. With the consent of the majority of the residents, these young men 'protect' the settlements during the night when thieves roam about. While their energy sometimes gets the better of them, they have a strong attachment to the settlements. When their Member of Parliament visits the Valley, which is frequently, he receives reports from the leaders of the settlements, inspects the self-help projects, watches the school children's progress, and supervises the distribution of skimmed milk for mothers and children. At times he will be found sharing a drink with selected members of the settlements while discussing the affairs of the people. Whenever he can help a job seeker to obtain employment, he uses all his influence to do so and his stature in the Valley increases. As their Member of Parliament, he has explained to the people the reasons for their being unemployed. He has repeatedly pointed out to them that they are not morally inferior although he is fully aware of their illicit activities. Residents understand the economic hardships they face but at the same time they do not feel themselves excluded from participation in economic and political affairs. Many of the more articulate residents of the Valley express the view that economic hardships make for a close community life, provided the people accept the authority and goodwill of their leaders. Some of the residents point to the numerous squatters' camps within the City of Nairobi as an example of how much worse the life of the people of Mathere Valley could be. They are quite right: as economic resources and opportunities diminish, the severity of adjustment to such conditions increases. The routine of individual and family life is then severely disorganized and the depth and extent of social relationships tend to contract, leaving the individual exposed and isolated.

A community of the poor avoids these difficulties as practically everyone is woven into a network of associations, both formal and informal, varying in depth and duration. Friendships and neighbourhoods flourish so that the sharp edge of dependency is replaced by a system of reciprocity and mutual aid particularly suitable to the conditions of the poor. Mathere Valley, however, is not a utopian community whose members distribute their collective wealth according to individual needs. Competition is extremely severe, both economically and socially, as the residents jostle for whatever economic and political advantage they perceive. At times there are strong factions in the settlements as residents make temporary or long-term alliances and personal tempers flare, fights break out and tensions linger. Most residents rarely challenge the authority of the local leaders but some reject it and thus jeopardize their continued residence in the Valley. A man who thus cuts himself off, and leaves the Valley for good, will almost certainly drift into one of the squatters' camps where his circumstances will be far worse.[9]

Summary and conclusion

The unemployed straddle the position between traditional and modern society and are a new segment of African society. Because they are increasingly detached from the traditional rural society, what remains of the working of this society applies less and less to them. Whatever traditional society might have to offer them cannot be reciprocated. Modern African society, which is organized more along universalistic lines, has no place either for the unemployed, lacking, as they do, education and skills. Under colonial administration African societies were drawn into modernization only as far as the colonial authorities desired it. Thus labourers were encouraged to migrate to meet the needs of new economic activities, but urban settlement, particularly in East Africa, was discouraged.[10] Under the rule of independent African governments, Africans are encouraged to take a rational and modernistic view of their individual and collective development, although the new national leaders are far removed from the life and the problems of the masses.[11] The place of tradition is judged by its contribution to solve the problems facing contemporary African society. Where tradition is an impediment it is subject to public criticism. Thus, Mr Tom Mboya, Kenya's Minister of Economic Planning and Development, addressing the East African Academy in September 1966, pointed to the African extended family as a threat to the new economy Kenya is trying to build.

> Growth depends on initiative and initiative can be badly stifled if the individual who makes the effort is required to share the rewards with many others whose claims can only be justified on moral grounds.
> In every part of East Africa one can witness the undesirable situation in which a member of a family whose income increases is suddenly and constantly besieged by demands for support from a large number of distant relatives.
> This continues to be part of our lives. It holds true of the small shopkeeper and the trained professional man. In social terms, such a man contributes to society in accordance with the patterns of an economy based on individual initiative but his rewards are severely limited by the traditions of a collective system at family level.[12]

However, what Mr Mboya neglected to discuss was that, were it not for the continued operation of this collective system at a family level, despite the modifications which have already taken place, the Government of Kenya would now be faced with an economic and political crisis which they might well not be able to keep under control.

The central importance of the rules of kinship, which have given African societies both their exact structure and their flexibility, are anchored on a wide range of particularistic relationships around which rural life is organized. The alleged flexibility of these rules, and the alleged adaptive qualities of African social systems, are not borne out when applied to the study of modern African society. This modernizing African society is unfolding according to a different pattern of social organization. The new groupings such as the unemployed, the trade unions, the co-operatives, and voluntary associations can only exist in a modern society, and are certainly a product of such societies, while they often maintain a pragmatically orientated tie with a more tradition-based social system.

NOTES
[1] This subject will be further explored in a forthcoming chapter on 'The poor in urban politics in Africa', H. J. Schmanur and W. Bloomberg (eds.), *Power, deprivation and urban policy*.

[2] See: M. Wilson and A. Mafeje, *Langa, a study of social groups in an African township*, Cape Town, Oxford University Press, 1963; B.A. Pauw, *The second generation, a study of the family among urbanized Bantu in East London*, Cape Town, Oxford University Press, 1963; J. C. Mitchell and A. L. Epstein, 'Occupational prestige and social status among urban Africans in Northern Rhodesia', *Africa*, **29**, 1, 22–40, (January, 1959).

[3] Field data notes, Nairobi, August–September 1966.

[4] In Kenya the following circular had to be issued as a result of pressure by those unemployed who had no highly placed relatives in government service to help them.

24 May 1966

SPONSORING OF CANDIDATES FOR EMPLOYMENT

It has been the practice in the Treasury and the Ministry of Economic Planning and Development to fill the vacancies in the grades of clerks, typists, stenographers, and the subordinate staff by employing persons, who have been introduced by officers working in these two Ministries or by engaging persons, who just happened to come to the Personnel Section at the time of the occurrence of the vacancies, looking for employment. This has given rise to a feeling among the unemployed that jobs in the Government are filled by candidates who are fortunate enough to have friends or relatives in influential places. In order to dispel such erroneous impressions and to ensure that all vacant posts in the above mentioned grades are filled entirely on the grounds of merit with no preferential treatment, the Minister for Labour has instructed all the Ministries that all vacancies in the above mentioned grades should be notified to the Employment Exchange so that workseekers registered there have the first chance of employment. This procedure will be followed very rigidly and therefore all the officers working in the Treasury and the Ministry of Economic Planning are requested to note that they will simply be wasting their time in introducing their friends and relatives to the Personnel Officer or other senior officers for employment in these two Ministries.

Any officer, who has a friend or a relative looking for employment should advise him to register his name with the Employment Exchange, which is situated on the Commercial Street in Industrial Area.

[5] Field data notes, *op. cit.*

[6] *Ibid.*

[7] *Ibid.*

[8] *Morning Post* (Lagos), 11 July 1966.

[9] Information to the contrary is provided by: H. Knoop, 'Some demographic characteristics of a suburban squatting community of Leopoldville: a preliminary analysis', *Cahiers economiques et sociaux* (University of Louvain), **4**, 2, pp. 119–46 June 1966.

[10] *East Africa Royal Commission* 1953–1955 *Report*, CMD 9475, HMSO London, 1955, p. 201.

[11] F. Fanon, *The wretched of the earth*, New York, Grove Press, 1966.

[12] *East African Standard* (Nairobi), 16 September 1966.

Workers in Mali

MAJHEMOUT DIOP

From Majhemout Diop, *Histoire des classes sociales dans l'afrique de l'ouest*, 1. *Le Mali*, Maspero, Paris 1971. (Translation © Heinemann Educational Books Ltd, 1974.)

The great majority of workers (77 per cent) are employed by the state. When one takes into account the fact that until 19 November 1968 the number of private concerns was kept to a quarter of their former size and their turnover to a sixth, one realizes the importance that the state took on as an employer of labour.

It is obvious that employment by the state instead of by private capitalist enterprises reduces the opposition between workers and employer. Especially as here the state is 'national', young and, moreover, socialist. Indeed, a state of this kind naturally relies on national solidarity against neo-colonialism and on the unity–not openly expressed but implied–of the working class in support of 'socialist construction'.

We see a sudden reversal of values in any clash of interests. In the past, the employer was private and foreign; and even when identifying himself with the state, that state was considered to be antagonistic and foreign. Today, the workers have to do with 'our state' and 'our government', African, negro, and socialist; and which no longer tolerates any shirking or evasion, any liberty other than unconditional support.

Any other attitude, says the state, is 'national treachery' and 'class betrayal'. The state alone, it proclaims, holds the truth to all things and to national and social justice; all that is asked of the workers is submission. If necessary, the means of coercion are at hand to remind them that 'no outburst will be tolerated and any crime will be severely punished'.

What kind of government is it? One of national union able to speak in the name of the 'micro-nation'? It becomes less so each day, by the very nature of things.

Is it a dictatorship of the proletariat or at least of the people, a dictatorship of the majority over a minority? The answer can only be: at no time has it been a dictatorship of the proletariat, and only for a short time a dictatorship of the majority.

The mystification arises from the fact that a social group adopted a ready-made ideology and in the name of sound ideas it carried out for its own benefit, knowingly or not, actions which were not always sound. And the more it carried out, the more it had to explain, the greater became the verbal out-pourings and the greater the 'leftist' language.

In the end, the governing group skipped over the stages and wiped out the national revolution, the democratic revolution.

Hardly had it buckled down to the socialist revolution than it exchanged that for a hypothetical cultural revolution. Or, to use a more down-to-earth expression, it swopped the boubou* for a Maoist tunic much too soon.

And of course the reactionaries still among the group went along with it all! So there was the revolution grossly misrepresented and discredited for a long time in the eyes of the people!

Pronounced backwardness of the workers

The percentage of skilled workers is very low, less than four per cent. Whereas unskilled labourers, the most uneducated class, make up about 60 per cent of the work force.

In the public service, foremen and trained personnel are found mostly in agriculture (over 40 per cent); there are 21 per cent in the mines, 20 per cent in transport, and only 0.6 per cent in the metal industry.

Moreover, the largest number of firms (36 per cent) are commercial concerns (private enterprise, 26 per cent; state-owned, 5 per cent; petrol, 5 per cent). Industrial concerns take second place with 21 per cent. But of these, 45 per cent are factories working for the food industry; if the concerns linked to agricultural production are added, the percentage rises to 60. These firms also account for 60 per cent of the total industrial turnover, whereas those in the metal industry–which amount to 10 per cent–account for only 8 per cent of the total turnover.

The lack of heavy industry, the preponderance of light industry linked to agriculture, and the fact that almost all the firms have come into being since Independence, are obviously factors contributing to the slow awareness among workers of their specific problems.

Insignificance of the female work-force

The percentage of women employed in industry is very low: only a little more than 3 per cent of the unskilled workers and less than 1 per cent of the trained personnel. What is more serious is that women workers are thought little of in most firms; fault is found with them because of their few qualifications, their erratic attendance, inability to adapt, etc. So there is a general tendency to dismiss women and take on men in their place.

A similar state of affairs is found among the labourers; despite no qualifications being needed, little more than 1 per cent are women. The civilizing contribution that a working wife could make to the home is thus reduced. And her understanding of workers' problems in a modern society and her support–even if only moral–of the workers' claims are bound to be lacking.

---

*voluminous garment common in West Africa (eds).

Ambiguous role of the foreign managerial staff

In the public service there are now only 3 per cent of foreigners among the trained staff; among workmen the percentage falls–naturally–to 0.26.

Yet in the private sector the number of foreigners employed is high, reaching 64 per cent.

The Africanization at the managerial level was politically justifiable and necessary to the consolidation of Independence, but it was often carried out in a suspect manner. People whose qualifications were inadequate were sometimes promoted through favouritism or political expediency. This partly explains the incapacity of the state administration and the public services, in marked contrast to the vigour of the private sector, for so much depended upon the ability and integrity of the senior staff.

The foreigners in the public sector, few in number and up against a general attitude of jealousy and distrust, rightly or wrongly, are therefore almost ineffectual. Whereas those in the private sector, much more numerous, manage affairs as they wish. They are most efficient in matters where Africa is being exploited, much less so in areas where the country should be given aid. Such is the ambiguous and striking nature of the presence of foreigners in senior positions.

Falls in the standard of living

Between 1947 and 1957 the SMIG* was multiplied by more than five; in the next two years (1957–59) by one and a half. But in the ten years 1959–69, with devaluation, it has been halved!

The resultant drop in income has not been equalled by a fall in the cost of living. On the contrary. Taking the annual rise in the cost of living as 5.4 per cent, over the past decade (1959–69) it has amounted to more than 50 per cent.

It is therefore easy to understand that the sacrifices demanded of the working classes, in conditions where their cost of living has practically doubled, have not been favourably received. Salaried employees in general, and the working class in particular, accepted heroically the many new taxes they had to bear, including a development tax and a special deduction from salaries in 1964–66. This was understandable in the years following Independence. In fact, after the break-up of the Mali Federation it was possible to mobilize, in the name of a national mystique, if not the whole population at least the workers in the towns. It is understandable, too, that the most aware among the workers were not indifferent to the development of socialism in the Mali Republic.

However, with the passing of time after the events of 19 August 1960, and the reconciliation with Senegal after the Kidira meeting in 1963, it became difficult to maintain the pressure of national claims. And the inequalities brought to light by certain scandals, the inadequacy of explanations and proposed solutions, made the exploitation of an egalitarian, socialist mystique useless or at least premature.

---

*official minimum wage (eds).

Yet it was in such inauspicious circumstances that a greater tax burden was laid upon the people. The increase in taxes for the fiscal year 1967–68 brought in 1500 million Mali francs, representing about seven per cent of all direct and indirect taxation (which accounts for some 30 per cent of the budget).

This was the reason why appeals to the working class were increasingly disregarded.

We shall see how and why the trade unions, which should have made relationships between the workers and the government easier, failed to carry out their role properly.

The workers advance

During the past decade the workers have nevertheless improved their position. Whereas the number of unskilled labourers remained the same from 1956 to 1967, that of salaried workers doubled. The figures are indicative of a betterment, as well as an increase, in this social class, because of the higher proportion of those with some education.

The growth of industry is, moreover, bound to result in a strengthening of the working class–a prospect which, within the framework of a socialist tendency, even an inconsistent one, cannot but alarm certain circles. For it is clear that, in such a climate, the workers were bound to become conscious of themselves as a class. Indeed, one could discuss at length the best conditions for a rapid development of working class awareness as such. Under the Mali régime prior to 19 November 1968, despite everything seeming an occasion prepared for taking the sting out of the growing opposition, there was nevertheless a climate propitious to the spreading of socialism in theory if not in practice.

Ultimately, the growth of industry coupled with the spread of Marxist-Leninist theories created at least a pre-revolutionary situation, though a revolution itself would be difficult in the particular circumstances prevailing in Mali. It is easy to understand that not everyone was pleased...

One can therefore be certain that inside as well as outside the country there were coalitions continually being formed to put an end to this state of affairs. And the more this continued, the more the régime hardened its position. And the people, from being enthusiastic at the beginning, soon became apathetic and then hostile. Conditions were not ripe enough for a change.

So it is difficult to affirm that there is a politically active working class in Mali. More problematical is whether it is sufficiently conscious to come to power, and even more so to wield and retain that power.

The fact is that the emergence of this working class in Mali is too recent. Even the most compact section, the railway workers, has not yet broken free from the office workers and other employees. In a society where the greatest ambition is to be a shopkeeper, everyone dreams of one day sitting behind his own counter; and many workers are no exception to this. On the one hand, very few of them have been reached by courses on politics and trade unionism; and on the other, socialism has never been supreme among the proletariat, far from it. The governing elements, while proclaiming themselves socialists, have never shown themselves over-zealous in the workers' cause. In other words, the workers have never been organized as such nor been ideologically prepared for considering themselves as an independent social class.

Lenin enjoined 'sustaining the general democratic struggle... without ever idealizing it by the use of little artificial words such as socialization, and without ever forgetting for a moment the necessity of organizing the proletariat of the towns and the countryside into an entirely independent social-democratic class party'.[1]

It must be admitted in all fairness that the break-up of the Mali Federation had disastrous and unexpected consequences for the working class in Mali. The withdrawal of the Mali frontier to beyond Faleme left the workers' capital, Thiès,* well outside it.

The socialist experiment in Mali continued without the participation of a working class, which was in any case almost non-existent as a force. It should be added that the party in power, the Union Soudanaise (US), had preserved a good deal from the 'tactical' withdrawal from the Rassemblement Democratique Africain (RDA) in 1951. The class struggle was theoretically put aside. Not until 1962 and the trade's demonstration was the antagonism of the social classes again brought into the limelight. Until the events of 19 November 1968 there seemed no real awareness that socialism in Mali involved, first and foremost, the mobilization and urgent organization of the workers, their effective participation in the country's affairs, and their access to positions of responsibility, and their presence in social bodies, in Parliament, and the government.

In a word, the socialist experiment in Mali was far from being orthodox. It took place without the 'working class of the nation', and therefore hardly with the participation of the international working class. It was certainly a novel and an interesting experiment in more than one respect. But that was far from sufficient, and the régime had to expect difficult times ahead.

Although those in power in Mali could not be classed as anti-proletarian, neither had they received the unconditional support of the workers. The most conscious of the latter regretted the monopolizing of responsible positions by the intelligentsia. The mass of the workers lost interest in a socialism that they barely understood anyway. Both moved further away from the governing class, and little by little came to liken the latter to one of the standard forms of African despotism.

The army seized power on 19 November 1968. We can now understand both the lethargy of those who had become disillusioned and ceased to believe in anything, and the enthusiasm of those who naively thought that a new golden age had arrived.

---

*A major railway centre in present-day Senegal (eds).

[1] Lenin, 'Petty-bourgeois socialism and proletarian socialism', *Complete works* IX.

PART V

Is there an African national bourgeoisie?
JACK WODDIS

From Jack Woddis, *New theories of revolution*, Lawrence and Wishart, London 1972.

Ledda[1] outlines five main groups of the African bourgeoisie–compradores who function as middlemen for the large foreign trading firms; indigenous entrepreneurs; a bureaucratic bourgeoisie emerging from the nationalist élites, and including both new political leaderships and former state functionaries; local planters; and feudal landlords. In some cases, he points out, these groups merge and become, in fact, a single capitalist class. But such a class, he argues, cannot be regarded as a 'national bourgeoisie' in the sense of 'a social force capable of producing a high level of development of a country's productive forces on the basis of *its own* choices'. The African bourgeoisie, he contends, is 'tied, body and soul, to foreign capital' and its interests 'cannot exist or be defended independently'.

Facts about the African bourgeoisie are by no means plentiful, but they are sufficient to enable one to judge to what extent an African capitalist class is developing, what are its main characteristics, and what role it is playing in the present phase of the African revolution.

The origins of an African capitalist class are generally to be found in trade. Export and import trade, of course, was firmly in the hands of the big imperialist trading companies even prior to the twentieth-century colonial system. Internal trade, however, gave scope for the emergence of African traders, especially in West Africa where palm-fruit production and processing was already in the hands of Africans and where local trading was already widespread.

In East and Central Africa, the lack of an immediate crop for export, and poor transport facilities compared with West Africa, delayed the emergence of African traders connected with the European market. Much of the trade fell into the hands of the Asians, who later expanded into cotton ginning and sugar plantations. European settlement in East and Central Africa meant that Europeans, too, monopolized certain branches of trade.

In West Africa, however, African traders had more opportunity, and with the coming of the lorry at the beginning of the twentieth century, a veritable revolution began to take place in African trading. Now it became possible to carry larger loads over longer distances in a shorter space of time; the interior could be more easily opened up to the trader; the village store could be set up and constantly re-stocked.

Some traders sell locally, others act as wholesalers, buying from the foreign importers and, with the aid of their lorries, selling up-country. Some traders in West Africa are also cocoa farmers, who utilize part of their profits from cocoa to launch out into trading, and, conversely, ploughing back some of their trading profits to expand their cocoa production.

From amongst these thousands of African traders a considerable differentiation has taken place. Studies by Peter Garlick of African traders in Kumasi and Accra show that amongst the 150 traders who are the biggest men in Kumasi, a turnover of £5000 to £20000 a year is quite common, and a number reach £100000 a year. Over 60 of these traders (at the time of the enquiry, 1959–60), were doing some direct importing from overseas, and most were employing up to three or four assistants (often relatives), and some were employing more. An analysis of 251 African traders in Ghana by Garlick shows six in the turnover class of £20000–£25000 a year, 19 between £25000 and £50000, nine between £50000 and £75000, four between £75000 and £100000 and six in the £100000 to £200000 class. A further 55 were between £5000 and £20000. This means a total of 44 out of 251 who could be classified as rich traders, and a further 55 as middle-size.

In his study on *Road Transport in Nigeria* (1958), E. K. Hawkins points out that while foreign transport firms dominate in the freight trade, African firms dominate in passenger traffic and in the carriage of internal trade. The African capitalist, says Hawkins, 'has asserted himself, notably in the field of road transport, but also in retail trade, buildings and contracting'. He further notes that 'a number of Africans have become prominent' in Nigeria in tyre retreading, woodworking, the supply of building materials, and printing.

A report on Senegal describes how the better-off cultivators are taking up trade, some of them having already given up cultivation in order to live entirely by trading. In Cameroun, the Bamileke are particularly active in trade; in some of the areas where they are heavily concentrated, a quarter of them are occupied in trading. Describing the activities of traders in the cocoa region of the Cameroun, Jacques Binet (*Budgets Familiaux des Planteurs de Cacao au Cameroun*), writes: 'The traders represent the wealthy section of the population.'

In general, one can say that an African industrial bourgeoisie does not yet exist. It is certainly the case that no large-scale industrial and factory production is in the hands of African owners. At the same time, a number of small-scale industries, owned by Africans, already exist in a number of territories, and in some cases are steadily growing. A study on the *Development of small industries in eastern Nigeria*, prepared for the United States Agency for International Development, estimates that small industry in Eastern Nigeria provides employment for approximately triple the number of people engaged in large-scale manufacture. In fourteen towns surveyed in the region, 10728 firms were recorded, employing 28721 workers–an average of 2.7 per enterprise. This average included the manager-owner and apprentices. Only 332, or three per cent of the 10728 firms, employed ten or more people; 55 per cent employed between six and nine; and as many as 38 per cent were one-man businesses.

Some of the African capitalists in Nigeria have diversified their efforts, acting as directors of British trading firms, exporting rubber and timber in their own right, entering industry itself with timber mills or rubber processing plants, and eventually employing several hundred production workers, shipping clerks, and so on. Some of these African capitalists, who commence as quite petty traders, evolve by stages into buying agencies in effect for the big foreign monopolies, subsequently emerging as direct exporters on their own account, accepting posts as directors of foreign monopolies, and then commencing their own manufactures. One can see, in this process, how inter-linked with foreign monopolies are these African capitalists, yet, at the same time, the different points at which they enter into competition with these very firms, both in trade and in manufacture.

In the majority of cases, the older capitalist sections have been joined by a new bureaucratic bourgeoisie, a stratum of career politicians–lawyers, civil servants, and other petty-bourgeois sections (sometimes sons of land-owners, traders, and richer farmers)–who utilize their new governmental and state positions to acquire wealth and economic position. As part of, but in some ways separate from, this bureaucratic bourgeoisie are the army and police officers, normally trained in Western military academies. Often, it is this new bureaucratic bourgeoisie which wields state power, sometimes in alliance with external imperialist forces. In his book, *Classes and class ideology in Senegal*,[2] Majhemout Diop, former General Secretary of the African Independence Party, argues that it is this bureaucratic bourgeoisie, numbering over a thousand, which has usurped political power in Senegal and is acting as an agency of neo-colonialism. The trading bourgeoisie in Senegal, says M. Diop, is negligible, and its income puts it rather in the category of a petty-bourgeoisie. African manufacture, in 1961, owned only 15 out of 320 enterprises in the country. Thus it is the new bureaucratic bour-geoisie which is the main obstacle to Senegal's advance. 'The bureaucratic bourgeoisie are the weeds on the fields of the nation', declares M. Diop. 'If our people want to live and survive they must uproot them from our native soil.'

In those new African states which are ruled solely by compromising sections of the African bourgeoisie, there is an open and obvious attempt to follow a capitalist path, to rely mainly on the growth of indigenous capitalist forces. Addressing the National Assembly of the Central African Republic on 16 October 1961, the President, David Dacko, declared himself in favour of 'a Central African bourgeoisie. That's what we have decided, because we think that that's what the future of our country will be. And I say to this Central African élite which is daily growing before our eyes: don't be ashamed to be bourgeois, don't be ashamed to become wealthy...'

Such conceptions are naturally encouraged by the imperialists who under-stand that these bourgeois forces can become a prop for continued imperialist exploitation. One important tactic of neo-colonialism which will influence the position of the African capitalist class is the drawing in of trading or bureaucratic capitalist sections into the apparatus and network of the big monopolies themselves. Thus the big imperialist trading companies, such as the UAC (United Africa Company), the SCOA (Société Commerciale de

l'Ouest Africain), and CFAO (Compagnie Française de l'Afrique Occidentale), as well as Cie du Niger Français, the main subsidiary of the UAC in
the former French territories in West Africa, Barclays Bank, and other major
companies, have deemed it necessary to 'bring in' the African, in some cases
offering him managerial posts, or even directorships, sometimes combining
this with abandoning a large sector of trade, especially in raw materials and
traditional consumer imports, to the African trader. The African traders
are still, to a considerable extent, merely agents of the big European monopolies from whom the goods for sale are imported and to whom in the last
resort, the raw materials produced in Africa are sold. But in general, the new
situation has favoured a further expansion and enrichment of the African
trader, especially the bigger ones who are already well-placed to take advantage of the new possibilities.

In Guinea the Government has kept a close rein on the African traders,
rightly regarding them as a base for reaction and counter-revolution. The
struggle there between the people and more forward-looking democrats on
the one hand, and the trading bourgeoisie on the other, has been a major
source of tension over the past few years. In 1962, Sékou Touré had to appeal
for 'revolutionary firmness' against the 'trading bourgeoisie'. The warning
was clearly necessary for, in 1963, when the Government introduced a ten
per cent tax on all sales, a number of traders went on strike. Sékou Touré,
in a message to the branches and committees of the Democratic Party of
Guinea (PDG), demanded: 'The traders must open their shops, or close
them for good.' The dangerous role of the trading bourgeoisie in Guinea has
been noted on many occasions by Sékou Touré, who has characterized it as
the base of all subversive, deviationist, and counter-revolutionary activities'.

President Sékou Touré has made it abundantly clear that these capitalist
elements in Guinea are not simply an economic obstacle to Guinea's advance.
These elements, he has said, are 'a primary form of the society of exploiting
capitalism, which is a natural ally of imperialism and neo-colonialism'. Thus
the leaders of Guinea have recognized that to give licence to such a stratum
would endanger national sovereignty, hamper economic progress, and prevent
Guinea's advance.

In Ghana, in the period prior to the *coup* against Nkrumah, there was a
considerable sharpening of the struggle between the most forward sections
who wanted to press forward and open the way to socialism, and those trading
and bureaucratic capitalist elements who wished to be the main beneficiaries
of independence and to drag their country along a capitalist road.

This nascent bourgeoisie was to be found not only in the so-called 'Opposition', but even within the Convention People's Party itself, and among the
Ministers. In his famous 'Dawn Broadcast', 8 April 1961, President Nkrumah
castigated the new bourgeois elements in Ghana society, who were utilizing
their state positions to enrich themselves at the expense of national development and the people's interests.

President Nkrumah's correct intention to 'smoke out the hoarders and
profiteers' did not succeed. The developing bourgeois elements, who had
been allowed to enrich themselves in the past decade, had no intention of
seeing Ghana travel towards socialism. Reactionary forces in Ghanaian

society, backed by foreign imperialism, and taking advantage of the failures of the Government, including its very failure to curb the nascent capitalist class whose greed and ostentation was arousing the disgust and anger of the whole people, reached out and struck down President Nkrumah's government[7] and the CPP. The aim of the *coup* was not to eliminate corruption but to swing Ghana away from her progressive path, and turn her into an ally of neo-colonialism. And this was so notwithstanding the fact that corrupt bourgeois elements were to be found in the topmost ranks of the CPP itself.

From the above facts one can draw certain tentative conclusions as regards the role of African capitalists.

1. Even before the winning of national independence, a stratum of African capitalists–mainly engaged in trading, transport, and farming–was beginning to emerge in most African states.

2. Though dependent on the big foreign monopolies (who were either purchasers of the peasant produce, or suppliers of the goods for sale by African traders), some sections of these African capitalists participated in the national movements. This helps to explain why it was possible for them, after independence, to emerge in a number of cases as the new rulers.

3. Since the winning of independence, *a national bourgeoisie interested in industrial development and the growth of the economy*, has begun to emerge in some instances. This section plays a progressive role, since it does not wish to see the national economy remain in the grip of imperialism. It has therefore thrown in its lot with the majority of the people who are struggling for economic independence and economic advance. The national bourgeoisie in Africa, that is to say that section of the bourgeoisie which is genuinely interested in national independence, national economic growth, the expansion of the internal market, and the creation of national industry, faces very great problems. Generally, it is economically weak, lacks capital, as well as managerial experience and knowledge as regards modern factory production, and has no body of skilled African workers and technicians ready at hand. For these reasons, it is in no position at this stage to initiate large-scale factory production itself–and understandably is often reluctant even to try. But, since it desires to see economic expansion and a growth in national production, it understands the need for and supports the idea of the state itself taking the necessary steps to create new national industries. It is this forward-looking section of the bourgeoisie in Africa which, in alliance with the working class, the peasants, and revolutionary democrats, is resisting imperialism and struggling against the intrigues of the compromising sections of the bourgeoisie.

4. In the most progressive states, the economic and political power of the *trading bourgeoisie* is being weakened by State economic measures (the setting up of state trading agencies, fiscal and tax measures, etc.), and this is leading to a sharp struggle with these elements since what is basically involved is the whole question of breaking decisively with imperialism, and opening the way to socialism.

5. On the land, while there is in many cases a significant growth of co-operatives, there is also a *considerable differentiation taking place within the peasantry* practically in every state, with the emergence of a small but clearly

defined capitalist stratum which exploits African wage labour.

6. The setting up of new states and new governments has meant the emergence of a stratum of *bureaucratic capitalists*, including army officers, which, when linked to imperialism, acts as its neo-colonialist agency. This stratum is sometimes in alliance with feudal forces, and usually with other sections of the African bourgeoisie, especially traders.

7. This total process is leading to the establishment not simply of sections of capitalists but of what can now be regarded in some African countries as *a definite capitalist class*, with common class interests expressed in its control of a political party, its domination over the state and government, and the growing cohesiveness of its economic and political power. In no case can one say that this process has reached an advanced stage, but it would be equally wrong not to note the tendency.

8. In all African states, both those which are under progressive leaderships and are cutting away from imperialism, and those which are under reactionary capitalist sections clinging to imperialism, *the internal class struggle is sharpening*. In reactionary states it takes the form of open class battles (strikes, demonstrations, and even the overthrow of governments), ranging from simple economic demands over wages, prices, etc., to the challenging of the whole direction of government policy. In the advanced states, it takes the form of economic and political resistance by the reactionary capitalist sections to the steps of the government and state which are aimed at the further unfolding of the national democratic revolution. In some cases, this resistance by the reactionary capitalist sections, acting in concert with imperialism, has been successful in overthrowing progressive governments, as in Ghana, Mali, and Uganda. Similar plots have been tried in Guinea and Congo (Brazzaville). The neo-colonialist counter-offensive which is now raging in Africa is based on an alliance between imperialism and indigenous capitalist elements in Africa who have a common interest in preventing African states from taking a path which would open the road to socialism.

When Ledda defines the national bourgeoisie as '*a social force capable of producing a high level of development of a country's forces*' it seems to me that he is, to an extent, confusing capacity with intentions, which arise from other objective factors. Certainly, among the groups he lists, some can be dismissed as outside the ranks of the national bourgeoisie, if one takes the term in its more normal sense as referring not to the whole indigenous bourgeoisie but to that section of it which is interested in controlling and expanding its own internal market (which necessitates an attack on, or at least a weakening of, feudalism, and competition and conflict with imperialism). Compradores and feudal landlords are not usually regarded as part of the national bourgeoisie. But can one so easily dismiss the African entrepreneurs, and even sections of the new bureaucratic bourgeoisie (which, to some extent, are to be distinguished from the older bureaucratic bourgeoisie reared by the colonial system)? And are not the petty-bourgeoisie, including sections of the peasantry, and sections of the élite, also linked to the aspirations of the national bourgeoisie?

Part of the problem arises from ignoring the present stage that Africa has reached, and misunderstanding the character of Africa's present revolution. Although the world as a whole is passing through a transition from capitalism to socialism, the African countries are at a very early stage of that process. They have, in the main, won their national independence, but the essential tasks of their democratic, anti-imperialist, anti-feudal, revolution remain to be fulfilled[3]–and some of these tasks, of course, may not be completed until the socialist stage is reached.

It is fashionable in some 'New Left' circles these days to emphasize the dependent and compromising character of the indigenous bourgeoisie, and even of the national bourgeoisie. In fact, this is usually cited in respect of all Third World countries as proof that there is no longer any possibility of a national democratic phase of the revolution but that the immediate aim must be a workers' and peasants' government. It is, of course, true that the advance of socialism and its increasingly decisive influence on world processes to some extent circumscribes the national bourgeoisie and limits its possibilities of an independent capitalist growth since its fear of the growing strength of socialism will tend to push it back into the arms of imperialism. But it is equally true that the very existence of a socialist system provides new possibilities for the national bourgeoisie to secure help in building its independent economy and in lessening its dependence on imperialism, and in this very process to come into conflict with the imperialist powers.

These two possibilities now before the national bourgeoisie are only another expression of the dual character of this bourgeoisie–and this, it should be said, is the nub of the matter. It is not a question as to whether the national bourgeoisie is on the side of the revolution or the counter-revolution– for, in a sense, the answer is both. And this was a point already emphasized by Lenin in 1920. Talking of 'a certain rapprochement between the bourgeoisie of the exploiting and colonial countries', he explained that as a result, while the bourgeoisie of the oppressed nation supports the national movement 'it at the same time works hand in glove with the imperialist bourgeoisie, that is, joins forces with it against all revolutionary movements and classes'.[4]

The whole point about the national bourgeoisie is that, like Janus, it faces two ways. As a bourgeoisie it is interested in exploiting its own workers and ensuring their submission to its domination. At the same time, its attempts to gain control over its home market and expand the national economy bring it into conflict with the big imperialist monopolies which naturally desire to maintain their dominant position in the market, and ensure that the economy of the given country evolves in accordance with their own profit-interests and not with the genuine development of that country itself.

Thus the national bourgeoisie finds itself in conflict both with its own workers and with the imperialists. Its very dependency on imperialism is a sign of its contradictions with imperialism. Its dependency is a form of its oppression at the hands of the big monopolies. However weak it may be, it would like to relax this grip. To do this it repeatedly makes use of the mass movement of workers and peasants, attempting to wield the movement like a big stick to win concessions for itself from the imperialists. But as soon as the workers and peasants begin to challenge the limits of the bourgeoisie's own aims, and start to press their own class demands, and even threaten to take over the direction of the struggle, the national bourgeoisie backs down in haste and will, at times, even turn to the imperialists for help in crushing the people's movement.

In China, the national bourgeoisie repeatedly sided with the revolution–and just as repeatedly abandoned it. Between 1924 to 1927 it was on the side of the revolution; from 1927 to 1931 important sections supported the counter-revolution. For a short period in 1931 it supported the national revolution–and then forsook it. From 1937 to 1945 it was once more on the side of the national revolution; and then in 1945, sections of it deserted once more. After the victory of the Chinese people in 1949, sections of the national bourgeoisie came back to the fold and played a positive role in building the new China.

No one would claim, for one moment, that the African bourgeoisie is analogous to that which existed in China. Even in Africa there is a considerable difference between the bourgeoisie that exists in Gambia–with less than half a million people–and that of Nigeria, with a population of some 50 million and far greater possibilities for the growth of a relatively strong bourgeoisie. It is correct to draw attention, as Fanon and Ledda have done, to the exceptionally weak and dependent character of the African bourgeoisie, but this factor itself does not justify a complete write-off of the national bourgeoisie in Africa. No matter how weak, how vacillating, how dependent, it has points of conflict with imperialism which can be used to further the national struggle. It is a commonplace of Marxism that revolutionaries should never ignore allies, no matter how weak, how temporary, how unreliable and how downright treacherous they may be. In this respect, despite its obvious weakness, the African bourgeoisie is no exception.

... Fanon's view of the path of the African revolution allows no room for an explanation of the progressive changes introduced into Ghana during Nkrumah's presidency or in Uganda under Obote, in Zambia under Kaunda, in Tanzania under Nyerere, and similar developments in some other African countries. Neither does it really explain why the *coups* took place in Ghana and Uganda (nor why they succeeded, which is another question altogether). Obviously neither in Ghana nor in Uganda were the workers and peasants in power, nor was socialism being built. It is equally obvious that those in power in these two countries were not the old feudal and compradore classes through whom imperialism formerly ruled directly over the territories. Simply to say that they were governments of the petty-bourgeoisie or of sections of the élite is only half an explanation. Clearly pre-*coup* Ghana and pre-*coup* Uganda, each in its own way, and the former probably more decisively than the latter, were weakening the old pre-capitalist structure, modernizing their countries, building new industry, creating a state sector of the economy, and loosening the grip of imperialism over certain sectors of the economy. In both cases, the government power represented the aspirations of the national bourgeoisie, even though it spoke often about building 'Socialism'.

The petty-bourgeoisie and educated élite in office is well-placed to evolve into a section of the bourgeoisie.[5] In taking important steps to build up the economy it is paving the way either for a transition to socialism–if the working people prove strong enough to take over power and carry through the changes still more fundamentally–or for the establishment of capitalism. The fact that the African entrepreneur has generally speaking proved too weak (lacking in sufficient capital, technical and managerial skills, qualified and trained workers, etc.) to build large-scale industry has meant that this task devolves on the state; but this does not rule out the further growth of indigenous capitalism. After the Meiji restoration in Japan, the state built up modern industries–and this paved the way for their being taken over later by the *zaibastu* and so making possible the growth of Japanese monopoly capitalism. Africa is not Japan. But the existence of an important state sector of the economy and the creation of state industries by no means rules out the growth of private capitalism, nor the possibility that, at a certain stage, the private sector will take over part or even all of the state-built enterprises. The overthrow of Nkrumah in Ghana, for example, was followed precisely by a partial sell-up of many of the state-owned enterprises, mainly to foreign firms.

No one should have illusions about the national bourgeoisie. It may be an *oppressed* bourgeoisie, but it is still a bourgeoisie. And as long as it plays a leading role in the African revolution it will prevent the transition to socialism. But if it is weak, so is the African working class which, in almost every African territory, has been unable so far to establish its own party, based on Marxism. This serves to underline the fact that Africa's road to socialism will not be easy or short. Enthusiasm for the socialist future should not be allowed to dim one's view of the stage one has reached, nor of the tremendous obstacles that have to be overcome. The economic, social, and cultural backwardness of Africa is itself a powerful argument for the revolutionary forces to utilize every potential for change, and to make use of every possible contradiction between the national bourgeoisie and the imperialists.

NOTES

[1] Romano Ledda: 'Social human and political struggle', *International Socialist Journal*, **14**, 22, 574–5,, (August, 1967).

[2] Majhemout Diop: *Classes et idéologies de classe au Sénégal*, Prague, 1963, pp. 51–61.

[3] In some cases, of course, even earlier forms of society have to be replaced.

[4] V. I. Lenin: 'Report of the commission on the national and colonial question', *Collected Works*, Vol. 31, p. 242.

[5] See, for example, Joan Bellamy: 'African élites: a study of Ghana', *Marxism today*, February 1967, pp. 37–43.

Class and status in contemporary Africa
IMMANUEL WALLERSTEIN

From Immanuel Wallerstein, 'Social conflict in post-independence black Africa: the concepts of race and status-group reconsidered', in Ernest Q. Campbell (Ed.), *Racial tensions and national identity,* Vanderbilt University Press, Nashville 1972.

Marx, in using the concept of class, distinguished between classes *an sich* and *für sich*. Weber repeated this distinction when he said: 'Thus every class may be the carrier of any one of the innumerable possible forms of class action, but this is not necessarily so. In any case, a class does not in itself constitute a group (*Gemeinschaft*)'.[1]

Why is it that classes are not always *für sich*? Indeed, why is it they are so seldom *für sich*? Or to put the question another way, how do we explain that status-group consciousness is so pervasive and powerful a political force, in Africa and throughout the world, today and throughout history? To answer that it is false consciousness is simply to push the question one step logically back, for then we should have to ask how it is that most people most of the time exhibit false consciousness?

Weber has a theory to account for this. He states:

As to the general economic conditions making for the predominance of stratification by status, only the following can be said. When the bases of the acquisition and distribution of goods are relatively stable, stratification by status is favoured. Every technological repercussion and economic transformation threatens stratification by status and pushes the class situation into the foreground. Epochs and countries in which the naked class situation is of predominant significance are regularly the periods of technical and economic transformations. And every slowing down of the change in economic stratification leads, in due course, to the growth of status structure and makes for a resuscitation of the important role of social honour.[2]

Weber's explanation seems very simple and makes class consciousness the correlate of progress and social change, stratification by status the expression of retrograde forces–a sort of vulgar Marxism. While one may agree with the moral thrust of the theorem, it is not very predictive of the smaller shifts in historical reality nor does it explain why one can find modern economic thrusts in status-group garb as well as mechanisms of the preservation of traditional privilege in class consciousness.

Favret gives us a clue in her discussion of a Berber rebellion in Algeria:

[In Algeria] primordial groups do not exist substantively, unaware of their archaism, but reactively. The anthropologist tempted by collecting traditional political phenomena is in danger therefore of a colossal misunderstanding in interpreting them naively, for their context is today inverted. The choice for the descendants of the segmentary tribes of the nineteenth century is no longer among ends–to co-operate with the central government or to institutionalize dissidence–for only the former choice is henceforth possible. The choice–or the fate–of the peasants of the underdeveloped agricultural sector is in the means of attaining this end; among which, paradoxically, is dissidence.[3]

Favret pushes us to look at claims based on status-group affiliation not in the intellectual terms of the actors in the situation, but in terms of the actual functions such claims perform in the social system. Moerman makes a similar appeal in an analysis of the Lue, a tribe in Thailand, about whom he asks three trenchant questions: What are the Lue? Why are the Lue? When are the Lue? He concludes:

Ethnic identification devices–with their important potential of making each ethnic set of living persons a joint enterprise with countless generations of unexamined history–seem to be universal. Social scientists should therefore describe and analyse the ways in which they are used, and not merely–as natives do–use them as explanations... It is quite possible that ethnic categories are rarely appropriate subjects for the interesting human predicates.[4]

Perhaps then we could reconceive the Weberian trinity of class, status-group, and party not as three different and cross-cutting groups but as three different existential forms of the same essential reality. In which case, the question shifts from Weber's one of the conditions under which stratification by status takes precedence over class consciousness to the conditions under which a stratum embodies itself as a class, as a status-group, or as a party. For such a conceptualization, it would not be necessary to argue that the boundary lines of the group in its successive embodiments would be identical–quite the contrary, or there would be no function to having different outer clothing–but rather that there exist a limited set of groups in any social structure at any given time in relation to, in conflict with, each other.

One approach, suggested by Rodolfo Stavenhagen, is to see status-groups as 'fossils' of social classes. He argues that:

Stratifications [i.e., status-groups] represent, in the majority of cases, what we call social *fixations*, frequently by juridical means, certainly subjectively, of specific social relations of production, represented by class relations. Into these social *fixations* intrude other secondary, accessory factors (for example, religious, ethnic) which reinforce the stratification and which have, at the same time, the function of 'liberating' it of its links with its economic base; in other words, of maintaining its strength even if its economic base changes. Consequently, stratifications can be thought of as justifications or rationalizations of the established economic system, that is to say, as ideologies. Like all phenomena of the social superstructure, stratification has a quality of inertia which maintains it even when the conditions which gave it birth have changed. As the relations between classes are modified... stratifications turn themselves into *fossils* of the class relations on which they were originally based... [Furthermore], it seems that the two types of groupings (dominant class and higher stratum) can co-exist for some time and be encrusted in the social structure, according to the particular historical circumstances. But sooner or later a new stratification system arises which corresponds more exactly to the current class system.[5]

In a later analysis, using Central American data, Stavenhagen spells out how, in a colonial situation, two caste-like lower status-groups (in that case, *indios* and *ladinos*) could emerge, become encrusted, and survive the various pressures at what he called class clarification. He argues that two forms of dependence (a colonial form, based on ethnic discrimination and political subordination) and a class form (based on work relations) grew up side by side and reflected a parallel ranking system. After independence, and despite economic development, the dichotomy between *indios* and *ladinos*, 'profoundly ensconced in the values of the members of society' remained, as 'an essentially conservative force' in the social structure. 'Reflecting a situation of the past... [this dichotomy] acts as a constraint on the development of the new class relations'.[6] In this version, present stratification is still a fossil of the past, but it is not so simply a fossil of class relations *per se*.

Another approach would be to see class or status-affiliation as options open to various members of the society. This is the approach of Peter Carstens. In two recent papers, one by Carstens[7] and one by Allen,[8] there is agreement that Africans working on the land in the rural areas should be thought of as 'peasants' who are members of the 'working class', that is who sell their labour power even when they are technically self-employed cash-crop farmers. But while Allen is concerned with emphasizing the pattern of tied alternation between cash-crop farming and wage-earning,[9] Carstens is more concerned with explaining the status-group apparatus of peasant class organization, or what he calls 'peasant status systems'.

Carstens starts with the argument that 'the retention or revival of tenuous tribal loyalties are resources available to persons to establish prestige or esteem'.[10] He reminds us that 'the same institutions that effected the hidden force that produced a peasant *class*, also created peasant *status* systems. For example... the surest way to achieve recognition, prestige, and esteem in the eyes of the ruling class as well as from the local peasants is to participate in the externally imposed educational and religious institutions.' It therefore follows that 'it is only by the manipulation of their internal status systems that they are able to gain access to other status systems which are located in the higher class. The strategy of status manipulation is best seen then as a means for crossing class boundaries'.

The strength of stratification by status can be seen in this light. Status honour is not only a mechanism for the achievers of yore to maintain their advantages in the contemporary market, the retrograde force described by Weber; it is also the mechanism whereby the upward-strivers obtain their ends within the system (hence the correlation of high ethnic consciousness and education, to which Colson called attention). With support from two such important groups, the ideological primacy of status-group is easy to understand. It takes an unusual organizational situation to break through this combination of elements interested in preserving this veil (or this reality—it makes no difference).

Weber was wrong. Class consciousness does not come to the fore when technological change or social transformation is occurring. All of modern history gives this the lie. Class consciousness only comes to the fore in a far rarer circumstance, in a 'revolutionary' situation, of which class consciousness is both the ideological expression and the ideological pillar. In this sense, the basic Marxian conceptual instinct was correct.

The African data re-analysed

Let us now return to the empirical reality of contemporary independent Africa in the light of this theoretical excursus. Independent Black Africa is today composed of a series of nation-states, members of the United Nations, almost none of which can be considered a national society, in the sense of having a relatively autonomous and centralized polity, economy, and culture. All of these states are part of the world social system and most are well integrated into particular imperial economic networks. Their economic outlines are basically similar. The majority of the population works on the land, producing both crops for a world market and food for their subsistence. Most are workers, either in the sense of receiving wages from the owner of the land or in the sense of being self-employed in a situation in which they are obliged to earn cash (and see farming as an economic alternative to other kinds of wage employment). There are others who work as labourers in urban areas, often as part of a pattern of circulatory migration.

In each country, working for the most part for the government, there is a bureaucratic class which is educated and seeking to transform some of their wealth into property. In every case, there are certain groups (one or several) who are disproportionately represented in the bureaucratic class, as there are other groups disproportionately represented among urban labourers. Almost everywhere, a group of whites lives, holding high status and filling technical positions. Their prestige-rank has scarcely changed since colonial rule. The local high rank of whites reflects the position of these countries in the world economic system where they are 'proletarian' nations suffering the effects of 'unequal exchange'.[11]

The degree of political autonomy represented by formal sovereignty enabled the local élites or élite groups to seek their upward mobility in the world-system by a rapid expansion of the educational system of their countries. What is individually functional in terms of the world-system is collectively dysfunctional. The workings of the world-system do not provide sufficient job outlets at the national level. This forces élite groups to find criteria by which to reward parts of themselves and to reject others. The particular lines of division are arbitrary and changeable in details. In some places, the division is along ethnic lines; in others, along religious; in others, along racial lines; in most, in some implicit combination of all of these.

These status-group tensions are the inefficacious and self-defeating expression of class frustrations. They are the daily stuff of contemporary African politics and social life. The journalists, who are usually closer to popular perceptions than the social scientists, tend to call this phenomenon 'tribalism' when they write of Black Africa. Tribal, or ethnic, conflicts are very real things, as the civil wars in the Sudan and Nigeria attest most eloquently. They are ethnic conflicts in the sense that persons involved in these conflicts are commonly motivated by analyses which use ethnic (or comparable status-group) categories; furthermore, they usually exhibit strong ethnic loyalties. Nonetheless, behind the ethnic 'reality' lies a class conflict, not very far from the surface. By this I mean the following straightforward and empirically testable proposition (not one, however, that has been definitively so tested): were the class differences that correlate (or coincide) with the status-group differences to disappear, as a result of changing social circumstances, the status-group conflicts would eventually disappear (no doubt to be replaced by others). The status-group loyalties are binding and effective, in a way that it seems difficult for class loyalties to be other than in moments of crisis, but they are also more transient from the perspective of the analyst. If the society were to become ethnically 'integrated', class antagonisms would not abate; the opposite in fact is true. One of the functions of the network of status-group affiliations is to conceal the realities of class differentials. To the extent, however, that particular class antagonisms or differentials abate or disappear, status-group antagonisms (if not differentials, but even differentials) also abate and disappear.

The usefulness of the concept of race

In Black Africa, one speaks of 'ethnic' conflict. In the United States or in South Africa, one speaks of 'racial' conflict. Is there any point in having a special word, *race*, to describe status-groupings that are the most salient in some countries but not in others (like Black African states)? If we were to regard each national case as discrete and logically separate, there would not be, since stratiffcation by status serves the same purpose in each.

But the national cases are not discrete and logically separate. They are part of a world-system. Status and prestige in the national system cannot be divorced from status and rank in the world-system, as we have already mentioned in discussing the role of expatriate white Europeans in Black Africa today. There are international status-groups as well as national ones. What we mean by race is essentially such an international status-group. There is a basic division between whites and non-whites. (Of course, there are varieties of non-whites, and the categorization differs according to time and place. One grouping is by skin colour but it is not in fact very prevalent. Another more common one is by continent, although the Arabs often lay claim to being counted separately.)

In terms of this international dichotomy, skin colour is irrelevant. 'White' and 'non-white' have very little to do with skin colour. 'What is a black? And first of all, what colour is he?' asked Jean Genêt. When Africans deny, as most do deny, that the conflict between the lighter skinned Arabs of northern

Sudan and the dark-skinned Nilotes of southern Sudan is a racial conflict, they are not being hypocritical. They are reserving the term *race* for a particular international social tension. It is not that the conflict in the Sudan is not real and is not expressed in status-group terms. It is. But it is a conflict which, though formally similar to, is politically different from, that between blacks and whites in the United States, or Africans and Europeans in South Africa. The political difference lies in its meaning in and for the world-system.

Race is, in the contemporary world, the only international status-group category. It has replaced religion, which played that role since at least the eighth century A.D. Rank in this system, rather than colour, determines membership in the status-group. Thus, in Trinidad, there can be a 'Black Power' movement, directed against an all-black government, on the grounds that this government functions as an ally of North American imperialism. Thus, Quebec separatists can call themselves the 'white Niggers' of North America. Thus, pan-Africanism can include white-skinned Arabs of North Africa, but exclude white-skinned Afrikaners of South Africa. Thus, Cyprus and Yugoslavia can be invited to tri-continental conferences (Asia, Africa, and Latin America) but Israel and Japan are excluded. As a status-group category, race is a blurred collective representation for an international class category, that of the proletarian nations. Racism, therefore, is simply the act of maintaining the existing international social structure, and is not a neologism for racial discrimination. It is not that they are separate phenomena. Racism obviously utilizes discrimination as part of its armory of tactics, a central weapon, to be sure. But there are many possible situations in which there can be racism without discrimination, in any immediate sense. Perhaps there can even be discrimination without racism, though this seems harder. What is important to see is that these concepts refer to actions at different levels of social organization: racism refers to action within the world arena; discrimination refers to actions within relatively small-scale social organizations.

Summary

In summary, my main point is that status-groups (as well as parties) are blurred collective representation of classes. The blurred (and hence incorrect) lines serve the interests of many different elements in most social situations. As social conflict becomes more acute, status-group lines approach class lines asymptotically, at which point we may see the phenomenon of 'class consciousness'. But the asymptote is never reached. Indeed, it is almost as though there were a magnetic field around the asymptote which pushed the approaching curve away. Race, finally, is a particular form of status-group in the contemporary world, the one which indicates rank in the world social system. In this sense, there are no racial tensions today within independent Black African states. One of the expressions of national identity, however, as it will be achieved, will be increasing international status-group consciousness, or racial identification, which would then only be overcome or surpassed as one approached the asymptote of international class consciousness.

NOTE

[1] Weber, Max, *Economy and society* (3 vols.), Bedminster Press, New York, 1968, p. 390.

[2] *Ibid.*, p. 938.

[3] Favret, Jeanne, 'Le traditionalisme par excès de modernité', Archives européennes de sociologie **VIII**, 1, 1967, p. 73.

[4] *Ibid.*, p. 167.

[5] Stavenhagen, Rodolfo, 'Estratificación social y estructura de clases (un esayo de interpretación)', *Ciencias politicas y sociales*, **VIII**, 27, 1962, pp. 99–101.

[6] Stavenhagen, Rodolfo, 'Clases, colonialismo y aculturación: ensayo sobre un sistema de relaciones interetnicas en Mesoamérica', *América Latina*, **VI**, 4, 1963, p. 94.

[7] Carstens, Peter, 'Problems of peasantry and social class in Southern Africa', presented at the Seventh World Congress of Sociology, Varna, Bulgaria, 13–19 September, 1970.

[8] Allen, V.L., 'The meaning and differentiation of the working class in tropical Africa', presented at the Seventh World Congress of Sociology, Varna, Bulgaria, 13–19 September, 1970.

[9] 'Wage-earners experience fluctuations in their living standards and employment whereas the peasant producers experience fluctuations in their living standards and the intensity of work. A depression in the living standards of wage-earners or in increase in unemployment, however, produces a movement of labour back to peasant production or is borne because the resources of peasant production exist as an insurance cover'. *Ibid.*

[10] Carstens, *op. cit.*, p. 9.

[11] For an elaboration of the concept and an explanation of its social consequences, see Emanuel Arghiri, *L'échange inégal*, Maspéro, Paris, 1969.

Class relations in a neo-colony: the case of Nigeria

GAVIN WILLIAMS

From Gavin Williams, 'The political economy of colonialism and neo-colonialism in Nigeria' (unpublished paper), Sociology Department, Durham University 1972.

The transition from the colonial to the neo-colonial political economy involves several changes in class relations, and in the political institutions and ideological legitimations through which they are mediated.

Expatriate domination of investment opportunities and sources of capital accumulation inhibits the accumulation and re-investment of capital by indigenous entrepreneurs who lack the resources to compete with vertically integrated multinational corporations.[1] Consequently, indigenous entrepreneurs became compradores i.e. intermediaries between expatriates and the indigenous polity and economy) and/or turned to the state as a source of capital. The increasing intervention of the state in economic life has caused it to control lucrative contracts and the disposal of monopolistic advantages. Consequently, politics has become the primary source of capital accumulation by Nigerians. Through the political process, professional men, bureaucrats, and merchants were able to accumulate capital and carve out monopolistic advantages for themselves within the neo-colonial political economy, and thereby form a 'bourgeoisie'.[2]

This is not to suggest that there is no conflict of interests between the indigenous bourgeoisie and the multinational corporations; the activities of the former continue to be determined by the activities of the latter. Conflicts over the scope of economic activity reserved to the indigenous bourgeoisie continue. But the contradictions between the pretensions of the bourgeoisie to autonomy and their dependence on a political economy dominated by foreign capital are firstly displaced on to the conflict of interests between African merchants and Levantines who most immediately stand in the way of the development of African entrepreneurs; secondly, the resolution of this contradiction requires the abolition of the neo-colonial political economy, on which the indigenous bourgeoisie depends for its share in the expropriation of the surplus. Thus the recent indigenization measures have readjusted the terms of the relations between foreign and indigenous capital, but in no way challenge the dominance of foreign capital in the Nigerian economy.

Businessmen are not the only indigenous beneficiaries of the neo-colonial political economy. The indigenous bourgeoisie has perpetuated the colonial administrative, salary, and tax structures, which are unrelated either to the needs of its citizens or to the resources of its economy, and are characterized by marked inequalities and a regressive incidence of taxation. Highly paid managerial posts with foreign companies create even more lucrative salaried opportunities for educated bureaucrats and exercise an upward pressure on senior administrative salaries. The incomes accruing to senior bureaucrats and their access to state resources and political influence facilitate their entry into business on favourable terms alongside politicians, merchants, army officers, and their respective wives, thereby assimilating them even further to the interests and objectives of the bourgeoisie as a whole.

The dependent character of the bourgeoisie restricts them to competing among themselves for the limited resources available within a neo-colonial political economy. This competition tends to take the form of a zero-sum game, modified by cartel-type arrangements where the competitors (defining themselves in regional, ethnic, and state terms) all seek to protect their own areas of activity. However, the unequal competition for resources at the federal level, in which all the contending parties were involved, ensured the instability of the successive compromises which the Nigerian bourgeoisie patched up on successive occasions in order to save the game itself. No impersonal rules governing competition over resources could be established to regulate the game where the differences among various regions and ethnic groups in access to resources, notably formal education, discriminates massively in favour of certain groups, and where the central aim of the game is to gain privileged access to monopolistic advantage through political power. The 12-state structure seeks to regulate the game by ensuring to each group an area of activity where it is protected from outside competition, and by increasing the number of contending parties to bring about a tendency towards an equilibrium of diverse alliances rather than the domination of a single party at the centre.

The bourgeoisie's ambiguous position within the neo-colonial political economy is expressed in its ideological ambiguity. Its nationalism is the outcome of its desire to appropriate resources back from the foreign expropriator; its commitment to freedom for foreign enterprise is the outcome of its concrete dependence on the neo-colonial political economy. National unity and reconciliation express its ambition to act as a hegemonic class, providing leadership at the national level and within the international arena; its particularism is the outcome of its inability to control the crucial productive resources of the economy, and hence the competition among the bourgeoisie for favoured access to scarce resources, as well as the need to manipulate particularist interests and sentiments among the poor to maintain its political domination.

The Nigerian bourgeoisie lacks the commitments of a religious, socialist, or nationalist character of the rationalizing, capital-accumulating, surplus-expropriating classes of Britain, Russia, Germany, or Japan during their period of industrialization. Perhaps it is this which lies behind the repeated call for a 'national ideology', which seeks to subordinate the energy of the people behind a single national goal. In fact, the Nigerian bourgeoisie do have an ideology, in the sense of a theoretical legitimation of the *status quo*. It is found in the concept of 'development', defined as 'that which we are all in favour of, and given statistical respectability in figures measuring the growth of the formal sector of the economy. The demand for Nigerianization gives it a nationalist colouring. But it stops short at the demand for expropriation of foreign capitalists, on whose activities the Nigerian bourgeoisie remains dependent. Thereby, the bourgeoisie's image of itself as providing national leadership is presented, with its contradictions abolished, and its immediate material interests preserved. What the bourgeoisie lacks, to use Mannheim's terminology,[3] is a 'Utopia', a set of ideas to inspire the transformation of the existing order and the liberation of human capacities.

The relations between the surplus producing and the surplus expropriating classes are changed by the transition to a neo-colonial political economy. As we have seen, this transition involved a change in the mode of agricultural exploitation, and an increase in the rate of exploitation of the agricultural surplus. As a consequence, the exploitation of the export-crop peasants *as a class*, sharing a common destiny, determined by the government's exercise of specifically political decisions (regarding the price of crops and the level of taxation), has become more clearly apparent to farmers. This has given rise to a specific peasant consciousness among the Yoruba cocoa farmers at least. Under conditions of falling crop prices, increasing taxes and inflation, it gave rise to the *Agbekoya* rebellion of 1968–69, which eventually forced the government to reduce taxes and withdraw its officials from the rural areas.[4]

The increase in the rate of exploitation of the agricultural surplus also deprived the urban petty-bourgeoisie (craftsmen and petty traders) of a significant part of their potential market. The consolidation of the intermediary position of the merchant bourgeoisie excluded them from direct access to expatriate firms for credit and supplies. The Nigerian merchants who partly displaced the expatriate trading firms tend to restrict the advance of credit to a limited network of dependents and to take over some of the middleman activities of the petty traders themselves.[5]

In more general terms, there has been a concern to increase opportunities in the formal sector of the economy at the expense of the informal sector, and thus to improve opportunities for those with education and other formal skills, at the expense of the illiterate. This discriminates against farmers and the petty bourgeoisie, and discriminates against women as a status group, since it limits opportunities in those sectors of the economy in which women are most commonly engaged, while creating opportunities in the formal sector, where women tend to be discriminated against.[6] While opportunities for education and thus for access to the formal sector of the economy have expanded dramatically, the rate of increase of opportunities has slowed down, while the size of the bourgeoisie and the number of its schoolgoing children has increased. Consequently, the level of education required for employment in the formal sector has sharply increased; the bourgeoisie, by virtue of the political, financial, and cultural resources at its disposal has been best placed to take advantage of the (subsidized) educational opportunities, thereby putting them ever further from the reach of the sons and daughters of the poor.

The expansion of the formal economy has drawn large numbers of young people into industrial and clerical employment. The market situation of industrial employees in the expatriate, capital-intensive part of the private sector differs from that of government employees (in general) in that wages are a relatively small proportion of total costs of production, so that employers can adopt more flexible wage policies than the government, and those employers (mainly Levantine and Asian) whose profits depend on low wages rather than on the productivity of their capital inputs and the purchase of intermediate goods from their foreign principals.

The attraction of both industrial and clerical employment has been in providing the income experience, and contacts which can be used contemporaneously or subsequently in independent economic activity. This, if anything, intensifies the wage or salary earner's determination to maintain and improve his real income and margin of savings, for both his immediate subsistence needs and family obligations, *and* his future trading opportunities are dependent on his maximizing his earning capacity in wage employment. A few manual workers with scarce skills (and some employees with relatively high levels of formal education) can sell their skills on a favourable labour market or look to promotion within their firm for advancement. For most factory workers, collective bargaining, supported where necessary by militant action, is their only weapon in protecting their real wage levels and their security of employment.

The social organization of industrial production, the concentration of factories in a few centres, the common and intractable problems of urban life, the common involvement of wage earners in a national system of wage determination, all produce a recognition among industrial workers of a common fate arising from a common class situation. Despite periodic wage increases, real incomes are continually being undermined by the structural inflation characteristic of neo-colonial underdevelopment. At least at the factory level, workers have the organizational resources with which to defend their own interests under their own leadership. The national system of wage determination had given them the issues (the demand for publication of the Morgan Commission award on wages in 1964; the implementation of the interim award of the Adebo [wages and salaries] Commission in 1971) on which to force a confrontation with the government and the employers.[7]

Clerical workers are usually concerned to defend and advance their real wages. Indeed, the tie-up between public and private sector wages through the 'system' of national wage determination is a major source of government concern about rising wages. But in view of the relative inflexibility of wages and salaries in the public sector, clerical workers are often as concerned about the regrading of posts as about changes in wage levels. Younger clerks look to further education as a means of advancement. They are often more concerned than are factory workers to seek the favour of their seniors (often determined or alleged to be determined by considerations of ethnicity and kinship rather than merit) in so far as their promotion structure is more favourable than that of factory workers. They also have greater security of tenure and better prospects of a gratuity which can be invested on early retirement in commercial activities.

How do the interests and characteristic forms of class-determined action of employees relate to those of the self-employed? In the short term, clerks and industrial workers both have an interest in raising the wage levels in the formal sector of the economy. This tends to push up urban prices to the advantage of some (but by no means most) craftsmen and petty traders, and to exert a squeeze on government revenues. Thus their immediate demands are distinct from those of the farmers, and of most craftsmen and petty traders outside Lagos who are more concerned with the level of crop prices. The dependence of clerks on government revenues for their incomes makes them ultimately dependent on the state's ability to expropriate an agricultural surplus adequate to meet its commitments. The very establishment of factory employment opportunities is dependent on the past and present exploitation of the rural producer and the consumer through the state and the market by government and expatriate firms. None of this confers on workers the right to engage in the 'discretionary consumption' which Saul and Arrighi impute to them, nor constitute them into a 'labour aristocracy'.[8]

The 'labour aristocracy' thesis argues first of all that *marginal* increments to workers' (money) wages are gained at the expense of the peasantry. This view is based on the following revealing assumptions: Firstly, it assumes that increased wages cannot be met out of the profits of entrepeneurs (which is ridiculous in the case of capital-intensive factories employing relatively cheap labour) or out of the consumption (in this case 'discretionary') of the élite. Secondly, it assumes that cuts to real wages would lead to a transfer of resources to the peasantry in the form of increased crop prices, lower taxes, and an improvement in the provision of rural services rather than by a transfer of resources to the surplus-expropriating classes. In fact, a decrease in the rate of exploitation of the rural producer depends, not on an increase in the rate of exploitation of the urban worker, but on the need to maintain at a minimal level the productive capacity of export agriculture and on the resistance of peasant farmers to their exploitation.

The complementary argument that 'development' (whatever that means) depends on keeping urban and rural wages down to facilitate savings and consequent investments (by the state, or by private capital) rests on the assumption that the surplus-expropriating class do save more than the expropriated *and* that such savings will be re-invested (and not expatriated) *in such a way* as to raise the productive capacity of the economy rather than to secure a corner on an established market.

The interest in such theories lies not in the validity of their assumptions but in their ideological import. The allegation that there is a conflict of interest between peasants and workers made by the bourgeoisie (and especially by their professional ideologues, the economists)[9] is a classic example of the 'displacement' of the 'primary contradiction' between the interests of the exploiting and the exploited classes on to a 'derived' contradiction between exploited classes.[10] It is certainly not a contradiction which is widely recognized among the exploited classes themselves, tied as they are to one another through family, lineage, and mutual support.[11]

The consolidation of the bourgeoisie, particularly in so far as they are involved in the formal economy, and have advanced through their command of formal education and formally acquired skills, has accentuated the differences between them and the poor and illiterate in terms of life style, patterns of interaction and patterns of residence. Interaction between rich and poor, even within the framework of kinship, is an interaction of unequals, and thus of patron and supplicant, where the patron, while meeting the appropriate conventions, remains in control of the situation by virtue of the superior resources at his command.

The attitude of all sections of the Nigerian poor to the rich is ambiguous. On the one hand the rich are admired as exemplifications of the success to which the poor aspire, and looked to (particularly among the petty-bourgeosie) for assistance with employment, credit, and political favours. On the other hand, they are berated for their selfishness in looking only to their own advantage and that of their immediate family, and depriving others of opportunities (and particularly, monopolizing educational opportunities) rather than helping them. Thus on the one hand, inequality is regarded as part of the natural order of things and privilege as a proper reward for investment, skill, and effort; on the other hand, we find such expressions of egalitarian values as 'our wives shop in the same market (as those of the rich)'.

We have already noted that the characteristic social relations of production in which the urban petty-bourgeoisie are involved preclude them from effective class action in their own interests. In certain cases, they have followed 'trickster'[12] populist leaders, to whom they have looked to favour them with a share of the resources appropriated by the bourgeoisie. Alternatively, they have sought individual advancement in relations of clientage to better placed patrons. By contrast, the social relations of production, distribution, and exchange in which the urban workers and the cash crop farmers are involved has produced significant class action on their part.

In taking political action in support of their immediate class interests, both urban workers and peasant farmers have regarded themselves as fighting for their rights in general, and thus in opposing the general unfairness of the existing order. In doing so, they provide a focus for the political consciousness of the urban petty bourgeoisie (and the food crop farmers) who lack the resources to articulate and enforce their own demands of their own accord. Thus contrary to the final thesis of the 'labour aristocracy' theorists, it is mistaken to regard the Nigerian proletariat at least as being quiescent, or only concerned with maintaining its alleged privileges against those more deprived than themselves.

At the same time, we must recognize the limited political capacity, at least thus far, even of urban workers and export crop farmers. At the end of 1971, the final Adebo award was widely recognized as favouring the bourgeois salariat at the expense of the less better off; but in the absence of 'rights' accorded to them by the declaration of an outside agency, the workers failed to confront the government collectively over this.[13] The cocoa farmers have shown that they have the consciousness and the determination to resist oppressive and forcible exactions. But on the crucial issue of the cocoa price, they remain by and large at the mercy of their rulers. Neither of them have the resources to intervene politically in the routine process of resource allocation. Nor do they have the resources, the education, and the *outside* leadership to articulate an alternative vision of society to that promised by 'development' ideology and to take over the economy and ensure that it is organized in their interests.

The contradictions of the neo-colonial economy[14]

Neo-colonial underdevelopment is characterized by 'uneven and combined' development of different modes of production, at the same time, within the same political economy. It is characterized by different sorts of contradictions. Firstly, there is a contradiction between the requirements of the development of peasant production, and the development of industrial production. Consequently, there are internal contradictions inherent in the development strategy itself, and between its objectives and the means adopted for their realization. The 'uneven and combined' character of neo-colonial underdevelopment generates a multiplicity of contradictions within the class structure, between the interests and objectives of the expropriators of surplus value, and of the surplus producers on whom they depend for their livelihood.

Neo-colonial underdevelopment is dependent upon the expropriation of the agricultural surplus for the capital and foreign exchange resources necessary to subsidize industrial investment. Not only do peasant producers and the consumer subsidize the initial development of manufacturing industry, but they are required to subsidize the *continuing* existence thereof Such subsidization takes the form of state provision of infra-structural investments and investment capital, over-valued exchange rates and fiscal and monetary policies designed to cheapen the cost of capital, and the capital-cheapening terms on which foreign state capital (so foreign aid) is transferred.[15]

Nor does the development of the industrial sector stimulate innovations in the mode of agricultural production by providing an expanding market for its products. As we have seen the import-substituting sector generates few backward and forward linkages within the underdeveloped economy itself; in particular, payments of profits and salaries are skewed in favour of expatriate and indigenous managers, whose consumption patterns are biased towards imports and goods with a high import content, and against the consumption of foodstuffs. The expropriation of resources from the rural sector of the economy, which are spent or re-invested, either abroad or in the urban sector, leads to a movement of skills and resources from the rural sector to the urban sector where they can now be more profitably employed, thus undermining the supply elasticity of the rural producer. In the absence of adequate credit, and often of adequate transport and marketing facilities, and in view of their low incomes, peasant producers are unable to adapt production flexibly to take full advantage of urban price fluctuations. Thus the industrial mode, far from stimulating the displacement of peasant agriculture by a more efficient mode of production is parasitic upon it, and undermines its productive capacity. At the same time, the industrial sector depends on the productive capacity of agriculture for its existence. Quite simply, it kills the goose that lays the golden egg. Only the windfall revenue generated by the oil industry has saved Nigeria from the fundamental crisis currently being undergone by the Ghanaians.

We have shown the crucial inherent contradiction in the strategy of neo-colonial underdevelopment, viz. it undermines rather than stimulates the productive capacity of agriculture on which it relies for its resources. Following on from this are the contradictions between its stated objectives[16] and the means adopted for its realization. In the first place, the diversification of the economy is aimed at reducing its reliance on export crops, and making Nigerian society more self-reliant. In the second place, the development strategy is aimed at increasing the productive capacity of the economy, so that it is sufficiently dynamic to engender its own development. In the third place, it is aimed at promoting the welfare of the individual, by establishing, in the words of the Nigerian Plan 'a just and egalitarian society', 'a land of bright and full opportunities for all citizens', and a 'free and democratic society'.

Industrial investment in a neo-colonial economy depends on capital-intensive technology developed to meet the needs of metropolitan economies–and corporations. This technology is imported into Nigeria by expatriate investors and suppliers. Multinational corporations apply to their activities productive techniques and techniques of management and organization which correspond to the abundant capital resources with which they are familiar. Such imports in turn generate a demand for technologically sophisticated machinery (and skills), which can only be met in the metropolitan countries and which consequently fail to develop for locally produced capital goods, thus maintaining the metropolitan investors' domination of the underdeveloped economy.

In order to attract foreign capital, government policies subsidize capital investment and facilitate its accumulating from Nigerian resources. This facilitates the outflow of resources in the form of profits and of payments for imports and services, and allows the demands of industrial production (largely expatriate owned) to become a first charge on foreign exchange resources to which industry makes only a very marginal contribution (in the form of import substitution) where it makes any contribution at all.

As we have seen, the neo-colonial strategy of development fails to increase the productive capacity and dynamism of the economy, since it depends on the shifting of resources from more to less profitable forms of activity (especially agriculture to industry, craft to factory production) through hidden and direct subsidies, and since it does so in such a way as to subordinate the economy ever more fully to metropolitan suppliers of capital, skills, technology–and markets.

Finally, the strategy both generates, and depends upon, an inegalitarian pattern of income distribution. As we have seen, wages and salary payments create far more significant forward linkages in the metropolitan economies than in Nigeria itself, owing to the patterns of consumption of those (mostly managerial staff, both expatriate and indigenous) to whom the largest share of the salary bill is paid. Import substitution is easiest in those industries producing for an élite market with patterns of demand similar to those of consumers in metropolitan countries. Furthermore, if a surplus is to be expropriated from workers and peasants by keeping their real incomes low, then only a privileged élite can provide a market for increased industrial output, and the political support necessary to sustain the political economy as a whole. Thus the inegalitarian income structure produced by the import-substituting sector, and the expropriation of peasant labour on which it depends, sustains the demand for imported goods, and for goods with a high import content (the so-called import-substitution goods), while reducing the potential demand for the output of the 'informal' (crafts, petty trading, and peasant) sector. Thus investment and production are orientated towards providing for the luxuries of the few rather than for the welfare of the many. The strategy of neo-colonial underdevelopment necessarily creates an unjust and inegalitarian society, which excludes the majority of its citizenry from significant opportunities, and requires the oppression of the producers who are subjugated to meeting its requirements.

Within the class structure, there are significant contradictions between the interests and objectives of the surplus-producing classes (notably the export-crop farmers and the urban workers), and of the surplus expropriators; of the national bourgeoisie and of the metropolitan companies who exclude them from access to significant opportunities and resources, and determine the scope of their activities; and of the petty bourgeoisie on the one hand and of the national bourgeoisie and the foreign companies on the other who deprive them of the resources and opportunities necessary for the development of their productive activities on the other. Each of these contradictions generates conflicts; the relation between these conflicts, as much as the course of each particular conflict, will determine the possibilities of the abolition of the neo-colonial political economy.

We have already argued that the dependence of the national bourgeoisie on the neo-colonial economy for its livelihood precludes it from either developing the productive capacity of the economy, or overthrowing the productive relations characteristic of neo-colonialism, of its own accord. Hitherto the intelligentsia, with its vested interest in and ideological orientation towards 'modernizing' policies, has by and large been successfully institutionalized within the neo-colonial institutions. Nevertheless, the contradictions between the bourgeoisie's nationalist, hegemonic ambitions and ideology and its dependent situation do create the basis for a radicalization of the intelligentsia; the potential for this must increase as successive policies fail to resolve the bourgeoisie's fatal dilemma, and as individual members of the national bourgeoisie find new opportunities increasingly closed off by those already established in the niches of the neo-colonial economy and administration. Herein lies the possibility, hitherto unrealized, for effective radical direction of the revolutionary forces of society.

We have also argued that the petty-bourgeoisie cannot constitute a class for themselves by virtue of the character of the productive relations within which they are involved. However, the appropriation of resources necessary for the development of their productive activities and their exclusion from various sorts of opportunities to which they have come to regard themselves as entitled, creates among the poor a general sense of the unfairness and impropriety of the existing order, and generates intermittent demands for the abolition of monopolistic arrangements (hoarding of commodities by merchants, for example), and of corruption and extortion of which they are most often the victims. The petty-bourgeoisie further share a dependence for their livelihood on the incomes of wage earners and export-crop farmers on whom they depend for their custom. They cannot generate a radical movement themselves, but they could provide one with followers.

The expropriation of the surplus value of peasant labour for industrial and administrative development has required an increase in the rate and a change in the mode of exploitation of the agricultural surplus. These changes have linked the peasant producer *collectively* (rather than individually through the market) to the political economy, and clearly revealed the extent of the exploitation of the peasantry. This has in turn generated a radical peasant consciousness and in a period of crisis, collective forms of peasant social organization which has given them a capacity to resist their exploitation. The development of industry has required the social organization of a proletariat, which has itself developed a consciousness of its class interests, and collective forms of social organization, which enable it to resist its own exploitation. It is these forms of social organization, generated by the social relations of production, distribution, and exchange in which peasant producers and urban workers are engaged, that the potential lies for the abolition of the contradictions of the neo-colonial political economy.

NOTES

[1] E. O. Akeredolu-Ale, 'Nigerian entrepreneurs in Lagos State', D.Phil., University of London, 1971.

[2] S. O. Osoba, 'Ideological trends in the Nigerian national liberation movement and the problems of national identity, solidarity and motivation 1934–45', *Ibadan*, 27, 1969.

[3] K. Mannheim, *Ideology and utopia*, London, 1940.

[4] C. E. F. Beer, 'The farmer and the state in Western Nigeria', Ph.D., University of Ibadan, 1971; Gavin Williams, 'The political consciousness of the Ibadan poor' in Emmanuel de Kadt and Gavin Williams (eds) *Sociology and development*, London, 1974.

[5] Williams, 'Political consciousness', *op. cit.*

[6] Dorothy Remy, 'Underdevelopment and the position of women: a Zaria case study'. (Unpublished).

[7] Adrian Peace, 'Industrial conflict in Nigeria', in de Kadt and Williams, *Sociology and development*, *op. cit.* See also the essays by Peace, Lubeck, and Remy in R. Sandbrook and R. Cohen, *The development of an African working class*, Longman, London, 1975.

[8] G. Arrighi & J. Saul, 'Socialism and economic development in tropical Africa', *Journal of Modern African Studies*, VI (1968). On the 'labour aristocracy' debate, see Peace 'Towards a Nigerian working class' in Sandbrook and Cohen, *op. cit.*, C. H. Allen, 'Unions, incomes and development', in *Political theory and ideology in African society*, Centre of African Studies, University of Edinburgh, 1972, and Robin Cohen, *Labour and politics in Nigeria*, Heinemann, 1974, and chapter 6, Peter Waterman, 'The labour aristocracy in Africa: introduction to a debate', *Development and change*, VI, 3, 1975, and sources cited by these authors.

[9] For example, W. Arthur Lewis, *Reflections on Nigeria's economic growth*, Paris, 1967, P. Kilby, 'Industrial relations and wage determination', *Journal of Developing Areas*, **I** (1967).

[10] These concepts are taken from Professor K.W.J. Post, *Arise ye starvelings! The Jamaican labour rebellion of 1938* (forthcoming).

[11] Peace, 'Industrial conflict', and 'Nigerian working class', *op. cit.*

[12] Post, *op. cit.*

[13] Peace, 'Industrial conflict' *op. cit.*

[14] I am indebted to Professor Post's discussion of contradiction in his book on Jamaica, though I have not followed it systematically in this paper.

[15] John F. Weeks, 'Employment, growth and foreign domination in under-developed countries', *Review of radical political economics,* **IV** (1972).

[16] Federal Republic of Nigeria, *Second national development plan, 1970–74*, Lagos, 1970, p. 32.

PART VI
Ideology: Ideas as a Material Force

The ideological deficiency, not to say the total lack of ideology, within the national liberation movements–which is basically due to ignorance of the historical reality which these movements claim to transform–constitutes one of the greatest weaknesses of our struggle against imperialism, if not the greatest weakness of all ... A full discussion of this subject could ... make a valuable contribution towards strengthening the present and future action of the national liberation movements.

A science of social control
BASIL DAVIDSON

From Basil Davidson, *The Africans,* Longman, London 1969.

The trouble about discussing religion is that most of us are against it. Since Bruno was burned at the stake and Galileo bullied into saying that the world was flat, rational and scientific thought about man and the world has known its enemy: God and the priests and all their works, the whole black cloud of canting obscurantists who have clogged understanding and persecuted knowledge for the sake of kings, popes, proprietors, or other baleful father-figures clinging to their privilege and comfort at other men's expense. If the liberal thinkers of the nineteenth century did not go as far as Marx and Engels in affirming that 'law, morality, religion are to (the proletarian) so many bourgeois prejudices, behind which lurk just so many bourgeois interests', they said much the same in their own context. They saw Christianity as a deplorable mystification, at best a mere vestige of primitive awe in face of the unknown, at worst an ingenious racket. Wrestling with it, they called for aid to 'primitive religion'. There they found 'a weapon which could, they thought, be used with deadly effect against Christianity', since 'if primitive religion could be explained away as an intellectual aberration, as a mirage induced by emotional stress, or by its social function', so too could 'higher religion' and the path thereby cleared to that extent of historical lumber.[1]

All this is may be very understandable. In any case it helps to explain why, again in Evans-Pritchard's words, the study of religion has remained 'an enormous and almost untilled field for research'. Even where studies were undertaken, they stemmed from a conviction that the subject matter was really superfluous to genuine social analysis. To these anthropologists 'religious belief was... absurd, and it is so to most anthropologists of yesterday and today'. This, too, is understandable. Even since the sixteenth century, the task of explaining the world has been the work of a science necessarily anti-religious because Christianity mutilated science. Today the battle is largely fought and won, but the attitude persists. Christianity has been diminished in the scientifically advanced societies to a merely personal prophylactic of individual rescue from isolation and alienation. It has lost its power to explain, and so its power to influence behaviour and has become a mere 'comfort', an eccentricity, a dying survival of a dead age. Consequently thoughtful men have sought–and clearly must seek–for other means of social control and personal reassurance.

Yet these attitudes, however meaningful in Europe, have just as clearly failed to close with the traditional African apprehension of reality. Explanations of African religion reduced to terms of 'superstition' or 'function' have left too much unexplained. It is now perfectly evident that far more is needed to elucidate why, for example, appointed ancestors should have become 'the jealous guardians of the highest moral values', that is to say, the axiomatic values from which all ideal conduct is deemed to flow'.[2] Superstition and function are partial explanations which point, in fact, to the greater residue of meaning that still remains in question.

When the lords of the Karanga carved their empire from the lands between Zambezi and Limpopo long ago, and built their stone dwellings at Zimbabwe, they set up a shrine to Hungwe, the fish-eagle, and erected soapstone effigies to the power they also called *Shirichena*, the Bird of Bright Plumage, or *Shiri ya Mwari*, the Bird of God. Attending this shrine the priest of the most powerful of the appointed ancestors, Chaminuka the 'great *mhondoro*', was required to interpret the meaning of the cries of Hungwe. Crucial decisions of state were influenced by what he said. For more than three centuries before 1830 it was to the spirit of Chaminuka, and its oracle the Bird of Bright Plumage, that the kings of the Karanga turned for guidance on their testing problems of state.

Now the old European explanations of the nineteenth century could have seen in this behaviour only a quaint foolishness engendered by the fogs of superstition, or else, yielding somewhat later to the facts, an in-built but arbitrary mechanism of social control. This has led to many misunderstandings: to the point, indeed, that 'most of what has been written in the past, and with some assurance, and is still trotted out in colleges and universities, about animism, totemism, magic, etc., has been shown to be erroneous or at least dubious' by modern anthropologists working from another standpoint, and in far greater possession of the facts.[3]

The point is that modern anthropologists in studying these societies have had to re-think what they mean by religion. For it has become clear that religion was, or is, far more than a mere 'comfort' or useful function in these traditional structures, based as they were on ancestral charters fashioned by the imperatives of daily life, and fastened by a corresponding moral order. 'Religion' in the sense we generally use it is really much too narrow a concept for application where all significant social and cultural patterns have been bodied forth in supra-sensible terms. We are in fact faced here with structures of belief which were not only mandatory in a social sense but also explanatory in a material one: and, as such, the basis for rational behaviour. What we call 'religion', in other words, was essentially the means of apprehending reality. Possibly, though not inherently, superstitious, and incidentally functional, it was basically a rational projection of consciousness according to its time and place.

When the priest of Hungwe interpreted the cries of Shirichena, the 'messages' he gave to the king of the Karanga were not, accordingly, a farrago of savage fancies. They were advice–obviously of a value depending on the wisdom of the priest in question–that was drawn from a particular study of reality; in this case, from a logically elaborated series of explanations about the way the world of the Karanga worked. However picturesque and peculiar his methods of conceiving such advice might be, the effective task of this priest was to safeguard community welfare and survival. His advice was therefore framed to ensure that behaviour stayed in line with the 'ideal equilibrium' of the ancestors: of those who had 'shown men how to live' in this land. That the advice might be couched in esoteric explanations of a bird's cries did not therefore mean that it was any the less concerned, in practice, with the social or cultural problems of the day. Just how practical such advice could be, and how closely the product of a weighing of realities, was shown with startling clarity later on when the priests of the Karanga advised revolt against European invaders, with whom, as they concluded, no peaceful action would any longer carry weight.[4]

Seen in this way, 'religion' in this context stands for an apprehension of reality across the whole field of life. This was the explanatory apprehension that produced its mandatory force. Out of it, in one way or another, there emerged what may reasonably be called a science of social control.

One may boggle at use of the word 'science' in these societies. Certainly they were pre-scientific in that, generally, their thought had 'no developed awareness of alternatives to the established body of tenets', and thus no urge toward systematic search for such alternatives.[5] Even so, this thought had a highly developed awareness of the practical possibilities of prediction arising out of observation: of what Lévi-Strauss has called 'the science of the concrete' [6] In fact it was copiously empirical in its approach to natural phenomena. Experiment, after all, had been its saving virtue from early times. Nothing else can explain the Africans' intense attention to the detailed knowledge of environment.

Their persistent classifying and naming of phenomena, whether known by observation or inferred by intuition, perhaps needs a little emphasis. The Dogon of the Western Sudan, for example, classify the plants they know in 22 chief families of which some are divided into as many as 11 sub-families, though according to criteria which might have surprised Linnaeus. The Karimojong can 'distinguish, as precisely as any outside professional observer, what the topographic features are that bear on a predictable water-supply', and name them accordingly; and 'for any herder, it is this "grid", applied to known stretches of territory with named pastures, that in part determines his movement plans over the year, and from one year to another'.[7] Lévi-Strauss remarks that the many known classifications such as these 'are not only methodical and based on carefully built-up theoretical knowledge. They are also at times comparable, from a formal point of view, to those still in use in zoology and botany.'[8]

Transposed to the wider field of social relations, comprehending natural relations, the same remark still holds good: thought remains concerned with prediction based on observation. The 'primary intention of much African thought', Horton has argued, 'seems to be just that mapping of connections between space–time phenomena which modern Christian thought feels is beyond its proper domain. Though, by the standards of the more advanced contemporary sciences, these religions could seldom provide value explanations or make completely successful predictions, there is a very real sense in which they are just as concerned with explanation and prediction as the sciences are'. So that 'the really significant aspiration behind a great deal of African religious thought is the most obvious one: *i.e.* the attempt to explain and influence the workings of one's everyday world by discovering constant principles that underlie the apparent chaos and flux of sensory experience.' In so far as we make 'this aspiration central to our analysis, we shall find ourselves searching for translation instruments not so much in the realm of Christian discourse as in that of the sciences and their theoretical concepts.'[9]

Horton goes on to urge, and I think that many modern anthropologists would agree with him, that traditional thought 'can be seen as the outcome of a model-making process which is found alike in the thought of science and in that of pre-science', taking pre-science to mean forms of empirical inquiry into the workings of the world that preceded any theoretical knowledge of material structure and process. To understand traditional politics, then, one must first understand traditional religion: only thus can the categories of description be grasped. Horton offers a parallel. 'A chemist, asked to give a thorough description of some substance in his laboratory, can hardly avoid mentioning such characteristics as a molecular weight and formula, which refer implicitly to a massive body of chemical theory' taken for granted. 'In the same way, an African villager, who is trying to describe what his community is, can hardly avoid implicit reference to religious concepts.'

Enough is understood about some African societies to demonstrate this in practice. Horton takes the case of a people among whom he has lived, the Kalabari of the Niger Delta, a fishing and trading community who have dwelt along the Atlantic creeks of southern Nigeria since unrecorded time, and certainly for many centuries.

Kalabari apprehension of reality supposes three kinds of Kalabari Core spirits. First of all, there are the spirits of the 'founding heroes' who first settled in Kalabari country and fathered their remote ancestors. These spirits are considered to be 'instruments of collective village welfare', since it is they who first framed the Kalabari way of life; and it is to them that one turns in matters affecting the whole community. Secondly, there are the ancestors of different Kalabari lineage segments, 'considered as instruments of collective descent-group welfare.' These are capable of being opposed to one another in defence of their respective living descendants, so that conflicts of interest at this level may have to be referred eventually to the spirits of the founding heroes. Thirdly, and in a way that the modern world will find attractively subtle and realistic, there are 'freelance spirits'–'water-people' who are thought to live at the bottom of the Kalabari creeks and who 'cater for individualist competitive aspirations'. The water-people are ready to confer their benefits on all comers on a scale proportional to offerings made to them, but they are not associated with any of the permanent social groupings in the community.[10]

One may note in this connection that the multiplicity of cults in any given society will depend upon the degree of competitiveness which the society can allow or afford. The more a system has scope for individual enterprise, the greater the number of cults will be. The Kalabari, with many opportunities for individualism deriving from their fortunate trading position in the Niger

Delta, have a multitude of cults; while the cattle-driving Karimojong, far away in their arid grasslands, have very few. Much the same is true of modern societies, as anyone will see who compares the pullulating cults of the motor car with complaints of 'lack of freedom' in societies which are short of consumer goods. The Kalabari, in this perspective, are far 'more free' than the Karimojong, though the Karimojong might not think so.

Although with many cults and much individualism, the Kalabari system is clearly neither chaotic nor arbitrary. It consists in a triangle of forces, with the spirits of the lineage ancestors 'underpinning the life and strength of lineages, bringing misfortune to those who betray lineage values and fortune to those who promote them', with the spirits of the founding heroes 'underpinning the life and strength of the community and its various institutions'; and, lastly, with the spirits of the water-people as the 'patrons of human individualism', as 'the forces underpinning all that lies beyond the confines of the established social order'.

Thus the Kalabari apprehension of reality–their religion and what flowed from it–composed a theoretical model of the workings of their world according to observed and meditated experience. A given people, that is, entered a given environment–the founding heroes of the Kalabari settling in the Delta–and there adjusted themselves to the needs of social growth. These needs they have codified in terms we call religious. And if we ask just *why* Kalabari thought should have taken a religious form, we are simply confused by the terms of our modern dichotomy: science–supernatural, reality–religion.

In traditional thought the dichotomy was not there, for the apprehension was a total one. This apprehension was concerned not only with what was, but also with what ought to be and why it ought to be. Its affect was mandatory, one may repeat, as well as explanatory. Things being as they were, such and such actions or ambitions were permissible, while others were not.

As organic aspects of the same necessary truth, means and ends were indivisibly conceived. Today in modern societies we have torn them apart; and the price of our progress is a split consciousness. 'Science' tells us what can be done but not what ought to be done or why it ought to be done: the mandatory moral issues are necessarily eluded, and scientists who raise them are likely to be chided for speaking out of turn. Otherwise the mandatory issues, the moral issues of choice that govern behaviour, are left to the promptings of whatever feeble residue of our own traditional morality there may still exist, at levels where it can really count, or else to sectional decisions about the 'national good'. And so we have a situation in which science predicts disaster with the continued spread of nuclear weapons, but the spread continues despite all lamentations because the mandatory moral force to stop it is no longer there. Whereas in African apprehension, persistently, the explanatory–mandatory duality of thought possessed its ultimate satisfaction in what was also its ultimate sanction: in conforming to prescribed behaviour as the only way of doing what was 'right and natural', of belonging to the 'community of the blessed', of flowering from the isolation of the one into the communion of the many.

If these ideologies are looked at in this way they will not present a paradise.

Reality was tough and tortuous. Many individuals will have fallen by the wayside, and whole communities engulfed themselves in ruin. Even where such ideologies were most successful in achieving social harmony, a heavy price was paid in conservative conformism. Just because they were total systems, their predictive capacities had to be hedged around with devices for explaining or ignoring failure, since their mandatory aspect depended on their explanatory–that is, predictive–claims: and these claims could not, in the nature of the systems, be 'wrong'. Putting it another way, the forms of social life could change, but not the content.

There is no case for gilding the past. But there is a case for understanding it. This approach will at least begin to make sense of what men actually thought or did, and why. It will help to drag us clear of swamps of mystifying verbiage, of bogs of boring paternalism and floods of flatulent speculation. Patiently pursued, it will elucidate all that enormously diverse range of 'founding myths' preserved by African peoples, such as the Lozi belief that descends from Mbuya whom God begot upon God's daughter Mwamba. It will explain why these ancestral charters held their force. It will open those 'social archives', as Leboeuf has called them, composed by the Dogon in the carving of sculptured masks at conscious intervals in time, or by the Sao and Kotoko in piles of polished stones which symbolized the vanished generations, or by others in other ways.[11]

Then much becomes clear. It becomes clear, for example, why these 'archives' were not conceived as records for the satisfaction of historical curiosity, and why they must offer pitfalls to uncautious analysts who take them at face value. It becomes clear why unfortunate kings could be omitted from remembered lists because they failed in battle, or otherwise upset the ancestral scheme of what should be and should not be; why new dynasties, fitting themselves into the charters of the dispossessed, were careful to 'rewrite' the past or else suppress it; and why, with the recent intrusion of a world of new ideas, the traditions often change again. D'Hertefelt has lately cited an illuminating case from Ruanda. There the ancestral charter of the Tutsi kingdom had long supposed strict hierarchical inequalities, but the ideas of national independence now spoke a different language. So the founding myths were re-interpreted during the 1950s in order to buttress with their force a premise, quite new for that stratified kingdom, according to which 'all Ruanda people are equal'–or, if they are not, then the fault lay with colonial rule. What had been in line with the 'right and natural' of the past was no longer so today, and the symbols accordingly required adjustment in their meaning.[12]

Yet the underlying significance of the symbols, of all such ideological data, did not change. They remained the embodiment of a specific world view, of an all round apprehension of how things were and ought to be. Where circumstances changed the symbols were adjusted, diminished, or extended– but in order to reaffirm the past and not in order to deny it.

In a related field the meaning of 'totems' and 'taboos' takes shape in the same perspective. These manifold differentiations and prohibitions were at one time regarded as mystical projections of the 'primitive mind', as phantoms deriving from aboriginal fears and fancies. Or else they were explained as more or less arbitrary aids to solving aboriginal problems: such as, in the matter of sharing out food, that one clan ate eland but not buffalo while its neighbour ate buffalo but not eland.

But totems and taboos can now be seen to display their true function as symbols deriving from a theory of social control. This theory was perfectly non-mystical in that it rested upon the observation of real phenomena; but it was couched in mandatory–moral terms. Within it, totems and taboos played the part of markers–symbolically embodied markers–along the boundaries of the 'right and natural', defining the theory and its system of control but also protecting these from all assaults of contrary phenomena. They are to be understood, accordingly, neither as mystical projections nor as acts of commonsense: not the first because they were codifications of the selective 'programme data' of the given social computation. Selective because they were designed to exclude events or actions which would threaten the system: programmatic because they aimed at the achievement of a desired ideal.

New research is getting us nearer to an understanding of all this. The Ndembu of north-western Zambia are undoubtedly among those who once would have been said to 'bow down to wood and stone', or at any rate to wood, and generally to suffer from a great deal of self-mystification. They attach a complex symbolism to three of their trees, the *mudyi*, the *muyomba*, and *mukala*. The *mudyi* and *muyomba*, which yield a milky latex when their bark is cut, are respectively associated with maternity and womanhood, and with the virtues of the ancestors: goodness and strength, generosity, long life, fertility. They also have to do with social harmony. Where the *mudyi* stands for the segmental unity of lineage or village, the *muyomba* 'represents a general unity–the unity of the moral order recognized by all Ndembu and sanctioned by the ancestor spirits'. The *mukala* tree, on the other hand, secretes a reddish gum. Ndembu associate it with blood and the properties of blood: with manhood and adult responsibility in society as a whole.[13]

So long as the key of the moral order was missing, these ideas could appear either as wild superstitions or as 'primitive customs' of merely arbitrary choice. In fact, Ndembu see them as a code–the phrase is that of Lévi-Strauss–which can 'guarantee the convertibility of ideas between different levels of social reality'. They even say as much. When Ndembu explain that the red gum of the *mukala* tree stands for blood, they call this symbol by a term in their language which means 'to blaze a trail'; so that a symbol is conceived as a tree-blaze or landmark, 'something which connects the known with the unknown', and thus links one level of apprehension with another.[14] But it is social reality with which this linking process is connected. The symbols are social symbols. They are intimately part of a determined socio-moral order.

This comes out insistently. Turner, who has studied the Ndembu, compares the initiation or other rites associated with these symbolic trees with sacraments which 'not only indicate inner changes of moral and social status, but also effect' such changes in the person conducted through the rites. 'Furthermore, like the Christian sacraments, they point to the past, present, and future, for they commemorate the first *mukanda* (in the series of circumcision or initiation rites), signify the various kinds of power they confer, and indicate the state of consummate manhood to come.'

'What actually happens' at these rites, or is seen to happen by the uninitiated observer, cannot therefore give any real description of them. Patient learning can alone do that, and it is only in recent years that any such insight has become available. As Ndembu see these rites, crude and simple though they may appear to others, 'each boy is sacramentally imbued with the whole Ndembu moral order, which is immanent in but also transcends the social order'–since by ancestral sanctions it controls the social order–'when he is circumcised under the *mudyi* tree of his mothers, passed over the tree of the ancestors (symbolized by a log of *muyomba*), and lodged finally on the tree of maturity (placed to rest and recover on a freshly cut branch of *mukala*)'.

Given the key of the moral order, other 'primitive customs' speak the same clear language. They too emerge as media 'for giving tangible substance to moral obligations', reflect 'a conviction that there is a moral order in the universe, and that man's well being depends upon obedience to that order as men see it', and appear as links in a chain of equilibrated relationships.

A number of African peoples have believed that their kings or ritual leaders must never 'die', and have gone to great lengths from time to time (it is difficult to know how often) to deal with the indisputable fact that they did die. Lienhardt tells how the Dinka say, they would dig a pit and place the dying Master on an *angareeb*, a type of bedstead of great antiquity in the Sudan. Then they would make a platform above this, using strips of hide, place a gourd of milk close by, and cover the whole with cattle dung.

Yet the dying Master of the Fishing Spear 'will not be afraid of death; he will be put in the earth while singing his songs. Nobody among his people will rail or cry because their man has died. They will be joyful because their Master of the Fishing Spear will give them life, so that they shall live untroubled by any evil.' So long as the Master still spoke, they would not cover up the grave. Only when he no longer replied to their words would they heap the dung upon his grave. 'And nobody will say "Alas, he is dead." They will say, "It *is* very good"'.

Now the inwardness of this rite was that the Masters of the Fishing Spear were concerned with matters pertaining to the condition and movement of the rivers which controlled men's lives in Dinkaland, and so were believed, in line with the Dinka apprehension of reality, to 'carry the life' of their people. This being so, a Master's natural death would symbolize death for his clan by means of one disaster or another. 'What (the Dinka) represent in contriving the death which they give him is the conservation of the "life" which they themselves think that they receive from him, and not the conservation of his own personal life. The latter, indeed, is finally taken away from him by his people so that they may seem to divide it from the public "life" which is in his keeping, and which must not depart from them with his death'. The ritual burial is 'associated by a wide range of associations with a social triumph over death and the factors which bring death in Dinkaland'. It is to be seen, in other words, as a conscious effort at control deriving from a given ideology, an ideology evolved in turn from ecological necessity and from Dinka means of meeting that necessity.[15]

Purposes varied. Other rituals belonged to other aspects of this 'pre-scientific' science of social control that were concerned with the endowment of authority. Whenever the emperor of Oyo died in old Yorubaland, appointed officials are said to have cut off his head; cleaned his skull, and taken out his heart. During installation rites the next emperor was obliged to sacrifice to Shango, a senior god, 'and was given a dish containing the heart of his predecessor which he had to eat'. A little later he was called on to swallow a portion of corn gruel from his predecessor's skull. These dramatic rites were occasioned by the need 'to open his ears to distinguish truth from falsehood', to give 'his words compelling power', and to assign 'to him alone the authority to execute criminals and his enemies at home, and to make war on enemies abroad'.[16] The point lay not in the gruesomeness, but in the mobilizing of chartered power behind the granting of a solemn office, thus guaranteeing legitimacy, as Fortes says, and imposing accountability on its proper exercise.

From this standpoint one may grasp why these societies needed many more rituals than ours. In our societies most individuals know their place by the influence of a process of differentiation effected by class, accent, education, income, professional affiliation, or some other fissile action of the social order. Rituals have fallen away, or have survived in affectionate gestures to an irrelevant past, as when budding lawyers in London have to 'eat their dinners' at an 'inn' which is no longer any such thing. But with these societies the situation was otherwise. They were faced with the task of creating a differentiation of roles and statutes from a more or less undifferentiated community of social equals; and then, afterwards, with the task of safeguarding these offices from disorderly infringement by persons who might otherwise be living in much the same way, or exactly the same way, as the office holders.

Summing up, religion in Africa appears in all its varied garb as the projection and affirmation of certain principles concerned with the evolution of society. Defined most simply, it is the selective codification for everyday life of the workings of the Principle of Good, of whatever guards or harmonizes with a system initially empirical but long since 'given', and of the workings of the Principle of Evil, of whatever undermines or goes against this given system. Hence the multiplicity of religions. Each society has necessarily required its own. And hence, too, the further elaboration into processes of what Turner has called 'social analysis': the application to oracles and the varied testing of reality against these twin Principles, against the truth or power of God and the Devil, in ways we call magical, in witchcraft and sorcery...

NOTES

[1] E.E. Evans-Pritchard, *Theories of primitive religion*, Clarendon Press, Oxford, 1965, p. 14.

[2] M. Fortes, *Oedipus and Job in West African religion*, Cambridge University Press, 1959, p. 53.

[3] Evans-Pritchard, *op. cit.*, p. 4.

[4] T.O. Ranger, *Revolt in Southern Rhodesia*, Heinemann, London, 1967, esp. ch. 6.

[5] C. Lévi-Strauss, *La pensée sauvage*, 1962 (*The savage mind*, London, 1966).

[6] *Ibid.*

[7] N. Dyson-Hudson, *Karimojon politics*, Clarendon Press, Oxford, 1966, p. 16 and p. 97.

[8] Lévi-Strauss, *op. cit.*, p. 67.

[9] R. Horton, 'Ritual man in Africa', in *Africa*, 2 (1964).

[10] Idem, 'African traditional thought and western science', in *Africa*, 2 (1967).

[11] J.P. Leboeuf, 'L'Histoire de la région tchadienne', in J. Vansina, R. Mauny and L.V. Thomas (eds), *The historian in Tropical Africa*, Oxford University Press, London, 1964.

[12] D'Hertefelt, 'Mythes et idéologies dans le Ruanda ancien et contemporain'.

[13] V.W. Turner, 'Ritual symbolism, morality and social structure among the Ndembu', in M. Fortes and G. Dieterlen (eds) *African systems of thought*, Oxford University Press, London, 1965; and 'Three symbols of passage in Ndembu circumcision ritual', in M. Gluckman (Ed) *Essays on the ritual of social relations*, Manchester University Press, 1962.

[14] *Ibid.*

[15] G. Lienhardt, *Divinity and experience: the religion of the Dinka*, Clarendon Press, London, 1961, p. 298.

[16] P. Morton-Williams, 'The Kingdom of Oyo', in D. Forde and P.M. Kaberry (eds) *West African kingdoms in the nineteenth century*, Oxford University Press, London, 1967.

Mahdism, Messianism and Marxism in the African setting
THOMAS HODGKIN

From Yusuf Fadl Hasan (Ed.), *Sudan in Africa,* Khartoum University Press, Khartoum, 1971.

I wish in this paper to raise, very briefly and inadequately, some questions about the relationships between these three types of revolutionary ideologies– Mahdist, Messianic, and Marxist–in the context of African history. I do not propose to limit myself exclusively to *bilad al-sudan*, since, while the Mahdist movements about which I shall have something to say arose mainly in that region, it seems useful to consider Messianic movements in a wider African context. It is, I realize, presumptuous for one who has done no original work in this field to attempt to say anything about Mahdism in this historic focus of the most important Mahdist movement of modern times. But I hope the attempt can be justified by the fact that so much interesting work has recently been done, or is now in progress, on the contribution of Mahdist and Messianic ideologies to new political and social initiatives in nineteenth and twentieth-century Africa. It may therefore be a good moment to look at some of the evidence in a comparative way. The footnotes will give some idea of the people whose researches I have leaned upon most heavily and from whom I have learned most.

Although there has been a tendency for Mahdist and Messianic movements, because they have emerged in different types of cultural setting (Islamic and non-Islamic), to be studied from somewhat different standpoints, it seems generally recognized that they have certain common characteristics. These might provisionally be listed as follows:

(1) The central role of the Messianic leader, prophet, or Mahdi.

(2) The millenarian expectations, or hopes, of the movement.

(3) The rejection of established authority, both religious and secular, as oppressive and illegitimate.

(4) The appeal to 'the masses' and the effort to mobilize them in support of the Mahdist–Messianic idea.

(5) Associated with this, the attempt to use the universality of the Mahdist–Messianic message as a means of overcoming traditional conflicts and antagonisms.

(6) The establishment of some form of continuing organization, based upon adherence to this ideology.

(7) The use of certain external symbols to express the common purposes and beliefs and distinctive character of the movement.

(8) The assertion of Puritan values in matters of personal conduct (abstinence, self-discipline, etc.); the rejection of 'the things of this world'.

(9) The situation of 'crisis' in which such movements tend to emerge.

Essentially both Mahdism and Messianism are ideologies which are, as Lanternari stresses,[1] particularly appropriate for 'the oppressed' in situations in which they have not only become conscious of oppression but are willing to respond to a movement which seems to offer a revolutionary way out: 'If the present belongs to the oppressors, the future belongs to us, the revolutionary community–and outside the community there is no salvation and no future.'

But, in spite of these basic resemblances, there are also some significant differences between movements that are generally described as 'Mahdist' and those described as 'Messianic'. In particular, Mahdist movements, emerging in societies which have been fairly effectively Islamized over a period of time, have had a well established body of Mahdist beliefs (or, as Holt prefers to say, 'a deposit of ideas and hopes... varying in their content and emphasis at different times and in different places'[2]) on which to draw.

There is, of course, an extensive literature relating to the general theory of Mahdism.[3] Apart from the traditional corpus of beliefs regarding the Signs of the Hour and the distinctive characteristics of the Mahdi, the aspects of this theory which would seem to be of most importance in the present context are:

First, the concept of crisis, during the period preceding the end of time in which the Mahdi will appear. 'Upheavals and dissension (*fitan*) will divide the Muslim community (*umma*) and lead to political strife, social disorder, and moral degeneration...'[4]

Second, the idea that the Mahdi, as the divinely guided one, in direct communication with God or his Prophet, can exercise a special revolutionary initiative in his interpretation of the Qur'an and the Sunna, unrestricted by the established *madhhabs*.[5]

Third, the idea that the Mahdi, as Ima, or ultimate Caliph of the Prophet, has the responsibility for conducting *jihad*, particularly against nominal and backsliding Muslims who reject his mission, and ensuring the universal triumph of Islam.

Fourth, the association of the appearance of the Mahdi with the approaching end of the world and a brief intervening Golden Age, during which he will 'fill the earth with equity and justice, even as it has been filled with tyranny and oppression'.

The Messianic movements on the other hand which have emerged in non-Muslim Africa have generally drawn their basic ideas either from the Judaeo-Christian tradition, or from 'traditional' African belief-systems, or, very often, from some combination of these. (Mahdist movements have naturally tended to show a similar kind of syncretism, combining pre-Islamic with Islamic elements in their ideologies.) But, while there is as ancient and important a 'deposit' of Messianic and millenarian ideas within the Christian as within the Muslim tradition, these have not in general been available to the membership of the various Christian churches and sects in Africa, in the modern period at least, in as well-defined and coherent a form as Mahdism. True, the ideologies of some African Messianic movements have been derived directly from a non-African prototype–as that of Kitawala, in the Congo and adjacent territories, was derived from the Watchtower, though with important variations and modifications.[6] But often, it would seem, the ideology has been worked out afresh by the movement through the application of certain basic concepts drawn from the Judaeo-Christian tradition–of a Messiah, of an oppressed people, of salvation as an event in historic time (not essentially different from political liberation)–to their own situation. The central idea is that the Kingdom of Heaven must be understood in a this-worldly, not an other-worldly sense–as a perfected social order, to be achieved in the very near future and enjoyed collectively by the faithful.[7]

Messianic movements in non-Muslim contexts would seem to differ from Mahdist movements also in that they are not committed to the same sort of attitude to institutions. It is an essential part of the Mahdist theory to regard *jihad*, in the sense of an armed revolutionary struggle, as the method whereby a perfected social order must be brought into being. Messianic movements on the other hand, while they may accept the view that the expected trans-formation of society depends upon revolutionary action on their part, may also regard it as dependent upon some cataclysmic external event which it is their duty simply to await.[8] In other words Messianism seems compatible, in some degree, with quietism as well as with activism. Similarly, at the level of objectives, Mahdist movements are committed to the idea of a Mahdist state, *i.e.* a perfected Islamic state, which they must seek to realize. Messianic movements are not necessarily concerned with state-building, though in practice this may become their objective. This, as Balandier points out in the case of Kimbanguism, follows logically from the interdependence of religious and political ends. The aspiration to establish a 'Congolese Church' cannot be separated from the aspiration to set up a 'Congolese state', detached from all forms of European control.[9]

Through history clearly Messianic movements, expressing millenarian expectations, have provided the oppressed in societies dominated, or strongly influenced, by Christian or Islamic ideologies with a particularly effective vehicle of protest. In such contexts a coherent, intelligible, and relevant system of revolutionary beliefs has been, so to speak, ready to hand. But such move-ments have been imported also in societies in which what may be loosely called 'traditional African systems of belief' have been dominant, and Islamic and Christian influences would seem to have been negligible. In this connection Terence Ranger's discussion of the part played by millenarian beliefs in the ideology of the Shona revolt of 1896–97[10], and John Iliffe's study of comparable aspects of the Maji Maji rising of 1905–07 are of particular interest.[11]

From this point there are various questions which it would be interesting to discuss. How far back in African history, or in the history of particular African regions, can Messianic–Mahdist movements be traced? How far did particular movements, separated in time and space, influence one another? In what kind of crisis situation did such movements tend to emerge? From what social groups did they draw their leadership and support? How significant a part did they play in the development of 'primary resistance', or proto-nationalist opposition, to European colonial régimes? How far have they influenced the theory and practice of modern political movements? In this paper I can only touch on such large questions in a very preliminary and inadequate way.

As regards this question of historical roots, in the Maghrib the Mahdist tradition is, of course, a very ancient one. Dr Holt has pointed out resemblances between the careers of Muhammad ibn Tumart, the founder of the Almohad movement, who assumed the Mahdiship in A.D. 1212, and Muhammad Ahmad, the Sudanese Mahdi, in the late nineteenth century.[12] But I know of no evidence of the circulation of Mahdist ideas or prophecies in *bilad al-sudan* at this early period. Indeed, it would follow from Ibn Khaldun's view, that within Sunni Islam, Mahdism is essentially a *popular* belief, 'commonly accepted among the masses of the people of Islam', that Mahdist ideas could not be expected to emerge in any significant way until Islam had become fairly widely diffused among the Sudanese masses.[13] Hiskett has suggested that 'the first written record... in Sudanese literature of the Messianic tradition, common throughout Islam', occurs in the following passage from the replies of Muhammad ibn Abd al-karim al-Maghili of Tlemcen to Muhammad Ture, the founder of the Askia dynasty in Songhai, (*c*. 1500 A.D.):

And accordingly it is related that at the beginning of every century God will send a learned man to the people to renew their faith, and the characteristics of this learned man in every century must be that he commands what is right and forbids what is disapproved of, and reforms the affairs of the people and judges justly between them, and assists the truth against vanity, and the oppressed against the oppressor, in contrast to the characteristics of the [other] learned men of his age.[14]

But al-Maghili, as Hiskett points out, seems clearly to be referring here to the historic function of the *mujaddid*, the renewer and reformer of Islam, who, according to tradition, appears at the end of every century, and not specifically to the Mahdi (though admittedly there is a certain overlap between the two ideas).[15]

At any rate by the turn of the eighteenth century Mahdist beliefs were sufficiently firmly implanted in the central Sudan, and sufficiently widely accepted, for 'Uthman dan Fodio to devote several of his works to their discussion.[16] Muhammad al-Hajj has pointed out that the growth of interest in Mahdism at this particular time was probably connected with the fact that the twelfth-century Hijra ended in A.D. 1785–86 and that, according to al-Suyuti (whose writings were widely read and respected in the Sudan), A.H. 1200 or A.H. 1204 were alternative dates for the appearance of the Mahdi.[17] He has also shown clearly the way in which what might be called 'latent Mahdism' persisted in the western and central Sudan throughout the nineteenth century. Hence it was natural that all the three major reforming leaders of the period–'Uthman dan Fodio, Shehu Ahmadu and al-Hajj 'Umar Tal–should have been associated in the public mind with Mahdist hopes and prophecies.[18] 'Uthman's own position (so far as I can understand it) seems to have been particularly interesting. He shared the widespread popular belief in the imminent appearance of the Mahdi and the approaching end of the world. At the same time he went to great pains to explain to the people that he was not himself the Mahdi, and precisely why he failed to meet the generally accepted requirements:

> Know, O my Brethren, that I am not al-imam al-mahdi, and I have never claimed the *mahdiyya*–even though that is heard from the tongues of other people. Indeed, I have striven beyond measure in warning them to desist from that, and declared its refutation in some of my writings, both in Arabic and 'Ajami... How can I claim the *mahdiyya* since I was born in *bilad al-sudan* in a place called Maratta and the Mahdi ought to be born in Medina?[19]

In his interesting Fulfulde poem, *Sifofin Shehu*, he takes the same general position, though mentioning 30 or more attributes of the Mahdi which he claims to possess.[20] But, while denying his own claims to the Mahdiyya, 'in the early stages of the *jihad*', Al-Hajj argues, 'the Shehu consciously emphasized the prophecies about the End of Time in order to instil into his followers the love of martyrdom and the renunciation of this transitory world'. And at his important meeting with the eastern leaders at Birnin Gada in the dry season of 1805–06 Muhammad Bello delivered a message from the Shehu 'about the approaching appearance of the Mahdi, that the Shehu's followers are his vanguard, and that this *jihad* will not end, by God's permission, until the appearance of the Mahdi'.[21] By 1808, when the main phases of the *jihad* had been successfully completed, he had shifted his ground, and presented in his *Amr al-sa'a* 'an apology for the confusion caused by his previous books and a warning against indulgence in extravagant prophecies'. In his *Tanbih al-fahim*, written in the same year, he subjected his former views on the imminent appearance of the Mahdi to severe self-criticism:

> What we used to mention again and again during the gatherings for preaching, that the time for the appearance of the Mahdi had come, was based on the assumptions of al-Suyuti. But, after investigation, we admit that we do not know the time with any degree of certainty.

And in 1814 his *Tahdhir al-ikhwan* was written specifically to refute the claims of the Tuareg Hamma (whom the Sokoto government later defeated and crucified) to the Mahdiyya.[22]

This evidence would seem to fit with the fairly generally accepted view of 'Uthman dan Fodio as essentially a middle-of-the-road reformer, as much opposed to the Leftist social-revolutionary ideas of Mahdism and Kharijism as to the Rightist opportunist attitudes of the 'venal mallams'.[23] At the same time it is natural that this reforming leadership should have been willing to promote and encourage Mahdist beliefs during the revolutionary phase of the *jihad*, when it was essential to mobilize the masses in its support, but should have found these expectations of a new world order an embarrassment, or even a positive threat to the régime, when it was attempting to consolidate the power of the Sokoto Caliphate on lines which offered relatively little prospect of fundamental social change. This dual attitude to Mahdism seems to have continued through the century. Since Mahdist beliefs remained current and officially approved it was necessary to keep the roads to the East, where the Mahdi was expected to appear, open. But active expressions of these beliefs, including attempts at mass migration to the East, were generally resisted on the ground that the time of exodus had not yet come, 'since there is still some good remaining among us'.[24]

Muhammad al-Hajj has shown very clearly how this two-way traffic in Mahdist ideas, between the central and the eastern Sudan, operated in the latter half of the nineteenth century–and has indeed continued down to modern times. What perhaps one needs most to understand is what was the nature of the crisis that stimulated the transformation of latent Mahdism into active Mahdism during the period from 1880 on–above all in the eastern Sudan, the only region in which an effective Mahdist state was able to estab-lish and maintain itself for a substantial period, but also generally, in many parts of *bilad al-sudan*. (It is odd that Holt, in his valuable study of the Mahdist state in the eastern Sudan, should have described it as 'an apparently isolated and anachronistic phenomenon'.[25] In fact it was far from isolated and not in any intelligible sense anachronistic.)

In a general way, no doubt, one can explain the activisation of latent Mahdist beliefs during this period by the increasing pressure of European imperialism upon the Muslim world and the economic, social, and political disintegration arising out of these pressures and, later, out of actual European invasion and occupation and the defeat or capitulation of Muslim govern-ments.[26] This, understandably, appeared to indicate the existence of the kind of crisis associated historically with the appearance of the Mahdi. (This identification had in fact already been made during earlier phases of European penetration into Muslim Africa: a Mahdist rising had occurred in Lower Egypt during Bonaparte's occupation;[27] 'Abd al-Qadir's revolt against French penetration into Algeria seems to have owed its popular support in part to Mahdist expectations.[28]) More study of the literature of the period would enable one to grasp in more depth and detail how the crisis presented itself to Muslims in different parts of *bilad al-sudan* at different phases of its development, and how far their reactions to it involved Mahdist ideas and symbols. We have poems of al-Hajj 'Umar ibn Abi Bakr al-Salghawi (of Ghana), for example, in which the European invasion of West Africa is associated with the conventional signs of the coming of the Mahdi.[29] At the level of practice Le Grip gives some rather fragmentary information, based mainly on Marty, relating to Mahdis who appeared during this period in various parts of the western and central Sudan and who led movements that provided, in one way or another, channels for 'primary resistance' to European imperialism.[30] But the whole subject requires much more investigation.

One important theme which is beginning to be more seriously studied is the impact of the Mahdiyya in the eastern Sudan on these various West-Sudanic Mahdist movements, particularly on the movements which emerged in the 1880s and '90s in the Sokoto Caliphate.[31] Here the situation involved at least four elements. First, there was the stimulus given to Mahdist beliefs by the successes of the Mahdi, Muhammad Ahmad, who in January 1883, after the capture of El-Obeid, opened correspondence with the rulers of

Sokoto and Bornu, demanding recognition and support (which they refused).[32] Second, there was the special position of Hayatu ibn Sacid, grandson of Muhammad Bello, with claims to the Caliphate, who identified himself with the Mahdist cause from the outset, and was appointed by the Mahdi (and confirmed after his death by the Khalifa) as his agent (*amil*), responsible for the affairs 'of all the people of Sokoto who were subjects of your great-grandfather, 'Uthman dan Fodio'.[33] Third, Mallam Jibril Gaini, a Fulani of Katagum, who described himself as *Amir al-jaysh* to Hayatu, established in about 1885 and maintained by military force an autonomous Mahdist state, based on Bormi in the Gombe region, on the Sokoto–Bornu frontier.[34] Fourth, the situation was transformed by the conquest of Bornu by Rabih ibn Fadlallah in 1893–94. Although Rabih's relationship with the Mahdiyya in the eastern Sudan, and in particular with the Khalifa, remained ambiguous, he clearly made use of Mahdist ideology and symbolism–'His army wore the Mahdist uniform, read the *Ratib*, and fought under a Mahdist flag.'[35] Initially Hayatu attempted to work in close association with Rabih, whose daughter, Hawwa, he married. Later he appears to have been kept virtually a prisoner at Dikwa, Rabih's capital, and was killed in 1898 by a force led by Fadlallah ibn Rabih when attempting to escape with the help of an escort provided by Jibril Gaini.[36] But during the period 1894 to 1900 Bornu was ostensibly a Mahdist state.

Against this background one can understand how the idea of *hijra* became associated with and re-inforced by Mahdist beliefs in the popular opposition to European–Christian rule which expressed itself in the final crisis of the Sokoto Caliphate. The choice of *hijra*, as opposed to collaboration with the Unbelievers, had already been made by Ahmadu Shehu, son of al-Hajj 'Umar and ruler of Segu, who, after Bandiagara had fallen to the French, had moved East with a considerable following to Sokoto, where he died in 1898.[37] His son, Bashir, together with a section of the ruling and scholarly classes from Sokoto and its dependent Amirates accompanied the legitimate (now officially deposed) Caliph, Attahiru Ahmad, when he opted for *hijra* after the fall of Sokoto in March, 1903. But what makes Attahiru's *hijra* particularly interesting historically is the scale of mass participation and support which it enjoyed, as Dr Adeleye shows from contemporary sources.[38] Hence the strengthened appeal, in a situation in which the country was now in actual occupation by the Europeans, of Mahdist ideas–reflected in the choice of the Mahdist town of Burmi as the place of refuge for Attahiru and his supporters and the base for their final stand against imperialism. At the battle of Burmi, on 27 July 1903, Attahiru (who, it is claimed, first accepted Mahdism) was killed with some 700 of his supporters. But the *hijra*, involving many thousands of Westerners, to the eastern Sudan continued, under the leadership of Attahiru's son, Muhammad Bello Mai Wurno (after whom their eventual town of settlement was named) and others. And within the British-occupied territories of the Caliphate a succession of Mahdist, or post-Mahdist, movements emerged–'the most celebrated... (being) that which culminated in the Satiru rebellion of 1906'.[39]

    If we turn from the Muslim to the non-Muslim world we can find a clear example of the use of messianic and millenary ideas to provide ideological

support for a movement of 'primary resistance' to European imperialism
in Ranger's admirable study of the Shona rebellion. Like the later Maji-
Maji rising in Tanganyika, he argues, the rebellion involved–

> ... defiance of a power which enjoyed great technological superiority
> and began with a superiority of morale based upon it and upon confidence
> in its ability to shape the world. The [African] religious leaders were able
> to oppose to this a morale which for the moment was as confident, if not
> more so, based upon *their* supposed ability to shape the world; and they
> were able to oppose to modern weapons the one great advantage that the
> Africans possessed, that of numbers.[40]

He goes on to stress the 'ambiguity' of the attitude of these resistance
movements to European ideas and technology. 'There is repudiation but
also desire; a rejection of white mastery but a longing for African control
of modern sources of wealth and power in an African environment... Mkwati
and Kagthi [religious leaders of the Shona rebellion]... were not reactionary
in the simple sense of looking to the restoration of the *status quo* of 1890;
their programme was in some ways revolutionary in its vision of a new society.'
In Mkwati's millenarian promises 'there was a strange mixture of return to
the past and control of the new'.

> Lobengula was to return from the dead–and to reign from Government
> House, Bulawayo. When Mkwati was trying to rally the north-eastern
> rebels in August 1896 it was reported that he promised them that they
> only "had to wait until all the whites are dead or fled and then they will
> enjoy the good things of the town and live in palaces of corrugated iron".
> "Directly the white men are killed", a police inspector was told during the
> Inyanga scare of 1903–04, "we will occupy your houses; all these nice
> things will be ours."[41]

There is, of course, ample evidence of the important part played by Messianic and Mahdist ideologies in the development of what may be loosely
called 'proto-nationalist' movements during the main period of colonial
domination.[42] Here again the use of these ideas as a basis for political action
seems to have been associated with situations of crisis, or situations seen
as such by substantial sections of the African masses, particularly the crisis
of the years immediately following the First World War. Tomlinson and
Lethem, in their interesting, if lurid and occasionally fantastic, report on
the history of Islamic propaganda in Nigeria, mention as one factor contributing to the revival and spread of 'Mahdist propaganda' during the period
1918–23:

> The widespread belief (not, of course, confined to Nigeria) that the end of
> the world, which is to take place in A.H. 1400 (A.D. 1979), will be preceded
> by the supremacy of the false prophet ("Dajjal" or Antichrist), followed
> by the second coming of Nebi Isa (Jesus Christ), after which all the world
> will be converted to Islam. It has been the practice of agitators of late to
> identify the European conquerors of Muslim countries with Dajjal.[43]

The content of this 'Mahdist propaganda' is described as including:

> The 'Vision of the Alfa Hashim', the Dajjal prophecies, encyclicals of the
> Mahdi, letters to Hayatu from the Mahdi and the Khalifa Abdullahi,

garbled versions of Abderrahman's visit to England,... old Fulani prophecies of the Fulani trek to the East, Muhammad Bello's prophecy as
to his son Sacid and his grandson Sacid, and Hayatu's upon his son Sacid
... Nonsense about 'the day' and the imminent appearance of Isa...[44]

While the eastern Sudan was regarded as the main source of Mahdist beliefs–
with the Hijaz as a secondary focus and the *haj* route providing the main
communications network–in a more confused and shadowy way 'Mahdist
propaganda' was thought of at this time as associated with Bolshevism, the
Third International, Egyptian nationalism, Pan-Islamism, and ideas of
'world revolution' in general.[45]

The Messianic movement associated with Simon Kimbangu and his success-
or prophets among the Bakongo, which is one of the best documented
among anti-colonial protest movements making use of an essentially Christian
ideology, was at the same time one of the most highly developed from the
standpoint of theory and most effective and stable in respect of its organization, maintaining itself through a variety of institutional forms over a period
of more than 30 years.[46] Balandier in his study of this movement emphasizes
the connection between its phases of greatest activity and situations of
particular crisis in Bakongo society:

> The moments of 'crisis' were coincident with the most violent protests
> on the part of the colonized society. In 1921–22, after the decline in the
> trade in export crops, the messianic movement known as *Kimbanguism*
> established itself in the areas around Brazzaville... After the 1929 crisis
> violent incidents occurred in Bakongo country and in various parts of
> Upper Congo. In this connection it is significant that the preacher and
> inspirer of the Sanga revolts was concerned to announce, after the expulsion
> of the Whites, a true Golden Age–'perpetual abundance of crops, game,
> and fish'. Official reports, dating from 1931, refer to 'the actions of sorcer-
> ers who take advantage of the economic crisis to spread the rumour that
> the Whites are growing weaker and have no more money', stressing at
> the same time the 'troubles' which threaten the Belgian Congo for the
> same reasons.[47]

However, one has not, I admit, made much progress towards answering
some of the crucial questions: What during this phase of history, the period
of the break-up of indigenous pre-colonial states and the imposition of
European-dominated colonial systems, was the nature of the crises which
led to the emergence of Messianic and Mahdist movements? Why have they
played a particularly significant part in the history of some societies and not
of others? At what point do the oppressed decide that oppression, or this
particular form of oppression, is no longer endurable, and turn to a revolutionary millennial ideology for a way out–since clearly no Messianic leader
can establish himself without a supporting popular movement? In this connection it is worth asking how important is the possession of a local tradition
of popular protest. In the case of the Mahdist movements which emerged
in the Sokoto Caliphate–Northern Nigeria during the late nineteenth and
early twentieth centuries, we have seen that these drew upon a deposit of
beliefs which had been in circulation in the region for at least a century.
Among the Shona there was a tradition of resistance to Portuguese pressures

going back to the early seventeenth century.[48] In the old kingdom of the Kongo there was a long-standing tradition of popular Christian heresies. At the beginning of the eighteenth century a Bakongo prophetess, Donna Beatrice, gave herself out to be St Antony, claimed to speak with God, prophesied that the Day of Judgment was at hand, and sent out her 'angels' as ambassadors through the country to summon the princes to San Salvador 'to restore the kingdom'. 'Almost the entire kingdom was disaffected and adhered to the Antonian sect.' Even after she had been condemned to death and burnt by the Portuguese, together with her principal 'angel', the movement remained a powerful force. Her supporters became 'more obstinate than ever'.[49] The existence of such traditions of protest within a particular society might seem to predispose its members to seek for a Messianic solution to the problems posed by modern forms of European domination.

It may help towards an understanding of the nature of the crises which have given rise to Messianic-Mahdist movements to note the distinction which Lanternari draws 'between movements generated by a conflict between societies or by the clash with an external force and those generated by dissensions within the pattern of one society', even though, as he says, 'we should view the distinction between external and internal motivation in a dialectical sense and not as a static condition'.[50] In other words, during the phase of history with which I am particularly concerned, Messianic–Mahdist movements were always directed partly against the external forces of oppression (Western imperialism, or its associated sub-imperialisms, and the dislocations, tensions, and problems to which it had given rise), partly against indigenous oppressive classes, interests, and institutions. Sometimes one aspect is more in evidence, sometimes the other. In the case of the Mahdist movements in the Sokoto Caliphate it would seem that the increasing economic difficulties of the free peasants and small gentry during the latter part of the nineteenth century were a contributory factor.[51] In the eastern Sudan Holt and others have stressed the importance of specific economic grievances associated with attempts to abolish the slave trade, supplementing and intensifying general popular opposition to the alien, oppressive, and un-Islamic régime of the *Turkiyya*.[52] Naturally, where Messianic-Mahdist movements occur in an apparently firmly established colonial situation, as vehicles for some form of proto-nationalism, as in the case of Kimbanguism and its successor movements, the main emphasis tends to be upon opposition to external oppression and its local agents:

> The Whites are about to be lost on account of the earning of money. Lord, pardon them that they may be saved.
> The chiefs are about to be lost on account of their money. Lord, pardon them that they may be saved.
> The police are about to be lost on account of the collecting of taxes, Lord, pardon them that they may be saved.[53]

As Lanternari mildly puts it–'Cultural conflict with the whites is by no means the only motivation behind the Messianic movements, but it is by far the most prevalent because of its disconcerting effects upon native society, culture and religion'.[54]

Clearly one should not attempt to be too rigorous in considering whether a given movement was or was not Messianic or Mahdist in character. Even in the case of Mahdism, where one might think it sufficient to apply the simple criterion–did this particular Muslim leader proclaim himself to be the Mahdi or not?–things are not necessarily altogether clearcut. One may be confronted with a popular protest movement in an Islamic frame of reference, such as the reformed Tijaniyya under the leadership of Shaykh Hamallah (the so-called 'Hamalliyya') in the Mali region during the inter-war period, which seems to have had most of the characteristics of a Messianic movement, as I have attempted to define them. Yet Shaykh Hamallah never (so far as I know) identified himself with the Mahdi, though he was certainly so regarded after his deportation by the French.[55] This kind of transformation of a given popular leader, after his exile, imprisonment, or death, into a Mahdi or Messiah is a not uncommon phenomenon: e.g., the transformation of André Matswa of Congo (Brazzaville), founder of *Amicalisme* in the late 1920s, from a secular political leader into 'Père Matswa' of 'Jésus Matswa', third person of the Kimbanguist Trinity and focus of the Matswanist Church, after his trial and first imprisonment in 1930, and even more after his death in prison in 1942.[56] It might therefore seem best to use the term 'Messianic movement' in a fairly general sense, recognizing that movements of many different types (including modern secular national movements) may reveal Messianic characteristics, reserving the term 'Mahdist' for movements whose leaders have claimed to be Mahdis (or representatives or agents of Mahdis) in the more strict and technical sense.

One needs to pay attention also to the later history of Messianic and Mahdist movements. There would seem to be a fairly general tendency for such movements, after their revolutionary phase has ended in defeat and repression and their millennial hopes have been disappointed, to adapt, or partially adapt, themselves, ideologically and structurally, to the new situation. The neo-Mahdist organization of the *Ansār*, which during the period of the Condominium developed as a quasi-*tarīqa*, is a case in point.[57] Kimbanguism–Matswanism during its later phase, as the *Mission des Noirs,* is an interesting example of a somewhat comparable kind of development, with its hierarchical, semi-military form of church organization (partly modelled on the Salvation Army), ethical and ritual prescriptions, calendar of holy days, sacred literature, esoteric interest in symbolic numbers, combined with its attitude of total rejection of the European Missions and the colonial state:

> Thus the symbol 12–a sacred number, which is expressed in the twelve 'persons' of Simon Kimbangu, the Council of 12 'apostles', the obligation to observe the 12 'days of grace' (the first 12 days of June), or in certain rules relating to personal hygiene (men had to cut their hair every 12 days)–was associated not only with Biblical tradition,... but with a whole network of activities in which the faithful participate...[58]

But this attitude of rejection and withdrawal may, of course, relate to all forms of secular politics, not merely to European-dominated politics; and the conflict between a Messianic Church that is committed to this kind of attitude and the nationalist party, once it is in formal political control of the state, may be even more sharp than with the former colonial administration–as in the case, particularly, of the Lumpa Church in Zambia.[59]

It is obviously difficult to try to answer large questions about 'historical significance' in relation to movements as complex and diverse as these, occurring in many different African territories, in very different kinds of historical context. None the less one can reasonably claim that these Messianic–Mahdist movements were important, both in themselves and as regards their influence on subsequent African history, in at least three ways.

First, through the universalism of their ideologies, and the forms of organization which they attempted to construct, these movements tried, with varying degrees of success, to provide a new basis of solidarity, transcending the more restricted ties of kinship, locality, ethnic or linguistic group, or pre-colonial state. This is a point which is constantly stressed by those who have studied specific movements: for example, Ranger, writing of the leaders of the Shona revolt:

> They were very successful exponents of a type of leadership which appears to have been associated with most of the striking attempts to solve, on however impermanent a basis, the greatest political problem of pre-colonial Africa; the problem of scale.[60]

Similarly Iliffe, on the organization of the Maji-Maji Rebellion:

> Since the object was to organize anew, it was not sufficient merely to revitalize structures and beliefs which often reflected those divisions which had previously hindered effective action. Rather, it was necessary to enlarge the scale both of resistance and of religious allegiance. The central figure in such an enlargement was the prophet, proclaiming a new religious order to supersede the old, a new loyalty to transcend old loyalties of tribe and kinship. German observers saw in Maji-Maji the signs of such a transformation. The *maji*–the water-medicine accepted by each rebel–united in common action peoples with no known prior unity.[61]

Compare also Balandier on the Kimbanguist movement among the Bakongo:

> ... The second remarkable fact [over and above its endurance through time] was its extension in space, which took less account of national than of ethnic frontiers. It expressed the profound reactions of a people who had rediscovered their sense of unity: the 'messages' circulated within the Congolese churches were described as 'bringing knowledge' to the faithful in the two Congos and in Angola. Unquestionably the movement for religious innovation lay at the root of a growth of 'national' consciousness. The new Church was the builder of social relationships, sought limits lying beyond the restricted framework of clan or tribe.[62]

The Mahdiyya in the eastern Sudan asserted its own form of Islamic universalisms:

> The fall of El Obeid opened to the Mahdi the prospect of a series of apocalyptic victories throughout the heartlands of Islam. The determination to undertake the conquest of the Sudan generally and then of the neighbouring lands was conveyed in the visionary form in which the Mahdi cloaked his decisions . . .[63]

True, this new revolutionary form of *casabiyya* was by its nature unstable and difficult to maintain over a long period. There was an understandable tendency, once the leadership had to confront the problem of constructing some kind of continuing system and preserving it against increasing internal and external pressures, to revert to reliance on those same traditional ties, loyalties, institutions, that the revolution had sought to abolish or transcend.

Thus Holt describes how the Khalifa Abdallahi, during the later phases of the Mahdist state, found himself obliged to depend increasingly upon Taʿīshi political support, while attempting to 'restore the administrative system... by bringing back the men and methods of the old régime and thereby much of the corruption, dilatoriness, and oppression which the Mahdi had hoped to sweep away'.[64] (Modern analogies will readily suggest themselves.) In his account of the Maji-Maji rebellion Iliffe refers to 'a third phase, in which the failure of the *maji* obliged the rebels to return to customary methods of tribal warfare... Thus the paradox of later nationalist movements, the need to use old loyalties in order to popularize an effort to transcend them, also characterized this earlier attempt to enlarge political scale.'[65] None the less, the mere fact of asserting a universal idea, as the basis for a new and more comprehensive form of organization, was itself of historical importance: 'God... has sent us a Saviour of the Black race, Simon Kimbangu. He is the leader and Saviour of all Black people, in the same way as the Saviours of other races–Moses, Jesus Christ, Muhammad, and Buddha.'[66]

Second, Messianic-Mahdist movements were in a basic sense forward-looking: they were 'movements of innovation looking to the future and the regeneration of the world'.[67] True, 'forward-looking' and 'backward-looking' are relative categories, and movements of popular protest and revolt normally contain elements of both. But what is significant about these particular movements is that they present a view of a future social order which is essentially different from any kind of society that has existed in the known or remembered past. They may refer back to the early Caliphate or to the state of man before the Fall; the Mahdi–Messiah may see himself as re-enacting the life and experience of the Prophet or Christ; or they may make use of concepts and symbols derived from traditional religion. But they were essentially different from those forms of resistance or rebellion whose primary object was to retain or restore the pre-colonial political and social order. The revolution, as they conceived it, must involve the total transformation of society, and of man as a social being; the assertion of a new ethic and a new basis for human relationships; the ending of all forms of oppression, not merely those specific forms of oppression associated with external domination or the colonial state.[68]

Third, Messianic and Mahdist movements have provided a structure of ideas and institutions through which 'the masses' have begun to play an active, formative, and conscious part in modern history. Not much work (so far as I am aware) has yet been done on the social composition of these movements, on the lines of the studies of other revolutionary movements in other historical contexts. In particular one is not clear about the relative importance of rural and urban components, or the part played (in the Congo or Nyasaland, for example) by migrant workers.[69] But in broad terms these movements would generally seem to have involved some form of alliance between large sections of the peasantry (including semi-proletarianized elements) and, in the case of the Sudan, the nomad population, with a revolutionary leadership drawn largely (like the *prophetae* in mediaeval Europe) from what one might call the underprivileged intelligentsia–Sufi shaykhs, small culamā, catechists, monitors, interpreters, clerks, and NCOs who had worked in the administrative, commercial or military sectors of the colonial apparatus.[70] It was essentially this literate leadership, with a grounding often in Islamic or Christian doctrine, which was able, as a member of the Khaki Movement (a successor to Kimbanguism) put it 'in various ways to "vana ngolo kwa bankwa brousse" (give power to the country people)'.[71]

The points of resemblance between the theories of Messianic and Mahdist movements and certain aspects of Marxism are evident enough, and have been discussed from various standpoints (though more often, I think, in a European than an African or Third World context).[72] These include the idea of history as involving a continuing conflict between oppressors and oppressed, and leading, by a process conceived as historically necessary, to the ultimate victory of the oppressed; the 'apocalyptic' idea of the just, or classless, society, based on the principle of 'to each according to his needs', as in some sense the goal of history; the idea of the total corruption and degeneracy of the existing social order, and the consequent necessity for the total reconstruction of all institutions, all aspects of human life and relationships; the idea of social change in a progressive direction as depending not simply upon providential guidance, or some cataclysmic external event, but also (in part, at least) upon revolutionary activism and the intelligent and continuing participation of the masses in the effort to transform the actual world.[73] The list, obviously, could be extended.

Of course, the points of difference between the two types of theory are also substantial and important. In part these arise from the fact that Marxism involves a much more carefully constructed, and objectively better grounded, method of historical interpretation and sociological analysis than the methods employed by Mahdist and Messianic movements. The classless society of Communism is conceived, not as imminent, but as realizable after a complex and protracted period of effort, conflict, and transition, involving many retrogressive as well as progressive phases–even though there have been moments in the history of the past hundred years when Marxists have in practice taken a somewhat millenarian view of the prospects of world revolution. Moreover bourgeois society, and even the colonial systems which Western bourgeois states have imposed upon the peoples of the non-Western world, are conceived as containing within themselves possibilities for the kind of total transformation of society in a Socialist (and ultimately a Communist) direction which Marxists believe to be necessary and desirable. 'Millenarian movements', Hobsbawm argues, 'share a fundamental vagueness about the actual way in which the new society will be brought about.'[74] But, while this contention is no doubt in general correct, I think he exaggerates the extent to which 'pure' millenarian movements have tended to adopt a passive, or 'waiting', attitude to revolutionary change: their 'followers are not makers of revolution. They expect it to make itself'. This is certainly not true of Mahdist movements, nor, I think, of most of the non-Muslim

Messianic movements referred to here.[75] They are closer to the classic Marxist position that revolution is at the same time historically necessary and dependent upon the beliefs and actions of revolutionaries.[76] Their difficulty was rather that of all Utopian movements: the lack of a clearly defined strategy of revolution, reliance upon a variety of methods–*jihad* or armed rebellion, magical-religious techniques (such as the *maji* water-medicine), *hijra* or withdrawal from the European-dominated political order, expectation of external support (e.g. from American Negroes)–inadequate to achieve their revolutionary objectives.[77]

Yet, when all this is said, it remains surely true that Utopianism, or 'impossibilism', is, as Hobsbawn suggests, in some degree a characteristic of all revolutionary movements, however 'primitive' or 'sophisticated' they may be in respect of their social theories or political strategies. 'Utopianism is probably a necessary social device for generating the superhuman efforts without which no major revolution is achieved.' It is essential for revolutionaries to believe that 'the ultimate in human prosperity and liberty will appear after their victories'.[78] It seems doubtful even whether the fact that, for participants in Mahdist and Messianic movements, 'the future' normally includes the prospect of the enjoyment of bliss in some form of other-worldly existence, while for Marxists it is *limited* to future phases of human history, makes all that practical difference. In both cases suffering, death, martyrdom are endured for the sake of a future which is believed to be their entire and sufficient justification. Hence the efforts of 'venal Mallams' among sociologists and political scientists to discredit revolutionary movements under Marxist (or partly Marxist) leadership on the ground that these are simply modern expressions of 'archaic' and 'primitive' millenarian ideas are otiose.[79] The resemblances, and the historical connections, between the two types of movement and ideology are a primary datum. But it is above all about this interesting question (which Hobsbawm has discussed in a European context) of the structural relations between millenarian and modern revolutionary movements that one needs to know a great deal more. How far, and by what kinds of historical process, have the one been transformed into the other–or provided necessary preconditions for the growth of the other? In the case of the Philippines the point has been made that the revolutionary Huk movement was able to stabilize itself most effectively in areas such as 'Laguna province, where the pre-war Sakdal movement (a messianic nationalist movement that staged an abortive revolt in 1935) had been strong'.[80] How far can comparable kinds of historical connection be traced in the African context?[81] Even where, as in the Sudan itself, there would seem to have been no significant structural relationship between the late nineteenth century Mahdist movement and the Sudanese Communist Party (which developed from quite different, and in some respects opposed, groups and interests), how far may the mere possession of a revolutionary millenarian tradition contribute to the growth of modern forms of revolutionary organization and consciousness?

NOTES
[1] Vittorio Lanternari, *The religions of the oppressed*, London, 1963, particularly preface and conclusions.

[2] P.M. Holt, *The Mahdist state in the Sudan*, Oxford, 1958, p. 22.

[3] See particularly Ibn Khaldūn, *The Muqaddimah* (trans. Franz Rosenthal, London, 1958), **II**, pp. 156–200, and references under *al-Mahdī* in H.A.R. Gibb and J.H. Kramers, *Shorter encyclopaedia of Islam*, Leiden, 1953, pp. 310–13, and in Muhammad Al-Hajj, 'The thirteenth century in Muslim eschatology: Mahdist expectations in the Sokoto Caliphate', Centre of Arabic Documentation, Institute of African Studies, University of Ibadan, *Research bulletin*, **III**, 2, 100–5, July, 1967.

[4] Al-Hajj, *op. cit.*, p. 100.

[5] Holt, *op. cit.*, p. 112.

[6] Robert Kaufmann, *Millenarisme et acculturation*, Brussels, 1964, chs IV and V, and George Shepperson, 'Nyasaland and the millennium' in Sylvia L. Thrupp (Ed), *Millennial dreams in action*, Comparative Studies in Society and History, Suppl. II, The Hague, 1962, pp. 148–56.

[7] Kaufmann, *op. cit.*, pp. 25–6.

[8] See particularly discussions of this question in Shepperson, 'The comparative study of millenial movements' in Thrupp, *op. cit.*, pp. 44–5, and E.J. Hobsbawm, *Primitive rebels*, Manchester, 1959, pp. 57–65.

[9] Georges Balandier, *Sociologie actuelle de l'Afrique noire*, 1st edn, Paris, 1955, p.455.

[10] T.O. Ranger, *Revolt in Southern Rhodesia, 1896–7*, London, 1967, pp. 346–54.

[11] John Iliffe, 'The organization of the Maji-Maji Rebellion', *Journal of African History*, **VIII**, 3, 502–12, 1967 and G.C.K. Gwassa and John Iliffe, *Records of the Maji-Maji Rising*, Part I, Historical Association of Tanzania, Paper No. 4, Nairobi, pp. 17–20.

[12] Holt, *op. cit.*, pp. 22–3.

[13] Ibn Khaldūn, *op. cit.*, pp. 156 and 195–7.

[14] Cited in M. Hiskett, 'An Islamic tradition of reform in the western Sudan from the sixteenth to the eighteenth century: *Bulletin of the School of Oriental and African Studies*, **XXV**, 3, 583–4 (1962).

[15] Al-Hajj, *op. cit.*, pp. 107–8.

[16] For a list of 'Uthman dan Fodio's Arabic work dealing with Mahdism and the end of the world, see Al-Hajj, *op. cit.*, p. 114.

[17] *Ibid.*, pp. 109–13.

[18] See John Ralph Willis, '*Jihād fi sabīl Allah*–its doctrinal basis in Islam and some aspects of its evolution in nineteenth-century West Africa', *Journal of African History*, **VIII**, 3, 401–6 (1967), and references there.

[19] 'Uthmān dan Fodio, *Tahdhīr al-ikhwān*, quoted in Al-Hajj, *op. cit.*, p. 111 (Cf. Murray Last, *The Sokoto Caliphate*, London, 1967), pp. lxxxi–lxxxii and 10.

[20] R.A. Adeleye, I.A. Mukoshi and others, 'Sifofin Shehu: an autobiography and character study of 'Uthmān b. Fūdi in verse', *Research Bulletin* (Ibadan), **II**, 1, 1–36 (January 1966).

[21] Al-Hajj, *op. cit.*, p. 109; cf. Last, *op. cit.*, p. 36.

[22] Al-Hajj, *op. cit.*, p. 110.

[23] E.g., Hiskett, *op. cit.*, p. 591.

[24] Saburi Biobaku and Muhammad Al-Hajj, 'The Sudanese Mahdiyya and the Niger–Chad region' in I.M. Lewis (Ed), *Islam in Tropical Africa*, Oxford, 1966, p. 429.

[25] Holt, *op. cit.*, p. 23.

[26] See Wilfred Cantwell Smith, *Islam in modern history*, Princeton, 1957, Ch. II. For a discussion of the local situation in the central Sudan see R.A. Adeleye, 'The

dilemma of the Wazir: the place of the *risālat-al-wazīr cila ahl al-cilm wa'l-tadabbur* in the history of the Sokoto Caliphate' in *Journal of the Historical Society of Nigeria*, **IV**, 2 (June 1968), and his *Overthrow of the Sokoto Caliphate, 1879–1903* (D. Phil. Thesis, Ibadan, 1967).

[27] Norman Daniel, *Islam, Europe and empire*, Edinburgh, 1966, pp. 98–9.

[28] Holt, *op. cit.*

[29] Al-Hājj 'Umar also criticized a certain Musa who was active in northern Ghana at the turn of the century and who claimed to be the Mahdi. See J.A. Braimah and J.R. Goody, *Salaga: the struggle for power*, London, 1967, pp. 191–2.

[30] A. Le Grip, 'Le Mahdisme en Afrique noire', *L'Afrique et l'Asie*, 18, pp. 3–16 (1952).

[31] See particularly the article by Biobaku and Al-Hajj cited above, which has been a point of departure for further work.

[32] P.M. Holt, 'The Sudanese Mahdia and the outside world', *Bulletin of the School of Oriental and African Studies*, **XXI**, pp. 276–90 (1958).

[33] MS., Sudan Government Archives, Khartoum, cited in Biobaku and Al-Hajj, *op. cit.*, p. 433; see also Al-Hajj, 'Hayātu b. Sacīd: a Mahdist revolutionary agent in the Western Sudan', (paper presented to the international conference. 'The Sudan in Africa', University of Khartoum, February, 1968).

[34] J.E. Lavers, 'Jibril Gaini: a preliminary account of the career of a Mahdist leader in North-Eastern Nigeria', Centre of Arabic Documentation. Ibadan, *Research Bulletin*, **III**, 1, 16–38.

[35] Biobaku and Al-Hajj, *op. cit.*, p. 434; see also G.J.F. Tomlinson and G.J. Lethem, *History of Islamic propaganda in Nigeria* (Reports, London, 1927).

[36] Al-Hajj, *Hayātu b, Sacīd*, p. 5; cf. Lavers, *op. cit.*, pp. 27–30.

[37] Last, *op. cit.*, p. 139.

[38] Adeleye, *op. cit.*, pp. 294–5.

[39] *Ibid.* and Tokena N. Tamuno, 'Some aspects of Nigerian reaction to British rule', *Journal of the Historical society of Nigeria*, **III**, 2 (December 1965), 291–3.

[40] Ranger, *op. cit.*, p. 352.

[41] *Ibid.*, p. 354.

[42] In addition to sources cited below see particularly Georges Balandier, 'Messianismes et nationalismes en Afrique noire', *Cahiers internationales de sociologie*, **XIV** (1953); Shepperson, *Nyasaland and the millenium* and (with George Price) *Independent African: John Chilembwe and the Nyasaland Rising of 1915* (Edinburgh, 1959); Michael Banton, 'African prophets', *Race*, **V**, 2, 42–55 (1963); T.O. Ranger, 'Connexions between "primary resistance" movements and modern mass nationalism in East and Central Africa', *Journal of African History*, **IX**, 3 and 4 (1968).

[43] Tomlinson and Lethem, *op. cit.*, p. 10.

[44] *Ibid.*, p. 72.

[45] *Ibid.*, passim.

[46] See particularly Balandier, *Sociologie actuelle de l'Afrique noire* and bibliography in 2nd (1963) edition; Efraim Andersson, *Messianic popular movements in the Lower Congo* (Studia Ethnographica Upsaliensia, **XIV**, Uppsala, 1958); and references in Banton, *op. cit.*

[47] Balandier, *op. cit.* (1955 edn) p. 55.

[48] Ranger, *op. cit.* (1967), p. 345.

[49] Andersson, *op. cit.*, pp. 244–5.

[50] Lanternari, *op. cit.*, p. 309.

[51] I owe this suggestion to Dr Murray Last.

[52] Holt, *op. cit.*, ch. I.

[53] Andersson, *op. cit.*, p. 276 (Sacred songs from Musana, 1930).

[54] Lanternari, *op. cit.*, p. 310.

[55] There is as yet no satisfactory study of the Hamalliyya. The relevant chapter in A. Gouilly, *L'Islam dans l'Afrique occidentale française*, Paris, 1952, remains useful. Amadou Hampaté Ba and Marcel Cardaire, *Tierno Bokar, le sage de Bandiagara*, Paris, 1957, contains interesting historical material, presented from a somewhat *engagé* standpoint. Jamil Abun-Nasr, *The Tijaniyya: a Sufi Order in the modern world*, Oxford, 1963, is disappointing.

[56] For André Matswa and *Amicalisme* see Balandier, op. cit., pp. 397–416.

[57] See, e.g., J. Spencer Trimingham, *Islam in the Sudan*, London, 1949, pp. 157–63.

[58] Balandier, op. cit., p. 450.

[59] Andrew Roberts, 'The Lumpa Church', in Robert Rotberg and Ali Mazrui (Eds), *Traditions of protest in Black Africa*, Harvard, forthcoming.

[60] Ranger, op. cit., p. 352.

[61] Iliffe, *The organisation of the Maji Maji Rebellion*, p. 502.

[62] Balandier, op. cit., p. 427.

[63] Holt, op. cit., p. 73.

[64] ibid., p. 246.

[65] Iliffe, op. cit., pp. 511–12.

[66] Balandier, op. cit., p. 431.

[67] Lanternari, op. cit., p. 322.

[68] See particularly Ranger, op. cit. (1968).

[69] Shepperson, *Nyasaland and the millennium*, *passim*.

[70] See particularly, Andersson, *op. cit.*, ch. VII; Balandier, *op. cit.*, pp. 401–3. Cf. Norman Cohn *The pursuit of the millennium*, London, 1962, pp. 314–18.

[71] Andersson, *op. cit.*, p. 151.

[72] See discussions, from very different standpoints, in Cohn and Hobsbawm, op. cit., Cf. also writings of Engels on this subject in K. Marx and F. Engels, *On religion*, Moscow, 1955.

[73] For texts illustrating Marx's approach to these theses, see T.B. Bottomore and Maximilien Rubel, *Karl Marx: selected writings in sociology and Social philosophy*.

[74] Hobsbawm, op. cit., p. 58.

[75] But Hobsbawm would presumably regard the movements considered here as holding 'intermediate positions' between 'the two extremes of the "pure" millenarian and the "pure" political revolutionary'. ibid., p. 59.

[76] Cf. G. Plekhanov, *Fundamental problems of Marxism* (trans. Eden and Cedar Paul, from the Russian edition of 1928, London, n.d.), p. 93: 'If I am inclined to take part in a movement whose triumph seems to me a historical necessity, this only means that I consider my own activity likewise to be an indispensable link in the chain of conditions whose aggregate will necessarily ensure the triumph of the movement which is dear to me'.

[77] For the idea of American Negroes as liberating agents and its possible connections with the influence of Garveyism, see Shepperson, *op. cit.*, pp. 153–4, and Andersson, *op. cit.*, pp. 250–6.

[78] Hobsbawm, *op. cit.*, pp. 60–1.

[79] See, e.g., Cohn, *op. cit.*, p. 309.

[80] William J. Pomeroy, 'Questions on the Debray thesis', *Monthly Review*, **XX**, 3, 38 (July–August 1968).

[81] In addition to Ranger's article, referred to above, John Saul's chapter, 'Africa', in Ghita Ionescu and Ernest Gellner (eds), *Populism: its meanings and national characteristics*, London, 1969, pp. 122–50, contains an interesting discussion of points which have some bearing on this question.

The impact of Stalinism on radical African socialists

YVES BENOT

From Yves Benot, *Ideologies des independances africaines*, Maspero, Paris, 1969.

The political and intellectual thought and attitude of most of the Africans whose work and actions have been a significant influence were developed and set before 1956, that is to say before the XXth Congress of the Soviet Communist Party, and in some cases even before the Second World War. In other words, their thought and attitude were for a long time marked by a particular period in the history of the international working class movement, and the ideological distortions this implied have left deep traces in Africa. To be fair, it should be remembered that Africans had to suffer from the crimes of colonialism, not those of Stalin; and it was clear to them–as it ought to be to any impartial observer–that the two had nothing in common, that the fight against the immediate enemy, the colonial régime, took priority over everything else, and that any comparison between the two was ruled out. Moreover, as no African political parties then existed,[1] militants had not been drawn into the backwash of the internal strife in the Communist movement, with its long chain of censures and expulsions. Stalin, and the whole period of his rule, represented for African patriots the example of both socialist enlightenment effected in conditions of under-development, and intransigence towards the colonial powers. Then again, in the eyes of the people of the Third World, 1956 was not so much the year of the XXth Congress as of the failure of the Franco-British Suez expedition and the decisive intervention of the Soviet Union: a reason for confidence and the certainty of victory which lasted until the Congo tragedy in 1961 and even until the Cuban crisis in 1962.

However, these considerations must not let us forget that Africans, too, have been influenced by what can be called the Stalinist way of thinking; and although at first, it was able to beguile them by its rigidity and certainty–and even to aid them in quickly determining a few principles of action, a few basic doctrines–it also resulted in leaving them helpless both in the matter of analysing specifically African problems and in the perspectives for the struggles to come after formal independence. This was for the same reasons that enabled Stalinism to be so beguiling. To give but two basic examples: This mode of thought had first codified and determined a schema of social evolution (with its five stages, primitive communism, slavery, feudalism, capitalism, socialism) which hardly applied to real conditions in Africa. It had at the same time codified and determined a model of socialist development, that of the Soviet Union, whose bloody and difficult battles took place in historical and social circumstances which, again, were not found in Africa. In general, Stalinism tended to reduce Marxism, and also the example of the Soviet Union, to a formula that was easy to grasp, certainly, but difficult or impossible to apply in different conditions. It should be added that the Stalinist system itself, the control of a single party, of the news media, and of statistical information (to mention but three aspects which are found in the independent African States), has not failed to impress and captivate African politicians. Understandably, those in power have found the system most convenient, and hence a suitable justification is provided for a system which has arisen in a very different context from that of the Soviet Union. And so great was the prestige of Stalin and his times[2] that the opposition often lays claim to the same principles.

NOTES

[1] The Communist study groups which existed in French-dominated West Africa between 1945 and 1950 were not comparable to a political party. On the other hand, in those years many Africans were members of the British, French, or Portuguese Communist Parties.

[2] The following little story seems to me significant. In November 1961, after the 22nd Congress of the Soviet Communisty Party, at which Kruschev had made public the main facts in the secret report of 1956, a Guinean activist asked me in anguish whether I too believed the revelations to be true. He still hesitated to believe it.

Populism and the aspiration for solidarity
JOHN SAUL

From John Saul, 'Africa', in G. Ionescu and E. Gellner (eds), *Populism: its meanings and national characteristics*, Weidenfeld and Nicolson, London, 1969.

It is important to note that whatever the weaknesses of the populist framework as a description of reality, ideas that may be called 'populist' serve wide-ranging purposes as political rallying-cries, both for those in power and for those in pursuit of power. The major aspect of such 'populisms', whatever amalgam of emphases upon the 'will of the people' and the 'defence against capitalism' any given example may represent, is the stress upon solidarity and the unity of vast sections of the populace that it provides: a 'populism' is thus a creed most attractive to leaders. In very many cases the stress upon solidarity will represent neither the real situation of the mass of the people, nor their views of that situation. Rather it will represent an aspiration to make a particular view as to the characteristics that unite people prevail over any continuing awareness of the elements that divide. Instead of assuming solidarity to be the actual norm, therefore, it is wiser to look to the tensions between various elements and various perspectives as defining the dynamic of any so-called 'populist movement'.

In so far as a populist ideology may thus represent the aspirations of people leading a particular African movement or state, it can be put to a number of uses. Here we move into the difficult region of 'intent' and one of the most most tortured questions will be to assess the sincerity of key actors when they advance such ideas. In the African case we can perceive, in the first instance, a real measure of *self-deception* among the leadership in their use of these notions. This was, to some extent, a legacy of the anti-colonial struggle. It was then as easy for the leaders, as for subsequent scholars, to overlook the diversity of elements constituting their movements and to subsume them within the analytical frame of misleading rhetoric. Nyerere himself has pointed this out succinctly: *Uhuru* provided a lowest common denominator for people with a wide variety of views as to what the future independent state should look like.[1] It seems probable too that much of the rhetoric of 'African socialism'–with its emphasis upon the automatic carry-over of traditional communalities to a modern Africa and the undifferentiated front to be presented to a rather hostile international economic environment–came rather easily to the lips of a leadership fresh to power and hot in pursuit of neutralism and a distinctive ideology.

It was only subsequently that the rather grimmer realities of induced internal differentiation and continued economic pressure from the outside began to demonstrate that choices would be rather more complex. Nyerere, for example, has moved from a reliance upon socialism as an 'attitude of mind' to be underwritten automatically by the continuing impact of the traditional environment, to a clearer statement in the recent 'Arusha Declaration' on socialism and self-reliance that it is also an 'ideology' to be learned and sustained.[2] And this has led in Tanzania to a growing emphasis upon the role of the educational system as an instrument for socialist education and to certain structural reforms. This sort of populist mode of thought exemplified by the creed of 'African Socialism' in a good many of its specific embodiments does have a continuing legacy for those in power, however, and tends to bring with it limitations: choices concerning the internal economic structure, as for example those relating to the modes of production to be fostered and encouraged, are blurred and subtle questions as to the costs and benefits for future social structure and national self-determination of various forms of possible compromise with the international market system are set aside. Solidarity is socialism, and real social trends which may be working against meaningful solidarity are lost to view.

Other leaders are rather more conscious of the loss of focus encouraged by the high-level of generalization of the populist framework. However it can then be transformed into an aspiration for solidarity useful to the interests of post-colonial élites–this is *interested, manipulative* populism. For a populist vision can divert attention from internal contradictions; used consciously, it may thus become a most conservative force, even a cynical cover for continuing privilege. Growing differentiation either between the élite and mass or within the rural community itself, as well as subtle compromises with international capital, can be masked behind a rhetoric of homogeneity and national interest. This has in fact become the underpinning for a number of self-indulgent one-party régimes; the manner in which emergent military élites, now so prominent a force in many African states, have found this appeal to the solidarities of the countryside attractive is also striking, in spite of their absence of interest in socialist aspirations, their most compromised position *vis-à-vis* external capitalism,[3] and their seeming reluctance to indulge in democratic experiments. Colonel Afrifa, prominent in the Ghanaian military leadership, captures something of this note in his recent book in commenting upon pre-*coup* days:

> ... perhaps people who lived in Accra or visited Accra would not have felt the suffering of the people who lived in the rural areas. Accra is organized in such a way as to give an impression of happiness and affluence; there were new streets and new lights, while vast areas of this country were planted with misery and suffering. I spent all my leaves at home on our farm, seeing and thinking about the helpless condition to which our people had been reduced. I became convinced that Nkrumah had failed the nation.[4]

And the extrapolation of similar themes and rationalizations for 'post-liberation' society has followed apace. Where 'populism' becomes the official ideology of states, more nuanced tests than ever are necessary to assess the degree of correspondence between its pretensions and the actual state of the rural masses.

There is one final possible use of 'populism' which must be mentioned all too briefly here. For 'populist' arguments and vocabulary that stress solidarity can be manipulated for ends beyond mere maintenance of power by ensconced élites. They can also be used as part of *a development strategy* designed to maximize the chances of economic breakthrough in a poor country and, therefore, even be intended to work for the well-being of the masses themselves. There is much scepticism about the capacities of a cap-italist route to development, a decision in favour of 'betting on the strong', to ensure sweeping economic success in the rural sector of backward societies; where so many need awakening to the potentialities inherent in a new way of life, premature differentiation may merely confront the vast mass with a local political environment manipulated by 'kulaks' and thus sap their interest and initiative. This is already a factor be reckoned with in Africa. On the other hand, forced march methods seem equally unattractive. The alternative, as Wertheim suggests, may lie in 'betting on the many', rallying the people 'through organization and intensive education toward efficiency and self-reliance'.[5] This is not an approach that assumes solidarity, but one that aspires to it and works to attain it. There are, in fact increasingly fewer African régimes that seem willing to choose to implement such an option, for it must involve some attempt to exemplify equality and independence in a convincing manner; in addition, like most 'populisms', such an aspiration carries its share of familiar ambiguities when brought up against complexities of the African context which we have seen. If implemented aggressively by a committed élite it is just possible, however, that it carries a promise of progressive results beyond that of more romanticized versions postulated upon pre-existent harmony and presumed egalitarianism.

NOTES

[1] See Julius K. Nyerere, *Freedom and unity*, Dar es Salaam, 1966.

[2] *The Arusha Declaration and TANU's policy on socialism and self-reliance,* Government Printer, Dar es Salaam, 1967.

[3] For a useful perspective on this phenomenon, see Roger Murray, 'Militarism in Africa', *New Left Review* 39 (July–August 1966), partially reprinted below, pp. 383–97.

[4] A. A. Afrifa, *The Ghana coup,* p. 95 London, 1966.

[5] W. F. Wertheim, 'Betting on the strong' in his collection of essays *East–West parallels,* pp. 276–7. The Hague, 1964.

Sékou Touré: the man and his ideas
R.W. JOHNSON

Originally published as 'Sékou Touré and the Guinean revolution', *African Affairs*, **69**, 277 (October 1970).

President Ahmed Sékou Touré of Guinea is indisputably Africa's senior radical leader still in power. But, for a number of reasons, both the man and his ideas remain somewhat obscure, particularly in the non-francophone world. We still have no biography of the man and only a few dated and fragmentary articles considering his early *idées majeures*.[1] It must be admitted at once that to fill this gap is a task much larger than can be performed by this article.

The period up to independence (1958)

First, a few biographical details. Touré was born in Faranah (Haute-Guinée) in 1922 of peasant parents. He is a Malinké and is of the same clan as the great Samory Touré who for so long led pre-colonial resistance to the French.[2] In the 1930s he came to Conakry to study at the Ecole Professionelle. Academically this was to represent the summit of his career, he did not go on to receive a post-primary, secondary, or university education. He is very largely a self-made and self-taught man–something which is virtually unique among the members of the political élites which have ruled West Africa in the last decade. On leaving school he held several lowly positions in the French Administration before becoming involved in the trade union movement (the *Conféderation Générale du Travail*, CGT) which he, virtually alone, founded in 1945–46 and which he dominated and led for the next 12 years.[3] He also was a founder-member of the *Parti Démocratique de Guinée* (PDG), the Guinean section of the *Rassemblement Démocratique Africain* (RDA), within which he played a second-echelon role until 1952 when he took over the Party's leadership. The PDG's period of political and electoral 'take-off' really dates from his accession to power within it, and well before independence was achieved in 1958 Touré had emerged as indisputably the dominant personality in Guinea, his position bolstered by a degree of popular and organizational support perhaps unique in West Africa.

In order to understand Touré's personal and ideological development we must first examine his period of trade union leadership. As Secretary-General

of the Guinean CGT, Touré was in continual contact with the French CGT
(he attended a Paris Congress of the CGT as early as 1946). It is undoubtedly
to this source that we must trace Touré's acquaintance with marxist theory
and communist organizational practice. Moreover, his later strong rejection
of all forms of racism, including theories of negritude, is probably also partially a product of the sympathy and support which he received from the French
metropolitan Left in this period.[4] But Touré's trade union experience was
of a more general importance as well. It was in this movement that he learnt
most of all that he still knows; this phase stands at the very centre of
his autodidactic career. One long quotation from the Touré of this
period will have to stand for a total impression. The subject is the duties of
trade union leadership:

> First of all you must thoroughly familiarize yourself with the *Code du
> Travail* and all other social legislation. *Responsable*, your bedside reading is
> the *Code du Travail* which you can never study enough. Its French, this
> beautiful language, has a finesse that will escape even those who suckled it
> with their maternal milk. *Responsable*, you have the duty of educating the
> masses; in order to educate them you must first educate yourself. That is why
> you must know all the rules and decisions which rule the world of work.
> You must be able at any moment to reply to the questions of comrades,
> even if they appear completely anodyne to you. . . . A lot of your comrades
> are illiterate. You must always read and explain social legislation and the
> trade union press to them.
>   You must never believe that ability resides solely in the so-called '*évolue*'
> element. In fact some of our best leaders are illiterates. Moreover, you will
> have noticed that they are the most able to sustain a discussion and can
> defend a cause or a thesis with rare aptitude. Notice too that they are seldom
> tricked for they often recognize a sincere man from his very first words. You
> must always take account of the opinions of illiterate comrades whatever
> their branch of professional activity. The majority of them have experienced
> concrete situations and their observations on them may well be highly
> consequential. The trade union leader who is most apt, best advised and
> the most *évolué* in every meaning of that word, is he who puts things at the
> level of all, so as to make better understood the aspirations of the masses
> with whose guidance he is charged. He must concretize the cause which
> he defends in all his actions and words so as to facilitate the workers'
> understanding of it.
>   We are all more or less presumptuous, more or less proud: we all believe
> ourselves already important. But pride and presumption are two vices that
> kill trust, esteem and sympathy. . . We must struggle against these internal
> enemies in order to deserve the trust of the workers. . . Our struggle does
> not consist solely in material demands, but also in raising the workers
> morally and professionally, in stimulating emulation and professional
> conscience, and in helping them struggle against their own weaknesses.
> The trade union leader is, then, a defender, a guide, and an educator of the
> masses. He must always bear in mind the fact that one false manoeuvre,
> one imprudent word, one gesture in a moment of anger and, moreover,
> every unreasoned act, compromises the whole of the movement which he
> represents.
>   It is in order to overcome these weaknesses in himself so that he may

become a fit leader of others, that the trade union leader must frequently and in a spirit of fraternal comradeship accept and even provoke criticism and self-criticism, correcting his own weaknesses and those of his comrades.[5]

Several themes which have continued to mark Touré's thought are already present here, notably his consciousness and populist rejection of the élitist presumptions of the educated *évolué* group constituting the political Establishment, Right and Left, against which he was ranged. Touré's stress on remaining in close sympathy and contact with the masses is merely the obverse side of his hatred of the group who made their possession, and his own lack, of French cultural finesse a reason for consigning him for many years to humiliatingly second-rank positions. The fact that in Guinea–uniquely in francophone West Africa–the independence 'inheritance' élite was *not* composed of men with a secondary or higher education was due to the fact that once Touré and the *petit-fonctionnaire* trade union-based group around him had attained power within the PDG, they were able to exercise a number of social controls to keep it. 'Keeping power' in this context meant either preventing altogether the otherwise inevitable yeast-like rise of educated *évolué* elements within the movement, or making their tenancy of power depend on a fairly explicit acceptance of these social controls.[6]

What were these social controls? The story of Touré's political career in the 1950s could really be summarized by saying that in the course of it he learnt, perhaps even over-learnt, two things. The first was that he could transform a political and even a social situation by the enthusiastic mobilization of large numbers of people. In particular this involved his encouragement and harnessing of the seething peasant discontent which provided the real motor of the PDG's development, eliciting mass response from the peasants to the Party's loose ideological definitions of their situation. Secondly, Touré learnt the virtues and power of organization: organization to sustain this mobilization and give direction to the movement thus created; and organization to institutionalize and bolster the power of personal leadership. In the period between 1946 and 1952 when the PDG had been led and run by *évolué* intellectuals, organizational coherence and discipline were at a discount. After 1952, under Touré, they were at a premium. Touré and the *petit-fonctionnaire* group around him exploited their organizational position, not only in the normal sense of enforcing discipline on men more educated than themselves, but also in order to multiply their organizational bases. Plural office-holding, indeed, became perhaps the most striking characteristic of Touré's group.[7] Thus when the 'intellectuals' again became important in the PDG in the later 1950s, they did so subject to the constraints of both organizational and ideological discipline. They had not only to accept but even to enunciate a populist rhetoric which explicitly devalued their own status as intellectuals.[8] By 1958 Touré had fairly thoroughly subjugated all possible rivals and established an apparently unchallengeable position of personal leadership.

Examination of Touré's role in pre-independence politics reveals a personal and ideological development of complex proportions. After an obscure early period (1945?–1948?) in which he held apparently orthodox marxist views, he moved towards a more *ouvrieriste* position, concentrating almost solely on trade union questions to the neglect of more overtly political ones. With his assumption of the PDG's leadership he veered towards a position that is perhaps best described as that of a radical populist–reformist, with his original marxist and even trade union background increasingly diluted and obscured. In the light of Touré's current stance–and of the PDG's re-writing of the 1950s period–it is as well to emphasize that Touré, as is clear in dozens of articles and hundreds of speeches, never seriously envisaged the possibility of violent revolutionary action in this period. Rather, his aim was to achieve power by whatever means were both possible and necessary, always acting within or on the margin of the institutional context provided by the French. He had, after all, no wish to see the PDG go the same way as the UPC (*Union des Populations du Cameroun*) in Cameroun.[9] On the other hand, he clearly aimed to achieve power while preserving as radical a party and policy as the situation would allow, thus hoping to retain the option of effecting radical change by the use of the power so achieved. This classic reformist tactic which just occasionally, due to the more militant attitude of the grass roots rank and file, seemed to be based on an implicit revolutionary threat, actually succeeded in Guinea; though this was largely because of the sheer historical accident of the quite unexpected abruptness with which independence was achieved.[10]

From independence to 1964

Given Touré's central personal position, the evolution of his ideas since independence conflates ineluctably with the evolution of official PDG policy in this period. Here it is important to take note of the emphasis laid officially– that is, by Touré himself–on the watershed of the *loi-cadre* of 8 November 1964.[11] Up to 1964, so runs the official view, the PDG followed an essentially reformist path, albeit a radical one, while since 1964 the Party has been transforming itself into a truly revolutionary *avant-garde* movement and it has become possible to speak of the 'Guinean revolution'. This distinction carries with it its own implied self-criticism, since the pre-1964 period was itself amply decked out in revolutionary phraseology and claims to revolutionary status and ambitions.

Nevertheless, an examination of Sékou Touré's writings–which have now reached 17 volumes[12]–does support the view that, in the realm of ideology at least, there has been a marked change since 1964. Gradually the forms of Touré's earlier radicalism have re-emerged; some ambiguous elements, such as the 'African personality', have virtually disappeared from view; and the marxist element has become more pronounced–though, as we shall see, Touré is still some distance from any of the various Marxist–Leninist orthodoxies.

There was little hint of such development in the first four volumes of Touré's *Works*. Indeed, the fact that these are the most widely known of his writings has itself become a source of confusion since they are so unrepresentative of Touré's contemporary position. In this early period attention is focused primarily on the meaning of independence. As early as March 1959, Touré had termed Guinea's acquisition of independence a 'revolution'. Apparently sensitive to Fanonist criticism, he denies that political violence is more than one of several possible revolutionary forms: the gaining of independence has resulted in a fundamental transformation of such proportions as to place Guinea in an objectively revolutionary situation (*Tome* 3, pp. 209–10). On the other hand he is concerned to emphasize the continuing nature of the anti-colonial struggle, not only in the sense of the completion of Africa's liberation but also in the sense of a still ongoing struggle in Guinea itself against the 'inherited structures of colonial domination'. In sharp contradistinction to those African leaders who saw independence as the fruit of a completed struggle, Touré insisted that independence was a purely instrumental acquisition. So, too, were democracy and national unity; to make them ends in themselves was as barren a doctrine as 'art for art's sake.' They were merely means towards social progress, towards the destruction of the old colonial 'structures of domination' and, above all, towards the decolonization of the minds, habits, and attitudes of the people, without which other forms of progress were impossible or illusory. A great effort of education, at once civic, moral, ideological, and national, must be launched in order to accelerate the normal course of history in Guinea. Yet the object of this enormous effort is still rather vaguely conceived as 'social progress'. The aim of socialism is entirely absent at this stage.[13]

The extent to which Touré's earlier marxism had been diluted and compromised is clearest when the question of social class in African society is considered. This question, indeed, provides a convenient touchstone for the measurement and evaluation of radicalism in Africa particularly in the early 1960s. One may use it to place all African ideologists within a four-point scale:[14]

(i) the Know-Nothing stage involving an attempt to deny the existence of significant social differentiation in African societies. Attempted by some political leaders in the early 1960s, it is clearly untenable for long;

(ii) a second stage in which it is acknowledged that a process of social differentiation and stratification has begun but in which it is insisted that the social conflicts thus occasioned are of a second order pressure group variety which may, indeed must, be reconciled in the interests of national unity or some other long-term goal;

(iii) a third stage in which it is frankly acknowledged that social classes proper with fundamentally opposed interests exist, but in which it is asserted that such conflicts, however bitter, may be due to the merely temporary strains of a particular historical period of, say, intensive 'modernization'. There is, it is claimed, both the tactical possibility and the strategic necessity of a pragmatic alliance of classes. Normally it has been the trade unions that have been asked or compelled to subordinate their class interests, but they may be asked to do this under either right or left-wing régimes, for technocratic, developmentalist reasons, or in the name of 'scientific socialism';

(iv) a fourth stage in which it is acknowledged that the social conflicts between different strata are of a fundamental nature, incapable of resolution. This necessitates the implicit or explicit taking of sides–theoretically, at least–for some groups and against others.

Briefly, the development of Touré's thought in the 1960s sees him move from (ii) through (iii) to (iv) though, to say the least, his thinking has moved a great deal faster than its political implementation. Thus when in 1959–60 Touré talked of the 'internal contradictions' within Guinean society, the contradictions with which he was concerned were idealist rather than social, sins of individual behaviour–'egoism', 'individualism', and 'opportunism'. It is hardly surprising that we should find that these sins are particularly liable to be committed by *déraciné* intellectuals with a 'superiority complex' (*Tomes* 1–2, p. 554, and *Tome* 3, pp. 161–8). Touré admits that social conflict is possible between the different '*couches sociales*', between, for example, peasants and traders on the question of free trade in rice; he warns *fonctionnaires* that resources are scarce; and he speaks of the danger that the fruits of independence will be confiscated by the few. But greed and selfishness, not class interests, are the true villains of the piece, and cultural and intellectual decolonization is the remedy.

It is, naturally, on the delicate subject of trade unionism that Touré makes his assumptions and position most explicit:

> In Africa, where class antagonism does not exist, where an identity of interest dominates merely occupational-functional diversity... the labouring masses must accordingly quickly comprehend the particularities of their situation as against that of the European working class. For them trade unionism must not be an instrument of class struggle but an instrument for harmonious evolution and rapid emancipation (*Tomes* 1–2, pp. 419–20).

Indeed,

> ... while marxism is applied in its doctrinal integrity by the international working class insofar as the class struggle is concerned, so we have amputated that element of it so that all the African *couches sociales* may work together in the general anti-colonialist struggle (ibid., p. 420).

On the other side of the coin he is equally clear, even to a trade unionist audience:

> The financial support of capitalism for which we appeal does not in any way compromise the mastery of the situation which we have acquired politically... We launch this appeal to Capital so that those who possess it may also, with complete solidarity, enter into collaboration with us (ibid., p. 426).

Even at this stage, however, the marxist origins of Touré's basic ideas are always evident. Indeed, there is always the suggestion that it is with a pragmatic reluctance that he abandons a more purely marxist approach. In time such an approach may become more clearly relevant, but in a sense the task is to prevent it from becoming relevant by halting social differentiation. At other times Touré appears to doubt whether such preventive action can be successful. And ultimately this more historicist view is dominant:

> Certainly, as our society develops, so it has a tendency to fragment itself into a more and more differentiated hierarchy. The scale runs from the plebeian element to the élite and the result is the dissociation of each element from that which precedes it and that which follows it, on the basis of the more or less accentuated contradiction between their interests. In the face of this hierarchical development there is a great temptation for each distinct

couche sociale to act in a 'cellular' manner–pursuing its own narrow interests rather than the common interest. Already (1959) one must observe–and one must deplore–that a very clear tendency towards crystallization is manifesting itself among the various layers of society. This egocentric phenomenon will of necessity continue, accentuating itself so that at least the most urgent of these (particularist) demands may be met, for it is undeniable that the man who is himself deprived is deaf and blind to the misery of others. There is in this tendency a social aspect which threatens to condition the political situation.

Thus one may fear, with justification, that this social mutation will have as its corollary the formation of a bourgeoisie, of a sort of aristocratic feudalism, the danger of which it is unnecessary to underline. As we have said, we reject the principle of class struggle, less through philosophical conviction than through the desire to save African solidarity at any price. For this [African solidarity] alone can lead us along our destined path, this alone is capable of preserving our originality and of imposing a respect for African Man' (Ibid., pp. 411–12).

The 'teachers' plot' and subsequent strikes of 1961 served to confirm Touré's ideas on these points even to the point of claiming that:

Should the class struggle appear in the Republic of Guinea–if we were to give leeway to egoistic interest groups, even trade union ones, they would form a reactionary class of a bourgeois sort (*Tome* 8, p. 296).

Indeed, he went even further, insisting that it was only counter-revolutionaries and the 'anti-Party group' who tried to substitute the notion of social classes for that of social differentiation endemic in all societies (*Ibid.*, p. 309). Only anarcho-syndicalists, he claimed, could believe that the principal contradictions facing Guinea were internal rather than those of the external struggle against imperialism (ibid., pp. 318–19). The fact was that colonialism had prevented the growth of a national capitalism or a national bourgeoisie in Guinea, and accordingly there could be no class struggle (ibid., p. 326).

At this point it appeared that Touré was moving clearly to the Right–there is little to separate the statements quoted above from positions later adopted by Mboya or Senghor. But in fact the long-term effect of the 'plot' was rather to dissipate the euphoria of the early independence period. As other real or imagined plots followed, the Guinean political climate tautened considerably, and the foundations of a formidable police and intelligence *apparat* were laid in place. Meanwhile Guinea's isolation within Africa and internationally deepened at the same time that the economy, labouring under an over-valued currency, hasty nationalizations,[15] inefficiency, corruption, and smuggling on a massive scale, plunged into ever more desperate straits. In the face of the first real signs of political disaffection and mounting apathy Touré's position hardened noticeably. He had always insisted, from independence on, that 'bourgeois democracy' was not applicable in Guinea, which was a *république populaire* (People's Republic), a democratic dictatorship. He now began to lay greater stress on the specifically revolutionary role of the PDG; disaffection must be expected and fought since 'every revolution creates its own counter-revolution'. The time for sentimentalism was gone–now was the time for 'la fermeté révolutionnaire'. 'L'ennemi de la fermeté révolutionnaire, c'est le liberalisme qui, de compromis en compromis, fait tomber un parti dans la compromission et l'anarchie' (*Tome* 9, pp. 144–7 and p. 151).

In some ways the period from 1961 to 1963 saw disaffection reach its height, particularly among intellectuals. Many French *progressistes* and foreign Africans who had come to Guinea after independence, full of enthusiasm for the new state and its régime, left in this period, disgruntled and despairing.[16] Many Guineans left as well, not only intellectuals but many thousands of peasants too, flooding into Abidjan and Dakar. Touré appeared to be building a regime of iron, and of smuggled cigarettes; and inefficient dictatorship in which austerity and corruption combined to provide the worst of both worlds. Such a view is, of course, still held by many.[17]

The *loi-cadre* of 8 November 1964 was essentially an attempt by Touré to halt this political and economic slide. Draconian new measures were introduced to curb corruption and to regulate commerce; in Conakry licences to deal in commerce were to be cut back by 80 per cent; all state and Party officials were to be submitted to examination of the sources of their income and possessions; all private import and export trade was outlawed; the PDG was entirely re-organized with work-place organization and a slimmed-down membership. Excluded from all Party responsibilities were all merchants and all those convicted since 1958 of theft, corruption, fraud, subversion, or racism. There followed a whole series of further decrees aimed at corruption among civil servants. Henceforth even the most senior Minister would have to prove his revolutionary militancy and vigilance in word and deed under pain of the most severe sanctions.[18]

This sharp turn to the Left is reflected in *Tome* 13, *L'Afrique et la révolution*. Using the same analytic base that he had earlier employed in his attack on the 'teachers' plot', Touré claimed that the measures were necessary to prevent a Guinean comprador bourgeoisie from becoming a full-blown national bourgeoisie:

> In Africa colonial intervention occurred during a feudal period which was still profoundly marked by a 'communocratic' spirit. The organization of the modes of production was still neither of the slave-based type, nor assimilable to the so-called 'Asiatic' mode. The despotism which characterizes feudalism only appeared after the colonial intervention and at its behest. *A fortiori* there was no bourgeoisie at all. In the absence of a national bourgeoisie one could not have a capitalist society. Moreover, colonialism, by its take-over of both land and men as means of production, hindered the formation of a bourgeois class. While a privileged social category (feudal chiefs, civil servants, and merchants) did appear under this omnipotent reign, it did so only very late and still possessed none of the means necessary for primitive capital accumulation, for these means were in the hands of colonialism or, at least, under its direct control. It is quite evident that this privileged national category was using our independence as a cover for transforming itself into a national bourgeoisie (*Tome* 13, pp. 110–11).

Guinea had moved from the stage of People's Democracy to that of National Democracy, by which was meant a régime intent upon preventing the emergence of antagonistic social classes by crushing the national bourgeoisie at the moment of its emergence (ibid., pp. 115–16).

For the first time Guinea's socialist option was affirmed, though Touré made it clear that he had doubts as to the applicability of the term. And, although *Tome* 13 concludes with an academic discussion of dialectical materialism, Touré's conception of socialism remained essentially idealist.

> Since the creation of the PDG we have always made clear, without hesitation or complexes, the aims of our actions. But we have always used the words 'socialist' and 'socialism' as little as possible. Often at (PDG) Congresses comrades have brought up the question and we have always replied that our basic philosophy of history did not allow us to consider capitalism or socialism as finalities. This being so, our revolutionary has aimed only at the well-being of the people... The question of our socialist perspectives is poorly framed. In every country there are capitalist and socialist perspectives which develop conjointly or separately... One may well ask whether it is possible to 'build socialism' in the conditions of an agricultural economy issuing from colonial mercantilism... We opt for the socialist system, that is to say that we devoutly desire the continued progress of social justice... The socialist revolution is first and foremost a heightened consciousness, a willing determination to see the good of all, a firm courage (ibid., pp. 171–3).

Here it may be as well to note that Touré's writings on semi-philosophical subjects such as this descend all too easily into self-repetitive generality and outright mystification. One must always remember that his printed word is merely transcribed platform oratory. He is at his best and clearest when he defines his positions in contradistinction to those of others; as when he analyses and condemns the concept of negritude as racist mystification,[19] or when he is analysing the incomplete and satellitic nature of 'independence' in so many African states. His often scathing clarity frequently deserts him when faced with the problem of conceptualizing or analysing original or purely Guinean phenomena.

The period since 1964

The major swing to the Left of 1964 has been followed in succeeding years less by important original ideological departures than by a process of continuous expansion, elucidation, and intensification of the 1964 theses. 1964 also marks a landmark, however, in the use of ideology as a form of social control. Hitherto, as we have seen, the dominant position of Touré's ideology had been used to disadvantage members of certain social groups in their public and political activities. Since 1964 ideology has increasingly become an instrument of control over *individuals* rather than groups. This has happened for several reasons.

The *loi-cadre* reforms of 1964 have never been fully or properly carried out, as Touré himself acknowledges. Since 1964 the disjuncture between what Touré says and what actually happens in Guinea has grown increasingly radical and severe–indeed, one has the impression that Touré has long ago run up against the outside limits of all that organization and exhortation to mass mobilization can achieve. At the same time Guinea's isolation within

Africa has increased enormously with the fall of the friendly Sierra Leonean, Malian, Ghanaian, and Algerian régimes and the weakened position of the UAR since the war with Israel. This isolation has, in turn, predictably intensified the domestic climate of tension and suspicion in Guinea.[20] This climate and the fact that Touré's ideology has far outrun both popular understanding and concrete every-day Guinean realities produce a situation in which hardly anyone in any position can feel safe from denunciation for ideological crimes such as the harbouring of counter-revolutionary sentiments. This is particularly so since Touré has continued to coin new watch-words so that 'what was progressive in 1964 may cease to be so in 1965' (*Tome* 13, p. 127). The need for vigilance is absolute since subversion is literally everywhere:

> ... subversion is not a material fact that one can show people. It is not an objective thing, it only has objective results. Subversion is part of one and it is in all of us, beginning with the Secretary General of the PDG down to the last militant who joins the Party as he strolls out of a meeting. Subversion inhabits every heart... (*Tome* 15, p. 39),

Naturally, the enemy has the sense to stay hidden:

> Embourgeoisement continues to make progress. Of course, a cadre will never say that he has become a bourgeois. But it is easy to detect it in his manner of speaking, in the way he discusses future possibilities, in the way he interprets facts, in the way he takes on a job, in the way he behaves himself in regard to the people. Of course, all this denounces him without his realizing (ibid., pp. 46–7).

If this sounds like a 'conspiracy theory of history' one ought to add that there are, indeed, many real enough conspiracies.

Implicitly, though not explicitly, the 1964 *tournant* revoked all Touré's earlier denials of the existence of social classes and of class struggle; the Party was summoned to revolutionary struggle against the bourgeois class. Since 1964 the principle of class struggle has been increasingly emphasized, particularly since the 8th PDG Congress in 1967. Moreover, Touré has made it clear that he views the problem of class struggle in both a national and an international context.

Domestically the lines of division have been somewhat clarified:

> The interest of the labouring masses... demands that the working class, the peasantry, and sincerely progressive elements effectively direct and control all the vital sectors of the national life and that the reactionary elements of the bourgeoisie, of the bureaucracy and of capitalism, even national capitalism, be thrown from all positions of influence, decision, and control... The class struggle hereby becomes the political form of practical explanation... The class struggle is a universal reality and historic necessity... Political organization, political and ideological education of the people, are the principal weapons in the struggle against the class enemy.[21]

Touré characterizes the 'class enemy' in several ways:

> Undoubtedly in these last few years a bureaucratic bourgeoisie has installed itself within the Party and in public administration and the State enterprises. It has spawned about itself a 'clientele' of merchants, *trans-*

porteurs, and rural land properietors–an embryonic national bourgeoisie–all as its dependants (*Tome* 13, p. 155).

But the real problem is a cultural one, of bourgeois and petit bourgeois aspirations:

> ... there are some who, victims of colonial petit bourgeois ideology, owing to their training as servants of colonialism, have never been able to regain their self-possession but have retained their old expectations, waiting for new masters able to provide them with the neo-colonialist crumbs to which they aspired during the colonial period and of which they have since been deprived... It is a petit bourgeoisie with an aberrant mentality, incapable of any creative or serious effort, while the European bourgeoisie, for example, was and still is tough-minded and ready for work. It is a petit bourgeoisie which has resigned itself, which is slothful, which is ready to sell the Nation to any imperialist power that presents itself, which is hypocritical and treacherous... it is a corrupted petit bourgeoisie... in fact a lumpen-bourgeoisie.[22]

Internationally Touré has moved towards a more 'Cuban' position. In several diplomatically explosive passages of his *Rapport politique* to the 8th PDG Congress he declared that *tiers monde* countries were now in the fore-front of the struggle against imperialism. Not only could one no longer believe that imperialism and capitalism would fall of themselves, but one could not rely either upon the Socialist great powers. It was, for example, not true that 'the British worker can wait upon the USSR or China to see the end of the exploitation to which he is submitted'.[23] Moreover, the Socialist powers were guilty of helping to uphold an international primary products price-system which merely institutionalized *tiers monde* exploitation.[24] The doctrine of peaceful co-existence was a reactionary and unacceptable compromise for it helped to freeze a world situation in which imperialism was still rampant.[25] Fruitful relationships between *tiers monde* countries and capitalist–imperialist ones were simply impossible–and, consistently, Touré gives a list of extremely restrictive conditions under which Guinea will be prepared to accept foreign aid.[26]

Although Touré's continuing exhortations to 'wage the class struggle to the death' and to 'deepen and radicalize the Revolution'–the general currency of his speeches since 1967–amount to little more than appeals for the execution of long-declared policy aims, there have been several ideological and organizational innovations in this latter period. Most notably these have included the declaration of a Socialist Cultural Revolution, the creation of a Popular Militia, the greater role given to the PDG Youth, the JRDA (*Jeunesse de la Révolution Démocratique Africaine*), and the institution of Local Revolutionary Power (PRL–*Pouvoir Révolutionnaire Locale*).

These innovations should not be allowed to obscure the continuities in Touré's thought. The counter-revolutionary bourgeoisie is still continually depicted in terms of armchair intellectuals with superiority complexes: 'The counter-revolution has installed itself in armchairs. It no longer lives in the (chiefs') huts from which it has fled. Now it lives in villas and civil service apartments...' (*Tome* 15, p. 45). Touré's marxism also still contains a strong voluntaristic element, only partially derived from occasional imitation of

Chinese models.[27] The counter-revolution is counter-revolutionary for the same old 'raisons de comportement individual'–'egoism', 'individualism', and so on. The Cultural Revolution, a massive campaign of orchestrated education and indoctrination, aims at changing the hearts and minds of the people in an entirely voluntaristic fashion. It is the same combination of education and organization, and continual re-organization, on which Touré has always relied. These factors were enough to bring him political success in the 1950s and to achieve independence in 1958–when an aroused and militant population, impressively organized and disciplined within the PDG, voted 'non'–and the walls of Jericho came tumbling down. One may doubt whether the barriers of poverty and corruption will fall in the same way.

Touré is doubtless aware of these considerations and there is an element of despair in these recent innovations. The Cultural Revolution is aimed particularly at the young through sweeping changes in the educational system which stress–to borrow the obvious Chinese analogy–the qualities of being 'red rather than expert'. It may well be that Touré has written off the present generation of office-holders and civil servants as irredeemably corrupted by colonialist ideology; hope lies with the younger generation who have come to maturity in the 12 years since independence.[28] Touré has certainly laid increasing stress on the role of youth in the revolutionary bloc of peasants and workers though of late there has been increasing stress on the vanguard nature of the working class–and the JRDA is now more in evidence in the streets of Conakry (performing police functions, for example) than is the Party proper. Similarly, the creation of the *Milice Populaire* (restricted to 20–30 year-olds) tends to assume that the Army is ultimately unreliable too. The PRL program, aimed at transferring a whole range of administrative functions from the State to local village Party committees, would, if successful, greatly reduce the power of the civil service bureaucracy which Touré has quite patently in large part written off.[29]

It is to be expected that, as with so many other of Touré's plans, projects, and slogans, these latest innovations will be at best partially fulfilled, particularly since enormous vested interests are at stake. It is difficult, however, to see what other course Touré could follow within the ideological limits he has set himself. The only obvious alternative would be to use openly Stalinist means to attain his objectives: the heightened and systematized use of discriminatory rationing, police and intelligence repression, and forced mobilization of labour. And he can rely neither on sufficient personal popularity nor an efficient enough repressive *apparat* to make this work for long.

At the moment he does seem to remain popular–impressionistically one feels he could probably win a free election easily enough, though not without significant opposition. This is no inconsiderable achievement for a radical leader in Africa who has already been in power for 13 years and who–it should be remembered–is still only 48. Provided that Touré retains his formidable health and physical strength, and his agility in thwarting both intra-and extra-Party challenges, it is conceivable–despite his currently critical situation–that he could remain in power for many years yet. But he has already taught us a good deal about the limits of the radical and the possible in contemporary Africa.

NOTES

[1] The best of which is 1. Wallerstein, 'The political ideology of the PDG, *Présence Africaine*, **12,** pp. 30–41 (First Quarter 1962).

[2] The belief that Touré is a direct descendant of Samory, widely current outside Guinea, is believed by nobody within the country.

[3] The best general background study of Guinean political history in this period is to be found in R. S. Morgenthau, *Political parties in French-speaking West Africa*, Oxford, 1964. The best existing biographical sketch of Touré–though it does contain some errors–is in J. Lacouture, *Cinq hommes et la France*, Paris, 1961.

[4] It is important to stress that the French Left which Touré has known is that which resides in Saint-Denis rather than on the Boulevard Saint-Michel. Interestingly, some of Touré's earliest major articles for the RDA paper, *Reveil*, consisted of primitive but bitter attacks on Sartre and the doctrines of existentialism—then a reigning mode of the intellectual Left and the *bête noire* of the French Communist Party.

[5] *L'Ouvrier* (a Guinean CGT paper edited by Touré), **37,** 17 July 1953.

[6] For an account of how Touré exerted control in a critical situation see R.W. Johnson, 'The PDG and the Mamou "deviation"' in C.H. Allen and R.W. Johnson (eds), *African perspectives*, Cambridge, 1970.

[7] On the political importance of this plural office-holding see *ibid.*, pp. 368–9.

[8] Since independence Touré's use of ideology as an agency of social control has taken on an entirely new dimension with his stress on the rediscovery of the African past. The continual public exaltation of Alfa Yaya and Samory Touré rather than, say, sophisticated café-society theories of negritude, or a technocratic stress on modernity and efficiency, allocates value to the heroic militancy of a popular past for which intellectuals feel the least affinity. The (by and large historically accurate) aspersions cast on these past heroes by contemporary Guinean intellectuals are not academic quibbles; they are a questioning of the hegemonic PDG ideology which has outflanked and displaced them.

[9] Here a radical popular movement adopted armed guerilla tactics and was bloodily crushed by the French. See 'Union des populations du Cameroun' (UPC) in *Cameroun Politics*, 1948–55, R.A. Joseph, unpublished B. Phil. thesis, Oxford, 1969.

[10] See G. Chaffard, *Les carnets secrets de la decolonisation*, **II,** Paris, 1967, pp. 165–268, esp. pp. 179–216.

[11] A.S. Touré, *8 Novembre 1964*, Imprimerie Patrice Lumumba, Conakry, 1965. The texts of the declarations on the *loi-cadre* are also reprinted in *Tome* 14 of Touré's *Works*.

[12] Further references to Touré's *Works* as given in the text and in footnotes, will be simply to the volume number.

[13] See p. 420.

[14] The scale is conceived for heuristic rather than historical purposes and the stages are set out more discretely than they may ever be in fact. In particular, stages (ii) and (iii) are frequently conflated, as they are for example in much Western contemporary pluralist ideology.

[15] Nationalization, which was always justified in radical–democrat rather than socialist terms, was in almost all cases followed by a steep fall in output. The great bauxite mining complex at Fria has not been nationalized and its continuing economic success remains crucial to the régime's solvency and, probably, its stability as well.

[16] This mood of despair is best expressed in B. Ameillon's *Guinée—bilan d'une indépendance*, Paris, 1963, a Fanonist–Maoist critique—which Touré has doubtless read.

[17] There are several anti-Touré front movements based on Senegal and the Ivory

Coast and a significant Guinean intellectual emigré group in Paris. These opposition groups are generally badly split—the Parisian group has a Maoist splinter. *Perspectives nouvelles,* the organ of the main Paris-based group, is a source of interesting though unverifiable information on contemporary Guinea.

[18] See *Tome* 14, pp. 331–408 for the relevant texts and the supplementary reform decrees of later weeks. A comparison of *8 Novembre 1964* and other sudden turns to the Left in Africa—Nkrumah's 'Dawn broadcast', and the Arusha and Mulungushi Declarations—would be a worthwhile subject for future research.

[19] *Tome* 13, pp. 191–3. One of the declared aims of the 8 November *tournant* was a relentless struggle against all forms of mystification—which included sorcery, witchcraft, maraboutism and racial versions of pan-Africanism and pan-Arabism. '*Technocratisme*' has been more recently added. This campaign was coupled with a massive literacy campaign, with a stress on literacy in the mother tongue (Soussou, Pular, Guerzé, Malinké, etc.) The de-mystification campaign has been more successful than most, the literacy drive less so.

[20] The impact of the Ghanaian and Malian *coups* was particularly great. Much of *Tome* 15 is taken up with considerations issuing from these *coups*. The attempted *coup* in Guinea in April 1969 saw the first official death sentences for political crimes meted out in Guinea since independence.

[21] A. S. Touré, 'Rapport politique et de doctrine', 8*éme Congrès National du PDG, Conakry* 25 *septembre–2 octobre* 1967, pp. 22–3.

[22] Touré, 'Rapport politique et de doctrine', *loc. cit.* p. 85.

[23] Ibid., p. 44. Touré's 'Rapport politique' was, as originally published, a diplomatically explosive document which led to protests from both the USSR and China. The official account of the 8th Congress was accordingly withdrawn from circulation and the account of it provided in *Tome* 16 omits all the more controversial passages.

[24] Ibid., p. 57.

[25] Ibid., pp. 45–48. Touré also denounces the Sino-Soviet split as a near-criminal irrelevance. Guinea sides with the Vietnamese against the USA and the NLF is normally cited as a paradigm model for anti-imperialist struggle. Characteristically and in company with China and Cuba, Guinea has refused to sign the Test-ban Treaty.

[26] Ibid., pp. 55–6.

[27] The extent to which imitation is conscious is a matter for debate, but one might list as possible subjects for such comparison *investissement humaine,* the de-mystification and literacy campaigns, Touré's conceptions of National Democracy and the compradore bourgeoisie and the Cultural Revolution. (One might also instance, more frivolously, Touré's budding ambition as a poet—most of the later *Tomes* include a number of his poems and some of them have been collected and published under the title *Poèmes militants,* Conakry, 1969. Unlike Mao's poetry, however, Touré's is exclusively political in content.) The régime has tolerated but not encouraged conscious popular imitation of Chinese models—Mao jackets, Mao buttons and so forth. Touré has refused an initiative to have a little Red Book of his quotations published.

[28] The first graduates of the Conakry Institut Polytechnique—the *Promotion Lénine*—were all made deputy-directors of State enterprises on graduation. Only students in advanced technical subjects such as engineering are now allowed to study abroad and even they must compulsorily work for one year in a factory as part of their course. Guinea is likely to have the first home-grown intelligentsia in Africa.

[29] On PRL see *Tome* 16, esp. pp. 46–109. On the Cultural Revolution see *Tome* 17, esp. pp. 210–309.

The rationality of the rich in Nigeria
OTONTI NDUKA

Originally published as 'The anatomy of "rationalization"', *Nigerian Opinion*, **7**, 1 (January 1971).

Ever since the announcement of the appointment of the Adebo Commission on the Review of Wages and Salaries a wave of excitement has been sweeping through the country. This is hardly surprising since vital issues are at stake: economic security, status, and prestige for some, bare subsistence for others, to name the most obvious. As we should expect, the various groups and individuals will have submitted memoranda and papers, replete with statistics and well marshalled arguments to the Commission, each generally in support of a claim for higher wages. Granted certain premisses, the arguments advanced by the various bodies and groups, including those submitted by the Committee of Vice-Chancellors, are logically impeccable–formally that is. As soon as the premisses and underlying assumptions of those arguments and representations are closely examined, however, grave doubts arise.

This paper sets out, in the first place, to examine some of the foundations and underlying assumptions of the existing wage policy–assumptions which the Adebo Commission is being invited to endorse. Whether the Commission can do otherwise is, of course, an open question. Even if we change the metaphor and regard the Commission's role as that of an umpire, it is obvious that it will be umpiring a game whose rules it did not make in the first instance. The problem then is: Can the Commission change the rules of the Nigerian societal game when, as Barbara Wootton has pointed out, the pattern of income distribution is essentially a political question and embodies a whole range of social valuations? That a change is called for, and the sooner the better, is the burden of the argument of this paper.

The two nations

The principles which guide or underlie human actions and relations take many recondite forms. On 13 June 1970, for instance, it was reported that at the I.L.O. Conference being held in Geneva the Commissioner for Labour, Chief Anthony Enahoro, appealed to the developed countries to remedy the imbalance in the terms of trade between them and the developing countries. Nearer home, one of the highlights of the present salaries and wages review exercise is the outspokenness of some of the military governors, among others, in the condemnation of the gross inequalities between the salaries, perquisites, and conditions of service of a privileged class of professionals (including army officers), top civil servants, the senior staff of the universities, top executives of public corporations as well as those of private commercial and industrial concerns, on the one hand, and the less privileged class of workers most of whom, in the words of the Morgan Commission, 'are living under conditions of penury'. Although it may not be immediately obvious, the imbalances pervading economic relationships at the international level are not unconnected with the inequalities existing at the national level.

Let us take the domestic inequalities. A few months ago, hundreds of sleek, new Mercedes Benz cars of the latest model were imported into Lagos. We know who rides in them now. At about the same time about a hundred Scania buses, diverted from a Scandinavian scrap heap and reconditioned, were shipped to Lagos. We also know for what classes of people the buses were bought and who rides in them now. Given the social and economic policies in operation in Nigeria, the purchasing of the Mercedes Benz cars and the Scania buses by the appropriate authorities was in each case a rational undertaking.

Similarly, in our would-be egalitarian society there are, all over the country, thousands of over-crowded primary schools, some in a dilapidated state, most of them ill-equipped and poorly staffed. There are also in existence a few select nurseries and private schools, generally well staffed and well-equipped, for the children of the well-to-do and of the privileged classes who can afford to pay the very high fees demanded. The proliferating of the latter type of educational institution is a phenomenon of the utmost sociological significance–a phenomenon whose political repercussion will become apparent in the not-so-distant future. That these patent inequalities in the provision of educational facilities make a mockery of the claim that equal educational opportunities let alone equal economic opportunities are being provided for all need not cost our astute planners a night's sleep. Why should they?

To these must be added the contrast between the excellent, even fabulous, living accommodation provided for the privileged class at nominal or subsidized rents and the over-crowded, squalid accommodation available at extortionate rents for the vast majority of people. The examples could be multiplied.

These contrasts, imbalances, and inequalities to which attention has often been drawn are integral parts of a way of life whose historical, economic and ideological foundations are traceable. Yes, ideological foundations! Although considerations, wrongly believing that such considerations are the stock-in-trade of Marxists, Communists, and their fellow-travellers, they least suspect, perhaps, that the ideological foundations of the capitalist system we are operating are clear enough for those who can see such things. The Committee of Vice-Chancellors were right enough to point out in a recent memorandum that 'salaries, wages, and other conditions of service should be determined within the framework of a well-defined ideological, political, and social programme for the whole nation'. But finding that such a programme would necessitate radical changes from 'the existing economic, political, and social systems', they join in the usual scramble for higher salaries.

Granted their premises and assumptions, the case they present for higher salaries and fringe benefits is virtually watertight. The basic assumption is, of course, that the *status quo* in the form of the existing salary relativities should be maintained. Needless to say, they have not avoided meddling with ideology, ill-defined though it may be.

The top Federal civil servants have gone a step further. They want the existing salary relativities to be altered–in their favour, of course. They have for long smarted under the 'invidious' system whereby a permanent secretary earns a Group 4 salary while a professional officer, technically responsible to him, earns a Group 3 salary. A lot of internal skirmishing has been going on over this issue for quite a long time. The Elwood Report is on their side in this connection. It is on record that they nearly succeeded, even at the height of the privations occasioned by the civil war, in having their way, but for the timely intervention of the Supreme Military Council. Nevertheless, armed with the devastating strictures of the Minority Report I of the Morgan Commission on Salaries and Wages (among other such adverse comments), a successful frontal attack was launched– thanks to the Ani Report on the inflated salary structures hitherto in vogue in the statutory corporations. It all looked so smooth sailing, so rational. One was left with the impression that the civil service salary structure is the acme of rationality, of equity even, to which all other salary structures should conform.

Veni, vidi, vici. Casting their imperious eyes across the national economic spectrum, the top civil servants could not fail to notice the irrationalities of the salaries and wages structure in operation in the private sector of the economy. An apt and revealing account (revealing in several ways) of what they saw is contained in the latter part of the paper presented by Mr P.C. Asiodu, permanent secretary, Federal Ministry of Industry, at the recent conference on administration and political development of Nigeria held at the Institute of Administration, Ahmadu Bello University, Zaria. It is presumably anomalous that some directors and managers of local firms, whose work is 'often merely supervisory' and among whom it is rare to see 'qualities of innovation and leadership comparable to what is demanded of and of necessity exhibited by, the best in the local services', should each earn as much as £10,000 per annum–that is, more than thrice the salary of a Federal permanent secretary. It should be noted, however, that there are by and large no such glaring disparities lower down the ladder between the salaries and wages paid in the public and the private sectors of the economy. Differences there are, but they are within reasonable limits. The effect of the glaring anomalies pointed out above is that they put into sharper focus the inequalities, the irrationalities, and the inequities pervading our national salaries and wages structure.

From what has been said above it was obvious that something had to be done to remedy the situation. The irrationalities of the salary structure of the statutory corporations had been successfully dealt with. Unfortunately those of the private sector did not seem to be amenable to frontal attack. It was a question of Muhammed and the mountain. Since short of nationalization of private concerns, the salaries of the top executives cannot be brought down, the obvious thing was to raise the top salaries in the public sector.

This is precisely what the Federal permanent secretaries attempted to do last year, when they were halted in their track by the Supreme Military Council.

One should bear such facts as the foregoing in mind in order to be able to read between the lines of the terms of reference of the Adebo Commission. The reference to such factors as the cost of living, the need to review salaries and wages periodically and keep them in proper national balance etc. are important and necessary, of course. It seems to me, however, that the crucial item of the Commission's terms of reference is contained in clause (2). While the preamble talks about the need to take into consideration the 'remuneration in posts with comparable responsibilities in the private sector', the Commission is in clause (2) enjoined 'to examine areas in which rationalization and harmonisation of wages, salaries, and other remuneration and conditions of employment are desirable and feasible as between the public and private sectors of the national economy'. The path which has been mapped out for the Adebo Commission by those who frame the policies of the Federal Military Government is clear enough. The interesting thing about the present salary and wages review exercise is to see how far, if at all, the Adebo Commission will be able to deviate from the path mapped out for it.

The reason why

In support of the stand of our advisers on national policy it should here be pointed out that the recent report of the British Civil Service restates the principle that the pay for posts should 'reflect the rate for the job on the basis of fair comparison with market rates for jobs of comparable responsibility and authority outside the service' (Fulton Report 1968, Section 214f). The point of mentioning this piece of evidence is that our civil service, which is the colonial legacy *par excellence*, is still largely modelled on the British Civil Service. What the principle is drawing attention to is, of course, equity in payment. But it is one thing to talk of equity in a society where the salary differential between the highest paid and the lowest paid groups of workers is of the order of 5:1; where the top executive, the professor, and the unskilled worker may ride to and from work in the same public transport while their children may attend the same primary schools; where the living accommodation provides the same basic amenities as regards lighting, plumbing, sanitation, etc. It is quite another matter to talk of equity in a society like ours where the salary differential is of the order of 50:1; where top people never ride in public transport (free cars, car advances, and basic allowances see to that); where the top people are necessarily segregated from their less fortunate fellow citizens, so that as regards living accommodation the privileged few, on the one hand, and the rest of the citizens on the other, might well be living in two different countries. The same goes for the educational facilities provided for the children of the one group as compared with the provisions made for the children of the other group.

In support of the gross inequalities prevalent in our society–inequalities which are a part of our colonial heritage–the privileged class argue as follows. In a society with a poorly developed public transport system the possession of a personal vehicle, virtually provided at public expense, is a necessity, not a luxury. Similarly, the public primary schools are of such poor quality that it is necessary, in a free country, to have select private schools suitable for the children of the privileged class. Needless to say, fees in these private preparatory schools are even higher than they are in the vast majority of secondary schools.

Although the foregoing and similar arguments are often presented with various refinements, they are basically rationalizations of indefensible inequalities whose historical antecedents are fairly well known. They err not so much in what they say as in what they omit to say. For instance, the privileged class is intelligent enough to know that the availability of car advances and basic allowances is a disincentive to the rapid development of an efficient public transport system. When Mercedes Benz and other brands of cars are available for the privileged class, few powerful voices will be raised against the purchase of a hundred scrapped and reconditioned buses. Similar arguments are applicable *mutatis mutandis* to the vogue of special schools and to the one-acre plots with Edwardian houses or houses of more recent vintage.

The logic of distributive justice

The argument of this article is not based on the assumption that it is desirable to equalize all incomes. Even in communist countries, salary differentials do exist, for such differentials, if they are within reasonable limits, are economically and morally defensible. One is bound to agree here with Professor Elliott Jaques that the real issue is not that of egalitarian versus differential distribution of income, but rather 'the degree and pattern of differentiation of income that is equitable under given economic conditions'. Those who submit 'learned' memoranda; those who talk about egalitarianism in one breath and about (upward?) rationalization and harmonization of incomes in another; and those whose privilege it is to adjudicate in such matters would merely be postponing the evil day if they failed now to examine critically the degree and pattern of differentiation of income that exists and to see how far considerations of equity could be made to play a part in determining the future pattern. The writers of the Second National Development Plan 1970–74 are merely pulling the wool over the eyes of the unsuspecting when they advise the mass of the people to wait until a large 'national cake' is baked before they can expect a sizeable share of it. But what is at issue is not the distribution of a non-existent cake but the *equitable* distribution of the loaves of bread that are available. Furthermore, the fact still remains that while the mythical cake is being baked the privileged class continue to eat 'imported cake' at the expense of the community. It is this pattern of distribution which needs to be critically re-examined.

What is called for, therefore, is a re-examination of the historical, economic, ideological, and other foundations of our habits of distribution–habits which, as Wootton rightly points out, profoundly affect the character of any society. For instance, a salary structure together with other perquisites and conditions of service which served the purpose of maintaining the imperialist agents in appropriate comfort and surrounding them with the aura and prestige commensurate with their role as the representatives of a superior, conquering race may be an anachronistic liability in the context of a would-be egalitarian society. Much less defensible is the further refinement whereby public officers are provided with advances with which they buy cars, are paid monthly car basic allowances, but never, except in very exceptional circumstances, use those cars for the performance of official duties, for which other official and chauffeur-driven cars are always available. This, mind you, is in a society where the vast majority have to queue daily for an hour or more before they can board overcrowded buses to take them to or from their places of work.

Of the many economic arguments which buttress the inequalities which characterize our pattern of distribution the one most frequently advanced is the need to attract and retain scarce talents. Thus while the top civil servant talks about crossing the road and having his value appreciate by £1000 or more, the university don talks of taking up more lucrative appointments in other countries. While such arguments are not without some force, it is doubtful whether the fabulous salaries and perquisites enjoyed by directors and general managers are explicable in terms of the scarcity of their talents. What the proponents of such arguments conveniently forget is that even where individuals did not enjoy any scholarship but paid their way all through their educational careers the financial contributions of the state towards the cost of their education are generally many times greater than those they and their families made. This is particularly true in the case of higher education. The distressing fact about the attitude of the presumably talented few is that they place the emphasis on how much of a comfortable living the society owes them and much less, if at all, on what service they should render to the society. Any under-developed country such as ours will make little progress so long as the highly educated class think more about imitating the consumption patterns of the developed countries and less about making the necessary sacrifices which are among the prerequisites of national development.

Now if we may believe P. E. Sigmund, Jr, a basic principle in the ideology of a developing nation such as ours is 'the absolute primacy of the goal of national development'. For our present purposes, we shall adopt Webster's definition of ideology as 'a system of ideas concerning phenomena, especially those of social life; the manner of thinking characteristic of a class or an individual'. The dominant ideology of present-day Nigeria–there are a number subsidiary ones–is a curious amalgam of multifarious principles. It is an amalgam of economic, political, ethical, religious, and other principles, albeit inadequately articulated and even less understood by the vast majority of the citizens. The background against which this ideology is to be understood is that of what Professor Elliott Jaques calls an 'under-abundant economy'. The society is capitalist in orientation, although the ghost of socialism stalks the political scene. Material wealth is the dominant value, the supreme object of individual and collective effort. The society, especially the privileged class, subscribes to the ethics of conspicuous consumption, the principles derived from the various religions being generally too weak to counteract the materialistic tendencies. The political principles are derived from democracy, even though political activities have been suspended and women were hitherto denied adult suffrage in certain parts of the country. Considerations of freedom, individual as well as national, and of equality (egalitarianism is the fashionable shibboleth) certainly find a place in such an ideology. The fault with the Nigerian society is not that it lacks an ideology but that it lacks a well-defined and viable ideology.

Who bells the cat?

From what has been said above one is bound to be sceptical about the outcome of the exercise being carried out by the Adebo Wages and Salaries Commission. If previous commissions provide any precedents there will probably be a general upward review of salaries and wages. That the lower income groups need such a relief, however shortlived it may be, is obvious. To maintain previous salary relativities the higher income groups will probably get a couple of hundred pounds each extra. Sooner or later inflation will wipe out a large part of the gain likely to be made by the lower income groups, unless a more determined effort is made to control prices and peg rents. The basic predictable outcome of the exercise is that unless there is a fundamental restructuring of the society, which means altering the basic distributive habits, the lot of the vast majority will not be appreciably better than it is.

It would, however, be a great pity if one's worst fears materialized. The pity of it all is that, after the eye-opening experiences of the civil war and presented with the opportunity of re-defining our national bearings during the ensuing period of planning and reconstruction, we are letting an opportunity slip by. Otherwise, what is one to make of the refusal of the Committee of Vice-Chancellors to recommend 'a radical change from the existing economic, political and social systems'? If during a military régime we are not in a 'revolutionary situation', when shall we be in such a situation? There is even a more lamentable aspect of the whole situation. One had thought that it was the duty and privilege of the intellectuals in our universities to define, re-define, criticize, and articulate viable ideological, political, and social programmes for the whole nation. From their attitude and utterances in this connection it seems that they are abdicating their responsibility.

Once again the top civil servants have apparently gone one better than their university counterparts. In the *Second National Development Plan* 1970–74 and in various speeches which they have composed for the Head of State, some national objectives have been outlined and appropriate references have been made to the need for building 'a just and egalitarian society'. While one does not doubt the sincerity of the Head of State in such matters one is sceptical of the actual intentions of those who formulate policies and are responsible for the details of administration. No one who has attended meetings of the Association of Senior Civil Servants (or those of university dons for that matter) and heard them discussing fringe benefits, etc. etc., will get the impression that they are particularly enamoured of the principles of social justice, and of distributive justice in particular. Yet, as Harold Laski pointed out long ago, 'it is the cumulative force of administrative acts which are the heart of the modern State', since 'principles (of justice and egalitarianism, for instance) may be invalidated by the method of their application'. Are those who, in an under-abundant economy are enjoying perquisites and a consumption pattern modelled on the standards of an abundant economy; those whose children enjoy educational and economic advantages which make a mockery of all talk about equality of opportunity, who are assiduously administering a nascent hierarchical society–are those individuals and officials really committed to social justice, to egalitarianism? One has great doubts, more so when the vast majority are being enjoined to wait until a larger national cake is baked before expecting to receive sizeable shares in the on-going acts of distribution.

We may in conclusion agree that the issues at stake involve rationalization and harmonization. The rationalization which is herein advocated is akin less to what the writers of the terms of reference of the Adebo Commission probably had in mind than it is to rationality in the true Weberian sense of systematic arrangement. It will involve an overhaul of the present pattern of income distribution not only as between the various groups of wage and salary earners but as between the modern and the traditional sectors of the economy, between the town and the countryside. It will involve waging a war against the irrationalities, and abandoning some aspects of our colonial heritage, however dear and favourable they may be to the privileged class. Taken to its logical conclusion all this will involve a *systematic* and *determined* restructuring of the society (not necessarily overnight) in the light of the principles of justice, freedom, and equality. The time to start the exercise is now, not the distant future. The question, then, is: who will bell the cat?

PART VII
Politics: Rulers, Masses and Political Power

... We think there is something wrong with the simple interpretation of the national liberation movement as a revolutionary trend. The objective of the imperialist countries was to prevent the enlargement of the socialist camp, to liberate the reactionary forces in our countries which were being stifled by colonialism and to enable those forces to ally themselves with the international bourgeoisie (...) in our present situation... there are only two possible paths for an independent nation: to return to imperialist domination (neo-colonialism, capitalism, state capitalism), or to take the way of socialism. This operation, on which depends the compensation for the efforts and sacrifices of the popular masses during the struggle, is considerably influenced by the form of the struggle and the degree of revolutionary consciousness of those who lead it.

Political implications of the development of peasant society in Kenya

COLIN LEYS

From Colin Leys, 'Politics in Kenya: the development of peasant society .
British Journal of Political Science, **1**, 3, 1971.

Since the nature of peasant society is that it provides a surplus for
the élite, the extraction of this surplus may, in the long run, generate
class consciousness and class antagonism on the part of the peasantry
towards the élite, creating opportunities for radical change in the
political system (not necessarily opportunities for the peasants, of course);
this is the essence of the question posed by Barrington Moore. In
this respect, what strikes one forcibly about the system of surplus extraction
as it operates in Kenya is its highly indirect, complex, and impersonal character. With few exceptions, the operation of the system does not focus attention
on any group as being either responsible for it, or beneficiaries of it; the
process is rather invisible. It is not just that there are no landlords; there
is no forced sale of produce at below market prices, either. To a large extent,
however, the terms of trade between the towns and the countryside produce
the same result. Profit margins in manufacture and large-scale commerce
are very high and salary and wage levels far above peasant income levels.[1]
In addition indirect taxes, paid largely by the peasantry and consisting mainly
of import duties, provide roughly half of the current revenue out of which
the civil service is maintained, also at incomes of which the lowest exceed
those of the majority of peasants.[2] Other parts of the salariat are supported
in the very large parastatal sector, numbering over 50 statutory bodies, and
in the co-operative movement, numbering 1900 primary societies, the operating expenses of most of these also being supported from cesses [taxes] on
agricultural products.[3] The distribution of government credit to the élite has
also to be taken into account in this connection; for instance virtually all
ICDC loans go to already prosperous businessmen (by peasant standards),
and under the first five-year development plan, credit for smallholders went
to the most prosperous three per cent of them.[4] Loans to the value of £800 000
given by the Kenya National Trading Corporation to African businessmen
had not been repaid in 1970, and similar problems of non-repayment were
also reported at the National Construction Corporation which advanced
funds to African building contractors.[5] In most of these transactions or
relationships, it is not apparent that the benefits accruing to the élite are

being provided by the peasantry, and it is probably significant that in the one or two cases where it has been obvious, there has been pressure to stop it. Thus in 1969 Graduated Personal Tax, a highly regressive form of direct taxation, was abolished prior to the elections for the lowest categories of taxpayers. The loan charges on settlement plots have also been seen as an unwarranted burden, to pay for land which many of the new settlers felt had never rightly belonged to the Europeans from whom it was bought, and repayment has never risen above 60 per cent of what was due.[6]

On the whole, then, the peasantry in Kenya are not placed in a position of obvious conflict of interest with other classes. There is no landlordism, no powerful, independent indigenous bourgeoisie, no radical proletariat. Marx's famous analysis of the inherent instability of the peasant-based régime of Louis Napoleon depended on the existence of an 'old order' for which the bulk of the peasantry yearned, while the revolutionary peasants were pushed by debt and hardship into an alliance with the growing revolutionary element among the urban workers; the régime was unstable because it represented

> not the revolutionary, but the conservative peasant; not the peasant that strikes out beyond the condition of his social existence, the small holding, but rather the peasant who wants to consolidate this holding, not the country folk who, linked up with the towns, want to overthrow the old order through their own energies, but on the contrary those who, in stupefied seclusion within this old order, want to see themselves and their small holdings saved...[7]

But in Africa there is no *old* order, strictly speaking, at the national level. The peasantry itself is part of a new order, and is far more independent of any other class than in any other historical setting hitherto considered in this connection. One cannot help feeling that in Kenya, at least, the character of politics will for some considerable time be determined by the fact that the peasantry as a class has not yet reached the limits of its development, and that the symbiosis between it and the emerging urban-based classes is not yet fully developed either. This symbiosis is mediated by the various kinds of client–patron ties which link peasants to the politicians in the towns locality by locality. This corresponds to the continuing importance of the clan or lineage as a unit of social organization; one might say that it is the characteristic mode of political self-expression of peasantries. The continuing vitality of clientelism in politics can be seen as a reflection of the failure of capitalistic development to transform social relationships by transforming the mode of production in an underdeveloped country. One might even draw a speculative parallel: on the one hand, the 'pyramidal' character of clientelist political structures, which consist essentially of unequal exchange relationships reproduced again and again at each level from the village up to the national party leaders and their lieutenants, and between the latter and the representatives of various kinds of power-holder in developed countries; and on the other, the structure of exploitative relationships portrayed by Frank between centre and periphery, from the metropolitan power down through the neo-colonial capitals to the rural townships and finally into the fields.[8]

But at a more tangible level, what does obviously stand out in the performance of the KANU leadership and the relations of the party to the electorate is its ambivalent, hybrid quality, combining the frank and officially sanctioned pursuit of private gain on the part of leaders with a good deal of sensitivity to peasant demands.[9] This sensitivity is due largely to the ties of kinship and locality which relate MPs to their constituencies. They are nearly all members of the urban élite, not peasant leaders, but they are still leaders of peasants, and they have not yet been allowed to forget this. The 1969 elections, which were held for no other reason than that the leadership, and perhaps especially the President, conceived of itself as deriving its authority from the peasantry, resulted in the defeat of half of the former MPs who stood again, and produced a parliament with a clearly renewed consciousness of peasant grievances, so much so that the President soon felt it necessary to castigate publicly MPs who complained too much and decried the progress that had been made.[10]

MPs act, of course, as agents to procure specific benefits for their constituents in the form of local projects and services, and finding jobs for their sons in town at the same time as this, by securing their own hold on office, makes it possible for them to secure profitable trading licences, loans, property options, etc. The stability of this system may depend on a good deal of false consciousness on both sides; peasants who credit MPs for getting them services from government which they have already paid for many times over, and which are taken for granted in the towns, and MPs who sincerely see themselves as champions of the rural poor. There is equally no doubt that the régime's ties with the better-off peasants are stronger than with the marginal peasants, through the links that exist between national politicians and the 'big men' in the localities, and that between the big men and the poorer peasants there is plenty of room for conflict; but whether this threatens the viability of the system in the short run seems doubtful. The problems of 'managing' this kind of relationship are not insuperable even when there is much more overt conflict of interest involved, as experience elsewhere shows. The *literati* may be co-opted by expanding the bureaucracy, or by channelling them into entrepreneurship; the use of patronage combined with efforts to re-orient secondary education towards commercial and technical subjects and the provision of credit and monopolies for new entrepreneurs are all devices which have been tried elsewhere; so is the use of political power to rule out ideological challenge to the régime. Moore's discussion of the various ways by which the imperial Chinese government tried to maintain its links with the peasantry also contains interesting points of resemblance; for instance the system of lectures to the peasants on Confucian ethics, which seems not unlike the regular lectures delivered by politicians and top civil servants on the themes of hard work, unity, honesty, etc., which are such a marked characteristic of the Kenya political style.[11] Moore, however, concluded that much the most effective link between government and peasantry was the clan, which strikes one as the most significant parallel of all.

In the longer run, however, it seems inevitable that the rate of population growth must (among other things) close the 'land frontier' and that the resulting social tensions will then be incapable of being resolved through the mechanisms of a loosely representative clientelist party. There is not much point in speculating about the political forms which might correspond to this situation, but it does seem worth while to draw attention to the most obvious points of potential friction within the system that has been sketched in this article; that is, besides the many points on which the present evidence is clearly inconclusive, there are some questions that suggest themselves as particularly important for testing the limits of the 'development of peasant society'.

The first and most obvious question is what the 'land frontier' really looks like, and what competition or conflict may develop over the land that is not already in African freehold tenure. We need to know much more about the real structure of the partnerships and companies and co-operatives that have bought and are buying the remaining large mixed farms and about the fate of the smaller estates (coffee, tea, or sisal) that have begun also to change hands. We also need to know much more about the indebtedness of farmers, especially the settlement scheme farmers, and the effects on their political consciousness of the pressure that has been exerted on them by the selective eviction each year of a few 'persistent defaulters' on debt repayment; for instance it has been reported that some settlers have resorted to the favourite Kikuyu device of oath-taking to try to build up solidarity for a collective refusal to repay.

Closely linked with the 'land frontier' question is the question of differentiation within the rural areas. One aspect of this is the great variations that exist between different regions and ethnic groups, owing to uneven rates of penetration of the money economy, and perhaps uneven distribution of benefits (school, settlement land, etc.) since independence. Even if the peasants of Kenya resembled a 'simple addition of homologous multitudes, much as potatoes in a sack form a sack of potatoes' we would have to start from the proposition that they formed a series of sacks, not one single sack. But even within a single locality and tribal area a process of differentiation is obviously taking place, even if it has not yet produced any major cleavages. The basis of it is freehold land tenure and access to education and jobs. People who got early access to schooling and employment have been best placed to get both additional land and better educational opportunities for their children subsequently. 'Progressive' smallholders are typically also small traders and it is typically these people whose sons are in secondary schools and these people who are purchasing additional small plots so as to leave each son a small-holding. Salaried employees typically aim to send their children to the 'high cost' (formerly European-only) schools in towns, which have better facilities and staff and much higher success records in public certificate examinations. In other words a cumulative process of differential recruitment into the salaried and land-owning classes is at work, whose consequences will be felt in the next generation much more keenly than they are now. At the same time, the apparent relative homogeneity of the life-styles of the peasant majority suggested both by existing statistics and casual observation may be a bad guide to current trends; for instance the difference between an income of £150 and £50 a year may be critical for the career prospects of one's children because of the heavy incidence of school fees, although people earning these different incomes may appear and even, as yet, feel, socially united. It would also be particularly important to know more about the effect of freehold tenure and land shortage on the traditional obligations which hitherto have assured landless families some access to cultivation plots on other peoples' land; in some areas it is said that people are becoming unwilling to recognize any obligations towards new applicants for such access.

A third and well-recognized set of questions concerns school-leavers looking for urban jobs which are no longer available, and the possibility that they may effect a link between other sections of the population–whether areas or social strata–which feel themselves underprivileged. It is estimated that half a million primary school children will leave school in the years 1970–74, almost all of whom will have to accept rural employment or self-employment, and a further 138,000 children will leave secondary school, of whom nearly half will not be able to find urban jobs. In April 1970 the formation of a 'School-Leavers Association' was announced in Nairobi and in June the Government decreed that all employers, including the civil service, must increase their work force by ten per cent by 1 September. Crowds numbering tens of thousands converged on Nairobi and Mombasa and other urban centres to register as job-seekers, leading to a tense situation and isolated disturbances. It was difficult to imagine that even 40,000 new jobs (i.e. ten per cent of enumerated employment only in firms with ten or more employees) would in fact permanently be created, and it soon became clear that most of those which employers actually offered would be on terms deeply dissatisfying to most of the would-be employees; e.g. low-paid agricultural estate labour. On the other hand, it was also clear that a very large portion of those registering were either married women or men already in employment, so that the real rate of unemployment defined as adult men without means of subsistence was perhaps only about half of the 200,000 plus who registered as job-seekers. What seemed likely, in any case, was that a majority of the unemployed secondary school-leavers, at least those who had passed their examinations, would be found employment, thus removing for the time being the possibility that such people might come to make common cause with alienated elements among the uneducated peasantry or with the marginal elements of the urban work-force, especially in Nairobi (for instance the victims of the Government's policy of destroying the 'shanty' homes of several thousand people in Nairobi during 1970). The Kenya Peoples Union, formed in 1966, had represented a potential alliance of this kind, combining an ideological appeal based on a partly socialist, partly peasant–populist programme with a practical appeal to ethnic solidarity among the Luo and perhaps some other ethnic groups which felt themselves deprived. The KPU was banned in October 1969 and its major leaders were detained. Others, however, mainly lesser leaders, were absorbed into the ruling party and within a year the principle of working within the existing system seemed to have been accepted for the time being in the areas of the KPU's former strength.[12] Meanwhile KANU seemed quite capable of adopting some elements of KPU's populist programme, for instance by eventually accepting some form of limitation on the size of land-holdings.[13]

It was a reminder that the questions raised above are essentially fairly long-term and that as writers such as Moore, Alavi, and Wolfe have shown, it generally requires a rare combination of tyranny and misery to produce a peasant revolt, let alone a peasant revolution;[14] short of which the clientelist political structures characteristic of peasant society have a resilience which can easily be underestimated.

NOTES

[1] Returns of 20–25 per cent per annum on capital invested are expected by most companies; see *Who controls industry in Kenya?* Report of a Working Party of the National Christian Council of Kenya, East African Publishing House, Nairobi, 1968, p. 155.

[2] Dharam P. Ghai, in 'Incomes policy in Kenya: need, criteria and machinery', Institute for Development Studies, Nairobi, Discussion Paper, June 1968, estimated average urban *unskilled* workers' wages at twice that of the average peasant household, even if the fact that the peasant figure represents the work of the whole family is disregarded (see pp. 2–3)

[3] G. B. Lamb's study of the Murang'a in his *Peasant politics,* Lewes, 1974, brings out the ways in which 'personal discounts' to committee members of co-operative societies on overpriced society purchases have also operated as an unofficial, not to say illegal, cess [tax] for the benefit of the local rich peasants who get onto the committees. See also John S. Saul, Marketing co-operatives in a developing country: the Tanzanian case', USSC Conference papers, December 1969, which describes a situation very similar to that in Kenya.

[4] *Development plan* 1966–60, p. 113.

[5] *East African Standard*, to February 1970, and 28 September 1970.

[6] *Department of Settlement five year review,* p. 36, Appendix F; the point was taken up by the Kenya Peoples Union in the 'Wananchi (People's) Declaràtion' in 1969: 'It is one thing to borrow and repay for productive assets, it is quite another to borrow huge sums to buy your own land back, and sums which promptly leave the country.'

[7] *The eighteenth brumaire of Louis Bonaparte,* Marx and Engels, *Selected works,* Moscow, Foreign Langauges Publishing House, 1962, p. 335.

[8] André Gunder Frank, *Capitalism and underdevelopment,* pp. 16–17. On party politics based on dyadic ties see Carl Lande, *Leaders, factions and parties: The structure of Phillippine politics,* Yale South-East Asian Studies Program, New Haven, 1965, and on clientelism generally see John Duncan Powell, 'Peasant society and clientelist politics', *American Political Science Review*, **LXIV**, p. 441, June 1970.

[9] Officially sanctioned in the sense that the President, for example, asked the then KANU backbench leader Bildad Kaggia in a speech in 1965 what he had done for himself, and cited other leaders of the nationalist movement who had acquired farms and businesses as examples to be emulated.

[10] See, e.g., his speech on Madaraka Day; *East African Standard*, 2 June 1970.

[11] Barrington Moore, *Social origins of dictatorship and democracy*, Beacon Press, Boston, 1966, p. 206.

[12] Most of the KPU leaders detained in 1969 had been released by the end of 1970 and Luo spokesmen had pledged that the remaining detainees would be loyal to KANU if they were released.

[13] Sessional Paper No. 10 of 1965 on *African socialism and its application to planning in Kenya* referred to the possibility of a ceiling on land holdings and the 1970–4 development plan stated that a limit would be imposed but made no further mention of it. Back bench MPs elected in December 1969, frequently called for such a ceiling and it was a major recommendation of the *Report of the Select Committee on Unemployment* (National Assembly, Nairobi, 3 December 1970), p. 11.

[14] Moore, *Social origins...*: *op. cit.*, H. Alavi, 'Peasants and revolution', *Socialist Register*, 1965, pp. 241–75, E.R. Wolfe, 'On peasant rebellions', *International Social Science Journal*, **XXI**, pp. 286–93 (1969).

Workers' control: the Algerian experience
IAN CLEGG

From Ian Clegg, *Workers' self-management in Algeria*, Allen Lane, London, 1971.

In just over five years the Algerian revolution had been recuperated, institutionalized, and then emasculated by a new bourgeois élite firmly entrenched in the state and party. The *comités de gestion* had been suppressed or existed in name only. *Autogestion*, once so proudly proclaimed as Algeria's contribution to the construction of revolutionary societies in the Third World, had given way to a banal state capitalism. The original leaders, of whatever political complexion, had been replaced by previously unknown careerists and bureaucrats. Abroad, the revolution that had fired so many failed to live up to their expectations and their attention drifted to other areas of struggle, spectacularized in their turn by the media. Algeria became yet another revolutionary failure.

The question of the actual nature of the Algerian revolution and, hence, the reasons for its defeat remained largely unanswered. The lessons to be drawn from the experience, and its relevance to revolutionary struggle as a whole, were not widely discussed except in terms of sectarian preoccupations. At this point the Algerian experience must be re-inserted into the historical and analytical process with which this book began. We are faced not just with the specific problems of Algeria but with the continuing dilemma of revolutionary authenticity in relatively underdeveloped societies and ultimately with the basis of authority in any revolutionary society.

The immediate misconception that must be corrected is that of the nature of the Algerian revolution. Many saw the violent resistance to colonialism and the ultimate achievement of independence as revolution. This is a profound error which can only lead to a misunderstanding of the subsequent events. What began in 1954, with the formation of the FLN and the declaration of armed struggle, was not revolution; it was the development of the fight for national independence on to an intense and violent plane. To term the struggle against colonialism as revolution is to mistake the nature and aspirations of this struggle. It is to confuse the identity of revolution as a class struggle aimed at the overthrow of pre-existing social, political, and economic structures with the attempt to replace them with structures more closely related to specifically national aspirations. Although a small section of the FLN in 1954 was influenced by socialist ideas, the aims of the majority were circumscribed by nationalism; their aspirations were rooted in traditional Arab, Berber, and Islamic culture. Algerian nationalism reflected the social and cultural Manichaeism forced on the country by a specific colonial enterprise. The appeal of the FLN, for the masses, was its aim to restore a historical, cultural, social, and political entity that had been destroyed with the defeat of Abdel Kader.

The extreme violence of the struggle gave expression to the violence already implicit in the relations between colonizer and colonized: a violence that was itself a product of the process and mode of colonization. It is this violence that largely created the myth of the revolutionary nature of the fight for independence. Fanonism, in particular, was responsible for the widespread misconceptions over the nature of the struggle. As we have seen, the struggle was seized in racial and cultural terms: the two communities, Muslim and European, faced each other as more or less homogeneous blocs. Apart from a few exceptions, class alliances between the communities did not exist; and where they had existed the war served to sever them almost completely. This gave rise to the attempted elision of a national with a class struggle through the identification of the European settlers as the oppressors and the indigenous population as the oppressed. Such reductionism had widespread appeal because of its apparent simplicity. But, despite the political and economic hegemony of the *pieds-noirs*, it is not possible to describe the war as a class war because of the existence of parallel class structures in the two communities. Although the settler proletariat were distinguished from the Muslim proletariat by their social and economic privileges, objectively they were in a similar relationship to both colonial and metropolitan capitalism.

Certainly the war contained overtones of a class struggle as a rising of the underprivileged and dispossessed. Mass support for the FLN in the early days came extensively from the traditional rural areas and its leaders were at pains to describe their struggle as peasant-based. It was in the countryside, with its consciousness of a past destroyed by colonialism, rather than in the towns that the FLN based both its military and political organizations. Despite this emphasis on the peasantry, dictated by tactical as well as ideological considerations, the struggle was national in orientation and extent. Members of all indigenous classes were fired by and, in varying degrees, took part in the revolt against colonialism. In seeking to overthrow French colonial hegemony the FLN was demanding the re-establishment of an Algerian national identity. Until the Tripoli meeting of the CNRA in May 1962 there had been no official expression of a socialist conception of the future, and even then it had a national rather than a class definition. The continued refusal of the FLN to accept the existence of classes in post-independence Algeria is a clear witness of an inability to define the social and economic contradictions existing within the indigenous population.

If the achievement of independence was not, of itself, a revolution, the occupation of the means of production by the workers and the formation of *comités de gestion* can be said to constitute the revolutionary aftermath of independence. It was the establishment of workers' management of the ex-*colon* industrial, commercial, and agricultural concerns that formed the revolutionary nature of independent Algeria. It was the proletariat rather than the peasantry who broke through the specifically national identifications of race and culture to develop a class action. The class nature of this action raises the question of the situation and nature of revolutionary consciousness both in Algeria and in similar societies.

Since the Russian revolution confused the identification of the revolutionary overthrow of capitalism as developing in advanced industrial societies, the left has been embroiled in controversy over the nature of revolution in non-industrialized countries. The classic, Europo-centric, Marxist thesis has been felt to be contradicted by a series of apparently successful peasant-based revolutions in largely non-industrial societies. This has given rise to an attempted re-definition of the exact class situation of revolutionary consciousness. While not producing a complete answer to this question, the Algerian experience is of great relevance.

The rejection or amplification of the classic definition of the proletariat as the sole negation of capitalism has been undertaken where there is a vast peasant majority or where the working class appears to be increasingly incorporated within capitalism. In non-industrialized societies this has led to the identification of a revolutionary consciousness among the peasantry, stemming from their participation in wars of national liberation and, to a lesser extent, class wars against a national bourgeoisie. The Fanonist ideology, as expressed in *The wretched of the earth*, identified the most dispossessed as the most revolutionary. Fanon, like Marcuse,[1] appeared to be able, at one stroke, to cut through the problem of the continuing absence of revolution in advanced industrial societies. By opposing the industrialized and colonizing to the underdeveloped and colonized, the class struggle assumed global proportions. The working class of the West became the bourgeoisie of the dispossessed of the third world. The appeal of this Manichaean division lay in its simplicity. For the 'wretched' it subsumed all local contradictions within a global contradiction; it removed the necessity for any critical analysis. For the intellectuals of Europe and the U.S.A. its attraction lay in the way in which it played on the guilt mechanisms of liberalism. The sordid abasement of Sartre in his introduction to *The wretched of the earth* has been paralleled by the stampede of American intellectuals to prostrate themselves at the altar of black power.

In discussing the value systems and consciousness of the peasantry, sub-proletariat, and working class of Algeria, I have attempted, in this specific case, to unmask the absurdity of this type of reductionism. Neither the peasantry, nor the truly 'wretched'–the sub-proletariat–can be said to have played an objectively revolutionary role in Algeria. The involvement of the population of the traditional rural areas in the independence struggle must be clearly separated from their passivity in face of its revolutionary aftermath. The peasantry were fighting for what they regarded as their inheritance: a heritage firmly rooted in the Arab, Berber, and Islamic past. Their consciousness was rooted in the values and traditions of this past and their aim was its re-creation. Revolution, as a concept, is alien to the peasant consciousness while their relationship to the environment remains one of passive endurance rather than active transformation.

The true, disinherited mass of Algeria, as in the rest of the Third World, is the rural and urban sub-proletariat. They exist in a half world that is neither the traditional nor the modern. They are denied the uneasy security either of traditional values of rural society or of employment in the industrial economy. This mass, spawned by demographic growth, changes in agricultural methods, by industrialization, war, and poverty, is involved in a desperate daily struggle for existence. For Fanon and for Marcuse it is this desperation and hopelessness which should drive the masses to revolt. Yet, as I have described earlier, it is this very desperation and extreme acculturation which deprives them of the ability to act on the external in a conscious manner. Subjectively, the sub-proletariat is not conscious of itself as a social organization: its total deprivation of social or economic self-identity makes of it a series.

Fanon, in particular, is at pains to emphasize the effect that participation in revolt has on the development of consciousness. For him, this experience breaks the chains of the psychological and social alienation forged by colonialism: the catharsis of violence liberates the individual and the society from the passivity engendered by the death of traditional cultural and social relationships. In *L'an V de la Révolution Algérienne*, he prophesies that the participation of Algerian women in the struggle against colonialism foreshadows their liberation from traditional male dominance. The fact that this liberation was not achieved after independence is symptomatic of the underlying fallacies of Fanonism. Neither the peasantry nor the sub-proletariat played any other than a purely negative role in the events after independence. Involvement in the revolt against the French did not transform their consciousness. Fanonism, with its abstract Manichaean division of the world, is pure ideology. It lacks a critical and dialectical analysis of the process of the formation of consciousness.

As ideology, Fanonism must be placed in a different context from the purely tactical or strategic identification of rural areas as a suitable operational base for guerrilla activity. The FLN, in Algeria, eventually achieved independence, not because the peasantry emerged as a successful revolutionary class but because France could only hold the countryside by an unacceptable expenditure of effort. Depending on their physical nature, rural areas can provide a suitable base for guerrilla activity. This does not mean that the rural population is involved as a conscious revolutionary force. As we have seen, the nature of their involvement is clearly dependent on the nature of the struggle. In Algeria the peasantry was deeply immersed in the attainment of national liberation because it promised a re-creation of a glorious past to which all their values were intimately related.

The desperation that drove the Algerian industrial and agricultural working class to seize the means of production must be qualitatively separated from that of the peasantry and sub-proletariat. The motivation of the workers in occupying and managing the *colon* farms and factories was extensively based on the purely immediate necessities of material survival. Despite the fact that they shared the same desperation as the mass of the population, the objective result of the workers' reaction to this situation was revolutionary. It cannot, however, be described as a conscious assumption of the historical revolutionary role of the proletariat. This fallacious interpretation led many to misconstrue the primitive nature of the seizure of the means of production as a sophisticated and mature revolt against capitalism.

It is in the objective relationship of the Algerian working class to the means of production that the key to their action lies. Unlike the peasantry and sub-proletariat, their relationship to the means of production was social rather than familial or individual. The social basis of the peasant economy is defined by a restricting relationship that pre-exists and encompasses the means of production–the extended family. Thus, although the peasant economy is apparently co-operative, the social relationships associated with it are not class-based. An industrial mode of production, despite the separation it engenders between individual workers, objectively creates an identity that transcends the boundaries of traditional relationships. The seizure of the means of production by the Algerian workers represented the subsuming of a series of individual motivations under a solidary, class action.

The contradictions of the Algerian revolution lay in the fact that it was not a conscious praxis. It was the practice of revolution with no concomitant theory. The class initiative of the workers must be considered in relation to their relative lack of revolutionary consciousness. Although able to embark on a class solution to their common desperation, they were not, at that point, capable of fully apprehending the meaning of their action. They were accustomed to using the self-definitional concepts of race and culture and not of class. The rapid imposition of bureaucratic controls on the *comités de gestion* and the development of an authoritarian state apparatus stems from the inability of the Algerian working class to grasp the immediate necessity of extending their revolutionary initiative further than the point of production. By the time this became apparent they had lost the initiative.

Besides the absence of a hegemonic consciousness, the Algerian working class was deeply inhibited by the contradictory nature of the party and state. For the mass of Algerians the FLN and the state under Ben Bella were cloaked in the mystique of the struggle for independence. They were vested with the authority and authenticity of success in the fight against colonialism. The Algerian working class found extreme difficulty in separating the nature of the FLN and its leaders during the war from their role after independence. The majority failed to see the full implications of their own actions: that the formation of the *comités de gestion* implicitly challenged the authority of the party and state. The tensions implicit in the tripartite division of workers' councils, party, and state in any revolutionary society were immeasurably increased in Algeria by the simple fact that the party and state were not products of the revolution.

Apart from some UGTA officials and some FLN militants, the Algerian nationalist movement was singularly unprepared to deal with the question of the country's future. During the war the heterogeneity of the FLN made agreement on anything outside the achievement of independence almost impossible. Despite its wide popular support, the FLN was never more than a loosely co-ordinated front for a wide assortment of political tendencies and personalities. It was not a socialist or a revolutionary party. Once independence was achieved it fell apart into a whole series of competing factions. The extent of its irrelevance to the immediate problems of Algeria was revealed during the summer of 1962. While the political and military leaders of the front were engaged in near civil war the working class was objectively turning independence into revolution. On his victory in September 1962, Ben Bella was forced to acknowledge that in many respects the Tripoli Programme had already been surpassed in actuality.

Many observers of and participants in the Algerian experience have located the failure of the revolution in the absence of an *avant-garde* capable of creating a theory and unifying this with the actions of the working class in a revolutionary praxis. The structure, function, and policies of the FLN in 1962 quite clearly defined it as other than an *avant-garde* party. After the factionalism of the summer it was patched up to represent more or less the same tendencies as before. In fact, at this point, no such *avant-garde* existed as a coherent force. Its elements were located in several centres: in the UGTA, in Boudiaf's PRS, the PCA, and in the FLN itself. Apart from the leaders of the UGTA, few of these potential elements had played any real part in the formation of the *comités de gestion*. The conditions of the war had in any case separated them from contact with the working class. Essentially they were split between those who saw that the front had become outmoded with independence and those who wished to use its national status as a vehicle. The banning of the PRS and the PCA and the defeat of the UGTA leadership in January 1963 effectively removed the immediate possibility of developing a legal political *avant-garde* outside the FLN. The establishment of the FLN as the single, official, authentic national party faced the *avant-garde* with the dilemma of opposition or entrism. Many, most notably the Harbi group, chose entrism.

The revolution at this point was incomplete. A sizeable proportion of the means of production had been seized by the workers but the state and party remained outside their control. This contradiction between the economic and the political manifested the underlying contradictions of the revolution. The *décrets de mars* and the *Charte d'Alger* were at one and the same time the measure of the success and failure of entrism. The *avant-garde* within the FLN could produce programmes and legislation but they were utterly incapable of carrying these through into practice. They did not control the party or the state and had no mass base among the working class or peasantry. As the counter-revolution gathered strength they were swept aside and only their texts remained as a memorial.

The public image of the Algerian revolution, created by the institution of *autogestion*, the *décrets de mars*, the *Charte d'Alger*, and a revolutionary foreign policy, masked the deeper realities of the unfinished nature of the class struggle. The Trotskyist-influenced *avant-garde's* attempt to create the revolutionary tripartism of councils, party, and state was meaningless as long as the party and state remained in the hands of a bureaucracy not only totally separated from the working class, but having different class origins. The lack of critical analysis of the modes of class formation stems, once again, from Fanonist-inspired simplifications. During the war, the internal class contradictions of the indigenous society were largely subsumed under the wider definitions of race and culture. To a large extent, the only social formations recognized as separate from the mass of Algerians were the remnants of the tribal–feudal leadership and the Francophile bourgeoisie. Through the identification of independence with revolution it followed theoretically that these feudal and bourgeois elements had been largely dispossessed and had become peripheral to Algerian social reality. The *Charte d'Alger* recognized the existence of social divisions within Algerian society but did not use the term class to characterize them. The bourgeoisie, the petit bourgeoisie and the bureaucracy are all defined as strata (*couches*) and not as classes.

This failure to identify the class characteristics, not only of the bourgeoisie but also of the new national bureaucracy, underlines the absolute necessity of rejecting the Manichaean vision of a global class struggle. It meant that the *avant-garde* within the FLN were unable to define the contradictions between the *comités de gestion* and the administration as part of an internal Algerian class struggle. In subordinating the *comités* to the administration, the *avant-garde* placed the whole revolution in jeopardy. The vision of the *avant-garde* was obscured by two analytical mystifications. Firstly they tended to accept the definition of the indigenous population as an undifferentiated mass in terms of its opposition to colonialism. Secondly, and more erroneously, they equated the seizure of the point of production with the seizure of the state. In their analysis, the fact that the means of production were largely in the hands of the workers prohibited the development of a national middle class. They were able to identify the emergence of a bureaucracy in Russia with interests opposed to the working class. But their answer to this problem lay in *autogestion* which, of itself, would remove the separation between the managers and the managed.

It is essential to the understanding of the failure of the Algerian revolution to realize that the bureaucracy acted as a class. It was sharply differentiated from the peasantry and the working class, and more narrowly from the classical bourgeoisie by the nature of its consciousness and by its relationship to the means of economic and political power. Although under *autogestion* the working class formally controlled the means of production, they did did not control the relations of production. The administration through their control of the mechanisms of finance and marketing were, in fact, able to determine the economic life of each enterprise. With the development of the *sociétés nationales* this control became total. The bureaucracy rapidly developed a hegemonic consciousness and within five years had carried through a successful counter-revolution.

The Algerian revolution was unfinished in the sense that the working class never seized the state and that the party was an appendage of this state. Not only did the entrist tactics of a section of the *avant-garde* fail to push the revolution any further than the workers had already objectively achieved in 1962; they also made the task of the counter-revolution immeasurably easier by handing the gains of the workers over to the state.

In respect of this analysis it is possible to identify three stages of class struggle in ex-colonial territories. The first, the struggle for national liberation, precedes the real development of class antagonisms. It is only after independence that the existence of contradictions over and above those of colonialism become explicit. The second is the conflict between the national bourgeoisie and the mass of the population ending in the seizure of the means of production. The third is the conflict between the working class (and peasantry) and the state and party bureaucracy, ending in the seizure of the state. The specific conditions of colonialism in Algeria made the near temporal elision of these first two stages possible: the third stage was not achieved. The seizure of the state does not depend on the existence of an *avant-garde*, either pursuing entrist tactics or as a party in its own right; it rests on the development of a hegemonic consciousness by the proletariat. Anything short of the full, conscious seizure of the mechanisms of the state and the economy by the proletariat leads to the development of a bureaucratic bourgeois élite within the state. In this situation both classic socialism and self-management can only represent both a recuperation of the class struggle and a mystifying obscuring of its very existence.

Before discussing the question of the development of a hegemonic consciousness and the role that *autogestion* may play in inhibiting this, the role of the economy in this process must be identified. In the Third World the economic situation of most countries and of their working class and peasantry is deeply antagonistic to the development of a full revolutionary consciousness and to its realization. The problem is situated around two major factors: the global economic dominance of neo-imperialism and the low level of material security of the mass of the population.

For Algeria, formal political independence did not bring economic independence from the metropolis. Not only was Algeria traditionally tied economically to France, but the relation was one of dependence. For most Third World countries, the Stalinist and Maoist solution to dependence on international capitalism remains a practical impossibility. They do not have either the manpower, the variety of mineral and agricultural resources, or the internal markets to attempt development in isolation. The imperialist expansion of Russia into Eastern and Central Europe after the Second World War and the subordination of the economies of this area is a clear measure of the difficulties of isolated development. At present the only possibility for the vast majority of underdeveloped countries is to maintain relations with international capitalism. It is to Western markets that their raw materials must be sent, and it is from the West that they must buy both industrial and consumer goods.

Clearly this relationship is an obstacle to the revolutionary development of the Third World but it is an error to suppose that it necessarily prevents the emergence of certain forms of socialism. Western capitalism will defend its direct holdings in ex-colonial territories and to a limited extent the nationalization of foreign-owned means of production is a blow against this form of capitalism. But the potency of such a step is severely reduced by the fact that it does not alter the overall economic relationship.

Algeria's nationalization of most important sectors of the economy aroused no serious opposition from any neo-imperialist power. The formation of the *sociétés nationales* in fact made relations between large international companies and the Algerian economy far simpler. Henri Alleg noted: 'The *sociétés nationales* are very suitable for dealing with foreign companies. In the recent period, as we have already seen, very many contracts have been signed with American, French and West German firms.'[2] Alleg goes on to enumerate the number of joint companies set up by the *sociétés nationales* and foreign companies. On one level it could be said that the *sociétés nationales* have prevented the large-scale penetration of the Algerian economy by Western capitalism. But the fact remains that substantial profits can still be made by foreign companies either through joint ventures or simple trading agreements with the *sociétés nationales*. American capital has no qualms about economic co-operation with Algeria; indeed the state pays a Chicago firm of consultants one million dollars a year to study the re-organization of the socialist sector.

Similarly, efforts at trade diversification are at best a simplistic view of the relationship with neo-imperialism. Algeria has attempted to break the near monopoly of trade with France and has succeeded in lowering the volume of trade, in both directions, from around 70 per cent to between 50 and 60 per cent. However, the bulk of this diversification has been towards France's other Common Market partners. The signing of contracts with Russia and East European countries has meant a rise in trade volume from almost nothing to five per cent. The logic of this move was expressed by the Algerian Minister of Trade when he announced: 'In fact these agreements are in the tradition of the Soviet government's and Soviet people's firm support for the strengthening of economic independence and the struggle against colonialism in all its forms and against imperialism.'[3] Basically all that this represents is diversification from one form of dominance to another. Soviet aid is largely restricted to the development of particular products which are in short supply within her own economy. Diversification only reveals the continuing subordination of the ex-colonial economy. The idea of exploiting intra-capitalist contradictions can give marginally greater room for manoeuvre but leaves the basic nature of the economic relationship unchanged. Trade with the Russian bloc can be used as a bargaining counter but even this can only mean continued subordination to the needs of other economies.

The global dominance of neo-imperialism and the historical situation of the majority of the underdeveloped territories as part of this system create a series of problems. Given that most of such countries are orientated towards the production of raw materials rather than either capital or consumer goods, any attempt to lessen this subordinate position entails the development of a comprehensive industrial infra-structure. Apart from large political and economic units, such as Russia and China, such an attempt is economic lunacy. National economic self-sufficiency and the concept of the siege economy is deeply reactionary in terms of the international division of labour made possible by advanced technology. A possible solution to the dilemma has been seen to lie in the formation of more comprehensive trade blocs in competition with neo-imperialism. However, this meets with the obstacle that the economies of the potential members of such a bloc are not complementary.

The political effect of economic subordination is seen to entail neo-imperialist support for either a national entrepreneurial bourgeoisie or, in its absence, a bureaucratic bourgeois élite, whether in civil or military form. It does not necessarily mean opposition to forms of state ownership and control of the means of production where this does not conflict with the interests of advanced monopoly capitalism. In fact the relationship can act as a positive incentive to the development of such forms of economic organization. The national need to avoid blatant neo-imperialist exploitation makes the creation of a unified form of economic organization a positive necessity. Although cloaked in the language of socialism, the development of such forms is more likely to be an expression of nationalism. Politically and socially, this economic centralism accelerates the development of a heterogeneous coalition of petit bourgeois and bourgeois elements into a fully fledged class. Thus, in the absence of a successfully concluded revolution, any attempt to reduce global contradictions by creating unified forms of economic organization leads to the intensification of internal class contradictions.

Autogestion, as visualized by the *avant-garde* in Algeria, represented a revolutionary alternative to this process. Vesting control of the means of production and, after a carefully supervised period, of the state, with the workers was designed both to avoid the development of a hegemonic bureaucratic bourgeoisie and to create the conditions for economic independence. The error of the *avant-garde* was, as I have stressed, to misconstrue the nature of the revolution. By identifying the events of 1962–63 as a revolution, rather than as the partial and hesitant onset of one, they were led to simplify the class structures of Algerian society. They also failed to appreciate the true state of the consciousness of the working class. The institution of a unified and unifying politico-economic structure above the point of production played directly into the hands of a petit bourgeoisie and bourgeoisie already partially seated in that structure. Before it had really taken place the revolution was institutionalized and reified into a series of symbolic forms.

NOTES

[1] Herbert Marcuse, *One-dimensional man*, London, 1964.

[2] Henri Alleg, 'Algeria seven years after: socialism or capitalism?', *Marxism Today*, **14**, 3, 8 March 1970.

[3] *El moudjahid*, 30 December 1968.

The Nigerian power élite, 1952–65
SEGUN OSOBA

From Segun Osoba, 'The Nigerian "power élite", 1952–65: a study in some problems of modernisation', History Society of Nigeria 16th Annual Conference, Ibadan, 1970.

Purely for reasons of analytical neatness and conciseness I would classify the Nigerian power élite into two broad categories: the business élite and the technocrats. The *business élite* comprised mainly those self-employed Nigerian men of substance who were in commerce or industry and were closely identified with the governing parties in the region or in the centre, or both. The *technocrats* included those Nigerians with considerable academic and professional training–the diploma holders–who worked in the public and quasi-public services, the big foreign firms, or were in full or partial self-employment as lawyers, doctors, pharmacists, insurance brokers, accountants, and engineering consultants. The ranks of both categories have grown rapidly since 1952 primarily, it would seem, because of the way in which government patronage and government decision-making have been deliberately used to favour them and foster their growth.

Government patronage and the growth of a business élite

It is true, as some foreign writers on Nigeria have shown, that as a result of the chronic shortage of imported consumer goods, a number of small-scale industrial concerns owned by indigenous entrepreneurs sprang up during the Second World War. The indigenous industries were especially in the spheres of food processing, leather works, and textiles. Such writers have therefore proceeded to date the period of the accelerated growth of the Nigerian business élite from the Second World War years.[1] There are, however, a few snags about this interpretation. It might be argued that these new industrial enterprises might have strengthened the competitive capability of some indigenous businessmen in the sense that they had acquired new skills and captured part of the Nigerian market for finished and semi-finished goods earlier monopolized exclusively by foreign concerns. It is doubtful, however, whether the number of indigenous businessmen with substantial capital and their share in the country's economy rose substantially during the Second World War and in the immediate post-war years. For one thing, it would appear as if the limited gains made by the indigenous business entrepreneurs in capturing a microscopic share of the manufacturing industry was more than offset by the ruin of many indigenous businessmen who, in the pre-war years had thrived on the export–import trade which suffered decline and fluctuation during the war years.

Furthermore, once the war ended and the normal flow of trade in and out of the country was resumed, the big foreign firms did not have much difficulty in recapturing whatever they might have lost to the indigenous businessmen during the war. This is clearly borne out by the fact that several of these unsophisticated indigenous industries had to close down or continue to run at a loss because their crude products could not compete effectively with the cheaper and finer articles being imported into the country by the foreign firms. A further evidence that indigenous Nigerian business enterprise did not make any permanent gains in the Second World War years is revealed in the disastrous fate which befell most of the Nigerian-owned banks, described by a top Federal Government official as 'mushroom institutions with signboards across derelict windows,'[2] which sprang up in the late 1940s and early 1950s and collapsed as speedily and chaotically as they sprang up. Although there was a substantial element of dishonest speculative enterprise in the mushrooming and collapse of some of these banks, many of them were clearly inspired by the desire to break the monopoly of foreign banking institutions and thereby liberalize the award of credit facilities to indigenous businessmen so that the latter might be able to take advantage of the new business opportunities that accompanied the end of hostilities. Even some of the most honest and efficient of these banks collapsed primarily because of inadequate capital, the cut-throat competition from the two giant British monopoly banking institutions (notorious for their discriminatory attitude to indigenous entrepreneurs on the award of loans) and insufficient experience and technical knowhow in the management of complex banking transactions–all clearly indicative of the enduring weakness of the indigenous business community.[3]

Consequently, the year 1952 marked a significant turning point in the fortunes of the Nigerian business élite, which was not only well represented in the majority African governments established in that year, but continued to play an increasingly significant role in all subsequent Nigerian governments and in the major political parties controlling the governments. All the governing parties, committed to a 'free enterprise' economic system, used their growing control of fiscal policies in the regions and the centre to create conditions favourable to the evolution of a Nigerian capital-owning class, which was unlikely to show political ingratitude and disloyalty to its benefactors. In a study of the economic attitudes of Nigerian businessmen, based on data collected in Western Nigeria but representative of the country at large throughout our period, two economists, S. P. Schatz and S. I. Edokpayi, made the following observation which is fully corroborated by empirical evidence:

A fundamental feature of Nigerian economic policy is the effort to develop the economy by encouraging Nigerian private enterprise. To this end the Regional and Federal Governments have devised many programmes, such as tax relief of various kinds, technical and managerial advice, and assistance, industrial estates, government patronage, the provision of credit, and many others.[4]

This statement, however, does not mean that the various Nigerian governments were interested in the indiscriminate promotion of indigenous private enterprise in Nigeria. On the contrary, as these two authors clearly show, the allocation of government business-aids was used in an essentially discriminatory manner to favour businessmen prominent in the governing parties or to win over to the government side politically influential businessmen. The bulk of the surveyed businessmen apparently representing the politically inconsequential ones and amounting to roughly 76 per cent, either found it difficult to secure these aids (favouritism, ignorance of the procedure, bribery and corruption among officials, red tape, and lack of co-operation featuring prominently among their difficulties), or were completely unaware that such government aid programmes existed at all.[5] This evaluation is substantially corroborated by a political insider, S.G. Ikoku, who was leader of the Opposition in the Eastern Region of Nigeria and a leading member of the governing party in Western Nigeria. He claims that one of the ways by which a 'privileged group' of Nigerian entrepreneurs emerged was 'through patronage (loans, contracts, bank credits, etc.) of the various governments to which they have attached themselves'.[6]

The case of government contracts, for instance, clearly revealed that politically influential Nigerian businessmen were anxious to take full advantage of this new source of wealth, and to press the governments through their representatives in the various legislatures to increase their share of government contracts. The climate of opinion in the Federal House of Representatives from 1957 to 1962 clearly revealed the intensity of the struggle of the business élite and the growing inclination of the Federal Government to pacify them. The budget session of the Federal House of Representatives in March 1957 witnessed an attack of unprecedented virulence against government discrimination in the award of contracts in favour of Levantine businessmen *vis-à-vis* Nigerians, and against the sharp and shady business practices among the former. Representatives E. O. Omolodun (Action Group), L. P. Ojukwu (N.C.N.C.) pressed that government should exclude foreign firms from transport contracts. Chief S. L. Akintola (Leader of the Action Group Opposition) called for the award of more substantial civil construction contracts to indigenous contractors and on the basis of parity of conditions with their Levantine counterparts, while R. A. Fani-Kayode (A.G.) and Maitama Sule (N.P.C.) buttressed these demands by joining actively in the fiesta of denunciatory campaigns against the monopolistic activities of Syrian and Lebanese entrepreneurs in Nigeria.[7]

That the government itself was disturbed by these criticisms was reflected in the frantic effort made by the Minister of Works, Alhaji Muhammadu Inuwa Wada, to explain the government's position:

Contracts are divided into different categories starting from category A to category G. Category A is £500 to £3000 and then it goes to category G which is over £100000. We have now registered with the Federal Government 182 African contractors and 25 expatriate contractors. Of the 182 African contractors 100 are all registered in category A. The trouble is that the Federal Public Works Department happens not to get much work in category A...

Now, Sir, I want to give some rather interesting figures. In 1954–55 12 contracts were let to African contractors to a value of £138,600 and last year, Sir,–the year for which I claim some responsibility, 1956–57–31 contracts were awarded to African contractors, to a value of £440,782.[8]

There is clear evidence that this official explanation did not satisfy indigenous business interests within and without the Federal legislature. Consequently pressure continued to pile on the Federal Government to the point that the Minister of Works had to give the House of Representatives in April 1962 a comprehensive account of what the government had done in the past to help indigenous contractors. The minister proudly announced that no expatriate contractor was allowed to tender for contracts worth up to £50 000. Furthermore, he asserted, for contracts

between £50,000 and £100,000... Nigerian contractors are given preferential treatment. If they compete with expatriate contractors and the difference in the price of tender between the Nigerian contractor and the expatriate contractor does not exceed a certain percentage, the contract goes to the Nigerian contractor. The percentage there ranges from $2\frac{1}{2}$ to 5 per cent. It is only in the highest categories... above £100,000, that we feel we should allow everybody to compete without any preferential treatment.[9]

This statement by the Minister of Works was partly a recognition of the sharp increase between 1957 and 1962 in the capital resources available to indigenous contractors, and in their competitive capability vis-à-vis their expatriate counterparts. It was also meant to assure his audience of government's contribution to this growth and its determination to continue to advance the cause of indigenous contractors in the future.

As in the case of contracts, buying agent licences–issued by the marketing boards controlled by the various Nigerian governments to businessmen dealing in the large-scale purchase of the country's export primary commodities like cocoa, groundnuts, palm products, and cotton–were used by the governments to build up and further enrich a growing core of indigenous businessmen who would loyally support the governments and parties that made them. Before 1952 this highly lucrative business was almost entirely dominated by the major European and Levantine firms with indigenous businessmen operating merely as their sub-agents. But after 1952, under pressure from the Nigerian business community and business representatives in the Regional and Federal Governments, African enterpreneurs progressively displaced foreigners as licensed buying agents for the marketing boards. By the early 1960s all but a handful of foreign buying agents had lost their licences to Nigerians. Even in Northern Nigeria, which was naively considered the last bastion of colonialism in Nigeria, by 1962, 44 of the 65 licences awarded by the Groundnut Marketing Board went to indigenous Nigerian firms.[10] There is no doubt that buying agent licences, like government loans and contracts, were almost invariably awarded to trusted and loyal supporters of the various governments.

It should, however, be noted that the granting of government patronage to party supporters carried definite and compelling obligations: such beneficiaries were expected to contribute substantially to party funds, use their wealth and influence to mobilize support for their parties in their various localities, and maintain unflinching loyalty to party leadership. If any of them failed to conform to this standard of behaviour, then he was immediately stripped of all the government patronage he was enjoying. A classic case was that of one L. N. Obioha, a wealthy produce buying agent in Eastern Nigeria and a leading member of the NCNC, who joined K.O. Mbadiwe and other 'rebels' in an attempt to push Nnamdi Azikiwe out of the leadership of the NCNC and the Eastern Nigerian government in 1958. The *coup d'état* failed and as soon as Azikiwe had mended his fences and consolidated his position, one of the first major actions taken by his government was to withdraw Obioha's buying agent licence. The licence was not restored to him until he and Mbadiwe, having sued for peace, were ultimately reconciled with Azikiwe in 1961. In 1965 I held an illuminating interview with a young indigenous businessman of substance dealing in pharmaceutical products and operating as a major supplier of these products to government hospitals and clinics. Asked whether he felt that party political considerations generally interfered with government action in helping indigenous businessmen, he answered with what struck me as unusual frankness:

Political interference is inevitable, and antagonizing the government is a luxury which a big businessman in any capitalist community cannot enjoy without disastrous consequences to his own interests.

All the Nigerian governments also had the habit of giving sinecure posts with inflated remunerations to many of their supporters, thereby affording such men the unique opportunity of accumulating investment capital at public expense in a country where capital was generally a rare commodity. To create 'jobs for boys' (in the popular parlance) the government established a whole series of public corporations, most of which were running up huge deficits and contributing little or nothing to the growth of the national economy. It did not worry the authorities that most of the chairmen and board members appointed to manage these corporations were not equipped either by training or experience to understand and effectuate what they were expected to do. A good example of the worthlessness of many of these public corporations, and the irresponsibility and purely mercenary outlook of those administering them was provided by the Nigerian National Press, publishers of the pro-government newsheets, the *Morning Post* and the *Sunday Post*. In April 1962, T.O.S. Benson, the Federal Minister of Information, questioned by one NCNC Member in the House of Representatives about the salaries of the directors of the National Press (at a time when it was sustaining huge recurrent deficits), could only answer apologetically in a rigmarole:

The Council of Ministers decided that the Directors should be paid £600 per annum and the Chairman and Managing Director £3,000 plus £600 allowance, plus free house, electricity, water, and the use of official cars... Under Clause 71 of the Articles of Association of the Company, the Directors are empowered to determine their own remuneration and at a general meeting in December 1961, they decided to increase the rate to £1000 per annum. This was done without prior consultation with me.

At the present moment, consideration is being given to examining the affairs of the Press in all its ramifications.[11]

Again in 1964 Mr R. A. Njoku, then Federal Minister of Transport and directly responsible for the Nigerian Railway Corporation, provided incontrovertible evidence that the Nigerian political decision-makers viewed appointments to boards of public corporations mainly as booty to be shared among their most loyal ethnic and party supporters. Accused of nepotism in appointing his brother, Bernard Njoku, to the board of the Nigerian Railway Corporation, he countered with a defence which any public figure outside Nigeria could hardly have permitted himself to make:

> Mr Njoku (according to his Minister-brother) is not only a party stalwart, but also a prominent, influential and wealthy man... he was not only chairman of the Agbala branch, but also chairman of the Divisional Executive of the NCNC in Owerri Division. The NCNC national president's campaign teams during the 1953 and 1954 general elections were housed by Mr Njoku... Mr Bernard Njoku was also chairman of the Oratta District Council and chairman of the Oratta District Union, and while in Lagos was also president of the Owerri Division Union.[12]

The contribution of foreign firms to the growth of an indigenous business élite

One other major factor in the rapid growth of the business sector of the Nigerian power élite was not unrelated to the change in the balance of political power, progressively in favour of indigenous Nigerians, from 1952 on. This was the growing willingness of the big foreign business concerns based in Nigeria to operate on the basis of fruitful collaboration with influential Nigerian businessmen. With the approach of independence the foreign concerns quickly saw the futility of their traditional policy of crowding Nigerians out of the most lucrative areas of business in the country. They now came to recognize that to be able to remain in business after Nigeria's attainment of independence, they would need all the goodwill they could muster among the Nigerian political decision-makers who, theoretically, could legislate them out of existence or cramp their style of operation by executive action. The foreign business concerns showed considerable perspicacity in identifying the growing business ambitions and the desire for wealth among many members of the up-and-coming Nigerian power élite, and they astutely pandered to these ambitions by entering into business partnerships with many politically influential Nigerians, whose active support and protection they sought to obtain by giving them a share, albeit a minor share, of profits which they earlier monopolized. This growing collaboration between the major foreign and indigenous business entrepreneurs was manifested in various forms:

(i) In the 1950s and 1960s it became fashionable to appoint Nigerians as 'honorary directors of foreign companies operating in Nigeria in order to make use of their positions in politics to further the interests of these companies'.[13] Such Nigerians, being used for 'window-dressing', were interested only in drawing their fat unearned directors' fees. Furthermore, being ignorant of the devious way in which foreign monopoly capital operated, and lacking any serious commitment to the nation's welfare, these paper directors constituted ready tools in the hands of those who paid them. It was not without good reason that some political insiders were beginning to get disturbed about the inevitable deleterious consequences of such clever methods of buying over some Nigerian businessmen. For instance, Senator Nwafor Orizu, in a debate in the Nigerian Senate in March 1961, lamented:

> The trend now is to call every company a Nigerian company. That is, somebody is appointed from outside, a Nigerian, one foolish man, who is usually given a big salary, so that they can call the company Nigerian. He has nothing to do with the company.[14]

(ii) One other familiar way of securing the goodwill of politically influential Nigerian businessmen is for foreign firms to hire from them their personal houses at specially inflated rates of rent. It was not unusual for these indigenous landlords to demand and get three to five years' rents in advance–amounting to a substantial capital which could be immediately re-invested to generate a self-multiplying effect. These Nigerian businessmen, some of them holding down top posts in Government, also enriched themselves by hiring out or selling outright their personal buildings, erected with financial assistance by their foreign friends, to the same Government at exorbitant rates. For example, in a House of Representatives debate on 16 March 1957, Jaja Wachuku, citing a concrete example of such dishonest transactions warned the Government that 'this racket of hiring buildings at exhorbitant rents from private owners should stop'.[15] Three years later, Dr Chike Obi, in his fiery maiden speech in the House of Representatives, for which he lost his party's whip, exposed two scandalous deals in which the Federal Government bought two buildings in Lagos at clearly inflated prices. One of the buildings, the Lion Building which now houses the Lagos State headquarters of the Nigeria police was bought from a Federal Minister at the colossal sum of £120,000. The other was bought from another businessman at the forbidding price of £381,000.[16]

(iii) Whereas up to the early 1950s the two British banking houses in Nigeria showed extreme reluctance in granting credit facilities to indigenous Nigerian businessmen, and were in the habit of repatriating their surplus funds to their headquarters in London,[17] as independence approached they too came to learn that, unless they won the goodwill of politically influential Nigerian businessmen, they could not continue to operate profitably and in safety. Consequently, these British banks began to liberalize the terms on which they gave loans to such highly placed Nigerian entrepreneurs. For instance, the Late Chief S. O. Sonibare, a very influential member of the Action Group, had a lot to gain from the changed attitude of generosity adopted by these banks on the eve of independence. By Sonibare's own testimony in 1962, it was a loan of some £250000, obtained from one of the two giant British banks in Nigeria, that he used in establishing his fabulous housing estate (Soni Investment Properties Limited) at Ikeja on the outskirts of Lagos.[18]

(iv) In view of the growing confidence between the big foreign firms on the one hand and the Nigerian business élite on the other, the former became increasingly disposed to appoint Nigerian businessmen with good political credentials as contact men in their bid for government contracts, as sub-contractors in the execution of major government contracts and as representatives and agents for metropolitan-based companies. Business partnerships between foreign and indigenous entrepreneurs in such activities as insurance, distributive trades, and manufacturing industries also mushroomed during this period. These partnerships were no doubt financially profitable to the Nigerian businessmen who were content to operate as juniors to their foreign principals, but they also helped to legitimize the foreign companies and to entrench them in their commanding position in the Nigerian economy.

Decolonization and the emergence of the technocrats as a significant section of the power élite

Nigerian technocrats–administrative, managerial, and various kinds of professional cadres, some of whom were in key decision-making positions–also grew dramatically in number and capital-owning capacity since 1952 when representative government was introduced into Nigeria. Even though most of them, being in government employment, could not engage directly in politics, a whole series of political decisions, or lack of them, had far-reaching implications for the development of this section of the Nigerian power élite.

Perhaps the most crucial factor in the numerical growth of those I have designated 'technocrats' for lack of a more precise term, was the overwhelming emphasis placed on the expansion of educational facilities by all the Nigerian governments from 1952 onwards. For instance, the Action Group government of Western Nigeria had to amend drastically in 1952 the first budget which it inherited from colonial officials to provide £80000 for 200 post-secondary scholarships tenable in British and American universities and at the Ibadan University College, whereas the original colonial budget did not make provision for even one scholarship.[19] This was the pattern of action adopted by all the other governments in Nigeria, with the result that by 1958– a period of six years–infinitely more had been achieved in educational development than during the 40 years or more of effective colonial rule preceding 1952.[20] A further measure of the increased tempo of educational development during this period is the substantial growth in public spending on education. Compared with the miserly sum of £8,324,000, the record investment by the colonial government, spent on education 1951–52, all the Nigerian governments put together invested £27,348,000 on education in 1962–63.[21] Higher and professional education also got a new fillip especially in the 1960s after the release of the reports of two Federal Commissions of Inquiry–the Harbison and Ashby Commissions–into the country's manpower needs in the high-calibre and medium grades. Whereas the total enrolment of

Nigerian's only university institution, Ibadan University College, had grown from barely 200 in 1948 to 1,024 students in 1959, by 1963 four new universities were already in operation and total enrolment of students in all five universities had jumped to 5,148 (an increase of over 500 per cent within four years)[22] a preponderant proportion of whom could only subsist in the universities on one form of scholarship or the other.

A direct corollary of, sometimes an impetus to, the rapid expansion of educational facilities by the Nigerian political decision-makers was the policy of Nigerianization vigorously pursued in the late 1950s and the 1960s by the various Nigerian governments under the strong pressure of public opinion. In consequence, during the decade of almost scrambled Nigerianization, many young Nigerians who had taken advantage of the new educational opportunities at the higher and professional levels were skyrocketed almost overnight into high positions in the public and quasi-public services, commerce, and industry–positions which earlier on had been almost exclusively held by expatriate British personnel. What is more important, the new occupants of these 'European posts', as they were popularly known in the hey-day of the colonial administration, merely inherited salaries and allowances designed originally for expatriate officials and which, by the general standards of poverty in the country, were inflated, unrealistic, and potentially disruptive of social and economic equilibrium in the country. The specially advantageous position in which this colonial salary structure has put these top 'senior service' men is clearly revealed by the fact that they constitute an increasing proportion of those Nigerians capable of speculating in real estate, which is a major 'money-spinner' in the big urban centres, and of investing capital in different forms of commercial and industrial enterprises.

Moreover, because of the government's lack of vigilance on, and concern for, the welfare of the masses of the Nigerian people, it was possible for some indigenous Nigerian professionals to exploit the defenceless common people and thereby enrich themselves. The most culpable in this respect were the medical practitioners and lawyers. Even doctors, working in state hospitals and generously paid by any standard in the world, often engaged in private practice, using government drugs and part of their official working time in treating their private patients. Sometimes, these state-employed doctors would even deliberately divert patients who had reported in government hospitals for treatment to their own private clinics; and any patient who refused to conform might be denied the medical treatment which he badly needed. A debate in the Federal House of Representatives in April 1962, when a number of Members severely criticized the malpractices among state-employed doctors and asked that their conduct be probed, revealed that the Federal Government was not unaware of these malpractices, but was rather determined to continue condoning them on the basis of a perverted kind of pragmatism. Dr M. A. Majekodunmi, the Minister of Health and lately a government-employed medical practitioner himself, in reply to Members' criticism, said:

> We hear of allegations of favouritism, malpractices of several kinds, and the like. But I would like to remind Hon. Members that the men and women who man our medical services are human beings with human

weaknesses like any Member of this House. They are Nigerians like ourselves, with attributes and moral values neither greater nor less than those
possessed by any Nigerian. No one can claim any perfection for them,
but the truth is that our medical services are at present hopelessly inadequate and when a commodity of service is inadequate, there is bound to
build up around it a black market.[23]

Private practice among state-employed doctors, lawyers, engineers, sur-
veyors, accountants, etc., often yielded untaxed incomes in excess of their
official salaries and constituted an important instrument of capital formation
and a reliable passport into the ranks of the emerging moneyed class, who,
by virtue of their wealth, also came to have considerable influence with the
political decision makers.

IV. The role and behaviour pattern of the power élite in the Nigerian political system

There is a general consensus about the smallness of the power élite in Nigeria
and other African countries, but there is no doubt that the role played by the
Nigerian élite in the life of the country in the period under review was out
of all proportion to its numerical strength. The Western-educated élite held a
commanding position in the government of the country from the local government level (except, perhaps, in the Muslim emirates) right up to the federal
level. It played the dominant role in the sectors of the national economy not
directly controlled by foreign business interests, it virtually monopolized all
the key decision-making positions in the regional and federal bureaucracies,
and exerted an unusually strong influence on the value orientation of the
people at large.

One major trend in the development of the Nigerian power élite was the
increasing bourgeoisification of its members–their obsessive concern with
acquiring wealth and the power which it could bring. Many of them were
perceptive enough to realize that, in view of the general poverty in the country
and the scarcity of capital, good connections with governments and the parties
controlling them were indispensable if their ambitions for wealth were not
to remain mere pipe dreams. This realization would seem to me to be a crucial
factor in explaining the over-developed sense of politicking to be found
everywhere among the various categories of the Nigerian élite. The essentially
business attitude which most of the élite developed to the affairs of the nation
meant that most of them devoted all their thinking and scheming to how well
they could do for themselves from the material resources available to the
whole populace.

In a situation like this there was no room for creative intellectualism or
idealism in Nigerian politics. The barrenness of the Nigerian power élite in
terms of viable political ideas during the period under study is proverbial–the
general rule among its members being expediency and pragmatism.[24] Even
in the university communities, where one would expect to find the flowering
of ideas and idealism, the students understood their studentship only in
terms of the diplomas or 'meal tickets' that came at the end of it,[25] while

members of faculty were in the main obsessed with the politics of promotion, overseas trips, and speculating in business. Making allowance for possible exaggeration, there is a lot of truth in Stanislav Andreski's assertion that: 'The most striking fact even about the African university teachers is that they are politicians much more than intellectuals.'[26]

The only objective way to understand this behavioural factor among the Nigerian élite is not to see it as a genetical or congenital trait, but as the product of a conjunction of objective social realities. The business or profit orientation to public affairs and its practical manifestations like kleptocracy, collusion with exploitative foreign business concerns, and fragmentation of the political culture of the nation on ethno-linguistic lines, were essentially symptomatic of a process of class formation among a disparate group of people, who found themselves in a position of political and economic advantage and intended to make the most of their advantageous position. It could be very misleading, for instance, to regard the intensification of ethnic antagonism among factions of the Nigerian power élite since the 1950s as inevitable because of the multi-ethnic nature of the Nigerian polity. The truth is that ethnic differences were artificially generated and magnified by political leaders anxious to carve up for themselves exclusive spheres of political and economic influence. The leaders of the three major political parties, the NPC, NCNC, and Action Group–NNDP who controlled the regional governments and vied for the control of the federal government were primarily concerned with monopolizing the access to wealth and power which the governments provided and with keeping out potential or actual rivals. When, therefore, as was their wont they tended to equate their private interests with the objective interests of their nationality groups, all they were doing was to exploit the sentiments of their groups to promote their private interests.[27] This was an understandable, though ultimately disruptive, gimmick to resort to in a situation where far too many desperately ambitious élitist elements were engaged in a 'more or less continual conflict over [scarce] material and symbolic resources'.[28] The ethnic factions among the Nigerian power élite were so blinded by considerations of private gain to be derived from pursuing a policy of ethnic exclusiveness, that they failed to realize that if they pushed this policy to the point of paralysing the overall Nigerian political system–as was the case in the crucial years of 1962–67–they might stand to lose even their ethnic empire.

Kleptocracy or institutionalized robbery of the state by its very custodians– an all-pervading phenomenon in the Nigerian political system–was another understandable, though suicidal, instrument used by members of the power élite to satisfy their ambitions for personal wealth and power. There is no doubt that there were material and psychological considerations which goaded highly placed Nigerians to indulge in different forms of graft, bribery, peculation, and straightforward looting of the public treasury. Many members of the top power élite were first-generation educated and prosperous men, having emerged from very humble peasant or working-class stock and from the most grinding and dehumanizing poverty. Psychologically, therefore, having emerged from such terrible condition of poverty and squalor, they could not contemplate with equanimity the possibility, for themselves or their progenies, of returning to that original condition. In their narrowness of mind, they did not see that the only lasting cure for their psychopathic fear of poverty was a wide-ranging exercise in social engineering and economic planning that would banish poverty on a country-wide basis. Their solution, which is ultimately futile, was to enrich themselves by any and every means. Many members of the élite also had immediate material motives for resorting to kleptocracy: the financial demands on them from members of their extended families in form of the school fees of the children of indigent relatives, the housing, feeding, and even clothing of poor or invalid relations, along with, in the case of politicians, the exactions of local men of influence in their constituencies, all meant that many members of the élite, with the best intentions in the world, could not live in style on their legitimate income. And living in style was clearly one of the main distinguishing features of the top Nigerian élite! Palatial residential houses, flashy and imposing cars, gorgeous apparel, lavish funeral, wedding and child-naming ceremonies, and parties, were among the luxuries which the typical Nigerian 'big man' considered absolutely necessary for the maintenance of a public image befitting his importance.

In a poverty-ridden and economically backward country like Nigeria, there is a high degree of correlation between the legitimacy of a political régime and its ability to convince the populace by action that it has the capability and the will to deliver the material needs of the people. This correlation is even more critical in these days of an explosion in mass media of communication when there is a dangerous crisis of expectation among the people, when, as a result of their growing knowledge about the living conditions in other parts of the world, the gap between what the people want here and now and what is realizable, given the country's economic backwardness, is becoming more and more unbridgeable. Members of the Nigerian power élite even in such a desperate and potentially explosive situation would not be guided by considerations of enlightened self-interest, which should have persuaded them to adopt policies that would enhance their tenure in office. On the contrary, members of this élite were noted for their unresponsiveness to popular demands and their infallibility complex–treating all oppositional groups as traitors who must be eliminated. In the Northern Region the invariable answer to all opposition, including the ill-used non-Muslim and non-Hausa–Fulani minority elements, was ruthless coercion. In the Eastern and Western Regions the answer to the same kind of opposition was a combination of demagoguery and coercion. The tragedy of the Nigerian power élite and of the country arose primarily from the obsessive concern of the Nigerian political decision-makers with the illusion of personal wealth and power to the extent that they did not fully appreciate the obvious fact that real power in any polity belonged to those who controlled the high points of its economy. Because the crucial control of the Nigerian economy continued to reside in the hands of foreign business concerns, backed by their home governments, the Nigerian power élite robbed themselves and their country of power and initiative without which Nigeria could not be modernized rapidly and efficiently. A statement made by Waziri Ibrahim, the Minister of Economic Development in Balewa's Government, during an economic debate in the House of Representatives in November 1961, is symptomatic of the tragic powerlessness, lack of confidence and enterprise of the Nigerian power élite right up to January 1966. Admitting that economic planning in Nigeria had been aimed to meet the requirements of the 'imperialists', Waziri Ibrahim, in a fit of hopelessness and capitulation, warned that if the government embarked on any drastic economic changes, the 'imperialists'–would use their vast propaganda resources against it.

> If we want to really set about improving the economy of our country in a particular way, they may say that we are Communists. They can make our countrymen suspect our every move. If they do not succeed by false propaganda, by calling us all sorts of names, if they fail to make us unpopular in order to win their case, they can arrange assassination. They can do it by poison or by setting our own people against us. They can go to any extent without discrimination.[29]

The plea for constructive and fearless action which a Member of the House, R. A. Akinjide, made as a rejoinder to Waziri Ibrahim's statement and which was the only escape route left to a régime that felt its doom hanging heavily on its head, seemed to have been lost on the government and its henchmen. Akinjide concluded his appeal thus:

> It is not enough to say that these people are there; we fear assassination; they will call us communists. We should not be afraid of these names. Let them call us whatever they like. As long as we satisfy the wishes and the aspirations of the indigenes of this country, I am sure that the Government has nothing to fear.[30]

Consequently, the members of the Nigerian power élite having, through their inordinate personal ambitions, reduced themselves to mere puppets of the so-called 'imperialist' powers were, like petty criminals belonging to a powerful underworld gang, mortally afraid of brutal reprisals from the big bosses on their becoming 'good guys' and of coming to terms with their people, the tragic victims of the predatory activities of the gang members at home and abroad.[31] This, in a way, would account for the initial outburst of euphoria, among the Nigerian people, that attended the collapse of the civilian power élite in January 1966 and the accession of the military to power. But has the old-style power élite been eliminated in Nigeria or is it merely lying low waiting for the return of civilian rule in 1976? If it comes back to power in 1976 will it have been chastened or will it merely pick up the strands where it left them off? What chances have the military rulers got to create a new élite or at least a new élite mentality? These are no questions for the historians, but are eminently suitable for speculating upon by the student of society and the citizens of this country concerned with its future.

NOTES

[1] See (i) L. N. Pribyitkovsky, *Nigeria v Borbe za Nezavisimost*, Moscow, 1961, pp. 41–3 and (ii) V. Makarov, *Nigeria (Ekonomitchesky Otcherk)*, Moscow, 1962, p. 119.

[2] A. A. Ayida: 'A critical analysis of banking trends in Nigeria', *Conference proceedings of NISER*, Ibadan, December 1960, p. 30.

[3] It is significant that the only three indigenous banks which survived this disaster were the ones in which the majority-African governments of the post-1952 period injected substantial funds. In fact, all three of them—the African Continental Bank, the National Bank and Agbonmagbe Bank (now Wemabank)—are now publicly owned.

[4] S. P. Schatz and S. I. Edokpayi: 'Economic attitudes of Nigerian businessmen', *Nigerian Journal of Economic and Social Studies*, **4**, 3, 257, (November, 1962).

[5] *Ibid.* pp. 260–1.

[6] S. G. Ikoku, *Nigeria for Nigerians: a study of contemporary Nigerian politics from a socialist point of view*, Lagos, 1963, p. 31.

[7] See H.R.D. 4/3/57, 1957/58 Vol. I p. 102, H.R.D. 20/3/57, 1957/58 Vol. II pp. 563–73 and H.R.D. 21/3/57, 1957/58 Vol. II pp. 594–6.

[8] H.R.D. 21/3/57, 1957/58, Vol. II p. 600.

[9] H.R.D. 16/4/62, 1962/63, Vol. II Col. 1846.

[10] *West Africa*, 24 March 1962, p. 313.

[11] H.R.D., 17/4/62, 1962/63 Vol. II. col. 1860.

[12] *Sunday Times* (Lagos, 5 April 1964).

[13] S. G. Ikoku, op. cit. p. 31.

[14] Quoted by H. L. Bretton, *Power and stability in Nigeria: the politics of decolonisation*/New York, 1962 p. 191, note 12.

[15] H.R.D. 16/3/57, 1957/58, Vol. II p. 456.

[16] H.R.D. 6/4/60, 1960/61, Vol. II, col. 798.

[17] See (i) W. Okefie Uzoaga, 'Bank money in Nigeria, 1950–62', *Nigerian Journal of Economic and Social Studies*, **6**, 1, 92–3 (March, 1964); and (ii) H.M.A. Onitiri, 'The Central Bank of Nigeria and the problem of domestic monetary stability', *Conference Proceedings of NISER*, Ibadan, December 1958, p. 84.

[18] *Daily Times* (Lagos).

[19] Obafemi Awolowo, *AWO an autobiography*, Cambridge, 1960, p. 49.

[20] Whereas in 1947 the total attendance in primary schools all over Nigeria was 609 353, by 1958 it had risen to 2 545 336 (an increase of over 400 per cent), with the more conservative Northern region registering an increase of over 300 per cent. Similar phenomenal growth took place in secondary and teacher-training sectors. For instance overall attendance in secondary schools rose from 9,908 in 1947 to 84,998 in 1958–a rise of about 850 per cent–with the North registering an increase of 1600 per cent. Figures computed from Otonti Nduka, *Western education and the Nigerian cultural background*, Oxford University Press, Ibadan, 1964, pp 73, 74, & 127.

[21] Figures computed from (i) J. S. Coleman, *Nigeria, background to nationalism*, Berkeley, 1963, p. 126, table 13 and (ii) *Statistics of Education in Nigeria*, Lagos, 1963, Series 1, **III** p. 70.

[22] Ibid. p. 21.

[23] H.R.D., 9/4/62, 1962/63, Vol. II col. 1145. See also H.R.D. 10/4/62, 1962/63, Vol. II col. 1275 ff.

[24] See Olusegun Osoba, 'Ideological trends in the Nigerian national liberation movement and the problems of national identity, solidarity and motivation, 1934–65: A preliminary assessment', *Ibadan*, 27 pp. 26–38, (October 1969).

[25] See Richard L. Sklar, 'Political science and national integration–a radical approach', *Journal of Modern African Studies*, **5**, 1, 11, (1967) where he characterizes

the 'majority of African students today' as 'first and foremost job seekers who aspire to well-paid, high-status, materially comfortable occupations.'

[26] Stanislav Andreski, *The African predicament: A study in the pathology of modernisation,* London, 1969, p. 141.

[27] Richard L. Sklar, 'Contradictions in the Nigerian political system', *Journal of Modern African Studies*, **3**, 2, 203 (1965).

[28] Walter E. Stewart, 'The study of constitutional law in the countries of the Third World'; Paper presented at the Annual Conference of the Association of Nigerian Law Teachers held at the University of Ife, Ile-Ife in March 1969. Mimeographed, p. 6.

[29] H.R.D. 17/11/61, 1961/62 Vol. IV col. 2987.

[30] Ibid. cols. 3028–9.

[31] Some foreign writers, however, displaying either total ignorance of the objective power situation in Nigeria, or blind prejudice in favour of the pro-Western and pro-capitalist orientation of the Nigerian leaders in the post-indepence period, ignore this crucial factor of the role played in political decision-making in independent Nigeria by the degree of physical and psychological coercion which the Nigerian leaders believed could be brought to bear on them from outside.

See for example (i) D. G. Anglin, 'Nigeria: political non-alignment and economic alignment', *Journal of Modern African Studies*, **2**, 2, 263 (1964) where he asserts:

'. . . in most cases, Nigerian leaders pursue the policies they do because, rightly or wrongly, they happen to believe in them'; and

(ii) C.S. Philips, Jr. *The development of Nigerian foreign policy*, Northwestern University Press, 1964, p. 144, where he sermonizes:

'Nigeria is as independent as any other African State. To charge that it is not independent when the decision-makers are making the decisions they want to make (even though conservative) is to imply that there is only one true way for an ex-colony to act.'

The social roots and political nature of military régimes

ROGER MURRAY

From Roger Murray, 'Militarism in Africa', *New Left Review*, 38 (July–August 1966).

If we look back over the past three years or so, we find the African situation characterized by three dominant and inter-related motifs: the unresolved problem of the South; the failure to convert the OAU into an effective or combative anti-imperialist instrument; and the trajectory of accommodation pursued by a majority of individual states towards the West, behind the screen of non-alignment'[1] and 'African socialism'. The connection between these phenomena is obvious enough. Régimes which have shown a genuine desire or capacity to attack the complex of reactionary interests in Southern Africa, to give a left-wing and positive content to the OAU, or to reject the conventional pseudo-independence resulting from the historical forms of the decolonization process and inherited material and human weakness, have been isolated. They have been unable to command a majority or devise an effective common strategy. Since 1963 (the Addis Ababa meeting), the political content and function of 'African unity'–*as embodied in the* OAU–has been unmistakable.[2] Autonomous action by more militant and leftist régimes has been undermined and compromised by this general context, and by the inability of most of them to sustain the risks and costs of a principled line. Algeria has become more heavily involved in its 'co-operation' with France. The Guinean economy more or less rests upon dollar infusions. Ghana has experienced a severe fall in cocoa prices, with its attendant financial and exchange difficulties. Mali and Tanzania remain too impecunious to contemplate permanent rupture with their neighbours.

Despite this general rightward current however, most of the post-colonial successor régimes have been unable to stabilize themselves, morally or institutionally. They have on the contrary displayed a fragility, incompetence, lack of authority, and corruption which rendered their function as political holding companies for foreign capital a good deal less effective than might have been wished. The 'fringe' costs of investment and economic activity have risen noticeably. One can understand, therefore, a certain convergence of pressures–internal and external–for a change of régime, or at least a rotation of personnel, in a number of countries.

This inherent instability somewhat weakens the assumption that a militarization of politics would not occur simply because political confrontations and contradictions are far less sharp than in Latin America or South-East Asia. It is, of course, true that communist and Marxist forces are feeble in most of Africa and, further, that the direct threat to vital property and strategic interests is relatively weak–partly because Africa, in any *comparative setting*, is not of central and predominating concern to advanced capitalism. But two further considerations should be borne in mind.

The first is that many of the African régimes are so insecurely established that not much is involved in overthrowing them *once a viable alternative is found*. In O'Brien's words in the article already cited, 'a relatively small expenditure of diplomatic, intelligence, and financial effort can secure gratifying results in re-aligning the non-alignment of governments in poor and weak states'. Given the single-party trend in most African states, the only obvious candidate for substitution is the army.

Secondly, while Africa as a whole is not a zone of primary importance in the international capitalist economy or the strategy of western governments, nevertheless major aggregates of capital investment *are* involved in Southern Africa taken as a whole (Congo, Zambia, Rhodesia, South Africa). Classically colonial in its origins, capital in this region has begun to show signs of mutation on the basis of surplus generated, generally towards more modern manufacturing activity and towards a re-definition of its relationship with the state. This has produced, in South Africa above all, a highly unstable equilibrium and contradictions between various segments of capital, internal and external, which are at the heart of the impasse of the liberation movement. These must be analysed fully elsewhere. For our purpose, what is necessary to stress is that nationalist encroachment southwards at a time when the future political outcome in the area has not been clearly determined necessitates a *co-ordinated imperialist strategy to keep control of the situation* on the part of the governments and competing private interests involved. This strategy must articulate both spatially and temporarily; embracing all 'independent' Africa (the OAU pressure group) and preserving a definite length of time ('breathing-space') in which to arrive at satisfactory accommodations.

Social situation

The fragility of authority in contemporary tropical Africa is, of course, related to the fundamental but unbalanced transformations of economy and society catalysed by administratively supported capitalism. Partial and unfavourable integration into the world market system has detonated a radical re-structuring of society and the emergence of contradictions which in most of Africa are only now beginning to crystallize: demographic surge, imbalance between education and employment opportunities, rural depopulation, widening income differentials and social fissures, volatilization of culture values, etc. It is pointless to illustrate this: any document will reveal the salient features of the situation.[3]

Unsurprisingly, almost all African countries are experiencing disequilibria, setbacks and, sometimes, wholesale failure in the management of 'their' economies and in the production of growth. Few of them have prospects of a sufficiently rapid growth and structural transformation of their economies to be able to negotiate this social crisis without resort to coercion. Some appear to be irremediably unviable: Dahomey, a monocrop economy–palm-oil–entirely dependent on French price and credit terms: 64 per cent of the budget is absorbed by administrative costs. Ghana, Nigeria, Dahomey, Congo–Brazzaville, Congo–Leopoldville, Hte Volta, all in their different ways, exhibit the explosive *social* consequences of economic mismanagement, deterioration or gross unevenness in spread of benefits: soaring debt (Congo–Leopoldville, Dahomey, Ghana, Nigeria), stagnating production (Congo–Leopoldville, Hte Volta), exchange shortage culminating in breakdowns in supply of essential commodities and producer goods (Ghana), glaring polarization of wealth (Nigeria, Congo–Leopoldville), conspicuous misdirection of resources (e.g. TV in Hte Volta and Congo–Brazzaville, prestige building in Dahomey, Nigeria, Ghana), and so on.

In this general sharpening of social contradictions, the potentially 'revolutionary' moment occurs with the passage from a corporate reaction of threatened groups (unions, farmers, traders) to some generalized perception of social structure and political power, however inchoate. This moment occurred in Congo–Brazzaville, Dahomey, Hte Volta, where military intervention was provoked (and in the Nigerian General Strike of 1964, where it was not).

It is striking, however, that the three territories where mass demonstrations and confrontations took place are small and comparatively untransformed societies in which a relatively clear-cut social and political situation presents itself;[4] whereas larger, more diffuse or imbricated situations–less susceptible of being taken into consciousness and totalized (Congo–Leopoldville, Ghana)–were the scene of putsches and feeble popular mobilization.

Only in these extremely retarded countries, lacking any significant sources of domestic capital formation and precipitated into 'independence' despite themselves, does the simplistic model of an 'administrative bourgeoisie' correspond to social reality. Here there is a fairly simple correlation between wealth and membership of the 'political class'–which is parasitic, concentrated, and identifiable. Further, the labour market is highly sensitized and politicized in these conditions–where government is the dominant employer and where the principal differential factor in the income structure is access to *undeclared earnings* (bribes, commissions, considerations, and outright embezzlement).[5]

Thus, the trigger of discontent and collective action in Dahomey, Hte Volta, and the Central African Republic was the unequal incidence of a suddenly initiated 'austerity programme', whose defining characteristic was a freeze or reduction in wages, striking especially at middle and junior government employees. One must recognize the ambiguous social import of these union-led agitations in Ouagadougou or Cotonou. Of course unionized labour in Africa–notably employees in the *fonction publique*–is relatively privileged: anyone with an urban wage is in some sense 'privileged' *vis-à-vis* rural masses still largely inserted into a subsistence economy with rudimentary market development (or *vis-à-vis* the growing unemployed and floating urban population, for that matter). But to invoke this comparison as the basis for imposing 'austerity' wage measures unaccompanied by *structural transformation in economic and political relations* is demagogic and mystifying. One has only to scrutinize closely the political credentials of those African leaders who play upon worker–peasant oppositions to confirm this.

The 'egoistic' oppositional action of urban wage-workers (and peripheral semi-employed) can debouch on to a genuine critique of the power system of post-colonial clientage–if the confrontation is sufficiently *sharp* and *sustained* and if it is relayed by groups with a wider social vision and programme (revolutionary intellectuals). This has happened only in Congo–Brazzaville, where new political forces (especially, youth and students) came to the fore in the *six-month period* commencing with the agitation to remove Youlou. In Hte Volta, the Central African Republic, the function of 'l' armée au pouvoir' has been precisely to abort the possibility–admittedly dim–of a radicalization along similar lines. These régimes have combined demagogy (sacrifice of individuals, abandonment of wage reductions) with disciplinary measures (creation of military tribunals, curfews, illegalization of meetings and, in CAR, indefinite postponement of the MESAN Conference) to contain the situation and *to prevent a reproduction of the radicalization which took place in Congo-Brazzaville*. The external policies of the military groups which assumed power in these countries–renewed affirmation of support for OCAM, spectacular anti-Chinese measures–merely ratify what is already evident from a study of their internal characteristics.

Political analysis

The general historical and societal setting underlines the fragility of institutions and the precariousness of authority in the present phase of decolonization. From our point of view, there are three facets of this structural weakness which are starkly revealed by the current wave of military intervention.

(*a*) *Presidentialism*. The concentration of multiple powers in the presidency, especially in the case of an Executive President, simultaneously Head of State independent of the National Assembly, and Head (or Secretary General) of the dominant national party.[6] It is clear that such a constitutional and political régime can facilitate a single, economical knock-out blow by a military insurrectionary group: in such cases, too, the junta merely inherits and employs for its own purposes the battery of powers formerly held by the elective president–executive instruments, rule by ordinance and decree, control over security network, foreign policy, etc. Equally, the absence of any functioning collective responsibility expresses itself in rapid switches of allegiance on the part of state and party officials to the new régime. The 'revolution' is a mere displacement of loyalties.

(*b*) *Atrophy and stratification of the party and mass organizations*. The use of administrative and police measures to pre-empt autonomous political life, and bureaucratization of assimilated organizations. Notably, steady elimination of oppositional or critical forces (parties, unions, student associations, etc) through patronage, illegalization, blackmail, decapitation, police harassment, and so on (Congo–Brazzaville under Youlou, Dahomey under Maga, Gabon under M'ba); administratively initiated single-party projects, superimposed from the summit (Congo–Brazzaville, Dahomey during the civilian inter-regnum of the short-lived Apithy–Ahomedegbe tandem); conversion of a dominant single-party with an original mass base into an administrative arm through its absorption into the state (CPP, MESAN) with concomitant decline in organizational vitality; creation of bureaucratic national union federations or *centrales* (Hte Volta, Dahomey, Ghana) acting as state agencies for labour administration and failing to command the genuine enthusiasm and determination of the workers. It is noteworthy that, among the cases cited, where internal resistance to a militarily effected transfer of power *has* occurred, it has not been the party or mass organizations which have acted in defence of the preceding régime or personalities, but tribal confrères of the deposed leader (Congo–Brazzaville, Dahomey, and N. Nigeria), or autonomous presidential security forces (Ghana), and gendarmerie (Central African Republic).

Mass demobilization and decline in attachment to the heroes and charlatans of the independence struggle is not hard to understand today. In most countries there is economic stagnation, urban inflation, ossification of the party, monopolization of the fruits of independence by a politico-administrative and commercial–contractor élite, functioning as contemporary compradors. The whole (often nepotistic) social formation comes to be regarded with irony and cynicism. All institutions are suspect (thus, for example, the attitudes provoked by the Nigerian Census and the Western Regional Elections of 1965; or by the privilege of parliamentary immunity from legal proceedings in Dahomey–the immediate origin of the demonstrations in Porto Novo and Cotonou in 1963 following the murder of a Goun sub-prefect and provisional release of the accused, a deputy).

The military élite is to some extent insulated from these high-living social circuits by its separate institutional and social setting (camps). It is thus relatively immune from the popular condemnation of waste and excess. It may easily put itself forward, or be propelled forward, in these circumstances as the only valid national force capable of cleaning up and restoring lost dignity. Thus, such pleasant spectacles as that of a Colonel Bokassa, nephew of Barthelemy Boganda and cousin of David Dacko, proclaiming in his message to the people: 'the bourgeoisie is abolished', while simultaneously expelling the Chinese from the Republic.

(*c*) *Domination by the capital in political life.* The high concentration of modern economic and administrative amenities at a single point: the national capital. Perfectly comprehensible as a phenomenon of partial and uneven development, its political dimensions and implications are particularly relevant here. All major institutions and leading personnel of government (ministries, national assembly, presidency), HQs of party and mass organizations, the technical and communications infra-structure of the modern state

(radio station, official press, airport, etc) are located there; while the hinterland, in many cases, continues to be *administered* from the capital. The possibilities for *coup d'état* afforded by this situation are considerable, whether
or not the capital city is 'unrepresentative' of the country as a whole.

Thus, the relative technical ease with which the coups over the past six
months have been carried out: the whole affair was decided (in Central
African Republic, Ghana, etc) in the capital city, by relatively small numbers
of disciplined men converging on key points–presidency, airport, radio
station, ministerial residences. In cases where popular mobilization had
already occurred (Congo–Brazzaville, Dahomey, Hte Volta) here too the
salient feature is that the political outcome was in effect decided by the interplay between the *strategically located groups*–urban workers, functionaries,
youth, 'forces of law and order', etc, in the capital. As Malaparte observed,
insurrectional efficacity has no need of numbers nor is it to be confused with
revolutionary mobilization.[7]

Officers as a political force

With the exception of the mutinies at the level of sergeant-major (Tanganyika,
Togo), the decisive military group are the officers–either commanding officers
counting upon vertical discipline to support personal assumptions of power
(Congo–Leopoldville, Hte Volta, CAR) or slightly lower echelon officers
(majors and colonels) acting as executive agents for, or to put pressure upon,
the supreme command (Ghana, Nigeria).

What are the relevant political characteristics of African officer corps?
Three features may be mentioned.

Firstly, *organization*. The general organizational attributes of modern
armed forces are fairly familiar: centralized command, hierarchy, discipline,
etc.,[8] comparatively speaking, the army possesses a definite institutional
solidity; but one should not exaggerate the capacity of African armed forces
at present. In most African countries, the organizational model remains the
Second World War infantry battalion; and even where subsequent modernization has occurred, the infantry remains the core formation. Specialized
experience among the first generation of African officers was accordingly
limited. The first wave of promotions was frequently drawn from the education and pay services (e.g. Mobutu, Ankrah). In the French army, experience
was slightly more diversified: both Bokassa and Lamizana are 'Anciens
D'Indo', where they had commands. A second generation of officers is now
in process of formation–younger men, more highly educated, without non-
commissioned experience in the colonial armed forces and trained as more
specialist and technically qualified cadres (Nigeria, Congo–Leopoldville,
Dahomey, Congo–Brazzaville).

It is particularly important to emphasize the growing corporate linkages
of senior and middle African officers. Apart from the possession of an *independent communications network* (radio, etc), there has been expanding opportunity for contacts between officers from different countries. This is afforded
by the creation of various specialized institutions of defence co-ordination

at a regional level–the Defence Commission of the OAU, the Afro-Malagasy Defence Organization, the Equatorial Defence Council, etc; and by the development of significant bilateral treaty arrangements for exchange of military missions and information (e.g. Ethiopia–Kenya). This corporate intercommunication helps to cast light on the remarkable 'imitation effect', whereby one intervention apparently triggers off another.

Second, *training* and *equipment*. The main orientation in educational and technical formation in most post-colonial African states still leans heavily towards the former metropolitan country, or its close associates (France, Britain, Belgium, Israel, Canada, W. Germany). In 1964, there were nearly 3000 French officers and NCOs seconded or contracted to the armed forces in independent African states (mainly training and advisory personnel), while 1500 Africans were undergoing training in France. In the same year, there were around 600 British officers and NCOs on secondment, and over 700 Africans training in Britain.[9] Approximately, one-sixth of Ghana's officer corps was trained at Sandhurst. Some 445 Congolese officers and NCOs have been trained in Belgium.

It is fairly easy to see the meaning of Gutteridge's proposition that, 'the armies of new states tend to retain their colonial flavour, their foreign advisers and their affinity with Europe longer than do the civilian public services...' Largely, this is a matter of the costs involved.[10] Thus, bilateral military treaties concluded by a number of francophone African countries with France relieve them of substantial training expenditure; but in return they are committed to France as a source of military supplies.

In this general process of military training and expansion, the really sensitive sector is the *equipment and development of specialized units*. In practice, large masses of infantry have not been used in the *coups* which have taken place; rather, it has been certain highly-trained and trusted élite corps which have been deployed–crucially, para-commandos, armoured units, motorized military police, etc (e.g. Congo–Leopoldville, Central African Republic, Ghana, Senegal). Engineer units took over communications in Ghana and Nigeria. Apart from the former metropoles, the following countries have concerned themselves with furnishing parachute units, airwings, engineers' companies and similar specialized units: Israel (Congo–Leopoldville), W. Germany (Nigeria), USA (Ethiopia, Congo–Leopoldville, Mali), and Canada (Tanzania). The training of the Central African parachutists (who played a key role in deposing President Dacko) at Bouar was in the hands of none other than Colonel Bigeard.

Thirdly, *ideology*. The terms for a discussion of the ideological universe of African officers can hardly yet be said to exist. Two things are obvious, however: the 'apolitical' tradition of men like Soglo ('the Dahomean Army is not Praetorian') or Aguiyi-Ironsi ('the army supports the government that is') has not stood up to post-colonial realities or prevented them from assuming political office. In part, this is due to the pressure of younger officers, politically and ideologically more permeable and volatile; but it is primarily because of the structural liability of power. As suggested, the situation is such that the political role of the armed forces will be actualized, willy-nilly.

The second observation concerns the inchoateness and primitivism of military consciousness (though sometimes no greater than that betrayed by some civilian 'professionals' of African politics, it may be added). How far does the military group have a programme? How far does it comprehend the mechanisms which have precipitated the crisis of authority? What is its understanding of the economic and political situation? What does it mean by promises of 'austerity', 'centralization', removal of 'arbitrary power'? These questions cannot be unequivocally answered at this stage. What so far seems common to the new ruling group is:

(i) A militarization of politics–that is, an attempt to structure political life on military norms and organization. Examples are the 'unitarian' system promulgated in Nigeria, the role of police stations in Ghana, the elimination of representative forms and substitution of a command hierarchy in CAR, Hte Volta, etc, forcible transfers of population in Congo–Leopoldville.

(ii) Heavy reliance on the civil service–both for day-to-day administration and for composition of the various special commissions set up to investigate the activities of public corporations, local councils, etc, to prepare revisions of institutional structures, etc. (e.g. Ghana, Nigeria, Dahomey). This has considerably strengthened the position of senior bureaucrats (principal and assistant-principal secretaries), and appears to reveal the pathetic programmatic weakness and susceptibility of the presiding military in major fields of decision: budget policy, investment code and commercial law, foreign relations, etc.

External pressures

Militarily, the present phase marks a changing equilibrium in Africa. First, 'colonial' forms of influence are definitely yielding to 'neo-colonial'. Bases are being wound up and are of declining (though not yet exhausted) importance to Western powers. Libya, Congo–Brazzaville and Ivory Coast have negotiated the withdrawal of British and French contingents; and a general process of regroupment and rationalization is under way. Notably, the large French military commitment is being drastically reduced: by a decision taken in July 1964, France's strategic presence will now be axed on three focal points–Dakar (Senegal), Fort-Lamy (Chad), and the Diego Suarez–Ivato complex (Malagasy). The phase-out has been sharp: in October 1964, the number of French troops was 35,000; in December 1965, 15,000; and by the end of 1966 will be 6,600. Reduction at this tempo has had disturbing side-effects: loss of military spending, discharge of colonial veterans (an important force in both CAR and Hte Volta, where *anciens combatants* number over 150,000). France still maintains its bilateral military treaties with eight African countries, but since the attempted *coup* in Gabon has refrained from open intervention in internal crisis situations, and seems unlikely to intervene again under similar circumstances. Apart from these French establishments, base facilities continue to be enjoyed by Belgium (which operates the Kamina airbase), the USA (Wheelus Field, Libya, and Debra Zeit and Kagnew communications centre, Ethiopia), and by the RAF in Libya,

Kenya, and Zambia, and the Royal Navy at Mombasa and Simonstown.

However, the truly contemporary modality of influence is clearly through the independent armed forces of the countries themselves, via expenditure on military aid and assistance, above all in the fields of training and equipment. This has been of prime importance in facilitating, for example, Mobutu's political promotion. Since 1961, the ANC has been systematically re-organized, first by the United Nations, whose military command (represented by the Moroccan General, Kettani) initiated both infantry retraining and creation of specialized units (armoured squadron, paratroops); and after 1963, by Belgium ('Opération Survie') and, increasingly, the United States. In 1965, for instance, while Belgium provided around one million dollars' worth of assistance, the USA gave grant-aid worth four million dollars (fiscal year 1964–65) and maintained a military mission of 26 persons. Throughout, this re-organization has been locally controlled by Mobutu.[11] The process is by no means complete (as the poor showing of ANC units in 1964–65 demonstrated); but a number of efficient operational units now exist.

Threatened interruption of the military re-training and build-up by Kasavubu, Kimba, and Nendaka (security chief, long involved in tense rivalry with military intelligence organization) was one of the causes of the November *coup*.

A second dimension of the situation is the growth of United States military expenditure and activity in the continent. One should not exaggerate this. It has been pointed out that, 'whereas ten per cent of America's general economic assistance is allocated to Africa, the percentage of her total military assistance programme directed there is only two per cent';[12] and it is of course true that compared with S. Vietnam, S. Korea, Taiwan, Turkey, Iran, etc., American military credits to African countries are trivial. Nevertheless, US expenditure has been increasing considerably since 1960 and is now not far short of the 40 million dollars spent annually by France. But American expenditure is far more highly concentrated than French, which is diffused throughout the francophone zone (though of course with greater fall-out to the three 'strategic' foci). We have already mentioned that American military aid to the Congo–Leopoldville quadrupled that of Belgium in 1964–65. The other outstanding beneficiaries are the 'historic' entities of Liberia and Ethiopia–the latter being quite in a class of its own. Between 1953–65, Ethiopia received over 80 million dollars of American grant-aid: more than all other African countries combined. In 1965–66, the American Military Assistance team to Ethiopia was 108-strong.

This selection is highly significant. Ethiopia and Congo–Leopoldville at present possess the largest (both in the region 30–35000), and potentially dominsting, armed forces in sub-Saharan Africa. Both are building up with new equipment, and are modernizing their military structures.

The total of American military personnel serving in Military Assistance and Aid Groups in Africa is around 250. A growing number of African officers are finding their way to the Staff School at Fort Leavenworth, Kansas. In a number of countries (e.g. Ethiopia, Senegal) the activity of the advisory groups clearly goes beyond traditional understanding of military objectives into the realm of the civic and social 'action' espoused by advocates of 'counter-insurgency' and military contributions to 'nation-building'.[13]

Congenital susceptibility to imperialist pressure stems, however, from the structural subordination of the under-developed, post-colonial regions within the world market system. Paucity of domestic capital formation, dependence on trade for budgetary revenue, absence of effective control over commodity prices, shortage of exchange, leave these countries wide open to externally catalysed political crisis. Here again, the United States as capitalist world-centre is playing a leading role through adoption of government policies which are subsequently mediated through the 'impersonal' mechanisms of international finance and commodity markets. There can be no doubt that a brutal hardening in US methods has occurred since the murder of Kennedy, expressing itself primarily in a clear determination to eliminate unreliable interposed agencies (the European colonial powers, flirting dangerously with new projects for the old continent).

This advance of US positions does not always require much in the way of direct 'contact' (primitive suborning) with local personalities by American diplomatic and para-diplomatic personnel (though in some cases of course it does–witness the activities of the 607 functionaries attached to the US Embassy at Leopoldville–Kinshasa). But in any event, the trend set in motion by US economic decisions is unmistakable. The case of Ghana is illustrative. Following Kaiser's large and profitable investment in the combined Volta dam and aluminium smelter (a project which had Kennedy's active support), a squeeze was put on the Ghana economy. Cocoa prices were falling very severely (from £352 a ton in 1957–58 to around £100 a ton in 1965), and shortage of foreign exchange would clearly jeopardize the well-advanced schemes for structural transformation of the economy towards state-controlled industrialization. Yet under Johnson, the US government took a consistently destructive line: it withheld investment and credit guarantees from potential investors, brought pressure to bear upon existing major furnishers of credit to the Ghana economy (UAC) to cut off, and negated applications for loans made by Ghana to American-dominated financial institutions (International Bank, IMF) and to the US direct (AID). Much play was made with the insolvency of many of Ghana's state corporations (the parallel condition of Nigerian public corporations received far less publicity), and with the verbal militancy of utterances by some CPP and Government figures. This aggravation of Ghana's economic difficulties provided a congenial context for military counter-revolution. This achieved, Ghana's demands for new loans as well as waivers on existing repayment were sympathetically and expeditiously considered by the IMF and the consortium of western creditors. The *political* objective of the State Department had been attained.

It is unnecessary to posit that a foreign government or agency is 'behind' every *coup* which occurs (in the sense of being privy to, encouraging, or subsidizing the conspiracy). It seems clear from the British reaction to the military takeovers in Nigeria and Ghana–Wilson's instruction to George Wigg to 'shake up' the intelligence services–that the appropriate sections in the British embassies in Lagos and Accra were trailing badly behind events or failing to evaluate correctly the information at their disposal. Similarly, there is no evidence that France was actively involved in the Dahomey, Central African

Republic and Hte Volta changes of régime. There is some evidence however of the intervention of Houphouet-Boigny in the Hte Volta–little more than a labour colony for the Ivory Coast plantocracy–by telephone call to recommend Yameogo to step down in favour of the extremely unrevolutionary Colonel Lamizana. There is nothing surprising in this: the shadow-play of neo-colonial politics is not merely performed, but also improvised, locally. In some cases, evidently, (e.g. the Congo) the 'intelligence' component in the events is rather considerable. But in any event, a few swift reassuring gestures–an address to the local Chamber of Commerce, ritual expulsion or denunciation of the Chinese, affirmation of a right-wing 'non-alignment' policy, etc.–will quickly convince Western governments, excluded from the actual machinery of the military plot by the technical need for clandestinity, that all is well.

With this general framework in which to situate the recent military interventions in sub-Saharan Africa a number of conclusions emerge.

General perspectives

Military interventions can be seen to have a dual function or possibility: either offering a political *alternative* (to civil war or internal oppression, economic collapse, anarchy, radicalization, left-wing advance, etc); or constituting a political *transition* (i.e. effecting a mere rotation of personnel or 'opening' a closed political situation). So far, however, only two interventions or applications of violence (very different in type) have opened the way to a revolutionary modification in political and social régimes; Congo–Brazzaville and Zanzibar. All the other cases confirm or announce adherence to a capitalist 'path of development'.

If we examine these interventions, what is striking is that–despite their original conjunctural variations or their technical and procedural differences–they converge towards an attempt to stabilize the situation for overseas capital and, in Nigeria, Congo–Leopoldville, and Ghana, for national capital also. The cases of Hte Volta, Central African Republic, and Dahomey may be quickly dealt with: poor countries where there was never much possibility that the military takeovers represent more than holding operations and reshuffling of personnel. (Despite General Soglo's ambitions, it is difficult to see any way in which he can hope to 'introduce a new style of politics in which the people will rally around a programme and not around personalities'.) The sense of the emphasis on economic development is quite clear.

The fact is that the politico-institutional structures of Congo–Leopoldville and the Nigerian Federation were incompatible with even minimal bourgeois rationality and efficiency, an impediment to contemporary forms of capitalist operation (as opposed to extractive enclaves). In Nigeria–a feudal-bureaucratic and political gang coalition whose domination was based on coercion and bribery; in the Congo–a permanent civil war situation, absence of effective civil authority, atrophy of production (outside the mining sector), and disaggregation of the internal market; in both, provincial autonomy and decentralization provided the legal–political framework for massive misuse of resources through local 'budgets' and economic agencies; in both, this state of affairs was increasingly felt as an impediment by local and foreign capitalists alike. Thus, the post-*coup* tendency towards centralization of powers, elimination or reduction of 'provinces' (with their attendant fiscal and economic attributes), and efforts to provide more propitious political conditions for capitalist exploitation and development: It has long been noted that Nigeria and the Congo–with their very considerable resources and potential internal markets–were by far the most significant economically of the independent African states.

The Ghanaian situation is more straightforwardly counter-revolutionary: it was not a case of political concentration and emphasis on increased agricultural production as a precondition of accumulation, but rather of re-converting on the basis of existing state accumulation. The *coup* has returned Ghana firmly into the capitalist orbit, and will doubtless encourage the re-formation of a powerful local bourgeoisie, especially in the commercial and distributive sectors, adventitious beneficiaries of prior-public policies and expenditure. 'Privatization' will proceed–it is already announced that nine of the state corporations are to be dismantled–and the whole long-term economic strategy of the CPP régime will be negated. In the immediate future, Ghana's economic policy will be effectively managed in the interests of the international condominium of creditors.

This fundamental and apparently unquestioned commitment of the military–police–civil service elements to a 'non-socialist path of development'[14] does not mean that there will not be certain collisions between the military leaderships and Western interests over the adjudication of spheres and profits between overseas and local capital. The case of the Congo is suggestive. Relations between Belgium and the Congolese régime have deteriorated rather rapidly since the initial honeymoon.[15] Sharp disputes have crystallized around the Congolese government portfolio, the statutes of SABENA and OTRACO, the legal siting of the major Belgian trusts operating in the Congo (important for both taxation and control of company policy), and Tshombe's cavortings in Brussels. These *contretemps* and some adjustments in favour of Congolese interests should not surprise or delude. Mobutu corresponds closely in fact to the type of the counter-revolutionary strong man with anti-imperialist coloration;[16] he is the exact antithesis of Tshombe, civilian and European to his marrow. Generals Ankrah and 'Johnny' Ironsi of course are made of feebler stuff.

The U.S.A.

The next noteworthy feature is the relative consolidation of US positions, as distinct from those of France, Belgium or Britain. (This may be confirmed by close examination of the whole pattern and direction of American investment trade with African countries–including the unliberated zones of Southern Africa.) For the moment, one indication must suffice.

Most of the new régimes have taken particular pains to win or reinforce American approval. Sinophobic pronouncements and actions provide the easiest and most vulgar form of international prostitution: what is interesting to observe is that this exhibition is designed to attract the American client rather than the British or French. Britain and more especially France maintain normal relations with China and are not concerned to align their former colonies on virulently anti-Chinese positions.

The principal local protagonist of vilification of China has been Ivory Coast president Houphouet-Boigny (although he is now being overtaken in this role by Kamuzu Banda). OCAM has provided the institutional setting for orchestrated denunciation of Chinese-inspired 'subversion' in Africa, and it is becoming apparent that it was not by chance that the Ivory Coast has chosen this way in which to express its 'independence' of France. Growing economic ties with the USA and W. Germany are the counterpoise to French military and economic disengagement in a number of francophone countries. Dahomey and the Central African Republic ruptured relations with China, and the representatives of Taiwan have opined that it is 'only a matter of time' before relations are established between Taipeh and Porto Novo; in the Hte Volta, there were no relations with China to be broken. For Ghana and Nigeria, too, the US is now the major economic factor to be reckoned with, given the urgent and crude financial needs of the new régimes, in pursuit of popularity. American penetration into the Congo (Rockefeller, etc) is such that one can assume that Mobutu, in his present dealings with Belgium, is playing the American card.

Domestic prospects and external support

The domestic prospects of the existing military régimes are directly linked to the external support they can obtain. The pattern of rule which is emerging is military–bureaucratic in type,[17] politically repressive, espousing conservative finance and free enterprise, culturally null. The formal homology between this pattern and the old colonial administration is striking: an irresponsible executive, feeble communication or consultation, departmental policy-making, proliferation of committees, sanctions against normal forms of political association.

How durable can all this prove? Since the general socio-economic and political (internal and international) conditions which facilitated intervention are likely to remain and indeed to aggravate, the military will depend heavily upon the complaisance of investors, donors and creditors if they are to avoid rapid and sharp increase in the dosage of violence by which they perpetuate their régimes. For the military 'rulers' are of course involved in a profound contradiction. If they take seriously their commitment to 'austerity' and retrenchment, they will inevitably attenuate their possible social and institutional supports. If they do not, economic and social tensions will merely worsen and they will be unable to fulfil their pledged historical function–to obtain more foreign investment and 'aid' for 'development'. Evidences of this dilemma are already accumulating.

Thus, the economic administrators and advisors of the new régimes in Ghana and Nigeria have hastened to conform to the 'orthodox' reactionary financial postulates of the IMF and IBRD: this has entailed abandonment of any original developmental strategy and a pathetic concentration on 'balancing' the budget. Casualties have been unavoidable. Current account spending has been pruned, especially in the fields of administrative and social welfare expenditure–i.e. the civil service (lower levels), education, health, and similar services. Half-completed schools have been abandoned, funds to hospitals and dispensaries cut back, and the axe hangs poised over the hordes of central, regional, and local government employees. Similarly, Mobutu's moves to reduce the number of 'provinces' (and their attendant parasitic bureaucracies) and to coerce urban populations back to the countryside are creating zones of social discontent. In the Hte Volta and CAR, on the other hand, no serious steps at all have been taken–beyond the creation of audit committees, and the abolition of polygamy (CAR).

The truth is that while the military may initially benefit from popular exhaustion and tacit or active support for the dismantling of sclerosed political institutions, it is unlikely to find a stable social–institutional base for its rule. It can be seen that clerical salariat, wage labour, students, and youth will gain no early benefits from military rule; and while commercial and farming bourgeoisie or senior professional and bureaucratic cadres (or even chiefs) may do so, this is a slender prop over the long term. No consistent mass base seems readily available given the policies to which the existing military leaderships are committed. Attempts to create *new political formations* to replace the parties as permanent institutionalized ratifications of the military régimes (as in Egypt) seem unlikely to meet with success. Much more likely is the development of *limited corporate forms of consultation* as in Dahomey, where the 'Comité de Renovation Nationale' on which military, regional, trade union, and youth interests are represented, serves the official purpose of 'guidance of government action and communication between Army and People'.

If military groupings try in these circumstances to pre-empt political life for any length of time, it is safe to predict the classic trajectory of internal degradation–*coup* counter-*coup*, assassination. This pattern is already discernible in the Congo–Leopoldville (and in Burundi), and the likelihood of such a historical sequence in Nigeria is obvious enough. Militarization of politics and politicization of the military will interact with one another. Divisions between generations and various military branches will concretize. Multiplication of intrigues and contacts will occur and a shifting kaleidoscopic round of military–civilian coalitions will preoccupy journalists and apparently constitute 'politics', until the whole system is contested by a disciplined revolutionary movement. One regularity will probably be visible: the rising curve of military expenditure, and the exclusion of the military from 'austerity' measures.

NOTES
[1] All too easily 'a reserve position in the international anti-communist strategy', as Conor Cruise O'Brien observed in his excellent article in the *New Statesman* (8 April 1966).
[2] To cite only the more glaring instance: the failure to respond effectively to the

Stanleyville intervention and the general impotence displayed over the Congo; the indiscipline and confusion over the sanctions policy and the methods of ending both secessionary and colonial rule in Rhodesia, which merely made embarrassingly public the weakness of the Organization–as strong as its most reactionary member. Again, exiled revolutionary and oppositional forces, committed to a responsible and consequent programme of political action against neo-colonial régimes have been muzzled by the 'syndicat des chefs d'Etat'; yet the Organization has quickly jumped to in affording recognition to new ruling groups which have simply imposed themselves by a *coup de force*.

[3] E.g. *The growth of the economy in Kenya*, 1954–62, Ministry of Finances and Planning, 1963; *The Report of the Morgan Committee on Wages and Salaries in Nigeria* (1964).

[4] Politics in countries such as Hte Volta or the Central African Republic (or Malawi) is still something of a family affair. The main actors in the Central African Republic, for example—the late President, Boganda, his successor Dacko, and the latter's successor, Colonel Bokassa—are all close family relatives: we might say they are members of a 'presidential lineage'.

[5] For some measure of the extent to which this had gone in the Central African Republic, for example, see the illuminating reports of Michel Legris in *Le Monde*, 5 January 1966; 'Esquisses centrafricaines'.

[6] This cumulation of powers has been described by a good number of writers. For an overall account, Jean Buchmann, *L'Afrique noire indépéndante*, Librairie Générale de Droit et de Jurisprudence, 1962.

[7] Curzio Malaparte, *La technique du coup d'état*, Grasset, 1931; see also D.J. Goodspeed, *The conspirators*, Macmillan, 1962. Two efforts to develop a 'theory' of the contemporary *coup* founded on empirical generalizations from several cases.

[8] See Finer, *The man on horseback*.

[9] M. J. V. Bell, *Army and nation in sub-Saharan Africa* (1965); and David Wood, *The armed forces of African states* (1966)–both published by the Institute of Strategic Studies, London.

[10] 'A useful guide to an understanding of the problem is that an infantry battalion organized and equipped on British colonial lines usually costs, in Commonwealth African countries, with the minor ancillary units necessary to its maintenance, from £1 million down to £600000 a year'. W. Gutteridge, *Military institutions and power in new states* Pall Mall, (1965).

[11] For some information on Mobutu's consolidation of power in the armed forces, see Crawford Young, *Politics in the Congo*, Princeton, 1965. Young omits to mention, however, the active support given by the CIA to this programme: see the *New York Times*, 27 April 1966.

[12] David Wood, *The armed forces of African states*, Inst. of Strategic Studies, 1966.

[13] For insight into this, see Charles Windle and T.R. Vallance, 'Optimizing military assistance training,' *World Politics* (October, 1962).

[14] There is no concrete evidence that the much mentioned younger 'radical' officers in Nigeria (Major Nzeogwu, etc.) are inspired by socialist ideas or by anything more than a vehement 'unitarian' consciousness, entirely in keeping with the aspirations of the Ibo bourgeoisie. They are in any case for the time being politically restricted. In the future, however, nationalist younger officers may be led by their experience towards left wing positions and a junction with the revolutionary fragments in the trade unions and the intelligentsia.

[15] As *Le Matin* of Antwerp put it, 'il faudrait un millier de Mobutu au Congo'

[16] See Lucien Rey, 'Persia in perspective–2', *New Left Review* 19.

[17] Given the present economic structure, administration and policies of these countries, it is confusing and inaccurate to speak of 'technocratic' direction.

The political strategy of guerrilla warfare
GERARD CHALIAND

From Gérard Chaliand, *Armed struggle in Africa*, Monthly Review Press, New York 1969.

There is no point in theorizing on the basis of a single experience and making of it a model having continent-wide, if not world-wide, validity; this would amount to underestimating specific conditions in individual countries. Nevertheless, some features revealed by an analysis of the struggle in Guinea seems to be a valid basis for a certain number of generalizations.

First of all, contrary to the theory of the *foco*, and above all contrary to the mechanical application of this theory[1] in a number of Latin American countries (Peru, 1964; Ecuador, 1962; Colombia, 1961; Paraguay, 1962; Argentina, 1964),[2] the PAIGC got underway only after a protracted phase of preparatory political work undertaken in view of special conditions obtaining in Guinea. Why?

It is not enough to say that support must come from the poor peasantry and the proletariat. It is still necessary to find out which are the most sensitized and easily mobilized sectors of the population, those having the strongest subjective and objective motivation to revolt. Experience has shown that it is not enough to assimilate the gist of revolutionary theory: beyond this, it is absolutely necessary to be able to determine the specific characteristics of the national realities in question. This is not the case in the leadership of many a revolutionary movement, inside and outside Africa.

Nor is it by any means an evident truth that the poor peasantry is spontaneously receptive or rapidly drawn to joining the ranks of the revolutionaries. There are blocks that retard the process. It is absolutely necessary in any given situation to find out what they are and what causes them, *before* having to overcome them.

Obviously, it is not a question of disputing the principle of armed struggle, which in many countries is the only possible way to change the existing social order. It is rather a matter of refining the technique of implantation as much as possible, of giving the struggle strong roots, which is the first phase of guerrilla war. Besides, at bottom the debate is not so much one of the pros and cons of implantation, but rather–the need for this being granted–of the most effective means of achieving it. The theory of the *foco* as systematized by the Cubans for the Latin American context has, among other merits, the advantage of bringing out into the open the political sclerosis of the many Latin

American Communist parties that are bogged down in legalism, electoralism–in a word, in reformism. This type of legalistic co-existence always turns out to benefit those who possess the instruments of power. The action of the Party, on the other hand–and sometimes its very survival–continue to depend on police and military repression or *coup d'états*.

Thus in Guinea armed struggle had been prepared for long before it began. This preparation consisted of reconnaissance in the field, together with political agitation and propaganda work. It is through this process that the PAIGC, forged between 1956 and 1959, tempered its steel between 1960 and 1962.

This usefulness of this political work in mobilizing the peasantry should not be overestimated. It is only the groundwork; it does not of itself win over the peasantry. From this standpoint, political preparation amounts to psychological mobilization, nothing more. It would be an error to think the contrary.[3]

However, without this preparation (and it can be made under arms) any guerrilla action runs the risk of being transformed into an isolated commando strike, whether launched from the other side of a frontier or from bases hidden in the mountains or in the forest. In either case the guerrillas are cut off from the people, whom they must avoid almost as carefully as the enemy; lacking political control of the villages, they have to beware of the agents the enemy has not failed to plant there. This, for example, is what has happened in Angola.

But the prime goal of this reconnoitering phase is to determine with precision which sectors, levels, etc., of this differentiated peasantry are the most conscious of existing oppression and therefore readily receptive to being mobilized against it. In other words, it is a matter of finding the tinder to strike the spark. This question requires the most meticulous attention and necessitates a real knowledge of specific local conditions. More often than not this is precisely what has been lacking.[4]

In 'Portuguese' Guinea, historical conditions have made the Animists the most easily mobilized part of the population. While engaged in the 'pacification' of the country at the turn of the present century, the Portuguese depended heavily on the Fulahs and re-inforced Muslim–Animist antagonisms by imposing Muslim chiefs on the Animists. They thereby succeeded in making the Muslim chiefs as a whole, and especially the Fulahs, a valuable auxiliary. The institution of chiefs naturally has deep roots, and it is not simple to tear away those who live under it.

Winning over a minority in order to make it an instrument of indirect domination is a classic historical phenomenon. On the other hand, the Portuguese invaders encountered stubborn resistance from the peoples of the Oïo forest, the Balantes, the Balantes-Manès–apparently less affected by colonialism–as well as the Pepels, who had formerly dealt in slaves with the Portuguese on a basis of strict equality, before they too were subjugated: all these were quickly mobilized for the armed struggle. It is first and foremost on these layers of the population, uninhibited by chiefs loyal to the Portuguese, that the PAIGC was able to depend, while at the same time steering clear of tribal problems and going on without hesitation to win over the

Mandjaks and the Mandingos and making a special effort to solve the Fulah problem.

At the same time, the PAIGC strove to unite the Cape Verdeans and the Guineans against Portuguese colonialism. The Cape Verdeans,[5] not being classified as 'natives', have often served as auxiliaries in the administration of other Portuguese colonies and have to a certain extent been instruments of indirect domination. But they also constitute (at least a large proportion of them) the stratum most conscious of colonial subjugation. And so the PAIGC has worked very hard to overcome any substantial divisions among these atomized groups that compose every colonialized society.

Naturally, there exists no single example of a national liberation struggle which has created absolute unanimity among the people. Even after seven years of war, the Algerian *harkis* still continued to fight against the FLN. Similarly, African mercenaries are found fighting on the Portuguese side. They do not form a distinct unit–there is no unity among African mercenaries–but are apportioned out in little groups in the colonial units as guides, interpreters, and soldiers. According to Portuguese deserters, their percentage is rather low.

The phase of primary mobilization enabled the PAIGC to determine, on the spot, where to concentrate its first efforts. In Africa the intellectuals who form the leadership core of a party all too often have little interest in the countryside–not that they fail to recognize its importance on paper; they simply do not have the taste for it personally and in fact feel definitively estranged from it. Too many parties in exile use up financial aid without being effective in the field, primarily because they are never to be found in the field. How are they to mobilize the peasants from whom they are so separated? And the struggle waged from a foreign exile offers them other advantages: far from being a renunciation, it is a means of social and financial advancement.[6]

Paralleling the problem of the psychological mobilization of the peasantry and of determining the sensitized sectors of the population, there is the problem of forming middle-rank cadres. Their number has generally been insufficient.

What is needed are cadres of middle rank from among the people, cadres who, once politically armed, can speak to the peasants in their own language, using arguments that move them and are a reflection of their day-to-day problems. The lack of such cadres is the tragedy of the great majority of abortive *focos* in Latin America.

Higher rank cadres generally, if not always, come from the lower middle class. Since the principal field of the struggle is the countryside, it is a good idea to have the middle-rank cadres come from there. It should be mentioned in this connection that it is important that the political education of these cadres be directly linked with their local reality and not be based on schematic textbook generalizations. For the most part, cadres sent to socialist countries for training–no matter to which one–receive a general theoretical education that needs thorough rethinking in the light of the realities at home before it can be put to use. It is up to the leadership to articulate theory in the light of practice. This is precisely what the PAIGC has been able to do, while at the same time itself training the maximum number of cadres. The training school for cadres organized by Amilcar Cabral at Conakry has been a prolific source of middle-rank cadres.[7] Mobilized by the agitation work being done in the countryside by already trained cadres, young people come for a political education adapted to their concrete problems, and having received it, go back into the *maquis* to carry on the job of agitation and mobilization.

The three features of the struggle we have just discussed are part of a single process and arise from the initial phase of guerrilla war–the phase of implantation, in which a liberation movement takes root among the people. This phase is difficult. The peasants, crushed by taxes and exploited though they may be, are still not in the position of having only their chains to lose. Repression, air-strikes, punitive expeditions ('sweeps', etc.) are bound to hurt them first. Obviously, the peasantry is going to be won over only by concrete achievements, such as abolition of the colonial tax and forced labour, or an agrarian reform carried out to meet local needs. But these acts by themselves are not decisive unless they are accompanied by tangible proof of the guerrillas' ability to fight against the colonial army and win. It is necessary to create an entirely new and favourable military situation if the peasants are to be drawn into genuine participation. Unless the guerrillas are capable of creating the conditions for the local defeat of the enemy, and, at least initially, of furnishing the peasants some degree of protection, the rebels will not have a following. The guerrillas must, in short, supply tangible proof that they are at least as powerful as the colonial army.

And so the phase of military implantation–once the preparatory political work has been completed–must be particularly dynamic: it should in fact be achieved in a lightning stroke, which naturally implies that while the political groundwork is being laid, specialized guerrilla commandos have been organized and trained. This, too, was done by the PAIGC.

The second phase of guerrilla war, that of its development, implies a considerable effort from the political standpoint alone. Gradually controlling greater and greater areas, more and more people, a liberation movement is faced with the necessity of doing a regular job of political indoctrination among the peasantry, so as to draw it fully into the struggle and raise the general level of political awareness. The best method seems to be to give maximum encouragement to the villagers' own organization of their villages, under flexible Party control. In our opinion, this work requires political commissars. If such officers are considered useless under the *foco* theory,[8] this stems from the fact that the *foco* rebel army consists solely of cadres from the urban petty bourgeoisie. This is not the case in Africa, it was not the case in China yesterday, nor is it the case today in South Vietnam.

Experience seems to show that a great deal of attention must be focused on preventing the guerrillas–at least a certain section of them–from becoming detached from the peasantry. Is the mere fact of having started the struggle on the behalf and in the name of the masses a guarantee against losing touch with them? Tribal and patriarchal structures in Africa create a tendency to accept unquestioningly the authority of the local leader. There is thus a tremendous temptation for certain local Party chiefs to display authoritarian tendencies when they have been given too much independence and not enough

Party supervision. The excessive independence allowed during the first year of the struggle in Guinea had already produced a few petty tyrants by the the time the Party Congress held in the *maquis* in February 1964 was obliged to get rid of them.

Naturally, there is no such thing as a dichotomy between the party and the guerrilla army. The guerrilla army is the party in arms. But care must be taken to maintain the closest possible symbiosis between army and people. There must be continuous interaction between leadership, cadres, guerrillas, and peasants through information, explanation, dialogue, and the exchange of criticism.

It is up to the leadership to insure the proper working of this process. There is no need to emphasize the fundamental importance of a unified leadership. Crisis at the top level of leadership is the beginning of a movement's decomposition. There is no point in agonizing over the role of the individual in history. An uncontested leader remains at the present time the safest way to insure the homogeneity of a party's leadership. This advantage is, to be sure, balanced by the difficulty of replacing him and by the fact that too often the solution both of complex and everyday problems is expected of him alone.

Despite the war and the discipline it implies, the right to criticism is the surest source of democracy: moreover, it permits the rapid correction of errors. Errors should be recognized and not hidden under the pretext that acknowledging them would help the enemy. What really helps the enemy is not so much the recognition of errors but the errors themselves. On a movement-wide scale, the fact of systematically masking errors, the refusal to let reality be known, ends in a 'bluff' disguised as psychological warfare. But whereas psychological warfare *accompanies* warfare, this kind of bluff becomes a substitute for warfare. A proof of the strength of the PAIGC can be seen in its willingness to display, through this book, its weaknesses together with its successes.

At the present time, the PAIGC has reached the second phase mentioned above. The revolutionary army is growing, with the village militias as an auxiliary. More than half the country has been liberated and the villages are politically organized. The peasants produce more rice than they did during the colonial occupation and they are feeding the combatants, furnishing them with information, and giving them their sons. The Party–absorbed though it is in waging the war–has sent four times as many children to school as the Portuguese did. In the south, people's stores have met the elementary needs of the population for goods it could not produce itself.

The Portuguese ground forces hardly ever leave their garrisons in the liberated regions. Since the summer of 1966, the PAIGC has successfully undertaken the destruction of isolated posts, the stoppage of all river traffic, and the liberation of the central region of Boe so as to link the two regions already under its control, and it has at the same time politically indoctrinated the newly liberated populations and assured the economic stability of these zones.

The PAIGC appears to be within reach of the highest point of the second, developmental phase.[9] It has passed from harassment to offensive action and to the destruction of isolated posts–which presupposes a relatively substantial concentration of material means. Will the PAIGC succeed, during the coming years, in moving into the final phase, the all-out, destructive offensive? Guerrilla warfare is in effect a transitory form of warfare; its rule is harassment. But to pass on to the destructive offensive, the rebels must be capable of striking the enemy in a decisive way at some given point. The Portuguese remain for the moment superior in numbers and in armament.

In the past 25 years, only three guerrilla movements–the Chinese, the Vietnamese, and the Cuban–have succeeded in achieving such results. It should be added that whereas in the neo-colonial context it is necessary to crush the enemy totally, in the colonial context the war of national liberation can, as in Algeria, culminate in independence through negotiation. If Portugal found itself obliged to go to the conference table, the military situation created by the Guinean guerrillas would permit them to negotiate from a position of strength.

The PAIGC bears a very heavy burden. Its future successes as well as its failures (in the context of independence as well as in the context of the struggle) will be extremely instructive for Africa, insofar as it has until now been able, through its struggle and the social goals that inspire it, to capture the rank of vanguard.

NOTES

[1] See A. Pumaruna, 'Révolution, insurrection, guérrillas au Pérou', *Partisans,* 31. [This article was published in the U.S. in *Treason,* **I**, 1, (July 1967).]

[2] Régis Debray, 'Le Castrisme: longue marche de l'Amérique latine,' *Les temps modernes,* January 1965. On the *foco* theory, see R. Debray, *Revolution in the revolution?,* Monthly Review Press, 1967. See also Henry Edmé, 'Révolution en Amérique latine?,' *Les temps modernes* (May 1966).

[3] 'In 1935 an army calling itself the Red Army arrived. It was in the countryside. The K.M.T. [Kuomintang] was in the towns. This Red Army made propaganda and told us: "The Red Army is good and we are going to divide up all the land and you won't have to pay taxes or rent to anyone any longer." It was in the month of February 1935 that I met communists for the first time... They came to us one night and told us: "We are propaganda makers for the Red Army and now you are to make a revolution." We replied: "All right, we will." But we didn't think they had any real power; they did not look as though they had and what could we poor farmers do? So we did nothing.

'But in March of that same year, they came back again. They called us all together for a meeting outdoors and told us to form a poor farmers' association and elect a leader...

'... To begin with, people were afraid of them and said that communists were murderers, but when they came here they were ordinary people and they always said: "Divide up the land and fight against landowners and despots." They talked a lot and held lots of meetings, and at the meetings we used to stand up and shout "Yes, yes!", but we did not really believe in them or that they had any real power.'
Jan Myrdal, *Report from a Chinese village,* New York, 1964, pp. 66–7.

[4] A fact which the Organization of Latin American Solidarity (OLAS) has re-cognized:

'A sociological investigation of anti-imperialist character is now underway in 20 Latin American countries. It is being carried out by the national committees taking part in the first conference of the Organization of Latin American Solidarity (OLAS).

'The questionnaire, covering six important topics, has been sent to progressive public figures, historians, sociologists, and others engaged in scholarly research, as well as to progressive organizations throughout Latin America. Several thousand persons in Cuba are presently engaged in this investigation, in which various organizations and institutions of the Revolutionary Government are participating under the guidance of the Communist Party.

'The objective of this OLAS project is to determine the actual situation in all countries involved as well as the degree and the forms of enemy penetration into Latin American society as a whole', *Prensa latina*, Bulletin No. 916, 5 March 1967.

A similar project was undertaken two years ago by the United States, with of course opposite ends in mind. The idea was, using investigations that can be characterized as 'sociological espionage' (Project Camelot in Chile, Simpatico in Colombia, etc.), to identify the discontented sectors and classes of the population and thus learn where to direct the greatest efforts to head off trouble.

[5] On this problem, see Dulce Almada, *Les Iles du Cap Vert*, PAIGC, 1962; and Gérard Chaliand, *Guinée et Cap Vert en lutte pour leur indépendance*.

[6] Here again we have the problem of the discipline and style of the party. And here again homage is due to PAIGC. Its foreign representatives have almost always been sober and hardworking militants who were seriously doing their job on a shoestring budget in such a way as to win the PAIGC the respect of militants in the countries where they have been assigned.

[7] A certain number of cadres have also been trained at the Université Ouvrière in Conakry.

[8] See *Revolution in the revolution? op. cit.* Similarly, according to the *foco* theory 'the rebel army is the nucleus of the future party'–which is highly improbable. The party, on the other hand, is very well able to form the core of the guerrilla army. It all depends, finally, on the nature of the party.

[9] At this level the important program arises of linking the rural struggle with the various forms of urban struggle. This is a problem of prime importance.

Tactical problems of the socialist option in Mali
MAJHEMOUT DIOP

From Majhemout Diop, *Histoire des classes sociales dans l'Afrique de l'ouest: 1, Le Mali,* Maspero, Paris 1971. (Translation © Heinemann Educational Books Ltd, 1974.)

One wonders what socialism meant in this situation. Was the choice inevitable? Was it dictated by entirely objective considerations? By class necessity?

Once these points are settled, another question arises: from the point of view here being examined (that of the class struggle) what were the chances of the socialist experiment succeeding?

To find an answer to these questions it is necessary to look back to the political situation in the Sudan* before Independence. There were then two political parties, the *Union Soudanoise–Rassemblement Democratique Africain* (US–RDA) and the *Parti Progressiste Soudanoise–Parti du Regroupement Africain* (PRS–PRA). These two opposed each other in the legislative elections of 8 March 1959. Below is a comparative table showing the social–professional status of the candidates in each list for the 4th constituency, which included the capital–in other words, the leaders of both parties.

Profession	US–RDA numbers	%	PRS–PRA numbers	%
Clerks and non-manual workers	17	89.4	17	89.4
Workers	—		—	
Farmers	—		—	
Traders	1	5.2	1	5.2
Others	1	5.2	1	5.2
Total	19	99.8	19	99.8

The percentages are exactly the same in each party: 90 per cent non-manual workers, 5 per cent traders, 5 per cent others and no farmers or labourers.

The question then arises: the occupational composition of the two lists being exactly the same, did the two parties represent merely a rivalry of personalities?

*i.e. the French Sudan, present-day Mali (eds).

Were they going to follow the same political line, since they represented the same social classes?

Ten years later, an answer is possible.

It is probable that if the PRS had come to power in Mali it would have pursued the same political line as the *Parti Populaire du Niger* (PPN–RDA) in Niger, that is to say more to the right, less radical, and less inclined to socialism. While in Niger, if the Sawaba–MSA* had remained in power its politics would have been little different from those of the US–RDA.

What can that mean, other than that it was not affiliation to the big federal organizations of the time (RDA, MSA, PRA) which determined political choices?

Then what was the cause of the different trends, towards liberalism in the one case and towards socialism in the other? What was the cause, in Mali, of the temporary defeat of the former and the victory–equally temporary–of latter?

There is a possible explanation.

A social class consisting of office-workers, teachers, doctors, and other non-manual workers, which had served its apprenticeship and been moulded under the colonial régime, was the only class capable of managing the social organizations and the state in most countries of Black Africa. And it took office everywhere when the colonial government withdrew.

However, this 'petty bourgeoisie', controlled by its most conscious elements, the intelligentsia, could not take the same political line everywhere. It split, in fact, into two factions, and one allied itself with the progressive forces and the other with the conservative. And what determined the victory of the one or the other was the harmony or connections between the traditionalists and the progressives within the 'nation'.

Here a classification becomes necessary. We can distinguish:

1. The conservative forces

These are conservative in the sense of being greatly attached to the traditional social order. They accept modernization only when it strengthens their position. They are bound to the colonial system in two ways, *politically* and *economically*, sometimes by one or the other, more often by both.

POLITICALLY

The traditional chiefs, all that remain of the old nobility, live mainly from their political posts, which have been left in their hands or granted to them. The modernization of the administration since Independence tends to make them redundant or at least powerless (in Senegal, Guinea, Upper Volta). They therefore oppose change and innovation.

ECONOMICALLY

The religious leaders (in Senegal) have no political posts or responsibilities. But they own land which they cultivate by traditional, outdated methods

---

*led by the radical Djibo Bakary, imprisoned by the ruling PPN after Independence (eds).

(voluntary work by Koranic students). So they fear the coming of the modern system of the paid agricultural worker.

The traditional traders (in Mali), like the religious leaders, wish to retain the archaic system of trading, and resist such modernization as the keeping of accounts, employment of salaried workers, proper shops, etc.,

2. The progressive forces

These are progressive in the sense that in both the towns and the rural areas they wish to make some sort of break with the past and at least to adopt modern methods of production. However, there are important differences between the various social classes and categories. From the point of view of their political leanings, they can be subdivided into those supporting capitalism, socialism, and those who are ambivalent.

PRO-CAPITALIST FORCES

Their activities fit into the capitalist system and so tend naturally towards capitalism. They are:

a) Planters. These are adapting modern standards or are inclined that way, and are engaged in single-crop production for export. They employ paid agricultural workers.

b) Haulage contractors, industrialists, businessmen, modern shopkeepers. Their production methods and business systems are modernized, and they are becoming increasingly capitalist.

AMBIVALENT FORCES

They do not seem to have any definite leanings, and are capable of violent swings in either direction. Moreover, some are modernized, others are still traditionalist, antiquated in their outlook.

The *modernized* are the intelligentsia, students, office-workers, and salaried staff. They are products of the new society, bound to modernism by their origins, their work and way of life. In this respect they are progressives. But having acquired advantages, they intend to increase them or at least to retain them. They are quite capable of making an ideological choice. And in theory there is no reason why they should not choose capitalism equally as well as socialism, both leading to progress by comparison with pre-colonial society. In either case, technocrats or bureaucrats, they could hardly lose.

The *traditionalists* are the peasants and farmers. On the one hand, as true representatives of pre-colonial society, they are imbued with archaic, conservative concepts. On the other hand, drawing their livelihood from new crops for industrial purposes, they have become part of the modern economy and they aspire to material improvements which will improve their production. They could therefore support the capitalists or the socialists, according to circumstances. But it should not be forgotten that peasant farming, such as it is here, leads more surely to capitalism.

SOCIALIST FORCES

The spread of socialism in the world and trade union activity in the world has resulted in impressing certain socialist ideas upon the working classes.

One can consider the workers—and these alone—as the only socialist forces. Brought into being by modern methods of production, and comparatively remote from the bush, they are to some extent open to, and approve of, revolutionary ideas. However, certain archaic ways of thought still persist and these sometimes cause the working classes to believe that revolution must be and can only be brought about–if at all possible–by others. They are thus led to adopt something of a wait-and-see attitude.

So much for the forces present in the political arena. Now let us return to the situation in Mali.

Here the two parties, PRS–PRA and US–RDA, were both controlled by the petty bourgeoisie, that is to say, the ambivalent, modernized forces, the intelligentsia and students, office-workers and salaried employees.

But the PRS was more alive to the problems of the conservative forces, the old-style traders and others, including some progressives tending towards capitalism. It follows therefore that the party should have been liberal in its politics. The US–RDA, on the other hand, being alive right from the start to the demands of the salaried workers, tended towards socialism.

Both parties, however, had direct links only with the salaried workers, through the urban social organizations such as trade unions, co-operatives and various groups. Neither had direct links with the country people. In Mali it was the traditional traders who, through their age-old connections with farming people and the traditional leaders in the villages, roused or at least interested the country people in the anti-colonial cause.

The misfortune of the US–RDA under the leadership of Modibo was to forget that it had no direct links with the country people; or at least, on becoming aware of the fact, not to have succeeded in establishing any links.

The error of the PRS in 1959 was to forget the workers, the trade union movement and their intense aspirations.

The fusion of the two parties later was therefore good and wise; and, although strengthening the controlling position of the intelligentsia, it re-created a correct balance.

But, as often happens when re-groupings take place, the ideology of one faction dominated all others, and the radicals increasingly imposed their views.

In the end, there was a complete break with the traditional traders and, as a result with the rural population.

As already noted, the intelligentsia, the governing class, had become indifferent to the mass of workers; and as a class it was too small and isolated to be able to govern the country much longer.

In fact, the whole question comes down to a matter of alliances between different social classes and categories. These alliances can be set out as follows:

FORCES PRESENT

Holding real power	C	{ Traditional tradespeople	}	Traditional
Reserve force		{ Farmers and peasants	} B	forces
Holding legal power	A	{ Intelligentsia	}	
Reserve forces		{ Office workers, clerks		Modern
		and salaried workers		forces

This shows a triple alliance which enabled a united front to appear. But there are essentially two alliances which have developed from a common struggle or common interests over a long period. These are the modern forces (A) and the traditional forces (C).

The third (B) is of a different nature, as it has not developed from a slow economic process. It is even an alliance between two forces which are antagonistic up to a point, the traditional and the modern. But it was made necessary politically by the struggle against colonialism, in other words by an immediate community of interests. So it will probably last as long as the community of interests remains. Such has been the case in the Ivory Coast, where the intelligentsia and the customary chiefs (who are often planters too) form an alliance of this B type. And in Senegal too, where the religious leaders (marabouts), who are big agricultural producers, have become associated with the intelligentsia.

In Guinea the B alliance is composed of the intelligentsia and the farmers. The C-type alliance is almost non-existent as the traditional chiefs have been practically eliminated.

In Mali the intelligentsia in power made the same choice as the intelligentsia in Guinea; and, as in Guinea, great efforts were made to 'conquer' the farmers and peasants. But, for reasons connected with pre-colonial and colonial times, these efforts failed to produce satisfactory results.

The alliances in the different countries can be summarized as follows.[1]

In the Ivory Coast

$$
D \left\{ \begin{array}{l} C \left\{ \begin{array}{l} \text{customary chiefs} \\ \text{farmers} \end{array} \right\} \\ A \left\{ \begin{array}{l} \text{planters} \\ \text{intelligentsia} \\ \text{office workers and others} \\ \text{workers} \end{array} \right. \end{array} \right\} B
$$

In Senegal

$$
D \left\{ \begin{array}{l} C \left\{ \begin{array}{l} \text{religious leaders} \\ \text{farmers} \end{array} \right\} \\ A \left\{ \begin{array}{l} \text{capitalists} \\ \text{intelligentsia} \\ \text{office workers and others} \\ \text{workers} \end{array} \right. \end{array} \right\} B \left. \begin{array}{l} \\ \\ \end{array} \right\} E
$$

In Guinea

customary chiefs (almost non-existent)

$$
A \left\{ \begin{array}{l} \text{farmers} \\ \text{intelligentsia} \\ \text{office workers and others} \\ \text{workers} \end{array} \right\} B
$$

As can be seen, in Guinea the B-type alliance is direct, uniting the governing intelligentsia with the farmers. Such a front has a better chance of lasting while no break occurs–although this is always possible–between A and B.

But it can also be seen that nowhere has a strategical alliance of workers and peasants taken place, not even where it was hoped to introduce socialism! Clearly, this type of alliance (worker–peasant) at the bottom, as opposed to an alliance at the top, represents lasting interests of communities with much in common, and looks beyond national liberation. The strategic aim of such an alliance was defined by Lenin: bourgeois democratic revolution or socialist revolution, according to the situation. Then he examined the tactical phases in each case and divided the social forces into three categories: forces revolutionary right to the end, unreliable revolutionary forces, and counter-revolutionary forces.

'The proletariat', wrote Lenin, 'must make the democratic revolution the whole way, bringing in the peasantry to crush the resistance of the autocracy and paralyse the uncertainty of the bourgeoisie. The proletariat must make the socialist revolution by bringing in the mass of the semi-proletarian elements of the population, in order to break the resistance of the bourgeoisie and paralyse the uncertainty of the peasantry and the petty bourgeoisie.'[2]

It would seem that no study of this kind has been made in Mali in particular, nor in Africa in general.

At the Congress held on 22 September 1960, almost a month after Independence, the Union Soudanois opted for the socialist road, in a situation that was difficult and complicated. But neither the *avant-garde* class nor the class enemy, nor the tactics, had been defined. Silence on these points was only to be expected, since at the time the class struggle was still being denied and the existence of classes was scarcely accepted.

Things were much the same in Guinea, except that there some slow, experimental progress towards socialist tenets had been made.

In many countries of Black Africa, therefore, a salaried class, the intelligentsia, had made use of other salaried people (office workers and employees) to seize power. The end of colonialism having been abrupt for various complicated reasons, the liaison of the intelligentsia with the rural masses could be made only through the intermediary traditional classes, who alone possessed the means. Thus the contribution of the farmers and allied classes was by weight of numbers, without necessarily going into action permanently. In short, they constituted a reserve force.

Consequently the traditional classes, who are able to arouse their interest in precise aims, if not to stir them up, emerged as the most influential social force.

This was certainly the case with the religious leaders in Senegal and the tradespeople in Mali, *who hold real power,* if not legal power. And when, in addition, these classes are endowed with vigour, like the Mali traders, they play a most important part.

In the pre-colonial period they endeavoured to gain complete power, and in Senegal they succeeded at Fouta and Ndakarou. They would apparently have succeeded in Mali too. They had very prominent positions in the old empires of West Africa. Later, the Djema at Timbuktu, the assembly of leading citizens, consisted largely of wealthy traders. If it had not been for French intervention, the régimes established by El Hadj Omar and Samory would have certainly taken the same direction.

When the intelligentsia is not the most influential force and yet refuses to govern through others, it is bound to enter into conflict with the forces which hold real power, if not legal power. In Mali it naturally followed that the intelligentsia, the governing body, came into conflict with the traders. It might have been possible to avoid the clash by a combination of the two forces, but that was far from easy...

The emergence of new powers in Africa has acted as a catalyst. Ten years of independence have done more to transform socio-professional groups into classes than three-quarters of a century could otherwise have done. And so the clash of class has become more open.

The governing intelligentsia is a bureaucratic caste with a strong dose of the petty-bourgeois mentality and all that is thereby implied of inconsistency, of hesitation, sudden retreats, and also of radicalism, leftist fumblings, and rashness.

The national democratic revolution–which is the only concern here–is constantly threatened by its originators, who speed up or slow down the historical process without taking into account the real facts of life.

As R. Ulyanovsky rightly said:

All anticipation, all acceleration of the revolution, all hasty proclamation of a change in the character of the class in power, of an immediate change in the hegemony of the proletariat, in the counter-revolutionary character of the national bourgeoisie in general, as well as any attempt to speed economic development by premature measures, or to apply arbitrary solutions to economic problems which are not yet mature, would be evidence of a tendency towards recklessness which could put at risk the whole progressive evolution of these countries. But just as much a risk exists in the degeneration of the bourgeois bureaucracy in power in a national democracy, in the loss of liaison with the workers, neglect of their social and national interests, underestimation of the party political role of the *avant-garde*, and in a willingness to rely exclusively on the officer corps, in a persecution of supporters of scientific socialism, and finally in speculation by some leaders of national democracy about divergencies within the Communist movement.[3]

Here in Mali, in this Africa said to have been decolonized in the 'sixties of the twentieth century, one should not (unless one accepts Cabral's notion of the suicide of the petty bourgeoisie as a class) ask for the impossible.[4]

NOTES

[1] This is simplified; to go into more detail would complicate things. For instance, there is the D-type alliance which is strong in the Ivory Coast, and the E-type which is gaining ground in Senegal.

[2] Lenin, 'Two tactics in the social revolution', *Complete Works*, **IX.**

[3] R. Ulyanovsky, *World Marxist Review* (Prague) 133 (September 1969).

[4] In his paper on the evolution of political ideology of African nationalism, L. Yablochkov wrote: 'In politically conscious circles, socialism is more often considered as a radical means of modernizing African society, that is to say first and foremost as a means of destruction of outmoded social and economic organization. The following question then arises: Can such ideas be adopted by a social class which is not interested in decisive changes probably resulting in wide modifications of its own situation?' *Report of the 2nd World Congress of Africanists*, p. 16.

Neo-colonialism, state capitalism, or revolution?

ARCHIE MAFEJE

From Archie Mafeje, 'The fallacy of "dual economies" revisited: a case for East, Central and Southern Africa' (duplicated), Institute of Social Studies, The Hague 1973.

The distinction between continuity and change is as elusive for the social scientist as is the distinction between immanent and manifest for the philosopher. 'Neo-colonialism' and 'revolution' are such terms. Yet in radical social science they have come to be used as antonyms. As a logical construct that makes perfect sense but, prescriptively and qualitatively, it carries certain disadvantages as shall be shown presently. Elsewhere we have argued that insofar as there is an objective contradiction between appropriation of surplus by international capitalism and the desire by underdeveloped nations to establish an independent base for internal appropriation and reproduction, there *is* a Third World. Otherwise we are unable to evaluate the historical significance of nationalist struggles and their success and we are, thus, liable to dogmatism and '*status ante*' reasoning. For that matter, the term 'neo-colonialism' is dangerous in its ambiguity. It suggests both change and continuity and the qualitative difference between the two is often lost in undue emphasis on the latter. While neo-colonialism can be rightly regarded as a revision of forms and methods of control to maintain the old dependency relations, it is equally important to bear in mind that it is *within the competence* of independent governments to counteract such manoeuvres. Wherefore, historically and qualitatively, a distinction must be made between colonialism, which was an unmitigated imposition, and neo-colonialism, which is a *contractual relationship* even if accompanied by very severe constraints. Independent governments can contract into or out of certain arrangements. In East and Central Africa we have the contrasting examples of Kenya and Tanzania, and Malawi and Zambia. Without imputing anything dramatic by these examples, they still provide a line of demarcation between a neo-colonialist and a more radical trend. As for revolution, that is a very big word and a few more things need to be said before we launch into a discussion on its prospects.

Even though neo-colonialism is seen as a continuation of a prior situation, experience has shown that the reverse could also occur. A formerly independent country, owing to the fragility of its economic structures, can easily been turned into a neo-colony by international finance-capital. America, a country which formally never had any colonies to speak of, through its imperialist economic penetration, has managed to create a number of neo-colonies for itself including Liberia and Ethiopia in Africa. Therefore, what is crucial here is not a colonial past but a *dependency social formation* which derives from basic structures which transcend the specifically colonial phase. That is why independence does not, *ipso facto,* imply a resolution of the contradiction between the capitalist mode of production and surplus appropriation at the centre and its negative dialectic at the periphery.

If there are three 'worlds', as we have asserted, then it need not be presumed that there are three ways of resolving the problem. In the present historical epoch there are *two* dominant modes of production, representing, theoretically, the universal contradiction between capital and labour and, that is, capitalism and socialism. But those who subscribe to this basic postulate, albeit while trying to avoid over-simplification, freely admit to the existence of an admixture of modes of production in underdeveloped countries. But as has been pointed out in Laclau's case, their basic problem is to say what this admixture amounts to. For writers such as Frank, who have been rightly criticized for over-simplification, it amounts to capitalism. The second problem is, irrespective of the genre to which the admixture belongs, why should not its existence be taken as *prima facie* evidence for the possible existence of other admixtures and, therefore, a third way to development? Once again we are treading on the treacherous ground between dogmatism and revisionism. It is often argued by social democrats that the existence of two opposing camps, capitalist and socialist, makes it possible for underdeveloped countries to leave their options open. As is shown by the affirmative chorus of 'non-alignment' or 'positive neutrality', probably this view is shared by the majority of leaders in underdeveloped countries. Is it opportunism or simply an illusion?

In a valiant effort to come to terms with some of the issues involved in the problematic of combined and uneven development, Samir Amin warns that:

> Modes of production... do not actually constitute historical categories, in the sense of occurring in a necessary sequence of time. On the other hand, social formations have a definite age, reckoned on the basis of the level of development of the productive forces. This is why it is absurd to draw any analogy between the same mode of production belonging to societies of different ages.

This would, conceivably, suggest a third possible route to development, depending on the social formations and the level of development of the productive forces. But then comes the more dogmatic point:

> It is necessary to emphasize that social formations are *concrete* structures, organized and characterized by a *dominant* mode of production which forms the apex of a complex set of subordinate modes. (ibid.)

The view expressed by Samir Amin that modes of production are mere 'abstractions', in contrast to social formations which are 'concrete', is very hard to accept if they, at the same time, 'organize and characterize' social formations. If by 'organize and characterize' is meant a *determinant* role then we have come full circle. While this might prove felicitous for the particular perspective we are developing, there are immediate complications which arise from Samir Amin's interpretation. Whereas his greater clarity on the question of social formations is an improvement on Laclau's position, his implicit association of the dominance of the capitalist system in Africa with the dominance of the capitalist mode of production *per se* detracts both from Laclau's valuable insight and from his own explanation for the existence of a distorted social formation in peripheral countries. It would seem then that in accepting Samir Amin's clarification on social formations, we must maintain Laclau's basic distinction on modes of production. As a logical development on that and in compliance with the historical circumstances of present-day underdeveloped countries, we must declare that there is *no third* route to development. If by second or first way to development is meant capitalism, then neither is there a second way as far as an historical logic can tell.

Historically, classical capitalism has been superseded by an international system of capitalist domination or imperialism which, in its wake, has brought about combined and uneven development. One of the implications has been the establishment of dependency relations whereby any attempt by an underdeveloped country (cf. Latin America) to emulate the capitalist model of development has opened the way to even greater ravages of the national economy by international finance-capital. This cannot be otherwise because, in the first instance, dependency implies inability to compete with patron countries and, in the second instance, patron status means a basic unwillingness to be equal. It is our submission that if the premise of inequality were to be surrendered by the developed countries, then imperialism would lose its meaning and opportunities for internal accumulation and progressive division of labour in dependent countries would be greatly enhanced. But then what would happen to the international market for capital? Supposing national governments in the exploiting world were prepared to make reparations by granting loans with no strings attached, would that bring to a halt the insatiable quest for *profits* by capital?[1] Here we touch on the central ganglion from which emanates both the external contradiction of the capitalist system and the internal contradiction of the capitalist mode of production itself. The question then is: Can any serious beginning towards development be made without its extirpation? It is apparent that advanced capitalism cannot be defeated on its own terms. It seems, therefore, that any country which tries to go against this logical deduction can only do so at the risk of accentuating internal underdevelopment and of exacerbating internal contradictions, which can only issue in violent repression by the comprador class in self-defence. Latin America is witness to this and some African countries such as the Ivory Coast, Kenya, Liberia, Sierra Leone, Gabon, and others might, over time, prove worthy contenders.

To disprove my theoretical pretensions, my critics will, no doubt, remember the case of Japan—a marvellous mixed blessing for the West. They might even be tempted to add to the list 'promising' examples such as Thailand, the Philippines, and South Korea. But then Japan is a perfect example for us, as it is neither an exception nor a contrary case to our argument.[2] Japan, having escaped colonial incorporation, never suffered underdevelopment or systematic distortion of its economic and social formations. On the contrary, whilst engaging intermittently in imperialist ventures in its own right else-where in Asia, it had full opportunities for internal accumulation and uni-form social division of labour. The Meiji Revolution in the 1880s was only an expression of an expanding internal accumulation, advancing labour differentiation and wages, and of the development of the internal market into all spheres of production, particularly agriculture. Happening at the end of the nineteenth and the beginning of the twentieth century as this did, for Japan the timing could not have been better. Genuine capitalist competition (as against modern monopoly) still obtained internationally and, above all, consolidation of market power in the hands of the leading capitalist countries had not yet become the rule. In her time, therefore, Japan was favoured by internal as well as external conditions which are not repeated anywhere else in present-day underdeveloped countries. It is only in that sense, and in no other, that Japan is an exception.[3] In the meantime the impact she has had on the international capitalist system can only be judged by the whinings of the older capitalist countries—Britain at first and America and the Common Market countries more recently.They have been forced to share *equally* with Japan what used to be their monopoly. This is not true of even the former British Dominions—Canada, Australia, South Africa, and New Zealand, which emerged more or less at the same time as Japan but had always enjoyed a white associate status and privileges.

Countries such as Thailand, the Philippines, and South Korea, which are often quoted as 'promising' examples in Asia, are not anything like Japan. Their apparent development has been a direct result of American policy in South East Asia. They are meant to be a counter-weight to communist count-ries in the area. The vast quantity of American 'aid' they have received since the Korean War could *not but have* made a dent in their economies. But the price has been increased dependence on America and diminished freedom to pursue independent internal policies. Therefore, in such cases the question of resolving the contradiction between the capitalist mode of production at the centre and its distorting social formations at the periphery becomes unrealizable and genuine development a receding goal. The creation of 'better off' underdeveloped states in carefully selected zones must be seen as a strategem best suited to serve the interests of the patron countries. Like the American 'non-communist belt' across South East Asia or the capitalist concentration on Kenya in East Africa, they act as bulwarks against 'com-munism'. Secondly, as has been pointed out by some writers such as Waller-stein, they forestall possible polarization between the 'have' and the 'have-not' nations within the capitalist system. In other words, they give a credi-bility to the capitalist model—a faith which is hardly justified by the historical experience of the last 25 years, or more in the case of Latin America. It is our contention, therefore, that the rise of many more possible Japans such as India, Mexico, or Brazil (to quote a few sleeping giants) would have negative implications for the first capitalist countries and imperialism in general.

State capitalism and revolution

In effect we have argued that in modern times the capitalist alternative is unfeasible because it leads directly to neo-colonialism or dependency and, therefore, ham-strung development. It makes it impossible to close the gap between capitalist appropriation and distorted social formations in under-developed countries. To straighten out their perverted social formations, the underdeveloped countries need to introduce a new social division of labour or a revision of production relations. But that cannot be achieved, *without* jettisoning the interests of foreign capital. Such a step is antithetical to the existing structural relations and, of necessity, provides the initial ground for their dissolution. It paves the way for a revolutionary transforma-tion. We see this as the only alternative to neo-colonialism or dependency. But that is more easily said than done. The question of *how* a revolutionary transformation can be implemented in an underdeveloped country still requires elucidation.

Revolution in general can mean any number of things. For our purposes we are going to focus on value and labour or their manifest forms, production relations and social formations. In economies such as the East African ones the cleavage between surplus appropriation by foreign capital and wages[4] as an index of internal differentiation of labour will have to be resolved. It can only be solved by dispensing with labour migrancy as a structural feature of the economy. The producers will have to be allowed to specialize wherever they are. In the present set-up they are unable to do so because neither the rural nor the urban sector affords them the necessary opportunities and secu-rity. That is a problem, not of income distribution as is often supposed, but rather of distribution of resources and discretionary power. Although gene-rally speaking access to land is not an acute problem in the area under consi-deration, access to land suitable for agricultural production under the present conditions of technological development among all producers is actually restricted.[5] Apart from the glaring inequalities in Southern Africa and Kenya, and in regions such as Buganda, Bukoba, Kilimanjaro, Rungwe, Iringa, Busoga, Bugisu, West Nile, and Ruwenzori, unequal distribution between richer and poorer producers is making headway; while in areas such as Burundi, Ruanda, and Kigezi pressure on the land has reached critical proportions. While that might not be detrimental from the point of view of production, as capitalists are quick to point out, structurally it is detrimental in a basically immobile, internationally dragooned economy. First, it creates a residual category of unemployed and *unemployable* individuals.

Second, as is shown by the rapacity and the corruption of the bigger farmers who normally dominate the co-operative movement, it hands over dis-cretionary power to those who have a vested interest in the present set-up. What is true of inter-regional inequalities is also true of intra-regional in-equalities. The labour-exporting regions are caught up in a vicious circle. Their lack of resources or inability to find an alternative way is not improved by labour exportation and importation of necessary goods i.e. they suffer progressive underdevelopment and are particularly vulnerable to the vicissi-tudes of unemployment.

Labour employment functions in direct relation to capital (physical and pecuniary). Control over capital is an infallible source of discretionary power. It is obvious that richer farmers and richer regions have what is denied to poorer producers and poorer regions alike, *viz.* the right to determine the allocation and utilization of capital on their own behalf. But, unhappily, in a structurally deformed economy such self-interest is incapable of bringing about any overall transformation of a system of which it is only a hand-maid. The incapacity, if not the underlying contradiction, is generally recognized by governments in underdeveloped countries and, hence, the universal acceptance of the principle of state intervention and a planned economy. Whether inspired by capitalist or socialist ideologies, such intervention aims at securing for the national government what we have referred to as discretionary power. It invariably involves reorganization of land use (land reform), if not its distribution and, at least, indicative planning by the government for the use of available capital resources. Willy-nilly, the national government becomes the greatest provider of capital and promoter of all kinds of development projects. Through foreign loans and national revenue, it becomes the biggest investor in the national economy. Irrespective of the intentions and the extent of government ownership in commerce and industry, such an involvement is in itself evidence of a categorical imperative in present-day underdeveloped economies. State capitalism is an unavoidable historical necessity in the circumstances of underdeveloped countries. In these countries it is only national governments that can protect and give to the economy the necessary boost. Without necessarily solving basic internal contradictions, they can eliminate the contradiction between distorted local social formations and distorting central capital by introducing a new social division of labour, whereby adequate employment opportunities and security are created for the now abused migrant workers in the rural economy itself which, contrary to prevailing dogmas, need not be dissociated from *industrialization.* Of necessity, all this would require greater access to resources, whether land or capital. But, in return, through expansive production and reproduction of both capital and skills, it would provide a better link forward with the urban industrial sector than has been the case hitherto.

Having denied the possibility of a capitalist transformation along classical lines in contemporary underdeveloped countries, we now seem to be giving primacy to state capitalism as a necessary stop-gap in the process of development. While it is fair to maintain a distinction, historically and operationally, between *laissez-faire* and state capitalism, it is absolutely necessary to recognize the inherently unstable or transient nature of the latter. In its early phase the state in underdeveloped countries, like the nationalism of which it is only a culmination, represents a united front of as yet ill-defined classes. To maintain its legitimacy, it has to act, and be seen as acting, on behalf of all the citizens. Sooner or later it falls a victim of rising but unfulfilled expectations. As all citizens are not equally placed, disillusionment among certain sections becomes rife and the government is called upon to make an unavoidable choice as to what class interests it is going to sponsor. More often than not the dice are cast in favour of the educated middle classes who, practically, control the instruments of government. If they win out in the ensuing conflict of interests, then state capitalism degenerates into a broker for private interests. As the functions of the political and bureaucratic élite and their usual discretionary consumption are not necessarily related to production in these countries and as whatever surplus appropriation there is depends on the maintenance of restrictive or unproductive social formations at the base, the system inevitably gets caught up in the same contradictions that state capitalism set out to obviate in the first place. Progressive and expansive capitalism once again becomes, logically and historically, an impossibility and consequently the economy is committed to indefinite semi-stagnation, as has been the case in the older underdeveloped countries.

The other alternative open to state capitalism is increasingly to intervene on behalf of the producing but underprivileged classes. Naturally, this would bring it into direct conflict with the middle classes and their foreign patrons, since it would alter radically existing opportunities for surplus appropriation—even though it would enhance opportunities for progressive social division of labour and quicker social reproduction. Secondly, its realization would be dependent on the amount of support the government commands among the peasants and the workers. This would presuppose a high level of political mobilization among the relevant classes by the leaders of the governing party. In this context it is important to note that it is not to be supposed that all sections of the middle class are incapable of transcending their class boundaries and engaging in radical or revolutionary political action. So far, even the more radical régimes in underdeveloped countries have been led by petty bourgeois elements. This pattern of development is, of course, not without its contradictions. For instance, whereas a fight against the middle classes will necesssrily involve a progressive diversion of national resources and assets away from them as a class to the nation as a whole, such a move does not in itself imply a similar transfer of discretionary power to the majority of the people nor, least of all, does it mean possession of requisite skills by the majority of the people to use it for the effective transformation of their society.

Underdeveloped countries are notorious for their low level of real capital among the general populace. In them industrial workers constitute an insignificant proportion of the population[6] and are, not too infrequently, inclined to be supportive of the urban social classes and their ideologies.[7] On the other hand, peasants who comprise the vast majority of the people and who invariably feel excluded from the benefits of modern life are usually deprived of education and technological knowledge and are often free of organizational and political skills on a large scale. While they seldom lend active support to their class enemies in time of crisis, in their private lives they are more liable to conservative rustic ideologies than the industrial workers are to conservative urban ideologies. These discrepancies and inabilities often oblige a progressive government to rely too heavily on its own cadres for development and thereby delay the emergence of an independent organizational capability among the peasants *and* the workers (whom they feel they must keep in check for the benefit of the peasants by curtailing trade union activity). In East Africa this is best exemplified by Tanzania.[8]

The entrenchment of state bureaucracy in underdeveloped countries is often attributed by some radical critics to bad faith, class conspiracy, or to historical inevitability in the absence of a formed industrial proletariat and the predominance of a conservative petty-bourgeois peasantry instead.

Questions of dogma aside, it may be pointed out that the experience of countries such as Russia, China, North Korea, North Vietnam, Cuba, Algeria, and Mexico confirms more than one thesis. Earlier, we contended that the processes of international surplus appropriation were such that producers in underdeveloped countries, whether urban workers, plantation hands, or part-time small producers, were subject to higher rates of exploitation by capital than in the metropolitan countries. Their active participation in nationalist struggles is evidence of their awareness of the contradiction between imperialist capitalism and its social formations in what has come to be seen as a Third World. Secondly, we argued that the kinds of labour mobilization that the would-be peasants have been subjected to through the system of migrant labour has brought them into direct confrontation with capital. Strikes by urban workers are generally acknowledged but, out of sheer prejudice or dogma whose roots are not far to find, less importance has been attached to the fairly widespread revolts by the peasants.[9] And yet this is another indication that the peasants are aware of the fact that they are being exploited by their own governments through the Marketing Boards or by the hierarchy of the co-operatives and middle-men.[10] They are also fully conscious of the exploitation they suffer as cheap, unskilled, migrant labour on the plantations and in the towns.[11] Contrariwise, their willingness to migrate on a massive scale for labour employment is further evidence that they are not half as land-fixed as adherents of classical theory would have us believe. In the light of these objective manifestations and the undeniable revolutionary capacity of peasants in countries such as China, Korea, Vietnam, Cuba, Algeria, and Mexico and most of Latin America in recent years, and in the war-ridden African territories of Guinea-Bissau, Angola, and Mozambique where there is hardly any 'proletariat' to boast of, it is foolhardy for anyone to assert inherent incapacity on the part of the peasants, without a careful investigation of their objective material circumstances and social quality.

Consequently, it is one of our main theses in this essay that the so-called peasants in underdeveloped countries are, historically, not only contemporaries of the workers in the developed countries but are also their identical objects i.e. they are objects of exploitation by the same international finance-capital. Theoretically, this is an exceedingly important point. Peasants in underdeveloped countries are not only subject to exploitation in the market as petty producers but are also objects of direct exploitation by capital as migrant workers or intermittent sellers of labour power. Objectively, this gives them the quality of semi-proletarians. Insofar as they would prefer to remain in the countryside but cannot afford it and insofar as they dream of high wages when they migrate to the cities but are unable to realize them because of lack of skills, subjectively they regard themselves as the least favoured category in society and say as much when interviewed. Above all, when we consider them as unskilled labourers in town we are struck by two things, at least, in East, Central, and Southern Africa. They are the majority and the worst-paid labour and yet they do the hardest jobs. In other words, they are the human industrial machines. Here comes the contradiction: they are the broad base of the industrial labour force, without themselves being fully industrialized or urbanized, thanks to their itineracy. Are they an industrial proletariat domiciled in the countryside or are they proletarianized peasants? However we look at it the proletarian part-quality remains and to me that is what seems to be of fundamental importance.

Among urban workers in developing countries there can be identified other categories of workers besides uneducated and unskilled migrants. These are the so-called white- and blue-collar workers. They vary in their occupations but have relatively high salaries as a common feature. They have been referred to by various names, 'labour aristocracy', 'salariat', 'sub-élites', or 'petit bourgeoisie'. These names are as nice as they are confusing. The simple fact is that all workers who receive high salaries do not represent the same phenomenon any more than all people who enjoy the same standard of living constitute a class. What is diagnostic is the way the income is derived. All *industrial* workers, irrespective of the level of their incomes, form a specific category by virtue of exchanging their labour power *with capital,* i.e. they produce surplus value and are, therefore, exploited. As long as they produce added value, in no way can they be said to be benefiting by the exploitation of the peasants. What cannot be determined with any objectivity, except in extreme cases such as South Africa, is the exploitative implication of the differential between the best and the worst paid among them. e.g. managers–technicians and the migrants workers.

An interesting and contrasting group which is more difficult to categorize is those workers who derive their livelihood from exchanging their labour power, not with capital, but with *revenue.* It is a well-known fact that bureaucracy is one of the greatest sources of employment in underdeveloped countries and that the service sector is the most expansive part of the economy. Whatever the qualifying arguments, it cannot be denied that labour exchanged with revenue cannot but detract from the revenue it is incapable of reproducing, i.e. it does not produce any added value. Similarly, services, with notable exceptions such as education, medical facilities, and public transport which produce value *indirectly*, promote more consumption than production. Insofar as this kind of labour depreciates existing stocks (in this case revenue), it has to be underwritten by a more productive type of labour such as the one mentioned earlier. In underdeveloped countries where up to 85 per cent of the national revenue comes from agriculture, it is obvious that bureaucratic and menial workers benefit by the exploitation of the peasants and the industrial workers. Therefore, the level of wages of the former category of workers can have extremely negative implications for the other workers. In *sensu stricto* it is this kind of worker which should be referred to as petit bourgeois, remembering that the petit bourgeoisie is an intermediate and dependent class. *Ipso facto* salary differentials among them matter very much as they are more arbitrarily determined and, most of all, predicate the individual's political allegiance. In Africa two factors are observable in this respect. Promotion in the bureaucracy is fastest and is accompanied by a disproportionate amount of political power. Secondly, the antagonism of the bureaucracy towards the peasants and the industrial workers (trade unions) is noticeable. More than the distinctions made here, particularly in regard to the lower end of the hierarchy, the theoretical point I wish to underscore is that the behaviour of the bureaucracy cannot be *objectified* except by relating it to the impulses of both the producing and the owning classes. In my view this puts class theory into perspective and disposes of the muddles of stratification theory.

In our quest for taxonomic categories we often dichotomize and impute differences in quality even in highly mediated situations. In most of Africa the difference in quality between the average industrial worker and the migrant worker is not half as stark as conventional theory obliges us to believe. The main reason is that half the time we are dealing with identical agents.[13] Even in those cases where workers can be described unambiguously as rural or urban, it is well to remember that, ontologically, contrasts are not necessarily contradictions. Therefore, in reply to the usual Trotskyite heresy about peasants and the revolution in underdeveloped countries, I would suggest that the rural and the industrial producers be treated as a continuum which is constantly re-inforced by the intermittence of a high proportion of their number. I would also insist that when we referred to them as allies, it should be out of recognition of this objective fact and not out of ideological expediency.

On the other hand, family continuity theories such as are advanced in the preceding paragraph should not, by the mere fact that they admit of a mean, be interpreted as a denial of the existence of contraries. While fully industrialized, highly skilled workers and partially industrialized itinerant workers in the countryside can be thought of as polar opposites whose mean is the field of graduation in which each sub-category is continuously interrelated with the other, dialectically it is as important to set up a further proposition which specifies the direction of the gravitation of such moments. As in any movement, members of a class are at different stages of becoming: there are advanced workers and there are less advanced workers. The fully industrialized workers represent the former but, without the less advanced rural workers, they are like a head without a body. In terms of strategy and perspective, the mandatory replacement of peasant ideologies with proletarian ideologies should be matched by a complete realization of the revolutionary potential of the so-called peasants. An absolute identification of taxonomic categories with actual human agents at different junctions in history must be abandoned once and for all. Similarly, the incautious reduction of strata, e.g. bureaucrats, technicians, and kulaks, into an identical class mainly on the grounds of their standard of living must be avoided as it obscures the major organizational issue, *viz.,* the uneven development of the proletariat in underdeveloped countries. If conservative in their praxis, can the advanced industrial workers be written off as sub-élites and, obversely, should similar behaviour by part-rural workers warrant their dismissal as petty bourgeois? In its generic sense the problem is one of determining which classes are dispensable and which are not. In our view, while bureaucrats and kulaks are dispensable, the same cannot be said of technicians and other highly skilled industrial manpower. Likewise, the vast supporting army of semi-skilled and unskilled migrants cannot be spared, if the great transformation is to take place. Therefore, when confronted with the problem of a divided working class in underdeveloped countries, we should not relapse into the easy language of metaphors. Objectively speaking, there are neither 'aristocrats' nor 'petit bourgeois' among those who suffer systematic extraction of surplus value in society. Vulgar praxis and income differentials are as old as the history of the working class itself, but they need to be acknowledged in order to be defeated. In Africa it is the more deprived, semi-proletarianized migrant workers who are a potential counter-weight to those elements among the industrial workers who are swayed by their immediate gains. Only when that balance is achieved can the antithesis to state capitalism and bureaucratic entrenchment become a reality.

NOTES

[1] The point here is, whether or not the greater volume of capital goes to the already developed countries, the underdeveloped countries are still severely constrained by the demands of foreign capital, however small relatively, and secondly, the net outflow of wealth they suffer through unequal exchange and repatriation of capital constitute a very high proportion of their meagre internal accumulation.

[2] As it is supposed to be in works such as E. E. Hagen, *On the theory of social change: how economic growth begins,* Homewood, Ill., 1962, R. P. Dore, 'Japanese industrialization and the developing countries: model, warning, or source of healthy doubts?' Institute of Southeast Asian Studies, Singapore, 1971.

[3] China, would have been another, if it were not for the different external conditions under which she operated in the inter-war period and the different system she evolved after the Revolution.

[4] Or the colonial wage structure between black and white in Southern Africa.

[5] The extent of free land in Africa is often confused with its availability for production, without confronting the pervasive problem of technological underdevelopment in the continent.

[6] While some older underdeveloped countries such Brazil and India have as much as 20 per cent of the population in urban employment, emergent African countries hardly approach ten per cent.

[7] As is evidenced by strikes, it does not mean that they are immune to exploitation nor are they ignorant of their class enemies in specific contexts. However, in Africa where competition is fairly low both in agriculture and in commerce, petty-bourgeois aspirations among blue and white-collar workers still hold sway.

[8] See. M.A. Bienefeld, 'Labour in Tanzania' in (eds) J. Saul and L. Cliffe, *Tanzania socialism, politics and policies,* Dar es Salaam, 1972.

[9] In Asia and Latin America the phenomenon has reached near-revolutionary proportions. In Africa noticeable instances have occurred in South Africa, in Kenya and in some West African countries such as Nigeria and Cameroon.

[10] Interviews during a field trip in Buganda in 1966–67 established this point beyond doubt.

[11] Field-work among migrant workers in Cape Town in 1961 and farm-labourers on the outskirts of the Elliot and MaClear Districts in South Africa in 1963 confirmed this awareness.

[12] In South Africa after $1\frac{1}{2}$–2 years I was able to interview in the Transkei, a rural area, the same men as I had interviewed in Cape Town. In Uganda before I had finished my 15-month survey some of the poorer farmers had disappeared to the city for employment or were commuting by bicycle.

PART VIII
A Bibliographical Guide

Christopher Allen is the compiler of *Radical Africana*, a bibliographical supplement to the *Review of African Political Economy*.

Radical themes in African social studies: a bibliographical guide

CHRISTOPHER ALLEN

PART I: INTRODUCTION

A. Selection and organization

Problems of selection in this guide arose from constraints imposed by the editors–length, language, availability, and scope–and by the material itself. Limitations on the number of items made it frequently necessary to choose between alternatives, and in each case I have preferred items that were more recently published, more readily available, and in English. I have included only material written in French or in English, as these are the main languages used in radical writing on Africa; and I have not included unpublished theses and papers, valuable though these often are. This guide was completed in March 1975.

Problems of *scope*, and of the material itself, overlap. Radical writing, and still more, Marxist writing, on Africa is very uneven in the fields that are covered, and in its quality. While francophone authors have tended to concentrate on methodology, political economy, and anthropology, writers in English have dealt far more with politics and policy issues. Neither group has paid much attention to institutional problems and to what may loosely be called problems of 'government', despite the importance, made clear by studies of the state, of understanding how institutions are used by certain socio-economic categories to reproduce wealth and power. This unevenness is reflected in this volume, and in order to begin to compensate for it, I have included some work that is not radical in intent, but which seems to me to be of major empirical value in understanding questions posed by radicals. The outstanding work of Polly Hill is one example, and Anthony Hopkins's *Economic history of West Africa* is another, despite its use of neo-classical economics and its neglect of French Marxist sources. Sections G and H in particular contain much material of this type (though of lesser standing than Hill and Hopkins), included for its usefulness in the study of radical themes, rather than for its direct contribution to radical work; the several articles by Rivière which clearly belong to the realm of bourgeois sociology, fall into this category. This may of course lead to a certain amount of theoretical and ideological confusion within this paper and on the part of those who find it helpful; but the earlier theoretical sections should counteract this. Readers will also notice that I have cited very little material from official Communist publications. This is in part because much of it is strident, misinformed, and irrelevant; but also because the material that is valuable is for the most part covered by more academic publications, which I have included.

The bibliography itself (see Part II) is *organized* by author and date of publication, rather than by topic, since too much material covers more than one topic. Instead, this introduction has been arranged along the same divisions as the book itself, with the addition of a section dealing with countries of particular interest and with revolutionary liberation movements.

B. Methodology, theory, and concepts

Programmatic statements by radical Africanists are harder to come by than their critiques of bourgeois methodology, but they occur in C. Leys 1975 and Brett 1973, as well as in a major series of articles of considerable generality by Abdel-Malek (1967; 1968; T[1]; 1970; 1971a). General overviews of the field are provided by Coquery-Vidrovitch (T), and by Augé 1972 and Copans 1974 (T); 1972[2], while Havens 1972 makes a rather mechanical but sympathetic comparison between methodologies on the basis of the problems each may be readily used to investigate.

For *critiques of anthropology*, see Copans 1974, Meillassoux 1972 and Augé 1972, for French material, and for English, Leclerc 1972, Goddard 1969, Banaji 1970, and Asad 1972. This last item, together with Buijtenhuijs 1972 and Magubane 1968; 1971, provides interesting case studies in the abuse of anthropology, a theme taken up for American work by Berreman *et al.* 1968, and Stavenhagen 1971. *Modernization theory* has been frequently exposed as inconsistent, inapplicable, and reactionary since Frank's early and famous attack in Frank 1970; useful recent articles include Bodenheimer 1970, Bernstein 1971, D. O'Brien 1972, and Kesselman 1973.

Apart from Weberian approaches (for which see Williams in Allen and Johnson 1970; Willame 1972), the only body of theory to be successfully applied in analysing the history and political economy of Africa is Marxism, which in the process has been somewhat revised and enlarged. The major contributions have been made by francophone Marxists; English Marxists have been a much smaller and less experienced group, and one that has dealt more with empirical questions suggested by Marxist theory than with the theory itself. A successful body of theory must begin by examining the nature of the international economy and the origins and dynamics of capitalism in Africa: *dependent peripheral capitalism*. Here the most important contribution is being made by Samir Amin (1973a; 1973b; 1974), who discusses both the nature of dependent peripheral capitalism and of the social and political structures associated with it; Floret 1974 is a brief critique. The latter arise

---

[1] (T)=this volume. Items included in this volume are cited at appropriate points in the introduction, but may not be listed below.

[2] Copans's numerous book reviews in French journals are not listed here but are excellent as both critical reviews and more wide-ranging though brief comments on questions of methodology and analysis; see e.g. *Cahiers d'études afr.*, 51 (1973).

from the articulation of pre-capitalist modes of production with the capitalist mode, principally but by no means entirely under imperialism and during the colonial period. Further treatment of the nature of dependent peripheral capitalism, and of *underdevelopment,* can be found in Frank 1970; 1974 (which is best criticized by Laclau 1971), in C. Leys 1975, and in Szentes 1971, a major work weakened both by its dualist descriptive framework, and by its uncritical treatment of economic relations with East European countries. Recent Latin American theoretical work is only rarely available in English, but T. dos Santos (1970a; in Bernstein 1972), Cockcroft *et al.* 1972 and Cardoso 1972 are useful; Warren 1973 provides a rather dated commentary and critique of uneven worth. Valuable surveys of the whole range of work in underdevelopment have been made by Ehrensaft 1971, and Riddell 1972, and of neo-Marxist theorizing by Foster-Carter in de Kadt and Williams 1974.

Pre-capitalist modes of production have unfortunately provided scope for the more mechanical forms of debate, and of application of models, among Marxists. Such work is, however, only parasitic upon the real debate and elaboration where the key figure has been Claude Meillassoux. In a series of articles (1960; 1965; 1971; 1972; 1973a; 1973b) he has elaborated his notions of pre-capitalist modes; they are applied in his book on the Gourou (1964). This work has been criticized, revised, and elaborated by his colleagues and pupils notably in Terray 1972 and Rey 1971; 1973; less significant is the debate with Deluz and Godelier 1967 and the general remarks of Banaji 1972. Unfortunately much of the fieldwork associated with this theoretical position is in mimeographed or unpublished form, but representative studies can be found in Dupré and Rey 1973, Rey 1969, Augé 1975, Pollet and Winter 1971, Willame 1971, and—of particular interest as an analysis of the dialectic of ritual and mode of production—Bonnafé 1973. Though part of a non-Marxist tradition, the work of Polanyi 1975 and Sahlins 1973 must be mentioned here as a valuable contribution to the general elaboration of theory.

Rather less productive, but also important, has been the discussion of the *Asiatic mode of production,* where the key figure has been (for Africa) Jean Suret-Canale (1961; 1966b). The debate has not centred on African data, but it is worth consulting the two collective volumes (*Recherches Africaines* 1967, CERM 1969) and Coquery-Vidrovitch (T) on the role of trade; *La Pensée* carried a great many other contributions, mainly in case study form, during 1964–69. For Marx and Engels on the subject, see Hobsbawm 1964, Terray 1972, and Krader 1973.

Further material belonging to this Marxist tradition may be found below; the rest of this section discusses particular concepts or micro-theories found in African studies. Treatment of *class analysis,* particularly in English, has been undermined by a tendency to attempt the application of existing models and specific, if related, versions (for attempts at this, see the work of Amin, Rey, and Arrighi and Saul). Despite this, there is much of value in the works by Balandier 1965, Rivière 1969, T. dos Santos 1970b, R. Cohen 1972, and Kitching 1972; Amin 1964 and Ledda 1967 discuss the issues more in terms of their immediate political implications. The colonial and post-colonial *state* is a badly neglected field, treated only—and rather obscurely—by Alavi 1972, and by C. Leys 1975, Saul 1974b, and Shivji 1976). Similarly, the notion of *political development* has been left largely to American ideologues; but see Rudebeck 1970; 1974, Cockcroft *et al.* 1972 and (in future) the as yet unpublished work of Roger Leys. Critiques of rival concepts are again more common; '*tribalism*' and ethnicity are dealt with by C. Leys 1975, Mafeje 1971, and–more kindly–by A. Cohen 1973 and Melson and Wolpe 1972. *Pluralism* is presented in the work of Kuper 1971; 1972, and dismissed by Wolpe in ICS 1971, Magubane 1969, Legassick (T) and Sklar 1967; there is, of course, a much broader debate concerning non-African material. '*Traditionality*' is now less favoured by non-radicals; explicit discussion in the context of case-studies can be found in Staniland 1975 on Ghana and Willame 1973 on Zaïre. Finally, *patronage* models have recently become more popular among non-radicals (see Lemarchand 1972a; 1972b, Sandbrook 1972), but have had much less critical attention (see Alavi 1973, Kaufman 1974). Among economists' concepts, *dualism* and *development* have been most influential. The latter has been mentioned above (see also Rimmer 1972 on the 'ideology of development economics'), while the former has been exposed by—among many alternatives—Mafeje in R. Leys 1973, Weeks 1971d; 1972, and Frank 1970.

C. History

Discussion of the problems of historical methodology, periodization, etc., has been carried on by Marxists largely in the context of other problems, as in work mentioned in Section B, while critical discussion of African historiography, which has concentrated on the issue of ethnocentrism to too great an extent, has been carried out mainly by non-radicals. To John Saul's useful piece on Tanzanian historiography (T) we may add Coquery-Vidrovitch 1969a, Holden in Allen and Johnson 1970, and Davidson (T). *Pre-colonial history* is covered in Rodney's stimulating and popular account (T) as well as in his earlier more academic volume on West Africa (1970). More succinct is Amin 1972, on 'underdevelopment and dependency'; his account is extended in Amin 1973a, and applied in Barm 1972, on the Senegalese Kingdom of Waalo. More narrowly economic are Hopkins 1973, Schnapper 1971, and Hymer's two pieces on Ghana (1970; 1971); for trade and markets see the key volume edited by Meillassoux (1971) and a recent article by Dupré 1972 and, on the slave trade, Rodney 1967 and Wolff 1974. 'Domestic' slavery itself is the subject of a recent collection edited by Meillassoux 1975, and of case studies by Meillassoux (in Meillassoux 1971) and by Bazin 1974. Nigeria is dealt with briefly by Ehrensaft (T) and Williams f.c.; East Africa in Lubetsky in VEA 1972, and in the unpublished work of A. H. M. Sheriff; and North Africa in Gallisot 1968a, 1968b.

The *colonial period* is better covered, notably by Rodney (T), Suret-Canale (T) and Amin 1972. Imperialism has been mainly dealt with by works without a specific African reference (for bibliographies see Lee 1972, Owen and Sutcliffe 1972), or by conservative historians. African material is discussed by Coquery-Vidrovitch 1970, Owen and Sutcliffe 1972, Emmanuel 1972, and

Hopkins 1968; 1973, *Colonial economic change* is covered for East Africa by
Brett 1973 and Wolff 1974, and for West Africa by Suret-Canale (T) and
Amin 1973b, with important case studies by Suret-Canale 1970 on Guinea,
Coquery-Vidrovitch 1972 and Rey 1972 on Congo-Brazzaville, Williams
f.c. Pearson 1971 on Nigeria, and Kay 1972 on Ghana (see also Rhodie
1968). Further south, Arrighi in Arrighi and Saul 1973, Phimister 1974;
in ICS 1974, and Emmanuel 1972 discuss Rhodesia, and Trapido 1971 and
Wolpe 1972 South Africa. *Colonial political history*, by contrast shows major
gaps, only partly filled by earlier works of 'official' Marxism, such as Boiteau
1958 on Madagascar, Sebag 1951 on Tunisia, and Ayache 1956 on Morocco.

Social history again overlaps with the anthropological material listed
earlier, and with some of the economic history (e.g. Meillassoux 1971).
M. Klein 1972 provides a general and pessimistic survey of the field, which
Amin 1973a and Davidson (T) cover in broad terms. Aspects of the growth
and activity of classes over time are discussed by Amin 1964, and by Diop
1971; 1972 for Mali and Senegal (see also Dème 1966). Rivière 1971a, and
Amin in Meillassoux 1971, discuss merchants in Guinea and Senegal, while
Kay 1972, Rhodie 1968, and Hill 1963 deal with Ghanaian cocoa farmers.
Nigeria is covered by Berry 1975, Osoba (T) 1969 and Cohen and Hughes
1971, and South Africa, in part, by Trapido in ICS 1973 and Bundy 1972.

D. The economy

The basic theoretical material on dependent peripheral capitalism is listed
in Section B. Detailed discussion of the contemporary workings of this form
of capitalism and of mechanisms of underdevelopment (trade, aid, etc.) is
common, but the great bulk is marked by strongly Fabian or sentimentalist
themes associated with centres for 'development, studies and relief organizations'. Both can provide much valuable factual data, but their contribution
to analytical work is ultimately minor. General accounts of *mechanisms of
underdevelopment* are best sought in Szentes 1971 and Amin 1974; also useful
is Weisskopf 1972. Surveys of African data occur in Nkrumah 1965, and
Green and Seidman 1968, and commentaries on the effect of association with
the *EEC* in Brown 1972 and Curzon 1971. Arrighi and Saul 1973, Girvan
1970, and Szentes 1972 deal in general terms with *multinationals,* while studies
of *foreign private investment* are provided by Schatz 1969, Van der Laar 1971,
Weinberg 1971, and Evans 1971. Vaitsos (1970; in Bernstein 1972) has dealt
revealingly with the real costs of *technology transfer*, patents, etc., covered
generally in Cooper 1973. Arguments for '*aid*' are entertainingly swept aside
by Byrese 1972 and Worsley 1972; case studies are made by Corbett 1973,
Fuchs 1973 and Suret-Canale 1974 for France, and Piret 1971; 1972 for
Belgium. Problems of *trade* and monoculture arise in Ofana 1967 and Essang
1967 who deal with cocoa, in Haslemere Group 1972 dealing with coffee,
and in Seidman 1971, who surveys the prospects for African exports; see also
Section H.

For *specific African economies* (also covered in Section H), see Suret-
Canale 1973; 1974, Amin 1970b; 1973b and Afana 1967 on West Africa

overall; Amin 1965 on Mali, Guinea, and Ghana; Amin 1967a on the Ivory Coast, also discussed by Green in Foster and Zolberg 1971, where it is compared with Ghana (covered also by Seidman 1969); Blanchet et al. 1974 on Senegal; and finally Kom 1972 on Cameroun. For central Africa, there is Amin and Coquery-Vidrovitch 1969 on Congo-Brazzaville, Sklar 1975 and Seidman 1973 on Zambia, and Sutcliffe 1971 and Arrighi in Arrighi and Saul 1973, on Rhodesia. Seidman's useful but dualist study (1972) discusses all three East African countries in detail; for further analyses consult Leys 1974, ILO 1972, and Van Arkadie 1970 on Kenya, Rweyemamu 1974, Thomas in UEA 1972, Yaffey 1970, and Green in Allen and Johnson 1970, on Tanzania (see also H. below); Ethiopia is briefly discussed in Bondestam 1974a. Finally, Amin 1970a examines North African economies.

Selection from among the numerous studies of particular aspects of African economies is difficult, and the list that follows is more arbitrary than usual, though I have tried to choose items dealing with limited topics of general significance. *Foreign firms* are discussed by Bonté 1975 and Campbell 1975 for francophone Africa, Gérard-Libois 1967 and Wolfe 1963; 1967 for Zaïre, and Sklar 1975 for Zambia; *indigenous capitalism* is analysed in general by Amin 1967b and Benot 1966; there are also case studies of Senegal and Ivory Coast by Blanchet *et al.* 1974 and Amin 1969a; 1967a, of Kenya by Leys (1974; in CAS 1972) and of Nigeria by Akeredolu-Ale (1972; in Williams f.c.) and Teriba 1972. *Banking* in Nigeria is covered by Oni 1966 and in Tanzania by Loxley in Uchumi 1972. Weeks 1971a; 1971b; 1971c, C. Allen in CAS 1972, and Amin 1969c assess the rationale and effect of *wage policies,* while Weeks 1971; 1973 covers '*unemployment*'. Shivji 1974 is a debate on the social and economic effect of *tourism,* while Tribe shows quietly but effectively the ways in which *housing policy* can benefit the rich (CAS 1972) and *suppliers' credits* enrich the supplier (Cohen and Tribe 1972). Van Arkadie 1971, Gershenberg 1972, Ryan 1973, Seidman 1973, Packard in Uchumi 1972, Shivji 1973 and Loxley and Saul 1974 all detail the many ways in which *parastatals and the public sector* can be used to prevent or undermine income redistribution and economic independence.

Rural economies have been brilliantly described in determinedly nonradical contributions by Polly Hill 1963; 1970; 1972, whose francophone counterpart might well be Pelissier, author of a massive text (1966) on Senegalese peasants; also worth mentioning in this context is the Berry book on Western Nigeria (1975). A rather erratic description and critique of postwar *agrarian policies* is contributed by Dumont and Mazoyer 1969, and further broad criticism is contained in the work of Meister (nd; 1971a; 1971b; 1972). Case studies which are concerned with this area are De Decker 1968 on Guinea and Senegal, Ernst 1975 on Mali, Dumont 1972 on Senegal, Green and Hymer 1966 on Ghana, R. Leys 1973 on East Africa, and Cliffe (and others) on Tanzania (Cliffe and Saul 1972, Africa Studiecentrum 1970, and RDRC 1974). For the '*green revolution*' see Cleaver 1972 in general and Stahl 1974 for an excellent Ethiopian case study. Another critique of capitalist agricultural 'development' in Ethiopia is provided by Bondestam 1974b, while further East African studies include Doornbos and Lofchie in Lofchie 1970 on *ranching,* Cliffe and Cunningham in Cliffe and Saul 1972 on *settle-*

ment schemes, and Leonard 1972, Thoden van Velsen in Cliffe and Saul 1972, and Raikes and Meynen in UEA 1972, on *extension workers*.

E. Social structure

Of the *general works* on class already mentioned, Kitching 1972, Cohen 1972, and Amin 1973a contain some empirical data on individual classes and territories. There is, however, little else available that does not either present class in terms of social stratification alone (as do almost all anglophone sociologists) or as a set of immutable and long-standing categories, as in the early work of Diop, whose later studies of Mali 1971 and Senegal 1972 are more sophisticated, though still faulty. Barbé 1964 provides an early and rather stereotyped collection of socio-economic data on African classes, while Arrighi and Saul 1973 try—as does Amin—to relate class categories to the nature of African economies. Other general accounts of some value are Williams in Allen and Johnson 1970 on Western Nigeria, Demunter 1972 on Zaïre, Seytane 1966, Kom 1972, and Duvignaud 1965 on the Ivory Coast, Cameroun, and Tunisia respectively. Abdel-Malek 1971b and UEA 1972 are very uneven but still useful sets of essays dealing with class issues.

The *urban poor* have recently received considerable attention, mostly as an unwelcome menace to political and economic stability. General commentaries are provided by Gutkind 1972, R. O'Brien 1973, and Armstrong and McGhee 1968, and town studies by Williams in De Kadt and Williams 1974, on Ibadan, Gutkind (T); 1973 on Lagos and Nairobi, Hart 1973 on Accra, Gibbal 1974 on Abidjan, and Jeffries in Sandbrook and Cohen 1975, on Sekondi. Attitudinal surveys have been made by Descloitres and Reverdy 1963 in Algeria, and Seymour in UEA 1972 for Lusaka. Earlier radical studies of *workers* suffered from their identification as a necessarily radical force, which later studies, notably Sandbrook and Cohen 1975, have shown must be proved rather than assumed. This volume contains studies of labour history by Allen (French West Africa), Iliffe (Tanzania) and Stichter (Kenya), to which should be added Van Onselen 1973; 1974 on Rhodesia, Joseph f.c. on Cameroun, and the painstaking account of pre-war Nigeria in Cohen and Hughes 1971. Good contemporary accounts are rare, but combine careful empirical work with sophisticated analysis, as in Peace in de Kadt and Williams 1974, Burawoy 1972a; 1972b, Grillo 1974, and Sandbrook 1974. Less weighty are Le Divelec 1967, and Pfefferman 1969. The concept of '*labour aristocracy*' is used and debated in Arrighi and Saul 1973, Peace in Sandbrook and Cohen 1975 and Jeffries f.c. Sandbrook 1974 provides additional empirical material from Kenya. '*Proletarianization*', another concept which has caused confusion but little useful debate, is demonstrated by Arrighi in Arrighi and Saul 1973 and Heisler 1970 for Central Africa, and discussed by C. Leys 1975; (T), McGhee 1973 and Storgard in R. Leys 1973. A third equivocal concept, the '*lumpen-proletariat*', treated as a potential revolutionary force by Fanon 1965 is more sceptically discussed by C. Allen 1972, Cohen and Michael 1972, and Worsley 1972b; some empirical data on its role in Kenyan politics can be found in Furedi 1973 and Mutiso 1971 (see also the novels of Meja Mwangi).

Discussions of *rural class relations* and their reproduction is much less common than empirical data on rural economies or demonstrations that peasant producers are not, after all, immutably conservative. The concept of *peasantization* is elaborated in Post (T) in particular, while important case-studies of rural class formation include Bundy 1972, Aronson 1971, Stavenhagen 1969, Chodak 1971, Copans 1972, D. O'Brien 1975, C. Leys 1975, Awiti 1973, Boesen 1972, RDRC 1974 and Oxaal *et al.*, f.c. Rural revolt is approached generally by Post (T), Wolf 1969, Davidson 1974, Kiernan 1970, and Alavi 1965; for case studies see Williams f.c., Fox *et al.*, 1965, Verhaegen 1965; 1967a; 1969, Fanon 1965, Saul 1974, and the material on liberation movements below.

Finally, the *bourgeoisie* and related groups. No single work devotes itself to such groups in general, though Amin 1967b; 1970; 1973 gives them more attention than do most general works. We must instead rely on case studies, such as those on the 'bureaucratic' or 'petty' bourgeoisie by Meillassoux 1970 on Mali, Ameillon 1964 and Rivière 1971c on Guinea, Cabral (T) on Guiné-Bissau, Marshall f.c. on Ghana, and Shivji f.c. on Tanzania. Entrepreneurs are mentioned above (Section D), and traders by D. O'Brien 1971a and Rivière 1971b. Capitalist farmers figure largely in C. Leys 1975, Amin 1967a, Marshall f.c., Awiti 1973, and Kamb 1974.

F. Ideology and consciousness

Despite their importance, these related topics have been little studied by radicals; sadly, many of the data in non-radical work are irrelevant and the product of dubious methodologies. Benot 1969 is the most sustained attempt to come to grips with both the official or state ideologies such as the variants of African socialism, and with the much weaker currents of radical thought. Rodinson 1974 discusses Islam, and Hodgkin (T) mahdism and messianism; also valuable for the latter is Fox *et al.* 1965. '*African socialism*' has often been exposed as a cover for non-socialist policies; representative studies are Mohan 1966, Marton 1966, and Mohiddin in UEA 1972, but there is as yet no adequate critique of Tanzanian *ujamaa*. More explicit examples of *ruling-group ideology* are examined by Prewitt in UEA 1972 which parallels Nduka (T), and by Osoba (T). The consciousness of the *urban poor* has been treated by Williams in de Kadt and Williams 1974, and Jeffries in Sandbrook and Cohen 1975, and that of *urban workers* by Peace, Lubeck, and others in Sandbrook and Cohen, by R. Cohen 1974 and by Van Onselen 1973. For the 'lumpen' see above (E). Finally, two unusual studies should be mentioned: Fougeyrollas 1970 is an attitudinal survey that asked the right questions of Senegalese social groups, and Althabe 1972 combines fascinating radical–utopian documents from post-independence Zaire with a rather pessimistic analysis. Individual African theorists (Fanon, Cabral and others, Nyerere, Nkrumah, and Touré) are dealt with below (Section H).

G. Politics, power, and institutions

This section lists those studies which (whether explicitly radical or not) seem to me to be most valuable for an understanding of the political process in post-war Africa in general and in those countries not separately discussed in the next section. It also includes material on a number of topics not covered elsewhere: unions and strikes, the military, women, and micro-politics (where the emphasis is on studies showing the genesis and reproduction of power and dependency relationships). To save space and reduce repetition, the text takes the form simply of a list by country or topic.

General	Hodgkin 1956; First 1970; Arrighi and Saul 1973; Munzer and Laplace 1966; Davidson (T), Copans 1972.
Cameroun	Beti 1972; UPC 1971; Joseph 1974, f.c.; O'Sullivan 1972; Woungly-Massaga 1971.
Congo-Brazzaville	Bonafé 1967, 1969; Terray 1964.
Ethiopia & Eritrea	Nicolas 1972; Lobban 1972; Halliday 1971.
Ivory Coast	Amin 1967a; 1973b; Staniland in Leys 1969, in Allen and Johnson 1970; M. Cohen 1973; Stryker in Lofchie 1971.
Kenya	Leys (T); in CAS 1972; 1975; Lamb 1974; Rosberg and Nottingham 1967; Wasserman 1973; Furedi 1973; Stichter in Cohen and Sanbrook f.c.; Okumu 1968; Murapa 1972; Mutiso and Godfrey 1973; Sandbrook 1974; Stren in UEA 1969; Ghai and McAuslan 1970.
Malawi	Ross 1967; f.c.; Mpakati 1973; Chipembere 1971.
Mali	Meillassoux 1970; Zolberg 1968; Hopkins 1972; Megahed 1970; Julis n.d.; Jones 1972; Ernst 1975; Amin 1965.
Nigeria	Post and Vickers 1972; Post and Jenkins 1973; Waterman 1971; Lucas 1971; First 1970; Vickers 1970; Melson and Wolpe 1972; R. Cohen 1974.
Senegal	Diop 1972; O'Brien 1967; 1971; 1975; Barker 1973; in Lofchie 1971; Foltz 1969; Schumacher 1974; De Decker 1968.
South Africa	Legassick 1974; in Harris, f.c.; Johnstone 1970; in ICS 1970; Wolpe 1972; in ICS 1970-74; Johns 1973; Asherson 1973; Turok 1974.
Zaïre	Merlier 1962; Verhaegen 1965; 1967a; 1967b; 1969; Gérard-Libois 1966a; 1966b; Weiss 1967; Fox et al. 1965; Willame 1972; Kamitatu 1971; Chomé 1973; Demunter 1972a, 1972b; Althabe 1972.
Zimbabwe	Arrighi in Arrighi and Saul 1973; Bowman 1974; Good 1974; Sutcliffe 1971; Emmanuel 1972; Wilkinson 1973; see also Section H.
Unions & Strikes	Sandbrook and Cohen 1975; Peace in de Kadt and Williams 1974; C. Allen in Allen and Johnson 1970; R. Cohen 1974; Burawoy 1972a, 1972b; Waterman 1973; Stren in UEA 1969; Sandbrook 1974; Mapolu 1972; 1973; Grillo 1974; Mihyo 1974.
Military	First 1970; Murray (T), Terray 1964; Martin 1973; Decalo 1973.

Women	Wipper 1971; 1972; in Cliffe *et al.* 1974; Mbilinyi 1973; Boals and Van Allen in Jacquette 1974; Ardener 1973; Rivière 1971d.
Micropolitics	Lamb 1974; Mutiso and Godfrey 1973; Schumacher 1974; Barker in Lofchie 1971; 1973; D. O'Brien 1971; 1975; Thoden van Velzen in Cliffe and Saul 1972; Holmquist 1972; N. Hopkins 1972; Vincent 1971; Derman 1972; Dunn and Robertson 1973; Cliffe *et al.* 1974; Staniland 1975.

H. Selected areas

These include those states whose claims to be implementing socialist policies are, or have been, considered sincere (Algeria, Ghana, Guinea, Tanzania; for Mali, on which little is available, see Section G), and those in which re-volutionary struggles are occurring (for South Africa, see G). With the first group, I have tried to include the same broad range of material as the biblio-graphy as a whole (excluding historical material), but with the latter group the emphasis is on the more theoretical and analytical material and not on 'news from the front', which is constantly changing, and which is indexed in *Radical Africana* (see Section I).

Algeria

Here one is overwhelmed by contemporary accounts of the war, the resulting debates, and the academic literature produced within Algeria. I have not tried to sort through these several hundred volumes in French, concentrating instead on items in English, dealing with Fanon and with *autogestion* in the main. Fanon's own work (1967; 1970a; 1970b) is clearly important, though often fallible on Algeria itself (Beckett 1973, Lucas 1972, Perinbam 1973) and debatable in his general theses (Nghe 1963, Beckett 1972, Staniland 1969, Worsley 1972b, Museveni 1971, A. Klein 1966). Useful accounts of the period before independence are in Lacoste *et al.* n.d., Wolf 1970 and Murray and Wengraf 1963; critical accounts of the last decade are given by Alleg 1970 and Maschino and M'Rabet 1972. Foreign investment is covered by Akkache 1971, workers' self-management by Clegg (T), and agrarian reform by Lucas 1973, Ollivier 1973, Agéron 1972, Duprat 1973, and Mazoyer in Dumont and Mazoyer 1974.

Ghana

Radical work on Ghana has centred on Nkrumah and his removal, though there is a certain amount on the equally important problem of the economy (Green in Foster and Zolberg 1971, Hymer 1971, Callaway and Card in Lofchie 1971, Seidman in UEA 1969, Miracle and Seidman 1970). Some of general works touch on the economy (Marshall f.c., Fitch and Oppenheimer 1966, Genoud 1969), the first of these being the best of three uneven accounts. Other general surveys of the CPP period include Davidson 1973a, which is best for the earlier part, Ikoku 1971, Owusu 1970, which is needlessly obscure but very useful, Murray 1965; 1967a (of which the same can be said), Kofi 1972 and the essays of Kraus and Kilson in Foster and Zolberg 1971. Narrower accounts are given by Ryan 1970a; 1970b and Kilson 1970 on the CPP, Rathbone 1968; 1973 on the social bases of the CPP, and Staniland 1975 and Dunn and Robertson 1973 on local politics. The political thought of Nkrumah, summarized in Nkrumah 1973 is discussed in many of the references above, and particularly in Mohan 1967 and *Présence Africaine* 1973 (see especially the articles by Hodgkin, and Martin, which was Genoud's pseudonym).

Guinea

Since independence it has become increasingly difficult to study Guinean politics, especially contemporary events. R. W. Johnson is preparing a massive political history until the appearance of which we shall have to be content with his all too few articles (Allen and Johnson 1970; T). The PDG is also discussed by Charles 1962 and Gastaud n.d., and recent history by Suret-Canale 1966a, Chaffard 1967 and Ameillon 1964. Suret-Canale 1970 is a monograph on the economy, and De Decker 1968 one on rural animation. Guinean sociology has been partially covered by Rivière 1971a; 1971b; 1971c; 1971d; 1973a; 1973b, who avoids the most politically sensitive aspects of his field (such as workers and unions, touched on briefly by Allen in Sandbrook and Cohen 1975).

Tanzania

More socialists have visited, studied, and arisen in Tanzania than most African states; conditions in the country and at the university seem to have encouraged them into greater intellectual activity and a corresponding level of publication (often, unfortunately, in mimeographed form for local use only). From among these I have selected material offering important general analyses of the Tanzanian polity and economy, and that dealing with problems of rural class formation and development policy. The key volume is Cliffe and Saul 1972, a collection of material from the 1960s, dealing with these and other topics; Saul in Arrighi and Saul 1973, has a long analytical article on the background to Tanzanian policies and the contradictions of their implementation, which Shivji 1976 comments on more forcefully, identifying what he calls the 'petty-bourgeoisie' as mainly responsible for the equivocation in Tanzanian socialism (for some data on this group, see McGowan and Bolland, 1971). Cliffe compares Tanzania with Kenya (1973), and shorter general comments are offered by Bhagavan 1972 and Hughes 1970. Overviews of the underdevelopment of the economy occur in Rweyemamu 1974, Cliffe 1973, Seidman 1972, and Yaffey 1970 (which concentrates on mechanisms of capital drainage). The problem of how to overcome underdevelopment is best discussed in Thomas in UEA 1972 and Uchumi 1972, the latter dealing with planning, also discussed by Leys in C. Leys 1969; other contributions come from Resnick in UEA 1970 and Helleiner 1972. The public sector B is discussed in Vchumi 1972 and Shivji 1976, but more centrally in Loxley and Saul 1974 and Shivji 1973; Loxley again, and Green cover technical assistance in Tandon 1973. Contributions to the debate on tourism have been edited by Shivji 1974.

Among urban strata, only workers have begun to receive adequate study, particularly in the work of Mapolu 1972; 1973, Bienefield in Sandbrook and Cohen, and Mihyo 1974. The study of rural stratification in Tanzania has been intimately linked to that of rural development policy, as is reflected in the publications which deal with both topics: RDRC 1974; Cliffe et al. 1974, Raikes in UEA 1973, R. Leys 1973, Boesen 1972, Brett and Belshaw f.c., Afrika Studiecentrum 1970 and Feldman in C. Leys 1969. Items centering on stratification do exist, as with R. Feldman 1974, R. Feldman in Oxaal et al. 1976, Shivji 1976, Raikes 1970, Gottlieb in UEA 1972 and Awiti 1973. Co-operatives are covered by Saul in RDRC 1974 and Cliffe and Saul 1972, ujamaa villages by Luttrell 1971, Huizer 1971, Shivji 1976, and Raikes in UEA 1973. Agricultural extension, lastly, occurs in the work of Thoden van Velzen in Cliffe and Saul 1972 and Raikes and Meynen in UEA 1972.

Liberation movements
A useful introduction to Portuguese colonialism has been recently published by Ferreira 1972, though it does not fully replace Anderson 1962, nor Boavida's 1972 history of Portuguese activity in Angola. The best and most readily available account of the genesis, history, and significance of the struggle in *Angola* is Davidson 1972, which is complemented by documents and interviews in Barnett and Harvey 1972 and by Marcum's 1969 account of the beginning of the struggle (see also Wheeler and Pelissier 1972). Participant accounts are given by de Andrade and Ollivier 1971 and de Pinto 1973, Portuguese counter-insurgency is discussed by Bender 1972, social change by Heimer 1973, and early divisions within the movement by Chaliand 1965. *Mozambique,* surprisingly, has very little analytical material, apart from Mondlane's 1969 participant account, the excellent essay by Saul in Arrighi and Saul 1973, and Museveni's overly romanticized article (1971). Interviews with Marcelino Dos Santos have been published by LSM in Canada (Box 338, Richmond, BC, Canada) and occur in much of the literature of the support groups (a list of which is forthcoming in *Ufahamu*); a recent interview of wide interest is M. Dos Santos 1973. For *Guiné,* the position is reversed, the late Amilcar Cabral having written extensively (1969; 1970; 1972; 1973a; 1973b) on revolutionary war, social structure, and problems of culture; a volume of his complete works is planned. Davidson again provides the best account of the struggle (1969b), and Rudebeck that of the process of political and economic reconstruction (1974; see also Davidson 1973b). Further material can be found in the special issue on Cabral of *Ufahamu*, **3**, 3, (1972), and in de Andrade's memoir 1973. *Zimbabwe,* where armed struggle has just begun (Good 1974, Wilkinson 1973) has no major analytical works. The origins of the existing movements are dealt with by Shamuyarira 1965, Chenu 1970, and Mevu and M'Gabe 1969, and the ZAPU viewpoint by Silundika 1974.

I. Further reading

'Keeping up with the literature' is best done by consulting *Radical Africana,* a regular bibliographical guide published with the new journal, the *Review of African Political Economy*, Merlin Press, London. This journal is the best source for radical analysis and commentary. Other valuable journals are *Ufahamu* (African Activist Association, UCLA) and *Maji-Maji* (TANU Youth League, University of Dar es Salaam), though in both cases some recent issues have been disappointing. Of the major socialist journals, *Monthly Review* (USA), *New Left Review* and *Socialist Register* (UK), and *Les Temps Modernes*, *La Pensée*, and *Partisans* (France) have most consistently carried useful material. Academic journals carry far too much that is dull, mediocre, and reactionary (though much of the list below is from such journals); the best are *L'Homme et la Société*, *Cahiers d'Etudes Africaines*, *Economy and Society*, the *Journal of Modern African Studies*, the *Canadian Journal of African Studies*, and the *Journal of Peasant Studies*, all of which are unfortunately very expensive. Among publishers three are outstanding: Monthly Review Press, Maspero and Anthropos, and two always good: Heinemann and Cambridge University Press. Finally, we may expect much more Marxist and radical material not only from Africa, but also from Scandinavia and West Germany.

Abbreviations

CEA	Cahiers d'Etudes Africaines
CIS	Cahiers Internationaux de Sociologie
CUP	Cambridge University Press
HS	L'Homme et la Société
JMAS	Journal of Modern African Studies
MR	Monthly Review
NLR	New Left Review
OUP	Oxford University Press
REVUE ALGÉRIENNE	Revue Algérienne des Sciences Juridiques, Economiques, et Politiques
SR	Socialist Register
TM	Temps Modernes

PART II: BIBLIOGRAPHY

ABDEL-MALEK, A.
1967   'Sociologie du développement nationale, problèmes du conceptualisation', *Revue de l'Institut de Sociologie,* 2-3, pp. 249–64.
1968   'Vers une sociologie comparative des idéologies', *HS*, 7, pp. 115–30.
1970   'Marxisme et libération nationale, position du problème théorique', pp. 256–90 of *Le centenaire du Capital* (Paris: Mouton).
1971a   'L'avenir de la théorie sociale', *CIS* 50, 23–40.
1971b   *Sociologie de l'impérialisme* (Paris: Anthropos).

AFANA, O.
1967

L'économie de l'ouest africaine (Paris: Maspero).

AFRIKA STUDIECENTRUM:
1970

Seminar on changes in Tanzanian rural society,
2 vols, (Leiden: Afrika Studiecentrum).

AGERON, C.R.
1972

'Agriculture socialiste et auto-géstion rurale en
Algérie', Compte rendu trimestrielle des séances
de l'Académie des Sciences Outremer, 31, 3,
499–524.

AKEREDOLU-ALE, E.O.
1972

'Environmental, organizational, and group
factors in the evolution of private indigenous
entrepreneurship in Nigeria', Nigerian Journal of
Economic and Social Studies, 14, 2, 237–56.

AKKACHE, A.
1971

Capitaux étrangers et libération economique:
l'expérience algérienne (Paris: Maspero).

ALAVI, H.
1965 (1973)

1972

1973

'Peasants and revolution', 241–77; revised version
in Imperialism and revolution in south Asia, ed K.
Gough and H.P. Sharma (New York: Monthly
Review).
'The state in post-colonial societies', NLR, 74,
pp. 59–81.
'Peasant classes and primordial loyalties', Journal
of Peasant Studies, 1, 1, 23–62.

ALLEG, H.
1970

'Algeria seven years after: socialism or capitalism?', Marxism today, 14, 3, 76–89.

ALLEN, C.
1972

'Lumpenproletarians and revolution', pp. 91–121
of Political theory and ideology in African society,
(Edinburgh University: Centre of African
Studies).

ALLEN, C. & JOHNSON, R.W.
1970

African perspectives (Cambridge: CUP.)

ALTHABE, G.
1972

Les fleurs du Congo, (Paris: Maspero).

AMEILLON, B.
1964

La Guinée, bilan d'une indépendence (Paris:
Maspero).

AMIN, S.
1964

1965

1967a

'The class struggle in Africa', Revolution, 1, 9,
23–47 (reprinted, 1969, by the African Research
Group, Cambridge, Mass.).
Trois expériences africaines de développement
(Paris: Presses Universitaires de France).
Le développement du capitalisme en Côte d'Ivoire
(Paris: Minuit).

1967b	'Le développement du capitalisme en Afrique noire', *HS*, 6, 107–119.
1969a	*Le monde des affaires sénégalaise* (Paris: Minuit).
1969b	'La bourgeoisie d'affaires sénégalaise', *HS*, 12, pp. 29–41.
1969c	'Levels of remuneration, factor proportions, and income differentials', pp. 269–93 of *Wage policy issues in economic development*, ed A.D. Smith (London: Macmillan).
1970a	*The Maghreb in the modern world* (Harmondsworth: Penguin).
1970b	'Development and structural change: the African experience', *Journal of International affairs*, 24, 2, 203–25.
1972	'Underdevelopment and dependence', *JMAS*, 10, 4, 503–24.
1973a	*Le développement inégal* (Paris: Anthropos); review by P. Hugon, *Revue tiers monde*, 15, 57, 421–34 (1974). English version forthcoming (Brighton: Harveste: Press).
1973b	*Neocolonialism in West Africa* (Harmondsworth: Penguin).
1974	*Accumulation on a world scale* (New York: Monthly Review); review by C. Palloix, *HS*, 18, pp. 197–208.

AMIN, S. & COQUERY-VIDROVITCH, C.
1969
Histoire économique du Congo 1880–1968 (Paris: Anthropos).

ANDERSON, P.
1962
'Portugal and the end of ultra-colonialism', *NLR*, 15–17.

ARDENER, S.G.
1973
'Sexual insults and female militancy', *Man*, **8**, 3, 422–40.

ARMSTRONG, W.R. & MCGHEE, T.G.
1968
'Revolutionary change and the Third World city', *Civilisations*, **18**, 3, 353–75.

ARONSON, D.R.
1971
'Ijebu-Yoruba urban–rural relationships and class formation', *Canadian journal of African studies*, **5**, 3, 263–80.

ARRIGHI, G. & SAUL, J.S.
1973
Essays on the political economy of Africa (New York: Monthly Review).

ASAD, T.
1973
Anthropology and the colonial encounter (London: Ithaca).

ASHERSON, A.
1969
'Race and politics in South Africa', *NLR*, 53, pp. 55–68.

AUGE, M.
1972   'Sous-développement et développement: terrain d'étude et objets d'action en Afrique francophone', *Africa,* **42,** 3, 205–16.
1975   *La vie en double* (Paris: Hermann).

AWITI, A.
1973   'Economic differentiation in Ismani', *African Review,* 3, 2, 209–39; see also *Maji-Maji* 7 (1972).

AYACHE, A.
1956   *Le Manoc: bilan d'une colonisation* (Paris: Editions Sociales).

BALANDIER, G.
1965   'Problematique des classes sociales en Afrique noire', *CIS,* 38, pp. 131–42.

BANAJI, J.
1970   'The crisis of British anthropology', *NLR,* 64, pp. 71–85.
1972   'For a theory of colonial modes of production', *Economic and political weekly,* **7,** 52, 1948–52.

BARBE, R.
1964   *Les classes sociales en Afrique noire* (Paris: Editions Sociales).

BARKER, J.S.
1973   'Political factionalism in Senegal', *Canadian journal of African studies,* **7,** 2, 287–303.

BARNETT, D. &
HARVEY, R.
1972   *The revolution in Angola* (New York: Bobbs-Merrill).

BARRY, B.
1972   *Le royaume du Waalo* (Paris: Maspero).

BAZIN, J.
1974   'War and servitude in Segon', *Economy and society,* **3,** 2, 107–44.

BECKETT, P.A.
1972   'Frantz Fanon and sub-Saharan Africa: notes on the contemporary significance of his thought', *Africa today,* **19,** 2, 59–73.
1973   'Algeria *v.* Fanon: the theory of revolutionary de-colonization and the Algerian experience', *Western political quarterly,* **36,** 1, 5–27.

BENDER, G.J.
1972   'The limits of counter-insurgency: an African case', *Comparative politics,* **4,** 3, 331–60.

BENOT, Y.
1966   'Développement accéléré et révolution sociale en Afrique noire', *La pensée,* 136, pp. 19–56.
1969   *Idéologies des indépendances africaines* (Paris: Maspero); see also *Revue tiers monde,* **15,** 57 135–70, (1974).

BERNSTEIN, H.
1971
    'Modernization theory and the sociology of development', *Journal of Development Studies,* 7, 2, 141–60.

1973
    Underdevelopment and development (Harmondsworth: Penguin).

BERREMAN, G.D. *et al.*
1969
    'Symposium on the social responsibilities of anthropologists', *Current anthropology,* **9,** 391–435.

BERRY, S.F.
1975
    Customs and socioeconomic change in western Nigeria (Oxford: O.U.P.).

BETI, M.
1972
    Main basse sur le Cameroun (Paris: Maspero).

BHAGAVAN, W.R.
1972
    'Problems of socialist development in Tanzania', *MR,* **24,** 1, 28–39.

BLANCHET, G et al.
1974
    Structures sociales et développement économique: la formation du capital en Sénégal (Dakar: ORSTOM).

BOAVIDA, A.
1972
    Angola: five centuries of Portuguese exploitation, (Richmond, Canada: Liberation Support Movement).

BODENHEIMER, S.J.
1970
    'The ideology of developmentalism', *Berkeley journal of sociology,* 15, pp. 95–137.

BOESEN, J.
1972
    Development and class structure in a smallholder society and the potential of ujamaa (Copenhagen: Institute for Development Research, Paper A72.16).

BOITEAU, P.
1958
    Contribution à l'histoire de la nation malgache (Paris: Editions Sociales) (see also his 'Mouvement national et problème des classes à Madagascar', *Cahiers du CERM,* 44).

BONDESTAM, L.
1974a
    'Underdevelopment and economic growth in Ethiopia', *Kroniek van Afrika,* 1, 20–35.
1974b
    'People and capitalism in the northeast lowlands of Ethiopia', *JMAS,* 12, 3, 423–39.

BONNAFE, P.
1967
    'L'apparition d'une nouvelle "classe" en République du Congo-Brazzaville', *Revue de l'Institut de Sociologie,* 2-3, pp. 321–36.
1968
    'Une classe d'age politique: la JMNR de... Congo-Brazzaville', *CEA,* 31, pp. 327–68.
1973
    'Une grande fête de la vie et de la mort', *L'homme,* **13,** 1-2, 97–166.

BONTE, P.
1975
    'Miferma', *Review of African political economy,* 89–109.

BOWMAN, L.W.
1974
Politics in Rhodesia (Cambridge, Mass.: Harvard University Press).

BRETT, E.A.
1973
Colonialism and underdevelopment in East Africa, (London: Heinemann).

BRETT, E.A. &
BELSHAW, D.G.R.
Forthcoming
Public policy and rural development in East Africa, (Nairobi: O.U.P.).

BROWN, M. BARRATT
1972
Essays on imperialism (Nottingham: Spokesman Books).

BUIJTENHUIJS, R.
1972
'Defeating Mau Mau', *Sociologische GIDS, 19,* 5-6, 329–39.

BUNDY, C.
1972
'The emergence and decline of a South African peasantry', *African affairs,* **71,** 285, 369–88, See also **ICS** 1973.

BURAWOY, M.
1972a
1972b
The colour of class in the copper mines (Manchester: Manchester University Press).
'Another look at the mineworker', *African social research,* 14, pp. 239–87.

BYRES, T.
1972
Foreign resources and economic development (London: Cass).

CABRAL, A.
1969
1970

1972

1973a

1973b
Revolution in Guiné (London: Stage One).
National liberation and culture, Occasional Paper 57, Program of East African Studies, Syracuse University.
'Identity and dignity in the national liberation struggle', *Africa today,* **19,** 4, 39–47.
Return to the source: selected speeches (New York: African Information Service).
'Fruits of a struggle; notes for a history', *Marxism today,* **17,** 1, 13–21 (and *Tricontinental,* 31).

CAMPBELL, B.K.
1975
'The French textile industry in West Africa', *Review of African political economy*, **1,** 2, 36–53.

CARDOSO, F.H.
1972
'Dependent, capitalist development in Latin America', *NLR* 74, pp. 83–95.

CAS
1972
Developmental trends in Kenya (Edinburgh University: Centre of African Studies).

CERM
1969
1970
Sur le mode de production asiatique (Paris: Editions sociales).
'Libération nationale, néocolonialisme, développement' *Cahiers du CERM* 76–79.

CHAFFARD, G.
1967

Les carnets secrets deta decolonisation, vol. 2, (Paris: Calmann-Levy).

CHALIAND, G.
1964

L'Algérie, est-elle socialiste? (Paris: Maspero), review by J. Leca in Revue algérienne, **5**, 1, 251–67.

1965

'Problèmes du nationalisme angolaise', TM, 231, pp. 269–88.

CHARLES, B.
1962

'Le parti démocratique du Guinée', Revue française de science politique, **12**, 312–59.

CHENU, F.
1970

'La difficile naissance de la guérilla rhodésienne', TM, 292, pp. 890–915.

CHIPEMBERE, H.B.M.
1971

'Malawi's growing links with South Africa', Africa today, **18**, 2, 27–47.

CHODAK, S.
1971

'The birth of an African peasantry', Canadian journal of African studies, **5**, 3, 327–47.

CHOME, J.
1973

L'ascension du Mobutu (Paris: Maspero).

CLEAVER, H.M. et al.
1972

'The contradictions of the green revolution', MR, **23**, 2, 80–128.

CLIFFE, L.
1973

Underdevelopment or socialism: a comparative analysis of Kenya and Tanzania (Brighton: Institute of Development Studies, Discussion Paper 33).

CLIFFE, L. & SAUL, J.S.
1972

Socialism in Tanzania, 2 vols (Nairobi: East African Publishing House).

CLIFFE, L. et al.
1974

Government and rural development in East Africa, (Nairobi: O.U.P.).

COCKCROFT, J.D. et al.
1972

Dependence and underdevelopment: Latin America's political economy (New York: Bantam).

COHEN, A.
1973

Urban ethnicity (London: Tavistock).

COHEN, D.L. &
TRIBE, M.A.
1972

'Suppliers' credits: Ghana and Uganda', JMAS, **10**, 4, 525–41.

COHEN, M.A.
1973

'The myth of the expanding centre: politics in the Ivory Coast', JMAS, **11**, 2, 227–46.

COHEN, R.
1972
1974

'Class in Africa: analytical problems and perspectives', SR, pp. 230–56.
Labour and politics in Nigeria, 1945–71 (London: Heinemann).

COHEN, R. & HUGHES, A.
1971
Towards the emergence of a Nigerian working class... 1897–1939, Birmingham University (Faculty of Commerce and Social Science Occasional Papers D7).

COHEN, R. & MICHAEL, D.
1973
'The revolutionary potential of the African lumpen-proletariat: a sceptical view', *IDS bulletin*, **5**, 2–3, 31–42.

COOPER, C.
1973
Science, technology and development (London: Cass).

COPANS, J.
1972
'Economies et luttes politiques de l'Afrique noire contemporaine', *L'homme*, 12, 3, 119–31.
1974
Critiques et politiques de l'anthropologie (Paris: Maspero)
Forthcoming
Stratification sociale et organisation sociale du travail agricole dans les villages wolof mouride du Sénégal (Paris: Maspero).

COQUERY-VIDROVITCH, C.
1969
'Anthropologie politique et histoire de l'Afrique noire', *Annales*, **24**, 1, 142–63.
1970
'De l'impérialisme britannique à l'impérialism contemporain', *HS*, 18, pp. 61–90.
1972
Le Congo au temps des grandes compagnies concessionaires, 1898–1930 (Paris: Mouton).

CORBETT, E.M.
1973
The French presence in Black Africa (Washington: Black Orpheus Press).

CURZON, G. & V.
1971
'Neocolonialism and the EEC', *Year book of world affairs*, pp. 118–41.

DAVIDSON, B.
1969
The liberation of Guiné (Harmondsworth: Penguin).
1972
In the eye of the storm (London: Longman).
1973a
Black star (London: Allen Lane).
1973b
'A report on the further liberation of Guiné', *SR*, pp. 283–302.
1974
'African peasants and revolution', *Journal of peasant studies*, **1**, 3, 269–90.

De ANDRADE, M.
1973
'Amilcar Cabral: profil d'un révolutionnaire africain', *Présence Africaine*, 86, pp. 3–19.

De ANDRADE, M. & OLLIVIER, M.
1971
La guerre en Angola (Paris: Maspero).

DECALO, S.
1973
'Regionalism, politics and the military in Dahomey', *Journal of developing areas*, 7, 3, 449–78.

DE DECKER, H.
Nation et développement communautaire en

1968	*Guinée et au Sénégal* (Paris: Mouton).
DE KADT, E. & WILLIAMS, G.P. 1974	*Sociology and development* (London: Tavistock).
DELUZ, A. & GODELIER, M. 1967	'A propos de deux textes d'anthropologie économique', *L'homme*, **7**, 3, 78–91; reply by Meillassoux, pp. 91–97.
DEME, K. 1966	'Les classes sociales dans le Sénégal précoloniale', *La pensée*, 130, pp. 11–31.
DEMUNTER, P. 1972a 1972b	'Le régime de Mobutu (1965–71)', *TM*, 308, pp. 1448–81. 'Structure des classes et lutte de classes dans le Congo colonial', *Contradictions* (Bruxelles), **1**, 1.
DE PINTO, R. 1973	*The making of a middle cadre*, (Richmond, Canada; Liberation Support Movement).
DERMAN, W. 1972	*Serfs, peasants, and socialists* (Berkeley; California University Press).
DESCLOITRES, R. & REVERDY, J.C. 1963	'Recherche sur les attitudes du sous-prolétariat algérien à l'égard de la société urbaine', *Civilisations*, **13**, 1–2, 30–76.
DIOP, M. 1971 1972	*Histoire des classes sociales dans l'Afrique de l'ouest*. I: *Le Mali* (Paris: Maspero). II: *Le Sénégal* (Paris; Maspero).
DOS SANTOS, M. 1973	'Frelimo faces the future', *African communist*, 55, pp. 25–53.
DOS SANTOS, T. 1970a 1970b	'The structure of dependence', *American economic review*, **60**, 2, 231–36. 'The concept of social classes', *Science and society*, **34**, 2, 166–93.
DUMONT, R. 1972	*Les paysanneries aux abois* (Paris).
DUMONT, R. & MAZOYER, M. 1974	*Development and socialisms* (London: Deutsch).
DUNN, J. & ROBERTSON, A.F. 1973	*Dependence and opportunity: political change in Ahafo*, (Cambridge: CUP).
DUPRAT, G. 1973	*Révolution et autogestion rurale en Algérie* (Paris: Armand Colin).
DUPRE, G. 1972	'Le commerce entre sociétés lignagères', *CEA*, 48, pp. 616–58.

DUPRE, G. & REY, P.P.
1973

'Reflections on the pertinence of a theory of the history of exchange', *Economy and Society*, 2, 2, 131–63.

DUVIGNAUD, J.
1965

'Classe et conscience du classe en Tunisie', *CIS*, 38, 185–200.

EHRENSAFT, P.
1971

'Semi-industrial capitalism in the Third World', *Africa Today*, 18, 40–67.

EMMANUEL, A.
1972

'White settler colonialism and the myth of investment imperialism', *NLR*, 73, 35–37.

ERNST, K.
1975

Tradition and progress in the African village (London: Hurst).

ESSANG, S.M.
1967

'The lessons of the cocoa crisis', *Nigerian Journal of Economic and Social Studies*, 9, 235–42.

EVANS, P.B.
1971

'National autonomy and political development: critical perspectives on multinational corporations in poor countries', *International Organization*, 25, 3, 675–92.

FANON, F.
1965
1970a
1970b

The wretched of the earth (London: MacGibbon and Kee).
A dying colonialism (Harmondsworth: Penguin).
For the African revolution (Harmondsworth: Penguin).

FELDMAN, R.
1974

'Custom and capitalism: changes in the basis of land tenure in Ismani, Tanzania. *Journal of Development Studies*, 10, 3/4, 305–20.

FERREIRA, E. de S.
1972

Portuguese colonialism from South Africa to Europe (Freiberg: Aktion Dritte Welt).

FIRST, R.
1970

Barrel of a gun (London: Allen Lane).

FITCH, R.B. &
OPPENHEIMER, M.
1966

Ghana: end of an illusion (New York: Monthly Review).

FLORET, J.
1974

'Samir Amin', in *Sous le drapeau de socialisme* (Paris), 62, 40–2.

FOLTZ, W.J.
1969

'Le Parti African de l'Indépendance', *Revue française des études politiques africaines*, 45, 8–35.

FOSTER, P. & ZOLBERG, R.
1971

Ghana and the Ivory Coast (Chicago: University of Chicago Press).

FOUGEYROLLAS, P.
1970

Où va le Sénégal? (Paris: Anthropos).

FOX, R.C. et al.
1965

'The second independence; a case study of the Kwilu rebellion in the Congo', *Comparative studies in society and history*, 8, 1, 78–109.

FRANK, A.G.
1969
1974

Latin America: underdevelopment or revolution, (New York: Monthly Review).
On capitalist underdevelopment (Delhi: O.U.P.).

FUREDI, F.
1973

'The African crowd in Nairobi: popular movements and élite politics', *Journal of African History*, 14, 2, 275–90.

GALLISOT, R.
1968a
1968b

L'Algérie précoloniale, *Cahiers du CERM*, 60.

'Essai de définition du mode de production de l'Algérie précoloniale'. *Revue algérienne*. 5, 2, 385–412.

GASTAUD, M.
n.d.

'Naissance et évolution du P.D.G.', *Cahiers du CERM*, 55.

GENOUD, R.
1969
1973

Nationalism and economic development in Ghana (New York: Praeger).
'Sur les révolutions partielles du Tiers Monde', *TM*, 328, pp. 884–911; comments by Delaforce, Rodinson, pp. 876–83, 911–18.

GERARD-LIBOIS, J.
1966a
1966b

1967

Katanga secession (Madison: University of Wisconsin Press).
'The new class and rebellion in the Congo', *SR*, 267–80.
'L'Union Minière', *Etudes Congolaises*, 10, 2, 1–47.

GERSHENBERG, I.
1972

'Slouching towards socialism: Obote's Uganda', *African Studies Review*, 15, 1, 79–96.

GHAI, Y.P. &
MCAUSLAN, J.P.W.B.
1970

Public law and political change in Kenya (Nairobi: OUP).

GIBBAL, J.N.
1974

Citadins et villageois dans la ville africaine (Paris: Maspero).

GIRVAN, N.
1970

'Multinational corporations and dependent-underdevelopment in mineral export economies', *Social and economic studies*, 19, 4, 490–526.

GODDARD, D.
1969

'Limits of British anthropology', *NLR* 58, 79–89.

GOOD, K.
1974

'Settler colonialism in Rhodesia', *African affairs*, 73, 290, 10–36.

GREEN, R.H. & HYMER, S.H.
1966

'Cocoa in the Gold Coast: a study in the relations between African farmers and agricultural experts', *Journal of economic history* 26, 3, 299–319.

GREEN, R.H. &
SEIDMAN, A.
1968

Unity or poverty? (Harmondsworth: Penguin).

GRILLO, R.D.
1974

African railwaymen (Cambridge: C.U.P.).

GUTKIND, P.C.W.
1972

'The socio-political and economic foundations of social problems in African urban areas', *Civilisations*, 22, 1, 18–34.

1973

'From the energy of despair to the anger of despair', *Canadian journal of African Studies*, 7, 2, 179–98.

HALLIDAY, F.
1971

'The fighting in Eritrea', *NLR* 67, 57–68.

HARRIS, R.
1976

The political economy of Africa (Cambridge, Mass: Shenkmann).

HART, K.
1973

'Informal income opportunities and urban employment in Africa', *JMAS*, 11, 1, 61–89.

HASLEMERE GROUP
1972

Coffee: the rules of neocolonialism (London: Haslemere Group).

HAVENS, A.E.
1972

'Methodological issues in the study of development', *Sociologica ruralis*, 12, 3/4, 252–72.

HEIMER, F.W.
1974

Social change in Angola (Freiburg; Arnold-Bergsträsser Institut).

HEISLER, H.
1970

'A class of target proletarians', *Journal of Asian and African Studies*, 5, 161–75.

HELLEINER, G.K.
1972

'Socialism and economic development in Tanzania', *Journal of development studies*, 8, 2, 183–204.

HILL, P.
1963

The migrant cocoa farmers of southern Ghana (Cambridge; C.U.P.).

1970

Studies in rural capitalism in West Africa (Cambridge; C.U.P.).

1972

Rural Hausa (Cambridge; C.U.P.).

HOBSBAWM, E.J.
1964

Preface to *Pre-capitalist economic formations*, by Karl Marx (London: Lawrence and Wishart).

HODGKIN, T.L.
1956

Nationalism in colonial Africa (London: Muller).

HOLMQUIST, F.W.
1972

'Toward a political theory of rural self-help development in Africa', *Rural Africana,* 18, 60–79.

HOPKINS, A.G.
1968

'Economic imperialism in West Africa: Lagos 1880–92', *Economic history review,* 21, 580–606: see discussion with Ajayi and Austen, ibid, 25, 2: 303–12 (1972).

1973

An economic history of West Africa (London: Longman).

HOPKINS, N.S.
1972

Popular government in an African town (Chicago: University of Chicago Press).

HUIZER, G.
1971

The ujamaa village programme in Tanzania: new forms of rural development (The Hague: Institute of Social Studies, Occasional Paper 113).

HYMER, S.H.
1970

'Economic forms in pre-colonial Ghana', *Journal of economic history,* 30, 1, 33–50.

1971

'The political economy of the Gold Coast and Ghana', in *Government and economic development,* ed. G. Ranis, (New Haven: Yale University Press).

HYMER, S.H. &
RESNICK, S.A.
1971

'International trade and uneven development', in *Trade balance of payments and growth,* ed J.N. Baghwati (Amsterdam: North Holland).

I.C.S.
1970–74

Societies of Southern Africa in the nineteenth and twentieth centuries, 5 vols. (London: Institute of Commonwealth Studies).

IKOKU, S.
1971

Le Ghana de Nkrumah (Paris: Maspero).

I.L.O.
1972

Employment, incomes and equality in Kenya (Geneva: I.L.O.). Reviewed by C. Leys in *African affairs,* 72, 289 (1973), 419–29.

JACQUETTE, J.S.
1974

Women in politics (New York: Wiley).

JOHNS, S.
1973

'Obstacles to guerilla warfare: a South African case study', *JMAS,* 11, 2, 267–303.

JOHNSTONE, F.R.
1970

'White prosperity and white supremacy in South Africa today', *African affairs,* 69, 275, 124–40.

JONES, W.I.
1972

'The mise and demise of socialist institutions in rural Mali', *Genève-Afrique,* 11, 2, 19–44.

JOSEPH, R.A.
1974

'Ruben um Nyobe and the "Kamerun" rebellion', *African affairs,* 73, 293, 428–48.

Forthcoming 'Settlers, strikers and *sans-travail:* the Douala riots of September 1945', *Journal of African history.*

JULIS, G. 'L'action des masses populaires au Mali', *Cahiers*
n.d. *du CERM,* 54.

KAMITATU, C. *La grande mystification du Congo-Kinshasa* (Paris:
1971 Maspero).

KAUFMAN, R.R. 'The patron–client concept and macro politics',
1974 *Comparative studies in society and history,* 16, 3, 284–308.

KAY, G. *The political economy of colonialism in Ghana,*
1972 (Cambridge; C.U.P.).

KESSELMAN, M. 'Order or movement? The literature of political
1973 development as ideology', *World politics,* 26, 1, 139–54.

KIERNAN, V. 'The peasant revolution', *SR,* 9–38.
1970

KILSON, M. 'Elite cleavages in African politics: the case of
1970 Ghana', *Journal of international affairs,* 24, 1, 75–83.

KITCHING, G. 'The concept of class and the study of Africa',
1972 *African review,* 2, 3, 327–50.

KLEIN, A.N. 'On revolutionary violence', *Studies on the left.*
1966 6, 3, 62–82.

KLEIN, M. 'African social history', *African studies review,*
1972 15, 1, 97–112.

KOFI, T.A. 'The élites and underdevelopment in Africa:
1972 the case of Ghana', *Berkeley journal of sociology,* 17, 97–115.

KOM, D. *Le Cameroun: essai d'analyse économique et*
1972 *politique,* (Paris: Editions Sociales).

KRADER, L. 'The works of Marx and Engels in ethnology
1973 compared'. *International review of social history,* 18, 2, 223–75.

KUPER, L. 'Theories of revolution and race relations',
1971 *Comparative studies in society and history,* 13, 1, 87–107.

1972 'Class race and power: some comments on revolutionary change', *Comparative studies in society and history,* 14, 4, 400–21.

LACLAU, E. 1971	'Feudalism and capitalism in Latin America', *NLR*, 67, 19–38.
LACOSTE, Y. *et al.* n.d.	*L'Algérie, passé et présent* (Paris: Maspero).
LAMB, G. 1974	*Peasant politics* (Lewes, Sussex: Julian Fried- mann).
LECLERC, G. 1972	*Anthropologie et colonialisme* (Paris: Fayard).
LEDDA, R. 1967	'Social classes and the political struggle', *Inter- national socialist journal*, 22, 560–80.
Le DIVELEC, M.H. 1967	'Les "nouvelles" classes sociales en milieu urbain: le cas du Sénégal et celui du Nigéria du Nord', *Civilisations*, 17, 3, 240–53.
LEE, G. 1972	'Imperialism', *Bulletin of the Conference of Socialist Economists*, 2, 1, 99–107.
LEGASSICK, M. 1974	'South Africa: capital accumulation and viol- ence', *Economy and society*, 3, **3**, 253–91.
LEMARCHAND, R. 1972a 1972b	'Political clientelism and ethnicity: competing solidarities in nation building', *American Political Science Review*, 66, 1, 68–90. 'Political exchange, clientelism and development in Tropical Africa', *Cultures et Développement*, 4, 3, 483–516.
LEONARD, D.K. 1972	'The social structure of the agricultural extension service in the Western Province of Kenya', *African review*, 2, 2, 223–43.
LEYS, C. 1969 1975	*Politics and change in developing countries*, (Cam- bridge: C.U.P.). *Underdevelopment in Kenya* (London: Heine- mann).
LEYS, R. 1973	*Dualism and rural development in East Africa* (Copenhagen: Institute for Development Research).
LOBBAN, R. 1972	*Eritrean Liberation Front: a close-up view* (Pasadena; Munger Africana Library Notes).
LOFCHIE, M. 1971	*The state of the nations* (Berkeley: University of California Press).
LOXLEY, J. & SAUL, J. 1974	'The political economy of the parastatals', *Review of African political economy*, 54–88, early version in *East African law review*, 5, 1/2.

LUCAS, P.
1971

'Nigérie: lutte de classe ou conflit "nationalitaire"?', *Revue française de science politique*, 21, 4, 881–91.

1972

'Déchiffrement dialectique de l'histoire et libération de la connaissance: Fanon et la lutte de libération algérienne', *Revue algérienne*, 9, 4, 1043–56.

1973

'Réforme agraire en Algérie', *HS* 27, 131–42.

LUTTRELL, W.L.
1971

Villagization, co-operative production, and rural cadres: strategies and tactics in Tanzanian socialist rural development (Dar es Salaam; Economic Research Bureau, Paper 71, 11).

MCGHEE, T.G.
1973

'Peasants in the cities', *Human organization*, 32, 2, 135–42.

MCGOWAN, P.J. &
BOLLAND, P.
1971

The political and social élite of Tanzania, (Syracuse University: Program of East African Studies).

MAFEJE, A.
1971

'The ideology of "tribalism"', *JMAS*, 9, 2, 253–61.

MAGUBANE, B.
1968

'The crisis in African sociology', *East African Journal*, 5, 12, 21–40.

1969

'Pluralism and conflict situations in Africa: a new look', *African social research*, 8, 529–54: comment by Van den Berghe, *ibid.*, 9, 681–89.

1971

'A critical look at indices used in the study of social change in colonial Africa', *Current anthropology*, 12, 4–5, 419–46.

MAPOLU, H.
1972

'The organization and participation of workers in Tanzania', *African review*, 2, 3, 381–417.

1973

'The workers' movement in Tanzania', *Maji-Maji*, 12, 31–43.

MARCUM, J.
1969

The Angolan revolution, Vol. 1 (Cambridge, Mass.: M.I.T. Press).

MARSHALL, J.M.
forthcoming

The political economy of dependence, Ghana, 1945–66, (Harmondsworth: Penguin); available in draft as an M.Soc. Sc. thesis, 1972, for the Institute of Social Studies, the Hague.

MARTIN, M.L.
1973

'Un aspect de l'insertion des militaires dans le processus de développement national en Afrique: étude de quelques contradictions', *Canadian journal of African Studies*, 7, 2, 267–85.

MARTON, I.
1966

'De la négritude au "socialisme africain"', *La pensée*, 130, 3–10.

MASCHINO, T.M. &   *L'Algérie des illusions: la révolution confisquée,*
M'RABET, F.   (Paris: Laffont).
1972

MBILINYI, M.J.   'Education, stratification and sexism in Tanzania',
1973   *African Review,* 3, **2,** 327–40.

MEILLASSOUX, C.   'La phénomène économique dans les sociétés
1960   traditionelles d'autosubsistence', *CEA,* 4, 38–67.
1964   *Anthropologie économique des Gouro de Côte
                         d'Ivoire* (Paris: Mouton); review by Suret-Canale
                         in *La pensée,* 135, 94–106.
1965   'Elaboration d'un modèle socio-économique en
                         ethnologie', *Epistemologie sociologique,* 1-5, 283–
                         308.
1970   'A class analysis of the bureaucratic process in
                         Mali', *Journal of development studies,* 6, 2,
                         91–110.
1971   *The development of indigenous trade and markets
                         in West Africa* (London: O.U.P.).
1972   'From reproduction to production', *Economy
                         and society,* 1, 1 93–105.
1973a   'The social organization of the peasantry: the
                         economic basis of kinship', *Journal of peasant
                         studies,* 1, 1, 81–90.
1973b   'On the mode of production of the hunting band',
                         pp. 187–203 of *French perspectives in African
                         Studies,* ed. P. Alexandre (London: O.U.P.).
1974   *L'esclavage dans l'Afrique précoloniale* (Paris:
                         Maspero).

MEISTER, A.   *East Africa: the past in chains, the future in pawn,*
n.d.   (New York: Walker and Co.).
1971   'Quelques problèmes de la recherche sociale et
                         sociologique appliqué au développement parti-
                         cipationist', *Genève-Afrique,* 10, 2, 5–67.
1972   'Characteristics of community development and
                         rural animation in Africa', *International review
                         of community development,* 27–8, 75–132.

MELSON, R. &   *Nigeria: modernization and the politics of com-
WOLPE, H.   munalism,* (East Lansing: Michigan State Uni-
1972   versity Press).

MERLIER, M.   *Le Congo de la colonisation belge à l'indépendance*
1962   (Paris: Maspero).

MEVU, M. & M'GABE, D.   'Zimbabwe: exploitation and liberation', *MR,*
1969   20, 10, 30–51.

MIHYO, P.B.   'The workers' revolution in Tanzaina', *Maji-
1974   Maji,* 17, 1–61.

MIRACLE, M.P. &
SEIDMAN, A.
1970
'Co-operatives in Ghana, 1951–65', *African ubran notes*, 5, 3 59–94.

MOHAN, J.
1966
'Varieties of African socialism', *SR*, 220–66.

1967
'Nkrumah and Nkrumahism', *SR*, 191–228.

MONDLANE, E.
1969
The struggle for Mozambique (Harmondsworth: Penguin).

MPAKATI, A.
1973
'Malawi: the birth of a neocolonial state', *African Review*, 3, 1, 33–68.

MUNZER, T. &
LAPLACE, G.
1966
'L'Afrique recolonisée', *Cahiers du Centre d'études socialistes*, 64–68.

MURAPA, R.
1972
'Neocolonialism; the Kenya case', *Review of black political economy*, 2, 4, 55–73.

MURRAY, R.
1965
'The Ghanaian road', *NLR*, 32, 63–71.

1967
'Second thoughts on Ghana', *NLR*, 42, 25–39.

MURRAY, R. &
WENGRAF, T.
1963
'The Algerian revolution', *NLR*, 22, 14–65.

MUSEVENI, Y.T.
1971
'Fanon's theory on violence; its verification in liberated Mozambique', pp. 1–24 of *Essays on the liberation of southern Africa*, ed. N. Shamuyarira (Dar es Salaam; Tanzania Publishing House).

MUTISO, G.C.M.
1971
'Fanon, Kathue, and the future of the African revolution', *Black world*, 20, 7, 69–80.

MUTISO, G.C.M. &
GODFREY, E.M.
1973
'The political economy of self-help; Kenya's Harambee Institutes of Technology', *Canadian journal of African Studies*, 8, 1, 109–34.

NGHE, N.
1963
'Frantz Fanon et les problèmes de l'indépendance', *La pensée*, 107, 23–36.

NICOLAS, G.
1972
'Protest in Ethiopia', *Ufahamu*, 2, 3, 39–70.

NKRUMAH, K.
1965
Neocolonialism (London: Nelson).

1973
Revolutionary Path (London: Panaf).

O'BRIEN, D.C.
1967
'Political opposition in Senegal, 1960–67', *Government and opposition*, 2, 4, 557–67.

1971   *The Mourides of Senegal* (Oxford: O.U.P.).

1972   'Modernization, order and the erosion of a democratic ideal: American political science, 1960–70', *Journal of development studies*, 8, 3, 351–78.

1975   *Saints and politicians* (Cambridge: C.U.P.).

O'BRIEN, R.C.   'Unemployment, the family and class formation
1973   in Africa', *Manpower and unemployment research in Africa*, 6, 2, 47–59.

OKUMU, J.   'Charisma and politics in Kenya', *East African*
1968   *journal*, 5, 2, 9–16.

OLLIVIER, M.   'Révolution agraire et mobilisation des masses',
1973   *Revue algeriénne*, 10, 1, 33–140.

ONI, O.   'Features of Nigeria's financial institutions: a
1966   marxist approach', *Nigerian journal of economic and social studies*, 8, 3, 383–402.

OSOBA, S.O.   'The phenomenon of labour migration in the
1969   era of British colonial rule', *Journal of the Historical Society of Nigeria*, 4, 4, 515–38.

O'SULLIVAN, J.   'Union des populations du Cameroun: a study
1972   in mass mobilisation', *Ufahamu*, 3, 1, 53–72.

OWEN, R. &   *Studies in the theory of imperialism*, (London:
SUTCLIFFE, R.   Methuen).
1972

OWUSU, M.   *The uses and abuses of political power* (Chicago:
1970   University of Chicago Press); review by J. Dunn, *Transactions of the Historical Society of Ghana*, 13, 1 (1972), 113–24.

OXAAL, I. *et al.*   *Beyond the sociology of development* (London:
1976   Cass).

PEARSON, R.   'The economic imperialism of the Royal Niger
1971   Company', *Food Research Institute Studies*, 10, 1, 69–88.

PELISSIER, P.   *Les paysans du Sénégal* (Sainte-Yrieix: Im-
1966   primerie Fabrègue).

PFEFFERMAN, G.   *Industrial Labor in the Republic of Senegal* (New
1969   York: Praeger).

PERINBAM, B.M.   'Fanon and the revolutionary peasantry: the
1973   Algerian case', *JMAS*, 11, 3, 427–45.

PHIMISTER I.   'Peasant production and underdevelopment in

1974   Southern Rhodesia', *African affairs*, 73, 292, 217–28.

PIRET, B.   *L'aide belge au développement* (Brussels: Vie
1971   Ouvrière).
1972   'L'aide belge au Congo et le développement inégal du capitalisme monopoliste d'état', *Contradictions*, 1, 1.

POLANYI, M. *et al.*   *Trade and markets in the early empires* (Glencoe,
1975   Ill.: Free Press); for discussion of Polanyi's entire work see S. C. Humphreys, in *History and theory*, 8, (1969), 165–212.

POLLET, E. &   *La société Soninke* (Brussels: Institut de Socio-
WINTER, G.   logie).
1971

POST, K.W.J. &   *Structure and conflict in Nigeria 1960–65*
VICKERS, M.   (London: Heinemann).
1973

POST, K.W.J. &   *The price of liberty* (Cambridge: C.U.P.).
JENKINS, G.D.
1973

PRESENCE AFRICAINE   'Homage to Kwame Nkrumah', *Présence*
1973   *africaine*, 85.

RAIKES, P.L.   *The historical development of wheat growing in*
1970   *Northern Mbulu District* (University of Dar es Salaam; Economic Research Bureau, Paper 70. 11).

RATHBONE, R.   'Education and politics in Ghana', pp. 21–30
1968   of *Africana Collectea*, ed. D. Oberndorfer (Gütersloh).
1973   'Businessmen in politics: party struggle in Ghana, 1949–57', *Journal of development studies*, 9, 3, 391–402.

RDRC   *Towards rural co-operation in Tanzania* (Dar es
(Rural Development   Salaam: Tanzania Publishing House).
Research Committee)
1974

RECHERCHES   'Premières sociétés de classe et mode de produc-
INTERNATIONALES   tion asiatique', *Recherches Internationales*, 57/8;
1967   review by Jean Copans, *L'homme*, 9, 1 (1969), 92–95.

REY, P.P.   'Articulation des modes de dépendance et des
1969   modes de reproduction dans deux sociétés ligna-gères', *CEA* 35, 415–49.

1971	*Colonialisme, neocolonialisme et transition au capitalisme* (Paris: Maspero).
1973	*Les alliances de classes* (Paris: Maspero).
RHODIE, S. 1968	'The Gold Coast cocoa holdup, 1930–31', *Transactions of the Historical Society of Ghana,* 9. 105–18.
RIDDELL, D. 1972	'Towards a structuralist sociology of development?', *Sociology,* 6, 1, 89–96.
RIMMER, D. 1972	*Macromancy: the ideology of development economics,* (London: Institute of Economic Affairs).
RIVIERE, C. 1969	'De l'objectivité des classes sociales en Afrique noire', *CIS* 47, 119–44.
1971a	'Les bénéficaires du commerce dans la Guinée précoloniale et coloniale', *Bulletin de l'IFAN,* 33, 2, 257–84.
1971b	'Les mécanismes de constitution d'une bourgeoisie commerçante en... Guinée', *CEA,* 43, 378–99.
1971c	'Comportements ostentatoires et style de vie des élites guinéenes', *Cultures et développement,* 3, 3, 415–43.
1971d	*Mutations sociales en Guinée* (Paris: Rivière).
1973a	'Genèse d'inégalité dans l'organisation sociale malinke', *Cultures et développement,* 5, 2, 279–314.
1973b	'Dynamique des systèmes fonciers et inégalités sociales: le cas guinéen', *CIS* 54, 61–94.
RODINSON, M. 1974	*Islam and capitalism* (London: Allen Lane).
RODNEY, W. 1967	*The West African slave trade* (Nairobi: East African Publishing House).
1970	*A history of the upper Guinea coast* 1545–1800 (Oxford: O.U.P.).
ROSBERG, C.G. & NOTINGHAM, J. 1966	*The myth of Mau Mau* (New York: Praeger).
ROSS, A. 1967	'White Africa's black ally', *NLR,* 45, 85–94.
forthcoming	*Malawi* (Harmondsworth: Penguin).
RUDEBECK, L. 1970	'Political development: towards a coherent and relevant theoretical formulation of the concept', *Scandinavian Political Studies,* 5, 21–63.
1974	*Guiné-Bissau: a study of political mobilization* (Uppsala: Scandinavian Institute of African Studies).

RWEYEMAMU, J.F. *Underdevelopment and industrialization in Tan-*
1973   *zania* (Nairobi: O.U.P.).

RYAN, S.   'The theory and practice of African one-partyism;
1970a   the CCP re-examined', *Canadian journal of
                African Studies*, 4, 2, 145–172.
1970b   'Socialism and the party system in Ghana 1957–
                66', *Pan-African journal*, 3, 1, 49–97.
1973   'Economic nationalism and socialism in Uganda',
                Journal of Commonwealth Political Studies, 11,
                2, 140–58.

SAHLINS, M.   *Stone age economics* (London: Tavistock).
1973

SANDBROOK, R.   'Patrons, clients and factions: new dimensions
1972   of conflict analysis in Africa', *Canadian Journal
                of political science*, 5, 1, 104–19.
1974   *Proletarians and African capitalism: the case of
                Kenya* 1960–72. (Cambridge: C.U.P.).

SANDBROOK, R. & *Towards an African working class* (London:
COHEN, R.   Longman).
1975

SAUL, J.S.   'African peasants and revolution', *Review of
1974a   African political economy*, 1, **1**, 41–68.
1974b   'The state in post-colonial societies: Tanzania',
                SR, 349–72.

SCHATZ, S.P.   'Crude private neo-imperialism: a new pattern
1969   in Africa', *JMAS*, 7, 677–88.

SCHNAPPER, R.   *La politique et le commerce français dans le Golfe
1971   de Guinée de* 1838 à 1871 (The Hague; Mouton).

SCHUMACHER, E.J. *Politics, bureaucracy and rural development*
1974   (Berkeley; University of California Press).

SEBAG, P.   *La Tunisie* (Paris: Editions Sociales).
1951

SEIDMAN, A.W.   'Prospects for Africa's exports', *JMAS*, 9, 3,
1971   409–28.
1972   *Comparative development strategies in East
                Africa*, (Nairobi: East African Publishing
                House).
1973   *Alternative development strategies in Zambia*,
                (University of Wisconsin: Land Tenure Center,
                Paper 89).

SEYTANE, S.   'Les classes sociales et les dirigeants politiques de
1966   l'ouest-africain', *Partisans* 29–30, 45–70.

SHAMUYARIRA, N.   *Crisis in Rhodesia* (London: Deutsch).
1965

SHIVJI, I.G.   'Capitalism unlimited: public corporations in
1973   partnership with multinational corporations',
                       African review 3, 3, 359–81.
1974   *Tourism and socialist development* (Dar es
                       Salaam: Tanzania Publishing House).
1976   *Class Struggles in Tanzania* (London: Heine-
                       mann). This contains *Tanzania: the silent class
                       struggle* (UEA 1970); republished with com-
                       ments, Dar es Salaam: Tanzania Publishing
                       House, 1973; and *The silent class struggle
                       continued* (Dar es Salaam: the author, 1973).

SILUNDIKA, G.   *Interview* (Richmond, Canada: Liberation Sup-
1974   port Movement).

SIMONS, J. & H.R.   *Class and colour in South Africa* 1850–1950
1969   (Harsmondsworth: Penguin).

SKLAR, R.L.   'Political science and national integration: a
1967   radical approach', *JMAS*, 5, 1, 1-11.
1975   *Corporate power in an African state* (Berkeley:
                       University of California Press).

STAHL, M.   *Ethiopia: contradictions in agricultural develop-
1974   ment* (Uppsala: Political Science Association).

STANILAND, M.   'Frantz Fanon and the African political class',
1969   *African affairs*, 68, 270, 4–25.
1975   *The lions of Dagbon: political change in Northern
                       Ghana* (Cambridge: C.U.P.).

STAVENHAGEN, R.   *Les classes sociales dans les sociétés agraires,*
1969   (Paris: Anthropos).
1971   'Decolonializing applied social sciences', *Human
                       organization,* 30, 4, 333–57.

SURET-CANALE, J.   *L'Afrique noire, occidentale et centrale,* 2nd.
1961   edition (Paris: Editions sociales).
1964   'Essai sur la signification sociale et historique
                       des hegemonies peules', *Cahiers du CERM,*
                       unnumbered.
1966a   'La fin de la chefferie en Guinée', *Journal of
                       African history,* 7, 3, 459–94; translated extracts in
                       African politics and society, ed. I. M. Markovitz
                       (New York: Free Press 1970).
1966b   'The traditional societies of tropical Africa',
                       Marxism today, 10, 2, 49–57; longer French
                       version in CERM 1969.

1970	*La république de Guinée* (Paris: Editions Sociales).
1973	*Afrique noire: de la colonisation aux indépendances* 1945–60, Vol. 1 (Paris: Editions Sociales).
1974	Difficultés du néo-colonialisme français en Afrique tropicale', *Canadian journal of African Studies*, 8, 2, 211–33.
SUTCLIFFE, R.B. 1971	'Stagnation and inequality in Rhodesia 1946–68', *Bulletin of the Oxford University Institute of Economics and Statistics*, 33, 1, 35–56.
SZENTES, T. 1971 1972	*The political economy of underdevelopment* (Budapest: Akademia Kiado). *Socioeconomic effects of two patterns of foreign capital investment* (Dakar: IDEP).
TANDON, Y. 1973	*Technical assistance administration in East Africa* (Stockholm: Dag Hammarskjold Foundation).
TERIBA, O. *et al*, 1972	'Some aspects of ownership and control structure of business enterprise in a developing economy: the Nigerian case', *Nigerian journal of economic and social studies*, 14, 1, 3–26.
TERRAY, E. 1964 1972	'Les révolutions congolaises et dahoméenes', *Revue française des sciences politiques*, 14, 917–12. *Marxism and 'primitive' societies* (New York: Monthly Review).
TRAPIDO, S. 1971	'South Africa in a comparative study of industrialization', *Journal of development studies*, 7, 3, 309–20.
TUROK, B. 1974	*Strategic problems in South Africa's liberation struggle* (Richmond, Canada: Liberation Support Movement) see also *SR* 1972 and 1973.
UCHUMI (Editorial Board) 1972	*Towards socialist planning*, Dar es Salaam (*Uchumi*, 1, 2–3).
UEA 1969, 1970, 1972	*Universities of East Africa Annual Social Science Conference: Proceedings* (published by the host institution in each year).
UPC 1971	*L'UPC parle* (Paris: Maspero).
VAITSOS, C.V. 1970	*The transfer of resources and preservation of monopoly rents* (Harvard University, Economic Development Report 168).
van ARKADIE, B. 1970	'Development and the mode of production', *East African journal*, 7, 8, 45–48.

1971	'The role of the state sector in the context of economic dependence', *Institute of Development Studies Bulletin*, 3, 4, 22–37.
van der LAAR, A. 1971	'Aspects of foreign private investment in African development', *Kroniek van Afrika*, 3, 159–76.
van ONSELEN, C. 1973	'Worker consciousness in black miners: Southern Rhodesia 1900–20', *Journal of African history*, 14, 2, 237–56.
VERHAEGEN, B. 1965 1967a, 1969 1967b	*Les cahiers de Gamboma* (Brussels: CRISP). *Rébellions au Congo*, 2 Vols (Brussels: CRISP). 'Les rébellions populaires au Congo en 1964', *CEA*, 26, 345–59.
VICKERS, M. 1970	'Competition and control in modern Nigeria: origins of the war with Biafra', *International journal*, 25, 3, 603–33.
VINCENT, J. 1971	*African élite: the big men of a small town* (New York: Columbia University Press).
WALLERSTEIN, I. 1972	'Social conflict in post-independence black Africa: the concepts of race and status reconsidered', in *Racial tensions and national indentity*, ed. E. Q. Campbell, Vanderbilt University Press.
WARREN, W. 1973	'Myths of underdevelopment: imperialism and capitalist industrialization', *NLR*, 81, 3–45; discussed by A. Emmanuel *et al. NLR*, 85, 61–104 (1974).
WASSERMAN, G. 1973	'Continuity and counter-insurgency: the role of land reform in decolonizing Kenya 1962–70', *Canadian journal of African Studies*, 7, 1, 133–48.
WATERMAN, P. 1971 1973	'Structure, contradiction and the Nigerian catastrophy: elements of an analysis', *Présence Africaine*, 77, 191–207. 'Communist theory in the Nigerian trade union movement', *Politics and society*, 3, 283–312.
WEEKS, J.F. 1971a 1971b 1971c	'The problem of wage policy in developing countries with special reference to Africa', *Economic bulletin of Ghana* NS, 1, 1, 31–44. 'The impact of economic conditions and institutional forces on urban wages in Nigeria', *Nigerian journal of economic and social studies*, 13, 3, 313–40. 'Wage policy and the colonial legacy', *JMAS*, 9, 361–87.

1971d   'The political economy of labour transfer', *Science and society*, 35, 4, 463–80.

1972   'Employment, growth and foreign domination in underdeveloped countries', *Review of Radical Political Economics*, 4, 1, 59–70.

1973   'An exploration into the nature of the problem of urban imbalance in Africa', *Manpower and unemployment research in Africa*, 6, 2, 9–36.

WEINBERG, W.R.
1971   'The costs of foreign private investment', *Civilisations*, 21, 2–3, 207–19.

WEISS, H.
1967   *Political protest in the Congo* (Princeton University Press).

WEISSKOPF, T.E.
1972   'Capitalism, underdevelopment and the future of the poor countries', pp. 43–77 of *Economics and world order*, ed. J. Baghwati (New York: Macmillan).

WHEELER, D.L. &
PELISSIER, R.
1971   *Angola* (London: Pall Mall).

WILKINSON, A.R.
1973   'Insurgency in Rhodesia 1957–73: an account and assessment', *Adelphi Papers*, 100.

WILLIAME, C.
1971   'Recherches sur les modes de production cynégétique et lignager', *HS* 19, 101–19.

1972   *Patrimonialism and political change in the Congo*, (Stanford, Calif.: Stanford University Press); review by B. Nimer in *International journal of African historical studies*, 6, 2, (1973), 315–34.

1973   'Patriarchal structures and factional politics; towards an understanding of the dualist society', *CEA* 50, 326–55.

WILLIAMS, G.P.
forthcoming   *Nigeria: economy and society* (London: Rex Collings).

WIPPER, A.
1971   'The politics of sex: some strategies employed by the Kenyan power élite', *African Studies review*, 14, 3, 463–82; see also *JMAS*, 9, 3. 429–42.

1972   'The roles of African women; past present and future', *Canadian journal of African Studies*, 6, 2.

WOLF, E.R.
1970   *Peasant wars in the twentieth century* (London: Faber).

WOLFE, A.W.
1963   'The African mineral industry: evolution of a supranational level of integration', *Social problems*, 11, 2, 153–64.

1966   'Capital and the Congo', in *Southern Africa in transition,* ed. J. A. Davis and J. K. Baker (New York: Praeger).

WOLFF, R.D.   *The economics of colonialism: Britain and Kenya*
1974   *1870–1930* (New Haven: Yale University Press).

WOLPE, H.   'Capitalism and cheap labour power in South
1972   Africa', *Economy and society,* 1, 4, 425–56.

WORSLEY, P.M.   'Aid or revolution?' pp. 603–609 of *Problems of*
1972a   *modern society,* ed Worsley, P. (Harmondsworth: Penguin) and pp. 43–61 of *The Times' History of our Times,* ed. M. Cunliffe, (London: The Times, 1971).

1972b   'Frantz Fanon and the 'lumpenproletariat', *SR,* 193–230.

WOUNGLY-MASSAGA   *L'Afrique bloquée: l'exemple du Kamerun*
1971   (Geneva: CIML).

YAFFEY, M.J.H.   *Balance of payments problems of a developing*
1970   *country: Tanzania* (Munich: Weltform Verlag).

ZOLBERG, A.R.   'The political use of economic planning in Mali',
1968   pp. 98–123 of *Economic nationalism in new states,* ed. H. G. Johnson (London: Allen and Unwin).

Index

African countries are given their modern names (i.e. Zambia); South Africa *is referred to as* RSA, *while the names* Egypt, Rhodesia *and* Madagascar *have also been retained.*